Judaism and Christianity

PERSPECTIVES AND TRADITIONS

Judaism and Christianity
PERSPECTIVES AND TRADITIONS

LUTHER H. HARSHBARGER

JOHN A. MOURANT

The Pennsylvania State University

With a Foreword by
Rabbi Benjamin Kahn

ALLYN AND BACON, INC.   BOSTON

to Marian

and Margaret

Foreword

THE western world today appears to be the scene of unprecedented interest in religion. This has not expressed itself particularly in attendance at religious services or in ritual observances. Even though there are statistics of increasing membership in churches and synagogues, the reasons for these may not necessarily be growth in religious conviction. The new interest in religion appears to view it as an intellectual concern and as a valid ingredient of western culture. There are more books on religion than ever before, many of them on best-seller lists. Protestants, Catholics, and Jews are more curious about each other's teachings and institutions, an interest which may also be a product of contiguity of cultures previously separated by chasms of prejudice. In western society the concept of religious pluralism now is accepted alongside that of cultural pluralism, the hallmark of a democratic society.

This trend is only in part a product of the new ecumenical spirit. Inter-religious dialogue antedates Vatican II, although it received great forward impetus from this important development.

In years past pleas for religious understanding were made on the grounds of the similarities among religions. Today we know that such grounds, whether in the religious, national, or racial realm, are relatively meaningless. Rather it is precisely the fundamental differences that establish a basis, as well as the need, for cooperation and understanding. The former basis is totalitarian, the latter is democratic.

Protestantism and Catholicism share many beliefs and traditions, but they possess basic differences in theology and institutions. Perhaps they may some day be resolved. Judaism and Christianity have many things in common; how could it be otherwise when one is the daughter religion of the other? Both are responsible for the ethicizing of man and society, and they share a common commitment to social change. They must work together to relieve the shame of the cities, to promote equal rights for all men, to bring meaningful peace to the world. Yet, their differences in theology, practice, and institution are fundamental, and in larger respects irreconcilable. Only on the basis of the recognition that these differences exist, and legitimately so, can religious dialogue acquire a dimension of validity and meaning.

There is a parallel in the evidence of the new interest in religion exhibited in the curricular offerings of colleges and universities. Higher education recognizes today that the university has the obligation to expose students to all the components of culture and civilization. They include the philosophy, sociology, and history of religion and basic ideas of religions, which are today woven into the university curriculum in both state and private institutions of higher learning. This new attitude is duplicated in the field of adult education, beyond the confines of the university itself.

The proliferation of courses in western religions has created the need for new textbooks, particularly in comparative religion. There is no dearth of excellent books on Christianity and on Judaism, respectively. There has been, however, a great need for a text which would approach their study on a comparative basis, as does this book by Professors Harshbarger and Mourant. Uniquely, this text places Jewish and Christian views side by side in respective categories (so to speak, in parallel columns), so that the reader can immediately perceive the similarities and the differences between the religious traditions in general terms and in particular details. This makes the book, in my opinion, a pioneering and highly significant contribution to the field of religious literature.

The authors have recognized that the unusual student will not be satisfied with a single text, and have provided him with excellent bibliographical references at the end of each chapter for further and more intensive study in areas of his special interest. For most students, however, the text alone suffices to give introduction and insight into the basic beliefs, practices, and institutions of Judaism and Christianity. I should add that the book would be no less useful in the field of adult education under both public and private auspices, as well as for teachers of pre-college courses in comparative religion which are being offered in religious schools and high schools.

The teacher of a course in which this is the text will want to encourage his students to supplement it by readings from original sources, ancient, medieval, and modern. He may also wish to invite into his classroom representatives of the several religious traditions to lecture from their own particularistic viewpoints, so that there can be direct confrontation of ideas and personalities. The students should be encouraged to make "field visits," with this volume in hand, to churches and synagogues, so that they may have direct experience of the institutions whose history and teachings are explicated.

Judaism and Christianity: Perspectives and Traditions is one of the best introductions I know to the implementation of inter-religious dialogue, through the medium of self-knowledge and knowledge of others. It is written with extraordinary scholarly objectivity, yet is infused with evidences of religious conviction. By its very nature it encourages free discussion and the expression of divergent views. It demonstrates an understanding of the historical process by which contemporary religions have come to be what they are, and takes into account the effect upon them of the intellectual and social conditions of successive eras. The recognition of the validity of differences in conviction, sorely needed in our time, is inherent in every page.

Professor Harshbarger and Professor Mourant have made it possible, through this text, to raise the level of teaching and study in the area of western religions, for the university student and for all persons interested in the search for truth in its many forms.

BENJAMIN M. KAHN

Preface

THIS book has been designed to meet the needs of those readers who wish
to gain a deeper appreciation of the basic issues and ideas that have
emerged within the Jewish and Christian traditions in the history of
western religion. Today it can no longer be assumed that the average
individual possesses an adequate background in the knowledge of the
Jewish and Christian traditions. Acquaintance with the Bible, let alone
an understanding and appreciation of its literary and religious content, is
no longer common. Acting on these assumptions we have endeavored to
provide an introduction to some of the basic issues and problems that have
agitated the Jewish and Christian traditions throughout western history.
Of necessity we have confined our treatment to Judaism, Roman Catholicism, and the major Protestant groups. As a text this book provides
sufficient material for an entire year's course that could serve as an introduction to religious studies, particularly if combined with additional
source readings.

This book originated in a television series entitled "Exploring Religious
Ideas: The Great Western Faiths" sponsored by the Center for Continuing
Liberal Education at the Pennsylvania State University. To the moderator
and initiator of that series, Professor Ralph Condee, the authors are grateful for his guidance at that time and for his many valuable suggestions.
Rabbi Benjamin Kahn, who writes the foreword to this volume, was a
participant in that series, and cooperated with the authors in formulating
the outline and the approach of the book. For his evaluation of the material
on Judaism and for his critical appraisal of the manuscript we are heavily in
his debt.

To Mr. Terry Foreman we are very grateful for his compilation and
writing of the glossary and for his reading and evaluation of the entire
manuscript. Acknowledgments are also due to Elizabeth Meek for research assistance; to Lyn Ayres, Gillian Masemore, Elizabeth Eliot Harsh-

barger, Helen Kaufman, and Judy Stewart for the typing of the manuscript. For financial assistance we are grateful to the Central Fund for Research of the Pennsylvania State University. Finally, for their reading of the manuscript and their many valuable suggestions and criticisms we are indebted to Professor Samuel S. Hill, Jr. of the University of North Carolina, Professor Carl Purinton of Boston University, the Reverend Gerard S. Sloyan of the Catholic University of America, and to Professor Robert Michaelsen of the University of California at Santa Barbara.

LUTHER HARSHBARGER
JOHN A. MOURANT

Contents

Judaism and Christianity

PERSPECTIVES AND TRADITIONS

Introduction: From Generation to Generation

JUDAISM and Christianity represent expressions of faith, symbols of reality, structures of thought and experience which have been meaningful in most parts of the western world for nearly four thousand years. Throughout their long history Judaism and Christianity have developed and formulated ideas and doctrines which have become the life, the heritage, and the traditions of the people in both cultures. This statement represents facts of incalculable importance. It means, first of all, that there are patterns of ideas which are windows through which the generations understand their world. Second, it means that these perspectives are structures of experience and tradition which focus on the value and meaningfulness of history. And, third, it means that these ideas and experiences provide a cumulative tradition by which each generation becomes aware of itself in new and often revolutionary ways.

Both Judaism and Christianity raise profound questions and place great weight on the importance of the intellectual enterprise. The efforts of the rabbis to spell out in detail the implications of the Torah text, and the history of creedal conflict in the Church—and the conviction that these endeavors were part of the labor of the Divinity—are evidences enough for the vitality of the intellectual tradition. Such an intellectual tradition is expressed in the ordering of the content of the faith which the traditions confess and maintain. Theology is the term usually given to such an enterprise—an enterprise both exciting and audacious, for it seeks to deal with the human condition in its historical and cosmic totality. None of the baffling questions of life and death, goodness and truth, or time and eternity escapes its purview. If, therefore, a religious tradition claims to be true it must make sense of the whole of life. Theological thought is not a special kind of thinking which deals with queer experiences belonging only to that strange, other world. What makes thought theological is its attempt to interpret the depths of ordinary experience. The demand of faith, as Augustine insisted, is the demand for understanding. Theological ideas therefore are the attempts to state what has been apprehended in man's experience, although the validity of that experience is not dependent upon accurate verbal expression, since men know more about the content of faith's demands than their intellectual systems can comprehend. Despite this fact, there are certain ideas which for particular periods in their history seemed not so much dogmas as inevitable categories of the human mind through which everything else was seen.

No dogma, however, ever expresses the whole truth. Indeed, it may even distort the truth, especially when it becomes static or an object of veneration. This is what the Bible calls idolatry, and indicates the validity of Judaism's habitual distrust of dogmatic formulation. Dogmas become particularly odious when they substitute defense and argument for interpretation. Yet dogmas as central elements in the coherent and cohesive experience of a group can have "elucidatory power" for human thought and conduct. An understanding of the importance of dogma and a distrust of any definition must always go hand in hand.

An authentic theology will attempt to provide an explanation of the human condition and its status without doing violence to man's reason, conscience, or heart. It will express the content of the tradition and interpret the faith in such a way that it brings belief into some intelligible order with man's knowledge and experience and enables him to relate his truth to his own experience in an understandable way. "The task of theology is to show how the world is founded on something beyond mere transient fact, and how it issues in something beyond the perishing of occasions."[1]

But ideas cannot have discontinuous modes of existence. The context of religious thought is culture and experience. An idea, a belief, or a value is never free from its historical and cultural forms. The questions men ask and the answers they give are conditioned by the thought forms, the language, and the ethos of the age in which they arise. Each idea comes clothed in the form of its society at any given time. This accounts for the fact that certain questions are possible only at certain times. All ideas have to be reformulated and rethought in every age and in the language and the cultural forms of that age. It is probably valid to say that truth is contained only in those experiences that can be expressed in different ways by various ages. Indeed, if one aspect of truth must be so expressed then the whole truth at any given time is expressed only on several levels together.

This observation applies with special force to the biblical religions, which are historical traditions unique among the religions of the world in the stress they place upon the importance of history and the lasting quality of the intellect. In this respect they are authentically western, and whether and to what extent that is a handicap or strength is not ours to judge. But the history of these traditions amply demonstrates that no idea is shaped in a vacuum. Rather each is an expression of fact and experience as it appears within a complex of ideas, a cultural sphere of thought. These traditions have shown amazing ability to create and express religious convictions of men in widely differing ideological and cultural climates. This historical observation has been corroborated by the works of such writers as Durkheim, Fraser, Weber, and Troeltsch. The biblical traditions ineluctably have adapted their ideas and doctrines to changing historical circumstances in a continuous effort to relate their primordial experiences and revelation to the conditions and needs of men.

Theology, then, exists in the context of history and is not just uninhibited speculation. History is the stuff of theology and beliefs presuppose knowledge of the past, dependent upon historical inquiry. Judaism and Christianity base themselves upon the significance of certain historical occasions which cannot be read apart from any other historical events. But beneath the surface of ordinary events there is an affirmation of the divine presence concealed in the totally profane. There, these religions maintain, God has spoken a word which is permanently valid for human existence, and his purpose from creation has remained essentially the same. The difference lies not in whether and how these events occurred, but rather in the way they are interpreted and in the significance attached to them. Interpretation is

. . . that subtle combination of insight into, and articulation of, the meaning of the experience that is so deeply persuasive and so widely accepted that it becomes a part of the common consciousness and passes into the realm of motivational myths. The experience of the Hebrew people in breaking away from Egypt, crossing the Red Sea, and entering into a land of their own was striking enough to be celebrated in song and story. But the important thing was that this happened to a people who had it in them to translate the experience into "the exodus." That made the difference between a merely successful rebellion of an obscure people and the myth of a chosen people that through all subsequent history has remained a pillar of fire by night and of cloud by day.[2]

Jews and Christians point to certain historical occasions which give all other events and periods their own meaning in terms of the biblical witness, the doctrinal tradition, and the living faith of adherents. But the task of the interpreter is not just the reconstruction of events. It includes also the penetration of their meaning and intention, identifying and elucidating situations and positions which made possible their appearance and triumph at a particular historical moment. Then these events become normative for the tradition, which functions as a symbol of a life orientation and sense of inherited historic mission, but which now provide meaning and motivation in changing and changed circumstances from generation to generation.

If we now understand that the content of these traditions is the very warp and woof of history, we can use the terms "sacred" or "religion" as ways of talking about the value and significance of this complex of events. "Sacred" symbolizes those critical points in their life experience through which Jews and Christians became aware of themselves in a new way. We need, of course, to be careful, for the term "religion" is employed in a variety of ways, and is so ambiguous in its meaning, so labyrinthian in its complexity as it is used in the contemporary world that it conjures up all sorts of images. Here we can describe, but not define, it as both *sui generis* (what it is in itself) and as pervasive in all aspects of human thought, life, and culture.

Religion refers to those dimensions of depth or height or ultimacy which inform the very heart of culture; to a transcendent reality present to the world. Whatever its other characteristics it is epitomized by Job's description of God being present, though in silence, in dread and fascination, and far beyond comprehension:

> dread came upon me, and trembling,
>   which made all my bones shake.
> A spirit glided past my face;
>   the hair of my flesh stood up.
> It stood still,
>   but I could not discern its appearance.
> A form was before my eyes;
>   there was silence, then I heard a voice:
> Can mortal man be righteous
>   before God?
> Can a man be pure before his
>   Maker?

(Job 4:14-17)

Somehow or other the term "religion" refers to God, and "God" is the reference in all life to the ultimate source of meaning, apprehended only indirectly through symbols of the finite world. While always transcendent and therefore unknown, reference to it is implicit in life, and wherever there is meaning it is present. It has also the character of immanence although it is not inherent in the sum total of things. Nonetheless it is manifested in every entity so that man can stand in some sort of response called "faith." Religion and faith represent a total attitude toward reality, not a theory of the universe, not a practice of detachment or escape, but a level of life which lies underneath or above the cleavages of theory and practice, sacred and profane, religious and secular. It is not one department of life, not even the most important. If there is religion at all it must mean the elevation of the whole of life into new modes, every natural activity caught up into the sphere of reality; a way of looking at experience as a whole and of interpreting the elemental facts of existence.

Of course, the expression of this experience is not wholly intellectual; perhaps not even primarily so. Such an experience uses myth, symbol, liturgical formulation, and the structures of worship. But history is the history both of the primordial experience of revelation and the interpretation of that event. It is the task of the tradition to reinterpret the revelation in such a way that its content and meaning can be grasped by other generations. So God reveals himself to man who proclaims it and writes it down for all to read, but the interpretation of the meaning of the event and of life itself is the result of, not identical with, the revelation. The Talmud, for example, can be understood as essentially the attempt of the rabbis to re-experience the original revelation, to confront future generations, and then to decide what is to be done in response. The same is basically true of the creeds of the Church. This is the theological enterprise and it points to the truth of Whitehead's statement that "the dogmas of religion are the attempts to formulate in precise terms the truth disclosed in the religious experience of mankind."[3] While dogmas grow out of particular situations which are unique and unrepeatable, the depths of the experiences they disclose are often best expressed in confessions, liturgical formulations, and prayer. However it is articulated the tradition will persist to the extent these forms continue to serve each generation as the ground of faith. A. J. Heschel speaks to the difficulty of describing the subtlety of these experiences. "The study of ritual is like phonetics, the science of sounds; the study of dogma is like grammar, the science of the inflections of language; while the study of inner acts is like semantics, the science of meanings." He adds, "We do not have words for the understanding of these moments, for the events that make up the secret history of religion, or for the records in which these instants are captured."[4]

Tradition, then, is the way to make the past relevant to the present and to provide a means whereby its personal appropriation becomes possible. But there is always a "generation gap" because each generation has its own secret understandings of the nature of things. Each generation differs in its elucidation of what it means to live, act, and feel. This perennial problem of existence usually reappears in sharpest form in periods in which the changes in the conditions of existence are so dramatic as to create the illusion that man's achievements can eliminate the perennial problems of the race. Why not cut entirely free of any appeal to the past and concentrate rather upon the contemporary world and experience? What could be more irrelevant, for example, than the age-old office of the liturgy? Yet by the simple, seemingly incongruous acts of kneeling in a cathedral chancel, or by a wayside altar, by chanting the choral antiphon, by reading and hearing the words of the Torah, the Law and Gospel, by the blessing of the bread and wine, men have spoken across the generations to their children and their children's children concerning their own responses to the mystery through which they found themselves—this mystery of the immanence of the past in the present, the mystery of identity—which gave meaning and direction to the whole of human life. Traditions can grow only through this succession of generations reaching out their hands to each other in the same spirit spanning the ages. Yet every generation is "the generation of those who seek . . . the face of the God of Jacob" (Psalm 24:6), but who have to understand anew the meaning of these crucial words and symbols.

This points to the central significance of prayer which Feuerbach said revealed the ultimate essence of religion,[5] and which belongs to the essential character of man, even though it may appear to be the least practical thing to do. Prayer is the act or stance through which man achieves a different dimension based upon his awareness of the holy, the means by which he clarifies his faith and the purposes of his existence through a response to mystery and beauty. Doubtless, if we knew how a man or civilization prays, or what he prays about, we could see not only the depths of religion but also the inner character of an entire people, an age, a type of culture.

While prayer is the central phenomenon in religion, its necessary and natural exercise, it is also the highest exercise of the rational mind. Continuity of the tradition does not mean that dogmas, confessions, and prayers do not change. Over and over again, history observes that the formulations and practices of yesterday no longer communicate because situations in which men find themselves have changed entirely. Although this does not necessarily invalidate these forms, communication requires the sharing of basic ideas and presuppositions which allow discourse to be intelligible. But presuppositions erode and new ones take their place. Words evaporate, become vague and indeterminate. In every generation the totality of the tradition hangs in balance. In every new situation and age it is not enough just to transmit and receive the tradition. Everything inherited must be won anew.

Traditions can be serious and worthwhile only insofar as a generation makes vital contact with them. However significant they have been in the past, man's own responsible participation in the life of the present is of decisive importance. In every generation every religious idea, symbol, and system is challenged as to its right to exist. This challenge raises questions for serious thought. It is the duty and privilege of each generation to handle the perennial problems of religion in the form in which the age presents the challenge. In the modern age the challenge has been primarily intellectual. The content of the traditions are to be studied for the sake of what they signify for truth and meaning, for the relation of time and eternity. This requires vital intellectual identification with them.

The function of the thinker is to focus the unorganized mental content of his time. This is not a passive function. Focus requires much more. The thinker gives thought fresh impulse and new perspective. Though rooted in the past he shapes the future. Though conditioned and limited by history he is not bound wholly by it. He can transcend history and time in proportion to the use of his power to think about them and to relate events to one another. We need not argue here the ageless question of the role of thought in human society and behavior to suggest that thought is not only conditioned by but can become the instrument of historical change. Whichever comes first, history requires the formulation of ideas. Nor do we need to argue that change is purely intellectual in cause. In every society, however, there is a thinking minority whose opinions and convictions become the unreasoned assumptions of the next generation. None of these ideas and values will continue long to inspire coming generations, however, unless they are communicated effectively; and they will not be communicated effectively if they are not communicated on an intellectual level.

To be sure, intellectual awareness alone is more likely to produce "debaters of this age" then it is saints and devout spirits. Personal piety and morality, liturgy and worship may exist in spite of intellectual deficiencies, but not for the culture and not for the next generation. Traditions need the power to understand the generation as the condition for a share in guiding it. This requires not only ardor but intelligence. There is no necessary conflict between strong belief and a scrupulous respect for intellectual and spiritual freedom. The time is long past when one need be victimized by the fashionable and superstitious dogma that one cannot be well educated, sophisticated, and participate fully in the thought and method of the modern age and still be religious. Piety may be the religion of the individual, but theology is the religion of the generations. In an age when religion raises questions for serious thought, all men have a moral obligation to be intelligent. This is man's unique quality and special strength. Pascal puts it best: "Man is but a reed, the weakest in nature; but he is a thinking reed. . . . Our whole dignity consists . . . in thought. . . . Let us endeavor to think well; this is the beginning of morality."[6]

Now a word about the organization of the book. We start with a general discussion of religion, its nature and meaning. The reader has already been introduced to the complexity of this discussion and will realize already that no definition will command general assent. We then describe the biblical religions as particular historical traditions in western religion. Chapters 2 and 3 are concerned with their historical context because Judaism and Christianity are historical religions not only in the sense that they have a history but in the sense that they take history with utmost seriousness.

In the next section we deal with certain basic ideas or concepts of the traditions. Biblical religions are religions of revelation. In Chapter 4 we discuss the meaning of revelation as a way of knowing by discussing models of revelation and inspiration currently operative in both Judaism and Christianity. Faith as the response to what is revealed is discussed in Chapter 5. The source, and some would say, the content of revelation is God. Chapter 6 deals with the questions of how God can be known to be and what he is like, according to these traditions. Here we explore biblical and classical as well as modern notions. In the third section we attempt to describe some of the implications of revelation for the meaning of human existence. Chapter 7 discusses the relationship of God and the world, including the troublesome questions of miracle and evil. The nature of man and his redemption is the focus of Chapter 8. The cardinal doctrine of the Messiah and the messianic hope is the theme which runs throughout Chapters 9, 10, and 11. In Chapter 9 the major point upon which Jews and Christians differ, the valuation of Jesus of Nazareth as the Christ (Messiah), is explored in historical and doctrinal context under the heading of The Christ Event and the Messianic Idea. Chapter 10 continues this discussion and its implications for the discrete historical developments of Judaism and Christianity under the rubric of The People of God. Chapter 11 discusses the meaning of history and the nature of the eschatological hope.

In the last section of the book we are concerned with the structures of the traditions in their organization (Chapter 12) and their ceremonies and liturgies (Chapter 13), and with how as institutions they are manifested as living religious traditions. Finally, in the Epilogue we explore Judaism and Christianity in their contemporary American setting, and the effect on them of the extraordinary heterogeneity of the American religious tradition.

Our method is descriptive, interpretative, and comparative. It is descriptive in that we have tried to portray accurately the facts and data and what each tradition has to say for itself. We have attempted to see these traditions as a coherent whole as well as to pursue disagreements. We have tried to describe accurately points of view as they arose in their own context—usually, in the case of ideas, at the point where the issues first developed—and then to relate them to the way the problems occurred later or in our own time. While the book is not a history of ideas, the ideas are always placed in historical and institutional context. The subjects we have chosen to discuss have more aspects than can be conceived or expressed here. Yet we believe that what we have chosen to discuss represents key problems in human existence as well as the central thrust of the classical periods of these two traditions. If anyone is distressed by the lack of emphasis on currently popularized theologies, we can only say that the present journalistic debates are not theology so much as the raw material out of which new theologies may arise. But in any case we would insist that they make no sense apart from an understanding of their historical roots.

The second element in our method is interpretation. This is apparent and inevitable in two ways. The selection of the subject matter and the way it is organized means that some interpretive principle is in operation. But beyond that we have tried to penetrate to the original intention of the ideas we discuss in the hope that we could then translate them into intelligible terms for the modern reader. Obviously, there is some risk in so doing, because the original ideas were formulated in a universe of discourse vastly different from the one which has been operative for us since the eighteenth century. This is only a dramatic illustration of the point we have made before. Revealing ideas can be known only in the categories of our own time and always in the concrete situation of man's life and understanding. If there are any absolute ideas they are always expressed in "earthen vessels," and must be re-expressed in every age. That is why the notion of finality must be abandoned.

Third, our method is comparative in the sense that it places the traditions of Judaism, Roman Catholicism, and Protestantism side by side. If the book has any distinctive quality it consists in this. Most books treat these traditions as discrete entities. To see their interrelationships one must read and compare at least three books. In this book the reader should become aware of the vast gulfs that separate these biblical religions, and yet discover their common ground and common documents. To overemphasize one at the expense of the other would be a serious mistake, however. From the inside the differences are all too apparent, while from the outside the two religions must appear as one. It may even be true that basic religious ideas appear in different guises in all the great world religions. Yet each system of thought and practice has its own texture and pattern, each tradition its own perspectives. Doubtless there is much that all have in common; certainly there is great differentiation. To ignore these differences is to overlook deep cleavages which existed in the past and to assume a similarity of outlook and doctrine which does not exist in the present.

The common sources and divergencies of Judaism and Christianity are determining factors in the history of their relationships to each other and to western culture. The thoughtful reader will become aware of amazing differences and similarities and sensitive to the fact that, among thinking men, these agreements and disagreements are not confined to institutional boundaries. He will see how some questions could arise in one tradition at a particular time and not in others, an illustration of the fundamental insight that given expressions of thought are possible only in given historical periods and cultures.

There are two conscious omissions. Certainly both Eastern Orthodoxy and Islam can lay claim to being biblical religions. On grounds of space and competence we have omitted discussion of Orthodoxy beyond historical mention. For those same reasons and one other Islam is not discussed. Our concentration has been on the west, with all the limitations that implies. We are aware of some of the contributions of Islam to western culture and religion, but among scholars there is some question whether the Islam can be discussed fairly as a western tradition. In any case, it deserves and demands much more space and competence than we can muster.

One final word. In writing this book we have become more vividly than ever aware of the ways in which Judaism and Christianity have penetrated the intellectual tradition of the west, and how alive they continue in the contemporary world. They have made history, and are still vibrantly relevant to the direction of the contemporary period. We hope that this book will serve to open a small aperture on some of the wisdom and insight of these ancient and classical traditions to members of a new generation who are in search of freedom, identity, and peace, and who will themselves be guiding future history. For this may be the generation of whom David Frishman wrote,

> . . . there will arise a new generation,
> A generation that will understand the meaning of redemption,
> A generation that will be redeemed.[7]

NOTES

1. Alfred North Whitehead, *Adventure of Ideas* (New York: Macmillan, 1933), p. 221.
2. Sidney E. Mead, *The Lively Experiment* (New York: Harper, 1963), p. 75. Copyright © 1963 Sidney E. Mead.
3. Alfred North Whitehead, *Religion in the Making* (Cambridge: Cambridge University Press, 1927), p. 47.
4. A. J. Heschel, *The Insecurity of Freedom* (New York: Farrar, Straus and Giroux, Noonday Press, 1967), p. 117.
5. Ludwig Feuerbach, *The Essence of Christianity*, trans. George Eliot (New York: Harper, 1957), p. 122.
6. Blaise Pascal, *Pensées* (New York: Random House, 1964), No. 347, p. 116.
7. Cited by Benjamin M. Kahn, "Freedom and Identity: The Challenge of Modernity," in *Tradition as Idea and Contemporary Experience* (Washington: B'nai B'rith Hillel Foundations, 1963), p. 12.

I

The Meaning of Religion

OUR study of religion in this chapter will be limited to an analysis of its meaning within the context of the Jewish-Christian traditions. In this analysis we shall consider some of the difficulties and complexities encountered in any definitions of religion, noting briefly some of the more representative definitions of religion that have been offered. The subjective and objective aspects of the meaning of religion will be set forth and developed, as well as the relation of religion to history and a somewhat detailed exposition of theology and its place in religion. Finally, a further clarification of the meaning of religion will follow from certain distinctions drawn between religion and philosophy, and religion and the natural and social sciences.

"Religion," like "democracy," is one of those words in our language of which all of us would profess to have some knowledge, but which we would find difficult to explain in a formal definition, that is, to express in a proposition the precise nature of our subject. Many of us would probably be more inclined to say, as did St. Augustine when asked for the meaning of "time," "if you do not ask me, I know." Whitehead reminds us that definitions come at the end of an investigation rather than at the beginning. And logicians and philosophers have considered it to be one of their purposes to substitute clarity for vagueness in our language. Assuming, then, that the word "religion" is vague, our procedure will be to eliminate as much vagueness as possible from its meaning. Any initial definitions offered may be treated as practical guidelines which will enable us to arrive at a more precise and descriptive account of the nature of our subject.

We must also observe that the diversity of religious beliefs held by man is matched only by the equal diversity that men so often give to the meaning of religion. Certainly it would be extremely difficult to obtain a general agreement upon any one formula for religion. Part of the difficulty in arriving at any general agreement is enhanced by the fact that religion is a very complex phenomenon, so closely related to the labyrinthian patterns and varieties of culture through which it is expressed that some have doubted whether there is any single phenomenon, type of experience, or ideological set of expressions that can be determinately and exclusively designated as "religion." What we shall attempt here is a description of religion as something unique and autonomous rather than the expression of some related discipline or a subordinate part of that discipline, such as for example, "religious philosophy" or "sociology of religion." Our task is a difficult one because religion is a pervasive human experience integral to the cultural framework of a given society; it is something social, it has a language of its own, it possesses a history, it originates in different ways, and it is a reflection of certain types of man's experience. To single out, then, that form of experience which is uniquely religious and that conceptual complex that is uniquely religious is not an easy task. Although the task is not necessarily lightened by beginning with definitions, at least a beginning may be made. Perhaps out of the contrasting definitions, the ambiguities, and the vagueness, we can successfully grope our way toward a descriptive account that will suit our immediate purposes and attain a more complete explication in the succeeding chapters of this book.

SOME DEFINITIONS OF RELIGION

ETYMOLOGICAL DEFINITIONS. Looking back to antiquity, one of the first definitions of religion is that given by Cicero: "Those who carefully took in hand all things concerning the Gods were called *religiosi*, from *relegere*."[1] Lactantius declares: "We have said that the name of religion is derived from the bond of piety, because God has bound and tied man to Himself by piety, since it is necessary for us to serve Him as Lord and obey Him as Father. Therefore, much better is the way in which Lucretius interpreted the name when he spoke of 'loosening the knots of religions'."[2] Augustine gives varying interpretations of religion, but he follows Lactantius when he observes that "Religion binds us [*religat*] to the one Almighty God."[3] Skeat, in his Etymological Dictionary, favors the position of Cicero when he notes that "religion probably has its source in *relego*, *relegens*, meaning attentive, studious."[4] St. Thomas Aquinas treats religion as a moral virtue and as a part of justice. He does not declare in favor of either of the preceding definitions but does declare that religion "denotes properly a relation to God."[5]

Taken in its etymological origins, there thus appears to be an ambiguity and an uncertainty concerning the meaning of religion. If we trace the word back to *religare*, we emphasize religion as a binding together. If we trace it back to *relegere*, the emphasis is upon careful and studious practice.

OTHER DEFINITIONS. In the West the term "religion" has come to mean a relationship between man and God, between the human self and some nonhuman transcendent entity, between the natural and the supernatural. In the East, such a relationship is more often described in terms of a "way." Thus we have *hodos*, or the way of the Pharisees. In the New Testament, Christianity is also called "the way." Buddhism is described as "the noble eightfold path," and the Japanese nationalist religion is called *Shinto*, "the way of the gods." *Tao* is Chinese for "way," and *Taoism* is a Chinese philosophy and religion based on the teachings of Lao-tse (sixth century B.C.). In the traditional Chinese notion religion means a guiding doctrine (*Chiao*). For Aquinas there is not merely a relationship to God but a purpose or goal implied in such a relationship. He stresses this aspect of the end of religion when he states: "Now moral virtues, as stated above, are about matters that are ordered to God as their end. And religion approaches nearer to God than the other moral virtues, insofar as its actions are directly and immediately ordered to the honor of God. Hence religion excels among the moral virtues."[6] Max Müller defines religion as a "perception of the infinite." Matthew Arnold terms it "morality touched by the emotions." Kant declares it "the recognition of our duties as divine commands."

These somewhat restricted definitions, and others like them, tend to single out certain aspects of religion. But in abstracting from the totality of phenomena that make up religion, they fail to yield the more complete description that would be desirable. On the other hand, there are some definitions that express perhaps more comprehensively some of the important characteristics of religion. For Paul Tillich, "Religion is the state of being grasped by an ultimate concern, a concern which qualifies all other concerns as preliminary and which itself contains the answer to the question of the meaning of our life. . . . the predominant religious name for the content of such concern is God—or gods."[7] This ultimate concern is present, Tillich maintains, in nontheistic religions or quasireligions directed toward the Brahma or to objects like nations, science, or a society.

Schleiermacher understands the religious relationship to be: "The consciousness of being absolutely dependent or, which is the same thing, of being in relation to God."[8] For Schleiermacher religion is fundamentally man's response to the relationships into which the whole of human nature is bound. It is a relationship that is given and best expressed by some inwardly appropriate reconciliation rather than through conceptual knowledge. Not that conceptual knowledge is lacking, but rather the relationship attains satisfaction in the religious situation of the creature who finds himself as a being whose existence at every level is implicated in the God relationship. Religion is thus an inevitable part of human existence, it comprehends the sense and the perception of the Infinite, an awareness of an Other upon which he is dependent.

Another, frequently quoted definition of religion is that given by Whitehead: "Religion is what the individual does with his own solitariness. It runs through three stages if it evolves to its final satisfaction. It is the transition. It is the transition from God the void to God the enemy, and from God the enemy to God the companion. . . . Thus religion is solitariness; and if you were never solitary, you were never religious."[9] These definitions emphasize the depth of the personal element in the experience and relationship that men call religion. In another work, Whitehead defines religion more fully as: ". . . the vision of something which stands beyond, behind, and within, the passing flux of immediate things, something which is real, and yet waiting to be realized; something which is a remote possibility, and yet the greatest of present facts; something that gives meaning to all that passes, and yet eludes apprehension; something whose possession is the final good, and yet is beyond all reach; something which is the ultimate ideal, and the hopeless quest."[10] This definition seems to catch up the paradoxes and ambiguities, the dimensions and complexities of religious phenomena in a most striking and adequate manner. Reinhold Niebuhr says of this definition: "The paradoxes are in the spirit of great religion. The mystery of life is comprehended in meaning, though no human statement of the meaning can fully resolve the mystery. The tragedy of life is recognized, but freedom prevents tragedy from being pure tragedy. Perplexity remains, but there is no perplexity unto despair. Evil is not accepted as inevitable nor regarded as a proof of the meaningless of life. Gratitude and contrition are mingled which means that life is both appreciated and challenged."[11]

For Judaism religion might be defined as "the knowledge of God" (*Da'at Elohim*). Such a knowledge of God finds its highest expression in the *Torah*, which may be taken more narrowly and literally as the Law given to Moses in the Pentateuch or more broadly and spiritually as the whole teaching of the Bible and the subsequent commentaries written upon it. Jewish religious teaching centers upon the Torah and its many precepts (*Mitzvoh*), for these are relevant not only to the individual but also to the whole social fabric of Jewish life. An excellent summary of religion is that found in Book 6:8 of the Prophet Micah:

> It hath been told thee, O man, what is good,
> And what the Lord doth require of thee:
> Only to do justly, and to love mercy, and to
> walk humbly with thy God.

Subjective Aspects of Religion

The various definitions and descriptions thus far given of the meaning of religion tend to emphasize or reveal primarily the subjective side of religion, which centers on the disposition on the part of the individual to acknowledge his dependence upon God. It emphasizes more man's emotions and feelings, his will rather than his intellect. It may issue in prayer and piety or in the theological virtues of faith, hope, and charity which express in one way or another man's acknowledgement of his dependence upon God, his love for God, and his aspirations toward God as the ultimate reality and the end of his existence. In a word, this subjective aspect of religion is caught up in man's religious response.

This response has certain qualities. First of all, it represents an experience *sui generis* in character: it is a religious experience—the human response to ultimate reality, to God as revealed. In a sense it is something that happens to men and to which they respond rather than something that men do. Tillich would say that man is grasped from beyond himself in such a way that the whole meaning of existence consists in responding to this object, and that this experience underscores the dependent, contingent character of existence. Tillich's point is reflected in a similar manner in Francis Thompson's *Hound of Heaven,* the opening lines of which are familiar to many:

> I fled Him, down the nights and down the days;
> I fled Him, down the arches of the years;
> I fled Him, down the labyrinthine ways
> Of my own mind;[12]

According to some, the initiative for the religious experience and man's response may be said to lie with God, for "we would not love God unless He first loved us." Others would say, "Seek Him where He may be found."

Historically religions are neither contrived nor invented. They happen as men respond to the reality upon which they are dependent. Such a response is the highest of all man's concerns. It is the worshipful awareness of standing in the presence of a mysterious reality—the Wholly Other —which overawes but at the same time fascinates and irresistibly attracts. The heart of the religious response is what Rudolph Otto terms the *mysterium tremendum,* the "numinous" which is accompanied by an utter sense of finitude, creaturehood, and dependence.[13] Confronted by such a reality, one is constrained to acknowledge its presence by a profound reverence called "religious awe." This combines responses of deep devotion and dread with even deeper responses of fascination and acknowledgement.

In his already cited definition of religion Whitehead comes close to describing the biblical understanding of the relationship of man to God: "[Religion] is the transition from God the void to God the enemy, and from God the enemy to God the companion."[14] By this he means that in the presence of the ultimate reality, the "numinous," man's first reaction is revulsion and flight. It is an unbearable experience for man to find himself face to face with an Other that is superlatively great and terrifyingly good. But the frantic effort to withdraw, to hide one's falsity and weakness from this searing blaze of truth, is swallowed up by an awareness that the Other confronting him is friendly to his deepest being. Hence, the God who appears at first as one's enemy turns out to be one's companion. This is the experience of *reconciliation* which is at once forgiveness, renewal, trans-formation, and rebirth, making possible the communion between man and the sovereign God. The initial *alienation* is overcome and the reconcilia-tion is made possible by the God to whom the individual responds. The result of an experience of this kind is an unreserved commitment called *faith*. This is more than mere intellectual belief. It more closely approxi-mates the trust we might place in a friend or a cherished cause. Such faith transcends all conditional commitments; it is a fundamental and complete reorientation of man's whole being. Achieved not merely by intelligence and good will but called forth by the transforming presence of the Other. The outward expression of such an experience of faith lies in acts of worship and devotion.

Second, this experience is pervasive. Religion is not just one aspect among the many aspects of life. Like the pattern in a mosaic, it is pervasive of life itself. Religion is not just a way of thinking, acting, or feeling; instead the whole person is involved to the depths of his being. In the religious response the totality of the human existence is involved. Religion is a complex rather than a simple phenomenon; it orients our behavior and taken in the full permeates our every action and thought. It may issue in the dedicated life, in the mystical way, in the unswerving faith and courage of the martyr. The religious experience and the religious response are re-flected in the various facets of a culture. Objectively such a response has political, economic, social, literary, and artistic implications and effects. In this manner it manifests itself in all aspects of human existence.

Third, the religious response integrates the complexity of human experi-ence and gives it meaning. Such a response is one of the distinguishing marks of the nature of man. Man alone of all creatures exhibits religious behavior. The religious response has something in common with the philosophical response. Both may raise such questions as "why am I here? What is my life all about? What is the meaning of my existence? What is truly real? What is the purpose of the world? Why is there evil? What is death?" Such questions are evidence of man's traits of self-awareness and self-transcendence from which the basic religious questions arise. Religion, then, is man's attempt to understand the ultimate meaning of his existence. Just how it differs in this respect and others from philosophy will be pointed out in the section on Philosophy and Religion.

Finally, we may observe that there are various objects that may be singled out for a religious concern. Any object invested with unconditional concern may be considered religiously significant. In the history of religion there is no object, no matter how bizarre or common, that has not been made the object of man's devotion and worship. As Luther puts it: "Trust and faith of the heart alone makes both God and idol . . . for the two hold close together. Whatever then thy heart clings to, relies upon, that is properly thy God."15 Feuerbach, in denying the reality and objectivity of any transcendent deity, declared: "*Homo homini deus est.*"16 By this he meant that the God of mankind is man and the worship of any divinity apart from man wholly an illusion. Such a belief in man or humanity as the only object worthy of man's religious devotion and worship is generally termed "religious humanism."

Whether this last type of religious concern can be truly identified with the meaning of religion is debatable. From the standpoint of the Jewish-Christian traditions such conceptions of religion lack many of the significant features of religion. For such conceptions tend to abstract certain qualities of the religious experience and to hypostasize them. Thus qualities found in the traditional conception of the religious experience, for example, enthusiasm, belief, fanaticism, and intensity of devotion, are identified with religion itself. Any object upon which such qualities are conferred thereby becomes a religion. We may, for example, describe an individual's devotion to the Nazi or Communist cause as religious. We may endow any form of nationalism with a religious meaning, merely because it partakes of that devotion, enthusiasm, fanaticism, and belief which are usually associated with religious behavior in the traditional sense. We can even speak of a religion of business, by which we would mean an individual's total and complete devotion to the world of business. The dedicated revolutionary, the ardent nationalist, the devoted humanist are all concerned with a certain kind of response by the individual, a concern for that which they regard as very real and all-important. Yet although we may describe their attitude as religious, it is diffcult to identify what they worship as religious in the traditional meaning of the term. Such forms of behavior are hardly consonant with Rudolph Otto's simple but quite adequate definition of religion as "the experience of the Holy." Certainly, "business," "Communism," "Nazism," "humanism" are not what is meant by the "Holy" no matter how intense may be the devotion and the belief. Finally, the error involved in these characterisations of the "religious" are due not merely to a kind of hypostasization of certain subjective factors associated with the religious experience, but also to an excessive concern with the response of the individual and an insufficient attention to the stimulus. Carried too far, this makes religion something purely subjective and thereby illusory in nature.

Objective Aspects of Religion

Whether we regard man as primarily a creature either of the will and the emotions or of the intellect, the response that man makes to a religious reality is not merely subjective. Eventually, his thoughts, ideas, feelings, and emotions must issue in certain forms of behavior. The religious response may be said to issue in the life of faith, the life of the intellect, and the life of the community. Although these categories may be logically distinguished, it is not to be thought that each is excluded from the other. Actually, there will be an overlapping that these three forms of response may take in the life of the individual. However, it is true that the emphasis upon any one form of response may be much greater for one individual than for another. The missionary and the mystic, for example, will have far less interest in the intellectualization of his faith than the philosopher or the theologian.

THE LIFE OF FAITH. In the expression of his faith the individual responds with worship and devotion. His life may be one long prayer, a religious life of contemplation in which every hour is marked out for divine praise and love. Or the overwhelming truth of his faith, the depth of his own conviction, may be transformed into the desire that others should enjoy the truth that he possesses. Such an individual seeks to convert others and to give them something of that love for God which he possesses so fully and feels so intensely. These expressions of the life of faith culminate in the life of the mystic or the life of the missionary. Following the moral imperatives of their faith, such individuals become saints.

Obviously, not everyone becomes a mystic, a missionary, or a saint. The expression of his faith by the individual need not require nor does it necessarily lead to such dedicated forms of the religious life. All truly religious men seek to follow the precepts of their faith, and to the extent that they do so they achieve a measure of sanctity. Similarly, one expression of the intensity of their religious belief is reflected in their concern to convert others to the faith they affirm. Finally, it is open to each individual to achieve something of the experience of the dedicated mystic.

THE INTELLECTUAL LIFE. In his intellectual life, the individual who responds to the religious experience with an act of faith must eventually give some form of explanation of that experience, either to others or to himself. The explanation he gives represents a conceptualization of the basic elements of that experience. It may consist in an attempt to explain by language and ideas the meaning of his faith and the nature of the religious experience. More ambitiously, perhaps, it may consist in the defense of his religious beliefs, in the development of *apologetics*. Again, the intellectualization of the religious response may lead to the development of *theology*, that knowledge about God—the object of his faith— that God has revealed. Finally, the concern of the individual may be directed to the establishment on purely rational grounds of what he has already accepted on faith—the existence and nature of God, the relation of God to the world and to man, in a word, the content of what has been termed *natural theology* and *theodicy*.

THE LIFE OF THE COMMUNITY. Finally, the religious response is manifested in the religious life of the community, for the individual and his experience is integrated with his membership in the social group. In the group certain characteristic forms of social expression are to be found. For the sake of brevity these may be characterized as *cultus, propaganda,* and *polity.*

(1) *Cultus* represents that form of organization or means by which the individual and the community may participate in the worship of deity. The forms of worship, the acts of homage to deity, may be many and varied, but all are designed to bring the individual into close relationship to his God. Verbally, the forms of worship may be represented by prayers, preaching, the singing of hymns, the reading of Scripture. The acts of worship may also consist in the performance of certain rites and cere- monies—acts of genuflection, the sign of the cross, bowing of the head, the silent prayer, and participation in the sacraments to name only a very few. All of these forms of worship and devotion are an expression of the faith of the individual and are representative of the liturgical life of the individual community, synagogue, or church. The sacraments, of course, are central in Christian worship, whether Catholic or Protestant. The nature of the sacramental act, for example baptism or the eucharist, is to effect a relationship between God and man, to bring man into the presence of God. Just how this is achieved, the precise meaning and function of each of the sacraments, and the differing interpretations of the sacraments will be examined later.

The employment of a liturgy can easily lead to an exaggeration of its importance. Undoubtedly certain forms of religious behavior—habitual ways of acting—can intensify our faith and makes us receptive to the acquisition of faith. In response to the question of how one might acquire faith, Pascal declared: "Endeavor then to convince yourself, not by increase of proofs of God, but by the abatement of your passions. You would like to cure yourself of unbelief, and ask the remedy for it. Learn of those who have been bound like you. . . . Follow the way by which they began; by acting as if they believed, taking the holy water, having masses said

"[17] Such actions Pascal believed create religious habits, they are occasions for faith, and they make the individual more receptive to God's grace.

One issue that emerges from these considerations is whether these ways of acting can be said to precede and create doctrine or to follow upon and reflect doctrine. Some historians of religion are inclined to accept the former interpretation. Among Christians, Catholics definitely accept the latter interpretation. Fr. Rondet states: "The Christian sacraments are not the result of a blind urge of the collective soul; they express the will of Christ, and even though later made more precise by the Church, this expression was from the first imposed on the mind and faith of pastors as well as of the faithful. But even when we remember this, it remains true that the liturgical life of the Church certainly implies a doctrine and indeed a theology."[18] And later in referring to the encyclical of Pius XII, he declares: "In the encyclical *Mediator Dei* Pius XII rejected a false interpretation of the principle, *Lex orandi, lex credendi*, showing that religious practice depends on doctrine and not *vice versa*."[19]

(2) *Propaganda*. In the nonpejorative sense, this term comprises those means by which the faith of the believer is extended, clarified, strengthened, and solidified. It includes *teaching, exposition, interpretation*, and *doctrine*. Extended primarily to the members of the community of the faithful, it is expressed in the education and spiritual nurture of the members of the group. Extended both to members of the group and to outsiders it may be regarded as *evangelism*. Addressed primarily to outsiders, it is embodied in *missionary effort*, in *proselytization*. There is some overlapping here, but in general the lines are drawn fairly accurately. Thus, propaganda includes *preaching*, and although preaching is an essential part of the Christian liturgy, it may assume a role of varying importance in evangelism and in missionary effort. Proselytization may run the gamut from such odd practices as giving the Saxon tribes shirts to persuade them to accept Christianity, to the more noble and self-sacrificing work of the medical missionaries. Teaching is also obviously embodied in education, evangelism, and most forms of proselytization. In Judaism the emphasis is more upon study as a mitzvoh and as a form of worship.

Teaching includes both the exposition and the interpretation of belief. In Judaism teaching has a place of central importance. It is especially well exemplified in the scriptural reading in the synagogue service and in the writings of the Talmud.

When teaching and its results issue in an accepted form represented by a structure of ideas accepted by the community, then we have *doctrine*. The development of such doctrine and its organization and defense is primarily the function of theology. Out of the controversies of theology and the development of doctrine may emerge certain formulations of belief that are regarded by the religious community as normative or obligatory for its members. Such formulations of belief are called *dogmas*.

(3) *Polity* represents the organization of the religious community. Through organization provision is made for the division of religious functions within the community. Thus religious functions may be entrusted to priests, deacons, elders, missionaries, rabbis, cantors, and lectors, among others. The polity of the religious community also provides for the continuity of the religious function, for example, ordination, or the laying on of hands. Through a religious organization an authoritative discipline may be provided by means of synods, councils, congregations, and hierarchies.

Two principal types of organization may be noted. One is the organization of the whole of the social community into a religious community. This is the pattern of *folk religions* in general as well as certain types of advanced religions, for example Judaism. In Judaism the term *synagogue* (from a Greek word meaning assembly) may refer to the building where Jews gather for worship or it may stand for any assembly or meeting of the Jews for worship purposes. In Christianity the term "church" (*Ecclesia*) may refer to the building in which Christians conduct their meetings, or it may refer to a group or aggregation of Christians. The latter sense is the more significant and admits of two distinctive interpretations. The Protestant interpretation is that the Church is invisible and comprised of all who believe in Christ. The Roman Catholic and Orthodox interpretation is that the Church is both visible and invisible, temporal and eternal. It is comprised here on earth of all who are its members, receive its sacraments, and obey its laws.[20]

RELIGION AND HISTORY

The objectification of the religious phenomena and the religious response always occurs within a particular historical context. As Eliade puts it: "Every manifestation of the Sacred takes place in some historical situation. Even the most personal and transcendent mystical experiences are affected by the age in which they occur."[21]

Judaism and Christianity represent particular responses to the Sacred, to a particular personal God, at a particular time and a particular place.

Whatever may be universally present in religion can be grasped only through an understanding of the historical identity of the particular religious faith that gives concrete form to the religious consciousness. Christianity, for example, is a historical religion in that it is the acknowledgement of God disclosing himself in relationship to the minds and hearts of persons who are related to the personal existence of Jesus of Nazareth. It is a divine disclosure occurring within a given historical time; it is the impact of the eternal in the instant of time, the presence of God in history.

Judaism has always possessed a very real apprehension of the manifestation of God in history. For Judaism such a manifestation takes its initial appearance in the covenant God made with the Israelites in which they are singled out as the chosen people of God. The close relationship thus established is further evidenced in such historical acts as the departure from Egypt, the wandering of the Jewish people in the wilderness, the triumphs of Judaism under King David, the captivity in Babylon, the return to Palestine. In all these historical events God is with the Israelities; and even in those instances in which it might be thought he had abandoned them, the belief of Judaism is that the events that followed were a punishment for their sins. For Christianity the whole course of the historical development in the Old Testament is continued and consummated in the New Testament. The events in the Old Testament it is believed typify and foreshadow the events of the New Testament. The coming of Jesus, the Incarnation, represents a fulfillment of the Law of the Old Testament, by which the grace of Christ completes that Law and gives it new meaning.

Thus both Judaism and Christianity recognize that their heritage of faith is defined by historical and physical boundaries occurring within a particular sequence of cultural histories. Acknowledging that the minds of men cannot comprehend the Holy of Holies, they nevertheless affirm that ultimate reality—God—appears in the very commonplaces of experience and that there is no history of experience without this ultimate depth or reference.

RELIGION AND THEOLOGY

Speaking in somewhat general terms, we may say that theology is the systematic and critical exposition, interpretation, and defense of what the religious believers or the religious community take to be the revelation of God. It is the knowledge men have of God through the act of God in revealing himself to man. Etymologically the term means simply the science or knowledge of God. Strictly speaking, theology is not any kind of knowledge one may discover concerning God. It is not a knowledge based upon the nature of things or a purely rational type of knowledge. Rather it is knowledge based upon God's revelation of the truth and the exposition and interpretation of that truth which is contained either in the Hebrew Scriptures and the Talmud which would comprise the basis of a Jewish thought, or in both the Old and the New Testaments which yields a Christian theology.

The term "theology" as we have been using it has no counterpart in the Hebrew language. It does not appear in the Bible or the Talmud. The greatest of the medieval Jewish writers are to be classified more as rational theologians than as theologians in the sense in which we have been using this term.[22]

Protestant Theology

For Protestantism, two main conceptions of the content of theology can be discerned in the modern period: (1) a theology concerned primarily with the impact of God upon man; and (2) one concerned primarily with the nature of man's religious response. The first is more closely akin to traditional conceptions of theology, in which the theologian's task is to expound and interpret the revelation of God to man as disclosed in the Old and New Testaments. This point of view was given a powerful restatement in Barthian theology in the first part of the twentieth century. For Karl Barth, theology is the systematic presentation of the Christian revelation and that revelation is the starting point of thought; the content of theology is provided objectively by an act of God Himself.[23] The second conception is represented in the work of Friedrick Schleiermacher at the beginning of the nineteenth century. Schleiermacher was influential in the development of liberal Protestant thought. Known as the "father of modern theology," he conceived the chief task of theology to be the systematic elaboration of the content of religious experience. The contribution of Schleiermacher was revolutionary for the time. He claimed that religion possessed a unique and independent nature, a valid and normative quality of its own rising out of man's experience of dependency upon God. Religion as the feeling of absolute dependence is the fundamental way of apprehending reality. A somewhat similar interpretation appears in the work of Nygren, *Religiost Apriori*, published in 1921. Nygren based his theological method upon that of Schleiermacher. To the extent that both men emphasize religion as a positive philosophical category, their conception of theology would appear to be closer to a philosophy of religion. This seems somewhat evident, considering Nygren's description of religion as "a necessary and universal experience, inseparable from the nature of man." Whether such an approach is to be regarded as stemming from religion as philosophy or religion *sui generis* is frequently difficult to say. However, the intention of such writers (and of many others within the Protestant tradition) in this conception of theology is to emphasize theology not merely as containing revelation, or based upon revelation, but as an essentially human response to such a disclosure. Both emphases are necessary. By and large, twentieth-century Protestant thought as represented in Paul Tillich, Reinhold and Richard Niebuhr, and others has been deeply influenced by both tendencies.

Theology, then, is concerned with the nature of the religious response and with the significance of the primary reality—the Word of God—that confronts man. Theological thinking is reflection upon and clarification of this experience. It is the disciplined and critical thinking of these men to whom has fallen the responsibility of guiding and vocalizing the common life shared by the believers. Just as philosophy has often been termed "the handmaiden of theology," so theology might be termed "the handmaiden of religion." An overemphasis upon the rational analysis of the human response to revelation leads to a confusion of theology with a philosophy of religion or philosophical theology. On the other hand, an insufficient emphasis upon the place of reason can lead to the destruction of theology and a reliance upon an irrational or blind faith. It is necessary to strike a proper balance between these two tendencies if theology as a science is to be preserved and made effective.

More specifically, Protestant theology may be divided into three main types:

(1) *Dogmatics,* or *systematic* or *confessional theology,* has for its primary concern the clear and articulate affirmation of what is believed to be true respecting God and man. On this point the philosopher Whitehead remarks: "The dogmas of religion are the attempts to formulate in precise terms the truth disclosed in the religious experience of mankind."[24] Schleiermacher called theology faith's descriptive science of itself. As descriptive theology it is the declaration in a highly articulated form of the faith of the Church in a particular age. It is the "science" that systematizes the doctrine prevalent in the Church at a given time. It is therefore the voice of the living historical Church with the responsibility of crystallizing the living consciousness of the church.

(2) Theology is also *interpretative* and *critical.* Theology as interpretative may study and set forth the meaning of Scripture and doctrine. As critical it performs the task of ecclesiastical criticism since essential religion can never be identified with any one denomination or generation but only with the entirety of all the genuine effects of the work of that tradition in history. This means a perpetual dialectic between the historical manifestation of the religion and the evolving canon of true religion by which the church and its theologians are guided. This sort of theology is sometimes

called *historical theology*; it seeks to display the development of belief current in any given age and to make plain the continuity of religious response and insight in the religious community throughout the years.

(3) A third type of theology is called *apologetic* or *philosophical theology*. The apologetic theologian seeks to make the fullest possible use of the competent understanding of the scientific and philosophical thought of his own age. He considers and makes use of the secular interests and presuppositions of those who criticize or oppose the faith of the religious community and of the common experience of men in all walks of life within and without the religious community.

One further development needs to be noted of Christian theology in general. As it has developed from thinker to thinker and from age to age in the life of the community, it has left behind it a residue of dogma or teaching doctrine. In Christian history this has come to mean authorized teaching—a body of officially approved theological statements that can serve as a norm for testing the continual process of theological development. Within any religious community whose members differ widely in individual experience and cultural backgrounds, there is bound to be a wide diversity of theological thought. When these different opinions come into sharp conflict, it is necessary for the *community* to decide what is normative as against inadmissible deviations. The usual agent in Christianity has been a council, assembly, or synod which have had to reach such decisions. On a world-wide basis these councils or assemblies have been ecumenical or universal synods comprising representatives of the Christian community at large. When a fresh dogmatic definition emerges from the deliberations of such councils, that definition comes to be the authentic landmark by which a future theological inquiry and construction can be guided. A dogmatic formulation of this sort is often called a *symbol* or *creed* or *confession*, adding nothing new to the thought of the religious community but rather defining the correct way of understanding what the church has already been accustomed to affirm. This task needs to be done anew in every generation. Building upon the heritage, each generation must articulate for itself the intention of theology as a whole. The long history of theology shows the constant correction of one generation by the next.[25]

Roman Catholic Theology

In the Catholic tradition any tendency to blur the distinction between theology and philosophy, to permit theological thought to transcend revealed truth and merge into a philosophy of religion, is restrained by the disciplinary role of the Church and by the long tradition within the

Church of sharply distinguishing between natural theology and dogmatic theology. Generally, the term "theology" taken without any qualification usually signifies that knowledge of God and divine things derived from a supernatural revelation and critically expounded and interpreted by trained scholars. Catholic theologians have customarily divided theology into the following groups:

(1) *Dogmatic theology* is concerned with certain theoretical truths about God and His relations with man. It embraces such subjects as Christology, the Trinity, redemption, soteriology, grace, the Sacraments, and eschatology.

(2) *Moral theology* is defined by Jone as "the scientific exposition of human conduct so far as it is directed by reason and faith to the attainment of our supernatural final end."[26]

(3) *Ascetical theology* is that branch of theology which is concerned with an exposition of Christian asceticism, with the practice of the Christian virtues and the exercises and other means of attaining Christian perfection. The *Imitation of Christ* by Thomas à Kempis and the *Spiritual Exercises* of St. Ignatius of Loyola are illustrative of this type of theology.

(4) *Mystical theology* is concerned with those acts and experiences or states of the soul which cannot be produced by human effort but are acquired by a secret operation known only by God. It strives for a pure knowledge of God by employing the active and passive purification of the soul, contemplation and the higher forms of prayer, and in general all the experimental means required to reach the ultimate mystical union with God in which the soul becomes one with God. It is well illustrated by *The Dark Night of the Soul* by St. John of the Cross. Sometimes mystical theology is identified with ascetical theology.

(5) *Pastoral theology* is a division of practical theology which is concerned with the qualifications and character of the priestly ministry. Its object is "to make priests 'the ministers of Christ, and the dispensers of the mysteries of God' " (I Corinthians 4:1). As such it naturally presupposes the application of all pertinent knowledge contained in the other divisions of theology, but especially of dogmatic theology.

In all these types of theology[27] within the Church there is still a diversity of opinion. More particularly in dogmatic and moral theology not every belief has achieved authoritative definition through the teaching of the Church. The formulation and clarification of doctrine, belief, and practice is a continuing process. This has been very much in evidence in recent times. A study of the achievements of the Second Vatican Council will reveal marked and sometimes radical changes in doctrine and practice. Considering the ever-changing climate of contemporary opinion, there will undoubtedly be many new pronouncements by the Church, particularly on the subject of moral theology.

RELIGION AND PHILOSOPHY

Philosophy and religion differ in their approach to God, in the means by which a knowledge of God is obtained, and in the nature of that knowledge. Philosophy begins with man or the universe; religion begins with God—as an experience and a revelation. For philosophy the approach is from man to God. The religious approach is essentially from God to man; it is God's activity in the world and in man that gives meaning to religion and creates the religious experience. For religion God is primarily a fact, a Person, the ultimately real. For philosophy God is an idea, a notion, a metaphysical necessity, an Absolute or an illusion.

The philosopher uses reason in his approach to God and he submits all truths, including those of religion, to a never ending dialectical inquiry and examination. The religious person relies upon the assurance and certitude given by faith. For the philosopher, faith is subordinated to reason, its truths are determined by reason, its insights clarified or rejected by reason. The philosopher's faith is a faith in reason—human reason. For the religious person, faith is a faith in the Divine Reason as revealed in the Divine Word. Hence the religious person will subordinate reason and philosophy at all times to faith, which is the ultimate arbiter of truth.

For religion the ways to God are manifold, for faith may express itself in diverse activities. The religious person relates to God through worship, prayer, sacraments, rites, moral behavior, church activities, etc. Religion integrates the whole being of man toward the attainment of God and a unity with God. Philosophy is largely restricted to intellectual activity. The philosopher is concerned more with the meaning of God, His existence and nature, as He is in Himself. Religion is more concerned with the meaning that God has for man. The approach of religion is existential rather than detached and objective. Philosophy has no cult, hierarchy, community, church, revelation, and authority by which religion effects and supplements more completely the relation of man to his God.

The philosopher's knowledge of God is more apt to be objective than experiential; it is discursive and limited in nature. Generally it finds expression in what is described as a negative theology or a metaphysics of analogy, the *analogia entis*. The philosopher may attempt to say what God is *not*, or strive to transcend anthropomorphic notions of God with a knowledge based upon the analogy of being. But either method of attributing abstract qualities to God lacks the intimacy of the knowledge of God that is contained in a profound religious experience or in the revelation of the Word.

Religion's knowledge of God centers around the paradox that God is most known and most unknown. He is most known because He has revealed himself to man in His creation in His Law and through His prophets; and more particularly for Christianity through His Son and in the Trinity. Yet even in speaking to man He remains "the hidden God," the *Deus absconditus* of the prophet Isaiah, YHWH the ineffable name of God which may not be pronounced by pious Jews. God is most unknown because of the infinite distance that separates Him from man and He is most known because He is immanent in the world. He is unknown because He is completely other than man, yet most known because through his grace He saw fit to create man in His image.

RELIGION AND SCIENCE

Etymologically the term "science" means knowledge. Traditionally it has come to be identified with certitude or necessary knowledge—for example that which exists in mathematics—or with the method by which knowledge is obtained. In either sense it has come to mean knowledge that is objective, precise, measurable, and demonstrable. Furthermore, it has been associated with certain methodological techniques, such as the laboratory and experimental verification. Perhaps the most important characteristic of science, especially in relation to our own topic, is that science is descriptive. It seeks to establish rules or laws which govern the behavior of phenomena. Science does not raise any form of normative inquiry; it is not concerned with values; it does not seek to show how things or persons ought to behave, but merely how they do behave. In contrast, religion is concerned with values, with the norms and the imperatives of the moral and religious life of the individual. Religion is prescriptive rather than descriptive. It states what an individual ought to do; it prescribes the rules which govern the conduct of the individual. Such rules or norms may be formulated in the religious injunctions of constituted religious authorities; or they may be made manifest, as in the Ten Commandments, in the Word of God. Such rules govern the duties of the individual toward others, toward himself, and toward God.

On the basis of these considerations it should be fairly obvious that religion is not a science. On the other hand, religion, or certain aspects of religious phenomena, or the religious life may be the subject of scientific studies. To illustrate this last point let us consider very briefly how such sciences as psychology and sociology deal with religious phenomena.

The *psychology of religion* has for its object the study of certain types of religious phenomena and their relation to human behavior. The psychologist may concern himself with religious conversions, mysticism, the nature of religious belief, or abnormal religious behavior. His research may be directed to the possibility of a correlation between religious conversion and neuroticism or between age and religiosity. Like Freud, perhaps, he may regard all religious beliefs as "illusions, fulfilments of the oldest and most insistent wishes of mankind . . . the universal obsessional neurosis of humanity"[28] which will be abandoned upon the attainment of scientific knowledge. Or, like William James, he may be more impressed with the reality of religious phenomena as evidenced in his famous study *The Varieties of Religious Experience.*

The *sociology of religion,* first developed in a systematic way by Max Weber, may be defined as "the study of the interrelation of religions and society with special emphasis on the typology of religious groups."[29] Wach adds that the sociology of religion is a descriptive discipline and that it can "supplement but can never replace phenomenology, psychology, or the history of religion, to say nothing of theology."[30] To the latter, he says, it leaves the norms and values which guide our lives and actions. More specifically, the sociology of religion would study such things as the function of religion in society, the social structure of religious organizations, the function of authority, the nature and different manifestations of the cult—family, racial, and national cults; the place of the seer, the reformer, and the prophet in society; and in general all the manifold interrelations between religion and social phenomena.

NOTES

1. Cicero, *De Natura Deorum,* II, xxviii.
2. Lactantius, *The Divine Institutes,* trans. Mary Francis McDonald. In The Fathers of the Church Series Vol. 49 (Washington, D.C.: Catholic University of America Press, 1964), pp. 319–320.
3. St. Augustine, *De Vera Religione,* 55. Translated by the authors.
4. Skeat, Walter W., *An Etymological Dictionary of the English Language* (Oxford: Clarendon Press, 1882), p. 500.
5. St. Thomas Aquinas, *Summa Theologica,* II–II, Q. 81, a. 1. Translated by the authors.
6. *Ibid.,* Q. 81, a. 6
7. Paul Tillich, *Christianity and the Encounter of the World Religions* (New York: Columbia University Press, 1963), pp. 4–5.
8. F. E. D. Schleiermacher, *The Christian Faith,* trans. H. R. MacIntosh (Edinburgh: Clark, 1928), p. 12.
9. A. N. Whitehead, *Religion in the Making* (New York: Macmillan, 1926, and Cambridge: Cambridge University Press, 1927), pp. 6–7.
10. A. N. Whitehead, *Science and the Modern World* (New York: Macmillan, 1958, and Cambridge University Press), p. 191.
11. Reinhold Niebuhr, *Christianity and Power Politics* (New York: Scribner, 1946), pp. 201–202.

12. Francis Thompson, *Complete Poetical Works* (New York: Modern Library, 1925), p. 88.
13. Rudolph Otto, *The Idea of the Holy*, 2nd ed. (London: Oxford University Press, 1952), p. 511.
14. Whitehead, *Religion in the Making*, p. 6.
15. Martin Luther, *Concerning Christian Liberty*, trans. R. S. Grignon. In Harvard Classics (New York: Collier, 1910), vol. XXXVI, p. 378.
16. L. A. Feuerbach, *The Essence of Christianity*, trans. Marian Evans (London: Kegan Paul, Trench, Trübner, 1893), p. 282.
17. Blaise Pascal, *Pensées*, trans. W. F. Trotter (New York: E. P. Dutton, Everymans's Library, 1941), p. 83.
18. Fr. Henri Rondet, S.J., *Do Dogmas Change?* A Faith and Fact Book (London: Burns and Oates, 1961), pp. 70–71.
19. *Ibid.*, p. 73.
20. A more complete account of "Synagogue" and "Church" and the differing interpretations of the latter will be found in Chapter 12.
21. From *Patterns in Comparative Religion* by Mircea Eliade, © Sheed & Ward Inc., 1958, p. 2.
22. For an excellent and readable restatement of his own theology, see Karl Barth, *Evangelical Theology: An Introduction* (New York: Holt, Rinehart, and Winston, 1963). Note especially Barth's emphasis on the "Humility" of theology.
23. Something of the contemporary Jewish position may be found in Arthur Cohen, *The Natural and the Supernatural Jew* (New York: Pantheon, 1962), pp. 301–305. Note especially his statement: "Theology is rather the science of sacred history. It sets itself but one task: to apprehend and interpret the presence of God in time and history" (p. 304).
24. Whitehead, *Religion in the Making*, p. 47.
25. The contrast between the Protestant and the Roman Catholic positions on the development of doctrine, the means for deciding what is authoritative in dogma, and the function of the community and the Church should be noted by comparing the thought developed here with that on the Catholic position as it is brought out more specifically in Chapter 12.
26. Heribert Jone, *Moral Theology*, trans. Urban Adelman (Westminster, Md.: Newman, 1951), p. 1.
27. Some Catholic theologians also list spiritual theology, speculative theology, positive theology, and historical theology.
28. *The Complete Psychological Works of Sigmund Freud*, trans. and ed. by James Strachey (New York: Liveright, 1961), XXI, 30, 44.
29. Joachim Wach, *The Sociology of Religion* (Chicago: University of Chicago Press, 1949), p. 374.
30. *Ibid.*

Select Bibliography

Augustine, St. *On the True Religion.* Trans. John H. S. Burleigh. Library of Christian Classics, vol. VI. *Augustine: Earlier Writings.* Philadelphia: Westminster Press, 1953.
Baeck, Leo. *The Essence of Judaism.* New York: Schocken Books, 1961. Paperback.

ELIADE, MIRCEA. *Patterns in Comparative Religion.* Trans. Rosemary Sheed. New York: Sheed and Ward, 1958.

GLAZER, NATHAN. *American Judaism.* Chicago: University of Chicago Press, 1957.

HERBERG, WILL. *Protestant, Catholic, Jew.* Garden City, N.Y.: Doubleday, 1955.

JAMES, WILLIAM. *Varieties of Religious Experience.* New York: Longmans, Green, 1902.

OTTO, RUDOLPH. *The Idea of the Holy.* Trans. J. W. Harvey, London: Oxford University Press, 1950.

SMITH, WILFRID CANTRELL. *The Meaning and Evil of Religion.* New York: Mentor, 1958.

UNDERHILL, EVELYN. *Mysticism.* London: E. P. Dutton, 1914.

WACH, JOACHIM. *The Comparative Study of Religions.* New York and London: Columbia University Press, 1958.

WACH, JOACHIM. *The Sociology of Religion.* Chicago: University of Chicago Press, 1944.

WHITEHEAD, A. N., *Religion in the Making.* New York: Macmillan, 1926.

GENERAL REFERENCE WORKS

A Catholic Commentary on Holy Scripture. London: Thomas Nelson and Sons, 1953.

The New Catholic Encyclopedia. Washington, D.C.: The Catholic University of America Press, 1967.

Encyclopedia of Religion and Ethics. Ed. James Hastings. Edinburgh: T. and T. Clark, 1908.

Encyclopedia of the Lutheran Church. Ed. Julius Bordensieck. Minneapolis: Augsburg, 1965.

HASTINGS, JAMES. *Dictionary of the Bible.* Rev. ed. New York: Charles Scribner's Sons, 1963.

Interpreters Dictionary of the Bible. New York and Nashville: Abingdon Press, 1962.

The Standard Jewish Encyclopedia. New-Revised. Garden City, N.Y.: Doubleday, 1962.

The New Universal Jewish Encyclopedia. New York: The Universal Jewish Encyclopedia, 1939.

HARTMAN, LOUIS. *Encyclopedic Dictionary of the Bible.* New York: McGraw-Hill, 1963.

II

The Historical Development
of Judaism and Christianity

IN this book we are primarily concerned with the varieties of the Jewish and Christian traditions as they are manifested in the contemporary western world and in particular as these traditions find their expressions in the United States of America. It is too often true that popular conceptions of religion in America recognize only three major faith traditions—Judaism, Roman Catholicism, and Protestantism—as the forms of religion in this country. Obviously this is a completely simplistic view of American religious thought, life, and institutions. The subtleties and diversifications are many. None—Jewish, Roman Catholic, Protestant, or any of the two hundred and fifty particular denominations—is monolithic in character, but is rather a composite of divergencies and manifoldness in doctrine and practice, cultural background and history. In no sense can the modern expression of these traditions be detached from their histories. While for the most part throughout the book we will be discussing the modern era, we will constantly be referring to the documents and forms of life and thought in the rich history of these traditions. However, in this chapter and in the one following it, we shall deal explicitly with their historical development.

Of religious traditions two histories can be written. One is the narration of actual fact which can be attested to by historical evidence, the narration of those political, social, cultural, and religious events which can be publicly discerned. The other is the history of meaning. The events are the same events, but their significance is understood from the inside, from the standpoint of a common memory or tradition. The historian as interpreter looks not only at the documents but at the contemporary situation behind the documents. So, for example, in Hebrew history there were many seminomads, like Abraham, wandering about the Fertile Crescent; this can be attested to by archaeological evidence. But there is only one "Call" to leave the homeland to serve God. There were other tribal confederations, but no other common conviction as at Sinai whereby a people covenanted with God. The historian must be concerned both with patriarchal legends as reflections of primitive history and with the significance they had for those who transmitted or recorded them. He wants to know how and why they were handed down.

Any "objective" history will record the fact of the existence of the Christian Church at the end of the first century of the Common Era, but the reasons for its existence are to be discerned within the Christian community; a scientific historian wants to discover the relationship of events or records to their primary environments. The primary environments of Judaism and Christianity are Israel and the Church, but neither existed in a vacuum. How did they influence the various cultures and in turn how were they modified by them and what is the basic core of the Torah or the Gospel underlying these changes?[1]

No history is simple or nonselective. There is always involved interpretation of so-called facts; and when interpretation is involved, there is a principle of selection, of necessity. Therefore, any history of Judaism and Christianity must not only take into account the external, historical evidence but also the evidence of the cumulative tradition[2] and the content of that tradition. The cumulative tradition is completely open for historical observation, but unless the content of the faith of that tradition is understood as well, the history will be seriously distorted. When we deal with biblical history, this problem is put in sharpest form. In the Exodus event or the Christ event, we are dealing with historical happenings for which there is very small historiographical evidence at best. However, it can be argued that the history of the Western world, and especially the history of Judaism and Christianity, cannot be understood apart from a thoroughgoing understanding of these events, however slim the historical evidence. Judaism and Christianity purport to be historical religions not only in the sense that they have a history like any of the world religions, but also in the sense that they take history seriously in insisting that the content of their faith and knowledge of God are associated with events that really happened in history.

This chapter deals with the historical development of Judaism and Christianity. It is an attempt at straightforward historical narrative in capsule form. It is a kind of précis, beginning as it does with recorded events dating back to the second millennium B.C.E. But the précis provides a historical locus for ideas discussed in later chapters. Here we trace Judaism from its primordial roots through successive crises until we see how modern Judaism was decisively affected by the beginnings of emancipation in the seventeenth and eighteenth centuries. We trace Christianity from its birth amid the cultural cauldron of the first century through the sixteenth century to the present day. The sixteenth century is the critical period of Christian history, for it determines the forms in which Christianity enters the modern era. This century marks the beginnings of Protestantism in its classical forms; modern Roman Catholicism was given definitive shape by the Tridentine Reform (Council of Trent, 1545–1563), a shape which underwent only minor change until the Second Vatican Council (1962–1965).

Chapter 3 covers the same ground, but now from a different perspective, from the inside, so to speak. It is concerned with sources and documents, the inner life, thought, and institutions of these traditions, with the "cumulative tradition." Here we trace "internal" history, how people in these traditions understood their relation to God and the world in successive generations; how their thought and life were defined, modified, and expanded, and why. In other words, it is an attempt at a history of meaning.

JUDAISM

The roots of contemporary Judaism may be traced from its primordial beginnings in Hebraism, beginning with the Call of Abraham (ca. 1750 B.C.E.)[3] (Genesis 12–50), through Yahwism and the giving of the Torah to Moses and the people (ca. 1250 B.C.E.); through biblical Judaism (ca. 400 B.C.E.) and the Mishnaic and the Talmudic periods (ca. 1st–5th centuries C.E.), through the Middle Ages to the beginnings of the modern period, which for Jews can be placed after the eighteenth-century enlightenment.

No history is simple, but Jewish history in particular is so varied and complex that it can scarcely be compressed into a portion of a single chapter. For one thing, we are dealing with a history of nearly four thousand years' duration and with people who have reacted and interacted with almost every cultural phenomenon of Western culture, for Jews have been dispersed through almost every culture of the world in the last 2500 years. Our interest, therefore, in Jewish history is not just with chronology and geography but with certain enduring ideas and motifs which have influenced Western culture. These ideas, of course, are religious in character, but a proper understanding of them requires some knowledge of the historical context.

The Biblical History

While the Classical Age of Judaism begins with Moses, it is said, and extends until the completion of the Talmud in the fifth century c.e., the first known Hebrew[4] is a nomad, one called Abraham, who with his family left the highly developed civilization in Mesopotamia around 1750 b.c.e. with one of the many waves of Aramaen migrations to settle in Canaan. This trek was to take him, his son Isaac, and his grandson Jacob from one end of the Fertile Crescent to the other (Genesis 12–50). Eventually, during the famine, Jacob's family migrated to Egypt, where, after enjoying initial favor under the Hyksos or "shepherd kings" (ca. 2214–1703 b.c.e.), they became slaves to the Egyptian Pharaoh. The stories of the patriarchs and ancestral fathers of Israel are steeped in legend, but they provide the prologue for the crucial event of Hebrew history, the deliverance from Egypt (ca. 1250 b.c.e.).

Under the leadership of Moses, a Hebrew of Egyptian upbringing, the Israelites, with a medley of other races, succeeded in escaping from Egypt into the desert (Exodus 1–18). After two generations ("forty years") (Exodus 19–Numbers 36) and a series of extraordinary events, they stood on the edge of Canaan ("the Promised Land"). Moses died and was succeeded by Joshua, who led the Hebrews in the initial successful penetration of Canaan (Joshua–Judges). Subjugation of the land was a slow and painful process lasting nearly 300 years until the establishment of the monarchy under Saul; and under Kings David and Solomon (1000–922 b.c.e.) Palestine became the Israelite empire.

Up to this point, we have been following the general lines of the traditional account as recorded in the Bible. Many would question the factuality of the patriarchs and even of Moses himself. The biblical account of entering the "Promised Land" is probably wrapped in folklore and legend. However, historical and archaeological scholarship[5] has thrown immense light on the biblical story. Enough evidence has been amassed to call for soberer judgments than the early enthusiasm of the proponents of biblical higher criticism had thought necessary.

In any case, we find in Palestine in the twelfth century b.c.e. a loose confederation of tribes each with its own chief, its priestly leader, sacred places, and traditions, occupying the hill country and unique from surrounding tribes only in religious cult. They worshiped a deity whose unpronounceable name was later written as YHWH. They also shared certain historical memories and traditions, although not all of them had taken part in these traditions. Their fathers had dwelt beyond the river Euphrates and had served other gods (Call of Abraham and the rite of circumcision). They had lived in Egypt and had escaped the oppressing power under the leadership of Moses (Passover), who had led them into a solemn covenant with YHWH (Sinai Tradition), who had in turn given them the land. It was the religion of Moses that had appealed to these seminomadic peoples and that proved to be the powerful centripetal force among them.[6] The power of this tradition is strikingly portrayed in Joshua 24.

At any rate, the Hebrew tribes developed an extraordinary sense of common destiny, and Moses is the central figure who looms as the first great prophet. He was not only important for what he was or did, but also for what later generations attribute to him.

Between the period of the conquest and the establishment of the kingdom the tribes were united by common shrines and religious observances and by a succession of charismatic leaders called "Judges." As the Hebrew tribes gained in strength and numbers, the need to consolidate their hold on the land was met by the creation of the monarchy first under Saul, then under David and Solomon.

The united monarchy lasted less than a century and was the first and last time that Israel appears as an important power upon the world scene until the middle of this century. Israel remembered the Kingdom of David, Jerusalem as Zion, the fortress city of YHWH, and the temple. These are the mighty themes in the people's consciousness, and ever after the Kingdom was thought of as a "golden age" and the Messiah as "the son of David."

Following the death of Solomon, the United Kingdom split into two kingdoms, north and south, Israel and Judah. Strategically located on the crossroads of the Middle East, these two small kingdoms became the buffer zone between successive ruling powers in Mesopotamia and Egypt and were drawn unavoidably into the power struggle. The northern kingdom fell to Assyria in 721 B.C.E., and the southern kingdom, after approximately one hundred years of vassal status to Assyria, fell to the Babylonians. Jerusalem was captured in 586 B.C.E., and the elite were carried into Babylonian captivity.

The historical importance of the period from David to the Exile does not rely on political history but rather on two striking developments. One was the development and the refinement of the ethical and moral traditions begun at Sinai, which through the centuries had been constantly revised and augmented, reaching its culmination in the seventh century in the book we know as Deuteronomy. The other was the rise of prophecy. Prophecy was a feature of Israel's life throughout its history. Moses was regarded as the prototype of the prophet, followed by such important seers as Samuel, Nathan, Elijah, and Elisha; but this movement was to reach its zenith in the eighth century, beginning with the writing prophet Amos and extending through the exile period to the anonymous prophet of the later sixth century B.C.E. whom we know as deutero-Isaiah. This unique phenomenon is native to Hebrew religion but flowers with amazing suddenness in this otherwise disastrous period.

The fall of Jerusalem is the great watershed of Hebrew history and religion. Israel ceased to be a nation in the normal sense, but it survived as a religious community. In 538 B.C.E., Cyrus, the Persian, the conqueror of Babylon, allowed the peoples who had been deported to return to their homes. The Israelites also returned, rebuilt Jerusalem, and resumed their way of life. The restoration took place chiefly under the leadership of Nehemiah and Ezra (ca. 50 B.C.E.). It is from this period that one can properly talk about Judaism, a religion differentiating a more or less discrete tradition. The walls of Jerusalem were rebuilt, and the second temple established.

If one looks for the motivation for the exiles' return, one cannot find them in the economic and political realms. One can only fully understand the attraction of Jerusalem in religious terms. The period associated with the name of Ezra sought to have the people renew the covenant which their ancestors accepted at Sinai, to purge the nation of the syncretistic practices they had acquired in the Exile, and to make religion effective in the daily lives of Jews. To accomplish these ends, the Ezraic period devised, developed, or strengthened three instruments which were to be important not only to Judaism itself but also to its two daughter monotheisms, Christianity and Islam. These instruments were the synagogue, the written scriptures, and the teacher of the Torah. The synagogue had developed during the Babylonian Exile as a place of study and fellowship. Ezra strengthened it as a place combining worship and prayer with instruction so that it was scarcely distinguishable from the academy. Further, there was a collecting and editing of the writings of the past, thus beginning the idea of a canonical system of scriptures, which was continued both by Christians and Moslems. The third element was the continuous education of ordinary people by two classes of scholars, the *rabbis* ("teachers") and the *soferim* ("scribes").[7]

In 332 B.C.E., Alexander the Great passed through Judea on his way to Egypt, and after two hundred years of Persian rule Palestine came under Greek control. When one of the Seleucid successors of Alexander attempted to impose the Hellenistic cultural uniformity upon Judah by suppressing Judaism, a revolution led by the Hasmoneans occurred. Under the leadership of one Judas Maccabaeus, the Syrian forces were defeated in December 165. He then cleansed and rededicated the temple in an event which is still commemorated in the feast of Hanukah.

While the biblical record breaks off at this point, the sequel to the revolt was the achievement of slightly more than a century of Jewish independence which was finally eclipsed by the Roman general Pompey in 63 B.C.E. After a century of great confusion, Jerusalem fell to the forces of Titus in 70 C.E., bringing to an end any form of Jewish national entity. A second desperate attempt at regaining independence under Bar-Kochba in 133 was brutally crushed. While the Palestinian Jewish society continued to develop for the next three centuries, its preeminence was rivaled and finally surpassed by the Babylonian community; flourishing Jewish communities continued in Rome and Alexandria.

Rabbinic Judaism

The earliest document of Jewish history, the Hebrew Bible, records the birth of the people of Israel and its slow growth into a small but cohesive ethnic religious group from the dim primordial beginnings with the patriarchs; through Moses and the Sinai covenant, which created a people; through the political development immortalized in the reign of David, which made Israel a nation. This was followed by the phenomenal prophetic impulse and the final development and codification of the Torah.

The period between 500 B.C.E. and 500 C.E. witnesses a new religious epoch. It is a period which thoroughly transformed biblical Israel and established postexilic Judaism upon later prophetic and Ezraic foundations. This metamorphosis was so thorough that its character remains practically unchanged until modern times. This talmudic or rabbinic Judaism is the abiding legacy to future generations of Jews throughout the world.

The Common Era

The century in which the eras divide is sometimes written about as though it were a very desultory period, when actually it was an age of great intellectual vitality marked by the proliferation of sects within Judaism and by the rise of Christianity.[8] The first century of this era is one of great historical uncertainty because the direct evidence available to us comes only from three sources which are naturally enough biased. These are, first of all, the early *Talmudic* writings, particularly the *Mishnah*, a code of law completed in the second century of the common era, and the *Midrash* and parts of the *Gemara*; secondly, the *New Testament*, which, while containing some anti-Jewish polemic, also preserves and places high value on much of contemporary Judaism; and Josephus' *The Jewish Wars* and *Antiquities*, which were published in the last decade of the first century.

Josephus tells us about four major parties in Judaism: the *Sadducees*, who had their origin in the temple hierarchy and formed the conservative and prosperous element of the Jewish community; second, the *Pharisees*, who were middle class, had a liberal interpretation of the Torah, and hoped to form a bridge between the ancient Torah of Moses and the requirements of the present; third, the *Essenes*, an ascetic sect about which we know more since the discovery of the Dead Sea Scrolls at the community of Qumran; and what he calls a *fourth philosophy*, probably meaning the Zealots, a group of very pious Pharisees who were motivated by an extreme hatred of the rule of Rome. Of the four parties, only the Pharisees survived in later rabbinic Judaism, the development of which reached its culmination in the Palestinian and Babylonian Talmuds, interpretations of the Mishnah, completed at the end of the fourth and fifth centuries respectively.

It is to this development of first-century Judaism that John the Baptist and Jesus of Nazareth properly belong. Their points of view must be understood in this light. Many of their concepts spring not only from the Hebrew Bible but especially from the interpretation and understanding of the Hebraic tradition which grew up in the period between the two Testaments. For example, the emergence of such concepts as the Kingdom or Reign of God, the Age to Come, the Son of Man, the Holy Spirit, and the New Covenant make this period extraordinarily important for understanding the development of Christianity. It seems entirely likely that John the Baptist belongs in some sense to the Qumran community, and that the teachings of Jesus owe much to the Pharisaic tradition. There is also the influence of the apocalyptic development in postexilic Judaism to which much of the New Testament owes its understanding of the coming age.

THE BEGINNINGS OF CHRISTIANITY
(ca. 25–125 C.E.)

It is against this background that Christianity began as a departure in the midst of an advanced and highly complex culture which would make any new movement composite rather than simple. Christianity began as a Jewish sect, centered in Jerusalem, and organized about a small group of followers of Jesus of Nazareth. It arose in Palestine first and developed rapidly among relatively unsophisticated people—in the New Testament they were called fishermen and not the intellectual elite. It presented itself not as an intellectual system but as a new gospel ("good news"). The startling fact is that within a hundred years Christianity became a highly intellectualized and disciplined faith of great proselytizing and organizing power appealing to the elite.

The exact historical facts are hard to ascertain. Whatever else may be true historically about the rise of Christianity in the first century, it is beyond historical doubt that at the end of the century there existed a Christian Church in most parts of the Mediterranean world claiming to have this new gospel. Why and how the Church was established is based upon the internal evidence of the New Testament. Apparently it grew up around the belief that Jesus had founded the new faith. This faith was centered in his life and death, and it was believed that he stood in the great prophetic line, speaking "as one having authority" in the manner of Elijah, Amos, Hosea, Jeremiah, and particularly deutero-Isaiah. To them, he spoke with the urgency of the apocalyptic seers, demanding speedy repentance and proclaiming hope for the downtrodden, because the reign of God was close at hand and the time was short; and apparently he believed that it was his mission beyond that of the prophets and the seers to usher in the new age as the suffering Messiah (anointed one) of God.

The Christian gospel had its rise in the recovery of Jesus' followers from the shock of their leader's death on the Roman gallows. There was an upsurge of confidence that he had risen and was alive, and the gospel and the vision quickly won over people like Saul of Tarsus and through them, at length, the Roman Empire. God was the gracious God of the New Age, long proclaimed by the ancient prophets but until now obscured. It was believed that He had shown Himself in a new guise, offering Himself freely to the whole world; that Jesus, as the Messiah, was the revealer and mediator of His love; and that though he had been crucified he was now alive by the power of God. In him, God was uniquely present; and thus, to a lost race, a new hope was opened which brought deliverance of death and entrance upon a new life "in Christ" initiating the kingdom which is just at hand.

Cultural Influences

To understand the character of early Christianity, however, it is necessary not only to understand the occasion of this new religious impetus, Jesus of Nazareth—but also to take into account the tributary cultural influences shaping the consciousness of his contemporaries through which his significance was to be interpreted. Four main cultural streams contributed to the form and content of early Christian life and thought.

The first was Judaism, which centered in its tenacious, distinctive monotheism: God was One, personal, transcendent, and the only God; the Torah was the revealed eternal word of God. Alongside rabbinic Judaism's characteristic interest in the affairs of this life, there were two special sorts of "otherworldly interests" which had developed among particular groups. First, there was the ascetic, contemplative way of Essene monasticism, which marked withdrawal from the turbulent scene. Second was the widely prevalent apocalyptic hope which had developed in late postexilic Judaism with special appeal to the underprivileged classes. Although the idea of the Messiah is anticipated in the classical prophets, this hope now proclaimed that a new age would come, the Reign of God would be made manifest against all oppressors through his "anointed one," "the Messiah," who would rule for God in righteousness, and the faithful of all time would be raised from the dead to share in the world to come.

But it was not only this Palestinian Judaism which led to the early development of the Church, but also Hellenistic Judaism. Its chief center was in Alexandria, Egypt. In the third century B.C.E. thousands of Jews had migrated to Alexandria, a newly established center of world commerce which was gradually succeeding Athens as the capital of Greek learning and Hellenistic civilization. Here the Jews had formed a community organization, speaking Greek and accepting Greek modes of life, and its thought represented a synthesis of Hebrew and Greek wisdom. The Greek translation of the Bible, known as the Septuagint, had become the authoritative sacred scripture of the Alexandrian and all Greek-speaking Jews; through this medium, the Jewish community had attracted many proselytes. It was in this atmosphere that some of the works later included in the biblical Apocrypha, such as the Wisdom of Solomon and the Fourth Book of Maccabees, had arisen. In fact, Jewsish-Hellenist thought at its best is represented by Philo of Alexandria (ca. 20 B.C.E.–42 C.E.), who tried to blend into a perfect harmony the Hebraic and Platonic thought that was to have great influence on Christian philosophy as it developed in later antiquity and the Middle Ages. This Hellenistic-Jewish thought of the Diaspora (Dispersion), influenced especially by Stoicism and Platonism, was the second main influence on Christian thought.

The third influence was oriental mysticism. While there was great conflict between Christianity and the mystery religions, largely of eastern origin, which fascinated the masses, they did have in common certain aspirations and certain practices. Among these were the quest for redemption from mortality and evil; a social fellowship in which slaves and free, male and female, were equal; the cult forms which centered about the passage of the seasons; the ancient figure of a dying and reliving God; and a fresh emphasis on individual salvation which was appropriated by virtual participation in such a god's death and rebirth.

Fourth and finally, Christianity was influenced by the practical discipline and genius of Roman culture, where personal morality was conceived in terms of responsible loyalty, and wherein authoritative social control had been wrought with insight and determination, epitomized by the *Codex Justinianus* (sixth century) which survived in both the East and the West for centuries as the Roman Law.

There was, of course, danger in this sort of amalgamation; and Christians had in the first century of the Church's existence the rather formidable task of differentiating themselves from the worlds of both paganism and Judaism, although they could never separate themselves entirely from either. For example, the early Christians discarded many of the cultic and halakhic (legal) requirements of Judaism, such as circumcision and food taboos, while retaining much of the morality of the Jews. They continued to worship the omnipotent, omnipresent, unique God of the Jews. From the Jews also they inherited the sacred books and the apocalyptic traditions. What they had assimilated of these strains they were to transmute into another religion which ultimately was to differ almost as radically from its sources as these sources differed from each other.

Thus it was that Christianity began as a Jewish sect and later claimed to be the new and true Israel. Beginning with the belief about Jesus as the Messiah, it now had become a religion about Jesus. For most of the first century, Christianity was indistinguishable from Judaism and was widely regarded as a Jewish sect. Judaism itself had been a religion of great missionary zeal, establishing synagogues all over the Mediterranean world, where there were both rabbinic Jews and Hellenistic Jews, or at least gentiles who had been affected by the message of Judaism. Paul, therefore, could use the synagogue as a place for his new message.

Through a successive series of persecutions, both Jews and Christians suffered martyrdom until Christianity emerged in the reign of Constantine as the quasiofficial religion of the empire.

During the first three centuries, the Christian community maintained a rather remarkable unity. However, from two directions there arose an urgent need to define more clearly what Christianity was. On the one hand, in order to recommend a new faith to Jews and pagans alike to whom the proclamations of Christians appeared either repellent or unintelligible, there was need for some common terms of discourse in the interest of mutual understanding and persuasion. Christianity had also to defend itself against the kind of hostile criticism and slander which is commonly experienced by an aggressive minority. This type of need brought forth the martyrs who simply witnessed to the true faith and the "apologists" who wrote the defenses.

The second need arose from the diversity and conflict within the Christian movement itself, which made it necessary to define and to enforce at various points an authorized version of Christian teaching over and against deviating groups who arose either as sectarians or heretics. Often the point at variance centered on the degree of church adaptation to the non-Christian environment. There were, for example, Jewish-Christians who continued their intense monotheism and devotion to the law who found it impossible to put Jesus Christ alongside God and impossible to regard the Torah otherwise than binding upon Jews and Christians alike. There were also bitter anti-Judaists, represented chiefly by Marcion and the Gnostics. Third, there were believers in charismatic prophetism or millennarianism (best represented by Montanus) who maintained that the age of the Holy Spirit had come, that direct revelation by God was the standard of faith.

The Church reacted to these and other irregular verions of the gospel in two ways. First of all, it met their reasoning with better reasoning, and the best exemplars of the "apologists" are Clement and Origen of Alexandria; and second, it met these variant enthusiasms with more and vigorous reassertion of the original revelation. This latter mode of defense will be examined more fully in Chapter 3; but for now we can say that it consisted of the tightening of church organization and discipline, the establishment of an authorized canon of authentic scriptures, and the development of formulations which gradually crystallized into "Rules of Faith" (creeds, symbols, and confessions) which were to define at contested points the correct interpretation of Scripture and the Church's tradition. This line of defense was to prove so successful that the early heresies faded by ca. 300 from major rivals of the Church to minor sects and were shortly left behind by the mainstream of Christianity.

But within the main body of the Church itself, still further divisions were to break out which required much more elaborate and precise statements as to the being of God and the person of Jesus Christ. This development, combined with the development of the Roman Empire, itself would have fateful consequences. In 313, Constantine I, ruler of the eastern half of the empire, and Lycinius, ruler of the west, issued jointly a proclamation—the Edict of Milan—establishing a provisional pluralism granting the church legal status on a par with other religions. In 324, when Constantine became ruler of the united empire, he proclaimed Christianity the official imperial religion. Constantine undoubtedly hoped that this would be a move toward political integration; but if he thought that Christendom would prove to be the cement of the empire, he was sadly mistaken. Soon after his enthronement the so-called Nicene controversy broke out, and under Constantine the first ecumenical (world-wide) council was called at Nicea (A.D. 325). This council affirmed a doctrine of the Trinity which proclaimed the full deity of the Son and his partaking of one essential being with the Father. The council set a fateful precedent for the future treatment of unorthodoxy as a political and not merely an ecclesiastical offense. Although there was near unanimity, the conflict continued and was not officially resolved until the Council of Chalcedon in A.D. 451. This council defined the authoritative doctrine of the nature of Christ (the "two natures" dogma). However, the controversy was to be continued in the east for another two hundred years, and the Latin Church was thereafter to follow a course of development of its own.

It may be useful to pause here to consider this development. It is customary to refer to *one* Church based on the dogmatic definitions of the first seven ecumenical councils. Actually, however, the present fragmentation of Christendom occurred in three stages at intervals of roughly five hundred years. The first stage occurred, as we have noted, in the fifth and sixth centuries as a result of this dispute over the nature of the person of Christ and resulted in the separation of the Nestorian and Monophysite churches. This isolated the churches of Assyria (Nestorian), Egypt, North Africa (Coptic), and the Far East, particularly in India (Mar Thoma), from the rest of Christendom. In fact, until the development of the ecumenical movement in the twentieth century, these churches had almost entirely passed out of western consciousness.

The second division is conventionally dated A.D. 1054 when an official letter (bull) excommunicating the members of the eastern Church was placed on the altar of Saint Sophia in Constantinople by the legates of the Roman Papacy, resulting in the division of the eastern (Orthodox) and Latin (Roman) churches. But historians now recognize that schism is not an event which can be precisely dated. It came as a result of a long, complicated process starting in the fifth century, and the fourth crusade in 1204 left no doubt that the Christian East and the Christian West were divided in two.

This schism, however, must be understood against a wider cultural and political background, since cultural and political estrangement can all too easily lead to ecclesiastical disputes. As we have noted, the Christian Church was born into a closely knit political and cultural unity. The Roman Empire embraced many national groups with a great diversity of language and dialect, but all were governed by the same emperor. There was a broad Greco-Roman civilization which at least educated people throughout the empire shared. Either Greek or Latin was understood almost everywhere, and many could speak both languages. This cultural unity was a great asset to the early development of the Church. But the factors uniting the Mediterranean world gradually disappeared, and the political unity was the first to disintegrate. After the time of Constantine, while the empire was still theoretically one, there was actually an eastern section and a western section with each under its own emperor. The problem of disintegration had been furthered by Constantine's establishing an imperial capital in the east at Byzantium. Succeeding emperors never attempted to bridge the gulf between the East and the West, so that by the time of the barbarian invasions (fifth century) the political unity of the Greek East and the Latin West was destroyed and never restored. As a result of the rise of Islam in the seventh century, the Mediterranean passed into the hands of Arab kingdoms, and cultural, economic, and theological contacts between the East and the West became exceedingly difficult to maintain.

Cut off from Byzantium, the western church leaders proceeded to legitimize the *Holy* Roman Empire by crowning Charles the Great, King of the Franks, as Emperor in A.D. 800. Instead of drawing Europe closer together, the creation of the Holy Roman Empire in the West only served to alienate the East and the West as never before. While a certain cultural unity lingered on, it was greatly attenuated, and the patience of the east was sorely tried with the advent of the Crusades in the eleventh to the thirteenth centuries. The theological result of this severance was that the Byzantines remained within their own world of ideas while theological development took a basically different form as scholasticism in the West. So cultural and political estrangement led to the final ecclesiastical dispute, climaxing in the event of 1054.

Two principal things then—the divergence between political development and theological construction—resulted in the final separation on matters of faith. Following the barbarian invasions of Rome, the cultural, spiritual, and political life of western Europe greatly disintegrated; and it is a notable historical fact that the Roman Papacy was able to act as the sole center of unity, which gave great incentive to its centralization to a degree unknown among the patriarchates of the East. Organizationally, there developed a monarchical form of church government in the West, and in the East, collegiality: the Pope considered his rank as superior to that of the other bishops, while in the east the Primate of Constantinople was viewed as a "first among equals," as his title indicates. The second difficulty had to do with credal development and a dispute centering around the validity of the ecumenical councils. The eastern Church recognized only the first seven as being truly ecumenical.

The third separation of Christendom came with the religious and cultural upheaval of the sixteenth century in Europe; to this topic we will return.

The Development of the Roman Catholic Church and Its Faith (ca. A.D. 400–1300)

The content of western Christian thought at the end of the Roman imperial era was essentially Augustinian. When Augustine died in 430, the Gothic invasions had already begun. The form which he gave to Latin theology was in general outline the form in which it was to be handed down to the high Middle Ages, with great influence on Thomas Aquinas as well as on the Protestant reformers in the sixteenth century.

The empire did collapse following the invasion of Rome in A.D. 410; and of all the institutions, it was the Church which came through the transition with the least complete disorganization and loss of prestige. When Gregory I became Pope in 590 the Church assumed under his leadership the task of salvaging and rebuilding in the areas of economic, social, and political no less than that of the moral and religious life. Monasteries became the outposts of civilization in Britain and on the western European continent. Churchmen took on administrative responsibilities for the maintenance of food supplies and of law and order. In fact, the Church was on its way to becoming another empire. The coronation by Leo III of Charlemagne as Emperor of the new Holy Roman Empire was believed to involve the subordination of the temporal to the spiritual power. This was maintained in a special way by Innocent III, the great Pope of the thirteenth century. Under him the papal monarchy achieved its greatest height. The Church became a state with its own law, a bureaucracy, a financial system, and even a military arm to enforce his policies. By skillful use of the *interdict*, which denied to whole populations under unfriendly rulers access to the sacraments, Innocent III was able to prostrate monarchs like Philip II of France. With the help of the Cistercian monks he extirpated the Albigensian heretics. Later he launched a crusade against heretics which created precedence for the establishment of the Inquisition.

Religious advances were made in the meantime along two lines. First, a new Latin translation of the Scriptures had been completed in 400 by Jerome, and this version came to be accepted in the west as authoritative; and the Vulgate, as it was known, came to be for the Middle Ages the scripture in which the initial revelation was enshrined (just as the King James version became that for later generations of English-speaking Protestants). Secondly, two western councils were held. The Council of Orange in 529 affirmed Augustine's doctrine of man's dependence on God for his salvation. On summons from Pope Innocent III the Fourth Lateran Council met in Rome in 1215. It was attended by emperors and kings, rulers and envoys from East and West and nearly one thousand ecclesiastical representatives. Among its several enactments of importance, including the minimal rubrics of yearly confession and communion, the most fateful was its definition of transubstantiation as the new doctrine of the Eucharist. (See Chapter 10.) These dogmas took their places alongside the doctrines of the Trinity and of the Person of Jesus Christ which had been confirmed in the fourth and fifth centuries as binding on all believers.

Monasticism

One of the most powerful factors affecting the advance and development of the western Church in its early years following the breakdown of the Roman Empire was the monastic orders. It was the monks of the west who were to preserve the culture of antiquity and to assume the initiative in education. For the conversion of the barbarians and the general direction of its missionary activities the papacy relied upon the monastic orders. Frequently the spiritual zeal and example of the monks led to needed reforms in both Church and state. And certainly not least in importance were the practical skills developed and taught by the monks to the common people, especially in the field of agriculture. In this early period of the history of the church we have space to single out just three names of primary importance: St. Patrick, St. Benedict, and St. Boniface.

Much legend, fiction, and truth has surrounded the career of *St. Patrick* (d. 461). He has been termed Irish, English, and Roman. In all likelihood he was not Irish. What we do know with some certainty is that for a period of thirty years (432–461) he devoted himself to the conversion of Ireland, which became, by the close of the fifth century, one of the strongest Christian countries. The monastic discipline imposed upon the country equaled in austerity that of the earlier desert monks of the Orient. But the most significant aspect of St. Patrick's conquest and influence rested more in the culture he established in Ireland and the missionary activity he initiated. With respect to culture, it has been said that the Irish monks were virtually the only scholars in Europe who had a knowledge of the Greek language and civilization. With respect to missionary activity, in the sixth century the Irish monk, St. Columba, led in the conversion of Scotland, and St. Columbanus and his Irish monks prevented the decay of the Church in France at the hands of the corrupt French monarchs. Under the leadership of St. Columbanus, Irish monasteries sprang up all over France; and in 615 at Bobbio in northern Italy he erected what was probably the greatest of all his monasteries.

In this same period another and more moderate type of monasticism—the Benedictine—came into existence and was to prove even more extensive and influential than Irish monasticism. *St. Benedict* (480–543) renounced the world at the age of fourteen. After living alone for some time in emulation of the ascetic life of the desert monks, he eventually established monastic order at Monte Cassino. To this monastery he gave a Rule that soon superseded all others and formed the basis for future monastic orders, for example, the Cluniac and Cistercian. This Rule is still the spiritual guide of the Benedictine order. The success of St. Benedict and the rapid expansion of his order was due largely to his own practical wisdom and his realization that the ascetic ways of the desert monks could not resolve the spiritual and social ills of the time. Moderation was the keynote of the Benedictine Rule. This is reflected in virtually all sections of the Rule and particularly in the statement that *laborare est orare* ("to work is to pray"). Even the discipline exercised over the monks showed moderation. There was no absolute rule by the abbot; rather it was the "Holy Rule" of St. Benedict in all its impersonality that was to guide the organization and the progress of the Benedictine monasteries as they sprang up all over Europe in the next few centuries. Before very long the Rule of St. Benedict had replaced the Rule of St. Columbanus.

More than any others, it was the Benedictine monks who taught Europe agriculture and preserved the learning of the past by copying the ancient manuscripts. And in a corrupt and insecure society, the spirituality and the devotion of the Benedictines to the Christian ideal provided Europe the spiritual leadership that was needed. It was from the Benedictine monasteries and their missions that there emerged in the eighth century such men as St. Bede, Egbert, and St. Boniface. The venerable Bede gave England its first history and established the rule of the Roman Church in England. His pupil Egbert founded the school of York, from which was to come Alcuin, the intellectual leader of France in the time of Charlemagne.

St. Boniface, from the south of England, was one of the great missionaries of all times. It was he who was responsible for the conversion of Germany and for the reformation of the Church in France. As legate of the Holy See and later as Archbishop he established churches in Salzburg, Freising, Ratisbon, Passau, Erfurt, Wurzburg, and many other places. He was martyred by the Frisians in 755. He was buried at the abbey church of Fulda, which he had founded and which is to this day an important center of German Catholicism.

Finally, in the medieval period, notice must be taken of the rise of the mendicant or "begging" orders, the Dominican and Franciscan friars. These orders differed from the older ones primarily in their endeavor to lead less secluded lives and to associate themselves more closely with the people by bringing them the gospel through their works of charity and their preaching and teaching. The Franciscan order was founded by St. Francis of Assisi (1182?–1226), whose Rule was approved by the Pope in 1223. At first the friars embraced a life of absolute poverty, but this was found impractical and the rule was later relaxed. The order grew with astonishing rapidity and members such as St. Bonaventure and Duns Scotus were prominently represented in the medieval universities. But the order was best known not only for its missionary activity in the Middle Ages but also for the conversion of much of America. The Dominican order was established by St. Dominic (1170–1221) in 1216. Like the Franciscan order, it was at first a purely mendicant order. It differs from the Franciscan order in the emphasis it places upon preaching and teaching. Called the "Order of Preachers" (O.P.), it too had astonishing success and spread rapidly throughout all of Europe. In the universities of the Middle Ages it was represented by such men as St. Thomas Aquinas and Meister Eckhart. The order was also prominent in the Inquisition.

THE RISE OF ISLAM

The seventh century saw the rise of a new world religion among the tribes of Arabia associated with the name of Mohammed (570–632). Within a century this force swept across the southern shores of the Mediterranean and up to the Pyrennees. Mohammed was profoundly influenced by Judaism, although he had no great ability for sophisticated theological speculation; and in many respects, Islam was very close to the eastern version of Christianity. The *Koran* taught not only the Virgin Birth and Christ's freedom from sin, but also regarded him as the God-appointed judge of mankind at the Last Judgment. There appears to be no accounting for the spectacular spread of Islam and for the hold it maintained on the minds of East and West; but its spread, so far as Judaism and Christianity were concerned, was not an unmixed evil. Mohammed had been in contact with the Jewish and Christian cultures in Jerusalem and Damascus, and he was deeply impressed with both religions and apparently wished to restore to them their pristine virtue rather than to found a religion of his own. Jews and Christians both rejected his version of the faith. Although Moslem rulers did not grant them equality with those who submitted to Allah, it was acknowledged that Jews and Christians were not idolaters and so were entitled to be protected subjects; thus began a long period of religious toleration.

The expansion of Arab power had two important effects on medieval Europe. One was the intellectual revival brought about by the flowering of Arab Spain and Sicily, in particular; but through the medium of Arab culture not only science, mathematics, medicine, and logic came to Europe but also the science and philosophy of Aristotle and his Neoplatonic commentators which heretofore had been available only in Greek and only in the East. Through the medium of Arab culture, the Hebrew language played the role of intermediary between Greek and Arabic, and Latin, which was the language of Christian scholarship. During the eleventh, twelfth, and thirteenth centuries, we have the splendid spectacle of Jewish, Moslem, and Christian scholars working together in the academies of Cordova and Toledo in Spain, the most advanced centers of learning in the West, trying to harmonize the orthodoxies of the Torah, the Koran, and the Christian Scriptures with the philosophical and theological insights derived from Aristotle. This enterprise culminated in the intellectual endeavor known as Scholasticism. The Sicilian court of Emperor Frederick II (1211–1250), was also a center of studies for Christian, Moslem, and Jewish scholars. In the field of religious thought, they were working on the primary problem of maintaining a tenable conception of the relationship between faith and reason, or knowledge and faith, or between revealed truth and truth discoverable by sense perception and the operation of the intellect. From this environment sprang Maimonides (1135–1204), the great medieval rabbinical scholar, philosopher, leader of Jewry, and physician. His writings encompass all these fields. In the Christian tradition, scholasticism reached full definition in St. Thomas Aquinas (d. 1274) whose philosophical and theological synthesis of faith and reason marked the high point of scholastic thought.

The second effect of Arabic expansion was the stimulation of the Christian Crusades originating in France and organized to drive the Moslems from the Holy Land. The Crusades were to have an enormous effect on the West. In spite of their barbarity and destruction the contacts between the crusaders and the Saracens in the Holy Land opened up medieval Europe and caused it to turn outward.

Medieval Judaism

In the meantime, centuries-old Jewish communities continued to exist in the East, particularly in Palestine and Mesopotamia, although the most active part of Jewry had become European. As we know, Jews had lived in Rome from the second pre-Christian century and in Spain from the first Christian century, first under the Romans, then under the Goths, the Moslems, and the Christians. They were known all over western Europe. Economically, they had undergone a transition. In antiquity and in the early Middle Ages, Jews were predominantly in cultural and artisan groups. Now they concentrated on business, petty trade, and money lending. This resulted from legislation which largely forced them into the ghetto and made usury a Jewish occupation since it was outlawed for Christians. The relationship of Christian to Jew in the Middle Ages is not an edifying one. One will recall the restrictive legislation, the pogroms, expulsions, and above all the establishment of the ghetto by the Fourth Lateran Council in 1215, which also forced Jews to wear yellow badges on their clothing for the sake of identification. A whole series of persecutions and indignities were associated with the relationship of Christian to Jew in medieval Europe, chief among which is the Inquisition and particularly the Inquisition in Spain, which resulted in the expulsion of the Jews from western Christendom in 1492.

Obviously, a vast gulf separated Judaism from her daughter religions, Islam and Christianity; but in spite of all this, there was a common ground and in the case of Christians a common document of faith, the Hebrew

Bible. Despite their treatment of Jews, the Christians still maintained that Jews had a place in the universal scheme of things, and the aim was not their annihilation but their inclusion in the Christian fold. Jews held that the Christian rejection of Israel was temporary; and Maimonides saw in Christianity and Islam the fulfilment of the historic mission of spreading essentially Judaic ideas in the world.

While the medieval Jew was dedicated to the transmission of the knowledge of antiquity, as we have noted, and for evidence of which we only need to point to such figures as Maimonides, Saadia, Gabirol, and Averroes, his main intellectual effort was directed toward the cultivation of Israel's law, piety, and wisdom. Medieval Jewry rests solidly on the foundation of Talmudic Judaism. Its emphasis on community organization and institutions, the cultivation of family life, the discipline of the law, and the use of the Hebrew language for study and worship connected the communities in various parts of the world. At the same time, it preserved continuity with the Hebraic past, strengthening the consciousness of the continuity and unity of Israel. Finally the messianic belief expressed their patient hope of redemption.

SCHOLASTICISM

At this point we need to retrace our steps to look at a development of great intellectual significance to which we have only alluded. Scholasticism marks a decisive turning point in the development of western philosophical and theological thought. The rise of cities in the eleventh century was a distinguishing cultural development from previous centuries, and with urban development arose cathedral schools and universities. What is commonly called Scholasticism is simply a mode of thought associated with these schools. The members of these early schools engaged in controversy over such issues as universals and the relationship of faith and reason. With the introduction of Aristotle in translation, later, these men were divided by questions such as the nature of man, the problem of knowledge, time and creation, and again in a new form, the problem of faith and reason. What was going on in cathedral schools was also taking place among Islamic and Jewish thinkers, as we have seen.

Prominent among the early Scholastics were Abelard, Anselm, Peter Lombard, Hugh of St. Victor, and John of Salisbury. A century later we find St. Bonaventure, Robert Grosseteste, St. Thomas Aquinas, Duns Scotus, and somewhat later still, William of Ockham. Just to mention these names is to indicate a lack of unity in medieval Scholastic thought. For example, the teachings of Aquinas were bitterly opposed by many of his contemporaries as being much too liberal, even revolutionary. A century later Duns Scotus was a major opponent of Thomism. Finally, there was the rise of Nominalism, the "Via Moderna" inspired by William of Ockham, who attacked Duns Scotus just as strongly as Scotus had criticized Aquinas before him. While Scholastic thought did not represent a unified system of thought, it did present a reasoned and comprehensive explication of Christian theology and philosophy in defense of the Church and its dogma. When, as with the Nominalists, it was felt that there was no basis for a rational theological set of affirmations, the teachings of the Church were accepted on faith. As Ockham might say: the Church teaches this, therefore I will affirm it; the Scriptures say . . ., therefore it is true.

The thirteenth century is often regarded as the high-water mark both for papal prestige and for the medieval synthesis in theology. Certainly with Innocent III the papacy had remarkable powers. As we have seen, however, the synthesis was not as monolithic as is commonly assumed. There is no denying the great achievements of the century in many respects, but some historians regard it also as a time of intellectual stagnation; the style of writing and thinking becomes rigid in its question-answer dialectic, theological problems become narrow, and Aristotelianism usurps the intellectual currents.[9]

However that may be, immediately following this century there was a wave of reaction and criticism mainly along three lines. First was the erosion of speculative theology under a variety of attacks by the literary humanists and mystical pietists. Second was the weakening of papal authority by the practical course of events including the rise of a new town culture and the "Babylonian captivity" (1309–1377), during which the popes lived at Avignon under the surveillance of the kings of France. And third and perhaps more fatefully was the translation of the Vulgate into the languages of the common people.

DEVELOPMENTS SINCE 1500

The period following the "golden age" of the thirteenth century brought sweeping changes in any event, both from within and outside the Church, which culminated in the sixteenth century. A period of exceeding complexity, the sixteenth century was marked by the spirit of adventure which led to the discovery of the New World, the rise of mercantilism, the intellectual flowering of humanism which was to make for radical reorientation of ways and directions of thought; and it brought about the breakdown of Europe and heralded the rise of national states. These changes brought reform, both Protestant and Roman Catholic, and the further splintering of the idea of Christendom, both religious and political.

Religious reform was in the air. It had already been foreshadowed in the twelfth century by popular revolts against the Church led by John Wyclif, in England, and especially by John Huss in Bohemia. The rise of piety and devotion within the Church which brought a desire to change the Church by calling individuals to repentance was represented by Savonarola in the fifteenth century in his attempt to convert Florence. Others such as William of Ockham, the great Nominalist philosopher, called for conciliar reform—the convening of a general council; still others looked to the Emperor for hope; and there were the advocates of the new learning as a means of bringing about reform.[10]

Protestant Reform

The first phase of the Protestant Reformation was a break with ecclesiastical authority on several fronts, occasioned by Luther's attack on commercialization of indulgences, the wholesale peddling of papal forgiveness from certain divine penalties. In a series of pamphlets and sermons (1520–1524) Luther set out what were to be the major themes of the movement: salvation is by faith alone; the Bible as the Word of God interpreted by individual conscience is the only infallible authority; there is a priesthood of all believers; and the Christian life is a sacred calling in both secular and sacred spheres. In public debate he attacked Popes and councils, and rejected all but two of the sacraments. Meanwhile the movement quickly spread, led by Zwingli in Switzerland, Bucer in Strasbourg, Farel and Calvin in Geneva; to the horror of the mainstream of protest, radical left-wing sects declared a new age of prophecy, claimed new revelations, and made a radical distinction between religion and culture.

In many ways, the sixteenth century paralleled the first centuries of Christianity. As in the early Church, so now enthusiasts had to be met with sound doctrine of revelation, organization, and discipline. Luther, in his own person, was the originating genius, and his German translation of the Bible had a powerful influence as an authoritative basis for belief and conduct. But systematic definition of doctrine and discipline had to await the second generation and people like Calvin and Melanchthon. Calvin's two great achievements—the *Institutes of the Christian Religion* (1536) and the disciplined church in Geneva—greatly influenced international Protestantism and through its Puritan form left an indelible mark on Anglo-American culture. New churches were formed, avowing to return to the "pure" church and doctrine of the apostolic age, rejecting medieval scholastic doctrine and decisions. Pauline and Augustinian views on man's sin and grace were reaffirmed. The ancient creeds, and the decisions of the early councils became the basis for new confessions and catechisms which were framed as rules of faith.[11]

English Reformation[12]

The English break with Rome is usually attributed to Rome's refusal to sympathize with Henry VIII's marital troubles. While this is entirely too simple, Henry's divorce does stand as the occasion of the break, which makes English reform unique in that its first break with Rome was a political move. Of course, religious divisions on the continent were associated with territorial divisions, but the first move there usually came from the religious reformers themselves. It is further significant that England was the largest political unit to secede at one time, an act which was probably decisive for the success of the Protestant movements.

The background of the English reform must be seen in the efforts of people like John Wyclif and the Lollards, popular preachers, and John Colet, Thomas More, and William Tyndale, linguists and humanists who represent the demand for a fresh understanding of the meaning of Christianity based upon new and higher principles of morality and on the rereading of the Scriptures. There had also been constant pressure to anglicize the Church to fit it more particularly to the needs of England.

The Elizabethan Age brought the Anglican Prayerbook and the Thirty-Nine Articles of Faith, both amalgams of Catholic-Lutheran-Calvinist-Zwinglian elements, as the theological standard for a broad-based church, open to all save "Romanists" and radicals, and relying upon the Bible, tradition, and reason for its religious authority. Serious moves for reform were to come later with the rise of Puritanism.

Roman Catholic Reform

The Roman Catholic response to this revolt was slow at first, but by midcentury it had become a full-fledged counterreformation. Sincere and liberal Catholics led by men like Contarini and Sadeleto, desiring moral and doctrinal reform within the Church, made the first moves toward reconciliation, hoping to win back the Protestants. At a colloquy at Ratisbon in 1541, both sides came close to agreement on fundamental issues. The failure of the colloquy changed the temper of reaction thereafter, and counterreform began in earnest. Inquisitions censored beliefs, conduct, authors, and books and suppressed variant doctrines. New monastic orders were formed—the Capuchins, the Theatines, and especially the Jesuits under the leadership of Ignatius Loyola. These engaged in aggressive educational and missionary activities. The Jesuits became the most effective teaching order in Europe and after the Council of Trent had the task of advancing the decreed dogma and defending the faith. With the Conquistadores, Catholic missionaries brought both Christian faith and civilization to the Americas and Indies and established the first settlements in Florida, California, and New Mexico. Beyond that, their work extended to Africa and Asia. "Between 1493 and 1620 Spanish and Portuguese missionaries changed the Christian map of the globe."[13]

The Council of Trent (1545–1563)

Finally, the Council of Trent was convened by Pope Paul III (1534–1549) to meet the challenges of the Protestants and to effect its own reforms. It met intermittently during the next eighteen years. The Council crystallized as dogma for the first time the major tenets of Scholastic thought which had been challenged by Protestants, published a Tridentine catechism, and decreed moral and financial reforms. In particular there were decrees rejecting the Lutheran doctrines of justification by faith alone and the depravity of man as insufficient, and affirming the council's own views of original sin stressing both God's grace and man's freedom. It affirmed the equality of tradition and Scripture as sources of Catholic faith. The Latin Vulgate became the only authorized version of the Bible. Primary emphasis was placed upon the authority of the Church itself. Further, the decrees confirmed the seven sacraments and the value of indulgences, and restated the belief in Purgatory.

Without much doubt the Council of Trent represents a decisive shaping of Roman Catholicism. It stated clearly and unequivocally the doctrines of the Church and it launched a successful counterreformation.

Eastern Orthodoxy[14]

The eastern and western churches had been divided since the capture of Constantinople by the crusaders in 1204. Now in the sixteenth century, the Orthodox Church was established only in Russia, and under Ivan III Moscow was thought of as the third Rome. Elsewhere eastern orthodoxy was under the hostile rule of the Turks. There was still great antipathy between Latin and Greek Christianity, although in this century young men from the Orthodox Church did come to study in Italian universities; and through this means, some of the modes and content of western thought seeped into the eastern tradition, for example, the seven sacraments and the notion of transubstantiation.

The Protestants welcomed friendly relationships with the East. Greek students also came to Tübingen and Geneva, and there was talk of the possibility of uniting Protestants and Orthodox. In the seventeenth century, there were cordial relations between the Archbishop of Canterbury and the Patriarch of Constantinople, and students were sent to Oxford and Geneva. But the contact between East and West was minimal; and while there was great antipathy between the Orthodox and Rome, the language and ethos and doctrine of the Protestants always seemed somewhat strange, if not erroneous, to the Orthodox. It is a historical fact of some importance that the Orthodox Church was unaffected by both the Reformation and the Counterreformation.

Judaism

By the end of the fifteenth century, the Jews were confined in western Europe to the ghettoes of Amsterdam and a few places in Germany, France, and Italy. The major populations were concentrated in two groups, the *Ashkenazim* ("German") in Poland, where, since the seventeenth century the *Hasidim* (a sect of "pious ones") have flourished; and the *Sephardim* ("Spanish") in Turkey, Italy, and Salonika. The most important intellectual center of Judaism was in Safed in Galilee under the leadership of Joseph Karo (sixteenth century).

The turmoil of the sixteenth century brought more tolerance of Jews, partly because of the split in Christendom and partly because of the rise of mercantilism. But it is an amazing fact of history that they continued to exist as Jews at all. In this period they were accused by Catholics of being pro-Protestant, because the reformers went often to Jewish quarters to study Hebrew and Jewish interpretations of the Scriptures, particularly at disputed points. Protestants were at first friendly, hoping to win Jews to their cause. When they insisted upon remaining Jews, they were vilified as never before; some of the most vitriolic denunciations came from Luther's pen. But they were sustained as Jews by their doctrines of the Messiah and homeland and their community organizations and way of life. Talmudic Judaism, as the universal tradition, gave fundamental unity in language and life to isolated Jewish communities; and Talmudic education within the ghettoes flourished, although they were insulated from the new trends of life and thought and were scarcely touched by the Renaissance.

The Modern Age

How can we evaluate the sixteenth century? To Protestants, the Reformation meant the restoration of the true Church. To the Roman Catholics, the Protestant Reformation was a revolt (not to say blasphemy). Coming at the end of the Middle Ages, both reformations were largely medieval in character, but still revolutionary enough to set the stage for modern development. In retrospect, the sixteenth century for Christians represents the watershed between the medieval and modern worlds and provides the context for understanding the basic religious forces of the modern era. Politically and ecclesiastically the tensions created led to the "thirty years" war. Although this conflict represents a complex mesh of religious, economic, and political causes, the Treaty of Westphalia did establish the religious lines of modern European states as they have persisted for three hundred years.

The general upheaval of the century also set in motion successive waves of critical reaction representing fundamental transformations in human life and thought. These movements were to call into question not only the authority of the Bible as infallible revelation and the authority of the Church, but also the validity of revealed religion at all. The science which rose with Copernicus, at which the reformers laughed and which Catholics condemned in Galileo, was to become a metaphysic with Descartes and Spinoza, a physical and mental world of unbending law. Enlightenment in the eighteenth century exalted reason over faith and asserted man's ability to understand his world without supernatural revelation. Religious views and convictions would become matters for searching inquiry. The application of historical method to the study of religion in the nineteenth century, not to mention sociological and psychological studies, saw the Bible as a growing record of religious experience at various levels of culture. Also Judaism and Christianity could be studied in comparison with other religions, and the extent to which they share a common experience and common ground with other religions became evident as never before.

Protestant and Jewish thought was greatly informed by this variety of intellectual movement and change, especially by men like the philosophers Hume and Hegel, Locke and Kant. Roman Catholicism did not escape this influence. Its reaction can be measured by the publication of the *Syllabus of Errors* in 1864 by Pius IX and by the dogmatic decrees of the First Vatican Council (1869–1870), which demonstrated the depths of the Catholic breach with modern thought.[15]

After Vatican I and the reign of Pius IX, however, a new age for the Church was opened with the election of Leo XIII. Much more the modern, Leo XIII was keenly aware of the social and political changes and undercurrents of the time, and he was determined to establish the leadership of the Church in a changing world. He was not a liberal but he saw clearly that the Church must live with liberalism, understand it, and, more importantly, demonstrate that the real guarantee of the liberty of the individual lay with the teachings of the Church. Leo XIII is best known for his great encyclicals: the *Aeterni Patris* of 1879, the *Immortale Dei* of 1885, and the *Rerum Novarum* of 1891. The first of these encyclicals recognizes the leadership in philosophy and theology of St. Thomas Aquinas. The *Immortale Dei* sets forth the basic doctrines of the Church on the relation with the state and certain practical principles for the guidance of the individual in his relation with the state. The last of the encyclicals, the *Rerum Novarum*, is probably better known than the others, for it seems more markedly liberal. It establishes the basic Catholic principles of a social philosophy. It has frequently been invoked to defend certain labor union ideals, such as collective bargaining and the living wage.

For Jews the enlightenment (Haskalah) is the watershed of medieval and modern worlds. It meant emancipation and changed the character of Jewish existence. The intellectual, social, and political unrest following the sixteenth century helped some to break the confines of the ghetto but political emancipation was signaled by the granting of political rights in France in 1791. Emancipation, however, brought the disintegration of these cohesive forces of Jewry which had sustained the community for centuries, and the modern Jew was challenged to reconcile religion with changing conditions of the modern world. Germany was the birthplace of Jewish enlightenment in the eighteenth and nineteenth centuries. The extent to which Jewish thought flourished in this atmosphere is represented by people like Moses Mendelsohn in the eighteenth century and Martin Buber and Franz Rosenzweig in the nineteenth and twentieth centuries.

Religion in America

Roman Catholics were the first to come to the North American continent, but their influence in the United States was to come much later in the great waves of immigration of the nineteenth century. Small numbers of Jews filtered to the American shores in the seventeenth century, but again the waves of the nineteenth-century immigration were to bring new forms of Judaism to the American shores. Calvinistic Protestantism in its English Puritan form was the first religious orientation to make an indelible impression upon American culture in the seventeenth century in New England, followed by the Anabaptists and Lutherans.

This complexity of religious backgrounds provided a new religious situation in history and the development of a special type of religious pluralism. America has Protestant traditions in every shape and form, the largest and most creative Jewish community in the world, the fastest growing and the most disciplined Roman Catholic community. It is against this background of diversity that the basic ideas of western religions, particularly in their American forms, have to be understood.

We should also remember that if the Reformation and Counterreformation caused a seemingly irremediable schism in Christianity, sealed by the dogmatic decrees of Vatican I, Vatican II with its *Aggiornimento* has provided the context for the breaches to be healed in the twentieth century. Protestant and Catholic thinkers are in dialogue as never before, and Jew and Christian live in increasing orchestration. In this atmosphere, we must examine both the distinctive characteristics and the common elements of Jewish and Christian thought.

NOTES

1. See H. R. Niebuhr, *The Meaning of Revelation* (New York: Macmillan, 1941), especially Chapter 2.
2. See Wilfred Cantwell Smith, *The Meaning and End of Religion* (New York: Macmillan, 1962), Chapters 6 and 7.
3. We will use the traditional Jewish terms for dividing the eras when the context is Judaism or predominantly concerned with Jewish history and thought. B.C.E.—*Before the Common Era*, C.E.—*The Common Era*, correspond to the conventional western, and Christian, division of time: B.C.—*Before Christ*, and A.D.—*Anno Domini*.
4. For an explanation of the origins of the term "Hebrew," see T. J. Meek, *Hebrew Origins* (New York: Harper, 1960, revised edition), pp. 6–7.
5. See *The Westminster Historical Atlas to the Bible*, ed. G. E. Wright and F. V. Filson (Philadelphia: Westminster, 1956) for details.
6. See W. F. Albright, "The Biblical Period," in *The Jews: Their History, Culture and Religion*, ed. Louis Finklestein (New York: Harper, 1949).
7. This development is discussed in more detail in Chapter 3.
8. Actually modern scholarship is discovering that postexilic Judaism is both more creative and variegated than has been commonly supposed. While it is probably true that much of the creativity shifted from Palestine to Babylon and Alexandria, it is inaccurate to draw very sharp distinctions between Palestinian and Diaspora Judaism since there is some evidence for considerable interaction between the two. Moreover, Palestine itself was "Hellenized" during this period by the Greeks and the Romans. Likewise, Christianity profited more than we usually assume from the rich diversity of Jewish thought in the intertestamental period and later. Our description here probably does not do justice to this development since there is still much to be written. For a start, however, see F. M. Cross, Jr., *The Ancient Library of Qumran and Modern Biblical Studies* (New York: Doubleday, 1958); Arthur Darby Nock, *Early Gentile Christianity and Its Hellenistic Background* (New York: Harper Torchbook, 1964); and W. D. Davies, *Christian Origins and Judaism* (London: Darton, Longman and Todd, 1962).
9. See for example Gordon Leff, *Medieval Thought* (Harmondsworth: Penguin, 1958), Chapter 7.
10. For the study of the sixteenth century, see Owen Chadwick, *The Reformation* (Harmondsworth: Penguin, 1964); E. H. Harbison, *The Age of the Reformation* (Ithaca, N.Y.: Cornell University Press, 1955); Harold J. Grimm, *The Reformation Era, 1500–1650* (New York: Macmillan, 1954).
11. See Hubert Jedin, *A History of the Council of Trent*, trans. Ernest Graf (London and New York: T. Nelson, 1957). For a most interesting discussion of the

Council of Trent one should consult the rare work of Paolo Sarpi, *The History of the Council of Trent*, 1676. No publisher given.

12. See William A. Clebsch, *England's Earliest Protestants, 1520–1535* (New Haven: Yale University Press, 1964); Leonard E. Elliott-Binns, *The Reformation in England* (London: Duckworth, 1937); Philip Edgecombe Hughes, *Theology of the English Reformers* (London: Hodder and Stoughton, 1965); F. M. Powicke, *The Reformation in England* (London and New York: Oxford University Press, 1941).

13. Owen Chadwick, *The Reformation, op. cit.*, p. 321.

14. See Ernst Benz, *The Eastern Orthodox Church, its Thought and Life*, trans. Richard and Clara Winston (Chicago: Aldine Publishing Co., 1963); Jean Meyendorff, *The Orthodox Church*, trans. John Chapin (New York: Pantheon, 1962); Timothy Ware, *The Orthodox Church* (Harmondsworth: Penguin, 1963).

15. See Edward C. Butler, ed., *The Vatican Council, 1869–70* (Westminster, Md.: Newman Press, 1962); J. B. Bury, *History of the Papacy in the Nineteenth Century* (London: Macmillan, 1930); E. E. Y. Hales, *Pio Nono* (London: Eyre and Spottiswoode, 1954).

Select Bibliography

Bainton, Roland H. *The Horizon History of Christianity*. New York: Harper and Row, 1964.

Bright, John. *A History of Israel*. London: Student Christian Movement Press, 1960.

Chadwick, Owen. *The Reformation*. Harmondsworth: Penguin Books, 1964.

Daniel-Rops, Henri. *Jesus and His Times*. New York: E. P. Dutton, 1954. 2 vols.

Dawson, Christopher. *Religion and the Rise of Western Culture*. New York: Doubleday Image Book, 1958.

Dillenberger, John, and Claude Welch. *Protestant Christianity Interpreted Through Its Development*. New York: Charles Scribner's Sons, 1954.

Epstein, Isidore. *Judaism*. Harmondsworth: Penguin Books, 1959.

Finkelstein, L., ed. *The Jews, Their History, Culture and Religion*. New York: Harper and Brothers, 1949.

Guignebert, Ch., *The Jewish World in the Time of Jesus*. Trans. S. H. Hooke. London: Routledge and Kegan Paul, 1939.

Manschreck, Clyde. *A History of Christianity: Readings in the History of the Church from the Reformation to the Present*. Englewood Cliffs, N.J.: Prentice-Hall, 1964.

Parkes, James. *A History of the Jewish People*. Harmondsworth: Penguin Books, 1964. Revised edition.

Pedersen, I. *Israel, Its Life and Culture*. New York: Oxford University Press, vols. I–II, 1926; vols. III–IV, 1947.

Petry, Ray G. *A History of Christianity: Readings in the History of the Early and Medieval Church*. Englewood Cliffs, N.J.: Prentice-Hall, 1962.

Roth, Cecil. *History of the Jews*. New York: Schocken Books, 1961.

Schuerer, Emil. *A History of the Jewish People in the Time of Jesus*. New York: Schocken Books, 1961. Abridged.

SCHWARZ, LEO, ed. *Great Ages and Ideas of the Jewish People*. New York: Random House, 1956.

TAVARD, GEORGE H. *Protestantism*. New York: Hawthorn Books, 1959.

WALKER, WILLISTON. *A History of the Christian Church*. New York: Charles Scribner's Sons, 1959. Revised edition.

WARE, TIMOTHY. *The Orthodox Church*. Harmondsworth: Penguin Books, 1963.

III

The History of Judaism and Christianity:

Sources, Documents, and

Their Interpretations

EVERY major religion of the world has its sacred books, or scriptures. Hinduism has its Vedas ranging from the Rg Veda through the Upanishads ("very words") and its great epics like the Bhagavad-gita; the teachings of the Buddha are enshrined in Buddhism's Dhamma/Dharma; and China has the great classics of Confucius. These constitute some of the interesting and better known religious books of eastern religions.

In this respect the religions of the Middle East and the West are not different from those of the East. Judaism, Christianity, and Islam are religions of the book. Their basic document is the Hebrew Bible (Tanakh), which Christians call the Old Testament. In addition each of the biblical religions has added its own distinctive documents to the primary one, through the pages of which they read the basic document. To the Tanakh Jews add the Talmud. Christians add the New Testament to the Old Testament, and Moslems add the Koran to both testaments. These are the source books of the traditions. To tell the fascinating and complex story of how these books came into existence and assumed their present form; how they became the norm and standard for these traditions; how they have been interpreted through the ages; and the problem of their interpretation in modern times will be our purpose in this chapter.

BIBLICAL SCHOLARSHIP[1]

Most of our understanding of the Bible is due to the research of modern biblical scholars. It sometimes comes as a surprise to many people, however, to discover that such research has been the activity of centuries. Since the time of Ezra (ca. 400 B.C.E.) critical study has been going on. One need only take note of the early work of Origen, Jerome, Jean Astruc, and Solomon Rashi and especially of the work of the Masoretes,[2] who from 500 C.E. onward concerned themselves with the safeguarding and transmitting intact of the traditional text.

But it is only in the modern era that so-called biblical criticism has revolutionized our understanding of the development of biblical literature. Based on studies in comparative religion, cognate languages, and archaeological discoveries, and using the tools of literary and historical criticism, scholars have demonstrated the composite character of early oral and written traditions, their commonalty and differences with Near Eastern lore, the authenticity and accuracy of the texts, and the ways other cultural influences have shaped the beliefs of Judaism and Christianity and in turn have been changed by them. From these studies we have learned that the Bible is historical literature in the sense that it takes history seriously because the God it portrays is associated with events that happen in real life. Not that these events are necessarily empirically verifiable, objective facts. Much of the literature is at the level of myth, saga, and legend. The Bible is rather concerned with the meaning of events, and this meaning is understood in terms of the social forms and structures of thought and experience related to that time and situation; moreover, it is expressed and articulated in the symbols and language of the idiom current at that time.

The biblical sciences enable us to see how the religious life and thought of peoples and traditions develop from a preliterary stage through oral traditions to an authoritative literary deposit. To these we will now turn our attention.

Oral Tradition[3]

Biblical scholarship has established that much of the literature was doubtlessly handed down orally from generation to generation for a considerable time before any attempt was made to set it down in writing. This is true with most national and religious literature. It must be remembered that in ancient times writing did not play the role that it does today. For the most part writing was the work of a specialist, a scribe, who worked for commercial concerns in temples making lists, drawing up formal documents, and the like, and who was also needed in the diplomatic and political affairs of a nation. Besides this, most emphasis was placed upon the oral transmission of historical and literary works. This may seem impractical to the modern Westerner, a slave to the technology of the written word; but he contrasts greatly with the ancient Oriental, who had tremendous power of memory not debilitated by literary crutches. The oral tradition was exceedingly important to ancient Israel, especially for the worship of the tribes and for instruction of the young; and the period from Moses to David is the period of oral tradition par excellence. This importance is stated succinctly by G. Ernest Wright:[4]

> Plato once said that the invention of writing was not necessarily the greatest of all good things in human culture. When writing was invented and widely used it tended to "produce forgetfulness in the minds of those who learned to use it," so that "they will not practice memory." The biblical world was dominated by genuine, living oral tradition whereby everything worthwhile was known and transmitted orally. Writing was not considered an independent word of expression. Literature and historical traditions such as descriptions of legal practice (laws), were put down on leather or papyrus only when there was a crisis of confidence, when faith in the spoken word began to waver, when there was fear that all might be forgotten.*

It need not be supposed that oral tradition was the only source of information, howbeit very important. There are written "sources behind the sources" of which there are several fragments noted in biblical passages.[5] These fragments consist of the court history included in II Samuel 9–20 and I–II Kings, regarded by many scholars as one of the best examples of Hebraic prose in the Old Testament and at least as sound a history as the writings of Herodotus; there are quotations from "The Book of the Wars of Yahweh" (Numbers 21:14) and the "Book of Jashar" (Joshua 10:13); and in addition to these historical fragments, there are known fragments of national songs such as the Song of Moses (Exodus 15:1–19) and the Song of Miriam (Exodus 15:21), oracles, curses and blessings, oaths and lyric poems. Nonetheless, one can say that the period before the monarchy was a preliterary one.

> . . . the historical song and the historical saga exist as spontaneous forms . . . of a popular preservation by word of mouth of "historical" events; such events, that is, as are vital in the life of the tribe . . . The saga is the predominant method of preserving the memory of what happens, as long as tribal life is stronger than state organization.[6]

This is true not only in Hebraic culture. The Homeric poems were also transmitted orally for generations and, as we shall see later, Jewish rabbis

---

* From *The Book of the Acts of God* by G. Ernest Wright and Reginald H. Fuller. Copyright © 1957 by G. Ernest Wright. Reprinted by permission of Doubleday & Company, Inc.

committed to memory the traditions of the Mishnah centuries before any of them were written down. The materials of the Christian Gospels circulated orally before they became memoirs. Today there are Arabs who can recite the whole of the Koran or Brahmins who know the Rg Veda[7] by heart, in fact who have never actually *read* the Rg Veda at all. It is a process similar to this we are describing with reference to the oral tradition of the Bible.

The point of oral tradition is that the stories, myths, legends, sagas, poems, and hymns are units of verbalization which arose spontaneously out of a living situation. While we often assume that myth, legend, and saga have no historical authenticity, these have, as they are employed in the biblical story, a popular form which tell us something about history that is often ignored by the modern historian who is only interested in the literary deposit. Legend can often communicate to us out of the past-as-experienced the internal meaning of events and happenings in a way that "scientific" history cannot.

Historico-Literary Tradition

A thoroughgoing historico-literary analysis reached its peak in the nineteenth century following the pioneering work of Spinoza, who, taking hints from some medieval Hebrew biblical commentators, argued that the Pentateuch in its present form could not have been completed by Moses, and suggested that it was edited by Ezra some 800 years later. In the nineteenth century Julius Wellhausen expounded the now famous documentary hypothesis which has had a seminal influence on all subsequent biblical criticism. In substance the Wellhausen theory asserted that within the Pentateuchal literature four strands could be found: "J," so called because it uses JAHWEH as the name for God, compiled ca. 950 B.C.E. in the southern kingdom; "E," which uses ELOHIM as name for God, a northern document, ca. 750 B.C.E.; "D" for the deuteronomic source epitomized in the Book of Deuteronomy and including the Books of Kings, dating from the deuteronomic revolution in 621 B.C.E.; and "P," for the priestly editors or redactors ca. 400 B.C.E. These four strands, according to the theory, were collated to form one body of literature which represents at least four and probably more separate written traditions.[8] This thesis is no longer accepted uncritically by any scholar. However, most scholars believe the Pentateuch to be a composite of the various strands of traditions drawn from very ancient documents and oral tradition all collated, examined, elaborated, and given final form in a period which falls perhaps sometime during the Babylonian exile and not later than the time of Ezra.

The Hebrew Bible (Tanakh)

With this brief introduction to biblical scholarship as background, let us
now look at the entire literary deposit of the Hebrew Bible. The literature
preserved by the Hebrew community is traditionally divided into three
parts: the *Law* or *Torah* (Torah means instruction or teaching but it is also
used for the Pentateuch; for its broader use, see p. 83), which comprises
the first five books (Genesis–Deuteronomy); the *Prophets* (*Nebi'im*)
comprising eight books (Joshua–Malachi); and the *Writings* (*Ketubim*)
comprising seven books (Psalms–Chronicles). This collection is called the
TaNaKh, so called because this combination of Hebrew consonants represent the first letter of each of the parts (see Table 1, pp. 70–72).

When we look at this collection from a literary-historical perspective
it can be described in the following manner. The literary deposit of the
Torah extends over a period of a thousand years. Most scholars agree that
the first written document probably comes from the period of Solomon in
the tenth century. The theory is that there appear to be three documentary
traditions comprising the historical strands. First, there is a document
covering the early history from creation to the Sinai covenant known as JE,
presumably edited in the period of the Babylonian exile (sixth century
B.C.E.). Second, there is the deuteronomic history of Israel covering the
period from Joshua to the end of Kings and including the Book of
Deuteronomy (ca. thirteenth to sixth centuries), which appears to have been
completed somewhere between 600–550 B.C.E. Third, there is the history of
Judah compiled by the Chronicler(s) (First Chronicles-Nehemiah) working from the older sources and completed by the early part of the first
century B.C.E.

Then there are four large scrolls (Isaiah, Jeremiah, Ezekiel, and "The
Twelve" or minor prophets) which are collections of sayings or sermons
and third-person history by the classical prophets collected by their disciples and compiled sometime in the fourth century. The third section, the
Writings, consisting of psalms, proverbs, and wisdom literature, have been
collected between the third century and 165 B.C.E. The book of Daniel was
the last book to be composed. In any case by 200 B.C.E. the historical and
prophetic books were in their present form; and the final form of the
Hebrew Bible was probably established not later than 100 C.E.

The New Testament

In our discussion of the oral tradition and historical criticism we have
focused so far on the Hebraic literature and traditions. A similar process

can be applied to the Christian literary deposit. In New Testament studies the scholars move on from literary or source criticism to what is now called form criticism (in German, *Formgeschichte*). Form criticism discerns in the literary shape of the synoptic gospels (Matthew, Mark, Luke), for example, clear evidences of material which circulated orally prior to its precipitation in writing.

It must be remembered that Christianity, like Judaism, developed in an environment in which oral traditions were flourishing; that tradition was a living power among the contemporaries of Jesus and Paul. As in the Tanakh, there are many traditions of stories, some of them conflicting. There are references to "received" traditions in the Acts, Pauline letters, etc. which provide significant clues to our understanding of the early development of Christian thought. Paul, for example, refers to such a "received" tradition concerning the origins of the central act of Christian worship, the Lord's Supper (I Corinthians 11:23–25). Again he refers to the traditions he received about Jesus' death and resurrection (I Corinthians 15) which provide the first written evidence of stories about the resurrection. There are divergent traditions within variations of form and content. At the end of the first century, Christian writers continued to use sayings traditionally ascribed to Jesus, even though they do not appear in the written text. From this one can conclude that the Gospels were almost certainly based upon oral traditions about Jesus which were widely circulated. The apostles and disciples told stories about Jesus in meetings in the synagogues or in small gatherings; what we likely have in the Gospels are their memorabilia.

According to form criticism, investigation of the literature derived from this material transmitted orally gives us five basic types of literary forms.[9] There are the *pronouncement stories* (e.g., Mark 2:1–3:6); *miracle stories* (Luke 7:11–17); the *Passion narrative* (John 18–20, and in all the Gospels), the earliest and longest continuous material to take shape; legends, myths, or *stories about Jesus* (Matthew 4:1–11); and finally, the *parable* (Luke 19:11–27). These literary devices and received traditions constitute what the form critics call the *kerygma* (proclamation).

When we come then to the written literature, these many traditions are melded into a composite literature which makes up the New Testament. The earliest writings are the Pauline letters, which can be authentically assigned to Paul, but they include at least the following: I and II Thessalonians, Philippians, Galatians, Romans, Colossians, I and II Corinthians, and Philemon (Table 1).

A second group of writings are the "synoptic" gospels of Mark, Matthew, and Luke, which arose between A.D. 66 and 85. These are collections of memoirs, remembered sayings, and events of Jesus' life and teaching, death and resurrection. The Book of the Acts of the Apostles also comes from this period, probably written by Luke as volume two to the

Gospel. Mark addresses his book to the problems of the Roman Church, Matthew to the Jewish community, and Luke to the gentiles. The fourth gospel, the Gospel according to John, is probably addressed to the Hellenic Jewish and gentile communities ca. A.D. 90–100. The fourth group is the Catholic or Pastoral Epistles dated between A.D. 90 and 150. And the fifth group includes the Epistle to the Hebrews and the eschatological Book of Revelation written ca. A.D. 90–100.

Now we have a literary deposit, both Jewish and Christian, but this deposit and the canon are not identical. In fact many other books were written but not included in either the Tanakh or the New Testament. There is a vast body of intertestamental literature called the *Apocrypha* and other writings called the *pseudopigrapha* not included in the Jewish canon. This is also true of both contemporary books and post-New Testament literature. These are disputed books which were excluded when the concept of a sacred canon began to take shape.

Canon, Creed, and Cultus

We have already noted the radical change occasioned in Hebrew thought by the Exile and the Ezraic revolution in the fifth century B.C.E. In the late fourth centure B.C.E., Judaism entered its Talmudic stage, which was to be normative for a thousand years until the end of the fifth century of the Common Era. During this period, Judaism became an universalist religion preaching to and converting Romans, Arabs, and Greeks. This "change from the religion-of-one-people to the people-of-one-religion enabled Jews and Judaism to transcend the limitations of land, language, and even conflicting economic-political interests."[10]

This startling development, however, should not blind us to the very serious difficulties Jewish leaders faced. During this period the new ideas filtering into the tradition left their mark in the profound changes in the eschatological views, the new forms of messianic ideas, the doctrine of retribution, particularly the insights of the apocalyptics, and the development by the Pharisees of the doctrine of the resurrection of the dead. Scattered Israel no longer had a geographic center, in relation to which the unity of the people could be defined. The temple gave way to the synagogue, the prophet and priest to the scribe and rabbi. Scattered as they were throughout the empire, the communities of the Diaspora developed a kind of syncretism. Moreover, within Judaism there were conflicting traditions which had introduced uncertainties into the religious and legal practices. The conflicts can perhaps best be illustrated by the differences between the schools of Shammai and Hillel concerning basic laws and their application in detail. Furthermore, the young Christian community had appropriated the Torah as its scriptures, and from the Jewish point of view it was misinterpreting its implications.

Within the Christian community a similar process was going on. The Rabbinic Age is, of course, the Age of Jesus, Paul, and the early apostolic fathers. Both the Jew and the Christian confronted a world permeated by pagan religion and philosophy; each had to define what differentiated him from the other and to define his own distinctive understanding. For Christians, the period after Jesus' resurrection required a basically different mode of thought than what had been possible during his life. Now they focused on Jesus as the object of faith and the central revelation of God. In confronting Palestinian Judaism they had to define the relationship of Christianity to the validity of the law and the meaning of monotheism. Confronting Hellenistic Judaism they had to speak of the gospel as higher wisdom and nevertheless define Christianity and its doctrine of salvation by faith in relation to the doctrine of wisdom currently abroad in Hellenistic Judaism. Moreover, they had to define the true faith of Christianity in response to a variety of professedly devout Christians who held divergent views that were later to become heresy. If this proliferation of beliefs were allowed to continue unchecked, the distinctive qualities of Christianity would disappear.

It is against this background that for the first five centuries we note a remarkably similar process going on within both Judaism and Christianity. Judaism was developing its normative form, and the Church was beginning to assume its shape and forge its thought. The three principal aspects of this process we shall label somewhat cryptically as Canon, Creed and Cultus.

Canon ("Measuring Rod")

The Canon is the technical name for the books making up the Bible. (Table 1). It is a list of sacred books separated from other literatures and considered especially sacrosanct. The very idea of a canon is something new. The conception apparently was established during the postexilic period when the Jews in Babylon and Palestine were industriously collecting sacred literature, editing it, and seeking to live by it. In its present form the Hebrew Bible consists of thirty-nine Books (Jewish Publication Society), divided among the Torah, the Prophets, and the Writings. The Protestant version (The Revised Standard Version) also has thirty-nine books, while the Douay and Confraternity versions (Roman Catholic) have forty-five. Both Protestant and Roman Catholic versions of the New Testament contain twenty-seven books. The difference in the total number

TABLE 1

CANONICAL LITERATURE OF JUDAISM AND CHRISTIANITY

JEWISH TRADITION: THE HEBREW BIBLE OF TANAKH	CHRISTIAN TRADITION: THE OLD TESTAMENT
The tradition of the Hebrew Bible has been stable since the first century c.e. The authoritative Hebrew text is the basic Masoretic Text (MT) of Ben Asher.	The order and "long list" of canonical works of the Catholic Vulgate tradition derives from the Septuagint with minor changes. The Protestant tradition kept substantially the Vulgate order, but returned to the Tanakh's "short list." The Catholic and Protestant versions compared here are the Jerusalem Bible (JB) and the Revised Standard Version (RSV) respectively.

I. *Torah*

  1. Bereshith ("In the beginning") [1]
  2. Shemoth ("[These are the] names")
  3. Wayyiqra ("And [Yahweh] said")
  4. Bemidbar ("In the wilderness")
  5. Debarim ("[These are the] words")

II. *Nebi'im* ("Prophets")

  A. The "Earlier Prophets"

    6. Yehoshua (Joshua)
    7. Shophetim ("Judges")
    8. Shemuel (Samuel)
    9. Melakim ("Kings")

  B. The "Later Prophets"

    10. Yeshayahu (Isaiah)
    11. Yirmayahu (Jeremiah)
    12. Yehezqel (Ezekiel)

The Pentateuch

  1. Genesis
  2. Exodus
  3. Leviticus
  4. Numbers
  5. Deuteronomy

Historical Books

  6. Joshua
  7. Judges
  8. Ruth
  9.–10. Samuel I & II
  11.–12. Kings I & II
  13.–14. Chronicles I & II
  15.–16. Ezra–Nehemiah [4]
  17. *Tobit* [5]
  18. *Judith*
  19. Esther
  20.–21. *Maccabees I & II*

13. Tere Asar ("The twelve" "minor"[2] prophets):
   Hoshea (Hosea)
   Yoel (Joel)
   Amos
   Obadyah (Obadiah)
   Yonah (Jonah)
   Mikah (Micah)
   Nahum
   Habaqquq (Habakkuk)
   Zephanyah (Zephaniah)
   Haggai
   Zekaryah (Zechariah)
   Malaki (Malachi)

III. *Ketubim* ("The Writings")

14. Tehillim ("Praises")
15. Iyyob (Job)
16. Mishle ("Proverbs of")
17. Ruth[3]
18. Shir Hashirim ("Song of Songs")
19. Qoheleth ("Leader of the Assembly" or Ecclesiastes)
20. Ekah ("How"; Lamentations)
21. Ester (Esther)
22. Daniel
23. Ezra-Nehemyah
24. Dibre Hayamim ("Chronicles")

Wisdom Books

22. Job
23. Psalms
24. Proverbs
25. Ecclesiastes
26. The Song of Songs (Song of Solomon)
27. *Book of Wisdom* (Wisdom of Solomon)
28. *Ecclesiasticus*

Prophetic Books

29. Isaiah
30. Jeremiah
31. Lamentations
32. *Baruch*
33. Ezekiel
34. Daniel
35. Hosea
36. Joel
37. Amos
38. Obadiah
39. Jonah
40. Micah
41. Nahum
42. Habakkuk
43. Zephaniah
44. Haggai
45. Zechariah
46. Malachi

TABLE 1 (Continued)

THE NEW TESTAMENT

The canon of the New Testament was crystallized during the first two centuries CE and has been normative for all Christians since.

Historical Books

1. Gospel According to Matthew[6]
2. Gospel According to Mark
3. Gospel According to Luke
4. Gospel According to John
5. Book of the Acts of the Apostles[7]

Didactic Works

6. Epistle to the Romans[8]
7.–8. I and II Epistles to the Corinthians
9. Epistle to the Galatians
10. Epistle to the Ephesians
11. Epistle to the Philippians
12. Epistle to the Colossians
13.–14. I and II Epistles to the Thessalonians
15.–16. I and II Epistles to Timothy
17. Epistle to Titus
18. Epistle to Philemon
19. Epistle to the Hebrews
20. Epistle of James[9]
21.–22. I and II Epistles of Peter
23.–25. I, II, and III. Epistles of John
26. Epistle of Jude

Apocalypse

27. The Book of the Revelation of John

[1] From the first words of the Hebrew text.
[2] So called because of the length of the books. All twelve were included on one scroll.
[3] The books Ruth-Esther are the Megilloth, the "Festal Scrolls" of the High Jewish festivals.
[4] The RSV separates these two books.
[5] Books appearing in the JB that are accounted apocryphal (noncanonical) by the Protestant tradition will be italicized.
[6] The Gospels of Matthew, Mark, and Luke are called the "synoptic" Gospels because they see the life of Jesus with "one eye" (*syn* + *opsis*).
[7] The book of Acts is a continuation of the narrative of Luke.
[8] The Epistles Romans-Hebrews were accounted the works of Paul the Apostle according to ancient tradition. Modern scholarship has contested this claim.
[9] The books James-Jude are called the "Catholic Epistles" because they address the whole Church.

is due to the acceptance by Roman Catholics of the Apocrypha. The canonical writings are those records of revelatory events which are received and accepted by any given religious community as central and as containing, therefore, the heuristic (interpretation) by which the life of that community is understood. The interpretation of these books generates a standard (canon) based on their antiquity, authenticity, and etiological and other significance by which all other writings are measured and by which faithfulness to the community and its beliefs are judged. Thus there must be some internal consistency in the deposit which both determines and is determined by the historical community and which, in turn, provides the standard for shaping the community.

The crystallization of the Judaic canon apparently began in the time of Ezra with the formation of the Torah books. The Pentateuch is absolute, if informal, by the end of the fourth century b.c.e. The prophetic books apparently were accepted into the canon by 200 b.c.e. and the writings soon after 100 b.c.e. In any case, the text of the Tanakh was carefully revised and standardized by the rabbis at the end of the first or early second centuries. Any writings after that period would have been strenuously opposed and would not have met the test of antiquity. The content of the Hebrew canon was probably given its final form by a council of sages at Jamnia (Jabneh) ca. 85–100 c.e.

The Talmud[11]

Supplementary to the written Torah was a substantial body of oral Torah, some of it of great antiquity; in fact, it was regarded as tradition received from Moses himself at Sinai. According to the *Sayings of the Fathers* (200 c.e.), "Moses received the Torah from Sinai and delivered it to Joshua and Joshua to the Elders and the Elders to the Prophets and the Prophets delivered it to the men of the Great Synagogue." A traditional legend had it that God had revealed two sets of laws to Moses on Sinai. One, on tablets of stone, was later transcribed word for word into the Torah; a second one, of equal importance, was whispered to Moses alone. This oral law, which provided specific elaboration of the Torah, consisted of two parts: the *Midrash* (from the Hebrew, meaning to teach, to investigate), which was both a *halakhic* (legal) and *haggadic* (homiletical) exposition of the biblical text itself and, therefore, constitutes a form of exegesis; and the *Mishnah* (repetition), which was law and lore independent of any scriptural basis. This kind of teaching activity had been carried on orally for generation after generation, lest it be confused with the written Torah if committed to writing. But such a mass of heterogeneous material has developed that no memory could be trusted, and in the midst

TABLE 2

THE AUTHORITATIVE POST-BIBLICAL LITERARY DEPOSIT
OF THE JUDAIC TRADITION

I. TALMUDIC LITERATURE
(TALMUD, "TEACHING, INSTRUCTION")

A. *Tannaitic Literature*

Oral tradition (*Torah be-al-Peh*), some of very ancient lineage, accumulated
and enlarged upon by the rabbis, especially Pharisees, the so-called *Tannaim*
("those who hand down tradition") during the period ca. 300 BCE–220 CE.

Mishnah ("repetition"): a technique and curriculum of comprehensive instruction in the Law (*halakha*) carried on in the Hebrew language, grouped in *Shas* (abbr. for *Shishah sedarim*, "six orders") and subdivided into 63 Tractates and 523 Chapters, definitively collated ca. 200 C.E. by Rabbi Judah ha-Nasi, b. 135. The Shas:

1. *Zera'im* ("Seeds"): agricultural regulations and the disposition of products (11 Tractates, 74 Chapters).
2. *Mo'ed* ("Festivals"): of the various religious celebrations (12 Tractates, 88 Chapters).
3. *Nashim* ("Women"): defining the social and religious role of women (7 Tractates, 88 Chapters).
4. *Neziqin* ("Damages"): civil and criminal jurisprudence (10 Tractates, including the famous *Pirqe Abot* ["Chapters or Sayings of the Fathers"], 73 Chapters).
5. *Qodashim* ("Holy Things"): of sacrifice and consecrated persons and things (11 Tractates, 91 Chapters).
6. *Toharot* ("Purities"): regulations governing ritual purity (12 Tractates, 126 Chapters).

Baraitha ("the extraneous one"): Tannaitic, extra-Mishnaic materials, rabbinical opinions, etc.

Tosephta ("addition," "supplement"): Judean Tannaitic materials from the Mishnaic tradition, quasidependent upon Mishnah though less extensive; also divided according to Shas.

Tannaitic Midrashim ("commentaries," "explications"): halakhic exposition on specific sections of the written Torah, compiled by the Amoraim, especially:

1. *Mekilta* ("measure," "standard") on Exodus.
2. *Siphra* ("The Book [of the School]") on Leviticus.
3. *Siphre* ("books") on Numbers and Deuteronomy.

B. *Amoraitic Literature*

Records of commentary on the Tannaitic authorities and written Torah by the *Amoraim* ("speakers"), rabbis of the *yeshiba* ("the Academy"), produced between the closing of the Mishnah and the fifth century c.e.

Gemara ("Completion"): commentary on specific Tractates of the Mishnah by the rabbis in the academies of Palestine (Jerusalem) and Babylonia (Sura). The former discussed many issues appropriate only to the Holy Land, but their discussions were briefer; the discussions of the Babylonian Amoraim are more exhaustive and more authoritative. The Talmuds proper are Gemara. Palestinian Talmud: discussions of 39 Tractates. Babylonian Talmud: discussions of 36 ½ Tractates.

Amoraitic midrashim were mostly homiletical and very haggadic in character. Several commentaries stand out:

Midrash rabba ("elder or greater commentary"): a series of commentaries on the important books of the Tanakh, especially:

1. *Bereshit Rabba* ("the great [commentary] on Genesis").
2. *Debarim Rabba* ("the great words") on Deuteronomy.
3. *Wayyiqra Rabba* ("Leviticus Rabba").
4. *Bemidbar Rabba* ("Numbers Rabba").
5. *Shemoth Rabba* ("Exodus Rabba").
6. *Rabbot* ("great [commentaries]") on the *Megillot* ("festival scrolls": Song of Songs, Ruth, Esther, Ecclesiastes, Lamentations).

Pesiqta (de-Rab Kahana) ("section") on Leviticus.

Tanhuma (rabbi's name) or *Yelammedenu* ("he may instruct us") on the whole Pentateuch.

Pesiqta Rabbati ("the great section") on Leviticus (a later work).

II. Later Authoritative Exegetical Writings

Responsa ("replies") of the *Geonim* (Rectors) of the Yeshibot of Babylonia during the Byzantine period and up until ca. 1040 c.e.

Mishnah Torah ("repetition of the law"): a monumental commentary on the Mishnah code by Moses Maimonides (d. 1204).

Arbah Turim ("the Four Towers") by Jacob ben Asher (d. 1340), editor of that text of Tanakh upon which the present Hebrew Bible and translations of the Old Testament are based.

Shulchan Aruch ("the Set Table") by Joseph Caro (d. 1575).

of the political and religious upheavals of the period the living tradition appeared to be dwindling with rapidity. Now the oral tradition takes on a new role: the task of interpreting the written Torah and of enlarging its domain by creative exegesis or interpretation. This use of oral tradition was one way to keep the revelation relevant to new problems and to new situations and to apply it to all phases of life, thus making Talmud a living legal document.

The corpus of the Talmud is based upon the Mishnah, which was crystallized by 200 c.e. as the normative code of Judaism. It is essentially halakhic (legal, lit. "walking") in character, but also contains haggadah (lit. "narration"), containing not only religion and ethics but maxims of worldly wisdom, philosophical speculations, tales of the past and visions of the future, and scientific subjects of all sorts. As time went on, new collections were added, and this intellectual activity was crystallized in the *Gemara* (lit. "completion"); so that the Mishnah and the Gemara constitute the Talmud ("teaching"), which is the interpretation and reinterpretation of the Torah to fit immediate situations. The dominant concern of the rabbis was to preserve inviolate the law and way of life against encroachments from alien cultures. Given once and for all by Moses, there could be no new laws. This meant that ancient laws had to be reapplied to new situations. The method used was casuistry. The idea was to abstract the real meaning and avoid novelties. The method characteristically repeated interpretations of their predecessors and then added new interpretations covering contingencies in their present life. The type of question is illustrated with the New Testament in the story of Jesus' discussion with the Pharisees concerning the plucking of corn on the Sabbath (Mark 2:23 ff.). To this end they built a "fence about the Torah" to aid men in their daily loyalties and to keep the core of the law inviolate against external pressure. The Talmud became and remains to this day the chief authority for traditional Jewish life. The Bible, of course, is the ultimate authority, but the Bible is understood as the Talmud interprets it.

The New Testament

For the early Church, "Scripture" meant primarily the Old Testament. Most of the Old Testament quotations in the New Testament are derived from the Greek translation, the Septuagint; but this is not surprising in view of the fact that the New Testament is written almost exclusively in Greek. Early Christian authors seem to have accepted the canon of the Old Testament as it was defined at Jamnia.

The formation of an authoritative body of New Testament writings is a process extending over at least two centuries. In this period, there are oral teachings, the preachings of Jesus and his apostles which were recorded in written form and circulated among the churches. Some of the writings were disputed, others accepted; some were regarded first as a key to understanding the Old Testament and then ultimately as equal to it, and finally in the process the writings as we now have them came to be regarded as inspired Scripture.

By a gradual process, mostly through use in the churches, particular books achieved the status of being circulated along with the Old Testament. By the end of the second century, all but seven books of the present canon were included. Ironically enough, the first canon to be published was by Marcion the Gnostic in A.D. 150, which included Luke and the Letters of Paul; but he was violently anti-Judaistic and excluded the Old Testament or any books that had a Jewish flavor. In response to this challenge, apparently, other canonical lists were drawn. In his Easter Letter in A.D. 367, Athanasius listed the present books as being part of the canon. Thus many lists circulated, but as the Church achieved clearer definition in its beliefs, discipline, and worship, a consensus developed. The criteria for selection are not always clear, but apparently the first criterion was the "eye witness" test: Was the book by an apostle or by a companion of an apostle? Since it was believed that the apostles were with Jesus, what they wrote could be taken as first-hand witness to the truth. The companions of the apostles would get the word directly from them. These writings representing close contact with the primary sources of revelation would given an authority which put them above the authority of such works as the Shepherd of Hermas, which at the time was quoted as a basis for authoritative teaching. Second was the criterion or tradition of acceptance: Were the writings in question faithful to the kerygma, and were they in general use?

In 1740, a Milanese scholar named Muratori published an eighth-century Latin manuscript which was believed to be a translation from a second-century Greek list of books. This list, known as the Muratorian Canon, is identical to the present one. (See Table 1.)[12] It is fair to assume that by the end of the fourth century the church had a rule which excluded a great multiplicity of the apocryphal gospels, epistles, and apocalypses which had proliferated everywhere. After these special revelations had been ruled out, there was one body of New Testament writings that could be regarded as authoritative.[13]

Creed

THE EARLY CHURCH.   A second way the challenges of the first century were met was the development of another set of canons, the *Rule of Faith (Regula Fidei)* or *Rule of Truth (Regula Veritatis)*. This Rule of

Faith was later to develop in the form of creeds, confessions, or catechisms. The Rule at first was not a set form of words so much as a standard group of ideas which were already to be found in the New Testament and which otherwise were expressed rather freely in a variety of ways. For example, one of the simple tests of orthodoxy in the New Testament is the confession, "Jesus is Lord," and everyone who made that declaration was recognized as having thereby said something essential. This Rule of Faith underlies many of the phases and sayings in the apostolic fathers, but at first it does not have a single, clearly recognizable verbal shape. Another example is to be found in Paul's first letter to the Corinthians: "For I delivered to you as of first importance when I also received, that Christ died for our sins in accordance with the Scriptures, that he was buried, that he was raised on the third day in accordance with the Scriptures," (I Corinthians 15:3–4). As Professor Robert M. Grant points out, this is obviously a "semi-credal formula not unlike what we later find in the developed creeds of the Church." Since it is received tradition, presumably authoritative explanations were already in vogue for the death and resurrection of Christ "in accordance with the Scriptures." Presumably this was an Old Testament reference, probably to Isaiah 53. "This is to say that the tradition which Paul has transmitted is not a simple 'factual account' although facts are undoubtedly involved; it is a factual account interpreted theologically with reference to the plan of God as revealed by the prophets."[14] Similar traditions are to be found throughout the New Testament, notably in the Book of Acts and the Gospel According to John.

The time came when a more elaborate form of words had to be employed in the baptismal confessions or as tests of authenticity when the Christians were under persecution. The term applied to these forms is *symbol*, a very interesting term coming from the word *symbolon*. This term referred to a bone or earthen disc or a rod broken in half so that one half could be given to a messenger who was trusted with a mission and the other half given to the one to whom the messenger is commended. The test of the messenger's authenticity was possession of the broken half of disc or bit of bone which would fit exactly into the half held by the other person. The term later came to be applied to any authenticating password, hence, to creeds or confessions which testified to the proper doctrine and genuine membership. This was a term rather regularly applied to forms of words which were required of each candidate for baptism at the time he was admitted into the Church by the fourth century.

These creeds or confessions were later developed to spell out the implications of Scripture; they were not meant to add to but rather to clarify what was implicit in the Scripture. At first, the form of thought in which they are cast is crude and naive, but gradually it becomes more sophisticated.

It may be instructive for our purpose to examine very briefly the most widely used symbol of the period—the *Roman Symbol,* which was to develop by gradual elaboration and expansion into what we know as the *Apostles' Creed.* In its present form, it has been familiar since the eighth century, passing into the Roman rite, providing the form of John Calvin's *Institutes of the Christian Religion,* and recognized by the reformers as a fundamental confession of the Christian faith. About the latter half of the second century, the Roman Symbol was known by persons as far apart as Irenaeus in Gaul, Tertullian in North Africa, and Marcellus of Ancyra (or Ankara, in Galatia). Its text has as its main structure an early threefold baptismal formula: "I baptize thee in the name of the Father and of the Son and of the Holy Ghost." Hence, there are three major divisions of the creed. A detailed analysis of the creed would take us too far afield.[15] However, briefly, this symbol is not only merely a convenient summary of Christian teaching; in actual fact it omits much that is fundamental to Christian teaching. But it is also polemical. The creed in its earliest formulation by the second half of the second century reads as follows:

> I believe in God, the all sovereign Father.
> And in Jesus Christ His Son
> The one born of Mary the Virgin,
> The one crucified under Pontius Pilate, and buried;
> The third day risen from the dead,
> Ascended into the Heavens, seated at the right hand of the
>   Father
> Whence he comes to judge the living and the dead.
> And in Holy Spirit, Resurrection of Flesh.

In this form, the creed appears as a polemic against the Gnostic heresy, which threatened to divide the Roman Church in half, and also against the heresy of patripassionism, the belief that it was God the Father who suffered on the cross. In the third century, we find another phrase inserted, "Holy Church," which apparently is to answer the sectarian view of the Novationists, the insistence that the Church and its bishops had to be morally blameless to be instruments of salvation. At a later date, the word "Catholic" was added to indicate the Church Universal as against the Donatist heresy in North Africa which so agitated Augustine. Also in the third century, the phrase "forgiveness of sins" was added to speak to the question of what should be done with Christians who have fallen into grave sins after baptism. Another phrase which appears in the Latin version in the eighth century is a curious statement, "He descended to the lower regions." This apparently was added sometime before 500. For the popular mind, this would mean Christ's conquest of the Devil. Later on, the term "Communion of Saints" was added to such terms as "The Resurrection of the Flesh."

So the Roman Symbol grew over some 500 years, being added to in specific places at specific times in response to particular doctrinal needs, until it reached the form called the Apostles' Creed.[16] The fact that this form was developed to meet the crude and simple heresies of the second and third centuries meant that subsequent more sophisticated and subtle heresies would demand more subtle credal formulas. New creeds were required, and new creeds were forthcoming.[17] Note that these formulas were intended to be commentaries on or interpretations of what was explicit and implicit in the biblical record. This was no problem so long as the formulas were in the Semitic idiom, but when the Church encountered the Hellenic world the terms of discourse changed to Greek categories. In this connection it is interesting to note that Athanasiums had great difficulty in the Nicene controversy because he used the term from Greek philosophy, *homolousios*, rather than a biblical term, to explain the consubstantiality of Christ with God.

In summary, we can say that the basic form and content of Christian thought was shaped by the eighth century. There were to be other elaborations and many other definitions of discipline, and of the nature of worship and the sacraments; but one can say that orthodox Christianity was fairly well defined through this credal process by the end of the Seventh Ecumenical Council (the Second Council of Nicea, A.D. 787).

JUDAISM.   This period of credal development in the Christian Church corresponds with the Talmudic Age. Is there any correspondence in these two developments? Are there similar symbols of belief verbally and authoritatively formulated in Judaism? On first sight, the answer appears to be an unqualified No. There is nothing in Judaism akin to the Roman Symbol or the Apostles' or Nicene creeds. Furthermore, no attempt at a creed was ever universally accepted. To be sure, Philo of Alexandria drew up a list of five points of essential doctrine, but this list had no influence on the main developments in Judaism. The most famous attempt was that of Maimonides in his commentary on the Mishnah in the twelfth century, in which he laid down thirteen principles as constituting the essence of Judaism.[18] This list was and still is very popular; and in the Middle Ages, there were many versions in rhyme recited by individuals and chanted in the synagogue. There is also a prose version in the Prayer Book. Here is one version of a hymn, in Zangwill's translation:

1. The living God, O magnify and bless,
   Transcending time and here eternally,
2. One Being, yet unique in unity;
   A mystery of Oneness measureless.
3. Lo, form and body He hath none, and man
   No semblance of His holiness can frame.

4. Before creation's dawn He was the same;
   The first to be, though never He began.
5. He is the world's and every creature's Lord;
   His rule and majesty are manifest
6. And, through His chosen, glorious, sons exprest
   In prophecies that through their lips are poured.
7. Yet never like to Moses rose a seer,
   Permitted glimpse behind the veil divine.
8. This faithful prince of God's prophetic line
   Received the Law of Truth for Israel's ear.
9. The Law God gave He never will amend,
   Nor ever by another Law replace.
10. Our secret things are spread before His face;
    In all beginnings He beholds the end.
11. The saint's reward He measures to his meed;
    The sinner reaps the harvest of his ways.
12. Messiah He will send at end of days,
    And all the faithful to salvation lead.
13. God will the dead again to life restore
    In his abundance of almighty love.
Then blessed be His name, all names above,
And let His praise resound for evermore.[19]

This may be said to be a kind of Jewish theology, but these thirteen principles were never formal articles. The very idea of a creed, in fact, led to a revolt against creeds and to what may be called the "dogma of the dogma-less-ness" of Judaism.[20]

To return to the Talmud, one has a feeling that the rabbis were doing for Judaism what the church fathers were doing for Christianity. While the rabbis never developed a systematic doctrine but rather thought of themselves as providing a running commentary on the Scripture, the Talmud is the repository of that tradition, and its authority is derived from the belief that its teachings and principles are a direct development of the Torah. Whatever concepts the rabbis had about God, revelation, man, Israel, or even about the Scriptures themselves were formally derived, they thought, from Scripture itself.

At the heart of the Torah, however, are five simple central events which are "symbols" of faith. These are (1) the call and promise to Abraham and the Patriarchs, (2) the deliverance from slavery and Egypt, (3) the Covenant at Sinai, and the election of Israel, (4) the Promised Land, and (5) the Davidic Kingdom. As there are semicredal statements in the New Testament, so there are liturgies and confessions in the Hebrew Bible which interpret the traditions. Among the oldest of these is one in Debarim (Deuteronomy) 26:5–9

A wandering Aramean was my father; and he went down into Egypt and sojourned there, few in number; and there he became a nation, great, mighty, and populous. And the Egyptians treated us harshly, and afflicted us, and laid upon us hard bondage.

Then we cried to the Lord the God of our fathers, and the Lord heard our voice, and saw our affliction, our toil, and our oppression; and the Lord brought us out of Egypt with a mighty hand an an outstretched arm, with great terror, with signs and wonders; and he brought us into this place and gave us this land, a land flowing with milk and honey.

There is also the sh'ma "Hear O Israel: the Lord Our God is one Lord" (Debarim 6:4). There are prophetic summaries as well as Psalms which celebrate these events.

Further, rabbinic Judaism has its own summaries. It is said that when a gentile came to the famous Hillel (first century B.C.E.) and asked to be taught the Torah, while he stood on one foot, Hillel replied, "What is hateful to thee do not do to your neighbor: That is the entire Torah, the rest is commentary; go and learn it." There is also Rabbi Simlai's summary of the law and 613 commandments:

Rabbi Simlai said: 613 commandments were given to Moses, 365 negative commandments, answering to the number of the days of the year, and 248 positive commandments, answering to the number of members of a man's body; then David came and reduced them to 11 (Psalm 15); then came Isaiah and reduced them to 6 (Isaiah 3: 15). then came Micah and reduced them to 3; then Isaiah came again and reduced them to 2 as it is said, "Keep ye judgment and do righteousness"; then came Amos and reduced them to one as it is said, "Seek ye me and live"; or one may say, then came Habakuk and reduced them to one, as it is said "the righteous shall live by his faith."[21]

But among these 613 precepts are ones concerning the existence of God and his unity, another is "being holy," which was, Maimonides said, the command to fulfill the whole law.

The Talmud is the instrument of survival and of development for Judaism. "Theological views" are incorporated in the Talmud as in the Bible. The oral law was understood as the explicit spelling out for new and changing situations what was only implicit in the written law. It was recognized as having its authority as from Moses. The oral law was written down in the Mishnah, and then the process started afresh. The Halakhah was the positive law, communal and obligatory. Haggadah is a kind of homiletical interpretation, a theory, which accompanies the Halakhah. It is, therefore, a kind of "theologizing," as is the Midrash, but it is not binding. Therefore, the thought and philosophy of Maimonides, as that of Rabbis Eliezer, Akiba, and many others, had tremendous influence on Jewish thought, not unlike the influence of the great individual Christian thinkers like Irenaeus, Augustine, and Aquinas in Christian thought. Not that the Haggadah is systematically unified; far from it. Yet the Torah as the fundamental concept of the Jew contains both the elements of the law (Halakhah), actual observance, and the Haggadah, a kind of rabbinical theology which interprets that law. Narrowly conceived, of course, it refers to the Pentateuch as a kind of pristine source of all tradition. But broadly conceived, Torah means any teaching which enables man to understand profoundly his relation to the God of Israel.

What the rabbis were doing during the first five centuries was to print central ideas indelibly on the character of Judaism: such ideas as the chosen people, the Holy Land, the belief in one God as against idolatry in any form, and the messianic hope and ideas of the world to come, which came to be part and parcel of the Talmudic heritage. They were, therefore, building a body of thought and law that would bind the Jews together as they went into the Diaspora and into the medieval period.

Cultus

The term cultus refers to the living tradition of the communities within which the canons are read and interpreted in an authoritative way, and to the organization or discipline which provides for the worship and practice of the community.

JUDAISM. We have noted that in the time of Ezra the prophet the original communication of the revelation gave way to the scribe. So after the destruction of the temple in 70 c.e., the priest gave way to the rabbi and the temple-worship to the Talmudic scholarship of the Diaspora synagogue. The rabbi was the chief authoritative person in the local community, not as a clergyman or priest but as a teacher. The *sanhedrin* (assembly), functioning as an academy as well as a legislative council, soon became the central religious authority charged with the task of teaching and transmitting the oral Torah and regulating the calendar of religious festivals. As a legislative council, it decided interpretations of the law and through this procedure the internal affairs of the community. The sanhedrin at Jamnia, which established the canon, is an example of the way the sanhedrin operated. It was headed by a patriarch (Palestine) and an exilarch (Babylon), who wielded great influence in the life of the Jewish community. Through its *nasi* (president) the sanhedrin represented the Jewish community to Roman authorities. The rabbis who codified the Mishnah were known as *tannaim* (teachers), and they were succeeded with the development of the Gemara by the *amoraim* ("reflect" or "speaker"). In short, the new nobility or aristocracy or authority was the scholar.

The institutional pillars became the synagogue and the academy. The synagogue had developed as an institution of the Diaspora and with the fall of Jerusalem became the focus of Jewish life, with its congregational meetings for prayer, instruction, and discipline. Even before the destruction of the temple, while the temple was still the proper center and every Jew paid his temple tax, the real center of religious life was in the synagogue. This was so true that the destruction of the temple, far from destroying religion, inaugurated a new period of vitality. The synagogue was not only a center of worship but was much more a center of instruction in the law combining secular and religious functions. A religious congregation was formed in the synagogue. The "house of study" became the "house of prayer" and the "house of assembly." Prayer in the synagogue took the place once held by sacrifice in the temple, and the *avodah*, the divine service, was associated with the *shekhinah*, the "dwelling" of God. Thus the cultus shifted from the temple to the synagogue, and a new distinction in Jewish worship emerged which was to have profound effect upon the pattern of Christian worship.

In addition to the synagogue, the academies became living intellectual centers and a means of communication to the masses. By developing a *kallah*, an assembly convened twice a year; they were able to keep the population in touch with the sources of law and moral teaching. "More than any other Jewish institution, the Synagogue can be credited with having assured the continuity of Jewish religious life after the second destruction."[22]

THE CHURCH.   Obviously, serious problems arise when a small local movement grows with rapidity, becomes a fellowship of different peoples, and then after a long period of persecutions and strife finally emerges as the religion of the empire. In this process, we see the Church become the embodiment of tradition and its custodian, thus the living source of its authority. Organizationally the power of the bishop of each congregation was growing, and at the same time the preeminence of the bishop of Rome was emerging.[23] As the Church was challenged, both by opposition from the outside and growing division from within, there came a need for the tightening of church organization and discipline. At the outset organization was informal, a kind of local congregational government. Where before almost anyone who felt moved by the Holy Spirit could speak and was freely permitted to do so, it became necessary more and more to give primary weight to messages of authorized spokesmen. These spokesmen were clergymen or teachers chosen by the congregations and regarded as the official representatives of the Church; and in the apostolic fathers we see more references to such matters as the need for obedience to the bishop and respect for elders. This was partly for the sake of peaceful ordered life but also partly to safeguard the living tradition against false teachers and fatal forms of infidelity. A need arose for a clear definition of forms of worship, especially the sacraments; so the Christian community developed regular forms of ordination, of church life, of closer control over the membership, and of the orders of worship. It should be noted here that the early forms of Christian worship, especially baptism and cate-chism, for example, follow the patterns established by Jewish missionaries of the Diaspora. The liturgies of the services, such as the reading and interpretation of the Scripture, stated prayers, and the reading of psalms, were modeled on the services held in the synagogue.

Bishops, presbyters, and deacons at first were local church officials; the bishops especially were responsible for authorized preaching and teaching the discipline of obedience. But the main concern of the bishops was the preservation of the unity and continuity of tradition handed down as it was believed from the apostles who were the eyewitness of the original revelation; and this tradition continued in unbroken succession of bishops in the leading churches.

When varying interpretations, all professing to be true, arose and these interpretations came into sharp controversy, it was necessary for the community to make decisions. When these decisions had to be made, the usual agent was a council (cf. Acts 15) widely representative of churches, assemblies, and synods on the local and regional levels; but when doctrine had to be defined, there arose the ecumenical ("universal") councils. The leaders of these were more likely to be theologically learned and very skillful defenders of particular views, but in local disputes the representatives were more likely to be concerned with practical activities and, therefore, could speak for all kinds of ordinary Christians. It was through a process like this that the Church could emerge from a small congregation to become the leading influence in the Roman empire; and after the destruction of the empire, the Church found itself organizationally in a position to be the primary power of bringing order out of the chaos of the early Middle Ages.

METHODS OF BIBLICAL INTERPRETATION

Up to this point we have concentrated on antiquity, for there, both in the Talmud and in the early Church, lies the base for all later developments. The period between antiquity and the modern period may be understood as one of elaborating and expatiating on doctrine, church discipline, and biblical understanding.

We need now to look at biblical interpretation as preparation for our later discussion, since the methods of interpretation are fundamental for the development of theology. The study of the Scriptures for both explicit and implicit meaning is characteristic of both Jewish and Christian exegetes. The Midrash is the search for a new meaning in Scripture in both haggadic and halakhic forms. To the Jewish thinker every word had been spoken by God, and, therefore, every single word had meaning—every jot and tittle—and there is no question of contradiction or authenticity. Within the Hebrew Bible itself one finds reinterpretations of major events. The prophets interpreted them (e.g., Hosea 11:1–4), and were in turn reinterpreted by the apocalyptic writers. The rabbis regarded every detail of Scripture as an archetype. If the plain sense of Scripture was obscured, they translated it into their own idiom; if details were omitted, they speculated.[24] The earliest Christians understood the Old Testament not from the text alone but also from this mass of haggadah and halakhah which had gathered about it in the previous three centuries, and both types of exegesis are to be found in the early Church.

Most of the New Testament writers stand within this tradition and interpret the Hebrew Bible literally. Jesus assumes its authority, and his teaching is rabbinic in form (Mark 10:19, Mark 2:27), and he does not hesitate to reinterpret passages in the tradition of the prophets. The most famous example is his use (in Mark 12:29 ff.) of the sh'ma, "Thou shalt love the Lord thy God . . ." which he joins with the law of love from the holiness code of Leviticus 19:18, "Thou shalt love thy neighbor as thy self."

The most obvious difference from the rabbis is the New Testament application of Old Testament prophecy to Jesus himself. This introduces a new approach to interpretation—the Christocentric principle. To Paul and other New Testament writers, Jesus is the promised *messiah* or "anointed one," in Greek *christos*; and therefore, the Scriptures are full of references to him. Paul finds Jesus' death and resurrection pretypified in Scriptures, apparently in Isaiah 53 and Hosea 6:2 or perhaps the Book of Jonah. Living after the death and resurrection of Jesus, they were able to discover many messianic allusions: Christ is the second Adam; the Church as the body of Christ is prefigured in the story of Israel; messianic references are found in the prophets Hosea, Micah, Isaiah, Jeremiah, and Ezekiel; Christ's passion is found in the story of the Pascal Lamb (Exodus 12); the account of the brazen serpent in Numbers 21:9 represents a type of crucifixion. Many of the parables have their forerunners in the Midrashim of Israel, and much of the imagery is based upon the Hebrew Bible. The Epistle to the Hebrews and the Gospel according to Matthew make the most of this typological and allegorical form. Another example is the Book of Revelation. The entire New Testament method of exegesis, including the typology and allegory, is based on the presupposition that the whole

Hebrew Bible looks beyond itself for its interpretation. These events were not recorded by the writers because they were fascinated with the past as such, but because the present and the past events had present and future significance. Therefore, they regarded the events recorded in the Hebrew Bible as prefiguration of the events in the life of Jesus and his Church. Thus was born a distinctively Christian type of biblical exegesis.

Senses of Scripture

As we have already indicated, the Scriptures appear to have more than one sense or level of meaning, and in the history of the interpretation of the Bible a number of methods have been developed to deal with each level of meaning. Any writing, of course, can be understood in several ways and may have a multiplicity of meanings. This is particularly true of the Scriptures since they are regarded as the work of God. There must be, some felt, a deeper meaning hidden within an obvious statement; in any case, there were a great many obscurities. The point is to find the whole meaning of the Scriptures.

The various senses of Scripture have frequently been elaborated into the typical, moral, allegorical, spiritual, mystical, figurative, anagogical, and accommodating. For our immediate purposes we might confine the discussion to two methods which were employed through the history of Judaism and the Church until the modern era. They are, first, the historical, literal, plain sense (*peshat*) and, secondly, the allegorical, spiritual, or typological sense. These two methods represent two early schools of exegesis: the first the school at Antioch and the second that at Alexandria. But a caution is in order. No neat dichotomy can easily be made. Biblical interpretation comes out of a living tradition and pristine meanings are not easily available. Sometimes passages are completely enigmatic. "Overmeanings"[25] supplant plain meaning. In an effort to interpret, many methods may be intertwined, as we shall see below.

ALLEGORY.   Allegory is as old as Greek philosophy, and its influence on Judaism and Christianity came chiefly through Stoicism. It was first used by the Stoics in an effort to harmonize the Greek myths, which were no longer believed, with their own philosophy. Philo and Origen are the classic exponents of this conception of the task of exegesis in the Jewish and Christian traditions. Philo used allegory in order to teach the Bible as the authentic document of the correspondence of Hebraic and Greek wisdom. For example, in his interpretation of the story of the three patriarchs, he found that the three men symbolically represent three types of man's relationship to God: Abraham is the symbol of man who knows

God through learning; Isaac through inspiration; Jacob through ascetic life.[26] But that the Talmudic rabbis also took great delight in the allegorical form is illustrated very plainly by their treatment of the Song of Songs, which was originally a compilation of blunt and impassioned love songs: the work was incorporated into the biblical canon only because it was read as a dialogue of love between God and the community of Israel. For the rabbis, the statement "Thy two breasts are like two fawns" meant "Thy two breasts are Moses and Aaron."[27] Christians have interpreted this same book as love between Christ and his Church. This method was also employed by Maimonides, the great medieval philosopher, in his effort to reconcile Hebraic faith and Greek wisdom as it was used by the *kabbalists* (mystics), who probed into the hidden mystic meanings of the sacred words not only of the Bible but of prayer and then enjoined concentration upon these meanings. And although Maimonides usually employed the rational method, he did resort to the use of allegory in his effort to reconcile Hebraic faith and Greek wisdom.

When we turn to the Christian use of allegory, it is surprising to discover so little of it in the New Testament. Paul uses it in Galatians 4:21–24, where he actually uses the Greek word for allegory and says that Genesis 16:15 and 21:2, 9 was meant *allegorically* by the writers; he indicates that Hagar and Sara are types of the two covenants. We have seen how the New Testament writers use typology, particularly with reference to the prefiguration of Christ and the Church in the Old Testament. Another example is St. John's use of the passage in Numbers 12:9: "Moses made a brazen serpent and set it up on a post and if anyone was bitten he looked at the serpent and was saved." John declares, "This son of man must be lifted up as the serpent was lifted up by Moses in the wilderness; so that those who believe in him may not perish but have eternal life" (John 3:14–15).

Some of the most famous examples of the use of allegory come from Origen in the third century. Origen was one of the first biblical scholars and critics. His greatest single work was the critical edition of the Old Testament which we now know as the *Hexapla* (the parts from *six* different manuscript traditions are arranged in parallel columns). He had learned Hebrew in order to read the Old Testament more intelligently and more accurately than if he depended wholly on the Greek translation (the Septuagint), and he intended to make Scripture the basis of all of his theological thought. To this end he consulted Jewish scholars in Caesarea.

Assuming the Scripture to be inspired, it needs to be interpreted, Origen thought, because there are places in it which are not only obscure but even absurd and offensive to the Greek mind. To meet the objection of his Greek critics, Origen undertook to interpret the Old Testament according to the Platonic principle, "Nothing is to be believed which is unworthy of

God." God is the very principle of good, and if one takes the Scripture as the word of God, then the Scripture must be understandable in such fashion that in no point will it contradict the essential goodness. Accepting that principle and following the precedence of Stoic interpreters of Homeric tales and men like Philo and Josephus as well as Paul, he regarded the Old Testament as displaying a number of levels of meaning. First, the simplest and most obvious level, is the physical or somatic level, the literal meaning of the text. He thought that most of the Bible would make perfectly good sense interpreted at this level; the historical portions give straightforward accounts and therefore may be accepted as a record of the events that took place in time and space. But second, there is a moral level. The record of events will carry with it ethical implications and the careful interpreter will try to make them clear. Third is the spiritual, allegorical level, and sometimes one will find a text which is interpretable only on this third ground. A commentator who is trying to get at not only the true text but the true meaning must be concerned, Origen thought, for all three of these levels of interpretation. In this he was following an ancient rabbinical tradition in modes of interpretation in which there were four types of exegesis based upon the Hebrew consonants in the word *pordes* ("garden"). P (*peshat*) means the literal; R (*remez*), that which is hinted at in the text, not immediately obvious, but also not completely devoid of some relation to the text. The D (*drush*) is a search or inquiry for deeper meaning; and S (*sod*) means a secret, esoteric, probably mystical interpretation.

In the Middle Ages the characteristic method of biblical interpretation was allegorical. In the late patristic period and in the Middle Ages, a system was developed according to which four meanings, and sometimes as many as seven, were to be sought in every text. There was a verse in circulation as late as the sixteenth century which illustrates these senses:

> The *letter* shows us what God and our fathers did;
> The *allegory* shows us where our faith is hid;
> The *moral* meaning gives us rules of daily life;
> The *anagogy* shows us where we end our strife.[28]

Professor Robert Grant shows how this applied to Galatians 4:22 ff:

For it is written that Abraham had two sons, one by a slave and one by a free woman. But the son of the slave was born according to the flesh, the son of the free woman through promise. Now this is an allegory: these women are two covenants. One is from Mount Sinai, bearing children for slavery; she is Hagar. Now Hagar is Mount Sinai in Arabia; she corresponds to the present Jerusalem, for she is in slavery with her children. But the Jerusalem above is free, and she is our mother.

"Jerusalem" could then be understood in four different ways: historically, the city of the Jews; allegorically, the Church of Christ; anagogically (spiritually), the heavenly city; tropologically (morally), the human soul. And Grant asserts that this fourfold understanding of the term was standard as late as in the early works of Luther and Melanchthon.

Thomas Aquinas, while mainly an exponent of the literal or historical method, was also fond of the nonliteral senses. For example, he thought that the locusts and wild honey that nourished John the Baptist (Matthew 3:4) point to the fact that his speeches were as sweet as honey but short as the flight of the locusts, and that his camel's hair garment represented the church of the gentiles.

While all of the Protestant reformers naturally insisted on a historical and grammatical understanding of the Bible, their exegesis was never merely historical. Luther, for example, insisted on the primacy of books which "preached Christ"; such a view required a typological understanding of the Old Testament, and often he used allegorical interpretation. While Luther claimed that he detested allegory, it was perfectly possible for him to use it on occasion. For example, in his *Lectures on Genesis,* he adopts the view of the ancients that the ark of Noah typifies Christ by whom we are saved from the flood. Yet for the most part he uses allegory in a less speculative way than was customary for medieval interpreters in that he insisted that Christ was the "rock" to break open the Scriptures. Calvin, likewise, most often insisted upon the plain sense of Scripture, but he uses typology to mark the relationship between the old covenant and the new, and in the *Institutes* the land of Canaan is a figure for eternal inheritance.

The allegorical method may seem strange, even crude and naive to us today, but in its time it served a very useful purpose. It saved both Judaism and the Church from crude anthropomorphisms and made it possible at critical moments for them to uphold the rationality of their tradition.

HISTORICAL METHOD.   The second method of biblical interpretation, the historical-literal, has a history like that of allegory. From the very beginning, the allegorical method encountered great opposition from parts of the Church and from the Jewish community. One of the centers of this opposition was the school of Antioch. There the Jewish community was prominent and influential, and the early Christian exegesis which comes from Antioch is largely derived from Jewish teachers. This school had great influence on later Christian exegesis through John Chrysostom, Archbishop of Constantinople, and on the later Jerome, the greatest exegete of the ancient Church. Jerome's most important accomplishment was the translation of the Old Testament from Hebrew into the Latin version known as the *Vulgate,* which was to become the authorized Roman Catholic version. This was a massive effort to discover *Hebraica veritas* for the good of the Church, and he frequently cites his Jewish teachers and rabbinic exegesis.

In the Middle Ages, great impetus was given to historical studies in an effort to have a sound intellectual understanding of the text. One of the most important biblical scholars who developed a style of commentary known as *peshat,* which is designed to get at the plain meaning of the text, keeping preconceptions at a minimum, was Rashi (1040–1109). Rashi endeavored to inquire into the grammar of each word and explain it to the best of his ability, and he produced scholarly aids for doing this which were widely used throughout the Middle Ages and which still are used today. Rashi's school of literal-rational exegesis had great influence upon Christian scholars, like Nicolas of Lyra and the Victorines (twelfth century). It has been pointed out that even in the midst of anti-Jewish enactments and riots of the early thirteenth century, when the Talmud and Rashi's commentaries were burned at Paris, Christians were busy translating parts of both.[29] This incident indicates something very important for our analysis, namely, that in the Middle Ages consultation with Jewish authorities was a common thing, chiefly because the study of the Scriptures took place in academies and schools associated with cathedrals and courts. As we have indicated above,[30] in the Islamic academies and in the courts, Jewish, Moslem, and Christian scholars very often worked together. Thomas Aquinas was a principal exponent of the importance of the literal sense of Scripture. He believed that we must be sure of what it says because Scripture alone is free from error; and while, as we have noted, he did not reject the allegorical interpretation, he insisted upon the literal sense as being primary.[31]

The works of Rashi and Lyra had great influence on the reformers, and they were to give great impetus to historical-literary studies; but the weight of the Reformation was also carried by the work of the humanists, especially Lorenzo Valla (d. 1457), John Colet (d. 1519), and Erasmus (d. 1536), who, by their philological studies in Greek and Hebrew, laid the foundation for a grammatical and historical understanding of the Scriptures. Luther himself claimed preference for the historical-literal interpretation, although he was not always likely to follow it, since he interpreted the Scriptures fairly freely in the light of his own belief in justification by faith. John Calvin insisted that the true meaning of Scripture is the natural and obvious meaning and that we should attempt to search out the meaning of the text as the Scripture writer understood it. This means employing historical data, humanistic learning, and philological and other aids.

The Problems of Hermeneutics

Hermeneutics is the methodology of interpretation. Technically it means the science of the interpretation of documents, and it particularly refers to biblical interpretation. *Exegesis* is the practical exemplification of the application of the rules of hermeneutics to the biblical text. The biblical exegete works on the materials of the Bible and offers his work to the theologian for explanation. However, the term "hermeneutics" may be applied to the interpretation of any written record of human thought and the exposition of the author's meaning in terms of our own thought forms. Therefore, the term applies not only to the biblical scientist, but to the theologian as well. *Heuristics* is the task of the systematic or dogmatic theologian who formulates principles or dogmas on faith and morals as he derives them from the text.

The Place of Tradition

Closely related to questions of exegesis is the problem of authority or the place of tradition. With variations of interpretation among Christians, the need arose for some authority to fix the meaning. While the allegorical method had assisted particularly in preserving an understanding of the Old Testament for Christians, it was only a stepping stone toward a definitive solution. The rabbis were perfectly clear about their understanding of the community as the bearer and interpreter of scriptural truths. Law was reinterpreted to meet the requirements of new situations by the authority of the community. Talmud and Midrash were the eyes through which Jews read the Scriptures. Authority lay both in the Scripture and in the tradition which interpreted Scripture.

Tertullian and Irenaeus both had written on the problem. It was Augustine who took the insights of Irenaeus and Tertullian and raised them to a higher level. Augustine himself had said that only when he discovered the allegorical method of interpreting the Old Testament was he able to become a Christian. The answer to the question for all three was the authority of the Catholic Church. Only the Church, preserved by apostolic succession, can properly interpret the Scriptures according to oral tradition as formulated in the Rule of Faith. For Augustine ultimate authority is twofold: first of all the Scripture itself, which proclaims the law of love; and second the tradition of the Church. This was to be given further exposition by the general principle of Vincent of Lerins. Faced with the problem of heretical aberration and with the fact that the complexities of Scripture permit many varying interpretations, Vincent said: "the line of the interpretation of the prophets and apostles must be directed according to the norm of the ecclesiastical and Catholic sense."[32] What is Catholic is what has been believed everywhere, always, by everyone. Roman Catholic exegesis has ever since relied strongly on the authority of the fathers as interpreted by the tradition of the Church.

The Protestant reformers, on the other hand, insisted on the right of the text literally interpreted to stand alone. The Church is not the arbiter of meaning; the "Word" is the Church's judge, as its authority is prior to the Church. To be sure, the teachings of the fathers are useful to lead us into the Scripture as they were led, but the Bible can be understood in terms of itself and no commentary by the fathers is necessary. The truth of one's understanding is confirmed by the internal testimony of the Holy Spirit.

Thus, in Christendom we have two diametrically opposed principles of interpretation. The division was sharpened by the Catholic Church's decision on authority at the Council of Trent, which was popularly interpreted to mean that the Church recognized two sources of revelation, the canonical Scriptures and the tradition independent of Scripture.

The problem does not arise in quite the same way within Judaism, because in Jewish tradition the Torah is not only the written Hebrew Bible but also the Talmudic writings—the oral Torah—and both are believed to be the sources of revelation. There is a unity of tradition. The Pentateuch, the prophets and writings, the Mishnah, the Midrash, the Talmud, rabbinic responses, Prayer Book, customs—all are part of tradition; and the whole of Judaism is explicit in its view that this is transmitted in a living chain of great teachers forming one unbroken succession from Moses. Though rabbinic interpretation is authoritative, its authority lies in the tradition; and where a particular teacher's interpretation achieves normative influence his authority is derived from his knowledge of the tradition. It does not lie in his person or office.

The Modern Problem

It would take us too far afield to discuss the history of the development of scriptural interpretation since the sixteenth century in any detail, except to say that from the sixteenth century on the conviction grew within the rationalist tradition that the interpretation of the Bible had to be made in the light of human reason. The most important systematic statement of this conviction was Benedict Spinoza, who in important ways is a forerunner of modern biblical criticism.

Modern biblical interpretation must take into account the very important fact that the fundamental thought forms since the eighteenth century are radically different than in any previous century. Both the basic theological formulations and biblical interpretation prior to the eighteenth century were carried on in a universe of discourse which has been drastically challenged in the type of thought that culminated in the nineteenth century. Prior to that time there were shifts and variations, to be sure, but they were all within an accepted framework. While the transition to the modern period is one of the most dramatic intellectual facts of history, one of the effects of this change is the fact that the study of the Bible left the control of the Church and moved again into the school. This had happened, as we have noticed, in the twelfth century, when biblical study was shifted from the cloister to the university. The rise of historical criticism, as represented by Spinoza, Ernest Renan, and Alfred Loisy as well as people like Lessing, Herder, and Wellhausen, was to affect Jewish, Roman Catholic, and Protestant studies of the Bible. But one of the startling facts of our time is the degree of consensus among all three traditions on historical studies. Once again, as in the eleventh century, Jewish and Christian scholars are working together in the same laboratories on the same text, and with a remarkable degree of unanimity so far as the historical understanding of the documents is concerned.

If we are right in the evaluation of the drastic change in intellectual development since the seventeenth century, then modern man has a new problem. To the ancient, it was evident that the Scriptures had been given by God to His Church, and the Torah to the rabbinic mind was the peculiar possession of Israel. Only those who stood in apostolic or rabbinic succession could interpret the sacred books or the traditions. This position was threatened with the rise of humanist scholarship, which reached its peak in the nineteenth-century critical movement. For our time, some historical and literary understanding of any ancient text, Bible or doctrine, is inevitable. But it requires us to take into account all the historical evidence, and this includes, as we indicated at the beginning of the chapter, the purposes for which the documents were written, preserved, and transmitted as well as a certain dialogue with the documents and their authors. This point of view was clearly recognized in the *Dogmatic Constitution of Divine Revelation* of Vatican II.[33] While emphasizing the inextricable relationship of Scripture, tradition, and the Magisterium (the Church's teaching organs) as the means by which the writings are transmitted, explained, and reinterpreted in each generation, Article 12 refers to St. Augustine's statement that God speaks in sacred Scriptures through men in human fashion. It then goes on to say:

The interpreter must investigate what meaning the sacred writer intended to express and actually expressed in particular circumstances as he used contemporary literary forms in accordance with the situation of his own time and culture.[34]

This means that much of the debate between Scripture and tradition is no longer necessary. When the reformers found a great gulf fixed between Scripture and tradition, they did not have the advantage of the modern interpreter; and therefore the Bible, and particularly the New Testament, had practically no historical context. But today we know a great deal about the background of the Bible by an intensive study of the ancient world, the Greco-Roman world; and in the last ten years this knowledge has been enhanced by the discovery of new documents such as the Dead Sea Scrolls. A modern interpreter, therefore, is not so much interested in a kind of vapid literalism or fanciful allegorical interpretation, either of Scripture or doctrine. His task includes

The determination of the text; . . . the literary form of the passage; . . . the historical situation . . . the meaning which the words had for the original author and hero or readers; . . . and also the understanding of the passage in the light of its total context and the background out of which it emerged.[35]

This means the total context, and part of that context is Israel and the Church. He will recognize that the canon is no earlier than the creeds or the cultus of the ancient Church, and thus enter into the biblical world through an understanding of the tradition. In other words, he will try to understand the intention of the document or doctrines not only in terms of the culture of their period but also in terms of the thought forms of the modern world.

There must be a constant dialectic going on between the contemporary interpreter and the ancient writer through the medium of the literary work. But it is fair to assume that thereby the intentions and understandings of both will be altered. The writer was a child of his time, as the interpreter is of another time. Although there is always "the peril of modernizing," modern insights may illuminate the exegesis as well as distort it. The modern interpreter committed to the historical method will attempt to see the literature in its historical setting, trying his best to understand it in the way that the writer intended or the first readers understood. This points to the importance of Rudolf Bultmann's method of "demythologizing," for example, with all of its attendant dangers.[36] It is natural for man to be nurtured in a sacred language, but it is important periodically to ask what that language really means. In this sense, "demythologizing" is a continually fresh interpretation of historical data (the New Testament in Bultmann's work) in terms of man's present ("Existential") situation. It is not enough to repeat over and over again sacred jargon. One must ask what the statements mean here and now. This has been the task of the great "apologists" in every age. In the twentieth century this effort marks the work of almost all of the outstanding biblical and theological scholars, Jewish and Christian. As John Knox, one of the very competent contemporary interpreters, puts it, the historian or hermeneuticist is not only a scientist, but an artist and a philosopher as well. "A good piece of historical writing is a picture, not a map; a living body, not a diagram; a full length portrait in color, not a list of dimensions or a thumb nail description."[37]

Heuristics

There is just one final word concerning the nature and validity of theological interpretation. It may seem on the pages to follow that we have forced on the material certain categories of interpretation as the foundation for the basic ideas. To a certain extent that is true. Religious traditions develop according to their own genius, and they must so be understood. It is true also that the theological enterprise is more congenial to the Christian traditions than to Judaism. Furthermore, there is always the danger of letting rigid theological categories—perhaps even dogmatic rigidity—set the terms of interpretation. We have taken the position that this in part happens anyway, consciously or unconsciously; if done consciously one has opportunity to curb unreasonable bias, perhaps even allow the emergence of some creative idea; if done unconsciously then both history and dogma, as someone has said, operate in us as fate.

For both Judaism and Christianity the community is the bearer and the interpreter of religious truth, although the folk character of Judaism has made it a more cohesive community historically. It is nice irony therefore to realize that this very cohesive community has encouraged the utmost freedom for individual interpretation, while the Christian community, with relatively more emphasis on individual salvation and destiny, has spawned periodically a rigid creedal allegiance and, historically, has been defensive about any form of heresy. Two things need to be said. First, Christianity, with all of its theological emphasis, has not been devoid of law, requirements, and discipline; while Jews, with their emphasis upon "the way," have still developed a massive speculative and mystical tradition. Second, the theological enterprise is becoming increasingly important to both traditions, and this is especially true of Judaism on the American scene. It is probably true that the leaders of Jewish communities have not encouraged the examination of the theological bases of Jewish faith, but it is becoming urgent for Jews to meet the modern world in categories that are understandable to the non-Jew; and this is especially important for the Christian understanding of Judaism.[38]

NOTES

1. There are many, many studies and surveys which could be cited, but for a summary see H. H. Rowley, *The Growth of the Old Testament* (London: Hutchinson's University Library, 1950), and H. H. Rowley, ed., *The Old Testament and Modern Study* (London: Oxford University Press, 1951). *The Interpreter's Bible* (New York: Abingdon-Cokesbury, 1952), Vol. I, has an excellent series of introductory articles. For a Roman Catholic perspective see *Biblical Criticism* in the Twentieth Century Encyclopedia of Catholicism (New York: Hawthorn, 1958).

2. The Masoretes (from *masora*, "tradition") are responsible for text division, verse division, as well as statistical devices, in the period between 500 and 1000 of the Common Era. An example of their work is their finding of the exact middle of the Old Testament in Jeremiah 6:7.

3. See Eduard Nielsen, *Oral Tradition* (London: Student Christian Movement Press, 1954).

4. From *The Book of the Acts of God* by G. Ernest Wright and Reginald H. Fuller. Copyright © by G. Ernest Wright. Reprinted by permission of Doubleday & Company, Inc. and Gerald Duckworth & Company Ltd., p. 33.

5. For an analysis of these fragments, see H. H. Rowley, *The Growth of the Old Testament*, pp. 37 ff.

6. Martin Buber, "Saga and History," *Moses: The Revelation and the Covenant*, published by East and West Library, London (issued in the U.S.A. as a Harper Torchbook, 1958), p. 15.

7. A Brahmin professor of our acquaintance claims that he learned not only the Rg Veda but the entire Vedas by sitting at his grandfather's knee and that he has never had need to refer to the text at all.

8. See Julius Wellhausen, *Prolegomena to the History of Ancient Israel* (New York: Meridian, 1957), for a full description. Naturally the theory is much more complex than this description. For a trenchant criticism of the Wellhausian hypothesis see Samuel Sandmel, "The Haggada Within Scripture," *Journal of Biblical Literature*, LXXX, part 2 (June, 1961), 105–122.

9. See Vincent Taylor, *The Formation of the Gospel Tradition* (London: Macmillan, 1953) and Alfred Wikenhauser, *New Testament Introduction* (New York: Herder and Herder, 1963), Leo Baeck, *Judaism and Christianity* (New York: Meridian and Philadelphia: Jewish Publication Society, 1959).

10. Gerson D. Cohen, "The Talmudic Age," in Leo W. Schwarz, ed., *The Great Ages and Ideas of the Jewish People* (New York: Random House, Modern Library, 1956) Chapter 7, pp. 143–44.

11. The study of the Talmud is highly technical and complex and requires special scholarship. For an introduction see H. L. Strack, *Introduction to the Talmud and Midrash* (New York: Meridian, and Philadelphia: Jewish Publication Society, 1959).

12. An English translation of this fragment is contained in Henry Bettenson, ed., *Documents of the Christian Church* (London: Oxford University Press, 1963), 2nd ed., pp. 40–41.

13. For a short but valuable discussion of the New Testament canon, see Robert M. Grant, *The Formation of the New Testament* (London: Hutchinson's University Library, 1965).

14. *Ibid.*, p. 55.

15. For an analysis see A. C. McGiffert, *The Apostles' Creed* (New York: Scribner, 1902).

16. The creed in its present form reads:
    I believe in God the Father Almighty, Maker of Heaven and earth:
    And in Jesus Christ His only Son our Lord: who was conceived by the Holy
    Ghost, Born of the Virgin Mary: Suffered under Pontius Pilate, Was crucified,
    dead, and buried: He descended into hell; The third day he rose again from the
    dead: He ascended into heaven, and sitteth on the right hand of God the Father
    Almighty: From thence he shall come to judge the quick and the dead.
    I believe in the Holy Ghost: The holy Catholic Church; The communion of
    Saints: The Forgiveness of sins: The Resurrection of the body: And the Life
    everlasting. Amen.

17. For example, the Nicene Creed (325) and the Chalcedonian Formula of 451.

18. The thirteen principles are: (1) God's existence, (2) unity, (3) incorporeality,
    (4) eternity and (5) exclusive claim to worship; (6) prophecy; (7) Moses' unique-
    ness among the prophets; (8) the law of Moses as in its entirety given by God
    and (9) its eternal immutability; (10) God's omniscience; (11) reward and punish-
    ment for sin; (12) coming of the Messiah; (13) resurrection of the dead.

19. Quoted from Leon Roth, *Judaism* (London: Faber and Faber, 1960, pp. 123–124;
    and New York: Viking Press).

20. *Ibid.*, p. 125.

21. *Ibid.*, p. 78–79.

22. Schwarz, ed., *The Great Age and Ideas of the Jewish People*, p. 168.

23. There is some historical dispute about the centrality of Rome in the early Church,
    and especially about St. Peter's relationship to it. According to Roland H. Bainton,
    only the lists emanating from the East make Peter a founder of the Roman
    Church, but not its first bishop. And he says, "that he was the first Bishop is
    rather a matter of faith than of historical demonstration." Roland H. Bainton,
    The Horizon History of Christianity (New York: American Heritage, 1964), p. 74.
    The first recorded reference to the Bishop of Rome as the heir of Peter, to
    whom Jesus had given the keys to bind and to loose, is by a Bishop of Rome,
    Callistus, in the third century. *Ibid.*, pp. 77; Chapter 2.

24. Louis Ginzberg, *Legends of the Jews* (Philadelphia: Jewish Publication Society,
    1919–25), 7 vol.

25. The term is Samuel Sandmel's and refers to a body of interpretative material
    which becomes the lens through which the Scripture is interpreted, i.e. Talmudic
    materials. See his "Jewish and Catholic Biblical Scholarship" in Philip Scharper,
    ed., *Torah and Gospel* (New York: Sheed and Ward, 1966).

26. See Nahum H. Glatzer, *The Rest Is Commentary* (Boston: Beacon, 1960), p. 113.

27. Cohen in Schwarz, ed., *The Great Ages and Ideas of the Jewish People*, p. 181.

28. Quoted from R. M. Grant, *The Interpretation of the Bible* (London: Adam and
    Charles Black, 1965), rev. ed., p. 96.

29. Herman Hailperin, "The Hebrew Heritage and Medieval Christian Biblical
    Scholarship," *Historia-Judaica* 5 (1943) pp. 133–54, quoted in "History of Inter-
    pretation of the Bible, Medieval and Reformation Period," by John P. McNeill, in
    The Interpreter's Bible, 1, 119.

30. Chapter 2, p. 49.

31. See Thomas Aquinas, *Summa Theologica* (New York: Benziger), I, Q 1, aa. 8,
    9, 10.

32. Vincent of Lerins, *Commonitorium*, ii(2), p. 3:17 Jêlicher.

33. See *The Documents of Vatican II*, Walter M. Abbott, S.J., General Editor (New
    York: America, 1966), p. 120.

34. As the editor of the documents points out in the footnotes, this and other state-
    ments in the decree echo both Augustine's "On Christian Doctrine" (III,
    18, 26) and Pius XII's encyclical *Divino Afflante Spiritu*, to which we refer below

(see Chapters 4 and 7). Here the Pope insists on the importance of (1) understanding the intention of the author, and (2) making a distinction in literary forms.

35. Samuel Terrien, "History of the Interpretation of the Bible, the Modern Period," in *The Interpreter's Bible*, I, 141.

36. See Hans Werner Bartsch, ed., *Kerygma and Myth* (New York: Harper Torchbook, 1961) and *Jesus and the Word* (New York: Scribner, 1958).

37. John Knox, *Jesus Lord and Christ* (New York: Harper, 1958), p. 65.

38. In this connection see the symposium on "The State of Jewish Belief" in *Commentary*, August, 1966.

SELECT BIBLIOGRAPHY

ADAMS, JAMES LUTHER. *Paul Tillich's Philosophy of Culture, Science, and Religion.* New York: Harper, 1965.

ANDERSON, BERNHARD W. *The Old Testament and Christian Interpretation.* New York: Harper, 1963.

BAECK LEO. *Judaism and Christianity.* New York: Meridian, 1958.

BAINTON, ROLAND H. *Christendom.* New York: Harper Torchbooks, 1964 and 1966, 2 vols.

BARBOUR, IAN G. *Issues in Science and Religion.* Englewood Cliffs, N.J.: Prentice-Hall, 1966.

CHADWICK, OWEN. *From Bossuet to Newman: the Idea of Doctrinal Development.* Cambridge: Cambridge University Press, 1957.

GLATZER, NAHUM, ed. *The Rest Is Commentary.* Boston: Beacon, 1960; and *Faith and Reason.* Boston: Beacon, 1963.

HARRELSON, WALTER. *Interpreting the Old Testament.* New York: Holt, Rinehart & Winston, 1964.

HARVEY, VAN A. *The Historian and the Believer.* New York: Macmillan, 1966.

LOEW, CORNELIUS. *Myth, Sacred History, and Philosophy.* New York: Harcourt, 1967.

NEUSNER, JACOB. *History and Torah.* New York: Schocken, 1965.

ROBINSON, JAMES M., JOHN B., AND COBB, JR., eds. *New Frontiers in Theology: The New Hermeneutics.* New York: Harper, 1964, vol. 2.

SANDMEL, SAMUEL. *The Hebrew Scriptures.* New York: Knoff, 1963.

SCHILLING, H. K. *Science and Religion.* New York: Scribner, 1962.

SMALLEY, B. *The Study of the Bible in the Middle Ages.* Oxford: Oxford University Press, 1941.

TAVARD, GEORGE. *Holy Writ Holy Church.* London: Burns & Oates, 1959.

TAVARD, GEORGE. *Transciency and Permanency.* St. Bonaventure, N.Y.: The Franciscan Institute, 1954.

TILLICH, PAUL J. *Perspectives on Nineteenth and Twentieth Century Protestant Theology.* N.Y.: Harper, 1967.

WRIGHT, G. E., and R. H. FULLER. *The Book of the Acts of God.* New York: Doubleday Anchor, 1960.

IV

Revelation

REVELATION is a primary term of crucial significance in Judaism and Christianity because it represents the starting point for the life and thought of these traditions, providing the context within which the basic ideas form some pattern of meaning in their cultus, creed, and conduct. Revelation is, so to speak, the epistemology (theory of knowledge) forming the content for major assumptions of the community which become in turn the subject matter of theological and intellectual reflection and development.

This chapter will discuss the meaning of revelation, describe some of the possible models for understanding its expression and content, and then explore the implications of each model for a theory of inspiration and their understanding in these traditions. We will then look at the important issue of the type of language which is useful in this context, and finally explore briefly the possibility of revelation in other religions.

THE MEANING OF REVELATION

The term *revelation* (Latin *revelatio*, Greek *apokalypsis*) literally means to unveil, to remove the covering by which something or someone is hidden and so expose it to view. It is the manifestation of something hidden which cannot be apprehended through ordinary ways of knowing. A revelation, then, is a special, extraordinary manifestation which removes the veil from something hidden in a special, extraordinary way.[1] This hiddenness is called a *mystery*, that is, something which transcends the act of seeing and which is inexpressible in ordinary language. One will not understand the depths of revelation unless one sees that whatever is essentially mysterious cannot lose that quality even when it is revealed. Mystery is not just some interesting possibility about which one will get knowledge later; it is an incomprehensible reality. When account is taken of all that is scientifically or philosophically knowable, there will still be mysterious depths that are unfathomable and inexhaustible. Thus, "Revelation is the manifestation of the ground of being for human knowledge."[2] This supposes that the truth about the ultimate meaning of existence undiscoverable by any human effort may be made accessible in revelation. It opens up the possibility that the mysterious reality by which man finds himself encompassed and the depths which are immeasurably beyond his sounding may at some point or other reveal their essential meaning. It is the claim both of Judaism and Christianity that this disclosure has taken place—that in a particular event or series of events the truth of what ultimately concerns man has been manifested.

It is the assumption of Judaism and Christianity that the proper subject of revelation is God in His being and His works. God reveals Himself, and man is dependent on His revelation of Himself for all knowledge of Him. Were there no revelation, God would remain absolutely hidden; because all human endeavors to obtain knowledge of God by independent inquiry are vain. But even in this self-disclosure, His revelation is fraught with mystery; for He reveals Himself as the Lord whose ways are higher than man's ways, and whose thoughts are higher than man's thoughts, so that even in His self-disclosure, He remains a hidden God (Isaiah 45:15). "It is essential to revelation that it elude our inquiries. To explain, to make it intelligible, transparent, would be to ignore it; in proving it, it would be reduced to insignificance. There is a partner to revelation with whose ways the mind's categories are incongruous."[3]

Divine-Human Dialogue

The Jewish-Christian view of revelation, of course, implies a particular view of the nature and acts of God. Here thought deals in polarities or paradoxes. The God of Israel and of Jesus Christ as reflected in the Bible and the Talmud is beyond the universe, yet enters into it. God is "Wholly Other" and yet is in relationship to the world He created, and man. Man must take His radical otherness and infinite distance seriously, and the only response to this is in terms of awe—awe before the majesty of God, Who is radically other than man. Nonetheless, this God deigns to speak to man.

He is the mystery, radically unhuman, yet reveals Himself to man. He is transcendent and immanent. The God who created the world, however, does not go into perpetual retirement; He enters into the world to confront a Moses, an Isaiah, a St. Paul, to single out Jewish or Christian communities. He enters into history, into the life of man, so that even the simplest and most ordinary person can stand before Him and know He is not distant but present. This Divine Being is not so ineffable as to be incapable of having intercourse with man. That would be to say that God cannot reveal Himself to men, or be recognized by them. God is unfathomable but not unknowable; and yet, about His disclosure there is always a kind of mystery. When a prophet of Israel had a vision of God and received His commission, it is said that "the house was filled with smoke" (Isaiah 6:4). Thus God reveals Himself by remaining partly veiled. For Christians, the clearest disclosure of God is in the Christ event; and yet, the revelation of God took place in such an improbable event that He remained, as Kierkegaard said, incognito. Who would have expected the awful majesty of God to reveal itself on Calvary?

The corollary to this polarity is this; although God is able to reveal Himself, He is able to do so only to a free and responsible finite being, who must of necessity receive and appropriate that revelation, or it does not take place. There is the divine-human dialogue: God acts and speaks; but there is no revelation until free men respond.[4] Until revelatory truth becomes truth for persons, nothing has happened. Organized religions come into being around people who have experienced this revelation, who have received it and appropriated it in such a way that they can communicate it to other people who in turn can say, "Yes, we have received this revelation too." That is the meaning of tradition: the handing down of the content of revelation by persons who are able to articulate the experience for the whole community.

As Tillich points out, revelation "is invariably revelation for someone in a concrete situation of concern."[5] In this sense, there is no such thing as "general revelation," although we will have occasion to qualify this statement. The point here is that revelation must both be given and received in particular situations and by particular persons or communities (special revelation).

What Revelation Is Not

Let us be clear about what revelation is not. First of all, it is not magic, divination, or augury. These most primitive definitions of the term represent the means by which men hope to discover the will of the gods through ecstatic states and ecstatic utterances, whether induced by omens or drugs or exercise. Nor does it mean predictive powers in the sense of foreseeing the exact form and shape and character of future events. This has very commonly been misinterpreted in the history of both the Jewish and Christian traditions, and it is significant that the Book of Daniel, and the Book of Revelation in the New Testament, have been very commonly interpreted this way by all sorts of eccentrics and cranks. Second, revelation, although it may be cognitive and rational, does not substitute for ordinary knowledge. It cannot be simply equated with discovery. Sometimes when some new knowledge hits us for the first time, we say, "It came to me as a revelation." But as understood in the Jewish and Christian traditions, revelation has to do with the ultimate and, therefore, does not give any knowledge that may be found out otherwise. That is, it is not a substitute for scientific knowledge, empirical investigation, intuitive insight, or philosophical discernment. Therefore, ordinary knowledge and revelatory knowledge do not come into conflict with what is true in either field, because they are in no way on the same level.

That this relationship of revelatory knowledge and ordinary knowledge has been misconceived is amply and unfortunately illustrated in the history of the relationship of science and religion. Sometimes religious traditions have attempted to sanctify particular philosophical world views or categories in the name of religion, identifying them with revelation. Whenever the religious institution has sought in the name of religion to maintain a particular view of knowledge against new knowledge, it has usually been defeated. Likewise, when science or philosophy have been tempted to make categorical metaphysical assertions on matters of theology, the statements are normally mistaken. Revelation provides that kind of knowledge which cannot be found out otherwise.

Natural Theology

We noted above that in one sense there is no such thing as "general revelation." We should note, however, that there has been in the history of religious thought a considerable body of opinion which holds that much can be known of God by "the light of reason and nature." Those who hold this view, known as natural theology, are interested in what can be known about God apart from special revelation. St. Thomas Aquinas wrote of "an assent by the natural life of reason and through created things to the knowledge of God"; and his views were characteristic of Scholastic thought, both Jewish and Christian. There are truths about the Divine Being which can be known by reason, and these truths are in principle accessible to all men who have the capacity to reason. St. Paul said, "God Himself has made it plain, for ever since the world was created His invisible nature, His everlasting power and Divine Being have been quite perceptible in what He has made" (Romans 1:19). John Calvin maintained that the knowledge of God is naturally rooted in the minds of men. He shows Himself in nature, in natural evolution, and in the history of mankind. While Aquinas believed that human reason could prove that God exists, he admitted it was a limited knowledge, as we shall see below. For Calvin, it has a negative value in that it leaves men without excuse, as St. Paul said; and unless they respond to this knowledge, it can only lead to their condemnation. But in general terms, this view has been held by Jew, Protestant, and Catholic at various stages in the history of these traditions.

The corollary of this view is, of course, that the ample spaces of nature, the whole of history, all of existence are media for the knowledge of God. The Psalmist says, "The Heavens declare the glory of God and the firmament showeth His handiwork" (Psalm 19). There is the rabbinic interpretation that Abraham came to his knowledge of God through an experience of nature. From the point of view of natural theology, the whole world process is potentially pregnant with divine meaning. As Tillich says, "There is no reality, thing or event which cannot become the bearer" of revelation.[6] He points to such possibilities even in stone, since the metaphor "Rock of Ages" is applied to God; sacramental elements of water, wine, and oil are to be seen in this light. But they are subject to a personal interpretation, and he maintains that natural revelation is a contradiction in terms, although there is revelation through nature. A positive point of view is seen in the writings of Martin Buber. Buber had learned from the Kabbalists of the sixteenth century that throughout the world there are sparks of the "Shekhinah," the divine presence, and that God can be encountered in all phases and aspects of life. He can be seen in everything, in people and things, and in organic and inorganic nature. Everything, in Buber's thought, can be a source of revelation.[7] The world is continually filled with the possibility of revelation because men are met by God not in extraordinary events, the unusual moment, the so-called mystical experience, but as the Hasidim had taught him, in the ordinariness of everyday life. Every moment, every day, everything, every event, though it may appear trivial, has the capacity to become the mediator of the "Eternal Thou." These media, of course, are signs only if they are understood as they are wont to be understood.

To sum up, there is in this view the dogma of the universality of man's awareness of God, which has both positive and negative implications, the truth of which men begin to understand wherever they think seriously and rationally about their experience. The God of Israel and of Jesus Christ is not without a witness anywhere; and in some important sense, all man's religious experiences have been responses to God in this universal revelation. Further, revelation of God is not confined to the so-called sacred but can also be in the "profane"—nature, history, and political events.

MODELS OF REVELATION

Traditionally, there have been two basic models for the understanding of revelation. First, revelation is viewed as a disclosure of supernatural truths; second, revelation is viewed as the self-revelation of the living God. The first point of view is characteristic of Scholastic thought, Roman Catholic, Protestant, and Jewish. The second position is exemplified also in Jewish, Neoreform Protestant, and Catholic personalist thought. This latter view generally stands in sharp contrast to the first one; and it insists that revelation does not consist of the communication of propositions or truths about God; rather it consists of the encounter of God with man through actual historical events. Within both these points of view, there are many variations and shadings; and our purpose now is to analyze and illustrate each position as it presents itself to modern thinking.

Revelation as Revealed Truth

For Scholastic thought, revelation consists of the communication of propositions about God to be believed. Aquinas, for example, defines revelation as "Divine truth which exceeds the human intellect, yet not as demonstrated to our sight but as a communication delivered for our belief."[8] This divine truth is contained in the Old and the New Testaments, which are the source books for the knowledge of revealed truth. The task of the theologian is to discover the meaning of these scriptural words and to arrange them and present them in the form of a complete system of dogma. This same principle was applied when the churches of the later reform identified revelation with the Scriptures. For traditional Jews, the Sinai Covenant is the revelation of laws and truths by which man lives. The moral imperative revealed by God is the content of revelation. The rabbis in postbiblical Judaism declared that the Torah represented the very word of God.

For Catholics and Jews, while it is clear that the Bible is a perceptible source of such knowledge, there is also the teaching of the oral or the unwritten tradition. This may refer either to the oral tradition related to the Bible or to the Church. Protestants, on the other hand, tend to reject unwritten tradition out of hand and apply the principle of *sola scriptura*— Scripture alone—as the source of revelation. As we have observed above, there is a great body of oral teaching in the Jewish tradition, based upon the interpretation of the biblical text and collected in the corpus of the Talmud and other bodies of literature. For the Catholic, there is a body of unwritten tradition inspired by the Holy Spirit and implicit in Scripture, which also represents the corpus of revealed truth. There are supernatural truths; for example, the doctrine of the Trinity or the Incarnation, which are not otherwise obtainable by reason and which constitute revealed knowledge and are preserved as dogma. We will now examine a Catholic point of view in some detail as illustrative of this position, and then we will turn to analysis of revelation as encounter.

A ROMAN CATHOLIC VIEW OF REVELATION.   Revelation in this view is that form of the divine activity that is manifested and established for man on the authority of God Himself. Such authority establishes the Bible as the *fact* of revelation, the means by which God has communicated His truths directly to man. The Bible, therefore, is a record of the activities and deeds of God; it constitutes a history of the salvation of man from the choice of Israel to the advent of Christ.

The primary instrument and source of revelation is the Bible, Scripture. For the Roman Catholic, the revelation contained in Scripture is supplemented by tradition. In content the two are in agreement. Tradition supplements Scripture by making explicit truths that are only implicit in Scripture. The Bible is an important source of revealed truths, of the Word of God in history. The reading of the Bible by Catholics and its importance for their faith has been increasingly and unanimously stressed in recent decades by Catholic scholars, theologians, bishops, and Popes. Beginning principally with the encyclical *Providentissimus Deus* of Leo XIII in 1893 and followed by the encyclicals *Spiritus Paraclitus* of Benedict XV in 1920 and *Divino Afflante Spiritu* of Pius XII in 1943, a great impetus was given to the importance of the study of the Bible by Catholics. The importance of this emphasis upon study is dramatically exemplified in the work of the Pontifical Biblical Commission, the Pontifical Biblical Institute, and the Biblical School of Jerusalem. The many new Catholic editions of the Bible, Catholic commentaries on the Bible, and in general the whole development of Catholic biblical scholarship characterizes this emphasis. Catholics maintain that Scripture is the absolute and supreme Rule of Faith, but that it is not the only rule that governs the faith of the Christian. To revelation the Catholic adds tradition, but not as equal in value or as possessing the same function.

THE MEANING OF TRADITION.[9]   In the Latin, *traditio* signifies something that is delivered, turned over, or transmitted. Generically and very broadly within the context of Christianity, tradition refers to the whole economy of salvation. Thus, God may be said to have *delivered* His Son to man for the salvation of man. Tradition in this sense was continued by the apostles, who transmitted the teaching of Christ to the community of the faithful, that is, the Church. That which is delivered or communicated is not merely a doctrine or teaching, but is inclusive of all that is requisite for the practice of such a doctrine, such as sacraments, liturgical rites and practices, ecclesiastical institutions and laws, and all that constitutes not only the Christian faith but also Christian life and practice.

More strictly, tradition may be said to signify the transmission of that which is unwritten. Congar notes that it was St. Basil in the fourth century who used the term *agraphos*, "unwritten," to characterize the nature of tradition.[10] Both Judaism and Christianity were at first represented only by oral tradition, Judaism as that which was taught by Moses and the prophets before such teachings were written down and became Scripture. For Christianity, the Gospel of Christ consisted at first only of that which was taught and preached by Christ and the apostles before it was written down. Although the Gospel was taught in conformity with Scripture, the Scripture in this case was the Old Testament. The Scripture of the New Testament came into being only when the apostles wrote down what had formerly been taught or preached by tradition.

Not only is tradition, the unwritten faith, prior to Scripture, but it is also revelatory of that which is implicitly contained in Scripture once the latter is constituted. As Charles Davis describes this relationship:

> The Bible originated in the life of a community. Israel with its living tradition and the Church with its living tradition came before the written Scriptures, which crystallized those traditions in the form in which they existed when the period of revelation was still open. This was the period of *traditio constitutiva*—tradition which was a process of revelation and which gradually built up or constituted the deposit of faith.
>
> The living tradition of the Church continues still and provides now the necessary context for the Bible. This is now *traditio continuativa et explicativa*, which adds no new revelation but which must remain permanently subordinate to the unchanging deposit of faith, taking this as its objective standard. It is this continuing tradition that interprets the Bible. The Bible does not stand on its own and was never intended to do so. It was given to be imbedded in the life of a community. The living teaching and witness of the Church alone gives the Bible its full intelligibility.[11]

Thus, all the truths of the Christian faith are contained either implicitly or explicitly in Scripture. The explicit testimony of Scripture may be drawn out through exegesis. Note that tradition is something that lives continually, that both the past and the present contribute to the future of the Christian faith. The truths transmitted in this way are not new, not supplemental, but an integral part of an eternal revelation continually made known to man. It is important to bear in mind that for the Catholic tradition is not something existing apart from Scripture and its truths. Tradition interprets and explicates Scripture and only in this sense may it be said to add to Scripture, thus giving the faith a continual wholeness. Blondel aptly expresses the meaning of tradition when he says:

> It is not merely an oral substitute for the written teaching; it retains its raison d'être even in matters where Scripture has spoken; it is the progressive understanding of the riches possessed objectively from the beginning of Christianity, held and enjoyed in a truly Christian spirit, and transformed by reflection from "something lived implicitly into something known explicitly."[12]

Tradition may be said to express itself in three principle ways:divine tradition, apostolic tradition, and ecclesiastical tradition.

The divine tradition embodies the actions and the teaching of Christ. Once these teachings and the principles expressed in his activities were put in writing by the apostles, Scripture came into being.

The apostolic tradition has for its subject those teachings and practices of the apostles that were not committed to writing. Congar states: "The apostles preached before they wrote (cf. I Cor. 15:1); they preached more than they wrote, and their letters speak of certain of their actions and speeches which are not recorded in writing (cf. I Cor. 11:34; Thess. 5:1–2; II John 12.)."[13]* And Congar adds that as examples of such traditions that the church fathers recognized, there were certain baptismal rites, infant baptism, the sign of the cross, prayer for the dead, various liturgical feasts and rites, certain eucharistic rites, the Lenten fast, and certain rules for the consecration and election of bishops. To these he says may be added the theory which ascribes an apostolic origin to the liturgical and disciplinary practices of the early Church. It should be observed that explicit statements in Scripture for all these apostolic traditions cannot be found, but it is maintained that they have an implicit existence in the Scripture. In a manner of speaking, they might be said to be analogous to mathematical theorems which are contained in their axioms and definitions but which must be made known through an activity of thought. Similarly, a tradition is contained in the basic truths of Scripture and developed therefrom.

In addition to the apostolic tradition, there are the ecclesiastical traditions. The best known of these traditions are such laws of the Church as the obligation to hear mass on Sunday and to receive communion at least once a year. These laws are written expressions or formulations of long-accepted practices within the Church, practices that have their foundation in Scripture itself. They are regarded as explications of the divine injunction regarding the Sabbath and of the apostolic tradition regarding the

* From the book *Meaning of Tradition* by Yves Congar, Trans. A. N. Woodrow. Copyright © 1964 by Hawthorne Books, Inc. Published by Hawthorne Books, Inc., 70 Fifth Avenue, New York, New York.

Last Supper. Another example is the organization of the Church, which is represented as a historical modification of a divine teaching and an apostolic tradition, that is, the primacy of St. Peter and the recognition of the priority of the see at Rome. All of these traditions are frequently so interwoven that it is difficult at times to distinguish them.

We have already observed that revelation in the strict sense was described as a more or less unique act, that it does not need to be repeated but was accomplished once and for all with the Word of God as given in the Old and New Testaments. The deposit of truth given in this way in Scripture is continued through tradition. Catholics maintain that the Church is of divine origin, that it came into being at the time of Christ and his apostles, and that it was given the injunction at Pentecost to transmit the divine truths necessary for the salvation of all men. What God founded through His Son is carried on through His Spirit. At Pentecost the Spirit descended upon the apostles and made them the means for the transmission of the message of Christ. That same Spirit is also within the Church throughout its history and enables the Church to carry the saving gospel of Jesus Christ to all men. Thus, given that tradition as the transmission of the Divine Word through the Gospel of Christ and the apostles, the activity of the Holy Spirit is essentially that of accomplishing or effecting that tradition through the Church.

THE CHURCH AND TRADITION.   The Church may be regarded as the entire body of the faithful, or it may be said to represent the leadership or hierarchy of such a group. In both respects, tradition plays an important role. The Church, for the Catholic, is an integral part of the community of the faithful and not something apart from it; its *sole* function is that of teaching and guiding the faithful. Related to the problem of tradition, this means that the transmission of tradition can be accomplished either through the instrumentality of the leaders or through the faithful themselves.

The *Magisterium*, or teaching authority, is that instrumentality by means of which the leaders of the Church accomplish tradition. The function of the teaching authority is that of maintaining or safeguarding the original deposit of revelation entrusted by God, of determining and judging with divine assistance what is valid and of value within tradition, and of defining infallibly the nature of that deposit or faith. Of primary importance is the task of safeguarding the faith rather than laying down new definitions of it. In fact, new definitions by the Church appear very infrequently and always involve considerable risk. The risk is that the dogma produced is imposed upon the faithful and may seem to be an addition to the faith, although it actually represents an interpretation of the faith. Of secondary importance is the evaluation and judgment that must be placed by the Church upon ideas and practices that have been transmitted by the doctors and fathers of the Church or by the faithful. As an example, the millennial theories of the second and third centuries, many of them frequently extravagant and unbelievable, must be judged on their correspondence with the basic faith of Scripture. Although the Magisterium is a means for the transmission of the faith, it is not the rule of that faith. In the words of Cardinal Cajetan, "Note well that God's teaching alone is really the rule of faith. Although the universal Church cannot err in her faith, she is, however, not herself the rule of faith: The divine teaching upon which she is founded alone is."[14]

Thus, the teaching authority of the Church is always dependent on the deposit of faith and all its interpretations of that faith derive their ultimate authority from the faith. Furthermore, in judging tradition the Church itself depends on that very tradition. To determine what is valid in tradition, the Church looks first for evidence of unanimity of belief with respect to a given idea or practice, for unanimity itself is a reflection of the activity of the Holy Spirit. The second recourse of the Church is to look to the monuments or witnesses of tradition, that is, to the dogmas and decrees of Popes and Councils, the opinions of the fathers of the church, and to the liturgy.[15]

The faithful—the individual Christians—share with the Magisterium the function of safeguarding and transmitting the faith. The relationship between the faithful and the Magisterium is a reciprocal one. That the faithful depend upon the Magisterium is clear; but it is also true that the response of the individual believer, his practice of Christianity, may profoundly move the Magisterium. A case in point would be the development of Mariology within tradition. For it was the devotion and practices of the individual believers that contributed equally if not more to the development of Mariology than did the pronouncements of theologians. The Magisterium is not independent of the faithful. Rather it is one with them in the community of the faithful—the Church.

Basically, then, Catholic theology maintains the absolute value of Scripture and the dependence of tradition upon Scripture. It holds that Scripture is the supreme rule of faith but not the only rule; tradition provides rules of faith that are only implicitly in Scripture. Tradition is more complete, because it is a living reality, whereas Scripture is fixed. Tradition lacks the autonomy and self-sufficiency of Scripture, although if there were no Scripture, tradition would be the ultimate rule for the Christian faith. The teachings of the Church are justified by Scripture, but tradition interprets and explicates Scripture. In brief, Catholicism seeks to maintain the unity of Scripture and tradition while yet distinguishing them. As Congar puts it:

Both Scripture and Tradition are necessary to arrive at a full knowledge of the saving deposit; they are two means by which the latter reaches us. However, the expression *two sources* should be avoided because it demands subtle explanations and would risk confining the theology of Tradition within a debatable position whose narrowness we are precisely trying to overcome.[16]

In conclusion, the work of tradition in relation to revelation is twofold: (1) to conserve and safeguard the truths of revelation, and (2) to transmit and to explicate those truths. The first task is the more important, yet it is of almost equal importance that the truths of revelation should grow and progress within time and the context of changing historical conditions. Both tasks must be accomplished: the former to preserve the faith; the latter to assure that the Christian faith is a living faith that can meet the needs of men of all ages. To emphasize the first task, to minimize or exclude all development on the grounds that it constitutes dangerous innovations, is to stultify faith. Emphasizing the second task excessively, in the name of "progress," may easily lead to the displacement of divine truths by man-made truths.

Revelation as Encounter and Event

In contrast to the first model, which understands revelation to be revealed truth, the second model does not see revelation as giving exact, clear statements, but asserts that ". . . there is no such thing as revealed truths. There are truths of revelation, that is to say, propositions which express the results of correct thinking concerning revelation, but they are not themselves directly revealed."[17] The essence of revelation is the "intercourse of mind and event."[18] Martin Buber expresses it this way:

My own belief in Revelation . . . does not mean that I believe that finished statements about God were handed down from Heaven to Earth. Rather it means that the human substance is melted by the spiritual fire which visits it, and there now breaks forth from it a word, a statement, which is human in its meaning and form, human conception and human speech, and yet witnesses to him who stimulated it and to his will. We are revealed to ourselves—and cannot express it otherwise than as something revealed.[19]

Man knows God in living encounter, in the meeting of one with the other. The heart of the experience is the event of man's confrontation with God and not any abstract formula or doctrine which may derive therefrom. The claim of revelation in this view is to provide an experience in which the whole of experience is seen in a new and different light. It is an "intelligible event which makes other events intelligible."[20] It provides insight into the pattern and relations of things and events.

This is the position held by Jews like Buber, Heschel, Herberg, Fackenheim, and many others, most Protestants in the Neoreform traditions, and Catholic personalists.[21] It commonly uses two modes of explication.

REVELATION AS PERSONAL ENCOUNTER.   First, revelation as the self-disclosure of God is understood, by analogy, as the communication between persons. God is so personally related to men that He can and does make Himself known and opens the eyes to see what they would not see were He not seeking them. God reveals Himself personally—as a man makes himself known to a friend—without violating personal freedom. The heart of the experience is confrontation and encounter where God is known in relationship to man. God takes the initiative, and man's act of faith is his response to this self-disclosure. This view of revelation follows closely Buber's seminal book, *I and Thou,* which conceives of all relationships as dialogical. A genuine "I-Thou" relationship does not communicate information but is self-disclosure received by an open self. A man can be known two ways: by objective observation of the sciences which study man as an object of physiological and anthropological sciences; but man can be known as a person only as he reveals himself to another. Only as a person "unveils" himself and takes the initiative and reveals his inner depths can he be known. How does he reveal himself? By words and acts, by speaking a living word—that is, by all modes of self-communication—by human interaction; we become persons as we are addressed and as we respond. When our acts are congruent with our words, revelation can be said to have taken place. What is communicated between person and person is something of the real self. Revelation takes place when two persons communicate in such a way that they each participate in the life of the other—that is, self-disclosure.

THE NAMES OF GOD.   This personal character of God's revelation is expressed by the *Names of God.* In Hebraic terms, the communication of a name is the way a personal being makes himself known to another. To a Hebrew, "a rose by any other name" would not be a rose, because the name is the essence of the being. "When God makes known His name to men, it means that He makes Himself personally known to them. Something resembling a formal introduction is recorded in Exodus 3:11–15, where the mysterious divine name is communicated to Moses."[22] This is the familiar story of the confrontation of Moses with God through "the Burning Bush."

But Moses said to God, "Who am I that I should go to Pharoah, and bring the sons of Israel out of Egypt?" He said, "But I will be with you; and this shall be the sign for you, that I have sent you; when you have brought forth the people out of Egypt, you shall serve God upon this mountain."

Then Moses said to God, "If I come to the people of Israel and say to them, 'The God of your fathers has sent me to you,' and they ask me, 'what is his name?' what shall I say to them?" God said to Moses, "I AM WHO I AM." And he said, "Say this to the people of Israel, 'I AM has sent me to you.' " God also said to Moses, "Say this to the people of Israel, 'The Lord, the God of your fathers, the God of Abraham, the God of Isaac, and the God of Jacob, has sent me to you': this is my name for ever, and thus I am to be remembered throughout all generations."[23]

In this theophany, God discloses Himself in the name YHWH, and He is experienced as the Deliverer of His people. As Murray puts it,

The text . . . contains a three-fold revelation—of God's immanence in history, of his transcendence to history, and of his transparence through history. God first asserts the fact of his presence in the history of his people: "I shall be there." Second, he asserts the mystery of his own being: "I shall be there as who I am." His mystery is a mode of absence. Third, he asserts that, despite his absence in mystery, he will make himself known to his people: "As who I am shall I be there." The mode of his transparence is through his action, through the saving events of the sacred history of Israel. However, what thus becomes known is only his saving will. He himself, in his being and nature, remains forever unknown to men, hidden from them.[24]

Murray's emphasis upon mystery and ineffability here is an important stricture against the easy analogical equation of the relationship of God with man, and man with man. Failure to observe the stricture has very often cheapened the "I-Thou" understanding of this relationship. God is known in His word and in His "mighty acts" in history. The prophets laid great emphasis upon the name YHWH as a way of portraying God's attitudes and his character in his works and relationships with men. To Isaiah, he is "the Holy One of Israel" (5:19). And deutero-Isaiah refers to a God who "hides Himself" (45:15). Thus, YHWH is a God not seen in himself but in his relationship to men. But not only is a being identified by his name. Knowledge of the name is not a matter of intellect only. In the biblical sense, it is an affair of the heart; and the heart is the center and source of man's inner life in the full complexity of thought, desire, and decision. The Hebrew word "to know" is also the word for sexual intercourse. Therefore, the knowledge of God is acknowledgement as well. As Murray says, "The knowledge of God is an affair not simply of cognition but of recognition."[25]

This same importance of the name applies to the New Testament as well. In the announcement of the birth of Christ (Matthew 1:18–25),

"You shall call His name Jesus, for He will save His people from their sins" (v. 21); the name, Jesus, has as its root, Joshua, which means "to rescue or to save" and which here is identified also with one the prophet had used, "Emmanuel" ("God with us," Isaiah 8:10). Again God is identified through Jesus as deliverer. St. Paul uses the same typology in Philippians 2:1–11: "Therefore God has highly exalted him and bestowed on him the name which is above every name" (v. 9). Thus in the typology of the Scriptures, there is a logic of response whereby God is known in His relationship to men by His name, that is, by personal identity in His self-disclosure. This point of view has been an integral part of the Jewish and Christian traditions through their history. Man can never find out God for himself. God can be known only where and when He chooses to reveal Himself. The first mode of thinking about revelation in this model is in terms of personal encounter.

REVELATION IN HISTORICAL EVENTS.   The second mode of thinking about revelation emphasizes the encounter of God with man through actual historical events, events which are pivotal points in the experience of a people and are apprehended as "the Mighty Acts of God." While all events of history may be full of meaning, there are special or key events in a people's history which are celebrated as giving clues to the meaning of that history. This point of view holds that all history has a central point from which meaning is derived. For Jews, such central points are the Call of Abraham, the complex of events around Exodus-Sinai, the Babylonian Exile and Restoration; for Moslems, it is the flight of Mohammed from Mecca; and for Christians, it is the historical appearance of Jesus Christ. Christ is for Christians the center of history, and the Christ event gives life ultimate meaning. Revelatory events are not peculiarly religious, mystical events. They can also occur in political struggles, national and cultural crises, or various critical moments in a history of a people. These are crucial events which are remembered.

THE EXODUS-SINAI EVENT.   For Israel, there are several critical historical points, but the prototype for them all is the Exodus-Sinai event. The "deliverance from Egypt" is the great watershed from which she derives a sense of identity and destiny. From the standpoint of the Hebrew Bible, it is not true that all moments are equidistant from God. There is the striking event which, by its creative power, constitutes a turning point in Israel's history. These turning points may be either when the people reach their peak, as in the Davidic Era, or in national disasters which open the people's eyes. The Exodus is the crux of Israel's history; all that precedes it and follows it is interpreted by its background. YHWH is the "God of Abraham, Isaac, and Jacob" and "the Holy One of Israel" and

"Emmanuel" ("God with us"). No event in the nation's history is to be compared to that mighty act. This theme with its accent on deliverance had a new flowering in the Exile; it occurs and recurs so that the past becomes contemporaneous with the present. In the Passover Rite, every Jew is bidden to regard himself as if he personally had been led by Moses out of the Egyptian bondage to the foot of Sinai to receive the Torah.

EVENT AND INTERPRETATION.[26]   It is not the historical event per se which is the content of revelation; it is the whole complex of events together with interpretation. "An 'event' is a syndrome (i.e., a running together) of facts and interpretation."[27] Revelation is given in historical events when the prophetic mind is present and able to interpret the event and its significance. Revelation results from "the coincidence of event and appreciation."[28]

History's moments of revelation are always marked by the appearance of prophets. The Exodus would not have been a moment of revelation without Moses. Isaiah saw God's sovereignty in the complex historical events of the Fertile Crescent. In the Exile, there was a Jeremiah, an Ezekiel, and a deutero-Isaiah to interpret its meanings. The interpretation the prophets placed upon these events was that they had been chosen, elected by YHWH, and were bound to Him in a covenant.

Prophets interpreted the events of Israel's tragic history as moments of engagement with God, Israel's judge and redeemer. According to their testimony, "to be chosen" by God was to be "known by God" and to be known by God was to be exposed uncomfortably to His penetrating judgements.[29]

Therefore, when the prophet says, "Thus saith the Lord," he is not being arbitrary. He is saying that he has been in communication with YHWH in such a fashion that his words become the words of YHWH, because he participates in the character of the Covenant, and that becomes revelation. The content of the Tanakh is, therefore, the articulation of the meaning and content of that experience; so that the Tanakh purports to describe accurately what YHWH has said because it is a faithful record of the experiences of Moses and the people at Sinai, and the prophets. Moreover, the Torah, as the understanding of the Covenant, does not restrict God's self-revealing to the Chosen People or to the prophets singled out for particular communications of His will. It witnesses that all mankind is within the scope and range of God's making himself known. It was the prophets who universalized the conception, not only of God's rule over the world, but also his purpose for and dealing with mankind. The symbolic account of God as Creator of mankind, and the myth of the Flood in which God is seen as Judge and Redeemer of the whole race, reflect the prophetic insight that what had happened to Israel was the clue to what God had done and had promised to do with the whole race and with all nations. They, therefore, saw themselves chosen, elected not to exclusive privilege but to the universal service and witness of YHWH to mankind. This is the core of the biblical revelation.

THE CHRIST EVENT.   For Christians, the center of history is the Christ event: the life, death, and resurrection of Jesus Christ. In Jesus Christ, they see the inauguration of a new epoch, "a new aeon" and "the new being." This new and special revelation is mediated through the long series of events in Jewish history. The epic escape from slavery in Egypt, the settlement in Canaan, YHWH's covenant with the nation, the destruction of Jerusalem and the exile of its leaders left Israel's hope unful-filled at the end of the prophetic era. The Hebrews cherished an expecta-tion of a Messiah who would restore them to the Promised Land. In the first century, the Church, through its apostles, thus interpreted the crisis of Jewish history, finding in Christ the clue to God's restoration and forgiveness of mankind in establishing the "new Israel"—the Church. "The time is fulfilled" (Mark 1:5). There is a "new covenant" fulfilling the old. Christ came not to destroy but to fulfill the law and the prophets (Matthew 5:17). He goes up on a mountain to give the new law (Matthew 5–7). He appoints twelve disciples for the twelve tribes of Israel, and he is the new Moses. In short, Christianity sees God's self-disclosure in Christ as the climax in the long process of revelation. This is dramatically illustrated in the story of the founding of the Church at Pentecost, when Peter is anxious to show how these events are related to Hebrew past (Acts 2). St. Paul sums up the meaning of history by saying, "For as in Adam all men die so also in Christ shall all be made alive" (I Corinthians 15:22).

THE WORD.   In prophetic history, the most common form of expres-sion for revelation is "the Word of YHWH," which came to the prophets as the interpretation of the situation or event. But the New Testament speaks of a person who was himself the Word. "The Word became flesh and dwelt among us" (John 14). For the Hebrew prophet, "the word" was not merely words; it also meant action and event. God speaks and it is done; He said, "let there be light: and there was light" (Genesis 1:3). And a most expressive description is that of deutero-Isaiah, "So shall my word be that goes forth from my mouth; it shall not return to me empty, but it shall accomplish that which I purpose, and prosper in the thing for which I sent it" (55:11). Thus, the apostolic interpretation was anticipated to some extent, when it affirmed that the Word can now be seen as well as heard. As Paul Tillich puts it,

Jesus also used the prophetic words. But, beyond this, his words are expressions of his being, and they are this in unity with his deeds and sufferings. Together, they all point to a personal center which is completely determined by the Divine Presence, by the "spirit without limit." This makes him Jesus the Christ. The WORD appears as a person and only secondarily in the words of a person. The word, the principle of the Divine self-manifestation, appearing as a person, is the fulfilment of Biblical personalism. It means that God is so personal that we see what He is only in a personal life.[30]

Thus, the early Christians experienced a new era symbolized in the Christian calendar, which divides time between B.C. and A.D.; and the Christian in the New Testament writes a faithful record of his understanding of this personal encounter he has had with God through the person and character of Jesus Christ. The New Testament becomes the record of the Christian's understanding of the revelatory acts and words of God. For him, no revelation is adequate apart from the Incarnation, which comprehends and sums up all experiences; and in the Holy Communion he reenacts these events in his own life.

To say that revelation is historical means that revelation occurs to particular people in particular places at particular times. For both Jew and Christian, the Word comes in the form of an interpretation of events and situations, and as a demand or challenge arising out of that situation, illuminated by these key events, events which are apprehended by faith as "Mighty Acts" of God.

THE INTELLIGIBLE EVENT.   This position receives particular clarity in H. Richard Niebuhr's formulation of it as the "intelligible event which makes all other events intelligible."[31] We have already referred to his understanding of the contrasting and complementary insights gained from internal and external history, of history as understood from the inside, and from the point of view of the participant and history as seen in detachment and as objective historiographical data. In terms of the self, it is the difference between autobiography and biography. "Revelation means for us that part of our inner history which illuminates the rest of it and which is itself intelligible."[32] This illumination enables one to discern a pattern of meaning not only in personal life but also in the history of the community of which he is a member; and it applies to events as they are known from the inside in contrast to the way these same events are understood from the stance of the detached observer.

Whitehead's doctrine of "occasions," as Niebuhr notes, points to the same understanding and provides a basis for interpretation of events. In his *Religion in the Making* Whitehead says,

Rational religion appeals to the direct intuition of special occasions, and to the elucidatory power of its concepts for all occasions. It arises from that which is special, but it extends to what is general.[33]

The "special occasion" for the Jew is the complex of events around the Exodus from Egypt and the giving of the law on Mt. Sinai, or the future coming of the Messiah. For the Christian it is the coming of Christ in whom he discerns the dramatic center or climax of his history. To these "special occasions" Jews and Christians appeal, and these events provide the context within which the basic concepts of the tradition can be explicated in such a way that they provide a pattern of meaning for the whole fabric of their history.

The significance of revelation in history is seen similarly in Paul Tillich's use of the terms "Kairos" and "Chronos."[34] Both terms are Greek words for time. Chronos (chronology) is calendar time through which history moves in linear fashion from a beginning point to an end, in which every moment is, as Ranke said, "equidistant from eternity." Kairos is the right or opportune time, a point in time of eternal significance, which intersects chronological time, giving meaning to the time process in such fashion that every moment of time receives significance. So certain events in history are of such crucial importance that they become the crucial myths to which the past points and from which the future receives its pattern of meaning. Every people's history has just such points. The crucial myths for Jews, as we keep saying, is the Exodus-Sinai event, and for Christians, the Christ event. These are the "intelligible event(s) which make all other events" in these histories "intelligible." This insight is caught in miniature in T. S. Eliot:

> Then came, at a predetermined moment, a moment in time
>   and of time,
> A moment not out of time, but in time, in what we call history:
>   transecting, bisecting the world of time, a moment in time
>   but not like a moment of time,
> A moment in time but time was made through that moment:
>   for without the meaning there is no time, and that moment
>   of time gave the meaning.[35]

THEORIES OF INSPIRATION

Every concept of revelation involves a view of inspiration, and this creates a new question for our time. To be sure, to the ancient Jew or Christian it was evident that the Scripture was given by God to the Church, and that the Torah, in which every word had been spoken by

God, was the peculiar possession of Israel. The New Testament reflects the Jewish tradition in the statement "all Scripture is inspired and helpful for teaching" (II Timothy 3:16). The Talmud expresses this point of view in commenting on the description of the death of Moses (Deuteronomy 34). The question obviously arises: How could Moses himself have written the story of his own death and burial? "The Talmud says that God was dictating while Moses wrote down the story of his death with a tear in his eye."[36] Philo of Alexandria could hold that the Holy Spirit uses the writer as a flute and breathes through him. To the writers of the New Testament, the Scriptures were authoritative and inspired, as they were to their contemporaries in Judaism.[37] Nevertheless that view did not preclude the possibility of judgment on the relative degrees of authority of certain passages. For example, Jesus himself makes such distinctions on cultic and religious prescriptions. Nor did he hesitate to use the method of prophetic reinterpretation. Of course, he was not a literary or historical critic; and therefore, to him Moses was the author of the Pentateuch as David was the author of Psalms, and the events of the Old Testament were real events. Yet the ancients had no mechanical theories about inspiration.

In the conception of inspiration as in revelation, again we can detect two points of view. There is first of all the Scholastic conception or model of revelation—Protestant, Catholic, or Jewish—which is generally accompanied by a theory of *plenary* ("complete") or *verbal* inspiration of the Bible. The second conception or model of revelation as encounter and event sees the Bible as the *record* of inspired events.

Plenary Inspiration

Since God speaks propositionally in the Bible and offers supernatural communication of information through the body of writings, and since God is omniscient, every word of the Bible must be infallibly true, equally inerrant, equally inspired. This view is, of course, accompanied by revealed dogma. In its extreme fundamentalist form, this view holds that the Bible has been dictated, as John Donne said, "By private secretaries of the Holy Ghost." Every incident is considered equally historical and factual whether it contains notions about the shape of the earth or insights into the nature of man and his relationship to God. In some Jewish Orthodox opinion, this viewpoint has been extended to the inspiration and infallibility of the Talmud and other rabbinical writings, especially those dealing with Halakhah.

Such points of view are always accompanied by a principle of interpretation. For the fundamentalists, it is the right of private judgment, although this judgment is always tempered by its particular theological presuppositions which very often are supported by equally rigid, rationalistic arguments. For the orthodox Jew, however, there is no room for private judgment, but the Word of God as interpreted by the scholars, that is, by the tradition. Most adherents of the view are tempered somewhat by the best scientific knowledge of our time, and they sometimes recognize that the Bible in its various parts is a composite work which reflects a long and immensely complicated process of literary construction and development.

THE ROMAN CATHOLIC VIEW.   Here again we will examine in more detail the Roman Catholic view as a model for this position. This point of view is by no means so monolithic since Vatican II and since Catholic biblical scholars have been encouraged to engage in the critical examination of the Bible. Nonetheless, for the Catholic, the Bible contains truths revealed by the Holy Ghost and transmitted in writing. Biblical interpretation is subject to the Church's authority. However, not all truths are contained in the Bible. The Church existed before the New Testament; in fact, it wrote the New Testament and decided the canon—which means that there was already a standard of faith and practice and authority superior to the New Testament. This authority existed in the teachings, liturgy, and councils of the Church and is attested by the living magisterium of the Church.

Recognizing that the canon of Scripture means that there is a collection of books which the Catholic Church has declared to be divinely inspired, what is the meaning of inspiration? What is its relationship to revelation? And what are the criteria for inspiration? In answering these questions, it is important to observe that although the Bible is held to be the Word of God, nevertheless it was written by men. Taken together these two factors reveal the basic nature of inspiration. Inspiration is a fact derived from Scripture itself: "Everything in the scripture has been divinely inspired . . ." (II Timothy, 3:16). "Yet always you must remember this, that no prophecy in scripture is the subject of private interpretation. It was never man's impulse, after all, that gave us prophecy; men gave it utterance, but they were men whom God had sanctified, carried away, as they spoke, by the Holy Spirit" (II Peter 1:20).

These scriptural statements demonstrate that inspiration is not mere dictation, that it refers to the whole of Scripture and not just to a part, and that it represents a division between the divine task of communicating the Word and the human task of incorporating that Word in the set of revealed truths called the Bible. This is also confirmed by tradition. The writings of the church fathers indicate clearly that they regarded God as the inspirer and the author of the Bible and that the sacred writers were the instruments of this authorship. Aquinas declares: "The Holy Spirit is the principal author of the Scriptures, men were his instruments" (Quod. 7, art. 14). And Leo XIII in his encyclical *Providentissimus Deus* states: "By supernatural power God so moved and impelled them to write,

He was so present to them, that they first rightly understood, then willed faithfully to write down, and finally expressed in apt words and with infallible truth the things which He ordered, and those only." This quotation from Leo XIII emphasizes the essential meaning of inspiration as a divine act, a supernatural influence of the Holy Spirit upon the human authors of the Bible.

Sometimes a distinction is made between active and passive inspiration. Such a distinction is helpful in developing further the nature of inspiration. Most authorities regard the influence of God or the Holy Spirit as active and positive. The individual human authors, however, are not left without any positive contribution of their own. They act freely and cooperate with the divine action in producing a coauthorship of the Bible. God as moving and inspiring man is the author of the Bible, but man as an instrument of God and responding to His inspiration is also the author of the Bible. Inspiration may be regarded not only as positive and active but as charismatic in the sense that man participates through inspiration in a gift of actual grace from God. The influence of God is both physical— exciting and moving the human authors to write—and supernatural, because the divine inspiration is a grace given by God to man.

Passive inspiration assumes God to be the sole author of Scripture and leaves nothing to the contribution of man. This interpretation of inspiration is generally rejected by Catholic scholars. This holds also for the view of those who declare that inspiration has a merely negative influence, that God inspires man only to the extent of preventing error from entering into the composition of Scripture. And the opinion that man is the sole author of Scripture and that God exerted no influence upon the human authors or at best merely a moral influence has always been rejected by Catholic theologians.

In this account of the meaning and nature of inspiration, two principal problems appear: (1) the determination of the contributions of man as the instrument of God or the Holy Spirit; (2) the effects of this division of labor upon the truth and interpretation of the Bible. Granting that God inspired the whole of the Bible and that the Bible as the Word of God is true, it is possible to circumvent many of the difficulties of interpretation and seeming errors by developing more the human elements involved in inspiration. Many apparent errors can be attributed to translations and transcriptions from the original text and to a confusion concerning the intentions of the human author, that is, whether he proposed to promulgate scientific truth or to proclaim in the language and thought of the time certain eternal truths. The example that comes most readily to mind would be the interpretation of the first chapter of Genesis. Confusions of this sort can be avoided when it is realized that the primary concern of Scripture is the inculcation of the basic truths of faith and morals rather than natural science and history. The human authors of Scripture frequently accommo-

dated the Bible to popular ways of thought. Certainly they did not have
the scientific knowledge we have today, and therefore they would not
express themselves in the language of the present. Difficulties of this sort
are not encountered in the historical books which the Pontifical Biblical
Commission regards as "really history and objectively true." Thus the
whole of the Bible is true, but the manner in which this truth is
exemplified depends upon the language of the human writer and the
conditions and ways of life in which he lived.

Sometimes the inspiration of Scripture is questioned upon the basis of
the resemblances between certain scriptural accounts and those found in
other ancient texts. Thus the Mosaic Law is compared with the Code of
Hammurabi, the story of the flood with similar Mesopotamian traditions,
Psalm 104 with the hymn of Akhenaton to the sun. Commenting upon
some of these comparisons, Msgr. Weber declares:

. . . it should be emphasized that these comparisons, which shed a powerful
light on the biblical texts and enable us to understand them, also throw into
relief the profoundly human and at the same time transcendental character of
the sacred books; for nowhere do we find what often disfigures ancient works;
complicated and extravagant notions, immorality or at least sensuality, and
above all the polytheism or at any rate pantheism in which pagan documents
are literally drenched. Yet our Jewish or Christian books are the product of a
people at a far lower stage of cultural development than the empires which
dominated the Near East in the centuries before Christ, or than Greek circles.[39]

This problem of the truth of Holy Scripture must always be judged in
the light of the basic principle that Scripture is the Word of God and that
God is never subject to error. As Fr. Benoit of the Biblical School at
Jerusalem puts it:

God cannot be deceived or deceive us. His word is always truth. So if he
moves a man to write in His name, he cannot allow him to teach what is false.
The charisma (grace or favor) of inspiration is necessarily accompanied by the
privilege of inerrancy. That is an article of faith which the Church has always
professed.[40]

Finally, we note by what criteria inspiration is determined, and the
distinction between the canon of Scripture and the inspiration of Scripture. The Catholic position is that the Church itself bears witness to what
is inspired in Scripture and that only in tradition can there be found an
adequate, objective, and universal criterion of inspiration. To base inspiration upon a subjective criterion, such as the enthusiasm of the individual
believer, engenders fallible belief and the substitution of private revelation
for public. The function of the Church here is well put by Cardinal Bea:

The Catholic position is that the formal witness of God to the inspiration of the Sacred Scriptures was revealed to the Apostles and handed down by them to the whole Church: that it has been preserved from error by divine ecclesiastical tradition, and is being legitimately proposed by the teaching office of the Church.[41]

That the criterion of inspiration is to be found in the Church is justified not only by the very nature of the inspired books but in the teachings of the fathers of the Church and in the actual practice of the early Church in distinguishing (canonically) the inspired books of the Bible from others proposed to it. The basic difference between inspiration and canonicity is interestingly put by Steinmueller in his assertion that God is the author of Scripture and the Church its publisher.

HEURISTICS.   Finally, there is the problem of discovering the true sense of Scripture; this is usually referred to as the science of heuristics.

Very briefly, the true sense of Scripture may be determined in two ways: first, by the employment in exegesis of philological and historical criteria. Here the concern of the scholar is to discover the meaning of statements in Scripture through the methods of historical research, linguistic analysis, contextual analysis, the "higher criticism," or by any other means. The second method of discovering the sense of Scripture is based upon dogmatic criteria and is limited to the determination of the truths of faith and morals, of dogmatic truths, that are to be found in the Bible. For Catholics, the authentic interpretation of Scripture in this sense is based upon the teaching authority of the Church. This prerogative of the Church has been limited by decrees of the Council of Trent and the Vatican Council to truths of faith and morals. This would imply that references in the Bible to scientific material and historical events and anything else outside the sphere of faith and morals would not be subject to the teaching authority or *Magisterium* of the Church. Where no specific interpretation or decree has been issued by the Church of statements in Scripture, then the individual may rely upon the authority of the church fathers, provided their interpretation is morally unanimous. When no interpretation by the church fathers and no specific interpretation by the Church is to be found, then it is necessary to follow that interpretation which is coherent with tradition.

The Record of Revelation

In contrast to the theory of plenary inspiration, the other model of revelation—the view of God's self-disclosure in personal and historical events—also has its implications for theories of inspiration. Since God confronts man through the meaning of events, the Bible is the report which powerfully conveys that meaning and conveys also the true revelation; and its writers can be God-inspired interpreters, while at the same time the records and writers are thoroughly human and fallible. Since the revelation came to living responsible human beings with whom God is in covenant relationship, the law, commandments, and teachings are the spelling out of the implications and understandings of this relation. Modern scholarship has shown how one may take the Bible with utmost seriousness as the record of revelation. It has shown how the findings of science and scholarship may be accepted and, at the same time, the Scriptures truly affirmed as the vehicle of God's Word. The Bible is not itself revelation but a humanly mediated record of revelation. It can be said, however, to be the revelation of God, not in the sense that it is under the direct dictation of God conveying absolute truth with no trace of error or relativity, but in the sense that it is something given to the chosen spirits of the race in their particular historical situations, who themselves were involved in the making of the history they are interpreting. An Amos, Isaiah, Jeremiah, Paul, or John, each has transmitted his understanding on the basis of profound insight. "The prophet is a person, not a microphone."[42]

This record is subject to the investigation of every relevant science. The books of the Bible can be studied as literary documents and, insofar as possible, their sources can be traced, their references to events can be checked by other historical references. They can be understood in terms of all the knowledge that can be gathered about the economic, political, social, or historical conditions of men and nations at a given time. Moreover, since they are written by men, they can be studied so far as data are available. There is a historico-literary science of the Bible, a psychology of religion of all peoples, a sociology of religion, of religious situations and social situations. From these studies, we know the Bible to be a veritable patchwork of documents, coming from the most varied sources and historical contexts; and this means that we must understand the variety of philosophical and scientific categories of the thought of the people who received the revelation.

Yet, the authority of the Bible is unique and indispensable.

. . . it is important not because it gives us knowledge of itself, but because it gives us knowledge of God acting on man and of ourselves before God; it gives us an understanding of the world in which we live; it gives us a meaning for an orderly view of life. Just as a scientist is under the authority of a method, a logic, and a discipline which identifies him as a scientist, so the Christian community is under the influential authority of Scripture which brings its moral identity into being. The community cannot think the mind of Christ without the training of Scripture; and it cannot know the God who calls it to responsibility apart from the study of Scripture. But Scripture always points to the authority which it mediates.[43]

The Bible and Tradition

When one says that revelation is historical, one means that it takes place within historic communities. The Bible is an account of some of the events in which God acted to make Himself known as these events were received and understood within the community of Israel and the community of Christ. The revelation could not have taken place without a community prepared to receive it. Therefore, in a unique fashion, the Torah is a product of the community of Israel and the New Testament the product of the Church. These communities wrote the Bible, and it has a normative character over these communities, because it represents the normative character of the classical period of these communities' lives. That is, the classical period of revelation is recorded in the Bible, but the academy and the church councils fixed the canon; and on the basis of the Bible, the revelation continues in Jewish and Christian history. Therefore, the tradition has authority along with the Scripture. But since there is only one Absolute authority—God—the Scripture has "mediate derived authority."[44] Nonetheless, it cannot be duplicated; and the Church, therefore, stands alongside the Bible as authority but also under the Bible. The Bible is unique, because it is the only record we have of the events which brought Israel and the Church into being; and it is through these two communities that its reality is continually renewed.

The Language of Revelation

When speaking of the self-disclosure of God or of the truths of revelation, it is of course impossible to be scientifically accurate. These truths are more like the truths of poetry than of science. Therefore, the language of religion is of necessity the language of metaphor, analogy, symbol, and myth. "The Torah is in the language of men."

The content of revelation can be described in propositional form, but the propositional forms are always human and symbolic; and they can be understood as having intellectual content in the context of some living experience. The problem for theology and dogma is the same. Dogma can be understood only as the intellectual framework of the living relationship with God. And if it is received only on a flat intellectual level as propositional truth, it is inevitably distorted and misunderstood. Dogmas are "our attempts to understand and define the meaning of the revelation; they do not belong to the revelation itself."[45] One therefore speaks of God mythologically and by analogy. If God be a living God, if there be any communication between man and God, this can only be in terms of a story—God spoke, He sent, He came. Such language cannot be exact and scientific; yet, it expresses truth, points to it, represents the truth to be seen. Myth as the account of an action of God (and this is exactly what it means) is the only way one can speak.

Since there cannot be such a thing as the plain, factual account of a divine act, theology is the attempt to make meaningful statements about the God revealed and the experience of that revelation. Its propositions are the reflections upon what has happened and of necessity make for some distortion. There is always the God above the God being described. Because God is ever the same the revelation is the same; but because men and ages differ, because insights and comprehensions vary enormously between man and man, culture and culture, age and age, revelation is never twice the same. God reveals Himself to man only insofar as man apprehends Him. The terms used in common point to a truth which in some degree man has seen.

The truth of this is nowhere better stated than in Marshall McLuhan's book, *Understanding Media:*

For myth *is* the instant vision of a complex process that ordinarily extends over a long period. Myth is contraction or implosion of any process, and the instant speed of electricity confers the mythic dimension on ordinary industrial and social action today. We *live* mythically but continue to think fragmentarily and on single planes. Scholars today are acutely aware of a discrepancy between their ways of treating subjects and the subject itself. Scriptural scholars of both the Old and New Testaments frequently say that while their treatment must be linear, the subject is not. The subject treats of the relations between God and man, and between God and the world, and of the relations between man and his neighbor—all these subsist together, and act and react upon one another at the same time. The Hebrew and Eastern mode of thought tackles problem and resolution, at the outset of a discussion, in a way typical of oral societies in general. The entire message is then traced and retraced, again and again, on the rounds of a concentric spiral with seeming redundancy. One can stop anywhere after the first few sentences and have the full message, if one is prepared to "dig" it.[46]

REVELATION IN OTHER RELIGIONS

There is no necessary reason to suppose that the revelation of God is in any way exclusive to the Jewish and Christian traditions. Most other religions, however, have no such sense of the presence of God in history; indeed, if God is acting in history, he must be acting in all of history, present in events whose meaning is only dimly discerned. Christianity, for example, has always maintained that without prior revelations the Christian revelation would not have been possible, since after all, it does come on the human scene rather late in history and could not have appeared without the prior Jewish revelation. "In many and various ways God spoke of old to our fathers," is the way the author of the Epistle to the Hebrews put it (Hebrews 1:18).

In the Biblical traditions, revelation is primarily conceived in a covenant relationship in the history of its peoples. According to a Talmudic saying, God is supposed to have said, with reference to Isaiah 45:19, "I have not spoken (the word of revelation) in secret. I did not reveal it in hidden places and in dark corners of the earth."[47] Thus Sinai becomes the place in which God reveals Himself to the world. There is no reason why other peoples could not have such relationships relative to their own history and culture. The notion that the knowledge of God is available to all men is symbolized in the Covenant of Noah (Genesis 9:8 ff.). In the Jewish tradition, this is regarded as the Covenant by which the fundamental moral commandments of God are binding upon all men.

Perhaps we are now in a position, in conclusion, to see how Jews and Christians maintain that revelation in their history is rational in the sense that it makes understanding of order and meaning possible. It makes sense to them, and faith is the response they make to that revelation and understanding. But that is the subject matter of the next chapter.

NOTES

1. Paul Tillich, *Systematic Theology* (Chicago: University of Chicago Press), I (1951), 108 ff. Copyright 1955 by the University of Chicago.

2. *Ibid.*, p. 94.

3. Reprinted with permission of Farrar, Strauss & Giroux, Inc. from *God in Search of Man* by Abraham Heschel, p. 221. Copyright © 1955 by Abraham Joshua Heschel. For an interesting and penetrating challenge to this point of view see F. Gerald Downing, *Has Christianity a Revelation?* (London: Student Christian Movement Press, 1964), pp. 193 ff.

4. Robert Gordis describes this relationship as "Cosmic Symbiosis." For him the process of revelation "depends both upon the unchanging source which is God and the finite imperfect recipient and mediator who is man." "A Modern Approach to the Bible," in Alfred Jospe, ed., *Jewish Heritage and the Jewish Student* (Washington, D.C.: B'nai B'rith Hillel, 1959), p. 102.

5. Tillich, *Systematic Theology*, I, 111.

6. *Ibid.*, p. 118.

7. For a fuller exposure to Buber's thought, one ought to consult his *I and Thou*

(New York: Scribner, 1958) which is one of the classics in religious thought in the twentieth century; and *Moses* (New York: Harper Torchbook, 1958) for his Biblical understandings.

8. St. Thomas Aquinas, *Summa Contra Gentiles*, IV, Chapter 1.

9. In much of the analysis of this difficult problem, we are heavily indebted to the excellent work of the Rev. Yves Congar, O.P., and his book *The Meaning of Tradition*, trans. A. N. Woodrow, The Twentieth Century Encyclopedia of Catholicism, Vol. 3 (New York: Hawthorn, 1964).

10. *Ibid.*, p. 20.

11. From *Theology for Today* by Charles Davis, © Charles Davis 1962, published by Sheed & Ward, Inc., New York.

12. Quoted by Congar, *The Meaning of Tradition*, p. 30

13. *Ibid.*, p. 37. The discussion in this section is heavily indebted to this book, especially Chap. 1, "Tradition and Traditions."

14. Quoted by Congar, *The Meaning of Tradition*, p. 68.

15. For further remarks on the Magisterium and the Liturgy, see Chapters 12 and 13.

16. *Ibid.*, p. 155.

17. William Temple, *Nature, Man, and God* (London: Macmillan, 1953), p. 317.

18. *Ibid.*, p. 316.

19. Martin Buber, *The Eclipse of God* (New York: Harper, 1957), p. 135. Reprinted with permission of Harper Torchbooks, Harper & Row, Publishers, Inc., New York.

20. H. Richard Niebuhr, *The Meaning of Revelation* (New York: Macmillan, 1941), p. 93.

21. M. Buber is cited above. See also: A. J. Heschel, *God in Search of Man*; Will Herberg, *Judaism and Modern Man* (Philadelphia: Jewish Publication Society, 1959); Emil Fackenheim, "The God of Israel: Can the Modern Jew Believe in Revelation?" in *The Sabbath as Idea and Experience: An Introduction to the Meaning of Jewish Life in Our Time* (Washington, D.C.: B'nai B'rith Hillel, 1962) pp. 57 ff.; in addition to John Courtney Murray cited below, see Gabriel Marcel, *The Mystery of Being* (Chicago: Regnery Gateway, 1960), 2 vols.; William Temple, *Nature, Man, and God*; H. R. Niebuhr, *The Meaning of Revelation*; Karl Barth, *The Doctrine of the Word of God* (Edinburgh: Clark, 1936); Emil Brunner, *The Divine-Human Encounter* (London: Student Christian Movement Press, 1944); Rudolf Bultmann, *Existence and Faith* (New York: Meridian, 1960); and Paul Tillich, *Systematic Theology*, Vol. I.

22. Alan Richardson, ed., *A Theological Wordbook of the Bible* (New York: Macmillan, 1956), p. 196.

23. For an excellent exegesis of this passage, see John Courtney Murray, S.J., *The Problem of God* (New Haven: Yale University Press, 1965), Chapter 1; and Martin Buber, *I and Thou*, pp. 110 ff., and *Moses*, pp. 49 ff.

24. Murray, *The Problem of God*, pp. 10–11.

25. *Ibid.*, p. 22.

26. For further explication of this notion, see H. Richard Niebuhr, *The Meaning of Revelation*, Chapter 2, where he makes the distinction between "internal" and "external" history and "history as lived and history as seen."

27. Tillich, *Systematic Theology*, III (1963), 302.

28. Temple, *Nature, Man, and God*, p. 315.

29. Bernhard W. Anderson, *Rediscovering the Bible* (New York: Association, 1951), p. 32.

30. Paul Tillich, *Biblical Religion and the Search for Ultimate Reality* (London: Nisbet, and Chicago: University of Chicago Press, 1955), p. 38.

31. H. Richard Niebuhr, *The Meaning of Revelation*, pp. 93–94.

32. *Ibid.*, p. 94.
33. Alfred North Whitehead, *Religion in the Making* (Cambridge: Cambridge University Press, 1927), p. 21.
34. See Paul Tillich, *The Protestant Era*, trans. James L. Adams (Chicago: University of Chicago Press, 1948), Chapter 3; and *Systematic Theology*, III, 369 ff.
35. From "Choruses from 'The Rock'" in *Collected Poems 1909–1962* by T. S. Eliot, copyright, 1936, by Harcourt, Brace & World, Inc.; copyright, © 1963, 1964, by T. S. Eliot. Reprinted by permission of the publishers.
36. Robert Gordis, "A Modern Approach to the Bible," p. 93.
37. See Chapter 3 above.
38. The Scripture quotations in this section are in the translation of Monsignor Ronald Knox, Copyright 1944, 1948, and 1950 by Sheed & Ward, Inc., New York. With the kind permission of His Eminence the Cardinal Archbishop of Westminster.
39. Quoted by Henry Daniel-Rops, *What Is the Bible*. In the Twentieth Century Encyclopedia of Catholicism (New York: Hawthorn, 1964).
40. *Ibid.*, p. 42.
41. Quoted by John E. Steinmueller, *A Companion to Scripture Studies* (New York: Wagner, 1941), p. 42.
42. A. J. Heschel, *The Prophets* (New York: Harper, 1962), p. xiv.
43. H. Richard Niebuhr, *The Responsible Self*. Copyright 1963 by Florence M. Niebuhr, used by permission of Harper & Row, Publishers, Inc.
44. *Ibid.*, p. 22. See also *Doctrine in the Church of England* (London: SPCK, 1928), pp. 27 ff.
45. John Knox, *Jesus Lord and Christ* (New York: Harper, 1958), p. 202.
46. Marshall McLuhan, *Understanding Media* (New York: McGraw-Hill, paperback ed., 1965), pp. 25–26.
47. Quoted from Adolph Lichtingfeld, *Twenty Centuries of Jewish Thought* (London: Beck, 1937), p. 47.

SELECT BIBLIOGRAPHY

BAILLIE, JOHN. *The Idea of Revelation in Recent Thought*. New York: Columbia University Press, 1956.

BAILLIE, JOHN, ed. *Revelation*. London: Faber & Faber, 1937.

BARTH, KARL. *The Doctrine of the Word of God*. Edinburgh: Clark, 1936.

BERDJAEV, N. *Truth and Revelation*. Trans. R. M. French. London: G. Bles, 1953.

BRUNNER, EMIL. *The Divine-Human Encounter*. Trans. A. W. Loos. Philadelphia: Westminster, 1943.

BUBER, MARTIN. *I and Thou*. New York: Scribner, 1958. And *The Eclipse of God*. London: Gollancz, 1953.

CONGAR, YVES M. J. *The Mystery of the Temple*. Trans. R. F. Trevett. Westminster, Md.: Newman, 1962.

DOWNING, F. GERALD. *Has Christianity a Revelation?* London: Student Christian Movement, 1964.

FARMER, H. H. *Revelation and Religion*. London: Nisbet, 1954.

GILSON, ETIENNE. *Revelation and Reason in the Middle Ages.* New York: Scribner, 1938.

HESCHEL, A. J. *God in Search of Man.* Philadelphia: Jewish Publication Society, 1955. And *Man Is Not Alone.* Philadelphia: Jewish Publication Society, 1953.

LICHTIGFIELD, A. *Philosophy and Revelation in the Work of Contemporary Jewish Thinkers.* London: Cailingold, 1937.

McDONALD, H. D. *Ideas of Revelation: an Historical Study,* 1700–1860. London: Macmillan and New York: St. Martin's, 1959. And *Theories of Revelation: an Historical Study,* 1860–1960. London: Allen and Unwin, 1963.

MICKLEM, N. *The Abyss of Truth.* London: Bles, 1956.

NIEBUHR, H. RICHARD. *The Meaning of Revelation.* New York: Macmillan, 1941.

RAHNER, KARL and JOSEPH RATZINGER. *Revelation and Tradition.* Trans. W. J. O'Hara. New York: Herder & Herder, 1966.

ROBINSON, H. W. *Revelation and Redemption in the Actuality of History.* New York and London: Harper, 1942. And *Inspiration and Revelation in the Old Testament.* Oxford: Clarendon, 1950.

V

Faith

ONE of the basic, and most complex, concepts of religious thought is that of faith. What the term means to both Judaism and Christianity will be our concern in the following chapter.

THE LANGUAGE OF FAITH

Probably the most serious difficulty faced in an understanding of faith is the determination of the proper meaning of the term "faith." Some typical lexical definitions of faith are the following:

faith. [. . . L. *fides, fidere,* to trust, confide in], 1. unquestioning belief. 2. unquestioning belief in God, religion, etc. 3. a religion or a system of religious beliefs: as, the Catholic *faith.* 4. Anything believed. 5. complete trust, confidence, or reliance: as, children usually have *faith* in their parents. . . . SYN. see *belief.*[1]*

Faith . . . L. *fidem,* f. root of *fidere* to trust. . . . 1. Confidence, reliance, trust. In early use, only with reference to religious objects. . . . b. Belief proceeding from reliance on testimony or authority. . . . 2. *Theol.* a. Belief in the truths of religion as contained in Holy Scripture or in the teaching of the Church. b. Saving or justifying faith, as a conviction operative on the

* From WEBSTER's NEW WORLD DICTIONARY of the American Language, College Edition. Copyright 1968, by The World Publishing Company, Cleveland, Ohio.

[131]

character and will . . . c. The spiritual apprehension of divine truths. Often
ascribed to the exercise of a special faculty in man, or to supernatural illumination. . . . 3. That which is or should be believed. . . .[2]

To disentangle the variety of meanings presented in the dictionary
definitions, we shall begin by considering how the terms "faith" or "belief"
may be used in the nonreligious sense, that is, how they may be applied to
objects and acts that fall outside the religious context. We shall also
assume for the moment that the terms "faith" and "belief" are synonymous.
Usually they are so identified, and little can be gained by undertaking the
elaboration of any fine distinctions between the two terms.

Very simply, then, "to believe" or "to have faith" means to accept or to
give assent to a proposition or statement offered by another person. Thus
someone may inform me that it is raining. Without any concern to verify
his statement I may simply accept it as true. I assent to his statement. I
believe him. I have faith that what he says is true. My reason for believing
him is undoubtedly the fact that I can verify his statement if I so choose;
knowing this, he is undoubtedly telling the truth. My belief in this particular instance is fairly certain. On the other hand, I believe that my grandfather died many years ago. I do not remember him or his death, but again
I have no reason to doubt what others have told me. I accept their testimony as true. Again, I may believe from my reading of history that Caesar
was assassinated. In this instance I believe upon the testimony and authority of historians.

Seeing and Believing

To clarify further the meaning of belief or faith, we shall distinguish
between the acts of believing and seeing. Suppose that I see you here and
now seated before me. This is clearly not a matter of belief or faith. To see
people or things is to be immediately and directly aware of their actual
existence. The word, testimony, or authority of another is not needed in
such instances. Seeing is never believing. I do not at the same time and in
the same respect both see you here before me and believe that you are
there. No purpose or necessity would be served by such a belief. In fact it
would not even make sense, for one does not believe what is actually seen.
However, if I were to leave your presence, I might subsequently believe
that you were still in the same place and that belief would be strengthened
if some one were to report to me that you were still there. My belief would
be even stronger if the report were made by someone I trust and had no
good reason to doubt.

There is another form of *seeing* that must be distinguished from believing. I may believe, for instance, in the truths attained in science and mathematics even though I may not be a scientist or mathematician, perhaps even being woefully ignorant of these subjects. I may not be able to follow at all the reasoning and the demonstrations by which truths in such sciences were arrived at. I do not understand or "see" the conclusions. Nevertheless, I can accept the conclusions or truths so demonstrated upon the authority of others. If an Einstein or a Newton were to instruct me of what is true in science, I would have little reason to doubt the truth of what either would say. I may not see how they arrived at their conclusions, but I recognize them both as men of authority in science and I have confidence or trust in what they say. Faith, then, is in one sense a form of knowledge. I know that something is so, not because I perceive it or because I can demonstrate it, but because I accept it upon faith. I believe that what is proposed to me may be seen to be true by another. My faith or belief is based upon the testimony, authority, confidence, trust, and reliance that I place in the word of another person.

The Content of Faith

The content of faith is *that which* we believe, that to which we give our assent. The content of our faith may consist of anything from a belief in physical objects and mathematical conclusions to statements about God and religious mysteries. Where the objects of our belief are gathered up in some unified and specific context, we may speak of faith as consisting of a set of doctrines, principles, or articles which determine in part the nature of faith and to which we give our adherence. Thus a person may subscribe to the principles of the Republican party, he may believe in the doctrines of the Keynesian economics, or he may accept the articles of incorporation of a fraternal society. In the religious context, a person may accept upon faith that which is held by a particular community of believers. A Christian can be defined as one who believes in the Apostles' Creed; a Roman Catholic as one who accepts the teachings of his church; a Lutheran as one who believes in the Augsburg Confession; and Reform Jews as those who believe in the tenets of Reform Judaism. Obviously, we shall be concerned primarily with religious faith, but it is also evident that the term "faith" may be applied to other than religious objects. Hence we may speak of "political faith," "economic faith," or "social beliefs."

That which is believed by the individual forms a most important part of the language of faith, for it is by means of this language that he is able to communicate with others in the community of believers and to establish a meaningful relationship with God. Such a religious language may come to have no real meaning for an individual. It may become a dead language as far as he is concerned, even though to the community it continues to have real meaning and vitality. Under such circumstances the individual may divorce himself completely from the community of believers—from Church or Synagogue—or he may hesitate to disassociate himself from the group. Through habit, custom, and authority he may continue to accept a faith that has lost all true vitality and meaning for him. He may simply find it convenient, expedient, or easier to "go through the motions" of believing.

On the other hand, the individual may come to understand and to appreciate more that faith which has been taught to him in the religious community to which he belongs. Religious activities and religious experiences may contribute to a more viable and living faith. The faith of the individual may be rendered more meaningful through application to everyday living. Yet the emergence of a more living faith may create certain tensions between the individual and the faith of the community. The seriousness of these tensions will determine his continued adherence to the authority of the community. He may feel that the faith of the community requires certain changes or reforms, and he may work within the community to bring those changes about and create what he considers to be a stronger faith. Or, overly impatient for change, he may break with the community entirely and bring upon himself the charge of heresy. In any event the language of faith may, for one and all, take on new meanings or reinforce old meanings.

THE LOGIC OF FAITH

The Propositions of Faith

If the language of faith seems baffling at times, it will occasion no surprise to learn that the logic of faith, the propositions that embody faith as religious knowledge and the certitude of that knowledge, also create no inconsiderable difficulty.

Taking the term *knowledge* in the broadest possible sense, faith may be regarded as a form of religious knowledge. It constitutes religious knowledge because the objects of faith are religious in nature. Knowledge is made up of propositions. The science or knowledge of chemistry consists of all those propositions comprising the subject of chemistry; that of political science, of the propositions relating to the political life and activity of a people. Similarly, the science or knowledge of faith will consist of all those propositions concerning God and His relations to man and the world. To mention a very few:

1. God exists.
2. The Torah is the Word of God.
3. Christ is God.
4. Isaiah was a Jewish prophet.
5. Moses was a historical person.
6. The Pope is infallible.
7. Good works justify no man.
8. There are no dogmas in Judaism.
9. God is eternal and infinite in nature.

These are just a few of the very many propositions that may be said to make up religious knowledge. They have been selected at random from different sources. Close examination will reveal some significant distinctions. Thus, propositions 1 and 9 are similar, and they differ from propositions 4 and 5, which are similar to one another. All these propositions in turn can be distinguished from propositions 6, 7, and 8. And finally, propositions 2 and 3 are markedly different from all the other propositions. Precisely how these propositions and others like them differ from one another and in what respect they all belong to religious knowledge will become more apparent if we divide all the propositions of faith into four principal categories: the *historical*, the *philosophical*, the *theological*, and the *acritical*.[3]

Propositions in the first category—historical propositions—offer little difficulty. These propositions usually assert the existence of a historical person or the occurrence of a historical event. To assert that "Moses existed," that "Christ preached in the temple," are historical propositions. They also form a part of our religious knowledge because they are propositions that make up a part of what we may accept upon faith. Such propositions belong to history as well as to religion. Those who do not profess a religious belief may accept or reject them upon the basis of historical evidence.

In the second category we have propositions comprising that part of our religious knowledge that may be said to be established by philosophical demonstrations. The propositions that "God exists" and that "God is One" may be entertained as the conclusions of philosophical arguments. Both Maimonides and Thomas Aquinas would agree that the proposition "God exists" can be logically demonstrated. Its truth, they held, is independent of revelation. It is also a proposition that an unbeliever could accept upon the basis of logic alone. And it is a proposition that is accepted upon faith by those unable to follow philosophical demonstrations. Obviously it is not a historical proposition.

Third, there are propositions which belong to theology. In our list they are represented by propositions 6, 7, and 8. Additional examples would be "There are seven sacraments," "Faith alone justifies," and "We must be

thankful to God for our afflictions." These propositions have little meaning unless one accepts the basic truths upon which they rest. Such
propositions, and countless others like them, constitute religious knowledge frequently designated as "systematic" or "sacred" theology. They are
based upon the acceptance of the Christian revelation or the divinely
revealed truths of the Hebrew Scriptures.

Finally, there are those propositions that transcend all historical or
factual reference and all philosophical and theological reasoning and
speculation. We have termed these propositions acritical because they are
over and beyond the ordinary propositions of theology. They are concerned
with those truths that constitute the basis of all theological reasoning and
speculation. In our list they would be represented by propositions 2 and 3.
Neither of these propositions can be demonstrated, and neither is a
historical fact. But both are believed by many persons, and a great many
other propositions have been deduced from them by theologians.

Contrast the statement of St. Peter: "Thou art the Christ," with the
statement of St. John: "And Jesus passing by, saw a man, who was blind
from his birth." There is a world of difference between the two statements. The last statement is historical and factual in reference. The first
statement is neither a factual reference nor a logical conclusion; it is an
affirmation of the truth to Peter that Jesus is the Messiah, that he has
actually appeared in history. Peter's statement has a value that is not
present in those propositions that we have described as historical, philosophical, and theological. The value is more than merely ethical. It is
religious in the highest sense, and its value is such that the individual who
believes it will find his whole life transformed by that belief. There are
many other propositions of a similar nature in the Bible. They form the
basis of our theologies and for a faith that possesses the highest value and
certitude for the individual believer. Some brief comments on the kinds of
certitude possessed by the propositions of faith will make these distinctions
clearer.

Certitude

The word "certitude" is derived from the Latin *cernere*, meaning to see
or discern. In this sense it would be related primarily to an assent by the
intellect to a given proposition. It has also been given the wider significance of including an assent of the will as well as of the intellect. In this
sense it embodies what is called a "whole-hearted" acceptance of a proposition, an acceptance in which our entire being responds positively and with
conviction to a truth proposed to it.

Of our four types of propositions we can distinguish among them the varying types and degrees of certitude they may be said to possess. Historical propositions will possess only that degree of certitude that is relevant to the subject matter and the method of inquiry. The propositions of history will be probable at best. They depend upon testimony and other forms of historical evidence. The flight from Egypt and the baptism of Jesus are propositions that will be accepted with varying degrees of certitude. For some they may be rejected entirely. On the other hand, we may accept such propositions and others like them not simply upon the basis of historical evidence but as comprising an integral part of the whole revelation of faith. We may base our conviction upon a supernatural revelation rather than upon natural knowledge. In this case the propositions may be said to possess a certitude that reflects the highest certitude of all—that of faith in the revealed Word of God.

The propositions of philosophy and theology possess a different type of certitude. These propositions rest primarily upon logical relations rather than empirical evidence. Philosophical propositions, such as "God exists," or "The soul is immortal," may be claimed to have a high degree of certitude because they constitute that kind of knowledge that is necessary, that cannot be other than it is. They resemble those propositions in mathematics and logic which, if we accept or intuit certain premises as true, are said to be necessarily true if our reasoning is valid. In a similar way philosophers have argued, from premises based upon the natural order of things, that God's existence and the immortality of the soul are necessary truths which reason can establish. However, the certitude of such conclusions has been challenged by other philosophers who reject the validity of the reasoning by which these conclusions have been established. In the Middle Ages, for example, Duns Scotus and William of Ockham rejected the validity of Aquinas' arguments for the immortality of the soul, although they upheld a faith in immortality. Those who reject the philosophical propositions of faith as certain may nevertheless accept such propositions upon the basis of faith alone. They may consider them to be acritical propositions, beyond the rational demonstrations of theology and philosophy.

The certitude of theological propositions depends upon the certitude attached to the basic premises of such propositions and the validity of the conclusions drawn from them. The certitude of theological propositions may be said to be higher than those of philosophy because their premises are based upon faith and the supernatural order, whereas the premises of philosophy are drawn from the natural order.

In Christianity certain basic truths of faith regarding grace have led to the development of a whole theology of grace in which there may be said to be a fairly large measure of agreement among theologians. On the other hand, from certain propositions in the New Testament concerning the "Blessed

Virgin," theologians have reached a sharp disagreement concerning her status and her role in the Christian faith. And from certain revealed truths in the Hebrew Scriptures, such as God's covenant with Israel and the Mosaic Law, Jewish thinkers have derived many varied conclusions regarding the relation of the individual to his God and to his fellow man.

We are now in a better position to evaluate that type of proposition we described as acritical. Since such propositions are neither factual nor demonstrable, their status and their certitude is quite different from the other three types of propositions. The proposition of the resurrection of the body is contrary to all natural law and phenomena. The proposition of the Trinity is a mystery beyond all rational understanding. Similarly, the notion of creation *ex nihilo* runs counter to explanations based upon physical laws. And the idea that Moses was divinely inspired points to an experience that transcends the ordinary and the natural and escapes the usual modes of certification. Such propositions seem to require a supernatural capacity rather than a mere natural capacity for truth, a divine illumination rather than a natural illumination of the mind.

Generally the certitude attached to these propositions is absolute, they are beyond all doubt to the believer. They transcend intellectual certitude; they depend upon something more than human reason. And their certitude is clearly beyond that which may be attached to historical evidence and human testimony. Suppose one asked why one believed in Christ. One might reply that one believes in him because of the testimony of the apostles, of what they reported concerning his teaching, his miracles, and his life. One accepts their testimony; does not doubt their veracity. But certitude here is limited to faith in the authority of the apostles, and by the fact that they were, after all, human and fallible. What one desires is a much higher and more direct kind of certitude, something more than reasonable motives for believing and something more than demonstrative arguments which may turn out to be invalid. One desires a certitude beyond all human questioning and fallibility, a certitude that wholly and completely transcends all other forms of knowledge. One looks for a certitude of faith from God and given by God. The certitude of acritical propositions, the highest propositions of all, is a certitude that God Himself gives to them. Such propositions involve far more than intellectual assent and certitude. They involve a faith that is inclusive of the whole being of the individual, a faith that may be expressed as a *response*, an *engagement*, and an *encounter* between the individual and his God.

FAITH AS A RESPONSE.   Faith may be considered as a response to revelation and a response of unreserved commitment on the part of the believer. Faith in this instance is not something that a person deliberately chooses as he would the ordinary preferences of everyday life. Rather, faith is the response that the individual makes to God's choice of him. One does not first choose God, but He chose man. The response is consequent upon God's Word and His revealed truth. The response of the individual to this choice of God leads to the total commitment of the individual. The response is complete and total because God has chosen all of him and not just a part. The whole nature of the individual responds with a trust and love for God because God's choice includes His trust and His love of the individual. It is in this sense that we may say that faith is all inclusive. Such a faith on the part of the individual possesses the highest possible certitude because it is not merely an assent of the intellect but something which encompasses and absorbs the whole being of the individual. Faith is the total response of the whole person: an act of both intellect and will.

FAITH AS AN ENGAGEMENT.   The conclusions reached in the preceding section also aptly bring out what is meant by faith as being an engagement. The term "engagement" best signifies that personal relation which is established through faith. In the religious sense, engagement always signifies a personal relation with another. Faith as an engagement means more than an intellectual assent to propositional truths, more than the communication of objective scientific truths to another. Such truths generally do not affect the personal life of the individual. To accept such truths does not lead to a reorientation of the whole life of the individual. In the language of some contemporary philosophers, faith is concerned with existential truths rather than essential truths. Faith centers upon the subjective rather than the objective, upon existence rather than essence.

This is why, when truth is embraced subjectively by the individual, when it penetrates the very core of his being and becomes a deep personal commitment, that we may speak of the individual's faith in such truth as one of engagement. For we mean that the whole life of the individual is committed through faith to that of another person. For the Christian the engagement is a personal one with Christ. To be engaged with Christ means to have faith in him, to identify one's life with his. Such an engagement of faith may be so total and so complete that the individual would willingly sacrifice his life and welcome martyrdom for Christ. In the Old Testament the classical example of this kind of faith was that displayed by Abraham. So great was the faith of Abraham, so complete his trust and confidence in God, that he would willingly sacrifice his son Isaac to God.

Faith as an engagement with God or with Christ may take many forms. Man may feel closeness with God and love for Him in an exemplification of that love for others. The depth of personal relationships with God may be experienced in the joy with which one carries out His commandments and in prayers to Him. For the individual whose faith is an engagement with Christ, the depth of his love for Christ and his commitment to his teachings may issue in a life that is entirely devoted to a spreading of the gospel to others. More simply, a personal engagement may be expressed in the individual's participation in the sacraments through which he enters into an active personal relationship with God. All of this is an experience of love on the part of the individual, an engagement of love that may lead the individual to a more ultimate personal union with God.

FAITH AS AN ENCOUNTER.   The preceding account of faith as an engagement implies a religious experience in which the individual *encounters* that being which is the object of his engagement. The notion of an encounter is again something of a highly personal nature. It lies at the center of a religious experience, an experience sometimes mystical, in which the individual is illuminated by God. The individual feels the very presence of God within him and to him. The religious encounter is not essentially different from the notion of an engagement; it simply stresses another aspect of the individual's personal relationship with God. The initiative in such an encounter is not that of the individual person. Rather, God Himself is moving the individual to faith. Faith as an encounter is not on the natural order because the initiative and the action is with God. The individual does not go out to meet God, rather He comes to the person in a religious experience. "No man can come to me unless the Father who sent me draws him" (John 6:44).

Finally, what we have termed the characteristics or the notes of religious faith enable us to sharpen the distinction between faith in the religious sense and our ordinary conception of belief. The Christian act of faith is customarily expressed in the phrase *"credere in."* The Christian and Jewish traditions apply such a formula to God and not to man or to things. The Christian act of faith is radically different than a simple belief. We can believe in many things and events and persons, but strictly speaking we have faith only in God. As St. Paschasius Radbert put it several centuries ago:

No one can say properly speaking, "I believe in my neighbour" or in an angel or in any creature whatsoever. Throughout Holy Scripture, you will find the correct use of this profession reserved to God alone. . . . We say, and rightly, "I believe concerning this man," as we say "I believe concerning God"; but we do not believe *in* this man, or in any other. For they are not themselves truth, or goodness, or light, or life; they do no more than participate in these. And that is why, when in the Gospel Our Lord wishes to show that He is of one substance with the Father, He says "You believe in God; believe also in Me" [John xiv:1]. For if He were not God, we should not have to believe *in* Him; by using this word He revealed Himself as God to His chosen ones.[4]

Thus far our analysis has raised a number of problems. One of these has been touched upon only lightly; it is now necessary to comment upon it in more detail. This is the problem of the origin and the possibility of faith. We have stated that faith comes from God, that it is a grace given by God. For the Christian this is developed in different ways. For the Jew the problem of faith is more complex and difficult to assess on a distinctively theological basis. Faith is more an act of the individual.

THE ORIGINS AND THE POSSIBILITY OF FAITH

The Christian View

Generally, Christians regard faith as a gift or grace of God extended to the individual in order that he may achieve a knowledge of God's truth and effect his own salvation. It is held that although the individual may pray for faith and prepare himself for the grace of faith, it is not something that he can achieve by his own efforts. Some Christians speak of faith as an "infused" grace, others emphasize that it is essentially a trust and confidence placed in God. Some maintain that in the relationship between the individual and God, the individual is wholly dependent upon God. Others argue that although the individual must depend upon God for faith, there remains the necessity of cooperation by the individual for the reception of faith. The further we pursue this overall problem, the greater will become the theological issues and differences separating the different Christian groups. Without attempting to describe all the different views, we shall restrict our analysis to some representative positions taken by Protestant and Catholic theologians.

Protestantism

We shall have a complete definition of faith, if we say that it is a steady and certain knowledge of the Divine benevolence towards us, which, being founded on the truth of the gratuitous promise in Christ, is both revealed to our minds, and confirmed to our hearts, by the Holy Spirit.[5]

This statement of John Calvin is typical of the Protestant conviction. For most Protestant believers, faith is in no sense a voluntary choice on the part of the individual. It does not arise out of human knowledge. Faith in its deepest sense is the turning of the life of the individual toward God, a redirection of man's very being, but the initiative is always with God.

Protestant thought emphasizes that faith is a confidence and trust that the individual places in God. And ever since Martin Luther, faith has been regarded by many as a means whereby the individual becomes justified and sanctified.

MARTIN LUTHER (1483–1547).   The classical expression of the Protestant conception of faith is that given by Luther in his work *Concerning Christian Liberty*. The position taken by Luther has been highly influential, and it is by no means as remote or distinct from the Catholic position as some might think.

Luther maintains that faith is a means whereby man is freed from sin. In faith God imputes righteousness to us and enables us to share not only in a fellowship with God but in the power of God. Through faith man is united to Christ and enabled to become a priest in Christ. To have such faith—which is possible only through the action of God—not only assures him of righteousness and eventual salvation, but it makes it possible to do good works. Thus Luther's position is not the denial of the value of good works but only the assertion that their value must proceed from faith. The following brief excerpts from his work will illustrate these points more clearly:

One thing, and one alone, is necessary for life, justification and Christian liberty; and that is the most holy word of God, the Gospel of Christ, as He says, "I am the resurrection and the life; he who believes in me, though he die, yet shall he live" (John xi. 25), and also, "So if the Son makes you free, you will be free indeed" (John viii. 36), and "Man shall not live by bread alone, but by every word that proceeds from the mouth of God" (Matt. iv. 4).

Let us therefore hold it for certain and firmly established that the soul can do without everything except the word of God, without which none at all of its wants are provided for. But having the word, it is rich and wants for nothing. . . .

But you will ask, What is this word, and by what means is it to be used, since there are so many words of God? I answer, The Apostle Paul (Rom. i.) explains what it is, namely the Gospel of God, concerning His Son, incarnate, suffering, risen, and glorified, through the Spirit, the Sanctifier. To preach Christ is to feed the soul, to justify it, to set it free, and to save it, if it believes the preaching. For faith alone and the efficacious use of the word of God, bring salvation. . . . For the word of God cannot be received and honored by any works, but by faith alone. Hence it is clear that as the soul needs the word for life and justification, so it is justified by faith alone, and not by any works. For if it could be justified by any other means, it would have no need of the word, nor consequently of faith. . . .

Hence a right faith in Christ is an incomparable treasure, carrying with it universal salvation and preserving from all evil, as it is said, "He who believes and is baptised will be saved; but he who does not believe will be condemned" (Mark xiv. 16).

From all this it is easy to understand why faith has such great power, and why no good works, nor even all good works put together, can compare with it, since no work can cleave to the word of God or be in the soul. Faith alone and the word reign in it. . . . It is clear then that to a Christian man his faith suffices for everything, and that he has no need of works for justification. But if he has no need of works, neither has he need of the law; and if he has no need of the law, he is certainly free from the law, and the saying is true, "the law is not laid down for the just" (I Tim. i. 9). This is that Christian liberty, our faith, the effect of which is, not that we should be careless or lead a bad life, but that no one should need the law or works for justification and salvation. . . .

This is a spiritual power, which rules in the midst of enemies, and is powerful in the midst of distresses. And this is nothing else than that strength is made perfect in my weakness, and that I can turn all things to the profit of my salvation; so that even the cross and death are compelled to serve me and to work together for my salvation. This is a lofty and eminent dignity, a true and almighty dominion, a spiritual empire, in which there is nothing so good, nothing so bad, as not to work together for my good, if only I believe. And yet there is nothing of which I have need—for faith alone suffices for my salvation —unless that in it faith may exercise the power and empire of its liberty. This is the inestimable power and liberty of Christians.

Nor are we only kings and the freest of all men, but also priests for ever, a dignity far higher than kingship, because by that priesthood we are worthy to appear before God, to pray for others, and to teach one another mutually the things which are of God.

. . . Thus a Christian, being consecrated by his faith, does good works; but he is not by these works made a more sacred person, or more a Christian. That is the effect of faith alone; nay, unless, he were previously a believer and a Christian, none of his works would have any value at all; they would really be impious and damnable sins. . . .

Since then works justify no man, but a man must be justified before he can do any good work, it is most evident that it is faith alone which, by the mere mercy of God through Christ, and by means of His word can worthily and sufficiently justify and save the person; and that a Christian man needs no work, no law, for his salvation; for by faith he is free from all law, and in perfect freedom does gratuitously all that he does, seeking nothing either of profit or of salvation—since by the grace of God he is already saved and rich in all things through his faith—but solely that which is well-pleasing to God.

We do not then reject good works; nay, we embrace them and teach them in the highest degree. It is not on their own account that we condemn them, but on account of this impious addition to them and the perverse notion of seeking justification by them. These things cause them to be only good in outward show, but in reality not good, since by them men are deceived and deceive others, like ravening wolves in sheep's clothing.[6]

Sören Kierkegaard (1813–1855). This Protestant theologian has probably exerted more influence on recent Protestant thought than any other single person. The originator of what has been called "existentialism," Kierkegaard analyzes faith from the existential point of view. He regards it as an encounter of the existing individual with the Paradox and the Absurd—with the fact that God came into existence as a particular man. As with the Lutheran doctrine, man is dependent on God and requires the grace of God, but in Kierkegaard's thought a greater emphasis is placed on the freedom of the individual. There is no concern to establish an intellectual relationship with God—faith is not a form of knowledge— but there is a very real concern to establish an existential relationship. God is our ultimate concern, as Paul Tillich has said. For Kierkegaard, faith is a means whereby the individual achieves the religious stage of existence; it is a leap, an encounter, and it always involves a deep personal relationship with God. It is also a means whereby the individual—to paraphrase the language of Kierkegaard—appropriates in passionate inwardness and subjectivity the eternal truth of God. But although God is not an object of knowledge, Kierkegaard was firmly convinced that God was real and that He had revealed Himself in history in Jesus Christ. "But he refused to refer to the reality of God and historical revelation as 'objective' because the latter word connoted for him demonstrable conceptual knowledge, an abstraction from passionate commitment, personal decision, and the 'I-Thou' encounter."[7]

The following passages will illustrate some of these features of Kierkegaard's notion of faith:

Christianity has declared itself to be the eternal essential truth which has come into being in time. It has proclaimed itself as the Paradox, and it has required of the individual the inwardness of faith in relation to that which stamps itself as an offense to the Jews and a folly to the Greeks—an absurdity to the understanding. It is impossible more strongly to express the fact that subjectivity is truth, and that the objectivity is repelled, repellent even by virtue of its absurdity. And indeed it would seem very strange that Christianity should have come into the world merely to receive an explanation; as if it had been somewhat bewildered about itself, and hence entered the world to consult that wise man, the speculative philosopher, who can come to its assistance by furnishing the explanation. . . . A believer is one who is infinitely interested in another's reality. This is a decisive criterion for faith, and the interest in question is not just a little curiosity, but an absolute dependence upon faith's object.

The object of faith is the reality of another, and the relationship is one of intense interest. The object of faith is not a doctrine, for then the relationship would be intellectual, and it would be of importance not to botch it, but to realize the maximum intellectual relationship. The object of faith is not a teacher with a doctrine; for when a teacher has a doctrine, the doctrine is *eo ipso* more important than the teacher, and the relationship is again intellectual, and it again becomes important not to botch it, but to realize the maximum intellectual relationship. The object of faith is the reality of the teacher, that the teacher really exists. . . . The object of faith is hence the reality of the God-man in the sense of his existence. But existence involves first and foremost particularity, and this is why thought must abstract from existence, because the particular cannot be thought, but only the universal. The object of faith is thus God's reality in existence as a particular individual, the fact that God has existed as an individual human being.

Christianity is no doctrine concerning the unity of the divine and the human, or concerning the identity of subject and object; nor is it any other of the logical transcriptions of Christianity. If Christianity were a doctrine, the relationship to it would not be one of faith, for only an intellectual type of relationship can correspond to a doctrine. Christianity is therefore not a doctrine, but the fact that God has existed.[8]

Kierkegaard's concept of faith as a "leap" we shall consider in some detail in the next chapter.

Catholicism

FAITH AS INFUSED.   The Roman Catholic position on the origin of faith is quite explicitly and authoritatively stated by St. Thomas Aquinas (1225–1274). Aquinas maintains that faith is essentially a grace that is infused in man by God. God is the cause and the beginning of faith. Faith is based on the divine truth and not upon the will of the believer. To believe depends upon the will of the believer only so far as he must assent to the truth proposed. However, the will of the individual must be prepared for such an assent through the grace of God. Since the truth of faith is above man's nature, his nature must be raised to things above his nature by grace. The grace of faith comes wholly from God, but God's work of grace affects our nature and renders it receptive to His grace, enabling us to assent to such grace. In a word, the power of grace gives us the ability to assent to God. "For by grace you have been saved through faith; and this is not your own doing, it is the gift of God—not because of works, lest any man should boast" (Ephesians 2.8–9). The following excerpts state most succinctly the position of Aquinas. They are taken from the question *Whether Faith is Infused into Man by God?*

I answer that, Two things are requisite for faith. First, that the things which are of faith should be proposed to man; and this is necessary in order that man believe something explicitly. The second thing requisite for faith is the assent of the believer to the things which are proposed to him. Accordingly, as regards the first of these, faith must needs be from God. For the things which are of faith surpass human reason, and hence they do not come to man's knowledge, unless God reveal them. To some, indeed, they are revealed by God immediately, as those things which were revealed to the Apostles and prophets, while to some they are proposed by God in sending preachers of the faith, according to Rom. x. 15: "And how can men preach unless they are sent?"

As regards the second, viz., man's assent to the things which are of faith, we may observe a twofold cause, one of external inducement, such as seeing a miracle, or being persuaded by someone to embrace the faith; neither of which is a sufficient cause, since of those who see the same miracle, or who hear the same sermon, some believe, and some do not. Hence we must assert another and internal cause which moves man inwardly to assent to what belongs to faith.

The Pelagians held that this cause was nothing else than man's free choice, and consequently they said that the beginning of faith is from ourselves, inasmuch as, namely, it is in our power to be ready to assent to the things which are of faith, but that the consummation of faith is from God, who proposes to us the things we have to believe. But this is false, for since, by assenting to what belongs to faith, man is raised above his nature, this must needs come to him from some supernatural principle moving him inwardly; and this is God. Therefore faith, as regards the assent which is the chief act of faith, is from God moving man inwardly by grace.[9]

Summing up further the Thomistic position, that which grace accomplishes with respect to faith is simply to enable us to assent to the truths that God has revealed to us. For revealed truths cannot be proved or demonstrated, they lack that evidence which is typical of those forms of truth verified by experience or demonstrated by reason. Faith is an act of the intellect moved by the will. That which moves the will is God, who in this manner leads us to a knowledge of Him and His truths. God Himself is both the motive and the object of faith; the reason why we believe and what we believe, so that faith attains to what our nature cannot attain, God in Himself. Thus faith is essentially supernatural; it is the effect of that divine grace which leads us to desire the revealed truths of God.

Roman Catholic theologians generally follow the position laid down by Aquinas, although there are certain differences with respect to the role of the intellect and the will among them. Augustinians and Scotists tend to place more emphasis upon the will rather than upon the intellect. These differences will become more apparent after we have examined the relation between faith and reason.

In general, Catholics and Protestants are agreed that faith is a gift of God, a grace whereby God enables man to grasp His revealed truths. The differences between the two groups lies largely in first, the greater importance and centrality in Protestant theology of man's justification by faith;

and second, the doctrine of faith as infused grace and its relation to the Catholic position on the sacraments. This last point will be developed in more detail in the chapter dealing with the sacraments.

Judaism

The faith of Judaism centers upon the reciprocal relationship that exists between God and man. Traditionally, Judaism has based this upon the belief that God has spoken to the individual and to the people of Israel as a nation, that He has established a special covenant with Israel, and that He has chosen Israel as His people. Thus Jews not only have the possibility of faith as individuals, but as a Jew he is one with his people whom God has chosen. In the relationship with God, man becomes a partner in creation. God has a need of man, just as man has a need for God so that he may become righteous and carry out the words of the Torah.

In the medieval period Jewish philosophers were just as concerned with the problem of the relationship between faith and reason as were Christian philosophers. They were also concerned to establish the content of the Jewish faith, the most notable example of which we have already described in Chapter 3 in the listing of the thirteen articles of Maimonides. Since the time of Maimonides, however, there have been many Jewish scholars who reject the notion that Judaism contains any dogmas except, as some have remarked, the dogma that there are no dogmas. Jewish scholarship has been much less preoccupied with theological issues and the development of a systematic theology than have Catholic and Protestant theologians. Orthodox Judaism continues to follow in the tradition of Maimonides. Conservative Judaism has yet to set forth precisely what constitutes the Jewish faith. Reform Judaism has issued a statement of the basic principles of Judaism, but not a theology of faith such as that found in Christianity. One reason for the difference between Christianity and Judaism on this issue is that Christianity has centered the notion of faith about that of salvation and the belief that faith is a grace or a gift of God. In Judaism, as for Luther, faith is primarily a trust (*Emunah*) or faith in God. There are no strict and formal articles of faith or creeds which must be accepted upon pain of excommunication. For Judaism faith is more a confidence in God, a consciousness of the intimacy of man's relationship with God. This should not be taken to imply that in Christianity there is no faith or confidence in God or that faith is not spoken of in this way. The relationship between God and man is just as close in Christianity, but in developing a theology of faith Christians have given primary emphasis to the notions of grace and salvation. For the Christian, faith in the Word of God is a means of salvation; for the Jew, faith is following in the ways demanded by the Torah.

Again, Judaism both past and present has been more concerned with the problems of the nature and maintenance of the Jewish culture and with issues of a practical nature. Judaism is concerned with moral issues, the problems of the community, with learning, with making God real and relevant in the life of the individual and the community. However, the theological problem of faith *per se* has attracted the attention of numerous Jewish scholars. Outstanding and representative here is *Abraham J. Heschel* (born 1907).

Heschel decries the efforts to treat religious belief conceptually. Using at times the language of existentialism he speaks of faith as a *response*, an *engagement*, a *leap of action*. Faith, he holds, centers in the religious experience of the individual, an experience of the ineffable mystery of existence. This somewhat mystical experience of the ineffable cannot be conceptualized or communicated. However, it is something of which we can be aware, and which may become the source of new insights and knowledge in religion. To say that faith centers in the realm of the ineffable does not mean that faith is no longer a trust in God or that we must accept blindly and fatalistically this realm of the ineffable. Man's freedom is never nullified. Rather, faith is just that freedom and power that man has to experience the ineffable, to believe in it so that he can transcend it. In this experience of the ineffable we attain the understanding that is given to us through revelation that God is and that He is concerned with man. Faith, then, is this awareness that the individual has for God as a subject that transcends the ultimate and ineffable mystery underlying reality. Faith is a response, but not a unilateral response. Heschel argues that unless God had first sought man out and revealed Himself to him in the Bible, man could not have responded to God: "Faith comes out of awe, out of an awareness that men are exposed to His presence, out of anxiety to answer the challenge of God, out of an awareness of being called upon. Religion consists of *God's question and man's answer*. The way *to* faith is the way *of* faith. The way to God is a way of God. Unless God asks the question, all inquiries are in vain."[10] Does this mean that faith in some sense, as in the Christian tradition, is a grace received from God, that man would not possess faith unless it were given by God? Not at all, according to Heschel, who is firmly within the Judaic tradition. Although God first seeks man, he has the power to seek Him, but not the power to find Him. ". . . the initiative, we believe, is with man. The great insight is not given unless we are ready to receive. God concludes but we commence. 'Whoever sets out to purify himself is assisted from above.'"[11]

The more practical aspect of faith is brought out in Heschel's description of the *leap of action* and the *engagement*. In the leap of action man comes to an understanding of the Torah, a perception of the spiritual meaning of its words through deeds. To live righteously brings man close to God and enables him to achieve a faith in God. "As for me, I shall behold Thy face in righteousness" (Psalms 18:15). Engagement is very similar in meaning. Heschel points out that the study of the Torah is one way of engagement by the soul. Worship is another. To perform acts of piety may lead to an attachment and a love for God, for it is in acts of piety that man fulfills the will of God and carries out His purposes and needs. Acts of piety do not necessarily lead to faith, to that vision, sensitivity, and attachment to God. But they prepare for those moments when through actions one attains faith. Faith is the outcome of a moral discipline, of religious acts of piety. As Heschel expresses it: "The gates of faith are not ajar, but the mitzvah is a key. By living as Jews we may attain our faith as Jews. We do not have faith because of deeds; we may attain faith through sacred deeds."[12]

FAITH AND REASON

Intellect and Will

It is necessary to look to the relation of faith or belief to the intellect and the will of man. This will give us a better understanding of the complex problem of the relation between faith and reason.

Faith may be taken as an essentially intellectual response by the individual, a response in which the intellect assents to or accepts a given proposition. On the other hand, in giving our assent to a proposed truth we may be moved to such an assent more by an act of will than of intellect. The will may be moved by practical considerations, it may be attracted by the desirability of a given truth. The motivation of an assent may be based upon the will, upon the emotions and feelings of the individual, upon the desire for the truth as good.

Accordingly, in the response of the individual in what we call faith, the emphasis may be placed upon either the intellect or the will. Both are present because both constitute the nature of the individual. The question of the priority of the one or the other is not an easy matter to resolve. It may be contended that the will is prior because to believe is essentially an act or a choice by the individual to accept that which is offered to his belief. On the other hand, it may be argued that before there is an act of will involved in faith, there must be a knowledge of that which is offered to the assent of the individual. This might seem to indicate a priority of intellect over will. But to give an intellectual assent implies the desire to give such an assent. Once more on the other hand, how can a person want or choose something without some knowledge of what he is choosing? And so the circle of the argument goes, leaving us perhaps with at least one definite point, namely, that the act of faith involves both intellect and will.

Thus, as an act of the intellect, faith involves an understanding of that which is to be believed; the intellectual assent is based upon the reasonableness of that which is to be believed. The will is required to act upon that which is offered for belief. The will commits the whole being to that to which the intellect assents as reasonable. Will lies at the very depths of moral and religious experience. It commits men to certain forms of action, leads to confidence or trust in persons; it engages the whole being, and through it one encounters most fully the source of faith to which intellect gives its assent.

We are now in a position to examine in more detail the specific relations that have been held to exist between faith and reason. Four principal relations have been noted. They are: (1) the supremacy of reason; (2) the supremacy of faith to the exclusion of reason; (3) faith over reason; and (4) faith and reason.

The Supremacy of Reason

This position maintains that the preeminent way to knowledge is that of discursive reason. Faith is not necessarily excluded, and religion may be accepted although its truths will usually be subordinated to philosophy or submitted to the criterion of reason. Generally this position has been held by certain philosophers and rejected by religious thinkers and theologians. Some typical representatives of this position are Averroes, John Locke, and Immanuel Kant.

Averroes (Ibn Roschd) (1126–1198) is known as the "Commentator" because of his commentaries on the works of Aristotle. Averroes regarded the philosophy of Aristotle as the final court of appeal in any dispute between the claims of faith and reason. The authority of Aristotle is higher than that of the Koran; the philosophy of Aristotle is the highest wisdom that can be achieved by man. Averroes did not reject religion; he regarded it more as a social necessity than as a truth. To show the relations among philosophy, theology, and religion he observed that all men could be divided into three classes. In the first class he placed the majority of men, who, he said, must rely upon the imagination for the attainment of truth. In the second class he placed the theologians, who argue dialectically for that which they believe. They are incapable of attaining the truths of philosophy, and the conclusions they reach are at best only probable. In the third class Averroes placed a very small minority of mankind—the elite group of the philosophers. Such men, he claimed, know those truths that the average man is persuaded of by the imagination and which the theologians reach by dialectic. However, only the philosopher can attain knowledge that is necessary and certain. The method that he uses to attain truth is that of scientific demonstration.

John Locke (1632–1702), the first of the so-called British empiricists, held a somewhat ambiguous position on the relation between philosophy and religion. He intensely disliked what he termed "enthusiasm" and the tendency of the times to accept private revelations. Although he did not question the possibility of divine revelation he placed rather strict limits upon it. Any so-called truths of revelation that were contrary to reason were to be rejected, for "faith can never convince us of anything that contradicts our knowledge." That reason is the final arbiter in any conflict between faith and reason is noted in his statement: "Whatever God hath revealed is certainly true. . . . This is the proper object of faith: but whether it be a divine revelation . . . reason must judge."

Yet Locke's position is far from being sceptical. He did accept certain revealed truths, for example, the immortality of the soul and the resurrection of the body. And he regarded such truths as the Incarnation and the Trinity as clearly transcending the competence of reason. But he was concerned to rationalize the truths of Christianity as he did in his book on the *Reasonableness of Christianity*, a work which did more to influence scepticism than to stimulate religious belief.

Immanuel Kant (1724–1804), like Locke, was concerned to apply reason to the understanding of Christian dogmas. Although he postulated the existence of God and the immortality of the soul from moral principles, his religious thinking clearly emphasized the supremacy of reason over faith. This is reflected in the title of his book *Religion Within the Limits of Reason Alone*. For Kant true religion meant little more than giving obedience to the moral law. As he put it: "Everything which, apart from a moral way of life, man believes himself capable of doing to please God is mere religious delusion and spurious worship of God."[13] Essentially Kant seemed indifferent to religious practices and religious creeds except where they might be justified by an appeal to the moral law or as acceptable to pure reason. Faith in God, even though reason rejects all arguments for His existence, may be justified on the basis of practical reason. But reason, pure or practical, is superior to faith and the arbiter of all truth.

Thus, the positions that fall within this relationship (the supremacy of reason) may not be sceptical; but once reason is made the judge of all religious truths, then the way is opened for the sceptical attack upon religion. Especially is this true once reason itself is attacked.

The Supremacy of Faith to the Exclusion of Reason

This position is known in the history of thought as *fideism*. The fideist accepts his faith blindly and unquestioningly; he rejects all appeals to reason, whether of philosophy or theology. There is simply no place for them in matters of faith. There is a scepticism here of the value of reason to attain any metaphysical or theological truths. This form of scepticism leads to the contention that the only certitude is to be found in the absolute power of God and in His Word as revealed in the Bible. No explanation is offered by the fideist as to what the meaning of the Bible may be with respect to an article of faith, or why the church may have arrived at a particular decision or definition of faith. Fideism is generally intolerant and overly defensive. It easily leads to the conclusion that since all knowledge and wisdom is to be found in Scripture, the study of profane literature is useless and unnecessary. A classical expression of this attitude of mind is the famous statement of the Latin apologist Tertullian (A.D. 160–240) *"credo quia est absurdum"* (I believe because it is absurd). He also remarked that "philosophers are the patriarchs of heretics" and that "philosophy is the work of demons." There is also the legend that the following dilemma posed by the Moslem conquerors led to the destruction of the Alexandrian Library in A.D. 640: If the books in the library are in conformity with the Koran, they are superfluous; if they are at variance with it, they are pernicious. But they must either be in conformity with the Koran or at variance with it. Therefore they are either superfluous or pernicious and may be destroyed.

In the early Middle Ages fideism is well represented by *Peter Damian* (1007–1072), who asserted in his treatise *On Divine Omnipotence:* "That which is from the argument of the dialecticians cannot easily be adapted to the mysteries of divine power; that which has been invented for the benefit of the syllogisms . . . let it not be obstinately introduced into divine law . . . let it [dialectic] be like a servant ready to obey her mistress."[14] Needless to say, Damian was quite hostile to all forms of profane learning.

In the early modern period fideism is well represented by *Pierre Charon* (1541–1603), a priest and a friend of Montaigne. Influenced by the scepticism of the latter, he tended to reject any rational approach to metaphysical and theological truths. Knowledge of the truth rests with God and in what He has revealed to man. *Blaise Pascal* (1623–1662) has often been accused of being a fideist, but the evidence of his writings, particularly his apologetics, seems to belie this accusation.

In our day the fideist position has been held by various types of Protestant fundamentalists, Jewish legalists, and Roman Catholic authoritarians.

Protestant fundamentalists insist upon the absolute authority of the Bible. The Catholic reactionary either misinterprets or exaggerates the principle of authority in the Catholic Church. The Orthodox Jew may insist upon the rigid observance of every detail of the Law.

Faith Over Reason: Credo ut intelligam

This view stresses at all times the primacy of faith over reason but does not exclude reason. Although reason is intimately associated with faith, reason plays a subordinate role. The relationship between the two has been expressed in the principle *credo ut intelligam* (I believe in order that I may understand). This principle forms an important part of the famous argument that Anselm developed for the existence of God. The meaning he gives to this principle is that if we are to understand an argument for God's existence, we must begin with an assent of our faith in God. Sometimes this principle is expressed in the statement *fides quaerens intellectum* (faith in search of understanding). The statement is Augustine's and means that faith is not an addition to knowledge, but its presupposition, a means by which truths can be adequately comprehended. Faith is the beginning of the knowing process, closely related to reason and including reason, for man is a rational being.

The importance of such principles is evident not merely in the realm of religious truth, but also in their application in the world of science and in everyday life. In science the uniformity and intelligibility of nature is accepted on faith. Upon this basis the scientist is prepared to carry on his inquiries and his search for truth. Whitehead has noted that the medieval faith in an orderly and providential universe strongly contributed to the modern scientific faith in the uniformity of nature. This example of scientific faith could be duplicated in many other areas. However, it should be observed that in any such instances we are taking the meaning of faith in its natural sense. But whether we are concerned with faith on the natural level or on the supernatural level, it is a necessary presupposition of knowledge, and it gives understanding to that which at first we simply believed.

AUGUSTINE ON FAITH AND UNDERSTANDING.   The position upon which we have just been commenting in an introductory fashion finds its finest expression in the thought of St. Augustine (354–430). Augustine's position is representative of the predominant view on the relation between faith and reason that was maintained throughout the greater part of the Middle Ages and which has extended down even to our own times. In addition to Augustine, such outstanding medieval philosophers and theologians as

Anselm, Bonaventure, and Duns Scotus accepted this position or certain variations of it. In modern times we find it represented by many early Protestant theologians and more recently by Richard Niebuhr, Reinhold Niebuhr, Paul Tillich, Karl Barth, and others.

In the Augustinian analysis the contrast is made between faith and understanding. Understanding (*intellectus* or *intelligere*) like reason (*ratio*) is contained within mind (*mens*), which may be identified with the highest functions of the rational soul (*animus*). Understanding may imply merely a knowledge of what the words of a statement mean; it may also include all that knowledge which reason obtains by its discursive activity as well as that knowledge which is arrived at intuitively.

Augustine defines faith as "to think with assent." Assent is an intellectual act; we cannot believe without some mental activity, we must have some understanding of that which is proposed to our belief. But to assent is also an act of will, the freedom to choose to believe or not to believe. Such freedom requires for Augustine the grace of God if the will is to have the power to believe. Faith, then, is an act of the whole man.

Although we are moved by the will and God's grace to faith, yet in faith there is knowledge, an intellectual awareness of that which is offered to the faith of the individual. Faith prepares the understanding, it anticipates knowledge and makes understanding itself possible by conferring an initial certitude upon it.

For a certain faith is in some way the beginning of knowledge; but a certain knowledge will not be made perfect, until after this life, when we shall see face to face (I Cor. 13:12). Let us therefore be thus minded, so as to know that the disposition to seek the truth is more safe than that which presumes things unknown to be known. Let us therefore so seek as if we should find, and so find as if we were about to seek. . . . Let us doubt without unbelief of things to be believed; let us affirm without rashness of things to be understood: authority must be held fast in the former, truth sought out in the latter.[15]

In this reciprocal relationship of faith and understanding there is no absolute separation. We are rational beings, we understand what we believe, and we believe in order that we may understand. Reason is never belittled by Augustine; it is present in faith. For faith is an assent of the whole man and the truth we assent to depends upon the grace of God. We must not only believe God, but we must believe on Him. And to believe on Him enables us to believe in Him. "What then is it to believe on Him? By believing to love Him, by believing to esteem Him highly, by believing to go unto Him and to be incorporated in His members. It is faith itself then that God exacts from us; and He finds not that which He exacts, unless He has bestowed what He may find."[16]

Finally, Augustine puts this entire problem of the relation between faith and understanding in terms of authority and reason: "Where, then, shall I begin? With authority, or with reasoning? In the order of nature, when we learn anything, authority precedes reasoning. For a reason may seem weak, when after it is given it requires authority to confirm it.[17]

For Augustine there can be no sounder principle than that authority should precede reason. It is through the authority of the Church that he is moved to accept the gospel. His reasons for accepting the authority of the Church are: the succession from St. Peter, the miracles which brought the Church into being, the consent of the peoples and the nations. For Augustine authority is represented by the Church, by Scripture, and by Christ. The authority of God is revealed in His grace. We accept the authority of faith because there are truths which must be believed if we are to attain a life of eternal happiness. To accept the authority of Scripture is to accept the revealed word of God, the truths that God has revealed in Christ and His Church.

Faith and Reason

SAADIA BEN JOSEPH AL-FAYYUMI (892–942). Saadia is the first great Jewish philosopher and in many ways he anticipates some of the solutions offered on the problem of the relation between faith and reason by Aquinas and Maimonides. The philosophical position of Saadia is developed within the context of the Torah and also of the Mishnah and the Talmud, both of which had been completed for some time. In one of his principal works, the *Book of Doctrines and Beliefs*, he endeavors to show that Judaism is essentially in harmony with reason, that Judaism is basically reasonable. He observes that there are three sources of truth: sense, judgment, and inference, and that these are common to all men. In addition Judaism possesses those truths given by divine revelation. He also points out that much of the Jewish faith can be shown to be in harmony with reason, although he does affirm that a rational argument for the messianic future must be replaced with simple faith.

A rational inquiry into religion is necessary for two reasons: first, to make known to ourselves that knowledge which has been given to us by the Prophets of God; second, to be able to refute our opponents. The function of reason is primarily to confirm the truths of faith that have been revealed by God. Since Judaism is so reasonable, the problem for Saadia is to show why revelation is necessary. There is no true conflict between faith and reason. The real conflict will be one between faith and false reason. Revelation is necessary because although reason can discover by itself such basic truths as creation, free will, the rational character of the Law, and the immortality of the soul, such speculative inquiry would require a great deal of time and we would have been deprived during that time of religious knowledge. Furthermore, many individuals are incompetent to carry out this type of inquiry or they lack the patience to do so. Hence, says Saadia:

> God (be He exalted and glorified) saved us quickly by sending us His Messenger, announcing through him the Tradition, and allowing us to see with our own eyes signs in support of it and proofs which cannot be assailed by doubts, and which we can find no ground for rejecting, as is said, "Ye yourselves have seen that I have talked with you from heaven" (Ex. 20.22). He spoke to His messenger in our presence, and He based on this fact our obligation to believe him for ever, as He said, "That the people may hear when I speak with thee, and may also believe thee for ever" (Ex. 19.9).[18]

Saadia concludes that we are obligated to accept revelation for it has been verified by the testimony of sense perception and the truth of tradition, oral and written. We must continue our inquiries until the truth of tradition has been verified by rational speculation. This will require patience on our part but we must abide by our religious truth until speculation has been completed. For some this may take a long time, but none shall be deprived of the truth of religion even though they are incapable of speculation.

THE THOMISTIC SYNTHESIS.   Like his illustrious predecessors and all great religious thinkers, Aquinas never overlooks the reality of the great disproportion that exists between the finite and the infinite. He does not denigrate faith to make a place for reason. Nor does he ever deny that faith is necessary for our salvation, or that there are truths that faith alone can attain. His real concern is to render a little more precise the distinction between reason and faith, a distinction that was too often blurred by many of his predecessors. At the same time he was very cognizant of the fact that not only is faith a gift of God; so too is reason. Hence the importance for him of delineating the province of reason, to show precisely what it can attain, and why it is never really in conflict with faith.

Aquinas was strongly influenced by the introduction of the Aristotelian philosophy in the twelfth century. He was quite impressed with the knowledge that is open to human reason and with the competence of human reason. He held that reason can not only establish the existence of God but also some of God's attributes, for example, that He is one, infinite, eternal. However, such knowledge is very minimal and negative compared to many of the positive truths that faith teaches and to the kind of knowledge that we shall be able to attain in the life to come.

The limitations of human reason are quite evident. Thus reason cannot prove the Incarnation, the Trinity, and other divine mysteries that completely transcend it. Even a truth such as the beginning of the world in time eludes rational demonstration.[19] But such a truth does not escape faith, for Genesis 1 says quite clearly: "In the beginning God made heaven and earth." Furthermore, we accept on faith what Christ has taught that we must do to achieve our salvation, and this is not subject to demonstration by reason. Finally, there are some truths which can be an object of faith for some and an object of reason for others. The uneducated man may accept the existence of God upon faith rather than attempt to understand a demonstration by reason for God's existence. On the other hand, the philosopher can prove by reason that God exists. So the same truth may be open to one individual on faith and to another through reason.

Aquinas held that there is no place for faith where reason understands. We cannot both know and believe at the same time. What one man knows by reason, another may understand through faith. But the same person does not at the same time hold upon faith what he demonstrates by reason. Of course, he may eventually decide that this demonstration of a truth was at fault and revert to a position in which he holds that truth by faith. Faith and reason each has a distinctive place, and each was created for a distinctive purpose. Both are given to man by God. Now since God cannot be subject to error and deception, there can be no incompatibility between faith and reason. Faith is the revealed word of God, and what God says cannot be false. Reason if rightly followed can yield only the true. Suppose, however, that reason teaches that which contradicts Scripture. In this case Aquinas would maintain that there is only a seeming contradiction. The word of God is absolute truth, and if reason teaches the contrary then reason must be at fault. In other words, error is possible for man but not for God. Our reason is fallible, but the revealed word of God is infallible. Any conflict between faith and reason therefore is only apparent and not real. An examination of the argument based upon reason (and which contradicts faith) will reveal its fallibility. As Aquinas puts it:

> From this we evidently gather the following conclusion: whatever arguments are brought forward against the doctrines of faith are conclusions incorrectly derived from the first and self-evident principles imbedded in nature. Such conclusions do not have the force of demonstration; they are arguments that are either probable or sophistical. And so, there exists the possibility to answer them.[20]*

It follows from this that for Aquinas as well as for his predecessors, faith is higher than reason. Faith exercises a transcendental influence upon reason, it guides reason and guards it from error and presumption. Speak-

---

* From St. Thomas Aquinas, *On the Truth of the Catholic Faith* (*Summa Contra Gentiles*), Book I, translated by Anton C. Pegis. Copyright © 1955 by Doubleday & Company, Inc. Reprinted by permission of the publisher.

ing of the importance of faith, Aquinas says: "It is also necessary that such truth be proposed to men for belief so that they may have a truer knowledge of God. For then only do we know God truly when we believe Him to be above everything that it is possible for man to think about Him. . . . Hence, by the fact that some things about God are proposed to man that surpass his reason, there is strengthened in man the view that God is something above what he can think."[21] And to curb presumption he says: "For there are some who have such a presumptuous opinion of their own ability that they deem themselves able to measure the nature of everything; I mean to say that, in their estimation, everything is true that seems to them so, and everything is false that does not. So that the human mind, therefore, might be freed from this presumption and come to a humble inquiry after truth, it was necessary that some things should be proposed to man by God that would completely surpass his intellect."[22]

On the other hand, Aquinas maintains that reason serves the very important function of explaining that which we believe. This explication of faith intensifies the strength of our faith. To understand that which we believe will surely give us a more satisfying and enduring faith. It will enable us to defend and to make more meaningful our faith. Thus reason supplements faith just as faith supplements reason. On the level of the intellectual disciplines this means that philosophy supplements the knowledge of theology, and theology that of philosophy. Faith and reason are each free within their respective areas, but the closeness of their relationship is exemplified in the way in which they supplement and enrich one another.

Faith, however, remains superior and for the reasons we have already outlined. In addition faith begins with God and descends to man, whereas reason begins with man and ascends to God. But even though the primacy of faith is maintained, a very high and significant place is given to reason in this relationship. This faith of Aquinas in reason is exemplified in the testimony he cites from Hilary's *De Trinitate*:

Enter these truths by believing, press forward, persevere. And though I may know that you will not arrive at an end, yet I will congratulate you in your progress. For, though he who pursues the infinite with reverence will never finally reach the end, yet he will always progress by pressing onward. But do not intrude yourself into the divine secret, do not, presuming to comprehend the sum total of intelligence, plunge yourself into the mystery of the unending nativity; rather, understand that these things are incomprehensible.[23]

PAUL TILLICH (1886–1965).   Among contemporary Protestant theologians, one of the most incisive analyses of faith and its relation with reason is to be found in Paul Tillich's *The Dynamics of Faith*.

The philosophical matrix of Tillich's theology lies in existentialism. For him faith means that ultimate concern which gives meaning to the whole of man's existence. He observes that the individual may have many concerns of a proximate and finite nature—health, life, family, politics. But man's ultimate concern demands a total commitment and promises a total fulfillment of all the aspirations of the individual. Such an ultimate concern cannot be met by any finite reality and it involves a response by the whole individual. "Faith," says Tillich, "is a total and centered act of the personal self, the act of unconditional, infinite and ultimate concern."[24] It is well exemplified in the great commandment of the Old Testament: "You shall love the Lord your God with all your heart, and with all your soul, and with all your might" (Deuteronomy 6:5). True faith is to be found in man's experience of the holy, in his total surrender to God as the symbol of man's ultimate concern.

Tillich maintains that if we grant that faith is the state of being ultimately concerned, there can be and need be no conflict with reason. The spiritual life of the individual person is a unity, and reason is that element within this unity which determines the nature of man—it gives him his humanity. Faith, therefore, would only dehumanize the individual if it were considered as opposed to reason. For it is only man, a rational being, who is capable of an ultimate concern, who can experience the holy, and who is a religious creature.

"Reason," says Tillich, "is the precondition of faith; faith is the act in which reason reaches ecstatically beyond itself. . . . Man is finite, man's reason lives in preliminary concerns; but man is also aware of his potential infinity, and this awareness appears as his ultimate concern, as faith. If reason is grasped by an ultimate concern, it is driven beyond itself; but it does not cease to be reason, finite reason. The ecstatic experience of an ultimate concern does not destroy the structure of reason. Ecstasy is fulfilled, not denied, rationality. Reason can be fulfilled only if it is driven beyond the limits of its finitude, and experiences the presence of the ultimate, the holy. . . . There is no conflict between the nature of faith and the nature of reason; they are within each other."[25]

Tillich next proceeds to show the concrete relation between faith as man's ultimate concern and reason in its cognitive function, that is, reason leading to knowledge in science, history, and philosophy. The meaning and dimensions of truth in these ways of knowledge is different from the truth of faith. Hence there can be no essential conflict between the two. The truth of faith has its own criteria and is not subject to the criteria of scientific knowledge. Similarly, scientific knowledge has its criteria and is not subject to the truth of faith. A like distinction holds for historical and philosophical truths.

The criteria of the truth of faith find their source in faith as an ultimate concern. Faith is true if it "adequately expresses an ultimate concern," and "if its content is the really ultimate."[26] The criteria of science have their source in observation, measurement, and the formulation and verification of hypotheses. Hence, as Tillich concludes, the truth of science and the truth of faith exist in different dimensions of meaning. Science cannot and should not interfere with faith and faith cannot and should not interfere with science.

This relationship between faith and science is exemplified in the early modern development of astronomy. The astronomer's concepts of heaven and earth, their place and relationship came into conflict with certain religious symbols which pictured heaven and hell as actual places above and below the earth. A false faith then came into conflict with scientific truth. On the other hand, when the modern empiricist reduces all reality to a mechanistic materialism, he denies any true reality to life and mind. He substitutes a scientific faith, the belief that our ultimate concern must be science, for that faith which is truly ultimate and infinite. In this instance a false faith based on science conflicts with the true faith of Christianity.

Between true science and true faith there is no conflict, although science may conflict with science, and faith with faith. If we examine the early struggles between science and religion over the origins of the world and of man we shall find that such conflicts were between fundamentalism and biblical literalism on the one hand and the claims of some scientists to the possession of ultimate and absolute truth on the other hand. However, between the religious conception of man and the scientific, there should be no conflict because the dimensions of meaning differ for each. Citing an example from psychology, Tillich observes that faith is concerned for the soul of man, for the meaning of his existence, and his ultimate destiny. Such concern is not the proper subject of psychology. Psychology as a science may or may not reject the notion of the soul, but in either case its real concern should be limited to that which is subject to scientific analysis. Failure to do so may lead to an expression of scientific faith rather than scientific knowledge. Criticizing Freud on this account, Tillich notes: "The naturalistic elements which Freud carried from the nineteenth century into the twentieth century, his basic puritanism with respect to love, his pessimism about culture, and his reduction of religion to ideological projection are all expressions of faith and not the result of scientific analysis."[27]

On the other hand, just as scientists must avoid projecting faith into science, so the theologians ought not to use scientific truths to confirm the truths of faith. Thus the truth of faith that we are free should not be supported by an appeal to the principle of indeterminism or the quantum theory. Such attempts to confirm the truth of faith by an appeal to science confuse the meaning of truth; they constitute an interference with the truths of science by the theologians. To attempt to confirm the truth of faith by the truth of science can only weaken the truth of faith.

KNOWLEDGE OF FAITH

How does the religious man know that he possesses faith? Few questions in theology have given rise to so many and such complex difficulties. We shall restrict our discussion to just a few of the major problems that arise out of this question.

One of the earliest and best responses to this question is that given by Augustine:

> Furthermore, the faith itself which everyone sees to be in his heart if he believes, or does not see there if he does not believe—we know in a different way; not as bodies which we see with our bodily eyes, and, through their images which we retain in our memory even think of them when they are absent; nor as those things which we have not seen, of which we somehow form thoughts from those things which we have seen and entrust to our memory, to which we may return when we will, in order that we may likewise see them there by recollection, or rather see their images, of whatever sort they may be that we have fixed there; nor as a living man whose soul indeed we do not see but conjecture from our own, and from the corporeal motions gaze also in thought upon the living man, as we have acquired knowledge of him by sight. Faith is not so seen in the heart in which it is, by him whose it is; but we know most certainly that it is there, and our conscience proclaims its existence.

> Although we are, therefore, commanded to believe for this very reason, that we cannot see that which we are commanded to believe; yet when the faith itself is in us, we see it in us, because the faith of things that are absent is present, and the faith of things that are without is within, and the faith of things that are not seen is seen; and yet it arises in time in the hearts of men, and if from believers they become unbelievers, it perishes from them.[28]

For Augustine faith is certain because we have a direct knowledge of our faith. It is something that is seen within, something that we are as immediately aware of as we are of our own self. Faith is self-validating; it requires no demonstration any more than the existence of the self requires demonstration. We may not see the object of faith—for example, God—but we do perceive directly that we have faith in such a being.

The view of Aquinas is not too different: "And if faith may not be known by exterior movements of the body, yet it is perceived by that in which it is, by the interior act of the heart. No one knows that he has faith, save in that he is aware that he believes."[29]

The certain knowledge we have of that which we believe is simply faith itself—an infused, supernatural faith bestowed upon us by God. Thus the motive of faith, the authority of the divine revelation, is obtained by a kind of supernatural perception. The certitude of faith is given by God, and is not the product of our reason or will.

However, a serious difficulty now appears. Can we truly say that one can be absolutely certain that he has faith any more than we can say that he is absolutely certain that he possesses grace? It is generally the opinion of theologians that men are not absolutely certain, but only morally certain, that we possess grace. If faith is a grace, can we truly ascribe to it anything more than a moral certitude? To assert that one has an absolute certainty is not only presumptuous but has the effect of canceling out the supernatural character of grace and faith. By any such assertion of a natural or human certitude God and His truths are brought down to the level of men's minds, whereas the function of faith is precisely to ennoble, to perfect, and to raise intellect to a level whereby with God's grace men can grasp His truths.[30]

Basically there would appear to be at least two solutions to the problem just raised. One is to maintain that one possesses the certitude of supernatural faith because God is intimately present in a mystical experience which accompanies knowledge of faith. The other solution is that man has a moral certitude of faith.

MYSTICAL CERTITUDE.   Many theologians are convinced that only by appealing to the mystical experience of the believer can we satisfactorily explain the knowledge of faith. Such an experience is not lacking in those positions we have described as taken by Augustine and Aquinas. Karl Adam declares that "the majority of Catholic theologians, St. Thomas, the most representative among them, Capreolus, his best commentator, Bañez, the leader of the Thomist school, Molina, the latter's great adversary, and many more, are in agreement that divine faith rests in the last analysis upon an interior and mystical illumination."[31]

And referring to a recent work by P. Roger Aubert on *Le Problème de l'Acte de Foi*, Fr. Trethowan observes:

P. Aubert puts the problem as follows at one point: "According to the most classical theology, the *motive* of *faith*, that is, the authority of God, can move us to assent only when we are convinced of this authority, and this evidence which is a prerequisite cannot have a 'scientific' character . . . Theology, he holds, is coming back to a recognition that it is the 'inner voice' which is the all-important factor of solution. Scheeben was one of the great labourers in this work of replacing in its position of honour the 'mystical' aspect of faith; for him the light of faith is a grace by which God makes himself known to the soul without intermediary, as being himself who speaks.[32]

MORAL CERTITUDE.   Other and equally influential theologians, for example Scotus and Suarez, maintain that at best we can have a moral certitude that we possess grace and faith. At the conclusion of a brief but excellent analysis of the position of Suarez, Mouroux states of that position: "Faith, in fact, is an obscure thing, as is proved by the case of the heretic, who believes he has faith when he has only opinion—'which would be quite impossible if he knew the nature of his assent, and its motive, clearly and intuitively. A fortiori, the proper mode of supernatural faith is too elevated and too hidden ever to be known by clear experience.' The conclusion is inevitable: it is impossible for the Christian to have a certain knowledge of his faith."[33]

Moral certitude is exemplified in the moral values we perceive as consequent upon grace. One delights in the things of the spirit, in charity and the love of God, in an experience of freedom from sin, etc. All of this may be said to convince one morally but not intellectually that one has the grace of God. Similarly, he may be said to be morally certain that he has the faith because he is able to obey God's commandments, to understand his teachings and to carry them to others, and simply because he is convinced beyond the shadow of a doubt of the truth he adheres to with his whole being.

Faith and Heresy

The term "heresy" is derived from the Greek meaning "an act of choosing." Among the early church fathers it was considered as "godless," as "alien to Christianity," and essentially as a form of belief that was disruptive of the unity of the Church. Heresy presents a problem for faith because the heretic is convinced he is right. Even though from the point of view of the nonheretic the heretic possess only a kind of psychological certitude, the heretic himself may claim the highest kind of certitude for his belief. Equally with the true believer he may claim a moral or mystical certitude of faith. The problem for the Christian theologian is to explain why the heretic is at fault and does not possess the certitude of faith.

The solution to the problem turns upon certain distinctions and theoretical considerations which involve very real difficulties and upon which there is no common agreement among theologians. The practical solution to the problem is another matter. The falsity of the heretic's claim to faith consists merely in showing how he has deviated from the accepted standards or norms of the Christian faith, for example, the Bible, the Church.

If the heretic alienates himself from such standards, then, despite his protestations, we can rightly judge that he errs in professing to have the true faith. For the faith he professes contradicts that which the Bible or the Church or both clearly state as God's Word.

For Judaism the problem of heresy is simpler and is almost entirely a practical matter. From its earliest history Judaism had to contend with deviations from the norms of Judaistic practices and beliefs: idolatry, immorality, mixed marriages, disrespect for rabbis. The basic method of dealing with nonconformity was the ban of excommunication (*cherem*). This disciplinary measure was also adapted by the early Christian Church, as St. Paul states in I Corinthians 16:22. In the medieval period excommunication often meant expulsion from the community ("great cherem") and was greatly feared by the Jews. The ceremony of excommunication, inquisitorial practices, and the various punishments meted out for heresy were similar in the medieval Church and Synagogue. With the beginning of the modern period the practice of excommunication waned, and today it is practically extinct within Judaism. Even in Christianity, where it is occasionally invoked, the penalties are by no means as severe as formerly. Heresy trials are relatively infrequent.

Some Consequences of Faith

First, we may observe that the consequences of faith issue in the good life since the man of faith is a man under commandment. Faith demands of him righteousness and justice as his unconditional duty, and the more nearly he realizes these commandments, the freer he is before God and man, and at a greater remove from sin.

For the Catholic, faith fulfills, completes, and enriches the life of reasoning by adding those truths that reason cannot attain. He believes not only that there is a God, but receives a deeper insight into the nature of God through the life and teachings of Jesus Christ. He takes as his rule of faith the historical creeds and finds in the Bible under authoritative interpretation a guide to the affairs of life. In the tradition of the Church he receives insight into the applications of Christian truths to the changing problems of the present. Through the sacraments he receives his spiritual nurture. His hope for a better life in the next world enables him to bear patiently the trials of this world and spurs him to works of charity that have merit for his ultimate salvation. Through faith he may draw upon the merit of his own good works as well as the treasury of merits built up by the saints through the ages and thus enlist their help in his fight against "the world, the flesh, and the devil."

For Protestant Christians the consequences of faith cannot be set forth quite as precisely because of denominational differences. For most Protestants the life of faith is a life that centers in the historical creeds and in the Word of God as given in the Bible. The life of faith for most would be a life reclaimed. A life in which he discovers that whereas formerly—without faith—the deepest and most crucial problems in his life eluded all right answer, now he finds that through the mercy of God and the faith of God he has the means to effect a complete reformation and reorientation of his life. Trusting in God and not just in himself, he has a new freedom and power to meet the problems of life. To cite again Martin Luther's famous paradox: "A Christian man is the most free lord of all, and subject to none; a Christian man is the most dutiful servant of all, and subject to everyone."

The faith of Judaism is more pragmatic and less theoretical in nature and scope. It emphasizes man's relation to his Creator, the covenant between God and man, the obligation of obedience to the mitzvoh of the Torah, and the faith in Israel as the chosen people of God. Good works are demanded of the individual. They consist in prayer, piety, study and learning, acts of justice and righteousness, the duty toward the neighbor, and the recognition of the obligations to the community ("Separate not thyself from the community," taught Hillel). Significantly, for Judaism faith is not a grace which makes possible the accomplishment of good works by man. Instead Judaism emphasizes more the freedom of man and the necessity for man to take the initiative in those actions which will lead to the good life and be pleasing to the eyes of God.

Throughout both the Jewish and Christian traditions there is the teaching that faith without works is dead, that it is idle to talk about having faith and at the same time to avoid responsibility and to be detached from the world. In all three traditions, faith received through God's unqualified acceptance of man frees him from fear and calculation, and sets him free to love his neighbor in a new way. As John Calvin put it: "They who are justified in true faith, prove their justification not by bearing an imaginary resemblance of faith, but by obedience and good works." For both Jews and Christians faith involves the whole person. Its gift is not something which we hold in our power, it is something which lives in man and by which man lives. Faith in God involves a permanent revolution of the mind and the heart, a continuous life which opens out into ever new possibilities.

NOTES

1. *Webster's New World Dictionary* (Cleveland and New York: World, 1962), p. 522.
2. *The Oxford Universal Dictionary* (Oxford: Clarendon Press, 1955), p. 670.
3. Adapted from Charles Sanders Peirce, who declared: "Critical Common-sensism admits that there are not only indubitable propositions but also that there are

indubitable inferences. In one sense, anything evident is indubitable; but the propositions and inferences which Critical Common-sensism holds to be original, in the sense one cannot 'go behind' them (as the lawyers say), are indubitable in the sense of being acritical." Justus Buchler, ed., *The Philosophy of Peirce: Selected Writings* (New York: Harcourt, Brace, 1940), p. 290.

4. From *The Splendour of the Church* by Henri de Lubac, S.J., 1956 © Sheed & Ward Inc., New York, p. 16.

5. John Calvin, *Institutes*, quoted by John Dillenberger, ed., *Handbook of Christian Theology* (New York: Meridian Books, 1958), p. 132.

6. Martin Luther, *Concerning Christian Liberty*, trans. R. S. Grignon. Harvard Classics Vol. 36 (New York: Collier, 1910), pp. 362–391.

7. David E. Roberts, *Existentialism and Religious Belief* (New York: Oxford University Press, 1959), pp. 84–85.

8. Sören Kierkegaard, *Concluding Unscientific Postscript*, trans. David F. Swenson (Princeton: Princeton University Press, 1944), pp. 290–291.

9. St. Thomas Aquinas, *Summa Theologica*, II–II, Q. 6, a. 1.

10. Abraham J. Heschel, *Between God and Man*, ed. Fritz A. Rothschild (New York: Free Press, 1959), p. 69.

11. *Ibid.*, p. 72.

12. *Ibid.*, p. 81

13. Quoted by Frederick Copleston, S.J., *A History of Philosophy* (London: Burns and Oates, 1960), VI, 344.

14. Quoted by Gordon Leff, *Medieval Thought* (Baltimore: Penguin, 1958), p. 96.

15. *The Trinity*, IX, 1, in M. Dods, ed., *The Works of St. Augustine* (Edinburgh, 1871).

16. *Tractate on the Gospel According to St. John*, in M. Dods, ed., *Works of St. Augustine* (Edinburgh, 1871), X, 405–406.

17. St. Augustine, *The Way of Life of the Catholic Church*, trans. Donald A. Gallagher and Idella J. Gallagher. In The Fathers of the Church Series Vol. 56 (Washington, D.C.: The Catholic University of America Press, 1966), p. 5.

18. Saadia Ben Joseph Al-Fayyumi, *Book of Doctrines and Beliefs*, ed. Alexander Altmann. From *Three Jewish Philosophers* (New York: Harper and Row, and Philadelphia: Jewish Publication Society, 1965), pp. 45–46.

19. Aquinas rejected the attempt of St. Bonaventure and others to demonstrate the beginning of the world in time, just as he rejected the arguments of Averroes and others for the demonstration of the eternity of the world.

20. St. Thomas Aquinas, *Summa Contra Gentiles*, I, 7, 7, trans. Anton Pegis. From *On the Truth of the Catholic Faith* (New York: Doubleday, 1955), I, 75.

21. *Ibid.*, I, 5, 3.

22. *Ibid.*, I, 5, 4.

23. *Ibid.*, I, 8, 2.

24. Paul Tillich, *Dynamics of Faith* (New York: Harper and Row, 1957), p. 8.

25. *Ibid.*, pp. 76–77.

26. *Ibid.*, p. 96.

27. *Ibid.*, p. 84.

28. St. Augustine, *The Trinity*, XIII, 1, 3, trans. Stephen McKenna. In The Fathers of the Church Series, Vol. 45 (Washington, D.C.: Catholic University of America Press, 1963), pp. 371–373.

29. St. Thomas Aquinas, *Summa Theologica*, I, 87, 2, ad. 1.

30. There is frequently apt to be a confusion between the motives of credibility and the motives of faith. The motive of faith is God Himself. The motives of

credibility are those reasons—prophecies, miracles, etc.—which prepare us for the reception of supernatural faith.

31. Quoted by Dom Illtyd Trethowan, *Certainty: Philosophical and Theological* (London: Dacre Press: A. & C. Black Ltd., 1948), p. 162.
32. *Ibid.*, p. 162.
33. From *The Christian Experience* by Jean Mouroux, Copyright Sheed & Ward Inc., 1954, p. 63.

Select Bibliography

AQUINAS, ST. THOMAS. *The Truth of the Catholic Faith.* Trans. Anton C. Pegis. New York: Doubleday and Co., 1955, Vol. I., pp. 15–76.

AQUINAS, ST. THOMAS. *Summa Theologica.* Edited and annotated by Anton C. Pegis. New York: Random House, 1945, II–II. Q. 1. a. 1, 4; and Q. 5. Q. 6, a. 1.

AUGUSTINE. *The Advantage of Believing.* Trans. Luanne Meagher, O.S.B. New York: The Fathers of the Church, Inc. Vol. 4, 1947. *Letter 120.* Trans. Sister Wilfrid Parsons. New York: The Fathers of the Church, Inc., 1953, Vol. 18.

BAILLIE, J. *Our Knowledge of God.* London: Oxford University Press, 1939.

BARTH, KARL. *Dogmatics in Outline.* New York: Harper and Brothers, 1959.

DANIÉLOU, J. *God and the Ways of Knowing.* Trans. Walter Roberts. New York: Meridian Books, 1957.

DARCY, M. C., S.J. *The Nature of Belief.* London and New York: Sheed & Ward, 1951.

FARMER, H. H. *The World and God.* New York: Harper and Brothers, 1936.

HESCHEL, ABRAHAM J. *Between God and Man.* Ed. Fritz A. Rothschild. New York: The Free Press, 1959.

KIERKEGAARD, SÖREN. *Concluding Unscientific Postscript.* Trans. David F. Swenson. Princeton, N.J.: Princeton University Press, 1944.

LEWIS, H. D. *Our Experience of God.* London: Allen and Unwin, 1959.

LOCKE, JOHN. *The Reasonableness of Christianity.* London: Adam and Charles Black, 1958.

LUTHER, MARTIN. *Concerning Christian Liberty.* Trans. R. S. Grignon. Harvard Classics. New York: P. F. Collier and Son, 1910.

MOUROUX, JEAN. *The Christian Experience.* Trans. George Lamb. New York: Sheed & Ward, 1954.

SAADIA BEN. JOSEPH (Gaon). *The Book of Beliefs and Opinions.* Trans. S. Rosenblatt. New Haven: Yale University Press, 1948.

SCHECHTER, SOLOMON. *Studies in Judaism.* New York: Meridian Books, 1958.

TILLICH, PAUL. *Dynamics of Faith.* New York: Harper and Brothers, 1957.

TRETHOWAN, ILLTYD. *Certainty: Philosophical and Theological.* London: Dacre Press: A. & C. Black, 1948.

VI

The Existence and Nature of God

THE subjects of God's existence and His nature lie within the areas of both theology and the philosophy of religion. The existence of God has always been a concern of the philosopher, and to a lesser extent so has the question of the nature of God. For the religious man, or the theologian, God is accepted as a fact, an original datum, an object of belief. For such individuals there is strictly speaking no problem of God's existence. On the other hand, the philosopher may argue either for or against God's existence.

With respect to the nature of God, the philosopher who rejects God's existence generally regards all attempts to describe God's nature as constituting some form of anthropomorphism. For the philosopher who accepts God's existence, the description of God's nature is usually limited to certain positive but minimal assertions based upon an analogy with the nature of man, or to certain negative assertions of what God is not usually embodied in what is called a negative theology. For the theologian or the individual who takes a purely religious approach to this problem, the nature of God is essentially revealed, and the evidence for such revelation is in Scripture. Here, although there is much concerning God that remains hidden or completely other than man, still there are the "names" of God, the manifestations of God to man, God's intervention in the history of man, His agreements with man, and—for the Christian—His Incarnation.

For the purely religious or theological approach we shall consider how God makes Himself known to man. For the philosophical approach we shall consider how man makes known the existence and nature of God.

Both of these approaches will be taken within the context of the Jewish and Christian traditions. The first will involve primarily some statement of what has been revealed to man. The problems arising from such statements will be essentially problems of interpretation, for the statements themselves are accepted as factual by the believer. The second approach will be based upon experience and reason and will involve the effort to establish either experientially or theoretically truths regarding God's existence and nature. The analysis that follows will be divided then into two major topics: the existence of God, and the nature of God. These in turn will be subdivided according to their treatment by both the theologian and the philosopher.

THE EXISTENCE OF GOD

How God Has Made Known His Existence

To the theologian and to one who takes a wholly religious approach to this problem, God makes His existence known to man by revelations, assertions, and manifestations. Thus God appeared to Moses in the form of the Burning Bush, and He spoke to Moses. Indirectly He made known His existence in the form of His emissaries or angels. His existence is proclaimed in His inspiration of the prophets and the writers of Sacred Scripture who regarded their words as God's Word. And God's many miracles, His various acts and interventions in the history of man, His covenants with man—all testify *that* He exists.

In the New Testament His existence is made manifest in the assertion of St. John: "In the beginning was the Word . . ." And far more concretely and personally, presenting us with a great mystery and paradox, there is the Incarnation of God Himself in the Person of Jesus His Son. God's existence is manifested in the faith and courage given to Moses, Aaron, Job, Joshua, Elijah, Daniel, and many others in the Scriptures. To St. Paul, God appears in the form of a great light on the road to Damascus. Nor does the testimony of God end with Scripture. Countless individuals since that time have testified how God made His presence known to them. To Augustine He is a voice in the form of a child crying "Take up and read! Take up and read!" (*Tolle lege, tolle lege*). To Joan of Arc, God appears through the "voices" of St. Michael, St. Catherine, and St. Margaret exhorting her to the liberation of France. For George Fox there are decisive "openings" in which God and His truths are directly revealed to his soul. And to all mystics God makes Himself known in their visions, their raptures, and their ecstasies. Finally, there is the often quoted state-

ment from Exodus 3:13 in which God declares explicitly to Moses that "I
Am Who I Am." The Torah reading gives:

> Moses said to God, "When I come to the Israelites and say to them 'The
> God of your fathers has sent me to you,' and they ask me, 'What is His name?'
> what shall I say to them?" And God said to Moses, "Ehyeh-Asher-Ehyeh"
> (variously translated as "I Am That I Am"; "I Am Who I Am"; "I Will Be
> What I Will Be"; etc.) He continued, "Thus shall you say to the Israelites
> 'Ehyeh ("I Am") sent me to you'" (Exodus 3:13–15).

It may be noted, however, that later on in this account a direct vision of
God is not permitted to Moses.

> He said, "Oh let me behold Your Presence!" And He answered, "I will make
> all My goodness pass before you as I proclaim the name Lord before you: I will
> be gracious to whom I will be gracious, and show compassion to whom I will
> show compassion. But," He said, "you cannot see My face, for man may not
> see Me and live." And the Lord said, "See, there is a place near Me. Station
> yourself on the rock and, as My Presence passes by, I will put you in a cleft of
> the rock and shield you with My hand, until I have passed by. Then I will take
> My hand away and you will see My back; but My face must not be seen"
> (Exodus 33:17–23).

The further significance of this passage and others like it will be noted
later when we treat more fully of the nature of God. At the moment we
cite it to show that although God Himself affirms His existence, *that* He is,
His nature or *what* He is remains hidden from man.

How Man Makes Known the Existence of God

We shall be concerned in this section with the different ways in which
philosophers and others have endeavored to show how the existence of
God may be presented for our intellectual assent or belief. We shall avoid
the use of the term "proof" because it implies often a more rigorous
mathematical type of demonstration than that found in most of the arguments or persuasions we shall describe. To simplify our presentation, with
the risk of some overlapping, we shall consider certain representative
arguments for God's existence from the metaphysical, the experiential, and
the existential points of view.

Metaphysical Arguments

THE AUGUSTINIAN ARGUMENT.   Augustine offered just one argument
for the existence of God.[1] He based his argument upon the notion of
truth, and it has been subject to different interpretations. Briefly para-

phrasing the argument, Augustine first shows that knowledge is possible and that the certainty we have that God exists is held at least by faith. Following the biblical injunction, "Except ye believe, ye shall not understand" (Isaiah 7:9, as rendered by Augustine), Augustine proceeds to show how we understand that which we hold by faith. He argues that we have a knowledge of mathematical and moral truths whose essential characteristics are eternality, immutability, and necessity. But that which is eternal, immutable, and necessary cannot be created by the finite mind of man or exist within the finite mind of man, for man's mind, as finite, is temporal, mutable, and contingent. Hence, eternal, immutable, and necessary truths exist above the human mind. And Augustine concludes:

> You conceded, however, that if I should show you something higher than our minds, you would confess that it is God, if there were nothing higher. Accepting this concession of yours I said that it would be enough if I should prove this. For if there is something yet more excellent than truth, that rather is God; but if not, then truth itself is God. Whether therefore there is this more excellent thing, or whether there is not, you cannot deny that God is, which was the question set for our discussion and treatment. . . . For God is; and He is truly and supremely. This, I think, we not only hold now undoubted by faith, but know also by a sure albeit still rather tenuous form of knowledge. . . .[2]

The argument may be briefly summarized in the following syllogism: Given that there is something above our reason then God exists. There is something above our reason; hence, God exists.

COMMENTARY

However we may interpret Augustine's approach to the existence of God, it must be fairly evident that the argument from truth is not demonstrative, as Aquinas was to point out later. Yet the different interpretations of the Augustinian argument are of interest, for they show clearly how religious thinkers react to all such philosophical demonstrations. It may be contended that Augustine himself never elaborated upon this argument because as a theologian he came to see that such arguments had little value in leading the individual to religious truth. In his own case, the existence of God was manifested as a direct revelation in a religious experience he describes so vividly in the famous garden scene of the Confessions. As a religious thinker rather than as a philosopher, Augustine came to emphasize and to establish the priority of faith for all Christians in the succeeding centuries. The attainment of truth and Christian wisdom follows the principle he laid down of *"Fides quaerens intellectam"* (faith seeking understanding). Thus his argument for the existence of God is essentially an explication of what has already been achieved through faith. To identify with God the eternal and immutable and necessary truths which the mind discovers can become possible only after God has first revealed Himself to us.

Some philosophers,[3] while admitting the deficiencies of the Augustinian argument, have endeavored to reconcile it with the Thomistic approach. This may take the form of showing that Augustine also favored a cosmological approach, that is, that he argued empirically from causes and effects in nature to the existence of God. Or it may take the form of showing that the Augustinian argument is similar to the Cartesian, in which it is argued from the idea of God as an effect to God as the cause of such an idea. We would maintain, however, that: "Augustine discovers God as present to the mind of man, but does not argue by means of a demonstration *quia* from the effects in nature to God as the cause of these effects. Rather Augustine sees all things as images and vestiges of God after he has discovered God within and present to himself . . . that this is a discovery of God rather than a demonstration of his existence."[4]

Whether or not the reader finds this an acceptable interpretation of Augustine will depend upon his own philosophical and religious position and his reading of the argument. The same will be true for the interpretations of some of the other classical arguments for the existence of God, particularly the justly famous argument of Anselm.

THE ONTOLOGICAL ARGUMENT OF ANSELM.   I do not endeavor, O Lord, to penetrate thy sublimity, for in no wise do I compare my understanding with that; but I long to understand in some degree thy truth, which my heart believes and loves. For I do not seek to understand that I may believe, but I believe in order to understand. For this also I believe,—that unless I believed, I should not understand.

.   .   .   .   .   .

And so Lord, do, thou who dost give understanding to faith, give me, so far as thou knowest it to be profitable, to understand that thou art as we believe; and that thou art that which we believe. And, indeed, we believe that thou art a being than which nothing greater can be conceived. Or is there no such nature, since the fool hath said in his heart, there is no God? But, at any rate, this very fool, when he hears of this being of which I speak—a being than which nothing greater can be conceived—understands what he hears, and what he understands is in his understanding; although he does not understand it to exist.

For it is one thing for an object to be in the understanding, and another to understand that the object exists. When a painter first conceives of what he will afterwards perform, he has it in his understanding, but he does not yet understand it to be, because he has not yet performed it. But after he has made the painting, he both has it in his understanding, and he understands that it exists, because he has made it.

Hence, even the fool is convinced that something exists in the understanding, at least, than which nothing greater can be conceived. For, when he hears of this, he understands it. And whatever is understood, exists in the understanding. And assuredly that, than which nothing greater can be conceived, cannot exist in the understanding alone. For, suppose it exists in the understanding alone: then it can be conceived to exist in reality; which is greater.

Therefore, if that, than which nothing greater can be conceived, exists in the understanding alone, the very being, than which nothing greater can be conceived, is one, than which a greater can be conceived. But obviously this is impossible. Hence, there is no doubt that there exists a being, than which nothing greater can be conceived, and it exists both in the understanding and in reality.

. . . . . .

And it assuredly exists so truly that it cannot be conceived not to exist. For, it is possible to conceive of a being which cannot be conceived not to exist, and this is greater than one which can be conceived not to exist. Hence, if that, than which nothing greater can be conceived, can be conceived not to exist, it is not that, than which nothing greater can be conceived. But this is an irreconcilable contradiction. There is, then, so truly a being than which nothing greater can be conceived to exist, that it cannot even be conceived not to exist; and this being thou art, O Lord, our God.

So truly, therefore dost thou exist, O Lord, my God, that thou canst not be conceived not to exist; and rightly. For if a mind could conceive of a being better than thee, the creature would rise above the Creator; and this is most absurd. And indeed, whatever else there is, except thee alone, can be conceived not to exist. To thee alone, therefore, it belongs to exist more truly than all other beings, and hence in a higher degree than all others. For, whatever else exists does not exist so truly, and hence in a less degree it belongs to it to exist. Why, then, has the fool said in his heart, there is no God, since it is so evident, to a rational mind, that thou dost exist in the highest degree of all? Why, except that he is dull and a fool?[5]

COMMENTARY

The determination of the validity or invalidity of this argument of Anselm is for the philosophers and logicians to decide. We simply offer it for acceptance or rejection by the reader and to show how one man argued very effectively for God's existence. Whether the argument is valid or invalid has divided philosophers since Anselm first proposed it. Thomists, Kantians, and Empiricists have generally rejected the argument on the ground that it constitutes an unwarranted passage from the world of thought to the world of reality. Scotists and Cartesians and the followers of Spinoza, Leibniz, and Hegel accept the logic of the argument, but usually with some modifications of their own. Among contemporaries an especially interesting statement on the argument is that given by Bertrand Russell in which he recalled: "the precise moment, one day in 1894, as I was walking along Trinity Lane, when I saw in a flash (or thought I saw) that the ontological argument is valid. I had gone out to buy a tin of tobacco; on my way back, I suddenly threw it up in the air, and exclaimed as I caught it: "Great Scott, the ontological argument is sound."[6]

Professor Malcolm's verdict is: "What Anselm has proved is that the notion of contingent existence or nonexistence cannot have any application to God. His existence must either be logically necessary or logically impossible. The only intelligible way of rejecting Anselm's claim that God's existence is necessary is to maintain that the concept of God, as a being greater than which cannot be conceived, is self-contradictory or nonsensical. Supposing that this is false, Anselm is right to deduce God's necessary existence from his characteristic of Him as a being greater than which cannot be conceived."[7]

The absorbing interest of philosophers in the dialectical aspects of Anselm's argument should not obscure the fact that the argument was essentially designed to persuade us of the basic truth of the existence of God and to render meaningful that which the believer holds upon faith. Furthermore, we must remember that Anselm was a monk and an archbishop as well as a dialectician. His own enthusiasm for dialectic in an age which had just rediscovered the importance of logic should not be exaggerated. For Anselm the religious interest was always uppermost. The argument that he offers begins with a prayer premised upon the famous maxim that unless we believe we shall not understand. In other words, the whole approach of the argument is through faith; the function of reason is merely to render intelligible that which is held in faith. Anselm is a profound Augustinian; to an Augustinian, God is present to the mind and the heart of the believer. Thus God already exists in the experience of Anselm, and the purpose of his argument is to make such an experience more meaningful to himself and to others who may share such an experience.

The persuasiveness of the argument and how much it proves will depend upon the individual to whom it is addressed. It is quite conceivable that an unbeliever might find the logic of the argument completely convincing but not accept God as having any meaningful reality in experience. An atheist could accept the argument yet continue to be an atheist. This is probably the position of Lord Russell if he still accepts the logic of the argument.

For one who believes in God there are two alternatives. He may find that the argument contributes nothing to his faith or to his conviction, on the ground that reason has nothing to do with the problem of God's existence. Like Pascal he may reject all rational appeals. On the other hand, like Anselm, Scotus, Descartes, and others, he may feel that the argument for the existence of God does make more meaningful that which is already accepted on the basis of faith.

THE FIVE WAYS OF AQUINAS
WHETHER GOD EXISTS

On the contrary, It is said in the person of God: *I am Who am* (*Exod.* iii.14).

I reply, There are five ways to prove the existence of God.

The first and more obvious way is from motion [or change]. We can certainly see that some things in the world are in motion. Now anything that is in motion is put in motion by something else. For nothing can be moved except it is in potentiality to that towards which it is moved; whereas a thing moves inasmuch as it is in act. For to move is nothing else than the reduction from potentiality to actuality. And this can be done only by something already in a state of actuality. Thus, that which is actually hot—such as fire—makes wood, which is potentially hot, to be actually hot, and thereby moves and changes it. Now it is not possible that the same thing should be at once in act and in potentiality at the same time. What is actually hot cannot simultaneously be potentially hot, though it can be potentially cold. Therefore, that which is in motion [or process of change] cannot itself cause that same motion [or change]; it cannot move [or change] itself. Hence, whatever is in motion [or process of change] must be moved [or changed] by something else. Now if that by which something is put in motion be itself put in motion, then this also must needs be put in motion by another, and that by another again. But this cannot go on to infinity, for then there would be no first mover, and consequently no other mover. For subsequent [intermediate] movers, move only because they are put in motion by the first mover; just as the stick moves only because it is moved by the hand. Hence we must conclude that there is a First Mover, not moved by anything else. This everyone understands to be God.

The second way is based upon the nature of the efficient cause. In the world of sense experience we find an order of efficient causes. There is no known instance of a thing being the efficient cause of itself, for this would mean that it precede itself and this is impossible. Now in a series of efficient causes it is impossible to proceed to infinity. For in such a series, the first is the cause of the intermediate cause, and the intermediate is the cause of the ultimate cause (whether the intermediate cause be one or many). Now to eliminate the cause is to eliminate the effect. Therefore, if you eliminate the first cause, there will be no intermediate cause and no ultimate cause. But if in the series of efficient causes one can proceed to infinity, then there will be no first efficient cause, nor any intermediate causes, and no ultimate effect. This is obviously false. Therefore, it is necessary to admit a first efficient cause which everyone calls "God."

The third way is based on possibility and necessity and it is as follows. In nature we find some things that can be but need not be, for they are found to be generated and to be corrupted, hence capable of being and of not-being. Now it is impossible that everything should be like this, for a thing which can not-be at one time was not. Therefore if everything can not-be, then at one time there was nothing. Now if this were true, even now there would be nothing in existence, because something that does not exist can only be brought into being by something already existing. Therefore if at one time nothing was in existence, it would have been impossible for anything to have come into existence; and thus even now there would be nothing in existence which we see is false. Therefore, not all beings are merely possible, but there must exist something whose existence is necessary. Now every necessary being either has its necessity caused by another or not. But it is impossible to proceed to infinity in necessary things which have their necessity caused by another, as was shown with respect to efficient causes. Therefore, we must admit the existence of a being having its own necessity and not receiving it from another, but rather causing in others their necessity. This everyone calls "God."

The fourth way is based on the gradation [of perfection] found in things. Some things are found to be more and some less good, true, noble, and so on. But "more" and "less" are predicated of different things insofar as they approximate a highest standard, as, for example, things become hotter the closer they approximate that which is the maximum or hottest. Hence, there is something which is truest, best and noblest, and therefore most fully in being. For Aristotle says that those things that are truest are the things most fully in being (*Metaph.* Ia, 1, 993b30). Now the maximum in any genus is the cause of all in that genus; as fire, which is the maximum of heat causes all other things to be hot (*Ibid.*, 993b25). So there must also be something which is to all beings the cause of their being, goodness, and every other perfection. This being we call God.

The fifth way is based on the governance of things. We observe that natural bodies, which lack knowledge, act for an end. For they act always or nearly always in the way which will obtain the best result. Hence it is clear that they achieve their end purposefully rather than by chance. However, nothing that lacks knowledge tends to a goal unless it is guided by someone with knowledge and understanding; just as the arrow requires an archer. Therefore all things in nature are directed to their goal by an intelligent being, and this we call God.[8]

COMMENTARY

The five ways have historical precedents. The first way is Aristotelian and the fifth way can be traced to Plato and beyond. The third way seems to have originated with Avicenna. The fourth way is frequently regarded as Platonic, and the second way owes much to Aristotle. The first three ways also appear in the work of the Jewish philosopher Moses Maimonides (A.D. 1135–1204). But although the five ways are not original with Aquinas, his statements of the arguments and his synthesis of the contributions of his predecessors represent a considerable achievement.

The five ways have certain common characteristics. They are all based on experience and proceed inferentially from certain facts in experience to the existence of God. Thus, in the first way, which Aquinas regarded as most evident because it began with that which is most evident to us—change or motion—the argument is from motion to God as the Prime Mover. All five ways make an explicit or implicit use of the causal principle—that every effect has a cause. It may also be noted that the possibility of an infinite regress is either implicitly or explicitly denied in each of the argument, and that with respect to the first and the third, the eternity of the world is assumed. And all the arguments merely conclude *that* God is, but make no inferences regarding His nature.

Regarding the demonstrative nature of the arguments, Aquinas refers to his arguments as demonstrative and distinguishes what he calls demonstration *propter quid* and demonstration *quia*. The former he rejects as being *a priori*, of beginning with the cause or with the idea of God, as Anselm does. The demonstration *quia* Aquinas accepts as more properly beginning with the effects, with that which is known to us in experience, and then proceeding to the existence of God as the cause.

Thomists have accepted the demonstrative character of the arguments, although they would acknowledge that the term "demonstrative" is not to be taken in any mathematical sense and that the arguments do not possess the rigor of mathematical demonstration. Jolivet qualifies the demonstrative character of the arguments in the following manner:

The *a posteriori* proofs of God, that is, those which proceed from the world to this first cause, have a unique character, which makes it impossible to equate them with demonstrations valid in the physical order. . . . For the term of the demonstration, God, remains always outside our grasp, beyond our power of experience: God appears as implied by what we know, but he is not grasped as an object of our experience. From this point of view he is an hypothesis, but a necessary hypothesis, without which nothing can be explained and everything becomes irrational. On the other hand the idea of God as such is, in a sense, previous to the demonstration, just as the hypothesis must precede the inductive process. The process of reasoning only serves to make explicit a sort of intuition, not of God in himself, but of the reasons which support the assertion of his existence.[9]

Some Thomists are of the persuasion that the five ways constitute formally valid syllogistic arguments. Fr. Garrigou-Lagrange constructs the following syllogism to illustrate this contention "*The world necessarily depends on an extrinsic first cause. Now we call the extrinsic first cause by the name of God. Therefore God exists.*"[10] However, as Fr. Illtyd Trethowan observes, although this is a valid syllogism it does not prove that God exists, because the first premise already contains the conclusion.[11] Other Thomists are content to show merely that the arguments constitute only valid inferential proofs which make use of analogous concepts. Thus D. J. B. Hawkins, a contemporary British philosopher, argues:

We know being as what is common to all things. . . . In reasoning about God we use the completely analogous concept of being and some other highly analogous concepts. Causation appears in experience in various forms . . . the recognition that being which is caused in any way presupposes totally uncaused being is followed, in virtue of the analogy or elasticity of being, by the recognition that uncaused necessary being can only be the infinite fullness of being. . . . The Thomist, then, holds that the use of analogous concepts does not vitiate his reasoning. There is sufficient community of meaning in their different modes of instantiation to make valid inference possible.[12]

This defense of the inferential character of the Thomist proofs would find contemporary philosophers ranged on both sides of the issue. The debate is undoubtedly an interminable one and we have no wish to prolong it. Perhaps in view of the controversy over all rational arguments for the existence of God, the reader may look with favor upon the following remarks of Jolivet:

. . . however valid the proofs of God's existence may be in themselves, absolutely speaking, they can only be valid *for us* in so far as we accept them on our side, with honesty, moral rectitude and purity of heart. The proofs are not compelling, as are proofs from experience. We can use an expression of Gabriel Marcel, and say that they are "ways of approach to the ontological mystery." That is undoubtedly why St. Thomas called them *viae,* ways or directions.[13]

Ways of Experience—The Experiential Arguments

By the ways of experience, we shall mean those arguments based upon man's experience of God. These arguments or approaches to God are not logical proofs; reason plays a secondary role in them in contrast to the types of argument previously considered. We shall divide the experiential ways into four major categories: the way of universal belief, the moral way, the mystical way, and the existential way.

UNIVERSAL BELIEF.   This way argues that the human race has always expressed a belief in God, that no race of people has been without some form of religious experience, or—as Cicero observed—that there is no nation so barbarous, and no race so savage, as not to be firmly persuaded of the existence of God. Calvin proclaimed that a sense of divinity is inscribed on every heart and that even idolatry exemplifies this. The belief in God, he held, is natural and indelibly impressed on the mind of man. The worship of God makes us superior to brute creation and leads us to aspire to immortality.

Now even though we grant the universal assent of all peoples to the existence of God, this does not prove that He exists, for peoples have frequently given their consent to ideas or beliefs that have turned out to be false. It is also true that in every age there have been apparently sincere atheists whose lives have been untroubled by any anguish of conscience or fear of the vengeance of Deity. Yet even though we allow for the exceptions, the general consent of humanity as a whole to the belief in God has been impressive, particularly if we argue that this belief has taken on a variety of different forms. Man's worship has included not merely the more primitive religious beliefs and the more sophisticated forms of monotheism, but has extended to such absolutes as Nature, the State, the Party. Man, it would appear, must worship, even though the old rites and traditions are transformed into new secularized absolutes. This is the value represented by the appeal to universal assent.

THE MORAL WAY.   This approach to God represents a more fundamental appeal to the experience of the individual than the appeal to universal assent. In the moral way we look more specifically to the values of the religious experience for the individual rather than to a consideration of the more general conclusions drawn from the experience of peoples. The moral way turns to the religious instincts and feelings of the individual; it predicates the existence of God upon such instincts and feelings. It considers the moral needs and requirements of the individual and shows that these can be met adequately only by postulating the existence of God. It does not reject reason but rather insists that we must look for God within the moral consciousness of man. This approach was strikingly put by Pascal in an often quoted passage: "The heart has its reasons, which reason does not know. . . . It is the heart which experiences God, and not the reason. This, then is faith: God felt by the heart, not the reason. . . ."[14]

And what "reasons of the heart" might lead us to the conviction that there is a moral order presided over by a providential and benevolent Deity who is concerned with our ultimate and eternal happiness? Few philosophers have expressed the convictions and hopes of man in this respect better than the great German philosopher Immanuel Kant (1724–1804) in his *Critique of Practical Reason.*

IMMANUEL KANT AND THE MORAL WAY.   In his moral philosophy Kant sought for a principle that would be as universal and certain for the regulation of our moral behavior as the laws of nature were for the behavior of physical phenomena. This principle Kant designated as the *categorical imperative*. It is a moral law and exists within each one of us; it has its source and its autonomy in the rational nature of man.

Kant developed three formulations of his categoriacal imperative, two of which will be sufficient for us to note. The first was expressed: "Act only on that maxim through which you can at the same time will that it should become a universal law." Thus, if a person were contemplating theft, analysis would reveal to him the contradictory nature of such an act, for he could not will that stealing should be a universal law which all must obey. This would render both stealing and property rights meaningless. The second formulation of the imperative may be expressed: "Treat every human being, including yourself, as an end in himself and not as a means to the advantage of anyone else." To treat anyone only as a means would be to disregard his rights as a person and to exploit him.

Kant felt that these dictates of practical reason—the categorical imperatives—could justify the existence of God as well as the existence of man's freedom and immortality. Thus, freedom is implied in the duty imposed by the categorical imperative, for if a man is obliged to do something, this must mean that he can do so. "Thou oughtest, therefore thou canst," Kant declared. Freedom, then, is a condition or postulate of the moral law. To show that we must have an immortal existence, Kant noted that the moral law imposed upon us the necessity to be virtuous in order that we might attain happiness. What Kant termed the *summum bonum* is that perfect good which includes both virtue and happiness. To attain the perfection of virtue and the perfect good is impossible, however, in the brief span of our lifetime. The attainment of our ultimate reward of happiness will be possible, then, only on the supposition of "the unending duration of the existence and personality of the same rational being, which is called the immortality of the soul." For those who obey the moral law, happiness should be their reward; for those who do not obey it, it appears wrong that they should prosper or be happy for their wrongdoing. To assure the individual of justice—that virtue will be rewarded and evil punished—it is necessary to postulate the existence of God. For God in His infinite wisdom and omnipotence will reward the just and punish the wicked in an eternal life.

COMMENTARY

It should be noted that the Kantian analysis does not establish God as a lawgiver. It only expresses our need to postulate God in order to render our moral life meaningful. Kant's argument is based upon the experience of the moral life and the meaning of moral obligation as it is found in the categorical imperative. For Kant the moral law is independent of theology; but once we accept the existence of the moral law and its obligations, we require God, freedom, and immortality.

THE MYSTICAL WAY.   With the mystical way the presence of God in the experience of the individual becomes more immediate and more intense. The ultimate goal of the mystic is a union with God, the attainment of God in this mortal life as well as in the life to come. For the mystic there is no inference to the existence of God, nor is God mediated through moral convictions, the requirements of a moral conscience, and a moral law. God's existence is apprehended by the mystic in a direct experience—an experience so complete, so absorbing and ecstatic, that it cannot be set down in words. Generally, the mystic way does involve a discipline and a method for the attainment of such an ineffable goal. Such a method and discipline has been called the "anagogic path." It is not open to all, but only to the professed mystics, to those who dedicate their whole lives to the worship of God. This does not mean, however, that the mystical experience cannot be attained by those who do not follow a dedicated life and discipline. This is certainly possible because the attainment of any union with God must be effected by God Himself. This is evident in the mystical experiences and conversions of Paul and Augustine, neither of whom in the strict sense were professed mystics, but both of whom nevertheless enjoyed the mystical experience of a direct apprehension of God.

The mystical experience may be described as the religious experience in its most intense form. Some, however, would identify it with any religious experience. This is why Rufus Jones in his writings on mysticism finds it to be more of a universal type of religious phenomenon. However, if we restrict the mystical experience only to the highest moments of the religious experience, then the pursuit of the mystical way to God is restricted to the few.

The validity of the mystical experience is something that we cannot here debate or resolve. Since the appeal of the mystic is always to his own experience, which is essentially incommunicable to us, we must either accept the report of his experience as sincere and honest or reject it as illusory or nonsensical. To illustrate the nature of the mystical way we shall summarize briefly some of the principal features of the mystical way of St. John of the Cross (1542–1601), one of the greatest of all Christian mystics.

ST. JOHN OF THE CROSS: THE PURGATION OF THE SOUL.   Using the word "night" to mean purgation or purification, St. John of the Cross shows how the sensual and the spiritual parts of the soul must be purified if the individual is to attain a union or spiritual marriage with God. Dividing the night of the senses into two parts, the active and the passive, he regards the *Active Night of the Senses* as that in which the soul with the aid of grace strives to mortify the senses, to avoid pleasure, to curb all desires, and to imitate Christ in all things.

The *Passive Night of the Senses* begins when God draws the soul out of the state of the beginner. This night is characterized by an activity of God in the soul in which the individual is led from a state of meditation to one of contemplation. The passive night is marked by the spiritual imperfections of the beginners—the satisfaction they take in spiritual works; their spiritual pride, a secret and concealed pride; their spiritual avarice marked by a neglect of spiritual duties; and their excessive interest in spiritual objects, such as rosaries and images. Spiritual gluttony—the sensible satisfaction derived from too many self-imposed penances—is also characteristic of this night of the soul.

The three basic signs of the passive night of the soul are: (1) the difficulty that the soul experiences in finding consolation in the things of God; (2) the "dryness" of the soul, that is, a lack of sweetness or satisfaction in meditations and prayers; and (3) the inability of the soul to meditate and to excite the religious imagination. All of these signs are a testimony that God is no longer working in us through the senses but is leading us into the life of contemplation.

After traversing the night of the senses, the soul must perfect its faith by a mortification of the spirit. In the *Active Night of the Spirit* the soul must be deprived of its own faculties, so that God can enter the soul completely. This means a purgation of the imagination, the memory, and the will. The imagination must be purged of the inclination to picture God. The memory must suffer a complete annihilation; it must be emptied so that God can replace memory. The will must be purified of the love of all temporal and moral goods, of virtues, and even of a love of supernatural goods. By this means all that will be left to love will be God Himself.

The *Passive Night of the Spirit* is a state for the proficients and requires years for attainment. It is a state of infused contemplation in which the soul lives by faith and in which God instructs the soul in all things and prepares it for the unitive life. "God now denudes the faculties, the affections and feelings, spiritual and sensual, interior and exterior, leaving the understanding in darkness, the will dry, the memory empty, the affections of the soul in deepest affliction, bitterness and distress."[15] This state of the dark night is a complete inflowing of God into the soul, purifying it and perfecting it in love. Such a state may last for some time, but intermittently. Eventually the soul dies to all that is not God and enters into the unitive life with God. In such a life, usually of brief duration, the soul becomes God by participating in God. Yet there is no loss of personality for the soul, for "the soul appears to be God, and God the soul." Such a union is ineffable; it "treats of things so intimate and spiritual that for the most part language fails in describing them."

THE EXISTENTIAL WAY.   This way has much in common with the moral way. It emphasizes the affective nature of man, his feelings and emotions. However, being essentially irrational in its outlook, it goes beyond the moral way in the greater emphasis it places upon the centrality of man's existence and the significance of subjectivity. By existence it means not merely that which is real in the older sense of the term, but the very mode of being of man himself. Existence is set over against essence, subjective truth is contrasted with objective truth, the irrational is opposed to the rational and the scientific. The primary concern of the existentialists is with the "existential" problems of man: with the meaning of life and death, of anguish, dread, and suffering, and of the alienation of man in a hostile world. Undoubtedly some of these features will be found in earlier religious thinkers. In a certain sense Augustine and Pascal may be regarded as existentialists. However, existentialism is basically a contemporary phenomenon originating in the revolt against the rationalism and absolutism of the nineteenth century. As a romantic and protest movement its concern was to establish the primacy of the person over the absolutism of the state and the objectivity of science.

Existentialism has taken two principal forms: atheistic existentialism and theistic existentialism. The former finds its best expression in the writings of certain philosophers, notably Friedrich Wilhelm Nietzsche (1844–1900), with whom the movement originated, and Jean-Paul Sartre (born 1905), its outstanding contemporary exponent. Occasionally certain religious thinkers find Nietzsche's dictum that "God is dead!" attractive and use it either to mean the death of religious faith or to express some form of the Apollinarian heresy. Theistic existentialism has been far more influential in the contemporary religious world and has had many exponents. Probably its two most justly recognized representatives are Sören Kierkegaard (1813–1855), the originator of existentialism, and Gabriel Marcel (born 1889), an outstanding Roman Catholic exponent of this form of religious philosophy, although theologians of all faiths have felt the impact of existentialism. Because of its importance and its influence we shall summarize briefly the position taken by its most outstanding exponent, Sören Kierkegaard.

Sören Kierkegaard and Theistic Existentialism.   Reacting to the philosophy of Hegel and Hegel's interpretation of Christianity, Kierkegaard emphasized the need of the individual to *be* a Christian rather than to speculate about Christianity. The significance of *being* a Christian led Kierkegaard to offer a dialectic of existence formulated in the three stages of the aesthetic, the ethical, and the religious life. A brief description of the dialectic and the three stages will afford a good introduction to Kierkegaard's existentialism.

The *aesthetic stage* or *life* is one of worldly pleasures, an exclusive concern with the finite and the temporal. It is a life of immediacy but also a life of melancholy mixed with frustration. In this stage one has no real commitments, existence is characterized by neutrality, and there is no true awareness of the moral life and the self. This stage will give way to a higher stage, the ethical, when the individual becomes aware of the aimlessness of his life and of the reality of good and evil. Only with the realization of his moral nature can the individual escape from this stage to the ethical.

In the *ethical stage* the real meaning of good and evil appears to the individual. He becomes aware of his moral obligations and duties and he endeavors to fulfill his moral potentialities in the social life around him. However, the individual may find it difficult to realize his moral potentialities. Thus, for Kierkegaard marriage was impossible. Furthermore, the ethical and what constitutes the duty of the individual may too readily be identified with the opinions of the masses. The paradox of the ethical stage is that it not only tends to enable the individual to realize his individuality but that it at the same time leads him to identify himself with the group. Thus the ethical becomes nullified. Only by relating himself to God rather than to the group can the individual attain true subjectivity and appropriate the ethical as something personal, secure from corruption by the crowd. The means of attaining this new relationship lies in the paradox of faith, which discovers the teleological suspension of the ethical.

In the *religious stage* Kierkegaard illustrates the teleological suspension of the ethical with the story of Abraham and Isaac. Abraham is called upon to sacrifice his son Isaac to God, but his hand is stayed by God. Here is a collision of the ethical with the religious. As Kierkegaard puts it: "The ethical expression for what Abraham did, is that he would murder Isaac; the religious expression is that he would sacrifice Isaac. . . ." There is a paradox of faith here, for, as Kierkegaard says: "It is a paradox which is capable of transforming a murder into a holy act—pleasing to God, a paradox which gives Isaac back to Abraham, which no thought can master, because faith begins precisely where thinking leaves off."[16]

Based upon faith, ethics becomes a religious ethics; it is concerned preeminently with the individual and his absolute relationship with God. The transition from the ethical to the religious stage is effected by what Kierkegaard calls the "leap." By this leap the individual attains the maximum stage of inwardness and freedom, for now as a religious individual he exists not in relation to the world or to the ethical as the universal norm, but only in relation to God. Furthermore, in the leap to the religious stage of existence the individual becomes conscious of himself as a sinner in the sight of God. The leap brings the individual to a new level of existence in which we find the opposition of faith and sin. In the religious stage the individual becomes fully aware that without God he can accomplish nothing, that he is nothing without God. Hence the dread of nothingness, which can be overcome or mitigated only by a faith in God. Such a faith establishes the sinner in a positive relationship with God, and the stronger the faith, the closer this relationship with God, the greater the enhancement of the self and the more marked the suffering of the individual which is a sign of the struggle to attain God.

Kierkegaard has much more to say on God, on man's relation to God, and on Christianity. However, this brief summary and paraphrasing of his dialectic of the three stages should be sufficient to show that for Kierkegaard God cannot be demonstrated to exist by reason; God is not an object whose existence can be proved. Rather God is a subject, and it is only through the subjectivity of the individual, his inwardness and affectivity, that God becomes meaningful and related to the individual. In conclusion, it may be observed that this existential way of Kierkegaard has much in common with both the ethical and the mystical ways previously described.

THE NATURE OF GOD

The God of the Philosophers

Now *that* God is, we may next ask *what* He is. Can God be defined? What meaning can we give to the word "God"? The answers of the philosophers or those speaking as philosophers are limited. Our account will therefore be content first with a very brief statement of some major theories concerning God's nature, and second with the methods used to arrive at the meaning we give to God.

Deism, derived from the Latin word *deus* meaning god, views God as wholly external and transcendent to the universe. Initially God is considered to have brought the world into existence; then He put it in motion; and finally He allowed it to run by its own mechanism. This is the meaning of *"Deus ex machina"* as representative of seventeenth-century and eighteenth-century deism. This view denies the existence of a divine providence or of any concern by God for the world. Generally the deists have rejected or rationalized Christianity. The following are representative deists: Matthew Tindal (c. 1656–1733), William Wollaston (1659–1724), Viscount Bolingbroke (1678–1751), Denis Diderot (1713–1768), and Benjamin Franklin (1706–1790).

Pantheism, from the Greek words *pan*, meaning all, and *theos*, meaning god, holds that God and the universe are one. Benedict de Spinoza (1632–1677) is an outstanding representative among philosophers of this viewpoint. Identifying God with substance, Spinoza conceived the world as participating in God's existence through the divine attributes and modes. God was conceived as the immanent and internal cause of all things. The world or universe has no separate existence from God but is closely bound to Him both causally and substantially. Everything flows from the necessity of the divine nature.

Among the Stoic philosophers God was conceived as universal reason pervading the entire universe. This reason or *logos* was also regarded by the Stoics as a kind of cosmic fire or fiery breath (*pneuma*).

Pantheism has frequently appealed to poets and essayists. Generally they emphasize the idea of God as the soul of the universe. Thus Carlyle asserts that "through every star, through every grass-blade, and most through every Living Soul, the glory of a present God still beams." And Emerson declares: "We see the world piece by piece, as the sun, the moon, the animal, the tree; but the whole, of which these are the shining parts, is the soul."[17]

Pantheism fails, however, because it explains the universe in terms of itself. A God who is completely immanent in the universe loses all meaning.

Theism has been frequently identified with deism, but more recently it has come to be identified with the Christian conception of God. Such a conception draws its inspiration from both the Old Testament and the New Testament. Theism looks upon God as One, as a Creator and a Person, as Transcendent and Immanent. From the philosophical point of view it endeavors to ascertain what man can know about God apart from faith and revelation. To this end it has relied upon the methods of negative theology and analogy.

Negative theology begins with the admission that God's nature is so transcendent that it cannot be circumscribed and comprehended by man. God cannot be defined, for to define Him is to limit His nature. This means, then, that we cannot say *what* God is. However, we may note to a very limited degree what He is not and thereby obtain some knowledge, however inadequate, of His nature. It is as though we were to describe a person as *not* being an Englishman, *not* a poet, and *not* a financier. This information tells us something of such a person, but precious little. Similarly we might indicate some of the usual attributes of God by saying that He is *not* in time, *not* material, and *not* finite, and from such assertions arrive at the notion of God as eternal, immaterial or spiritual, and infinite. In his *Summa Theologica* Aquinas makes a number of deductions of such a nature based on his arguments for the existence of God.[18]

One of the best expressions of the negative attributes of God is to be found in the work of the famous Jewish philosopher and theologian Moses Maimonides (1135–1204):

Know that the negative attributes of God are the true attributes; they do not include any incorrect notions or any deficiency whatever in reference to God, while positive attributes imply polytheism, and are inadequate, as we have already shown. . . .

The negative attributes, however, are those which are necessary to direct the mind to the truths which we must believe concerning God; for, on the one hand, they do not imply any plurality, and, on the other, they convey to man the highest possible knowledge of God; e.g., it has been established by proof that some being must exist besides those things which can be perceived by the senses, or apprehended by the mind; when we say of this being, that it exists, we mean that its non-existence is impossible. We thus perceive that such a being is not, for instance, like the four elements, which are inanimate, and we therefore say it is living, expressing thereby that it is not dead. We call such a being incorporeal, because we notice that it is unlike the heavens, which are living, but material. Seeing that it is also different from the intellect, which, though incorporeal and living, owes its existence to some cause, we say it is the first, expressing thereby that its existence is not due to any cause. We further notice, that the existence, that is, the essence of this being is not limited to its own existence; many existences emanate from it, and its influence is not like that of the fire in producing heat, or that of the sun in sending forth light, but consists in constantly giving them stability and order by well-established rule, . . . we say, on that account, it has power, wisdom, and will, i.e., it is not feeble or ignorant, or hasty, and does not abandon its creatures; when we say that it is not feeble, we mean that its existence is capable of producing the existence of many other things; by saying it is not ignorant, we mean "it perceives" or "it lives"—for everything that perceives is alive—by saying "it is not hasty, and does not abandon its creatures," we mean that all these creatures preserve a certain order and arrangement; they are not left to themselves, or produced aimlessly, but whatever condition they receive from that being is given them with design and intention. We thus learn that there is no other being like unto God, and we say that He is One, i.e., there are not more Gods than one.[19]

The negative way clearly establishes the transcendence of God, but this can create a difficulty. For it makes God a being "wholly other" if the method of negation is pursued too far. God then becomes a mystery, a *deus absconditus*, a being completely incomprehensible. But if God is so utterly different, so "wholly other" than the world and man, what remains in common between man and God? How can man worship and love and trust such a being? Such questions easily come to mind when we read in Meister Eckhart (1260–1328), the great German mystic, the following words:

If I say God is good, it is not true: I am good, God is not good. I say more: I am better than God is, for what is good can become better and what is better can be best. But God is not good, therefore he cannot be better; and since he cannot be better, therefore he cannot be best. These three: good, better, best are remote from God who is above all. And if, again, I say that God is wise, it is not true: I am wiser than he. Or if I say, God is a being, it is not true: he is a transcendental essence, a super-essential nothing. St. Augustine says, "The finest thing a man can say of God is that he is silent from consciousness of interior fullness." Wherefore hold thy peace and prate not about God, for prating of him thou dost lie, committing sin. If thou wouldst be free from sin and perfect babble not of God. Neither know anything of God, for God is beyond knowledge.[20]

Analogy (*analogia entis*) as a method in Christian philosophy and theology is more frequently used to supplement the method of negative theology. Analogy as a method tries to show how we may apply the same term to God that we apply to man without falling into an anthropomorphism. It seeks to maintain the transcendence of God yet bring God into closer relations with man. The method would establish a similarity or proportion between man and God on the grounds that what is said of man in a limited and less perfect way may be said of God in an unlimited and perfect way. Thus, we may say that man is good, that man possesses life and intelligence. Similarly we may apply the same terms to God. We may say that God is good, that God possesses life and intelligence. However, the goodness, life, and intelligence that we predicate of God is not predicated of Him in the same sense that we apply such terms to man. God's life, goodness, and intelligence are the same yet also different from such attributes that are applied to man. In effect, analogy means that which is somewhat the same and somewhat different.

The basis of the analogy or proportionality of the attributes we ascribe to God and man may be said to lie in the causal relation. Given that effects resemble their causes and that God is the cause of all, then everything that exists bears some resemblance to God, although it is not the same as God. This does not mean that in relation to man God is merely a superhuman being. We do not merely magnify the attributes of man and then predicate them of God. This would be anthropomorphism, and the doctrine of analogy seeks to avoid any such extreme. It seeks a middle way between an extreme negative theology on the one hand and an anthropomorphism on the other. As Copleston expresses the issue:

It would appear . . . that the theistic philosopher is faced with a dilemma. If he pursues exclusively the negative way, he ends in sheer agnosticism, for he whittles away the positive meaning which a term originally had for him until nothing is left. If, however, he pursues exclusively the affirmative way, he lands in anthropomorphism. But if he attempts to combine the two ways, as indeed he must if he is to avoid both extremes, his mind appears to oscillate between anthropomorphism and agnosticism.[21]

Whatever the difficulties may be, the doctrine of analogy does attempt to say something meaningful in a logical way of the nature of God. By emphasizing the radical difference between man and God it expresses the transcendence of God. Through the similarities between man and God it would establish God's immanence. Philosophically it may be said to be an expression of the scriptural teaching that God became man and that man was created in the image of God.

The God of Scripture

In Scripture God reveals His nature to man in many different ways. The revelation of God's nature is generally given in dramatic and historical form. There is no systematic, theoretical, or philosophical representation of God's nature.

The dramatic account is represented by the manner in which the writers of the Bible speak to God and are spoken to by Him. God is encountered by the individual; He is seen by the individual in various manifestations; He makes known dramatically and emphatically His omnipotence and His wisdom to the individual. The relationship between God and the individual is direct and personal. The historical account of God's nature is represented in the history of the relations of the Jewish people and God and in the life of Christ.

The many attributes ascribed to God in the Old Testament (or the Hebrew Scriptures) reappear of course in the New Testament. The New Testament as a fulfilling of the Old Testament adds to our knowledge of the nature of God, principally in the mystery of the Trinity. We shall merely note in what follows some of the principal attributes of God as they are revealed in both the Old and the New Testaments. A much more complete study of some of these attributes or names of God, such as God as Creator, and God as the Trinity, will be developed in later chapters.

GOD AS ONE.   In the Old Testament the God of Judaism, the God of Abraham, Isaac, and Jacob, always appears as *one* God. "Hear, O Israel! The Lord is our God, the Lord alone" (Deuteronomy 6:4-5). This is a ringing affirmation of monotheism and it will be repeated in many ways in the Old Testament and find emphatic expression in the Jewish liturgy.

GOD AS PERSONAL.   The God of Scripture is constantly addressed as "Father." He enters into a covenant with His people. He is a lawgiver; through His commandments He establishes a moral relationship with the individual and the nation. All these are the acts of a person and the expression of an ethical monotheism which is a basic characteristic of Judaism and one of its most significant contributions to western religion. In the New Testament, God as Person appears in the Incarnation, in the mission of Christ, in his moral teachings and in his close relationships with his disciples. He enters into history as a concrete, living, individual Person.

GOD AS CREATOR.   "In the beginning God created heaven and earth." These opening lines of Genesis testify to our faith in God as a *creator*. This is a truth held in faith by both Jews and Christians. For Judaism and Christianity it is not a philosophical problem, but simply the recognition that all the universe is the work of God. The meaning of creation is essentially to bring into being from nothing. As a creator God is concerned with His creation. He conserves the universe in being and His providence extends to all of it. If His providence were removed from the universe it would return unto the nothingness from which it was created. "He . . . hangs the earth upon nothing" (Job 26:7).

From the revelation of God as the Creator of the universe there follows His omnipotence, His transcendence, and His eternity. All these are attested to by Scripture. And all things are subject to Him and to His will. He destroys the Egyptian hosts, parts the Red Sea, causes the walls of Jericho to fall, and in many other ways intervenes in the history of the Jewish people to effect His purposes. The transcendence of God does not place Him beyond the world, nor does His immanence identify Him with the world. The opening words of the Lord's Prayer expresses this thought, for it says, "Our Father who art in heaven," thus emphasizing in the reference to our "Father" the nearness of God and in "heaven" the remoteness of God.

GOD AS REDEEMER.   The God of the Old Testament is also a God of justice and a God of mercy or love. As a just God He will reward the good and punish the wicked, and His justice will ultimately prevail. As the God of mercy He appears as a Redeemer, who, though judging humanity, is also concerned to redeem it from its sins and effect its salvation and ultimate happiness. In the New Testament God as a Redeemer appears in the Person of Christ who came into the world and suffered and died upon the cross in order to effect the redemption of man. Justice required that the original sin of man against God be propitiated. But it was the great and all-encompassing love of God that led Him to the Incarnation of His Son. Through him God's grace and love would be offered to all men to bring about their redemption, salvation, and ultimate happiness.

GOD AS SPIRIT.   In the Old Testament God's transcendence to the world of nature implies that God is a purely spiritual being, free from all the weaknesses and limitations of matter and the flesh. God is essentially an incorporeal being. The spirituality proclaimed of God lies at the source of the injunction against graven images.

This Old Testament account is supplemented in the New Testament. Here God as Spirit appears in an entirely new and radical form. He is God as the Holy Spirit, the Spirit of the mind, the person, and the work of

Jesus—the Spirit that descended upon the apostles at Pentecost, the Spirit that continues as the very soul of the Church to the present time. To emphasize that God is the Holy Spirit is to emphasize the immanence of God; the Holy Spirit is the Spirit of Truth that proceeds from the Father.

GOD AS THE TRINITY.   The preceding description of God as the Holy Spirit leads directly to the most important and fundamentally Christian conception of God, namely, that God is three Persons in one Godhead. This is a conception that baffles all explanation, and Christians hold it to be a mystery accepted solely upon faith. Although a mystery it is a very explicit doctrine in the New Testament. There are any number of statements by Jesus in which he teaches of the existence of the Trinity. Just before his ascension he instructed his apostles to go out into the world and convert all people, "baptizing them in the name of the Father, and of the Son, and of the Holy Spirit" (Matthew 28:19). He speaks frequently of God as the Father; when he departed from his disciples he said: "I am ascending to my Father and your Father, to my God and your God" (John 20:17). At the close of his life, Christ spoke of the Holy Spirit. He refers to Him as the Paraclete, the Comforter. He is to complete the work of the Christ and of John: "And I will pray the Father, and he will give you another Counselor, to be with you for ever" (John 14:16). And: "But the Counselor, the Holy Spirit, whom the Father will send in my name, he will teach you all things, and bring to your remembrance all that I have said to you" (John 14:26).

NOTES

1. St. Augustine (A.D. 354–430) is one of the great church fathers and undoubtedly the man who did more than any other person to create a Christian theology and to determine the direction of Christian thought. One of the great seminal thinkers of all times, his influence persists to the present. The argument we are summing up is taken from the *De Libero Arbitrio*, Book II, written around A.D. 387–388.
2. St. Augustine, *Freedom of the Will*, trans. Carrol Mason Sparrow (Charlottesville, Va.: The University Press of Virginia, 1947), Book II, 15, 39.
3. Notably E. Gilson and C. Boyer. See John A. Mourant, "The Augustinian Argument for the Existence of God," in *Philosophical Studies* (Maynooth, Ireland, 1963), XII, 98–100.
4. *Ibid.*, p. 99.
5. From St. Anselm, *Proslogion*, trans. Sidney Norton Dean (La Salle, Ill.: Open Court, 1903), pp. 6–9.
6. Bertrand Russell, "My Mental Development," in P. A. Schlipp, ed., *The Philosophy of Bertrand Russell*, published 1944 by The Open Court Publishing Company, La Salle, Illinois, p. 10.
7. Norman Malcolm, "Anselm's Ontological Argument," *Philosophical Review* (January, 1960, Ithaca, N.Y.: Cornell University Press). See the issue of January, 1961 for a number of criticisms of Malcolm's position.

8. St. Thomas Aquinas, *Summa Theologica*, I. Q. 2, a. 3.
9. Taken from *God of Reason* by Regis Jolivet, vol. 15, of The Twentieth Century Encyclopedia of Catholicism; © 1958 by Hawthorn Books, Inc., 70 Fifth Avenue, New York, 10011, pp. 10–11.
10. Quoted by Illtyd Trethown, *The Basis of Belief* (New York: Hawthorn, 1958), p. 46.
11. *Ibid.*, pp. 46–47.
12. *Ibid.*, p. 49.
13. Jolivet, *God of Reason*, pp. 10–11.
14. From *Pensées*, by Blaise Pascal, translated by W. F. Trotter. Copyright 1941 by E. P. Dutton & Co., Inc. Reprinted by permission of E. P. Dutton & Co., Everyman's Library and J. M. Dent & Sons Ltd. No. 542.
15. St. John of the Cross, *The Collected Works*, trans. David Lewis (London: Baker, 1889), II, 98.
16. Sören Kierkegaard, *Fear and Trembling*, trans. Walter Lowrie (Princeton, N.J.: Princeton University Press, 1941), pp. 38, 78.
17. Both of these quotations are cited from George C. Hackman, Charles W. Kegley, and Viljo K. Nikander, *Religion in Modern Life* (New York: Macmillan, 1965), p. 205.
18. Aquinas, *Summa Theologica*, I. QQ. 3–12.
19. From Moses Maimonides, *Guide of the Perplexed*, trans. M. Friedländer (London: Trübner, 1885), pp. 210–212.
20. From Eckhart's sermon on "Renewal in the Spirit," No. 99, Pfeiffer Collection (London: Watkins, 1924).
21. F. C. Copleston, "The Meaning of the Terms Predicated of God." From *Contemporary Philosophy*, by Fr. Copleston. Copyright 1956 by Newman Press. Reprinted by permission of Newman Press and Burns & Oates, Ltd., p. 96.

Select Bibliography

Augustine, St. *Freedom of the Will*. Trans. Carrol Mason Sparrow. Charlottesville, Va.: The University Press of Virginia, 1947.

Baillie, J. *Our Knowledge of God*. London: Oxford University Press, 1939.

Casserly, J. V. Langmead. *The Christian in Philosophy*. London: Faber, 1949.

Farrer, Austin. *Finite and Infinite*. London: Dacre Press, 1943.

Flew, Anthony and A. McIntyre. *New Essays in Philosophical Theology*. New York: Macmillan, 1956.

Hartshorne, Charles. *The Logic of Perfection*. La Salle, Ill.: Open Court, 1962.

Robert M. Grant. *The Early Christian Doctrine of God*. Charlottesville: University Press of Virginia, 1966.

Hawkins, D. J. B. *The Essentials of Theism*. London: Sheed and Ward, 1949.

Jacobs, Louis. *Principles of the Jewish Faith*. New York: Basic Books, 1964.

Jolivet, Regis. *The God of Reason*. Trans. Dom Mark Pontifex. New York: Hawthorn Books, 1958.

KAPLAN, MORDECAI M. *Meaning of God in Modern Jewish Religion.* New York: Behrman House, Inc., 1937.

KIERKEGAARD, SÖREN. *Philosophical Fragments.* Trans. David F. Swenson. Princeton, N.J.: Princeton University Press, 1951.

MAIMONIDES, MOSES. *The Guide for the Perplexed.* Chicago: University of Chicago Press, 1965.

MASCALL, E. L. *He Who Is.* New York: Longmans, 1943.

MASCALL, E. L. *Existence and Analogy.* New York: Longmans, 1949.

MURRAY, JOHN COURTNEY, S. J. *The Problem of God.* New Haven: Yale University Press, 1966.

TRETHOWAN, ILLTYD. *The Basis of Belief.* New York: Hawthorn Books, 1961.

VII

God and the World

THE casual observer of the Jewish and Christian traditions might well conclude that the doctrine of creation is the foundation and end of their thought and devotion. On the very first page of the Bible he could read: "In the beginning God created the heavens and the earth" (Genesis 1:1) and near to the last page, "I am the alpha and the omega, the beginning and the end" (Revelation 21:6). In the *Sabbath and Festival Prayer Book* (p. 5) he would read, "Let us bend the knee before the Lord our maker" (Psalm 95) and hear the Jew pray, "Lord of the universe, we lift up our hearts to Thee who made heaven and earth" (Union Prayer Book, p. 10), and the whole service would indicate that the Sabbath is the climax of creation.

Likewise, in Christian circles, he would hear the Gospel read: "In the beginning was the Word, and the Word was with God, and the Word was God. He was in the beginning with God: all things were made through Him, and without Him was not anything made that was made." (John 1:1–3). In the *Venite* he would hear the worshiper sing, "O come, let us worship and fall down and kneel before the Lord our Maker." In the *Jubilate Deo* he would hear that "It is He that hath made us and not we ourselves." In the first line of the Christian Creed—the Apostles' or the Nicene—he would hear a confession of faith in "God the Father Almighty, Maker of heaven and earth."

The observer would be correct in his judgment of the importance of the doctrine of creation, for it is this doctrine which expresses both the transcendence and the power of Almighty God, and, at the same time, His intimate relationship to the world and men.

[194]

WHAT THE IDEA OF CREATION IS ABOUT

God, as Creator of the world, is the presupposition of all other basic ideas in Jewish and Christian thought. It is therefore inextricably inter-related with revelation, redemption, history, and eschatology. "The Biblical doctrine of the creator, and the world as His creation, is itself not a doctrine of revelation, but it is the basis for the doctrine of revelation."[1] Paul Tillich says that "the doctrine of creation is the one on which the doctrines of the Christ, of salvation and fulfillment depend. Without it, Christianity would cease to exist as an independent movement."[2] It is likewise central to Jewish thought. Judging from the hundreds of pages of interpretations of Jewish ideas which are based upon the biblical stories of creation, the entire structure of Judaism seems to stand or fall on the seminal teachings of this doctrine.[3]

The doctrine of creation, as a basic description of the fundamental relationship between God and the world, is related to the question of the meaning of history and the destiny of human life. The full scope of this doctrine is described no better anywhere than in Paul Tillich's statement:

The doctrine of creation is not the story of an event which took place "once upon a time." It is the basic description of the relation between God and the world. . . . All three modes of time must be used in symbolizing it. God *has* created the world, He *is* creative in the present moment, and He *will* creatively fulfil his *telos*.[4]

Tillich goes on to describe these modes of time as "originating," "sustaining," and "directing" creation, which means that the doctrine of creation subsumes also the idea of preservation or continuing creation and the idea of providence. In this chapter, then, we will examine this doctrine by first of all looking at the biblical setting, then examine some of the major affirmations of the doctrine in Jewish and Christian thought, and in some further detail look at special problems, the problem of miracle and the problem of evil.

The Biblical Setting

In the logic of biblical experience, creation is a prelude or prologue to covenant history. "Chronologically, the creation myths are late in the history of culture. They appear at a point where the interpretation of life and history of a nation or empire becomes related to a vaguely discerned universal history."[5] Soteriology is prior to creation in consciousness. Biblical scholars long have recognized that the comprehensive statements about the creation of the world are in later texts. There is no reference to creation in the oldest cultic credo (Deuteronomy 26:5 ff.). Faith in the God Who made the heavens and the earth is later than faith in the God Who brought His people out of Egypt.

This does not mean that early Israel was unaffected by the cultural environment, which was literally saturated with creation myths, or that the people of Israel did not venerate Yahweh as the Creator of the world in their early history. It certainly must have occurred to them to connect Yahweh with the heavens and the earth—sun, moon and stars, animals, fertility, vegetation. Nature more often exists in the form of a miracle which provides a suitable setting for the fulfillment of the Covenant: the Red Sea permits the Israelites to escape and destroys Pharoah's armies; the waters of the Jordan divide to allow the conquest of Canaan; and the Song of Deborah (Judges 5) says that the stars in the heavens fought alongside the Israelite troops. Nor is the Old Testament unaware of the idea of a cosmos, of the universe organized with wisdom in which each thing has its own place and is produced in its own time. Why had God created the world? The Old Testament answers, He created it for the Covenant. The connection of the God of the cosmos with Israel's history is relatively late in the prophetic era of Hebrew religion. Deutero-Isaiah is the first prophet to connect the idea of divine sovereignty over Israel's historical destiny with the notion of the majesty of a divine creator of the world (Isaiah 40–55). The comprehensive statements, therefore, about the creation of the world by Yahweh are found in deutero-Isaiah, the priestly document, some Psalm, and the wisdom literature. But even in a prophet like deutero-Isaiah, the Creator seems to stand in a subordinate position to the Redeemer, "He who created the heavens," "He who created you, who formed you," are connected with "Fear not, I redeem thee." Deutero-Isaiah obviously sees creation as a saving event. To be sure, Yahweh created the world; but he created Israel too, and the two creative works are almost made to coincide (Isaiah 51:9 ff.). But this interest in saving history is by no means confined to deutero-Isaiah. This same understanding lies at the basis of the creation stories in Genesis, which make it clear that creation is part of the aetiology of Israel.

The Covenant is possible, however, only within a framework of creation. This is why Karl Barth in his work on creation characterizes the Old Testament idea of creation in these words: "The covenant is the goal of creation, creation is the way to the covenant." And his material is arranged under two headings, (1) the Covenant, the internal basis of the creation; (2) the Creation, the external basis of the Covenant. For Barth, also, the idea of creation is secondary to that of the covenant, of which it is both condition and consequence.[6]

This idea that God is the Creator because He is the God of the Covenant, and the God of the Covenant because He is the Creator, is "Christianized" in the New Testament. If the first covenant was possible only within a cosmic framework, that is also true for the "new covenant" in Christ. Christ is identified with creation (John 1:3), "for in him all things were created in heaven and on earth, visible and invisible . . . all things were created through him and for him" (Colossians 1:16). As the covenant is the destiny of creation, so Christ is the crown of creation and the fulfillment of its hidden destiny. The wisdom which was present at the beginning of the universe is manifest in the crucified and risen Christ, and this will be fully revealed at the end of human history. For the Christian to say that the universe has been created by Christ and for Christ means that the wisdom and love as revealed in him were present at the creation of the world, and therefore the idea of creation is inseparable from that of redemption and of final restoration.

Creation Stories

The biblical account of creation in any large corpus is found in the first and second chapters of Genesis, the first book of the Bible. Clearly, here are two very different pictures of creation (one, Genesis 1:1–2:4a, and two, 2:4b–25), moving in two completely different thought forms, and, to the casual reader, full of contradictions. In the light of biblical scholarship, we now know that these two distinct stories come from periods roughly five hundred years apart and reflect the cosmology and theology of the periods from which they came.

The earliest story is the Yahwist (J) account (2:4b–25). Its literary form dates from the tenth century B.C.E. A charming, naive account of creation, it stands as a theological prelude to a larger work, an epic which reads history backward from the Davidic era, with the Exodus event as the fulcrum of history. Yahweh's covenant with Israel is seen in the perspective of His purpose for all men. Yahweh, who brought Israel out of Egypt, is God of all mankind, and the story of this relationship must be seen in a cosmic setting and in the context of the universal history of mankind. To do this, J employed a number of ancient folktales and wove them into a central theme.

The later story (Genesis 1:1–2:4a) is from the priestly writers, dating approximately from the fifth century B.C.E. Pfeiffer calls the priestly history Midrash, or historical commentary, on the embryonic Pentateuch which consisted of the documents JED.[7] Like the Yahwist, in the tenth century, the priestly editors, from the perspective of the fifth century, look back to the beginning. They see the history of revelation—the origins of the chosen people and their institution—from the creation to the conquest of Canaan, unfolding in four successive eras or dispensations, each era having its own privileges and duties.[8] The beginning of the first dispensation is placed right before the Yahwist's story of Paradise. But unlike the earlier story, the priestly story reflects a long history and has all the marks of intense theological reflection occurring over a period of many generations.

It would be tempting to analyze the two accounts in great detail, but since our purpose is to discover the intent and significance rather than to exegete them, we must confine this analysis to a few examples. As we have already indicated, there are dissimilarities of vocabulary, style, and point of view in the two stories. The first conspicuous difference is in vocabulary. The P account uses the term "God" from the Hebrew word, "Elohim." J uses a double term, which is translated in the Revised Standard Version as "the Lord God." This is the combination of the Tetragammaton (lit. "four letters") YHWH and Adonoy (Lord). Further, the words "create" and "make" are used in P, while J uses "form" (lit. "to model") and a verb meaning "to build." In P the beasts are "of the earth," and in J, "of the field."

The second difference has to do with the order of creation. In J the earth's original state was that of waterless waste, a desert, and there is no time reference. Man is made in midpoint out of dust, a garden is created for his delight, including trees and beasts and birds, and woman is finally created out of man. In P, on the other hand, the original state of the earth is a watery chaos, and out of this chaos God made the four parts of the world—light, firmament, sea, and land. Then in every part of the world He placed the appropriate inhabitants: the heavenly bodies are attached to the firmament; in the air below the firmament are birds; in the sea, marine animals and dragons; and on the earth there are living creatures, animals, and finally man. All of this takes place within a time span of six days; and the work of creation consists of eight distinct acts, or nine if the creation of man is separated from the creation of animals, or ten if the creation of vegetation is counted as a separate act. There is a certain inconsistency in this arrangement, but the inconsistency apparently concerns the P writers less than the importance of the establishment of the Sabbath on the seventh day.

There is also a difference in the conception of man.[9] In P male and female are created "in the image of God," while in J woman is created in order to provide a companion for man, other animals not being fit. Both accounts agree, however, that (generic) man is the apex of creation, assuming that man is the purpose of creation and is to have dominion over it. In J man is the midpoint around which God constructs his world, while in P he is the apex of a sort of cosmological pyramid. Man also stands in a unique relationship to the Creator: the rest of the works of creation are more remote from Him, descending in order to the abysmal chaos. The plants and animals are related especially to the ground, although the animals receive a word of blessing; but no level of creation intervenes between man and God. Indeed, man, for whom the world was made, alone has an immediate relationship to God; the pattern out of which man is made is taken from the heavenly world above, and he alone of all the creatures is not created by fiat. There is no explanation for the meaning of "image of God," but etymologically it apparently refers to the whole of man and not only to the spiritual and intellectual aspects of his being. In fact, the words probably relate first and foremost to the bodily form (grace, nobility, and majesty) with which he has been endowed (see Psalm 86).

The J narrative is a more unsophisticated account, which pictures Yahweh in a much more personal and intimate way. Yahweh the Creator shapes man like a potter out of the ground and breathes into him His own breath from His own mouth. Here the implication is clear: Life is possessed by man only by virtue of that breath. Without that breath he would simply fall back into a state of dead matter. Also woman is designed to be a mate "corresponding to him," like him but not identical with him, rather a counterpart. She also is distinct from the animals and was immediately recognized as Adam's counterpart. Von Rad describes this male and female complement thus:

> So is elucidated the age-long urgency of the sexes for one another, which is only appeased when it becomes "one flesh" in a child; for the woman was taken from the man, and they must in consequence come together again. The Yahwist's story of creation practically issues in this aetiological explanation of the power of Eros as one of the urges implanted in man by the creator himself (verse 24f.) and so gives the relationship between man and woman the dignity of being the greatest miracle in the history of creation.[10]

The differences between the J and P accounts are obviously very great, coming as they do from completely different milieux. They are not only different in vocabulary and in content, but in total concept. At first sight this is no more clearly seen than in the description of God. In the J story, God is seen strolling through the garden in the cool of the evening. While it is deceptive to talk of "God walking in the cool of the day," the statement does vividly symbolize the truth that man is addressed by God and is lonely and lost apart from personal relationship with his Creator, that God is not an impersonal force in nature. He is the holy and transcendent God who nevertheless enters into a personal relation with man in history. In describing Yahweh, the Yahwist finds his most apt imagery in the human realm. God is not an abstraction or feeling, but a personal living reality who cannot be less than the personal reality of man, whom He has created and for whom He has high purposes. He is concerned with His creation, he respects the freedom of man, His will for man does not annul the human will. In fact the J writer thinks of Yahweh almost in corporeal terms, or at least with some embodiment which we regard as personal.

The P writer, on the other hand, sees a supreme and absolute sovereign. God is the one and only God in existence. He is the God of Israel, He is the God of the nations, and He is the creator of heaven and earth, the source of all life. The differences, in fact, between the two accounts are the differences between the tenth century and the fifth century. Because the P writers had the benefit of the insights of the prophets and the sages of Israel, they articulated a much more sophisticated notion of the transcendent deity, of creation by divine fiat.

The J account is a much more primitive tale, but it is very similar in intention. It is a more intimate story, using highly personalized and unabashedly anthropomorphic terms: God does not create the world by fiat, but He labors in creation; He himself plants the garden; seeing His creatures' loneliness, He gives them names. (As we noted above, the giving of a name identifies the essence of the very being which is named.) In fact, the J account understands man as the object of God's love and the partner, almost, in creation.

Actually, the Yahwist account is not an account of creation at all, but is an unsophisticated description of human origin and destiny in its relationship to Yahweh. J is much more interested, in the later stories (Genesis 3–11), in accounting for the sins of man and the fall of civilization. (For example, he makes the observation that there is a gradual deterioration of man: the more clever and adaptive he becomes, the more he turns against the order established by his Creator and toward social anarchy, a serious existential problem of the day.) He is interested in etiology, although this is not his main concern; he is trying to explain persistent and common questions of origin, as for example the relationship of men and women; nature; sex; pain and childbirth; the origin of music.

The P writer is also interested in etiology, but of a different sort. He is concerned to ground in creation the sacred institutions of the Jewish commonwealth. He therefore connects Jewish festivals with the works of God:by giving the luminaries the task of fixing the calendar, particularly the sacred seasons, and by his ingenious assembly of the eight creative acts into six days, he is able to give the Sabbath a cosmic origin and to establish a basis in creation for the dietary laws.

Apparently the priestly editors (the latest editors of the Hebrew biblical literature) deliberately put their relatively more refined and sophisticated notion of God and creation and man as a preface to the more primordial account. Their purpose must be understood in the light of their understanding of the history of Israel: the first eleven chapters of Genesis set the story of Israel against the background of all creation and in the midst of universal human experience. Thus they demonstrate that the history of Israel is inseparably related to the history of the world. Israel existed prior to the Covenant but, like the universe, it was in chaos: it too was "without form and void." And as Yahweh by His word called the cosmos into being, so too had He created Israel.

Myth and Saga

We should not have difficulty in recognizing that in these stories of creation we are dealing with saga or myth, not with literal history or scientific fact. The center of interest is not a cosmology or even cosmogony. Even less are the biblical accounts anticipations of the findings of modern geology or astrophysics. To be sure, the priestly account of creation, for example, is related to the cosmological knowledge of *its* time and appears to be in harmony with the scientific world view of the day. The biblical editors borrowed freely from the common sources of mythology in antiquity, and the creation account has its beginnings in and bears strong resemblances to other ancient myths of creation, especially the Sumerian *'Enuma 'Elish*. But theological refinement purges from the Hebraic account the gory struggles and sordid biological detail of the Babylonian Marduk-Tiamat cosmogony; yet the cosmology of the biblical writers was essentially that of Babylonian origin, the most advanced of the time.[11]

The universe was conceived as a three-storied structure, "heaven above, earth beneath and waters under the earth" (Deuteronomy 5:8; see also Job 38 and Psalm 104). The firmament is pictured as a vault, a great cupola which covers the earth. Above it was water, held there by the firmament, which is equipped with openings from which the water could fall below. Without this vault the world would be flooded by the waters and the world would return to chaos. The planets, sun, moon, and stars serve to reckon time; their significance lies in the fixing of the calendar. In this context, the P account of creation is both religious and scientific, and these two motifs are so interwoven that there is no tension between them. "In the scientific ideas of the time, theology had found an instrument which suited it perfectly, and which it could make use of for the appropriate unfolding of certain subjects—in this case the doctrine of creation."[12]

The fact that there are two different stories from different historical periods based on different cosmologies should give us a clue for our modern understanding. The stories deal with the religious aspects of nature and existence and use contemporary scientific world views as carriers of that meaning. The "science" is not a necessary part of the meaning. So the priestly writers, from the stance of the fifth century, could underscore the validity of the faith of the Yahwist in the tenth century, independent of the contradictory scientific views. Their basic themes are unaffected by the dimensions of time and space, the place of the planet in the universe, or the shape of the earth, flat or elliptical. The Creator God is independent of changes in the cosmological views, but at the same time He does not dictate any particular scientific view as necessary to His revelation.

The basic question still remains in any system—the question of understanding the relationships of God to the world and of the world to men who dwell there. There is no evidence that the immense increases in our scientific knowledge place us in a more or less advantageous position than that of the biblical writers. It is therefore futile to allegorize these stories by finding in the six days of creation the geological ages (in any case, the Hebrew word for day, *yom*, means from sundown to sundown). Efforts either to defend the authority of the stories by attempting to harmonize them with the modern scientific mentality or to dismiss them as prescientific superstition miss the essential affirmation of creation. The biblical story is an affirmation of the meaning of existence, not a scientific description of how the universe appeared out of nothing, evolved, or developed. That description can be given only by science, and scientific views will change with advance in scientific methods and tools of investigation. Pope Leo XIII essentially affirmed this point of view in his encyclical *Providentissimus Deus,* in which he said explicitly that the biblical account was not intended to reveal the truths of science. He went on to say that when the sacred writers speak of the visible world, they speak of it as men of their time spoke, and in language intelligible to the people of their time.

In a chapter on "Creation and Time," Erich Frank clarifies this view:

> The idea of creation does not infringe upon the precincts of natural science. It is a religious idea, and its realm is so far removed from that of science, that a confusion of the two spheres would endanger not only scientific understanding, but religious truth as well. . . . Scripture was concerned with religion, not with science; it is meant to reveal religious truth, rather than to transmit exact knowledge.[13]

THE IDEA OF CREATION

In attempting to elaborate the meaning of creation, we must keep firmly in mind the biblical and theological emphasis upon mystery. When concepts of this sort are discussed the mind very quickly exceeds the limits of its imagination and realizes that it is dealing with something utterly mysterious and beyond the limits of rationality. It is also true that the idea of creation rather naturally inspires ingenious imagination and conjecture about various cosmogonies. And although meaningless speculation on this matter has always been discouraged in the Jewish and Christian traditions, there is, nonetheless, a voluminous midrashic literature on the process of creation. In one midrash a Roman matron asks the rabbi: "In how many days did the Holy One, blessed be he, create his world? He said to her: In six days. She said to him: What has he been doing since that time? He said to her: The Holy One, blessed be he, is sitting and making ladders."[14] To the question, "What did God do before he made heaven and earth?" Augustine took great delight in saying that "he was preparing hell for pryers into mysteries."[15] Luther said that God sits in the primeval forest and cuts whips for people who ask foolish questions! Sirach warns: "Do not inquire into what is beyond your understanding . . . thou hast nothing to do with the study of mysteries." And in the same vein he continued, "for man has many strange notions and falls constantly into error."[16]

Anyone acquainted with the intellectual and scholarly traditions of Christianity and Judaism will realize that this is not a prohibition against inquiry, but is rather an effort to avoid vulgar misunderstandings. All Jewish and Christian thinkers were and are aware of the fact that the idea of creation, like the idea of God, is based on religious faith and revelation rather than on profound intellectual reasoning. No matter how hard one tries to find intellectual justification for religious assumptions, creation remains an utter mystery beyond human understanding—the miracle of all miracles. "By faith we understand that the world was created by the word of God" (Hebrews 11:3), and this faith and reflection resulted in an idea which is peculiar to Judaism and Christianity. Therefore we have to ask in a serious vein, what does it mean to create?

At the beginning of this chapter, we said that the doctrine of creation is a description of the fundamental relationship between God and the world. It deals not only with origination, but also with the sustenance and direction of the universe, and is, thereby, related to the questions of the meaning of human history and the destiny of human life. Now we wish to look more specifically at some principal implications of this idea. We will treat the idea of creation in its originating and sustaining aspects under the following headings: (1) God as the source of all there is (*creatio ex nihilo*), together with the possible alternatives to this view, and (2) continuing creation.

Creatio ex Nihilo

The first affirmation is that God alone is the source of all there is. God wills all existence and brings it into being out of nothing as a purposive act of His free will and love. According to the rabbis, God alone made the world and by His word were the heavens and the earth simultaneously and perfectly fashioned. According to St. Paul, God "calls into existence things that do not exist" (Romans 4:17b).

What does it mean to create? The history of the answers to this question shows a remarkable unanimity in spite of wide varieties of cultural contexts and philosophical concepts. Creation means absolute origination. While this assertion is not incontrovertibly clear in the Genesis stories, the logic of the biblical views does come naturally and finally to be elaborated into the doctrine of *creatio ex nihilo* (the bringing forth of something from nothing).[17]

The first specific reference to the doctrine *creatio ex nihilo* is in the apocryphal book, II Maccabees 7:28: "Consider the heavens and the earth . . . and know that God has not made them from existing things" (KJV). To express God's activities as Creator, the biblical writers used analogies such as the architect who lays the foundation and supervises construction (Psalms 24, Isaiah 45:18); the potter who molds the clay (Genesis 8:2, Amos 4:13), or the father who begets children (Job 38:28, Psalms 92:2). There is, however, a creative activity peculiar to God (*bara*) in which He creates all that is original, unforeseeable, and not realizable by man (Jeremiah 31:22, Psalms 51:2, Psalms 104:30). It is superior to any human creation, a complete and perfect work. For deutero-Isaiah, God is no longer the artificer who forms formless stuff, but is the source of every aspect of existence. He "lays the foundations of the earth." This point of view has been maintained consistently in the whole history of Jewish and Christian thought.[18]

Jewish thinkers from the prophets through Maimonides to modern Jewish thinkers like Heschel, Fackenheim, and Buber, and Christian thinkers from Irenaeus through Calvin to the Niebuhrs and Tillich, maintain that creation is an act of God's will deliberately performed out of His freedom and His unlimited powers.

As a theory of origins, *creatio ex nihilo* cannot be demonstrated. As a deduction it may, in fact, even sound absurd, but it must be understood as a primary statement arising out of faith and reflection. Aquinas says that creation cannot be proved demonstrably because faith is of things which do not appear. But that God is the creator of the world in such a way that the world began to be is an article of faith. The limits of the world is known only by revelation, and hence cannot be proved demonstrably.[19] Guided by faith and reflection, the biblical and theological view is that God is the Creator of the universe; that it is a real creation, which is to say that the universe and men themselves exist because of God's personal will and deed. The world is in existence because God so intended it.

We need, however, to explore further what the possible implications of this statement of faith are. Here, as elsewhere, when dealing with ultimates we can sometimes best understand an idea when we see what it intends to exclude and, beyond its negative intention, what it expresses or defends. Throughout their history, Judaism and Christianity have been faced with alternatives to this assertion which have at one time or another been declared heretical.

Alternative Views

What are these alternatives? They are emanation, dualism, pantheism, and deism.

First and foremost, the formulation *creatio ex nihilo* stands in marked contrast to the Latin maxim, *ex nihilo nihil fit* (roughly, "nothing comes from nothing"). In this view, all coming into being is from some other being; matter and form exist from all eternity. Aristotle's world, for example, is the world of eternally existing substances, and the only function of God is to initiate movement or change. The eternal existence of the universe is the result of the inexorable laws of nature. Therefore God has no freedom; God is also bound by these laws. The biblical formulations stand in even greater contrast to the neo-Platonic theory of emanation, according to which the world proceeds from God somewhat necessarily through a succession of causes and effects, to successively higher realms of value, until the highest value of body and matter is reached. For the Greek classical tradition, God did not really create the world out of nothing; He transformed the chaos into a cosmos. Thus he was an artificer, an architect who shaped the world out of the everlasting matter which was there and which He had not created.

Second, there is *dualism* in a variety of forms. In its Zoroastrian and Manichaean forms, good and evil are coequal, competing with each other for the soul of man; or, God is the principle of form battling against formless chaos; or, He is spirit struggling against the intractability of matter. Classical dualism presupposes two eternal principles of good and evil.

Third, there is *pantheism*, which assumes that the cosmos and God are identical and coeternal, one substance. For example, in some forms of Hinduism God is identified with the world and man in such a way that the divine Brahma, who dwells also in man, is both the worshiper and the worshiped, not only the hearer of prayer but the prayer itself. The whole of things is God. Person and world are illusions, and the true goal of existence is absorption or annihilation. In mystical pantheism, the finite dissolves into the infinite, and man loses his humanity and the world its real existence.

The fourth alternative is *deism*. The deistic creator is a first cause which, having caused the world, goes into perpetual retirement. God provides a universal system of natural laws and leaves man in human solitariness, as though the universe were a huge and intricate but divinely controlled machine, after the analogy of the watchmaker and the watch.

Against the maxim *ex nihilo nihil fit*, the Jewish-Christian view maintains that creation is not the result of some idea, fashioned from already existing material. God in His creative activity cannot be thought of as working merely with material which is already there prior to and independent of Himself. Were that so, He would not be the sole primary reality, and there would be another primary reality not derived from His divine will, but providing the stuff upon which the divine creativity alone would work. But everything in the completest and strictest sense depends upon Him. As Philo put it, "God, when he gave birth to all things, not only brought them into sight, but also made things which before were not. Not just handling material like a demiurge, an artificer, but being himself its creator."[20] This stands in opposition to any theory of emanation whereby the forms emanate from eternal ideas. God would in that case have no freedom but would be bound by law. Thus the world is the product of cause and effect, of necessity. But for the biblical tradition God is not merely the former of the formless stuff, or the fashioner of the raw material which He found. He creates out of nothing.

Here is the substance of the Jewish and Christian idea of the source of creation—radical monotheism.[21] The radical monotheist asserts that God literally created from nothing all the materials, all the shapes of creation, with the unique power of creativity not given to any creature, even man. To say that God is "the creator of heaven and earth and all things visible and invisible" means that the universe in its entirety is not self-explanatory or self-existent, but dependent upon the creative act of the eternal God. Creation owes its existence not to itself but beyond itself. Nothing in the world is absolute. A Christian book of the second century thus interprets the First Commandment: "First believe that God is *one*, who created and formed all things, who called all things from nothing into existence, who, Himself incomprehensible, comprehends all in Himself." The primary affirmation of the idea of creation emphasizes that God is not the first principle from which the origin of the world can then be deduced. He is the creating Will. Finite beings receive their being not out of some substance, divine or antidivine. "They receive it through the Word, the will of God and its creative expression."[22] God "calls" the world into being, as the Psalmist sang, "By the word of the Lord the heavens were made, and all their host by the breath of his mouth" (Psalms 33:6). This means further, as Tillich goes on to point out, that everything that is created is derivative and therefore dependent upon this creative will, and it follows that everything which God creates is thereby good. To these two important implications of *creatio ex nihilo* we now turn.

CONTINGENCY.   If God is Creator, then the world and men cannot have their origin in themselves but must be relative and contingent. As

Calvin indicated, to say that God is creator means that we receive everything from his hands.[23] The world is finite and limited. God is the Creator
of the universe, it is a real creation. When, therefore, Jews and Christians
assert that God is the Creator of the world and men, they mean that it and
men exist because of God's personal will and deed. The idea is not a
cosmological theory but the expression of man's dependence upon God,
the consciousness that he is a creature before God. God is other than his
creation. Unlike the pantheist, God "is the place of the world, but the
world is not his place," the rabbis said (Genesis Rabbah 68:9). Out of His
compassion He bestowed existence. Though He pervades the universe, He
transcends it. The universe cannot contain Him. God is not completely
identical with the universe, for if everything is God, then there is no god.
"Our world is not strong enough to carry the weight of an intrinsic
divinity."[24] That God "dwells on high" (Psalms 113:5) but nevertheless
created the world is a paradox which is essential to biblical faith. This does
not mean a depreciation of the world; quite the contrary. The positive
value of the world is derived, it has a value conferred upon it, and it is
relative to the One to whom a value can be ascribed. Augustine most fully
understood this distinction between the derived and the underived world
by pointing to the inner evidence of creation itself: "Behold the heavens
and the earth are, they proclaim that they were created; for they change
and vary. Whereas whatsoever hath not been made, and yet is, hath
nothing in it which before it had not; and this it is to change and vary.
They proclaim also, that they made not themselves; 'therefore we are,
because we have been made; we were not therefore, before we were, so as
to make ourselves.' "[25]

Furthermore, Augustine's words point to a character of reality which has
great significance. Creation means

that free and individual beings are brought forth, or, from the point of view of
the Creator, it signifies that he has infused his own being into another thing
which thereby has taken on an independent existence of its own and may later
on itself become productive. Thus the idea of creation, although transcending
experience, serves to explain the world as it really is in its twofold character of
individual autonomy and universal dependence.[26]

In other words, it is of the very nature of creation itself that the Creator
set over against Himself something which has self-determination, something which functions according to the law of its own being and has an
independent reality of its own. Once the Creator has made the created
thing, it has, by the very reason of its existence as a creature, some degree
of self-determination. The created thing is given a character and an
identity of its own, and it fulfills its function in keeping with the law of its
own being.

Every level of the creation has a peculiar nature and character of its own. In the subhuman creation there is an element of self-determination analogous to human freedom, an element which fulfills the function of this order of being in the continuous expression of its structure. Here we see especially how Judaism and Christianity are distinguished from pantheistic religions or from the mystic flux, for both of which god is in everything and everything is in god, and creator and creation are substantially one. Christianity and Judaism are particularly emphatic in this regard in their doctrine of man. He is made *imago dei* and charged with dominion over the earth (Genesis 1:28). On the one hand, he recognizes that life is framed by infinity and eternity, that life is absolutely dependent. On the other hand, he is conscious that although he has been created, he is expected to create. Thus we confront another paradox, so eloquently stated by Leo Baeck: "Man is created and yet he creates; he is a product and yet produces; he belongs to the world and yet is above it; his life exists only through God and yet possesses its independence."[27] Man, though made in the divine image, remains a creature. He is neither a fragment of divinity nor potentially divine. Yet by that consciousness he is able to transcend the universe and gain knowledge of the world that belongs to him; ". . . he gives meaning to the world through his action. He has received his life but he has to fulfill it."[28] Though creation is vast beyond all knowledge and comprehension, so far beyond human conception that it made Ben Sira cry out, "What is my soul in a boundless creation?" (Ecclesiasticus 16:17), it is in man alone that the universe becomes conscious of itself. Astronomically, man is a speck, but he is also the astrophysicist.

In this light let us look again at the two maxims: *creatio ex nihilo* and *ex nihilo nihil fit.* As we pointed out, *creatio ex nihilo* may be logically absurd, but it does point to the limits of rationality in dealing with the mystery of creation. As Reinhold Niebuhr[29] rightly indicates, it is not in conflict with the slogan which deals with the chain of natural causation within the temporal process, an arena in which man's creativity properly finds expression. Within this arena man understands, cultivates, creates, acts on a world unfashioned or in process of being fashioned. He makes things that were not there before—a symphony, a home, or a machine.

When, therefore, Judaism and Christianity speak about the universe being a creation, they really mean *creation.* They do not mean just an emanation, a manifestation of God; they mean that the universe has real existence distinct from God, with real self-determination on every level. Though God is infinitely distant, and though man and the universe are derived and contingent, there is still a relationship between the two. It is through this relationship that creation is confirmed in its finiteness and man in his humanity. This relation is symbolized in the Covenant for the Jew and in the Incarnation for the Christian.

ESSE QUA ESSE, BONUM EST.   The other implication of radical mono-theism is the *essential goodness* of the whole of creation. As opposed to any moralistic dualism, which affirms two principles of good and evil, a good god and a demonic god, radical monotheism asserts *esse qua esse, bonum est*—whatever is, is good—and thereby denies that the tragic antinomies of existence are integral to creation. Each thing is good in its particularity, and all things are good with reference to each other. As John Calvin put it, even a sinner is good and can be good for others in some ways that the righteous cannot be; even the most ruinous of men ravaged by sin can be noble, for one can never erase the *imago Dei*, the goodness in creation or in man. Therefore, man's life is placed in a cosmic setting which has meaning in the universal scheme of things. Not only is all existence bestowed and therefore contingent, but it is also fundamentally good.

"And God saw that it was good," is a constant refrain in the Genesis story; surveying all that he had made, God said that "it was very good." The biblical tradition maintained the goodness of creation precisely on the grounds that it was created by God as the "theatre of his glory" (Calvin), which is really to say, for the exercise of his creativity. As Rabbi Akiba says, "whatsoever the merciful one does, is for the good." This rules out from the start any denial of the meaningful existence of the world and every form of radical pessimism. The world exists, it is real, and it is good.

This belief in the essential goodness of creation is one of the unique marks of the Jewish-Christian view of creation. In most great religions and philosophies there is usually one aspect of existence which is the enemy, the foe, the meaningless part of human life and of the cosmos. For some of these religions the enemy is materiality and physicality themselves. These are things to be fled from, escaped from, or to be put aside. Sometimes this materiality as the thing to be escaped from is conceived more generally as the time and space limitation of finiteness, creatureliness. The doctrine of creation affirms that all existence is fundamentally and basically good in its concreteness and its individuality, in the differentiation of human beings into male and female, bodiliness, physicality, the earth, rocks, trees, water —all these are good. It was brought into being by God out of nothing, and it is maintained in being by God.

It must be admitted, however, that both historical Judaism and espe-cially historical Christianity have had to struggle hard to maintain this doctrine of creation. Historically, both have been infiltrated by world views such as Manichaeism and neo-Platonism, which have compromised the purity of the conviction. What Archbishop Temple maintained about Christianity is equally true for Judaism, namely, that "it is the most avowedly materialist of all the great religions."[30] Christianity's own central saying, "the Word became flesh and dwelt among us" (John 1:14) should underline the belief in the ultimate significance of the historical process and the goodness of matter and its place in the divine scheme of things.

Even in its finite inferiority the finite may be good; "more than this, its goodness as the finite is directly related to this infinite qualitative difference which distinguishes it from God."[31] Time may be limited and transitory in the light of eternity, but it is good as a gift from the One who is before the human past, the One who will be when all the presents have become pasts. The radical monotheist has "the confidence that whatever is, is good because it exists as one thing among the many which all have their origin and being in the One—the principle of being which is also the principle of value."[32] All times, events, and things are good because in them God acts as the intelligible structure of every event. As W. H. Auden puts it:

> Space is the whom our loves are needed by,
> Time is our choice of how to live and why.[33]

Continuing Creation

The second major affirmation of the idea of creation is that creation is continuing. Not only does God originate; He also sustains the cosmos and history. In sharp contrast to deism, the relationship of God to the world is not conceived in terms of the watchmaker and the watch, or the engineer and the machine. It is not that God once in 4004 B.C. created the universe and then left it to run by itself as though it were a huge, intricate, and finely constructed machine. He is not the First Cause aloof and untouched by the ordered processes, a process which rational man can observe and define and obey. Against deism, Judaism and Christianity affirm that God is eternally the Creator and sustainer of the universe; that apart from his eternal creativity the world would pass out of existence. God is eternally creating the world and seeing that it is good.

God is thus not only the sole Creator. He alone upholds the creation and maintains existence by His immutable will and power in everything that is. God creates, provides, makes, sustains, and maintains. This implies that creation is never quite finished, so that we should never be surprised to discover that there are new galaxies, new forms of man, new forms of the world as a part of this continuing creation. In scientific terms, therefore, it is not only that we are discovering galaxies that we did not know about before, but that new galaxies are in fact being created and others being destroyed, so that the process of creation and death is a continual process in the whole cosmos.

This view is in accord with the biblical picture of a continuing creation. In St. Paul's Epistle to the Romans, we have such a picture of creation, which, instead of being perfect, is frustrated and incomplete, subject to frustration by God, and instead of being acted upon by God from the outside, is in itself in travail, awaiting birth and being assisted in its agony by God's spirit (Romans 8:20 ff.). And this view is in accord with the vision of the prophet Isaiah, who said, "The Lord is the everlasting God, the Creator of the ends of the earth. He does not faint, or grow weary; his understanding is unsearchable" (Isaiah 40:28). "For behold, I create new heavens and a new earth" (Isaiah 65:17). And as Johannes Kepler is supposed to have said, "The works of God are worthy to behold." Man is here entrusted with a cosmic mission, for the "cosmos is not a phantasmagoria devoid of coherence, order, and meaning, but it expects from us, in a profound participation of hope, to be in its turn interpreted and revealed."[34] The world is not absurd. Everything in it implies an intention, betrays a meaning.

Creation, therefore, as Judaism and Christianity understand it, means that existence is given, first of all; and second it means that existence is sustained in what is called the doctrine of divine preservation. "Creation and preservation," according to the Prayer Book, belong together. The rabbis said, "He makes the world new every day."

THE GOAL OF CREATION

Closely allied to the idea of continuing creation is that of the goal or end (*telos*) of creation. God not only originates and sustains, but also *directs* his creatures. God continues to sustain the world, and His activity in history and nature is unceasing. There is history because there is a unity between creation and the future. The rabbis had a saying that "At the creation of the world King Messiah was born" (Pesiqta Rabbati 2b). In theological terms this affirmation establishes the historical meaning of creation and deals with three special problems connected with the question of God's relationship to the world: the idea of providence, the problem of miracle, and the problem of evil.

The Idea of Providence

A discussion of providence or predestination always arouses fervent debate about free will against determination, the absolute sovereignty of God versus human freedom. The term (*pro-videre*) is ambiguous in meaning since it has the double connotation of foreseeing and foreordering. If these are understood in any absolute sense then God either becomes an omniscient spectator, knowing all, but not interfering with the autonomy of creation; or a designer who has planned everything that happens. In the first, creaturely freedom remains but divine power is reduced to finitude. In the second, freedom vanishes and providence is inexorable fate.

Biblical thought does not dwell on the problem in terms common to our favorite modern dilemma. It notices but rejects the horns of the dilemma. In the prophetic literature, for example, nations and kings are instruments of divine providence, which uses them to punish Israel. Yet they remain free and responsible agents, hence are to be punished for their sins (Isaiah 10:5–34; Isaiah 44:24–45:13; Jeremiah 25:9 ff.). Rabbinic literature also recognizes this paradox, but the theological problem of freedom of the will did not arise until the tenth century with persons like Saadia, who listened to the Moslem debates on predestination. Human action may limit or expand, strengthen or weaken God's power by obedience or disobedience, they thought, but not literally. Here is a symbolic effort to understand the paradox. Man must stay with the double truth; in the words of Rabbi Akiba, "Everything is foreseen and freedom of choice is given" (Sayings of the Fathers III: 19). The implication is that history is solely in God's hand, even when man has a share in its making. To say both that man is capable of choosing and acting on his decision and that all things are ordained and exercised by God in His wisdom and righteous will does not appear to be questioned. Even when the issue became a matter of dispute between the Pharisees and other sects, the Pharisees still maintained that providence did not deprive a man's will of its own impulse to act. Man in his righteous acts is a partner in the realization of his destiny, but his sin and evil would never be able to destroy it. Finite actions alone cannot assure direction of history. Heschel sums up the rabbinic understanding in these words: "We are free to choose between good and evil, we are not free in having to choose. We are in fact compelled to choose. Thus all freedom is a situation of God's waiting for man to choose."[35]

Nor is the understanding of providence any less paradoxical in the New Testament. The Sermon on the Mount lays impossible moral demands upon man, yet it assures him of the solicitous concern of providence (Matthew 5–7), to the point of prodigality. Augustine sums up this extraordinary idea of a God Who demands perfect obedience yet supplies it himself. "Give what thou demandest, and command what thou wilt."[36] That no human action can thwart God's directing creativity is dramatically demonstrated to Christians in the scandal of the crucifixion. We have already noticed the embarrassing disappointment with which the early Christians experienced the humiliation of the cross (Chapter 2). It was the worst thing that could happen through the acts of men. Christians, however, came to believe that it was the best thing that ever happened in the providence of God, driving them thereby to think anew about the problem of God's sovereignty in the world (cf. Acts 2:23). They came to believe that whatever comes is from God, by God's appointment—good, evil, injury—not simply in the sense of some mechanical necessity, but freely through the spontaneity of creatures in such a way that all things work together for good (Romans 8:28).

Medieval thought is more speculative. Maimonides, following Aristotle, thought that a general providence is sufficient for the subhuman creation. But against Aristotle's view that in human affairs everything is due to chance, he argues for an individual or special providence for man. Against the Islamic view that all is directly caused by God's will and intention, he maintains the theory of man's free will as a principle of the law of Moses. Moreover, an intelligent providence "is related and closely connected with the intellect, because providence can only proceed from an intelligent being, from a being that is in itself a most perfect intellect."[37] Therefore, providence is not the same thing for all men, but is in proportion to their intellectual endowments. The prophets, for example, are the greatest beneficiaries.

By divine providence, Thomas Aquinas understands the eternal plan of all things in the divine mind, a plan according to which all earthly things are directed or tend to their final end. The basis for this divine providence is the truth that God is the cause of all things and the cause of all that is good in the universe. And since God created in accordance with the divine intellect, there will be some plan or order of creation and the attainment of the divine purposes of the universe in the divine mind. This implies intelligence in nature and God is that intelligence. The goodness and purpose of such an order in nature is the work of God. To effect this there must be a divine plan or divine providence for all things. Such a divine plan, moreover, extends to all things because God's causality and His creative power extend to all things, to the totality of existing things in the universe; so such providence in the divine wisdom may permit evils or defects in existing beings in order that the perfection of the good of the universe can be brought about. Thus evil has a place within the divine providence or the divine plan of things. If there were no evil in the world, much good would never come about, he argues. Pain, for example, can be regarded as a necessary evil to effect the greater good—the preservation of life.

For John Calvin, God is the Creator of the world and its absolute master; permanently and universally active in the world, its perpetual governor and guardian. God's providence works in three ways: (1) in the order of nature, through which He operates in conformity to the laws which He imposes, (2) by special providence, which has particular application to man, and (3) as governor, by which He is present to and acts upon both the elect and the nonelect. Like Augustine and Thomas, Calvin was inclined to believe that predestination was a particular application of the general notion of providence, concerned with each individual. But in any case, providence is God's permanent and universal activity: "When we speak of the providence of God, this word does not signify that He, remaining idle in the heavens, watches over what is happening on earth; rather he is like the captain of a ship, holding the helm in order to cope with every event."[38] Everything that happens in the world is directly through the direct causation of providence, with particular care for each creature. According to their natures, all species have secret guidance and are directly subject to God's will. This is true both for individuals and societies. Consciously or unconsciously, they are directed by God. History, and particularly revolutions, are eloquent testimony to God's power, which at every moment determines history and its vicissitudes. Providence is concerned not only with believers or the Church. On the contrary, God uses the wicked in such a way that they execute His judgments. But God is not the author of evil, and the evil-doers are responsible for their actions. He applies this to Judas in particular in much the same way as we have seen the problem resolved in Isaiah. Here again the paradox is apparent.

From what has been said about the paradoxical character of providence, it should be clear that it cannot be understood in a deterministic way, as though by some design all was decreed before the foundation of the world. In both Judaism and Christianity the issue is more subtle. Neither determinism nor indeterminism is an adequate description of what has been a basic experience in the great representatives of western religion (for example, Isaiah, Paul, Augustine, Thomas Aquinas, Maimonides, Luther, Calvin). Providence and predestination are ideas by means of which these men and their followers have been lifted above the uncertainties of freedom and the contradictions of history to a "transcendent necessity." But this sort of bondage is not mechanical necessity; they have been under a command, or partners in a covenant, by means of which their humanity was confirmed. They have "a calling" (a very important element in predestination) which can be rejected or fulfilled. So there is a mutual relationship between divine providence and finite man, despite the paradox of that assertion. Providence is not interference, but creation. "It is the quality of inner-directedness present in every situation."[39] Those who emphasize most this "unconditioned dependence" on God, for example Calvin and the Puritans, and Jews throughout the ages, have been the greatest activists in history. The world—all of it—has been the warp and woof of the concrete action of God. This discernment of the transcendent immanent in the universe, in a vertical-horizontal relationship, lends to nature and history an incomparable intensity and significance which confirms the autonomy of the creation and the humanity of man. "God's directing activity works through the spontaneity of creatures and human freedom."[40] And this provides an unshaking confidence and meaning "because, beneath all the process of becoming is the woof of that which everlastingly persists, in which it may be said with equal truth of all that comes into being, that it already is."[41] This does not mean that an understanding of the meaning of history and nature is or can be complete. Both the disclosure of meaning and the meaning itself is fragmentary until an eschatological dimension comes into view. Jewish faith looks, then, to a messianic future, and the Christian to redemption and the eschaton (end of history) which will be discussed later.

The Problem of Miracle

WHAT IS A MIRACLE? According to Webster's dictionary, the term miracle has three definitions: (1) it is an extraordinary event taken to manifest the supernatural power of God fulfilling his purposes; (2) it is an event or effect in the physical world, deviating from the laws of nature; or (3) it is an accomplishment or occurrence so outstanding or unusual as to seem beyond human capacity or endeavor. That these are definitions commonly used no one would deny. Presumably the average man, asked to describe a miracle, would define it as divine intervention into a closed system of causation, roughly understood in terms of Newtonian physics. This is not a very profound definition from the religious and theological standpoint. In fact, this sort of definition, along with the innumerable miracle stories in all religions, make the term somewhat misleading and even dangerous for religious thought.

St. Augustine said that "a miracle is not contrary to nature, but to what is known of nature."[42] Following this remark, two comments are in order. First of all, it is inappropriate to use the term "miracle" for events which are astonishing for a certain time, but by later scientific discovery seem to be ordinary events. Thus from the standpoint, say, of primitive man, a record player would be a terrifying miracle, as would the cure of certain deadly diseases, which still strikes modern man as miraculous. There is obviously much in nature which, from our very limited knowledge, may be deemed miraculous in these terms, and from the standpoint of science, certain things which appear to be miraculous today may not appear to be at all extraordinary to the scientists of tomorrow. Thus, miracle is commonly taken to mean that which occurs according to the operation of those laws of nature which are as yet unknown to us.

NATURAL LAW. The second definition of the term miracle has to do with what we mean by natural law or laws of nature. In recent history man has passed from a natural world of appearances which appear to be invisibly controlled by caprice or spirits through Newton's fixed world of causation to the universe of quantum mechanics. If, therefore, we mean by the miraculous an event transcending the known laws of nature, we have to bear in mind that these so-called laws have a way of being altered from one scientific generation to another. In modern science nature is not known as a completely fixed system, but leaves room for novelty. Therefore, miracle is not necessarily an untenable conception. Indeed, the pace of scientific knowledge has been so rapid since the nineteenth century that the extraordinary soon becomes ordinary knowledge and we fail to see that nature itself is one vast miracle and becomes an increasingly astonishing miracle with every new discovery. Each one of us, as a matter of fact, in our personal lives, repeats that miracle. We stand at the point where a miracle comes into being, and, after the event, we call it natural. We more than men in any other period of history, should be able to recognize the truth of Augustine's remark:

> Is not the universe itself a miracle, yet visible out of God's making? All the miracles done in this world are less than the world itself; yet God made them all, and after a manner that man cannot conceive nor comprehend. For though these visible miracles of nature be now no more admired, yet ponder them wisely, and they are more astonishing than the strangest: for man is a greater miracle than all that he can work.[43]

THE BIBLICAL VIEW.   From the standpoint of biblical and post-biblical men, much of the above discussion about miracle would be completely irrelevant. They did not think that way at all, let alone think in terms of closed systems of causation. They would never have arrived at a conception of miracle in any sense of the word as defined above. For the ancient Hebrew, God's power has no limit but His will. He can do anything He wishes, and His powers in nature are exercised directly. When the Psalmist sang, "The heavens declare the glory of God and the firmament shows his handiwork" (Psalms 19:1), he meant quite literally that God was exercising his majesty directly. Notions about the laws of nature, the regularity of nature, the uniformity of nature, never entered his mind. Natural forces were simply the ordinary ways of God's working. For him God was free to act in extraordinary ways or ordinary ways, one way being just as natural as the other. Since he had no contrasting conceptions of nature and supernature, all events could be the immediate work of God.

If the Hebrew talked about miracle, he meant some extraordinary phenomenon which was exercised for a special purpose (see the fascinating story of Elijah and the prophets of Baal in I Kings 18), but this was not described as at variance with nature or transcending or suspending the ordinary ways of nature's working. These astonishing acts were thought to be wrought neither for mere wonder nor were they mere magic, since they served the intelligible purposes of the Divine Will. There had to be religious interpretation of the occurrence. If the Hebrew made a distinction, it was something like this: the greatness of God was manifest in the ordinary course of nature, the goodness of God was peculiarly revealed in miracle as faith could interpret and appropriate the event. The greatest display of both God's power and His goodness, apart from the miracle of creation itself, was the miracle which took place at the Red Sea. The Psalmist sang:

> Our fathers, when they were in Egypt,
>   did not consider thy wonderful works;
> they did not remember the abundance of thy steadfast love,
>   but rebelled against the Most High at the Red Sea.
> Yet he saved them for his name's sake,
>   that he might make known his mighty power.
> He rebuked the Red Sea, and it became dry;
>   and he led them through the deep as through a desert.
> So he saved them from the hand of the foe,
>   and delivered them from the power of the enemy.
> And the waters covered their adversaries;
>   not one of them was left.
> Then they believed his words;
>   they sang his praise.
>
> (Psalms 106:7–12)

On this miracle faith dwelt.

For the rabbis, the age of miracles was not past. It was true there were no signal events, but greater than the deliverance at the Red Sea would be the deliverance still to come. In the meanwhile, miracles would continue on an individual scale, and if they appeared to be less frequent, it was because the people were less worthy. On this level, there was no greater miracle than God's constant provision for man's needs, nor was this preservation less wonderful than the cleaving of the Red Sea.

The talmudic literature is replete with stories of healings, exorcisms, and prayers for rain which were considered the ordinary operation of God's providence. In fact, some of the rabbis compared the miracle of rain in answer to prayer to the miracle of the resurrection still to come. Both had been wrought and will be wrought by the hand of God.[44]

In the New Testament there are three words for the term miracle (actually a comparison of the King James Version and the RSV shows that the translation "miracle" occurs much more rarely in the RSV than in the King James Version). The Greek words for the term are *semeion*, which means a "sign," something which signifies, gives a signal for, points to, but is itself part of that to which it points. The second word is *dynamis* (the word from which our term "dynamic" comes), meaning "power," that is, the manifestation of power. This is sometimes translated as "miracle" or "the working of miracles." A miracle is an act of power. The third term is *teras*, which means "wonder." "Wonderful" means that reality which, when it is experienced, fills one with wonder. It may be an extraordinary or ordinary event, but in and through the event or the personality of the acts or the words, there appears something which evokes in one awe, amazement, or reverence—wonder. In biblical terms, then, a miracle is a sign or sign event which manifests the power and goodness of God in such a way that it evokes a response of awe, reverence, and amazement—and faith— on the part of man.

Wonders and signs, of course, are not necessarily acts of divine power. They may be acts of demonic powers. Satan as well as God can work miracles. In both the Hebrew and Christian Scriptures there are evidences of differing interpretations about the same object or facts as seen by different people. For example, Jesus was called by some who saw his acts "the incarnate Son of the living God" and by others "Beelzebub" who "casts out demons." The content of "miracle," then, is not a kind of wand-waving magic by which God or Christ coerces man into believing. Miracles are given only to those for whom they are sign events, that is, to those who receive them in faith. There are no coercive wonders or objective miracles. These are contradictions in terms. Many times when Jesus was asked for a coercive sign, he refused to give it: "I will give you no signs save the sign of Jonah," which is the sign of repentance; and repentance means turning to God. He did give signs or perform sign events; in fact everything that he did, including the Sermon on the Mount, his healings and ultimately his death and resurrection, are signs for Christians through which he manifested himself as the incarnate Son of God to those who believed; but these were not compelling or coercive signs. For Jesus, they were simply the intention and direct action of God.

A MODERN POINT OF VIEW.   It is often said that modern man can no longer believe in miracles, and this is probably very true if miracle is interpreted as supernatural interference in the natural process. But from what we have said, this would make God a sorcerer and magician. In this light we can also see that what modern man regards as natural law is not of particular importance. The things that are important are what power appears and manifests itself through what event. As we have seen, since miracle does not destroy the stable structure, either of reason or of the natural order, such events can be put to the test of scientific analysis, psychological or physiological, and certainly historical investigation is both possible and necessary. Such analysis can undercut superstitions and demonic interpretations of miracle and revelation and become the allies of religion and theology in the battle against distortion of genuine under-standing. But, since the true meaning of miracle is an event in and through which God reveals himself, evoking a response, such investigation could not reveal the true meaning of the event.[45] A genuine miracle could still be, however, an astonishing event that is unusual and shaking, which would point to a mystery of God and be received as a sign event by those who have faith.

Further we can be relieved of the burden of thinking that God is particularly, exceptionally, or exclusively known only through those events which, from the standpoint of our present knowledge of what we call natural law, are inexplicable. God may appear and the miracle may happen in an incident or event which is completely explicable from the standpoint of our present scientific knowledge. It is possible for modern man to believe that the universe is neither a closed system of laws into which God must intervene if He would divert its movement, nor something which has no independence in itself, no autonomy or inner direction or law of its own, through which God moves even as man moves his body. To deny such a possibility would be, in the logic of Jewish and Christian thought, a denial of the freedom of the creation and the freedom of God. Was it not John Donne who said that nature is the common law by which God governs us? And if that is so, miracle is God's prerogative.

Emil Brunner, a Swiss theologian, makes this point unmistakably clear:

To deny the reality of miracle would be to deny the freedom of God, of the God who is the Lord of the whole world. To see this God at work, who is the free Lord of the world which He has created, means encountering miracle, whether this miracle of the divine action works through the laws of nature not outside them. . . . The freedom of God is a vital concern for faith, but it is no more and no less concerned with what is called "miracle," or the so-called "miracles," than with the working of God through the constancy of nature and its laws. As against the Deistic view we would say that God is actively at work even where no "miracles" occur; as against the Pantheistic view we would say, that God's working is not confined to the sphere of natural causality. Both the "ordinary" and the "extraordinary" action of God is equally wonderful; for everything that God does is wonderful, for those who see that it is *God* who does it.[46]

The Problem of Evil

Of all the problems which provoke man to philosophical speculation and thoughtful reflection, none has greater impact or more disturbing effect on him than the problem of evil. While evil has always been a persistent challenge to men's philosophy and faith, it confronts twentieth-century men with especial poignancy and force. This century, which has seemed to many to be the zenith of western man's aspirations, has also been an era of seemingly endless wars which have killed more people than all the previous centuries of the common era. It is a century symbolized by totalitarianisms, concentration camps, the death of more than six million Jews, and countless refugees wandering homeless across the world. All of those events associated with the name Auschwitz still pass human understanding, and certainly have shaken Jewish existence to its core. How then can Jews and Christians talk about the essential goodness of the world and history and of a God who acts in history and nature as the intelligible structure of every event?

Now, as in all times, we are faced with the question of how to account for the evil in the world if there is a good and powerful God. Man has been aware of two distinct categories of evil. The first may be called physical or natural evil, because it represents some deficiency, disorder, or deformity in the natural order of things. It may be blindness or lameness, monstrosities and abnormalities, death and destruction, tornadoes or floods. The second type of evil is moral evil, which is to be found in the actions of men, such as war, crime, perfidy, and sin. Of these two kinds, the first seems the more evidently disastrous, primarily because it appears to be beyond the control of man and is more clearly a product of natural forces. Moral evil, though certainly the more serious of the two, more often seems the lesser evil, perhaps because it is more clearly the responsibility of man and therefore something that presumably could be evaded.

Where does evil come from? Epicurus, the Greek philosopher, formulated the problem as a tough dilemma: "God either wishes to take away evil and is unable; or He is able but not willing; or He is neither able nor willing." Similarly modern philosophy states the problem as a metaphysical conundrum: If God is omnipotent, He could prevent evil if He wished. If God is perfectly good, He would wish to if He could. Thus, if God exists and is both perfectly omnipotent and perfectly good, then there exists a being who could prevent evil if He wished, and who would wish to if He could. If this is true, how is it that there are so many evils in the world?[47]

Doubtlessly, every person in the course of his life has been confronted with the logical rigidities of this seemingly insolvable dilemma which calls everything into question. Has anyone succeeded in wholly grasping the monstrous evil in the actual world? What believer has not rebelled against its existence to the point of doubting the existence of a good and powerful God? Faced with this dilemma men frequently have assumed that one or more of the traditional attributes of God—His wisdom, mercy, or power—must be deleted or curtailed.

It may come as a shock to many people to discover with what amazing honesty this problem has been faced in the biblical literature. To be sure, the Bible incorporates each and every theological argument conceivable, but it also portrays vividly the cry of resistance and rebellion of the human spirit confronted with the enormity of suffering and evil in life and society.

> As God lives, who has taken away my right,
>   and the Almighty, who has made my soul bitter;
> as long as my breath is in me,
>   and the spirit of God is in my nostrils;
> my lips will not speak falsehood,
>   and my tongue will not utter deceit.
> Far be it from me to say that you are right;
>   till I die I will not put away my integrity from me.
> I hold fast my righteousness, and will not let it go;
>   my heart does not reproach me for any of my days.
>   (Job 27: 2–6)

One expects to hear this kind of language from the Book of Job, which is popularly conceived as the book that deals with the problem of suffering, but this protest literature is not confined to Job. In the Book of Genesis, Abraham intercedes for the city of Sodom which the Lord is about to destroy. He protests by saying, "Wilt thou indeed destroy the righteous with the wicked? Suppose there are fifty righteous within the city; wilt thou then destroy the place and not spare it for the fifty righteous who are in it? Far be it from Thee to do such a thing, to slay the righteous with the wicked, so that the righteous spare the wicked! Far be it from Thee(!) Shall not the Judge of all the earth do right?" (Genesis 18:23–25). This voice of rebellion is authentic and is not considered blasphemous. (One must remember that this literature is canonized.) Out of deep personal anguish the sufferer defies but does not deny the attributes of God. Again, this defiance is not limited to the biblical literature. This same spirit can be illustrated in the Midrash, the Talmud, medieval poetry, indeed from antiquity to the present day.

A Variety of Answers

Let us still put the question, how do we account for the existence of evil? There are several possible approaches to this question. Before proceeding to enumerate them, however, let us keep in mind that any view on this problem necessarily involves a notion of the existence and nature of God and such other questions as the problem of human freedom and determination and the problem of redemption and eschatology.

One approach to the problem is to *deny its existence*. In this view, evil is an illusion which results from our imperfect way of looking at reality, the seeming disorders and evils of the world are evaluations introduced by men whose perspective is necessarily limited and finite. If one could see the whole world process in a flash of insight, one would recognize that things which appear to be evil from man's limited and confused point of view, are really right and necessary parts of the whole. For example, there are, after all, occasional discords, jarring in themselves, which are necessary to the perfection of a symphony; or there are dark streaks of color, which appear to be ugly as seen apart from the context, but nevertheless are indispensable elements in the masterpieces of art. There are two difficulties with this view: first, such a solution is not very likely to appeal to the sufferer from a painful disease or the victim of injustice. He is likely to get little comfort out of the fact that his misfortune is necessary to the grand harmony of things. Second, If the word *evil* means anything in the ordinary sense, then it is surely false to deny that it exists. One would have to assume that what has been taken to have happened, has not, in fact, happened. But who can deny the existence of an earthquake or a tornado, or a concentration camp? Surely it is clear that men do what is wrong and suffer.

A second answer that has been given traditionally is that evil is the result of, or *punishment for,* sin and wickedness. This answer is based upon a theory of retribution and is expressed often in biblical writings, particularly in the Book of Job and in the Deuteronomic literature. Actually, this does not so much speak to the general problem of evil as to the problem of the suffering of the righteous. If a man suffers, the argument goes, obviously there is a good reason: "If a man sees that painful sufferings visit him, let him examine his conduct" (B'rakhot 5 a). If a self-examination fails to reveal a man's moral failure, then as a final result he may attribute his evil situation to God's chastisement. A variation of this point of view is the theory of reincarnation in some eastern religions—according to our deserts we will be reborn into the next cycle, perhaps in some other form (a slave, or a spider!) and will continue to be reborn until our sins have been expiated and we have achieved release from the karmic cycle or wheel of rebirth.

In the rabbinic literature there are many modes of punishment for transgressions, such as disease, war, accident, and sentence by tribunal, but all can be traced somehow to the just exercise of divine will. In the rabbinic period and after the destruction of the temple, when Jewish courts could no longer decree capital punishment, the rabbis contended that punishment would continue through natural agencies: "He who would have been sentenced to stoning, falls from the roof; he who would have been decapitated is either delivered to the [Roman] government or robbers come upon him; he who would be sentenced to strangulation is either drowned or dies from suffocation" (K'tuvot 3 a, b). Were this true, then one would expect evil in the world to be in proportion to actual wrong-doing. The innocent would not suffer at all and the particularly wicked or evil individuals would suffer most. In fact, this is not the case. If we look at the adult world, or even to young children who are not notably exempted from the most painful diseases, famine, or terror, and, if this punishment is distributed by God, then He must be an unjust judge and therefore cannot be good. This point of view was categorically denied in the New Testament by Jesus when he was asked after he had healed the blind man, "Who sinned, this man or his parents . . . ?" Jesus' reply was, "It was not this man that sinned, or his parents, but that the works of God might be manifest in him" (John 9:2). This is a puzzling reply, but does emphasize the unequivocal rejection of the view that the evil was a punishment for wickedness.

A third possible answer is a *dualism*, which holds that the world process must be seen as a gigantic struggle between the twin powers of good and evil. This is the view known as Manichaeism, a heresy very popular in St. Augustine's time. The Manichaeans held that God is responsible for all the good in the universe, but that evil should be attributed to a supremely evil being or principle. Some religions still represent history as the battleground of the good and evil gods. A variation upon this same theme is the tendency to personify the struggle between God and His supernatural adversary, Satan, who has as his vocation the frustration of the purposes of God at every point.

St. Augustine, like the rabbis before him,[48] rejected this point of view and we can allow his answer to stand in response to this perspective. Augustine answers that there is no being contrary to God, the Supreme Being and author of all being whatsoever. God could not share the order in creation of the universe with another being and still be the omniscient and omnipotent Creator. Since all beings are created by God Who is infinitely good, then all that God creates must be good. There cannot be two competing and divine powers. From the Jewish and Christian stance, all forms of dualism are unsatisfactory, because there cannot be two ultimates: if reality is ultimately good, how did evil obtain a foothold in the universe; if it is bad, where did the good come from?

Similarly, and fourth, the Jewish and Christian stance rejects all form of thought which *deny that evil constitutes a real problem*, whether this be an atheism that posits a rudderless world in which God is utterly irrelevant to any proper explanation of history, or a pantheism that identifies God with a nature that reigns with an indiscriminate hand. In both these points of view, moral distinctions between good and evil, order and confusion, are simply dismissed as human biases or as man's anthropocentric tendencies. If the ultimate principle of things is simply blind force or chance or any irrationality, then is it not true that the direction of the universe is bound to be indifferent to the aims, aspirations, sufferings, and values of mankind? As Bertrand Russell puts it in his *Philosophical Essays:* "Blind to good use, reckless of destruction, omnipotent matter rolls on." If this be true, has man any consolation when catastrophe befalls him, except perhaps the thought that catastrophe does not know that it is crushing man? This seems not so much a meeting of the problem as avoiding it. What does one do with the problem of good? Why should there be goodness at all in such a world as ours, and how does one explain the instance of good? Yet, judging from his actions, a person like Bertrand Russell does have very firm convictions about what the good is.

The possible solutions we have outlined must stand as examples of man's anguished attempt to answer this age-old problem. We could cite many other answers, such as: without evil and suffering, we would not receive the necessary discipline to make us fit for the afterworld; pain performs a useful and beneficial function—and it is a necessary means to good, or we could say that it is an unnecessary though actual consequence of good, or that it is an incomprehensible mystery and must forever stand as a paradox and contradiction and difficulty. We mention these possible answers in brief not because they are useless; they may even be helpful and they are points of view to which men return constantly.

A MYTHOLOGICAL-SCIENTIFIC INFERENCE: THE "FALL" OF NATURE. Before we discuss the classical attempt to deal with the problem of evil, we may with some profit examine a notion which has been lurking in the back of men's minds for centuries. Does the myth of the "fall," either before or after the creation of the world, have any meaningful relation to the problem of evil? Does this myth include the natural order as well and point to the possibility of a metaphysical catastrophe in nature? At first this may seem like a fanciful notion, but it has been suggestive to men since the biblical era. There are hints of it in the story of creation (Genesis 1) and in the New Testament. The biblical epic suggests the notion that while creation was a victory over the hostile powers of chaos, the created universe no longer exists in the state in which it came forth from the hands of its Maker. Because of the sin of man "the ground is cursed," and there is biblical man's notion of the constant threat of the "watery chaos." Paul talks about "the whole creation . . . groaning in travail . . ." (Romans 8:22); "For the creation was subjected to futility, not of its own will . . ." (v. 20). But if the universe in some mysterious way has shared in the fall of man, so it will have a share in redemption.

This has been a profoundly serious question throughout the centuries, especially since Origen, who in the second century was influenced by Plato's *Timaeus.* It has recently been raised again by European theologians. Giovanni Miegge, a distinguished Italian theologian, provides a picturesque description:

. . . the powers of chaos, in the biblical picture of the universe, remain subdued, but not destroyed, in the margins of created world; they bear down upon it as a constant threat, from which only the faithful will of the creator avails to save it day by day and hour by hour . . . He [God] opposes the limits which they shall not pass to the "great waters" of chaos, which break in vain against the limits of His dry land—dry land only because He maintains it as such. Life flourishes on the borderland of death; being finds room to expand in the margins of non-being; but it can flourish, and expand with confidence only because the faithfulness of God keeps at a distance negation, death and non-being. In this narrow space, on the very edge of negation, the joy of created beings can find the expression, the power and the goodness of the Creator can be extolled.[49]

This may be a serious question, although of course, we are now thinking on the level of myth and we have no means of knowing to what extent the world beyond man can be regarded as having been altered in its structure by the fall, however we may understand the "fall."

Interestingly enough, however, a very similar notion has received some scientific attention from historians of science and at least one contemporary anthropologist. Professor Loren Eiseley suggests that there has occurred a rift or schism in man's endeavors that affects aspects of history and nature; there is a kind of involution of the human drama which has had a catastrophic effect on nature. He quotes Thomas Beddoes:

> Nature's polluted,
> There's man in every secret corner of her
> Doing damned wicked deeds.
> Thou art come of old world
> A whory, atheistic, murdering star

and he adds, "This is the dark murmur that rises from the abyss beneath us, and that draws us with uncanny fascination."[50] In another connection he writes:

It is with the coming of man that a vast hole seems to open in nature, a vast black whirlpool, spinning faster and faster, consuming flesh, stones, soil, minerals, sucking down the lightning, wrenching power from the atom, until the ancient sounds of nature are drowned in the cacophony of something which is no longer nature, something instead which is loose and knocking at the world's heart, something demonic and no longer planned—escaped, maybe— spewed out of nature, contending in a final giant's game against its master.[51]

However fascinating or significant these attempts at explanation are, they are, on the whole, of second magnitude when compared to the durability and usefulness of the classical answer which has been a mainstay of Jewish and Christian explanation.

THE CLASSICAL ANSWER.   The classical answer in the western intellectual tradition was stated by Augustine, and his answer was representative of a large part of medieval thought, both Jewish and Christian. Aquinas was largely dependent upon Augustine for his point of view, and Jewish philosophers like Maimonides, Saadia, and Abraham Ibn Daud, although not directly dependent upon Augustine, used the same kind of argument.

Augustine's answer is that evil is a lack, a deprivation, but that with the exception of God, evil can be found only in a substance that is good. Hence, good can exist without evil, but evil cannot exist without good. There cannot be a lack of privation without the existence of any being which, insofar as it is, is good.[52] For example, blindness is an evil, it is a lack or privation of what we know and expect a being to possess. But blindness, insofar as it has any existence, must exist in a being that is otherwise good. Examples could be easily multiplied here. Cancer is regarded as an evil: we cut it out, but we do not destroy the individual in whom the cancer exists, or regard him as evil. Furthermore, evil can affect creatures, in either the physical order or the moral order. Moral evil is a deficiency in will, a corruption of will, a privation of that which one would expect to find in a rational creature. The evil man is one who lacks the ability to choose rightly and to choose the good.

If we ask what is the origin or course of evil, the answer must be the good. As we have seen above, Augustine declares the world to be created and it is created qualitatively good, but not perfectly good, since only God can be perfectly good in the sense of being immutable. God's being is necessary being; the being of the world is contingent being, and therefore imperfect being. Whatever is natural, whatever exists at all, is so far good. Evil is to be found only in a situation in which there is a lapse toward nonbeing, or in which falsification or distortion has come into the good creature. Augustine maintains that the only way that falsification or distortion can come into such reality is through the deliberate act of a finite being who is free to act in a way which affirms falsity. God cannot do that. Inanimate things, plants, and animals cannot do it. Only angels and men have that sort of freedom. Unfortunately, according to Augustine, the angels first and then the parents of the human race did precisely that, and evil is now here. Nonbeing is not evil, but it is the intrusion of nonbeing into the realm of being which is. It is the failure on the part of what is real, a defect or decline or lapse in the direction of nonbeing. Since evil is therefore a function of free will, by the created order of things only men and angels have this function. Against the Manichaeans, Augustine argued that there is no evil principle in nature in the very existence of the world. Evil cannot be located in the natural order, it can only be thought of as a function of free choice and only man has that choice; therefore evil comes into the created world through man. Evil cannot exist alone, it must always exist in some being and all being created by God is good. Rational choice, the very finest manifestation in man of the beneficence of God, is the doorway for evil to enter the world.

Still one may ask why man could not have been created in a state of relative perfection, so that he would not be subject to nonbeing, illness, disease, and death. According to Augustine, this was man's original state, but by the exercise of his finest powers, evil has resulted. Of course, logically God might have created man wholly good, which is to say, incapable of any moral action or decision, but would the world thereby have been better? That is, God, if He had wished, could have created automatons who could not have caused Him or the world any trouble; but automatons are incapable of any kind of moral action, and therefore of any immoral action, and therefore of any act of good. In any case, it is not self-evident that a world where men were incapable of moral action would be any better than a world where men can be morally offensive.

But still we may ask, Why this particular creation and not another, a different order of nature? Why not a better world all around from our point of view? One answer Augustine gives is that we are too prone to consider all nature as merely a convenience for ourselves. "What is more useful," he says, "than fire for warming, restoring, cooking, though nothing is more destructive than fire burning and consuming? The same thing then applied in one way is destructive, but when applied suitably is beneficial. We must not listen then to those who praise the light of fire, but find fault with its heat, judging it not by its nature but by their convenience or comfort." In a different context H. H. Farmer rather amusingly says, "It is only because the fire can be relied on to boil the kettle, and the sound waves to carry our speech, that we can indulge in that highly personal activity called a tea-party."[53] Augustine multiplies examples, but the point is that we ought not to judge things by our own narrow perspective. That what appears evil or disorder to us, not only may be permitted by God but ordered by Him for the fulfillment of greater good than we can comprehend. He adds that we are too prone to jump to conclusions regarding what we consider evil.

THE PRINCIPLE OF PLENTITUDE.[54]   The medieval Jewish philosophers also often chided man for egocentrism in believing that the world was created for his benefit. Man's self-centered view would have limited the universe to those things which are serviceable to him, but according to the principle of plentitude, which they invoked, there flowed out of God's infinite being an inexhaustible perfection, a chain of being, in which every conceivable diversity of potentiality existed. Maimonides used this same principle somewhat impersonally by discussing what man calls the destructive evil, death. He said, ". . . in accordance with the divine wisdom,

Genesis can only take place through destruction and without destruction of the individual members of the species, the species themselves would not exist permanently."[55]

To sum up, therefore, Augustine seems to argue that evil comes into the created world through the wrong exercise of the rational choices of man. Through his degradation and loss of status, he is in the created order the most terrible creature and he has released a potentiality for terror and destruction upon the earth which no other creature can emulate, just as he had the potentiality for creative meaning, actualizing the good which no other part of the creation could provide. Now through man, creation in reverse, so to speak, can reach a magnitude of evil which is unique by reason of his great capacities for free choice.

This point of view Luther and Calvin would applaud. Reinhold Niebuhr emphasizes the same point. Niebuhr maintains that the various accounts which attribute sin or evil to inertia in nature, the hypertrophy of impulses, or to ignorance miss the essential point, namely, that evil "arises from the very freedom of reason with which man is endowed." Sin is the consequence "of the freedom by which man is able to throw the harmonies of nature out of joint." Evil is therefore not a defect in nature but rather the harmony of nature is disturbed because man tries to "make himself, rather than God, the center of existence. It is not a defect of creation but a defect which becomes possible because man has been endowed with a freedom not known in the rest of creation."[56]

THE JEWISH-CHRISTIAN STANCE.   None of these attempted explanations should be taken to mean that Jews and Christians believe they have any final answer to the problem of evil. On the contrary, in fact, the entire literature points to the incomprehensible mystery of the immensity of moral and physical evil and its overwhelming and tragic consequences in human history. The existence of evil and suffering as a brute motive force is an exhibition of the presence in our existence of that which is beyond man's control, and it is in response to that fact that most men are defined as selves, have their characters shaped, and even develop their whole ethos. The existence of this demonic force in human history has been and is for Jews and Christians as well as for all men both a theoretical and existential argument against belief in a creating and providential God.

Nonetheless, Jews and Christians affirm that evil is not a part of God, or even a part of essential man. The goodness of creation, as well as the presence of evil, must be seen in the larger context of the creating, sustaining, directing, and redeeming activity of God Who is not only the beginning but also the end (the alpha and the omega); and only the end can reveal the full significance of the beginning. Apart from this conviction they would agree that "life is a flash of occasional enjoyments lighting up a mass of pain and misery, a bagatelle of transient experience."[57] In fact, the providential character of Judaism is a lasting example. The persistent existence of the Jewish people throughout all efforts to effect "the final solution," and the central act of the Christian drama (the Crucifixion) shows how dastardly evil can defeat the purposes of God, but that defeat also proves to them that God cannot be ultimately defeated. As Reinhold Niebuhr puts it, ". . . it is God's nature to swallow up evil in himself and destroy it. Life in its deepest essence is not only good but capable of destroying the evil which has been produced in it."[58]

The Risk of Creation

Niebuhr's statement is a way of saying that creation involves real risk. This may also be what Dietrich Bonhoeffer meant by the "weakness" of God Who places Himself at the mercy of the world. But this "weakness" is also God's strength, and it is precisely when He appears in weakness that He manifests His invincible strength.[59] The vision of creation includes also the vision of evil and of grace. If there is real risk and real cost to God, there must also be a tragic element in the creative process in which man, history, and nature share. Hence the ambiguity in the actual picture of the world we know.

This was implied earlier in this chapter in our description of the idea of creation as the originating, sustaining, and directing activity of God. Creation is not a static notion of a God Who set things in motion at a beginning, nor is it a notion of merely random creativity. Creation does not produce a ready-made and perfect world, but rather perfection must be attained. This means at least two things. First, the idea of creation includes the ideas of providence, reconciliation, and the consummation of creation. The idea of providence, however, is not to be understood in deterministic fashion as a divine decree before the foundation of the world. There is always an element of contingency. Therefore, providence includes reconciliation whereby the antinomies of existence are healed, imbalances redressed, alienations overcome, and creation brought to perfection. These are not to be seen as successive acts of God, but rather as moments, so to speak, of one act. That is why Jewish and Christian thought has always connected the ideas of creation, redemption, and eschatology. It was the genius of the biblical writers to understand that God's reconciling activity was from the beginning and inseparable from His creating activity. Hence in the conflict of good and evil—in the tension between what is and what ought to be—they could expect that "The Lord shall be king over all the earth; on that day the Lord shall be one and his name one" (Zechariah 14:9). Second, it means that man is to be "entrusted," to use Calvin's terms, with responsibility for creation and his own existence. Creation does not mean "a Divine Despot and a slavish Universe."[60] Man does have freedom and responsibility, though his "boundaries are fixed" and he cannot break those boundaries or reverse the trend of creation.

This belief in God's creativity and governance is not a matter of metaphysical speculation but is an act of faith. Since the actual state of existence is always ambiguous, it is a belief held often in the face of contradicting facts. It is not obvious that "in everything God works for good" (Romans 8:28), nor was it obvious to Paul. The idea begins as an act of faith and hope, not as speculation about the nature of the world. This way of stating the issue may help to overcome some of the confusion and logical rigidity surrounding much of the thought about metaphysical attributes of God in which it is sometimes suggested that God is in some kind of inner conflict between His power and goodness, transcendence and immanence, and His justice and love. Many sensitive spirits have been troubled by this problem. Creative attempts have been made to explain these seeming contradictions. We need only mention in passing Whitehead's "primordial nature of God," Alexander's theory of emergence, Brightman's "surd" and Einstein's "finite" God.

For a faith founded existentially, terms like omnipotence, omnipresence, and omniscience are symbolic terms to describe personal experience with the "Incomparable." "Omnipotence" does not refer to a capricious despot who has the sheer power to do anything, but rather is the guarantee in faith that with God nothing is impossible; it is not an irrational force that can break out in any direction, but is an ordered power with a self-imposed limitation. "Omniscience" implies freedom from the narrow limitations characteristic of human knowing, that nothing is absolutely hidden, and is directed toward the most secret attitudes of men (Psalm 51). "Omnipresence" does not mean either that God is endlessly extended in space, diffused like an ether, or limited to one place. At the same time God transcends the world as much as he is immanent in it. Religious thought must stress the symbolic character of all such temporal and spatial symbols. Terms like "beyond," "outside," or "other" point to God's self-sufficiency, His relation to but not identity with the world, His unknowability except by analogy.

The heart of the creation faith for Jews and Christians lies in a courageous trust in Him who will ultimately resolve the paradoxes of history. The power and the pathos of this trust are magnificently illustrated in this statement:

God is disclosed as the Creator—the one in whom power is manifest, but goodness is uncertain. He is disclosed in the Son, as God with us—the one in whom goodness is present, but power is dubious. He is disclosed in the Holy

Spirit—the one whose presence is manifest, but whose ultimate nature is shrouded in mystery. The Bible shows us in the Incarnation that that power is goodness and goodness is power; our Christian faith and life are based upon the apprehending of this goodness and power of God.[61]

While Jewish faith would not express itself in this triadic manner, the spirit is much the same. The mystery of life can be faced only in personal reliance and trust in a powerful God who in ways past comprehension holds the destiny of the world in control:

Where God's power does not seem to be in accord with His goodness, it is still proper to trust in Him. He whose infinite energy and inscrutable purposes uphold the vast creation can be relied on to sustain our little lives.[62]

NOTES

1. Reinhold Niebuhr, *The Nature and Destiny of Man* (New York: Scribner), I, 133.
2. Paul Tillich, *Biblical Religion and the Search for Ultimate Reality* (Chicago: University of Chicago Press, 1955), p. 35.
3. See Louis Ginsberg, *The Legends of the Jews* (Philadelphia: Jewish Publication Society, 1919–1925), 7 vols.
4. Paul Tillich, *Systematic Theology* (Chicago: University of Chicago Press), I (1951), 252–253. Copyright 1955 by the University of Chicago.
5. Reinhold Niebuhr, *Faith and History* (New York: Scribner, 1949), p. 36.
6. See Karl Barth, *Church Dogmatics: A Selection* (New York: Harper Torchbook, 1961), pp. 150–151.
7. R. H. Pfeiffer, *Introduction to the Old Testament* (New York: Harper, 1948), p. 188.
8. These four dispensations are (1) from creation to Noah, (2) from Noah to Abraham, (3) from Abraham to Moses, (4) Moses to Joshua. See *Ibid.*, pp. 188–189.
9. To be discussed in greater detail in Chapter 8.
10. Gerhard von Rad, *Old Testament Theology*, trans. D. Stalker (Edinburgh: Oliver and Boyd, 1962), I, 150.
11. See J. B. Pritchard, *Ancient and Near Eastern Texts Relating to the Old Testament*, 2nd ed. (Princeton, N.J.: Princeton University Press, 1956), pp. 60–72.
12. Von Rad, *Old Testament Theology*, I, 148.
13. Erich Frank, *Philosophical Understanding and Religious Truth* (London: Oxford University Press, 1956), p. 56.
14. Pesikta de-Rav Kahana 11b–12a.
15. St. Augustine, *Confessions*, trans. E. B. Pusey, XI, 14:7
16. See G. F. Moore, *Judaism* (Cambridge: Harvard University Press, 1958), I, 383 ff. for documentation.
17. Whether creation was *ex nihilo* or formed from the chaos of previously existing matter, eternal or created, did not excite great discussion in the Palestinian school of the rabbis: See Moore, *Judaism*, I, 381. See also Edmund Jacob, *Theology of the Old Testament* (New York: Harper, 1958), pp. 136 ff.

18. There are some notable exceptions. It is true that some Jewish thinkers and some of the early church fathers were tempted to think about the universe and man in Greek rather than Hebraic terms. For example, Justin Martyr, Clement of Alexandria, and Origen believed there was a plurality of worlds and that God is eternally the Creator, which means that one must think of there having always been a created world. There is a rabbinic reference to God Who keeps "creating worlds and desolating them" until He "created these worlds of heaven and earth" (Genesis Rabbah 9:2). Philo most of the time speaks of God as the artificer, the demiruge, notions which presuppose the eternal existence of matter. In Moses Nahmanides (13th century), there is an interesting variation on this theme: "the true interpretation of the *nayaseh* (let us make) is that God created *ex nihilo* only on the first day and then he used the elements which he had created on the first day." See Nahum Glatzer, *Faith and Knowledge* (Boston: Beacon, 1963), p. 51.

19. See St. Thomas Aquinas, *Summa Theologica*, I, 46, 2. (New York: Benziger Bros., 1912).

20. Philip, *De Somniis*, I, 13, 76, quoted from Erich Frank, *Philosophical Understanding and Religious Truth*, op. cit., p. 75.

21. See H. Richard Niebuhr, *Radical Monotheism and Western Culture* (New York: Harper, 1960), Chapter 2.

22. Paul Tillich, *Biblical Religion and the Search for Ultimate Reality*, p. 36.

23. John Calvin, *Institutes*, I, 16, 4, John T. McNeill, ed., *Library of Christian Classics* (Philadelphia: Westminster, 1960), 2 vols.

24. Giovanni Miegge, *Visible and Invisible* (London: Mowbray, 1958), p. 116.

25. St. Augustine, *Confessions*, XI, 276.

26. Eric Frank, *Philosophical Understanding and Religious Truth*, p. 62.

27. Leo Baeck, *The Essence of Judaism* (New York: Schocken, 1958), p. 121.

28. *Ibid.*, p. 121.

29. Reinhold Niebuhr, *Faith and History* (New York: Scribner, 1949), pp. 46–47.

30. William Temple, *Nature, Man and God* (London: Macmillan, 1953), p. 478.

31. Miegge, *Visible and Invisible*, p. 116.

32. H. Richard Niebuhr, *Radical Monotheism and Western Culture*, p. 32.

33. "For the Time Being," from *The Collected Poetry of W. H. Auden* (New York: Random House, 1935), p. 447.

34. Denis de Rougement, *Man's Western Quest* (London: Allen and Unwin, 1957), p. 120.

35. Reprinted with permission of Farrar, Strauss & Giroux, Inc. from *God in Search of Man* by Abraham Heschel, p. 412. Copyright © 1955 by Abraham Joshua Heschel.

36. St. Augustine, *Confessions*, X, 29.

37. From Moses Maimonedes, *Guide for the Perplexed*, trans. M. Friedlander. Dover Publications, Inc., New York. Reprinted through permission of the publisher. 2nd rev. ed., p. 288. See Part III, Chapters 17–21 for the full discussion.

38. John Calvin, *Institutes*, I, 16, 4. op. cit. There is a popular notion held by many historians that predestination was the central idea in Calvin's thought. To many thoughtful scholars of Calvin, however, this is clearly not true, as a study of the various editions of the *Institutes* will show. See François Wendel, *Calvin: The Origins and Developments of His Thought*; trans. by Philip Marret (N.Y.: Harper, 1963), ch. 2.

39. Tillich, *Systematic Theology*, I, 267.

40. *Ibid.*, III, 372.

41. Miegge, *Visible and Invisible*, p. 104.

42. St. Augustine, *The City of God*, trans. Gerald G. Walsh and Grace Monahan.

In the Fathers of the Church Series, vol. 14 (Washington, D.C.: Catholic University of America Press, 1952), XXI, Chapter 8.

43. *Ibid.*, X, Chapter 12.

44. For documentation see Moore, *Judaism*, I, 377 f.

45. See Maimonides' interesting argument for miracles in *Guide for the Perplexed*, Part II, Chapter 25, pp. 199 and 200. He concludes, "Accepting Creation, we find that miracles are possible, that Revelation is possible, and that every difficulty in this question is removed."

46. From *The Christian Doctrine of Creation and Redemption*, by Emil Brunner, translated by Olive Wyon. Published in the U.S.A. by The Westminster Press, 1952. Reprinted by permission of The Westminster Press, and Lutterworth Press, London.

47. For a concise selection of readings in the philosophical approach to this problem, see Nelson Pike, ed., *God and Evil* (Englewood Cliffs, N.J.: Prentice-Hall, 1964).

48. The rabbis speak frequently against this theory that life is divided between two forces, good and evil. While it may provide a simple answer to the problem of evil it does so at the expense of the singularity of God. "All things in the universe come in pairs—heaven and earth, sun and moon, Adam and Eve, this world and the world to come—Only God is one and alone in the universe" (Deuteronomy Rabbah II, para. 31).

49. Miegge, *Visible and Invisible*, p. 120.

50. Loren Eiseley, "Man: The Lethal Factor," in *American Scientist*, March, 1963.

51. Loren Eiseley, *The Firmament of Time* (New York: Atheneum, 1960), pp. 123–24.

52. St. Augustine, *Confessions*, Book II; *City of God*, Book 19.

53. H. H. Farmer, *God and Men* (London: Nisbet, 1948), pp. 38–39.

54. The formulation, "the principle of plentitude" is Professor A. O. Lovejoys' in *The Great Chain of Being* (New York: Harper Torchbook, 1960), p. 52. He uses the term, first found in simpler form in Plato, to mean "that no genuine potentiality of being can remain unfulfilled, that the extent and abundance of creation must be as great as the possibility of existence and commensurate with the productive capacity of a 'perfect' and inexhaustible source, and that the world is the better, the more things it contains."

55. Maimonides, *Guide for the Perplexed*, p. 269.

56. Reinhold Niebuhr, *Beyond Tragedy*, (New York: Scribner, 1937), p. 11.

57. Alfred North Whitehead, *Science and the Modern World* (New York: New American Library, Mentor, 1958), p. 192.

58. Reinhold Niebuhr, *Beyond Tragedy*, p. 168.

59. Dietrich Bonhoeffer, *Letters and Papers From Prison*, ed. Eberhard Bethge, trans. R. H. Fuller (London: Student Christian Movement Press, 1953), p. 164.

60. Alfred North Whitehead, *Adventures in Ideas* (New York: Macmillan, 1933), p. 32.

61. H. Richard Niebuhr, *The Responsible Self* (New York: Harper, 1963), pp. 24–25. This statement is from the excellent introduction written by James M. Gustafson.

62. S. S. Cohon, *Judaism: A Way of Life* (New York: copyrighted 1948 by the Union of American Hebrew Congregations), p. 66.

Select Bibliography

BRUNNER, EMIL. *The Christian Doctrine of Creation and Redemption*. Philadelphia: Westminster Press, 1952.

CALHOUN, ROBERT L. *God and the Common Life.* Hamden, Conn.: The Shoe String Press, 1954.

CHALMERS, R. C., and J. A. IRVING. *The Meaning of Life in Five Great Religions.* Philadelphia: Westminster Press, 1965. See Emil Fackenheim, "Judaism," Chapter IV.

The Confessions of St. Augustine. Trans. E. B. Pusey. London: J. M. Dent & Sons and New York, Dutton, 1949.

EISLEY, LOREN. *The Firmament of Time.* New York: Atheneum, 1960.

FARMER, H. H. *The World and God.* London: Nisbet, 1942.

FRANK, ERICH, *Philosophical Understanding and Religious Truth.* New York: Oxford University Press, 1945. Chapter 3.

GILKEY, LANGDON. *Maker of Heaven and Earth.* New York: Doubleday, 1959.

MILLGRAM, A. E., ed. *Great Jewish Ideas.* Washington, D.C.: B'nai B'rith, 1964.

MUCKENHIRN, SISTER M. CHARLES BORROMEO, C.S.C. *The Image of God in Creation.* Englewood Cliffs, N.J.: Prentice-Hall, 1963.

SAYERS, DOROTHY. *The Mind of the Maker.* New York: Meridian Living Age Books, 1956.

VIII

The Nature and Redemption of Man

THE nature of man may be approached from many different perspectives. The physical sciences regard man as merely another part of the whole complex or mechanism of inanimate nature. Biology is concerned with man's place and development in the world of living matter. The social sciences look to the economic, political, and social behavior of man. The religious conception of man, however, is vastly different, for it is grounded neither in the observations and the methods peculiar to the sciences, nor on the speculations and analyses of the philosopher, but on what it is believed God has revealed to man of his nature. The teachings of Christianity and Judaism on the nature of man in part derive from the descriptions of the creation and fall of man given in the first three chapters of the Book of Genesis. However, the interpretation of Genesis in both Judaism and Christianity is by no means uniform. Jewish thinkers offer radically different interpretation of the Genesis narrative on original sin than that usually agreed upon by Christian theologians. And among the latter there are differences with respect to man's original state and the extent and the effects of the fall of man. Furthermore, Roman Catholic thought has generally found expression within the great traditions of Augustinianism and Thomism.

The philosophers representing these traditions have used philosophy as a vehicle for the explication of what they consider to be revealed truths. Usually this means that within Augustinianism, Platonic or neo-Platonic ideas have left their mark upon Christian concepts. In Thomism, Aristotelian ideas have found their way into the explication of theological truths.

To a fairly considerable extent Thomistic teachings on the nature of man have more or less supplanted the Augustinian teachings with Roman Catholic circles. But there is always the possibility that the Thomistic explication may give way to a new set of philosophical concepts either in our own day or in the future. This sort of divergence within Roman Catholic teaching and interpretation of the nature of man finds similar parallels within Protestantism. In early Protestantism, Lutherans and Calvinists looked back to Augustine and the church fathers as the source of their inspiration and for their theological guidance. Later Protestantism came to be influenced more by such philosophers as Kant and Hegel. Today both Catholic and Protestant theologians have felt the impact of the existentialist philosophies in their interpretation of the nature of man.

In the analysis that follows we shall give our attention largely to the theological considerations on the nature of man. Philosophical concepts and traditions will be used primarily to develop the conception of man as a composite creature, to discern more precisely what is meant by such terms as soul and its relation to the body, and to bring out the meaning and significance of man's freedom. The theological analysis will be concerned principally with the created nature of man, the interpretation of original sin, and an account of the fall of man and its consequences. The whole of the analysis that is to follow may be regarded as an extended commentary and explication of the biblical narratives on the creation and the fall of man. To follow more readily this explication we shall preface our study of these narratives in each instance with the pertinent chapters and verses from Genesis. Thus on the creation and nature of man we shall look to the relevant verses in Genesis 1 and 2. For the fall of man our commentary will be based on the relevant verses in Genesis 3.[1]

THE CREATION OF MAN

[26]Then God said, "Let us make man in our image, after our likeness; and let him have dominion over the fish of the sea, and over the birds of the air, and over the cattle, and over all the earth, and over every creeping thing that creeps upon the earth."

[27]So God created man in his own image, in the image of God he created him; male and female he created them. [28]And God blessed them, and God said to them, "Be fruitful and multiply, and fill the earth and subdue it; and have dominion over the fish of the sea and over the birds of the air and over every living thing that moves upon the earth." [29]And God said, "Behold, I have given you every plant yielding seed, which is upon the face of all the earth, and every tree with seed in its fruit; you shall have them for food. [30]And to every beast of the earth, and to every bird of the air, and to everything that creeps on

the earth, everything that has the breath of life, I have given every green plant for food." And it was so. ³¹And God saw everything that he had made, and behold, it was very good. And there was evening and there was morning, a sixth day—(Genesis 1:26–31).

⁷Then the Lord God formed man of dust from the ground, and breathed into his nostrils the breath of life; and man became a living being. ⁸And the Lord God planted a garden in Eden, in the east; and there he put the man whom he had formed. ⁹And out of the ground the Lord God made to grow every tree that is pleasant to the sight and good for food, the tree of life also in the midst of the garden, and the tree of the knowledge of good and evil.

¹⁵The Lord God took the man and put him in the garden of Eden to till it and keep it. ¹⁶And the Lord God commanded the man, saying, "You may freely eat of every tree of the garden; ¹⁷but of the tree of the knowledge of good and evil you shall not eat, for in the day that you eat of it you shall die." . . . ²¹So the Lord God caused a deep sleep to fall upon the man, and while he slept took one of his ribs and closed up its place with flesh; ²²and the rib which the Lord God had taken from the man he made into a woman and brought her to the man. ²³Then the man said, "This at last is bone of my bones and flesh of my flesh; she shall be called Woman, because she was taken out of Man." ²⁴Therefore a man leaves his father and his mother and cleaves to his wife, and they become one flesh. ²⁵And the man and his wife were both naked, and were not ashamed (Genesis 2:7–9; 15–25).

COMMENTARY ON GENESIS 1.   The verses cited from Genesis 1 give a much more sophisticated account of the nature of man than do the verses in Genesis 2. In Genesis 1 there is a greater emphasis on the dignity of man and his closeness to God. Genesis 1 presents man as the *imago Dei*, as created in the image of God. The narrative in Genesis 1 has usually been termed the "priestly" narrative; apparently it was composed several centuries after the narrative presented in Genesis 2. The latter account is generally designated as the "patriarchal" or "Yahwist" narrative, as described in Chapter 7.

The idea of man as being created in the image of God has an added significance when we recall that in the Hebrew tradition of this time the conception of God as One, as a Moral Person, as Omnipotent and Omniscient, had been well established. Such a conception of God[2] has important implications for the nature of man. For as an image of a God Who is omnipotent and omniscient, Who possesses a moral perfection and a spiritual nature, man could be said to share in similar qualities. Thus man possesses a spiritual nature; he is essentially a moral being; he has the potentialities of wisdom and power (he has been granted dominion over nature by his creator, Genesis 1:26). In a word, man participates in the divine attributes because he has been created in the image of God. In this narrative there is no omission of the physical nature of man. It is mentioned briefly in verses 27–28: "male and female He created them. And God blessed them, and God said to them, "Be fruitful and multiply, and fill the earth and subdue it; . . ." Man is a composite being, he is both body and soul, but the soul as life or spirit[3] is that higher nature which conforms to the notion of man as an image of God.

COMMENTARY ON GENESIS 2.   An interesting observation about this version of the creation of man is that it virtually reverses the order and the emphasis on the creation of man that we have just noted in Genesis 1. In Genesis 2 God is pictured as creating man from the dust (some versions give "clay") of the earth. Significantly in this account the beginning of the creation of man is with the body. God may be pictured as a potter fashioning man from the clay or soil of the earth, a notion not uncommon to many primitive religions and mythologies. The term "clay" or "soil" has an added significance in this account, for in Hebrew *adama* means earth. Out of it "man" (*adam*) is formed.[4]

Once the body of man has been created in this fashion the patriarchal narrative then proceeds with a somewhat physicalistic and mythical description of how God created the soul of man. God breathes into man the "breath of life." This breath or *Ruach* designates the soul. In early Judaism the soul is frequently designated as *Nephesh*, *Ruach*, and *Neshamah*. Each of these terms is identified with the notion of a vital or living element without which man cannot survive. This notion of the soul or spirit[5] of man as the breath of life still connotes something physical. The distinction of the physical and the spiritual appears more sharply at a later time, and it may be said to be representative of a higher stage of intellectual sophistication. Even in the writings of many of the early church fathers there is much evidence of their inability to think and write in other than materialistic terms; this is particularly true of some of the descriptions of the Millennium given by Irenaeus and Tertullian. It should also be noted that the authors of Genesis are concerned to represent certain basic truths to a people who at this stage of development can best understand religious truths in the form of poetic imagery and myths, in concrete rather than abstract terms. This is especially evident in the account in Genesis 2 of the creation of both Adam and Eve. Hence it would be a mistake to expect in the Genesis narratives the kind of sophistication we find in the great philosophers and theologians.[6]

INTERPRETATIONS OF THE GENESIS NARRATIVES.   In the interpretations of both narratives, some theologians stress their mythical or legendary character; they look to the meaning of the myths rather than to the notion of revealed truths. Other theologians may stress a more literal and fundamentalist interpretation, and others again reject any historical interpretation of Genesis in favor of the existential. On the whole, theologians accept the mythical character of certain parts of the Genesis narratives but stress the truths that the myths reveal. For example, they would accept the account of Eve being tempted by the serpent as a myth but would consider that such a myth contains a profound truth concerning man. With respect to the stories of creation occurring in six days and of man being created from the "dust" or "clay," theologians would reject any purely literal interpretation of this account of creation. Also, they would probably agree that the biblical myths or narratives in Genesis 1 and 2 wish to assert at least three things about the character of man: (1) man's self-transcendence as expressed in the "image of God"; (2) man's creatureliness or weakness, symbolized by his origin from "dust" or "clay"; and (3) that evil in man is the consequence of his unwillingness to acknowledge this dependence.

Roman Catholic theologians are generally committed to an acceptance of the historical element in the account of Adam's creation: Adam is accepted as an historical individual. Most Protestant and Jewish theologians would hold that the myth of the creation of man symbolized man's solidarity with other men as signified in the name Adam taken in the collective sense and meaning both man and mankind. A similar point would be made with respect to the fall of Adam. In biblical and theological terms such stories, they would say, represent the dramatization of the human situation. They are stories in which each man can find himself portrayed; if the portrayal is faithful, it is just as important to the fact as any art or science. This is the importance of the biblical myth. For many thinkers, then, the *imago Dei* is a mythological way of conveying the fact that every man stands related to his Creator, and through this bond with every other individual. Hence creation lays upon each individual a three-fold demand; he is made for God, for other people, and for himself; the living out of these relationships becomes his daily burden as well as his opportunity.

Within Judaism similar differences of interpretation of the Genesis narratives may be found. Generally, however, all divisions of Judaism recognize in these narratives not only a testimony of the divine omnipotence, omniscience, and infinitude, but the affirmation of the God idea as a fundamental religious truth for all mankind. The interpretation of the narratives with respect to the nature and the fall of man will be brought out more fully when we consider the Jewish rejection of the doctrine of original sin.

Finally, what is fundamentally true and meaningful in these narratives is that man was created by God and that he has both a physical and a spiritual nature. Just how the physical and spiritual nature of man is to be explained is the task of the theologian; to this problem we now turn.

The Physical Nature of Man: The Body

A fairly common error committed by some writers is to assume that in the Jewish and Christian view of the nature of man, the body is essentially evil and the source of man's sinfulness. The source of such a misconception lies in the extremes of asceticism practiced by some of the early Christians and in the influence of Orphism and Platonism. There is no denying the fact that some early Christian ascetics regarded the body as something evil, as a hindrance to the perfection of their spirituality. The Orphics held a doctrine that the soul had fallen from an original divine state. In the *Phaedo* of Plato we are told that the body is the "prison-house" of the soul. For Platonists the soul, considered far superior to the body, was generally viewed as prevented from attaining the highest wisdom and its true destiny by an enforced existence in the body. Such derogatory conceptions of the body—and they are common to many pagan religions—is quite the opposite of the teachings of Judaism and Christianity. The best affirmation of the true view of Judaism and Christianity is to be found in the last verse of Chapter 1 of Genesis, in which we are told that "And God saw all that He had made, and found it very good." This verse is frequently cited as the source for much of Jewish and Christian optimism. It is upon this basis that Augustine rejected the Platonic account of the nature of the body as evil. It should be noted that the Christian account also differs most significantly from the Platonic in that the whole person, both body and soul, is resurrected. Christian teaching has generally opposed any radically dualistic doctrine of the nature of man. It insists that man is a person, a composite creature, but essentially one. Needless to say, any wholly materialistic view of the nature of man is rejected by Christianity. In Judaism there has generally been less tension in the relation of the soul and the body. Judaism accepts both the spiritual and the material and has probably been more successful in avoiding the extremes of asceticism that have sometimes characterized Christianity.

What, then, is the peculiar function of the body from the religious point of view? In what respects has the Creator endowed the body as good?

First, the fact that the body was created by God, whether directly or indirectly in some evolutionary process, ennobles the body. This inherent nobility of the body is enhanced by the fact that it is the "place"[7] of the soul and shares in the existence of the soul. In the reciprocal relation between soul and body, the body is not only made truly a body by the presence of the soul—for without the soul it could not function as a true body—but the body in turn contributes to the activity and the perfection of the soul. By the soul we mean not only that which gives mere life (*anima*) to the body, but that which gives intellectual or rational life. In its higher activity, soul may be identified with mind.

It is through the body that we first become aware of ourselves, of others, and the world about us. The need to satisfy physical wants and desires leads to the love of self and to the love of others. This kind of love has often been identified with the Greek notion of *Eros*. Based upon the passions and the carnal desires of the individual, it may be regarded as an obstacle to the attainment of truth and wisdom and the higher spiritual values. Consequently, for some Greek philosophers the body was regarded as an evil. For Judaism and Christianity the body has always been considered as good because it was created by God.

The body may also be said to be the source of knowledge, for it is through the information provided by the senses that the soul is able to form ideas, make judgments, and attain knowledge. The senses form the basis for our communication with one another. By the use of signs and sounds and gestures and with the development of language we come to know one another. Through such knowledge and the extension of the love of that which is best in ourselves we achieve friendship. This may be regarded as a kind of spiritual love in which the welfare of another becomes our own welfare, for, as Aristotle observed, a friend is another self.

Among Christian writers a distinction is sometimes drawn between *Eros*, representing physical love, and *Agape* as a spiritual or Christian love. Some hold that such a distinction makes it impossible to effect any reconciliation between self-love and the love of God. *Agape*, it is said, does not admit self-love. Others, however, maintain that with the grace of God man can again achieve the love of that which is best within him and become once more a true image of God. In loving himself he can also love God. Man's love is said to be ecstatic, for he is taken outside his false self, his unlikeness to God, and restored to the proper image of God which sin had destroyed. Hence no real opposition exists then between the love of self and the love of God. As William of St. Thierry puts it:

When Thou lovest us, Thou lovest us only for Thyself, wherefore the perfect law of justice forbids us too to love anything beyond Thyself. And certainly, if but great grace be granted he who loves God may go so far that he loves neither Thee nor himself for himself, but both Thee and himself for naught but Thee. And so he is reformed in Thine image, to which indeed Thou didst create him, Thou, who in the truth of Thy sovereign nature, and in the nature of Thy truth, canst love nothing, neither man, nor angel, nor Thyself, but for Thyself.[8]

The importance of the physical nature of man, of the body, is also verified in certain verses of both the Old and the New Testaments.

Genesis informs us that man has been given dominion over creation: "And God said, Behold I have given you every plant yielding seed which is upon the face of all the earth, and every tree with seed in its fruit; you shall have them for food" (Genesis 1:29). And Eden is an earthly paradise and the pleasures of it are given to man. "And the Lord God had planted a Garden of Eden [delight], in the east; and there he put the man whom he had formed" (Genesis 2:8). Finally, in the New Testament we have the revealed truth of the Incarnation: "And the Word became flesh and dwelt among us" (John 1:14). Part of the tremendous significance of this mystery is that God chose to be born of a human body and that He took on a human body. No higher tribute could be paid to the essential nobility and goodness of the human body than this.

The Spiritual Nature of Man: The Soul

The basic distinction between body and soul is that of matter and spirit. Or, man is both an individual and a person. His individuality may be said to have its source in his physical nature, his personality in his spiritual nature—the soul. To say that man is both an individual and a person does not mean that he is two separate beings, but rather that his individuality and his personality are two aspects of one being. Man, then, is a composite being. By reason of his body, his material nature, man as an individual is rooted in the world about him. By reason of his spirit, his soul, man shares in the divine life and is dignified by such participation. As an image of God he is, like God, a person.

The source for some of these distinctions we have just drawn is in the Aristotelian philosophy of Aquinas. Very briefly, such a philosophy holds that man as a composite creature is made up of matter and form. Matter is represented by the body, and it is matter that individuates man. Form is represented by the soul, and it is the soul—more specifically the rational soul—that endows man with his essential nature. In the union of the soul and the body, the soul does not depend upon the body for its existence, and it survives the death of the body. Soul and body are incomplete substances, but united they form one substance. This conception of the relation of soul and body is based upon the Aristotelian principle of *hylomorphism*—that all nature is composed of matter and form.

For the most part Roman Catholic theologians follow this Thomistic explication of the scriptural truths concerning the nature of man. To some extent Protestant thought may find a certain sympathy with this kind of philosophical explication, but for the most part Protestant theologians, and also Jewish thinkers, are not overly concerned with a technical or philosophical explication of the problems of the soul and the body and their interrelationship. In place of the Aristotelian terminology of matter and form, they are more apt to speak of the psychosomatic unity of man. But whatever the semantic differences in explanation may be, the more important point is that all would agree upon the essential unity of man.

Within this context it is important to recognize that sin is not merely an act of the body or the failure of spirit or soul to control the impulses and desires of the body. Sin may also be considered as an affliction of the spiritual nature of man, an act of the soul itself by which man rebels against God. If we accept the distinction of sins, those of the spirit are far more serious than those related to the body and its appetites. Gluttony is a sin, and so is intemperance, but they are of much less serious import than the sins of pride and blasphemy.

Despite the essential unity of man, there is a basic contradiction or polarity in man's nature. Man is of this earth as evidenced by his bodily nature, but his spirituality, his rational nature, is the link he has with divinity. As such man is only too apt to be torn by the contradictory impulses of his nature. We are reminded here of the statement of the Apostle Paul:

For I know that nothing good dwells within in me, that is, in my flesh. I can will what is right, but I cannot do it. For I do not do the good I want, but the evil I do not want is what I do. Now if I do what I do not want, it is no longer I that do it, but sin which dwells within me.

So I find it to be a law that when I want to do right, evil lies close at hand. For I delight in the law of God, in my inmost self, but I see in my members another law at war with the law of my mind and making me captive to the law of sin which dwells in my members. Wretched man that I am! Who will deliver me from this body of death? Thanks be to God through Jesus Christ our Lord! So then, I of myself serve the law of God with my mind, but with my flesh I serve the law of sin (Romans 7:18–25).

Through his spiritual nature man endeavors to transcend his earthly nature, his lower self; he strives to imitate the divine image within him. Yet he does not know how, for he cannot comprehend that which is wholly above him. Reinhold Niebuhr contends that the spiritual nature of man points to a dimension of reality that man can neither comprehend nor express. He points out that the spiritual nature of man is most evident in man's disinclination to accept any anthropomorphic conception of deity and his willingness to place his faith and trust in a God that transcends human nature. Thus man is created in the image of God, but in no sense does God reflect the nature of man. That man was created in the image of God means not only that in some sense man participates in the divine nature, but also that man may achieve something of the divine; that through his faith, his reverence, and his devotion to God man realizes his spiritual nature. And by fulfilling his own spiritual nature in a harmonious relation with God he can extend that relationship to others. Spirit in man is not merely the essence of his being but his aspirations, his potentialities, and his ultimate goal. As Brunner states it: "Man is a 'theological' being; that is, his ground, his goal, his norm and the possibility of understanding his own nature are all in God."[9]

The views that we have just outlined are not contradictory, but are merely different ways of emphasizing certain basic truths concerning the nature of man that Catholics, Protestants, and Jews would accept. That is, they all accept the transcendent importance of the spiritual in man and the implications of this for man's freedom. They accept the place and the function of the body and its importance in the makeup of the individual. And however they would conceive the composite nature of man or explain the unity of the physical and the spiritual—the relation of body and soul— they would agree that man is essentially a person, created by God in His image. The most significant aspect of man's spiritual nature they would maintain is man's freedom, for it is this more than anything else that constitutes man as a moral person.

The Freedom of Man

Undoubtedly the most significant attribute of man is his possession of freedom or a free will. Without the freedom to choose between good and evil, man can hardly be said to be a moral person. Yet some have main- tained that man has no freedom, that he is utterly and completely deter- mined in all that he does—that if we knew all that there is to be known about an individual and his environment we could predict with scientific exactitude precisely what his every course of action would be. This position is usually designated as *determinism*. In opposition to it is the theory which holds that man is free, although not unqualifiedly so. This position is generally known as *indeterminism*; it affirms the freedom of the will. Determinism is usually based upon a naturalistic conception of man; it regards man as but another aspect of a world that is both materialistic and mechanistic. Indeterminism stresses the spiritual aspect of man's nature. Generally it holds that there is more than mere nature, that there is a supernatural order as well as a natural order. Obviously, this position lends itself to ready acceptance by most religious believers. The indeterminist will also argue that it is because of his spiritual nature that man is free. It is claimed that it is the very essence of the spiritual to be free, whereas to be wholly material means to be essentially determined and limited in activity. The things of nature and all creatures below man have no ability to exercise any freedom of choice. Like machines or robots they follow not their own purposes but the purposes or aims of that which made them.

In a very penetrating statement Gregory of Nyssa says, "our spiritual birth is the result of a free choice, and we are in some sort our own parents, making ourselves what we wish to be." Man, then, is the only creature that can make such a choice; man in a very real sense determines himself to be. It is this act of freedom that reveals our spiritual nature, for spirit is never confined, limited, or determined.

In philosophical circles the debate between determinists and indeterminists is perennial. We have no intention of attempting to resolve the issue, and we do not believe that either position can yield a demonstrative proof. It would seem, however, that there is sufficient evidence to warrant a reasonable belief in indeterminism, and we will set forth very briefly some of the evidence for such a belief. Fundamentally, indeterminism appeals to the experience of the individual. The current development of existentialism reflects this conviction that freedom is experiential, for much of existentialism was a reaction against both scientific and historical determinism. Based on introspective considerations, the appeal to experience means simply that all of us at some time or another, frequently or infrequently, are aware of our freedom; we feel that we are free. And we express this conviction in our language. We believe that we have been *responsible* or *accountable* for our successes or failures. We feel *remorse* or *regret* over past actions, and this would seem to imply that we believe we *might* and *ought* to have acted otherwise than we did.

Even the analysis of the word "ought" would appear to imply that the power of deliberate choice belongs to the rational person. For to what other purpose would we say to an individual, "you *ought* to do this" or "you *ought not* to do that," unless we believe that he could or could not do the one or the other? "Ought" implies "can," as Kant long ago pointed out, and the very real difference that exists between religion and ethics on the one hand, and science on the other, lies in the fact that the one *prescribes* what individuals ought to do whereas the other *describes* how they behave.

It should be noted that the appeal to experience in defense of indeterminism also serves to lend some support to the determinist position. For undoubtedly we do feel at times that we were under compulsion to act as we did, that our actions in fact were determined by circumstances beyond our control. This in no way contradicts or disproves indeterminism, for the indeterminist would be the first to admit that man is not always free, that man's freedom is not absolute. The indeterminist merely denies absolute determinism while insisting upon the necessity of freedom to give real meaning to the religious and moral conduct of the individual.

The relation of this issue of indeterminism to the religious point of view is of vital concern. For almost all great religions, even including such non-theistic religions as Buddhism, have been concerned with the problem and have affirmed the indeterminist position. Some branches of Islam, however, have stressed a fatalistic attitude. And within Christianity the position of the reformers was in varying degrees deterministic. Thus Calvin moved from faith to a doctrine of double predestination. He held that from all eternity God has elected some men for salvation and willed others to damnation:

Predestination we call the eternal decree of God, by which he has determined in himself, what he would have to become of every individual of mankind. For they are not all created with a similar destiny; but eternal life is foreordained for some, and eternal damnation for others. Every man, therefore, being created for one or the other of these ends, is, we say, predestined either to life or to death.[10]

Luther's position on man's freedom is less extreme. Although he denies the freedom of the will he seems to limit the denial to our ability to will for faith. On the other hand, the concept of the depravity of the human will does seem to lend weight to a nullification of human freedom. One of Luther's characteristic statements on the problem of freedom is the following one from his work *The Bondage of the Will:*

I could wish, indeed, that we were furnished with some better term for this discussion, than this commonly used term, *necessity*, which cannot rightly be used, either with reference to the human will or the divine. It is of a significa-tion too harsh and ill-suited for this subject, forcing upon the mind an idea of compulsion, and that which is altogether contrary to *will*; whereas, the subject which we are discussing, does not require such an idea: for Will, whether divine or human, does what it does, be it good or evil, not by any compulsion, but by mere willingness or desire, as it were, totally free. The will of God, nevertheless, which rules over our mutable will, is immutable and infallible. . . . And our own will, especially our corrupt will, cannot of itself do good; therefore, where the term fails to express the idea required, the understanding of the reader must make up the deficiency, knowing what is wished to be expressed—the immu-table will of God, and the impotency of our depraved will; or, as some have expressed it, the *necessity of immutability*, though neither is that sufficiently grammatical, or sufficiently theological.[11]

Religious indeterminism emphasizes the freedom of man. This is the position held by most Christians, who believe that man can accept or reject the grace offered to him by God for his redemption and salvation. Judaism emphasizes the freedom of man. It believes in man's self-motivated "return" to God, Who in turn chooses to receive the penitent. Some typical expressions affirming this conviction in man's freedom are the following:

I call heaven and earth to witness against you this day, that I have set before you life and death, blessing and cursing; therefore choose life, that you and your descendants may live, loving the Lord your God, obeying his voice, and cleaving to him; . . . (Deuteronomy 30:19–20).

Everything is foreseen [by God], yet freedom of choice is given (Aboth III, 19).

God, then in the beginning had given man a good will: He had made him in it, without which he could not continue in it, if he will; but the will itself to continue was left to man's free choice (Augustine).

SIN AND THE FALL OF ADAM

The belief that man is free leads to the more difficult and serious problem of explaining moral evil, or sin. Few would question the existence of evil, moral or physical, but the reconciliation of the fact of evil with the goodness and omnipotence of God presents many difficulties. In the analysis that follows we shall consider only the problem of moral evil.

Philosophers have offered different solutions to this problem. In Greek philosophy we find that sin is often equated with error. The implication drawn from this is that if man possessed the necessary knowledge he would naturally be virtuous, that with knowledge he could avoid all evil and always do what is right. But the religious experience, and indeed the moral experience of most of us, would challenge such an explanation. For we often feel that even though we may know what is evil, we cannot help but choose the evil. And if we are deeply religious, we become aware of our need for some kind of divine assistance to avoid the temptation to evil.

Other philosophers would argue that man is constantly making physical, moral, and scientific progress. Many of the philosophers of the Enlightenment and of the nineteenth century contended that the cultivation of reason and the development of science would alone be sufficient to bring about man's moral regeneration and perfection. Premising their prophecies upon the ultimate perfectibility of man, they envisioned economic and social utopias, brave new worlds. They based their hopes on the attainment of such goals upon man rather than upon God. In the light of the world's present ills, it would seem that such views reveal a rather exaggerated optimism. To place so much confidence in man brings to mind the warning of Jeremiah: "Cursed is the man who trusts in man" (Jeremiah 17:5).

The religious position is not one that can be demonstrated. It is a position that may be accepted on faith. It may be argued, however, that it presents a rather realistic view. It accepts man as free and as created in the image of God. But it also recognizes that since man is only a finite creature and lacking the perfection of God, man is subject to sin. The freedom of man inevitably leads to a choice between good and evil. To prevent man from choosing evil, God would have had to create man as a mere robot without the freedom of choosing the good, but then man would no longer be man. To the objection that man would be better off if he were not free, Augustine replied that free will is a perfection in man and that God should be praised for having given it. "We must not blame God," he says, "for having given man eyes, if man often uses these to serve some base passions."

The problem of moral evil as it concerns the three great western faiths, hinges on the interpretation of the Genesis narratives and the analysis of sin as it appears in these narratives.

GENESIS 3

[1]Now the serpent was more subtle than any other wild creature that the Lord God had made. He said to the woman, "Did God say, 'You shall not eat of any tree of the garden'?" [2]And the woman said to the serpent, "We may eat of the fruit of the trees of the garden; [3]but God said, 'You shall not eat of the fruit of the tree which is in the midst of the garden, neither shall you touch it, lest you die.' " [4]But the serpent said to the woman, "You will not die. [5]For God knows that when you eat of it your eyes will be opened, and you will be like God, knowing good and evil." [6]So when the woman saw that the tree was good for food, and that it was a delight to the eyes, and that the tree was to be desired to make one wise, she took of its fruit and ate; and she also gave some to her husband, and he ate. [7]Then the eyes of both were opened, and they knew that they were naked; and they sewed fig leaves together and made themselves aprons.

[Following God's judgment of the serpent, Eve, and Adam, the narrative resumes.]

[20]The man called his wife's name Eve, because she was the mother of all living. [21]And the Lord God made for Adam and for his wife garments of skins, and clothed them.

[22]Then the Lord God said, "Behold, the man has become like one of us, knowing good and evil; and now, lest he put forth his hand and take also of the tree of life, and eat, and live for ever"— [23]therefore the Lord God sent him forth from the garden of Eden, to till the ground from which he was taken.

The Jewish Version of Sin

The Jewish view differs sharply from the Christian in that it does not recognize the notion of original sin or the doctrine that man has inherited sin. It does not interpret the Genesis narratives of man's temptation and sin as constituting a fall. Perhaps partly in reaction to the Christian doctrine, Judaism accepts a much more radically optimistic view of the nature of man. As the Talmud puts it: "at a man's birth, God decides if he will be weak or strong, wise or foolish, rich or poor, but not if he will be good or bad." The denial of original sin does not mean, however, that there were no consequences to the sin in the Garden of Eden. It was the cause of the death for Adam and all mankind. Similarly, the sin of worshiping the Golden Calf affected future generations. "There is no generation in which there is not an ounce from the sin of the Golden Calf" (p. Taanit 68c).

Judaism recognizes that the action of Adam and Eve was essentially an act of disobedience to God. It looks upon sin as rebellion, and it interprets the Genesis narratives as embodying profound truths which are not necessarily historical. The basic truths revealed in the Genesis story of creation pertain to man as the highest form of creation, man's responsibility to his fellow men, man's power to choose between good and evil. There have been many religious thinkers and philosophers in the history of Judaism who have concerned themselves with the question of the problem of evil in the universe, but as a whole Judaism is more concerned with the ways in which evil may be eradicated; it believes that the good for man "is to perform the *mitzvoth,* the commandments of the Torah."[12] In contemporary Jewish thought, few have expressed the Jewish doctrine of sin and man's moral relation with God better than Leo Baeck:

The more man learns about himself, the more clearly he is conscious that he comes short of what he is meant to be as the image of God, a man pure and free. And this consciousness becomes clearer still, because it proclaims not only the human limitations which cause him to come short of what is demanded, but also the fact of his guilt. For he can also resist the commandment ["Thou shalt love the Lord thy God with all thy heart, and with all thy soul, and with all thy might." (Deuteronomy 6:5)] and refuse to walk in the way of God. He can deny the holy: he can choose what displeases God: sin can enter into his life. And each sin he commits is his sin. This is another feature that is peculiar to Hebrew religion. Disdaining all the mythological explanations of sin, and rejecting all theories that attribute sin to Fate, it emphasizes the personal part played by man in his sin and the personal fate which he brings upon himself by sinning. Keenly and clearly felt as are the links that connect the days and the generations of men, the influences of environment and heredity, the weaknesses, temptations, and difficulties of life, little is said about sin in the abstract, about original sin or inherited sin. The emphasis is on personal sin: "Thou hast sinned: it is thy sin." It is not Fate, but the individual man that is here involved. The word "sin" is the word of judgment concerning the personal act. The responsibility lies with man.

This raises the most important question presented by the religion of Israel, Is not the soul, created pure by God, rendered impure by sin? And does not man, created free, forfeit by reason of his sin the liberty that was his? Does he not, indeed, cease to be a child of God? This question is answered by the characteristically Hebrew conception of conversion or return—the Biblical word for it is often wrongly translated by "penance"—and of the reconciliation which is brought about by the return. This means that man is never a lost soul; it is always open to him to begin afresh and to get back to the path of life. In the words of the prophet, he can "make for himself a new heart and a new spirit" (Ezek. xviii, 31)—"new" is another characteristic Bible word—and thus recover his purity and his liberty. Or, as the Talmud says, "Seeing that he makes his behavior new, God makes him a new creature"; he is born again; his life is given to him anew. This Bible teaching contradicts all theories of fatalism.

The religion of Israel thus proclaims how the merciful, pardoning God, the God of righteousness and of love, receives back man thus reconciled. But this reconciliation is not conceived as being exclusively the work of grace. It means here more than a miracle of deliverance wrought for one of the elect. It lays the emphasis on the decision made by man and on the path that he now treads. It was his sin; it is his return. He may and ought to have faith in the forgiving God, but this faith alone cannot guarantee his reconciliation. The sole guarantee of that is his own actual return. The deliverance in question is not a deliverance from the world and from life in it: it is a reconciliation of man's will with God; an at-one-ment, a coming to be at one, a condition in which man "makes God's will his own."[13]

Another excellent version of the Jewish doctrine is that given by Eliezer Berkovits.[14] He notes that the answer to the question of sin in the Jewish tradition is the *yetzer ha-ra'*, the evil inclination. Man's heart is "evil from his youth" (Genesis 8:21) and the rabbis maintain that the youth of a man begins with the separation from his mother's womb. A man can refrain from evil, therefore, only if God has compassion on him: "For he knoweth a *yetzer*; he remembereth that we are dust," (Psalms 103:14). Yet this evil inclination enables man to marry, build houses, beget children, apply his trade or profession. That is, it is a necessary ingredient in life *per se* related to the desire to survive, however difficult of fulfillment. It is an affirmation of existence, also a potential source of evil as well as of pride and rebellion. Control of this *yetzer ha-ra'* is a condition man never reaches, and it is the plight of all men, high or low. In fact, the greater the man the more powerful will be the *yetzer ha-ra'*, and the closer he will stand to spiritual disaster. The good inclination is the *yetzer tov*, but the *yetzer ha-ra'* seems to be more powerful. Yet despite the strength of the evil inclination and the fact that it is an inherent part of man's nature, no man is ever bound to sin. He may be frequently tempted, but if he falls he is solely responsible. As God said to Cain: "Surely if you do well, will you not be accepted? And if you do not do well, sin is crouching at the door; its desire is for you, but you must master it" (Genesis 4:7).

The Christian View of Sin: Felix Culpa

Among Christian thinkers there is a considerable area of agreement on this problem as well as certain marked differences. Both Roman Catholic and Protestant theologians accept both the fact of moral evil and the Genesis narrative as a way of accounting for man's present moral state. Traditionally they both accept the conception of original sin and the doctrine of the fall. Some moderns find this notion of original sin offensive and unjust. But as Niebuhr points out, even the Jewish doctrine of the "evil inclination" (*yetzer ha-ra'*) which is a part of the heritage of man is similar in some ways to the Christian dogma, yet the two traditions differ radically in their interpretations of the ways in which man achieves salvation and release from evil. The Jewish tradition simply denies original or inherited sin and affirms that man can conquer evil and achieve the good solely through his own free actions. The Christian tradition accepts original sin and maintains that such a concept explains man's potentiality toward evil, and that man's inclination toward evil is empirically verifiable. For Christianity, however, the release of man from such evil inclinations cannot be effected by man alone. Rather man must have the grace of God to do the good and to achieve salvation.

Other aspects of the doctrine of original sin bring out certain differences between the Catholic position and the Protestant, although it is extremely difficult to generalize about *the* Protestant or *the* Catholic position. Protestantism has probably been more influenced until recently by the "higher criticism"; it also tends to emphasize more the mythological element in Genesis than does Catholicism. Catholic theologians certainly insist upon the importance of the literal meaning of Scripture, and so do many Protestant theologians, but not to the exclusion of other senses that Scripture may reveal.[15]

Monogenism and Polygenism

A more marked difference between Roman Catholicism and Protestantism occurs on the question of whether all human beings have descended from a pair of ancestors (monogenism) or from many different ancestors (polygenism). In biblical terminology the distinction is between the interpretations of the term "Adam" as referring to a given individual or to mankind as a collective whole. Are Adam and Eve just one pair from whom all have descended, or are the terms "Adam and Eve" descriptive of a multiplicity of pairs from whom all mankind take their descent? Scientific evidence favors the hypothesis of polygenism by the evolutionary development of man. Protestant theologians, except for a very few fundamentalists, find no difficulty with the theory of evolution in relation to the doctrine of creation. Nor do Catholic theologians, except on the issue of monogenism vs. polygenism. Both theologians find the evolutionary explanation of man's physical nature quite acceptable so long as the creation of his spiritual nature in the image of God is maintained. Precisely how and when the creation of the spiritual nature or soul is effected in conjunction with the evolution of the physical nature is a problem that has divided theologians.

On the issue of polygenesis, many Jewish and Protestant theologians generally accept this theory and the meaning of "Adam" as referring to a collective mankind. Catholic theologians, and some Protestant theologians, maintain that none of the commentators on Scripture accept polygenesis and that a correct exegesis yields only the conception of Adam as an individual man. As an instance of this disagreement, Protestants sometimes interpret St. Paul's account of Adam as identical with what St. Paul calls "the old man," that is, as representative of man collectively before the saving grace of Christ effected the "new man." Roman Catholics reject this interpretation; they point out that on very specific occasions St. Paul refers to Adam as the forefather of mankind. Thus in Romans 5:12 he states, "Therefore as sin came into the world through one man . . ." This idea is reiterated in other verses in the same chapter.

The encyclical *Humani generis* of Pope Pius XII, published in 1950, states:

There are other conjectures about polygenism (as it is called) which leave the faith no such freedom of choice. Christians cannot lend their support to a theory which involves the existence, after Adam's time, of some earthly race of men, truly so called, who were not descended ultimately from him, or else supposes that Adam was the name given to some group of our primordial ancestors. It does not appear how such views can be reconciled with the doctrine of original sin, as this is guaranteed to us by Scripture and tradition, and proposed to us by the Church. Original sin is the result of a sin committed, in actual historical fact, by an individual man named Adam, and it is a quality native to all of us, only because it has been handed down by descent from him.

On the other hand, the Catholic paleontologist Teilhard de Chardin, who seems to be a champion of polygenism, observes that one of the difficulties of monogenism in the strict scientific sense is that it leaves open the whole question. He states: "Thus in *the eyes of science,* which at long range can only see things in full, the 'first man' is, and can only be, *a crowd,* and his infancy is made up of thousands and thousands of years." To which he adds in a note the following remark: "That is why the problem of monogenism in the strict sense of the word . . . seems to *elude* science as such by its very nature. At those depths of time when hominisation took place, the presence and the movements of a unique couple are positively ungraspable, unrevealable to our eyes at no matter what magnification. Accordingly one can say that there is room *in this interval* for anything that a transexperimental source of knowledge might demand."[16]

Most Roman Catholic theologians would infer from this statement that since science cannot establish monogenism, and since polygenism is not an established fact, our only recourse is to turn to revelation. This is why the papal encyclical just quoted does not mark out a new doctrine or offer a new definition but merely reasserts the traditional interpretation of Genesis.

Original Sin

Both Protestant and Catholic theologians are inclined to follow Augustine's interpretation of original sin as constituted by man's pride and disobedience. They may express their conception of this sin in various ways: as a loss of faith in God, as the rebellion of man and the exaltation of his own righteousness, as the disruption of man's spiritual unity, as the lack of trust in God's Word. Since Augustine's description of the nature of original sin is still one of the best, we can do little better than quote briefly from him:

Our first parents fell into open disobedience because already they were secretly corrupted; for the evil act had never been done had not an evil will preceded it. And what is the origin of our evil will but pride? For "pride is the beginning of sin." And what is pride but the craving for undue exaltation? And this is undue exaltation, when the soul abandons Him to whom it ought to cleave as its end, and becomes a kind of end to itself. This happens when it becomes its own satisfaction. And it does so when it falls away from that unchangeable good which ought to satisfy it more than itself. This falling away is spontaneous; for if the will had remained steadfast in the love of that higher and changeless good by which it is illumined to intelligence and kindled into love, it would not have turned away to find satisfaction in itself. . . . The wicked deed, then—that is to say, the transgression of eating the forbidden fruit—was committed by persons who were already wicked. That "evil fruit" could be brought forth only by a "corrupt tree." But that the tree was evil was contrary to its nature; for certainly it could become so only by the vice of the will, and vice is contrary to nature. Now, nature could not have been depraved by vice had it not been made from nothing. Consequently, that it is a nature, this is because it is made by God; but that if falls away from Him, this is because it is made from nothing. But man did not so fall away as to become absolutely nothing . . . but to approximate to that. And therefore the Holy Scriptures designated the proud by another name, "self-pleasers." For it is good to have the heart lifted up, yet not to one's self, for this is pride, but to the Lord, for this is obedience, and can be the act only of the humble. There is, therefore, something in humility which, strangely enough, exalts the heart, and something in pride which debases it. This seems, indeed, to be contradictory, that loftiness should debase and lowliness exalt. But pious humility enables us to submit to what is above us; and nothing is more exalted and above us than God; and therefore humility, by making us subject to God, exalts us. But pride, being a defect of nature, by the very act of refusing subjection and revolting from Him who is supreme, falls to a low condition; and then comes to pass what is written: "Thou castedest them down when they lifted up themselves." . . .

In short . . . what but disobedience was the punishment of disobedience in that sin? For what else is man's misery but his own disobedience to himself, so that in consequence of his not being willing to do what he could do, he now wills to do what he cannot? For though he could not do all things in Paradise before he sinned, yet he wished to do only what he could do, and therefore he could do all things he wished. But now, as we recognize in his offspring, and as divine Scripture testifies, "Man is like to vanity." For who can count how many things he wishes which he cannot do, so long as he is disobedient to himself, that is so long as his mind and his flesh do not obey his will?[17]

EXTENT OF ORIGINAL SIN.   Differences also appear among the opinions of Roman Catholic and Protestant theologians concerning the extent of man's fall and the interpretation of the guilt of all men in Adam's sin. In the early Protestant tradition (and this was to be repeated more or less in Jansenism),[18] it was held that man's fall resulted in his complete corruption, intellectual as well as moral. Some consequences of this were the denial of man's freedom, the need of an irresistible grace for salvation, and the Calvinistic doctrine of double predestination.[19]

The Roman Catholic position, with the exception of Jansenism, has traditionally held that man's nature was wounded by the fall but in no way completely corrupted. As Jean Mouroux expresses it:

The sin of Adam involved the human race in a cleavage between creation and adoption: God continues to give life, but no longer his life. Every man born into the world is no longer all that God wishes him to be. . . . Though man's essence remains intact, henceforward his nature is wounded. He has no longer the power to move towards his predestined goal, he is too weak and blind to endure the divine presence which is henceforward his nourishment and true delight. He is incapable of that act of union with God which would restore him to life, and he can only fall back upon himself, shut off from his fellows and from God.[20]

Roman Catholic theologians also portray the fall of man as a fall from a state of physical, moral, and intellectual integrity to his present natural state. Their commentary on Genesis 3:16–19 usually depicts the truths contained in the narrative in the following fashion. Originally Adam was given sanctifying grace, perhaps created in grace. Such grace enabled him to share intimately in God's life. This participation in the divine life was thereafter to be found—apart from Jesus—only in the Blessed Virgin, who "is full of grace." From the sanctifying grace which Adam received there followed many God-given attributes and privileges. These are usually spoken of as the preternatural gifts of Adam. Four in number, they are: (1) the gift of immortality, of physical integrity, and freedom from pain. This is confirmed in St. Paul's statement that it was only through Adam's sin that death came into the world. And the Genesis verses imply that before sin Adam (and Eve) lived without toil and pain; (2) the gift of moral integrity. In his original state man's desires and passions were always subject to reason; his will was always directed to good, and there was no inclination to evil. In short, man possessed perfect moral equilibrium; (3) the gift of intellectual integrity. Man shared in the divine wisdom and there was no inclination to error; (4) the gift of what we shall term "supernatural integrity," by which we mean that in his original state man was capable of performing supernatural acts and that he could have achieved eternal life unaided. This would follow from the fact that he possessed sanctifying grace and shared in the divine life.

TRANSMISSION OF ORIGINAL SIN.   Finally, there is the question of the transmission of original sin. Catholics and many Protestants would follow the reasoning of St. Paul, who concluded that we are all subject to original sin, not because personally we have all sinned, but because death is common to all men, hence original sin is also common to all. The entire statement of St. Paul, well worth quoting, is to be found in Romans 5:12–26:

Therefore as sin came into the world through one man and death through sin, and so death spread to all men because all men sinned—sin indeed was in the world before the law was given, but sin is not counted where there is no law. Yet death reigned from Adam to Moses, even over those whose sins were not like the transgression of Adam, who was a type of the one who was to come.

But the free gift is not like the trespass. For if many died through one man's trespass, much more have the grace of God and the free gift in the grace of that one man Jesus Christ abounded for many. And the free gift is not like the effect of that one man's sin. For the judgment following one trespass brought condemnation, but the free gift following many trespasses brings justification. If, because of one man's trespass, death reigned through that one man, much more will those who receive the abundance of grace and the free gift of right-eousness reign in life through the one man Jesus Christ.

Then as one man's trespass led to condemnation for all men, so one man's act of righteousness leads to acquittal and life for all men. For as by one man's disobedience many were made sinners, so by one man's obedience many will be made righteous. Law came in, to increase the trespass; but where sin increased, grace abounded all the more, so that, as sin reigned in death, grace also might reign through righteousness to eternal life through Jesus Christ our Lord.

At the beginning of our analysis of the Christian view of sin on page 251, we used the phrase *felix culpa*. Now on the basis of St. Paul's account, and especially verse 17, "If, because of one man's trespass, death reigned through that one man," we can see the full significance of this phrase. Adam's guilt was a "happy guilt" because it led eventually to God's redeeming grace through Jesus Christ and our eternal salvation.

With reference again to this quotation from St. Paul, it should be observed that the apostle reiterates fairly frequently that the guilt of mankind as a whole is a common guilt. The original guilt or sin is Adam's, but men have inherited that sin even though personally they did not commit Adam's sin. But men are aware of the consequences—death, pain, moral turpitude. The fact that men are not personally responsible for Adam's sin may cause most Christians to feel that there is a serious injustice here. Why should men share in Adam's guilt, and why does the justice of God insist that they also share in all the consequences of Adam's act? To this there can be no rational or scientific explanation. It is a mystery which Christians accept on faith. As Pascal puts it: "Certainly nothing offends us more rudely than this doctrine; and yet, without this mystery, the most incomprehensible of all, we are incomprehensible to ourselves. The knot of our condition takes its twists and turns in this abyss, so that man is more inconceivable without this mystery than this mystery is inconceivable to man."[21]

As we have seen, most Christian theologians, Catholic and Protestant, accept original sin in all men as a common heritage derived from Adam. Few theologians make any effort to show more precisely just how original sin might have been transmitted, and they are inclined to interpret its transmission mythologically. Occasionally, however, efforts at explication have been made. We know, for example, that at one time Augustine was inclined to the view that all souls were generated in Adam. Since sin has its origin in the rational soul, this would readily account for the inheritance of original sin from Adam. At one time this view found some favor in the early Church and came to be known as *traducianism*.[22] However, this doctrine had materialistic implications, and Augustine eventually rejected it in favor of the special creation of the soul, even though this latter doctrine made it very difficult to explain the transmission of original sin.

An excellent commentary on this entire problem is provided in the following statement by Aquinas:

In endeavoring to explain how the sin of our first parent could be transmitted by way of origin to his descendants, various writers have gone about it in various ways. For some, considering that the subject of sin is the rational soul, maintained that the rational soul is transmitted with the semen, so that thus an infected soul would seem to produce other infected souls. Others, rejecting this as erroneous, endeavored to show how the guilt of the parent's soul can be transmitted to the children, even though the soul be not transmitted, from the fact that defects of the body are transmitted from parent to child. Thus a leper may beget a leper, or a gouty man may be the father of a gouty son, because of some seminal corruption, although this corruption is not leprosy or gout. Now since the body is proportioned to the soul, and since the soul's defects redound into the body, and *vice versa*, in like manner, say they, a culpable defect of the soul is passed on to the child through the transmission of the semen, although the semen itself is not the subject of guilt.

But all these explanations are insufficient. For granted that some bodily defects are transmitted by way of origin from parent to child, and granted that even some defects of the soul are transmitted, in consequence, because of a defect in a bodily disposition, as in the case of idiots begetting idiots, nevertheless, the fact of having a defect by the way of origin seems to exclude the notion of guilt, which is essentially something voluntary. Therefore, granted that the rational soul were transmitted, from the very fact that the stain on the child's soul is not in its will, it would cease to be a guilty stain binding its subject to punishment; for, as the Philosopher says, *no one reproaches a man born blind; one rather takes pity on him.*

Therefore we must explain the matter otherwise, by saying that all men born of Adam may be considered as one man inasmuch as they have one common nature, which they receive from their first parents; even as in civil matters, all who are members of one community are reputed as one body, and the whole community as one man. Indeed, Porphyry says that *by sharing the species, many men are one man.* Accordingly, the multitude of men born of Adam are as so many members of one body. Now the action of one member of the body, of one hand, for instance, is voluntary, not by the will of that hand, but by the will of the soul, the first mover of the members. Therefore, a murder which the hand commits would not be imputed as a sin to the hand, considered by itself as apart from the body, but is imputed to it as something belonging to man and moved by man's first moving principle. In this way, then, the disorder which is in this man born of Adam is voluntary, not by his will, but by the will of his first parent, who, by the movement of generation, moves all who originate from him, even as the soul's will moves all the members to their actions. Hence the sin which is thus transmitted by the first parent to his descendants is called *original*, just as the sin which flows from the soul into the bodily members is called *actual*. And just as the actual sin that is committed by a member of the body is not the sin of that member, except inasmuch as that member is a part of the man (for which reason it is called a *human sin*), so original sin is not the sin of this person, except inasmuch as this person receives his nature from his first parent (for which reason it is called the *sin of nature*, according to *Ephes*. ii. 3: *We . . . were by nature children of wrath*).[23]

THE REDEMPTION OF MAN

The meaning of redemption, like that of sin, reveals major differences between Judaism and Christianity. For Christianity the meaning of redemption is caught up in all the many facets of Christology. Since Judaism does not accept Jesus as the Messiah, redemption for Judaism will be meaningful only within another context. The account that follows will seek to avoid a repetition of those aspects of redemption which will be considered in more detail in the chapters on Christology and Eschatology. Here we shall merely note briefly a few of the more general aspects of redemption.

Christianity and the Redemption of Man

For Christian theology it follows as a consequence of original sin that to be redeemed man needs the grace of God. To be redeemed means to be restored to our original state of friendship with God: it means to be freed from the bondage of sin and this is our salvation. Luther's conception of the "bondage of the human will" meant simply that without God's grace man cannot will his redemption through faith. Redemption through grace is common to both Catholic and Protestant theologians, regardless of other differences that have appeared on related subjects, for example, justification, freedom, or faith and works. And in speaking of the redemption of man they mean the redemption of all men. All men are sinners because of Adam's fault, and all will be saved through Christ. "For as by a man came death, by a man has come also the resurrection of the dead. For as in Adam all die, so also in Christ shall all be made alive" (I Corinthians 15:21–22).

The Christian conception of redemption can be more clearly understood by comparing it briefly with the Pelagian notion of redemption. Pelagius (A.D. ?360–431?) rejected the doctrine of original sin. He held that man was inherently good, that the sin of Adam was not transmitted to posterity, and that the universality of sin among men is due more to Adam's bad example than to the taint of original sin. The rejection of the death of man through Adam's fault entailed that the redemption of man does not require the atoning effect of Christ's sacrifice. Thus Pelagius rejected any need of man for the grace of God. He believed that such grace would limit man's freedom. He held that man could work out his redemption solely through his own efforts. In combatting this view, Augustine did not deny man's freedom. "Freedom," he said, "is sufficient for evil; for good it is not enough unless it be empowered by the Omnipotent who is good." Augustine held—and his solution is generally accepted by most Christian theologians—that grace gives man the power (*libertas*) to choose the good and to effect meritorious actions. Grace begins in faith, and through grace man achieves a spiritual rebirth. Such grace enables man to be righteous, but the initiative is with God. The source of that grace and redemption lies in the Incarnation and in the sacrifice of Christ.

The mystery of the Incarnation is an expression of the divine love, the supreme act of charity by God, in which He became the God-Man, Jesus Christ. This will be examined more closely in the chapter on Christology. For present purposes the significance of the Incarnation is its expression of the great love that God has for man, a love that led God to assume the whole nature of man—both soul and body. This act on the part of God as the Redeemer gives added emphasis to what was pointed out earlier concerning the essential goodness of the human body and the unity of man's nature. This assumption of human nature is expressed in the words of St. John: "And the Word became flesh and dwelt among us" (John 1:14). In these words the apostle stresses the goodness of the body but without denying the soul, for the Word assumed both the body and soul of man. This assumption of human nature by God also reveals the humility of God. As Trinité points out: "St. John wished to intimate that the Incarnation befitted the work of redemption. Since man was wounded in his flesh, he would be healed by the flesh of the Word. 'This was something the law could not do, because flesh and blood could not lend it the power; and this God has done, by sending us His own son, in the fashion of our guilty nature to make amends for our guilt. He has signed the death warrant of sin in our nature (Rom. 8:3).' "[24]

The redemption of man through the Incarnation culminates in the supreme sacrifice of the God-Man. "As man, Christ became our sacrifice and redeemed us with his blood . . . as God, it is through him that we are forgiven our sins and freed from the guilt of sin."[25] The full meaning of the sacrifice of Christ on the cross, whether it was the only means by which man could be freed from death and sin, the merit and satisfaction of Christ's sacrifice, the curious conception of Origen that Christ's soul was paid as a ransom to Satan that man might go free—these are but a few of the questions that can better be answered only after a thorough study of Christology. We may conclude with a point that is less moot among theologians, namely, that the redemption of Christ is universal, that it was intended for all men. "[God] desires all men to be saved" (I Timothy 2:4) and "And he [Christ] died for all" (II Corinthians 5:15).

Judaism and Redemption

The idea of redemption in Judaism is highly complex, because it includes the redemption of the individual person, the redemption of Israel, and the redemption of the whole world. Redemption as a doctrine develops within the history of Israel and gives both substance and hope to the history of the Jewish people. Basically significant is the fact that redemption centers upon both the individual and the people. In Judaism the individual is closely identified with Israel as a people and a nation.

Rabbi Isaac Luria (1514–1572) held that Israel is one body and that each Jew is a member of that body, hence the sin of each is the responsibility of all. The redemption of the individual is effected by his individual deeds of righteousness and by his participation in the liturgy of the High Holy days, particularly in the recitation with the congregation of the long litany of the Confession on the Day of Atonement. "Repentance, Prayer, and Righteousness" are the preconditions of redemption for the individual. By expiating his sins and righting the wrongs committed against others, he will win God's forgiveness. And by his own goodness he will contribute to the moral progress and redemption of his own people and of all peoples. Luria makes the interesting observation that the dispersion of the Jews was intended for the salvation of all men, for thus the purified souls of the Israelites can be united with others and free them from evil.

The redemption of Israel in history has its source in the covenants God made with Noah, Abraham, and Moses; it has its end in the final redemption of Israel and the world by the Messiah.[26] Through the covenants the people of Israel became the chosen people of God and the instruments of divine providence. Such covenants enjoined that the people of Israel must be just and righteous, that they must honor God and live by His law—the Torah. In return for their obedience they will be blessed by God and will prosper. If they sin or disobey God they will be punished. The exilic periods in Jewish history are periods in which God has judged and punished Israel. They are followed by successive redemptions of Israel through the intervention of divine providence. Redemption requires not only God's providence, but also an expiation by the people themselves for their guilt.

This belief in redemption eventually led to the formation of the doctrine of the Messiah. The term "messiah" means "one who is anointed" and in the Hebrew Scriptures the Kings Saul, David, and Zedekiah are called "messiah." The first conception of the Messiah, then, is that of a political leader, another great king who would restore the glory of Israel to that which it had enjoyed under David. In the next stage of the development of the doctrine, this notion of a great king is coupled with the idea of the spiritual regeneration of the people of Israel. With the coming of the Messiah a reign of peace and justice, an era of blessedness will be ushered in for Israel. Gradually this conception of a national Messiah gave way to the conception of a Messiah who would not only lead the children of Israel to their greater glory but who would also inaugurate the redemption of all mankind. This seems to be the clear message of the prophet Zechariah:

> Thus says the Lord of hosts: Behold, I will save my people from the east country and from the west country; and I will bring them to dwell in the midst of Jerusalem; and they shall be my people and I will be their God, in faithfulness and in righteousness.
> Thus says the Lord of hosts: In those days ten men from the nations of every tongue shall take hold of the robe of a Jew, saying, "Let us go with you, for we have heard that God is with you" (Zechariah 8:7–8, 23).

The redemption effected by the Messiah is this-worldly rather than otherworldly. Such a redemption will come as a climax to Jewish history. Israel will not disappear but will be redeemed by the Messiah, who, as a human person will establish the Messianic kingdom in which God's truth and goodness will extend over all mankind.

The emphasis that Jewish writers place upon the freedom of the individual gives the individual an active role in redemption. Through his moral actions the individual purifies himself and establishes a close relationship with God. God becomes his goal, but the initial activity in this relationship is with the individual. On the other hand, Jewish writers do emphasize that redemption depends upon the divine providence. It is God working in history and not the individual who will bring about the redemption of Israel. In Christianity redemption proceeds wholly from God. The individual is free but God's grace is the determining factor in his salvation. In Judaism man remains free, but it is God who determines the logic of history and the ultimate miracle of the Messiah. Nevertheless, the actions of the individual will have an indispensable effect. The good man can and does affect the moral progress of the group and so advance the progress of mankind toward the messianic kingdom. One of the rabbinic teachings is quite explicit here: "The Messianic redemption will come in its time, regardless of what men do, but if men prove worthy, the Lord will hasten it" (Sanhedrin 98a). Thus the redemption of the individual in this life will be limited to his reconciliation with God through the expiation of his sins. But through his individual redemption, his own spiritual regeneration, the individual contributes to the spiritual regeneration and eventual redemption of all mankind. It is in this manner that Judaism endeavors to reconcile the role of the individual and of God in redemption.

A particularly fine expression of the hope of Israel for redemption is contained in an ancient prayer, the Alenu:

We therefore hope in thee, O Lord our God, that we may speedily behold the glory of thy might, when thou wilt remove the abominations from the earth, and the idols will be utterly cut off, when the world will be perfected under the kingdom of the Almighty, and all the children of flesh will call upon thy name, when thou wilt turn unto thyself all the wicked of the earth. Let all the inhabitants of the earth perceive and know that unto thee every knee must bow, every tongue must swear. Before thee, O Lord our God, let them bow and fall; and unto thy glorious name let them give honor; let them all accept the yoke of thy kingdom, and do thou reign over them speedily, and for ever and ever. For the kingdom is thine, and to all eternity thou wilt reign in glory; as it is written in thy Law, the Lord shall reign for ever and ever. And it is said, And the Lord shall be king over all the earth; in that day shall the Lord be One, and his name One.

NOTES

1. The selections from Genesis have been taken from the Revised Standard Version.
2. Usually termed "ethical monotheism."
3. Although the early Israelites undoubtedly believed in immortality, their understanding of the notion of "spirit" was limited to that which could be known by sense perception, hence the identification of spirit with "breath" or that which gives life to a being. This may also account for the lack of any description of the creation of the angels. St. Cyril of Alexandria thought this omission was because the knowledge of the incorporeal was too subtle to be understood by the peoples to whom the narrative was addressed.
4. The terms "soil" or "clay" would seem to be better adapted than the term "dust" for the explanation of the creation of the body. Note that Eve is fashioned from something even more solid and concrete, namely, the rib of Adam.
5. Observe the use of the term in Ecclesiastes 3:21.
6. Aquinas notes that "Moses was speaking to ignorant people, and that out of consideration for their weakness he put before them only such things as are apparent to sense." (*Summa Theologica*, I, Q. 68, a. 3.) Anton C. Pegis, ed., *Basic Writings of St. Thomas Aquinas* (New York: Random House, 1945).
7. "Place" should be taken in a figurative rather than in a literal sense. The soul does not occupy a place as do physical beings; the soul is not extended or physical but somehow it is present to and within that which is physical.
8. Quoted by M. C. D'Arcy, S.J., *The Mind and Heart of Love* (New York: Meridian, 1956), p. 110. This work should also be consulted for its excellent and exhaustive analysis of *Eros* and *Agape*.
9. Emil Brunner, *The Christian Understanding of Man*. An Oxford Conference Book (Chicago: Willett, Clark, 1938), p. 42.
10. John Calvin, *The Institutes of Christian Religion*, trans. John Allen (Philadelphia: Presbyterian Board of Education, 1936), III, xxi, 5.
11. Martin Luther, *The Bondage of the Will* (Grand Rapids, Mich.: Eerdmans, 1931), pp. 40–41.

12. Saadia Ben Joseph (882–942) held that all creation is designed for the good of the creature, and especially for man. Even suffering has a positive value and will be compensated for in the life to come. The great Jewish philosopher Maimonides held that evil was a privation of the good and generally speaking his philosophy is more optimistic than that of Saadia.

13. Leo Baeck, *God and Man in Judaism* (New York: Union of American Hebrew Congregations, 1958), pp. 46–49.

14. See Eliezer Berkovitz, "When Man Fails God," in E. Millgram, ed., *Great Jewish Ideas* (Washington, D.C.: B'nai B'rith, 1964), Chapter 11.

15. Thus the serpent symbolizes Satan, the tree of life, immortality.

16. From *The Phenomenon of Man* by Teilhard de Chardin, copyright © 1959 by Harper & Row Publishers, Inc. Reprinted by permission. Published in England 1955 by Wm. Collins Sons & Co. Ltd. Reprinted by permission. P. 186 and note 1.

17. St. Augustine, *City of God,* XIV, Chapters 13, 15.

18. From a Catholic heresy which had its source in the writings of Cornelius Jansen (Jansenius) (1585–1638). Although Jansen did not expressly deny the freedom of man's will, he restricted it to a freedom from external constraint. He rejected the idea of sufficient grace and denied that Christ died for all men.

19. Calvin has often been interpreted to mean that man has become so completely corrupted through original sin that he has lost all freedom and has become the slave of sin. From this it followed that man's salvation can only be attained by the irresistible grace of God given through Jesus Christ. Calvin maintained that it is God's freedom to elect whom He will for salvation and that from the beginning He has willed some individuals to salvation and some to damnation. Calvin justified double predestination on the basis of God's omnipotence, spoke of it as "God's awful decree," and believed that it could be supported by Scripture. Most theologians have long since given up this extreme position of Calvin.

20. Taken from *What Is Man?* by Rene Le Troquer, P.S.S., vol. 31 of *The Twentieth Century Encyclopedia of Catholicism;* © 1961 by Hawthorn Books, Inc., 70 Fifth Avenue, N.Y.C., p. 87.

21. Blaise Pascal, *Pensées,* trans. W. F. Trotter (New York: E. P. Dutton, Everyman's Library, 1941), p. 144.

22. From *traducere* (to carry over), and meaning that the soul as well as the body is inherited from the parents. The opposed doctrine is known as *creationism.*

23. St. Thomas Aquinas, *Summa Theologica,* I–II, Q. 81, a. 1.

24. Philippe de la Trinité, *What Is Redemption?* trans. Anthony Armstrong in *The Twentieth Century Encyclopedia of Catholicism,* Vol. 25 (New York: Hawthorn, 1961), p. 53.

25. St. Thomas Aquinas, *Comm. in Col.* 1, lect. 3, n. 28.

26. Since the doctrine of the Messiah and the messianic kingdom will be treated more fully in the chapter on Eschatology, we shall touch upon it only very briefly here.

SELECT BIBLIOGRAPHY

AUGUSTINE, ST. *City of God.* Trans. Gerald G. Walsh and Grace Monahan. The Fathers of the Church Series, Vol. 14. Washington, D.C.: Catholic University of America Press, 1952. Chapters 13 and 14.

BRUNNER, E. *The Divine-Human Encounter.* Philadelphia: Westminster Press, 1951.

GILSON, ETIENNE. *Elements of Christian Philosophy*. Garden City, N.Y.: Doubleday, 1960, pp. 203–260.

HERBERG, WILL. *Judaism and Modern Man*. Philadelphia: Jewish Publication Society, and New York: Meridian Paperback, 1959.

LEVINE, H. L. "The Experience of Repentance." *Tradition*, Fall, 1958.

LOHSE, BERNHARD, A *Short History of Christian Doctrine*. Trans. F. E. Stoeffler, Philadephia: Fortress, 1966.

LUTHER, MARTIN. *The Bondage of the Will*. Grand Rapids, Mich.: Erdmans, 1931.

MILLGRAM, A. E., ed. *Great Jewish Ideas*. Washington, D.C.: B'nai B'rith, 1964, Chapters 10–12.

MOUROUX, JEAN. *The Meaning of Man*. Trans. A. H. G. Downes. New York: Doubleday, 1948.

NIEBUHR, REINHOLD. *Nature and Destiny of Man*. New York: Charles Scribner's Sons, 1941.

SCHECHTER, SOLOMON. *Some Aspects of Rabbinic Theology*. New York: Shocken Books, 1961. Paperback.

TRINITÉ, PHILIPPE DE LA. *What is Redemption?* Trans. Anthony Armstrong, O.S.B. Twentieth Century Encyclopedia of Catholicism, Vol. 25. New York: Hawthorn Books, 1961.

IX

The Christ Event
and the Messianic Idea

IN this chapter we shall attempt to discuss with some detachment the central point of issue between Jews and Christians: the doctrine of the Messiah and the Christian evaluation of Jesus of Nazareth as the Messiah. Happily, this "problem" can now be discussed in a much clearer atmosphere than would have been possible a century or more ago. In recent years there has been a developing positive climate seldom known during the previous centuries of the Common Era, and seldom allowed by the Christian majority. Yet discussion still must proceed with considerable delicacy because the critical schism in which Judaism and Christianity broke with each other has left a wound, particularly on the body of Judaism, which the tragic experiences of the centuries has not yet permitted fully to heal.

Much of this history is, of course, due to ignorant and superstitious stereotypes we have no need to describe here. But not all stereotypes in error have come from ignorance. In the most learned theological circles many of these stereotypes still prevail, and it is possible to read in the most scholarly tomes, either Jewish or Christian, distortions or at least misreadings of the first-century Jewish matrix from which Christianity originated which are no longer defensible on historical grounds. These interpretations are often influenced by dogmatic considerations, consciously or unconsciously. These dogmas, whether simple or sophisticated, continue to control much of the Christian attitude toward Christian origins in relation to Judaism.

A typical (and composite) description runs something like this: The Old

Testament is important as historical preparation for the decisive events of the New Testament which gather up the hopes and aspirations of the Old Testament to bring fulfillment to the history of Israel. The history of Israel is important, therefore, as the prehistory of Christianity. Whereas, up to and through the Exile, the prophets developed the highest conception of God known to man, when prophecy ceased Judaism walled itself off from the rest of the world and lapsed into narrowness and exclusiveness, attempting to save its life by punctilious observance of the Law. The revelation was frozen into final form, needing only the clever legal casuistry of the scribes and Pharisees to make clear its implicit meaning. But this left only a haunting expectation and desire on the part of the people, and the achievements of pre-Christian Judaism were largely sterile. Out of that ferment, however, Christianity arose to give coherence to its various streams. Into this swamp of legalism, God sent His Son for the salvation of the world. Jesus of Nazareth, the utterly unique one, gave and taught a new and superior religion—the gospel of love—in place of the Law. Judaism's rejection of Jesus was the final repudiation of the task God had given to His chosen people. There came then the catastrophe of A.D. 70, the destruction of the temple, by which God, through the Romans, executed his judgment on a barren Judaism. The New Testament, therefore, is the reassertion of the authentic Old Testament tradition, as opposed to the rabbinic distortion of it, for the New Testament reaffirmed the primacy of Gospel over Law, the basic importance of redemptive history, and the Hebraic doctrine of man.

The basic outline of this description remains to this day pervasive in much of the Christian argument and, naturally enough, affronts Jews as a caricature of their faith.

An equally narrow view can be found within Judaism. This stereotype (again a composite) runs something like this: While Jesus belongs within the Jewish tradition as a courageous witness to truths which were by and large enunciated and accepted by his contemporaries, it is on Paul and his dogmatizing that one must place the blame for the severance of Jesus and his followers from the light of Israel. Henceforth, the most important ideas of Christianity were essentially antirabbinic and *goyische* (gentile). Christianity is a "romantic" religion of faith and dogma, replete with the mythical and miraculous, concerned with the world beyond, seeking ecstatic abandonment and lacking any strong ethical impulse. With Paul, convert to mystery and sacrament, Christianity accepted the inheritance of the Greek and Oriental mysteries with their cultic deities, holy consecrations, and atonements. By the grace of a god who walked the earth, man is united with his god, redeemed from primordial sin and original guilt, and thus related to the world beyond. By fusing the mysto-magic of the mysteries with the secrecies of Jewish wisdom, the Judaism of Paul and paganism became one, so that time is fulfilled, not in waiting for the Messiah, but in the mystery of the sacraments. Thus Christianity becomes the religion for those faint and anxious minds who are looking everywhere for strength and by which they receive redemption from the world and liberation from death.

That both views, however pervasive in each tradition, are profoundly mistaken can be shown by some understanding of a major strand of biblical-rabbinical-historical scholarship in the last fifty years which has provided the basis for correcting these essentially erroneous attitudes. It is not necessary—and not our purpose—to explore all the vagaries and labyrinthian ways of historical and biblical scholarship to recognize that popular Christian caricatures of rabbinic Judaism are gross oversimplifications and misinterpretations of rabbinic thought. Nor can Jewish interpretations of Christianity overlook the historical fact that not only Jesus but also Paul and the bulk of Christian literature, stem from and remain within a distinctly Jewish milieu and share much in common with rabbinism. Indeed, the whole Christological development within Christianity must be seen in its original and Jewish context. At the center of Christian origins there is the messianic issue—a Jewish doctrine. (After all, "Messianic" in Greek is "Christian," as "Christos" is the Greek translation of "Messiah.") It is no exaggeration to say that Christianity began as a sect within Judaism and by and large remained in and integrally related to its source for most of the first century. It is, therefore, utterly impossible to understand Christian origins apart from an understanding of Judaism in Palestine and in the Diaspora.

THE HISTORICAL MATRIX[1]

Rabbinic Judaism

The period surrounding the division of the eras is one of such exceeding perplexity that there is much we know little or nothing about. The first century c.e., especially, was an age of transition with many crosscurrents. But in the period 200 b.c.e.–200 c.e., Judaism was so alive, so progressive, and so agitated by controversy that under its roof many contrasting views could be held, and Christianity at the beginning simply added one more detail to a situation already singularly variegated. Rabbinic Judaism, which George Foot Moore called "a monument of the Pharisees,"[2] and which was the shaper of normative Judaism, was a movement under the aegis of which many new ideas entered the thought and practice of Judaism. While Pharisaism originally aimed at a separation from the nations, with a corresponding maintenance of strict purity and cohesion of the Jewish community by "building a fence around the Torah," its umbrella was broad enough to include many diverse elements, even the sectarians (see Chapter 2).

Theologically, the Pharisees seemed able to absorb apparently contradictory trends. On the one hand, there was a universalism stemming from the prophecy of deutero-Isaiah proclaiming that God only was worthy of mankind's worship. On the other hand, with the Apocalyptic they could proclaim the coming day of the Lord when all nations would be subject to the Torah and the Son of Man would reestablish Israel and crush Rome. Many of the basic ideas which were to enter the Christian stream of thought—resurrection of the dead, the Messiah, the Kingdom of God, the primacy of the commandment to love God and one's neighbor, as well as speculation about wisdom, angels, and demons—are products of Pharisaic thought.

This variegation is dramatized by the diverse flow of literature. There are the Tanakh with the Torah, cultus, prophets and their promises, and psalms, proverbs, and wisdom literature pointing toward an age to come— eschatology and messianism. There is a literature of apocalyptic intensity and vitality which pictures adherents living in obedience to the Law, but also in intense anticipation of the age to come. In addition to a vast body of intertestamental literature, there was the oral Torah, nonbiblical midrashic law and lore, which was to develop into the talmudic writings.

Although rabbinic Judaism struggled manfully to maintain the purity of the Torah, alien cultural accretions were unconsciously absorbed in their thought and vocabulary. Even Palestinian Judaism was "hellenized" to a degree unsuspected some years ago. This is true to such an extent that no superficial distinctions should be made between Palestinian and diaspora Judaism.

Christian Origins

These first-century developments naturally enough had their influence on primitive Christian thought, as the New Testament makes perfectly clear, and we now have a new picture of the Christian debt to Judaism, for it derives its spirit and impetus from its rabbinic context.

Within this context Jesus, Paul, the apostles, and the thought and life of the primitive Christian community must be seen and understood. They belong to a first-century Palestine in the same thorough-going way that anyone belongs to his age and culture. Jesus was, in every feature and trait of his character, a Jew of his period and locale, sharing Jewish thoughts and hopes; they, in turn, were anchored in the Tanakh and rabbinic interpretations of the time. His disciples came from his own people and shared with their contemporaries the hopes in the coming Messiah. Paul, too, must be understood as the Jew he was and never ceased to be. Standing within the pale of Judaism, his thought was essentially rabbinic and his ideas to a considerable degree remain within Jewish compass.[3] The early Church not only understood its historical continuity with Israel, but its self-understanding and interpretation of its faith was articulated to the world in the language of Judaism. This Semitic substructure of Christian thought persisted even through the Nicene period down to the present day.

Naturally there are profound differences, even irreconcilable antagonisms, between the nascent sect and its mother religion, but there were many profound differences in the total phenomenon of Judaism of the time, and it is against this background that we must attempt to understand the historical Jesus, the development of the primitive Church, and particularly the development of its thought about the nature of Jesus as the Christ.

Living within the same milieu, a dialogue continued between many Jews and Christians for decades. There were hundreds of points of contact, quite obviously, between Jews and the early circles of Jesus and his disciples, and nowhere is this more true than with the thought and practice of Paul, the normative figure for early Christianity. Precisely where New Testament Judaism stops and Christianity begins is difficult to indicate. But as time went on the two movements separated and recognition of the common heritage was subordinated to a concentration upon points of difference. These points of difference included judgment about the place of the Law, the importance of the Church as the new Israel, exegesis of the Scriptures, and many others. But of course the central point of difference was then, as it always has been, the evaluation of Jesus of Nazareth as the Messiah. And it is therefore probably at the point where Christian interpretation, after his death, placed more than human significance on Jesus' person and career that the schism occurs.

Conceptions of the Messiah

It is difficult to be precise about Jewish conceptions of the Messiah in the first century. The idea has its roots in the Tanakh, especially with the prophets. The Messiah would be a second David, indicating political messianism. There were hints of a suffering Messiah as described in Isaiah 53, but this was by no means a popular notion. Another and more popular notion was the apocalyptic one associated with the figure of the Son of Man in Daniel and the fourth Ezra: a "man from heaven," a transcendent messenger at whose coming the entire world would be transmuted and who would inaugurate the Messianic Age. It is a composite doctrine, with several notions which overlap: ". . . the resentment of Rome, speculation on the incidents of the coming day of God's judgment, and belief in a resurrection were the several streams that flowed together to form the messianic doctrine."[4]

The universalism heralded by the prophets and associated with the Son of Man received articulation in the identification of the Torah with wisdom (Hokhmah). Hokhmah (Proverbs 8:12) is a world-creating force, the power by which the cosmos came into being. Thus the Book became a cosmic force and later on in the Hellenistic writings is identified with the Logos, God's creative thought, with existence since time eternal. Along with this universalism also was eschatological messianism—the doctrine of the Messiah and "the days to come"—which was inherited from the prophets but which was especially enunciated in the apocalyptic literature. Rabbinic thought became preoccupied with both "this world" and "the world to come" so that the Messiah, like the Hokhmah, becomes a cosmic principle, dwelling in God from the beginning of time and ready to descend on the day of fulfillment. The rabbis said that "the name of the messiah" was in the mind of God before creation, but God had not yet revealed it. As time went on, the doctrine of a Messiah was increasingly endowed with eschatological features.

Certainly messianic speculation was rife.[5] When Jesus proclaimed that "the time is fulfilled and the Kingdom of God is at hand" (Mark 1:14–15), he was apparently voicing a widespread belief that the year 5,000 of creation would usher in the sixth millennium—the age of the Kingdom, associated with the coming of the Messiah. The "days of the Messiah," brief or long, would usher in the millennium and in any case would mean the destruction of Rome. It is this belief which led Rabbi Akiba to champion the cause of Bar Kochba in 135 c.e. Around this event there appear to be the same sort of chiliastic expectations as appeared in the Christian expectation with the first and second advents of Jesus (see Chapter 11).

That the followers of Jesus accepted him as the Messiah, a messiah whose purpose was redefined both by himself and by them, remains the most profound, perhaps impassable gulf between Judaism and Christianity. Judaism was and is unable to believe that its expected Messiah has already come in the historical Jesus, because the signs and promises related to the Messiah's coming have not been fulfilled. For decades Jews who did accept Jesus as Messiah remained within Judaism, and it was within that matrix that they developed their understanding of his role as one who ushered in the new age and who would usher in the final age.

It is to a consideration of the Christian claim that we now turn.

CHRISTOLOGY: THE MEANING OF THE CHRIST EVENT

Strictly speaking, Christology is that part of Christian thought concerned with the revelation of God in Christ, his work and person. It has been expressed traditionally in the idea of the Incarnation. Technically, Christology—the study of the person of Christ—is to be distinguished from *soteriology*, which refers to the study of the saving work of Christ and which is described in detail later in this chapter, p. 287. A sharp distinction between the two ideas, however, would be misleading, since in Christian thought they are inextricably linked. In this chapter we will use the terms Christology and soteriology as ways of interpreting the meaning of the Incarnation, or the Christ Event.

What Is the Christ Event? (Incarnation)

We mean by the Christ Event a syndrome of actual historical events occurring in, through, and around a person which resulted in the creation of a new community as the locus for a new ordering of relationships. There are at least three parts: first there is the *historical* Jesus, the Man from Nazareth, the events in his life, his teachings, his death and resurrection. Second, there is Jesus as *the Christ* or Messiah. Who or what was he (Christology: Christ-theology)? What did he do (soteriology)? That is, how was he or is he to be interpreted? Third, there is the *community*—the Church, which came into existence with or as a result of the event and the person. This third category will be discussed in Chapter 10. The Christ Event or Jesus Christ, then, means to Christians these three things: event, person, community.[6]

The New Testament is the literary deposit of the memory and experience of the early Christians. Were one to read the New Testament carefully, one would get a threefold impression, as John Knox puts it so vivdly: "Jesus was for its writers an object of memory, of present experience, and of theological reflection." That is, "He was remembered," "He was known still," "He was interpreted." And these three things "represent aspects of one unified meaning . . . actually memory, religious faith and theology were fused indissolubly."[7] The whole New Testament tradition is written from the standpoint of the community of faith, brought into existence by the impact of God upon man through the historical figure of Jesus of Nazareth, understood as Messiah (in Greek: *Christos*). Therefore everything that is said about a Jew named Jesus is formed and shaped by this understanding; the New Testament is written from within and by reason of the resurrection experience. The biblical authors are misunderstood if they are conceived as modern historiographers trying to provide a detailed and accurate hour-by-hour, event-by-event account of Jesus, or even the broad outlines of his life and death, for biographical and historiographical purposes. They experienced a central historical event and this event is a cluster or complex of closely knit events which include the character, life, death, and resurrection of Jesus, the response of loyalty he awakened, the coming of the Spirit, and the creation of the community. These events belong together and form an "indivisible historical moment," and a gestalt of meaning. They paint a portrait of this man as he is received and understood.

Jesus of Nazareth

Knowledge of the historical Jesus depends almost exclusively on the synoptic Gospels (Matthew, Mark, Luke), but not on John, which is of a different literary genre and the product solely of seasoned theological reflection. But the nature of these sources does not provide us with the historical and psychological evidence which would enable the writing of a biography of Jesus' life against the background of the history of his age and of his people. A biography in this strict historical sense is therefore an impossible achievement. For example, little is known of Jesus' early life, or the order or even the length of his public career. Jesus wrote nothing so far as we know. There are no diaries of events or utterances, no travelogues, not a single word or document that is not overlaid with interpretation. We do not have a photograph of "the historical Jesus." As Professor Lightfoot put it, "for all the inestimable value of the gospels, they leave us little more than a whisper of his voice; we trace in them the outskirts of his ways."[8] Nor are there any clear indisputable references to the historical Jesus or to the Church outside of Christian sources. The history of Jesus is not to be found in documents or the annals of Rome or the Jewish historical writings. World history in general took scarcely any notice of him. The few non-Christian sources can be quickly noted and contribute almost nothing to knowledge of the historical Jesus. Even the Jewish sources are strangely silent, with no reference to the crucifixion or the early Church, and such replies to Christian assertions as there are in the Talmud are so oblique and metaphorical that their relevance escapes the student, although there must have been many disputes and disputants.[9]

This should not, of course, discourage one from raising the historical question. Indeed, for two hundred years this investigation has been going on, with the surprising result that no one is in a position to write a life history of Jesus. Such attempts as have been made reveal how much each author brought the spirit of his own age to bear on the presentation of the figure of Jesus. There have been many "quests" of the historical Jesus, and Albert Schweitzer reviews them in his monumental work, *The Quest of the Historical Jesus.* A historian's first duty, as F. C. Birkett pointed out in the preface to that work,[10] with the gospels as with any other ancient document, is to interpret it with reference to its own time. The proper reading of the gospels will be that which explains the course of events in the first and second centuries rather than that which applies twentieth century canons to first century documents, persons and events. Schweitzer reviewed the nineteenth-century efforts in this direction, but the twentieth century has its "new Quests."[11]

Nor do the Gospels justify historical scepticism. Rather they depict, in a fashion very different from the one customary for us to expect in historical documents, the historical person with the utmost vividness. While they do not seek to reproduce a biography in historical and psychological dimensions, they do speak of history as occurrence and event and thus give abundant evidence of such history. In this respect, they are at least as reliable as other ancient documents and yield more than negligible historical facts which require respect.[12] But there is no way to make an authentic separation between "the Jesus of history" and "the Christ of faith."

It is quite possible to piece together certain formal facts of Jesus' career. First of all, the assertion "he never lived" can be denied unequivocally. The fashionable pursuits under such titles as "Jesus, Fact or Myth," "Jesus, Fact or Fiction," or "the Historical Jesus and the Christ of Faith" are now seen to be both foolish and futile endeavors. Nor is the attempt to associate the Christ myth with the cultic deities such as Isis or Mithras any more successful, because these cultic deities were not historical persons actually remembered, whereas there is no doubt that "the Lord Christ" is the historical *Jesus.*

"FACTS" OF JESUS' CAREER. From the historical point of view the childhood and adolescence of Jesus are obscure. The birth narratives of Matthew and Luke are much too overgrown by legend and by conceptualization to be useful for historical purposes. Their importance, as we shall see, lies in a different area. He was born in all likelihood somewhere between 6 and 4 B.C.E. and died sometime between A.D. 28 and 33.[13] Jesus is apparently at home in semipagan and despised Galilee; his native town is Nazareth. His family belong to the Jewish part of the population; his father—as well as he—was apparently a carpenter. We know the names of his parents, Joseph and Mary, and something about his family. His native tongue is the Aramaic of Galilee, although as one with rabbinical training, he must have understood also the ancient and current biblical language, Hebrew.

He began his public ministry following the work of John the Baptist, at the age of approximately thirty (Luke 3:23). He was baptized by John the Baptist, an occurrence the historical validity of which is underscored by the fact that this was embarrassing to later Christians. The estimates of the length of his public career vary from one to three years and there is no reliable chronology. These "facts" tell us little of significance about his life, save that he was in every way a child of his age, thoroughly imbued with Jewish religious tradition, though attempts to associate him with one of the sects—Zealot, Essene, or Pharisaic—have never been demonstrated.

Jesus as Teacher and Prophet.   The simplest way, perhaps, to understand the main thrust of Jesus' teaching is to accept the contemporary judgment of him as one who continued the prophetic tradition and lived as a "rabbi" (Mark 9:15), teaching in the synagogue and gathering around him a small circle of students and followers. In methods of argument, in turn of phrase, in the use of proverbs and parables, and in the content of his teaching he is closely related to the sages and rabbis of his day. For example, to the question, "Which is the chief commandment?" (Mark 12:28–34), which was often discussed among them, his answer— love God and neighbor—is from the Tanakh (Deuteronomy 6:4–5; Leviticus 18:19).

That there is nothing unprecedentedly unique in his ethical teachings has long been recognized by almost all scholars. Klausner says, "throughout the Gospels there is not one item of ethical teaching which cannot be paralleled either in the Old Testament, the Apocrypha, or in the Talmudic and Midrashic literature of the period near the time of Jesus."[14] But historians also contend that there is something unique in the combination and principle of selectivity, in the concentration of ethical teachings. "Jesus," to quote Klausner again, "condensed and concentrated ethical teachings in such fashion as to make them more prominent than in the Talmudic Haggada and Midrashim, where they are interspersed among more commonplace discussions and worthless matter."[15] The distinction lies then in the characteristic emphases and organization, and especially in the personality of the teacher and his convictions about his relationship to God.

Motifs in Jesus' Teachings.   We can indicate here only the main lines of Jesus' thought. Most analysts find three foci: God as sovereign and father; the coming of the kingdom; and the will of God.

The presupposition at the center of his seeking is the overarching majesty and saving power of God, Who is at the same time the infinitely merciful Father. Here his thought is identical with the prophetic heritage and with contemporary Judaism. God created the world and men according to His will, and He is personally related to them. While God is remote,

He is at the same time near, holding in His hands the destiny of the world, His people, and each individual. His power, knowledge, and care rule with calm impartiality, sending rain on the just and the unjust and extending to the humblest creatures, even to the smallest detail. His patience, however, is not indifference. He is a terrible judge as well as creator and sustainer, and therefore is to be feared far more than those who kill the body. At the same time He is ready and eager to forgive those who are penitent. More than that, He is ready to seek out men as a shepherd searches for a lost sheep, or as a father meets an errant child.

The concrete focus of his trust in God is formed by his expectation of the coming kingdom and its moral import. The kingdom, of course, is already existent. God reigns perpetually above and the kingdom is now and always present; but this reality is about to be made visible on earth. "The time is fulfilled, and the kingdom of God is at hand; repent and believe in the gospel" (Mark 1:14). What the kingdom means, whether imminent or delayed, will be discussed further in Chapter 10. Here we need only to indicate that the kingdom's imminence involves a searching ethic, immediate, urgent, and uncompromising in its demand for perfection. Primary stress is laid on repentance and trust, rather than on ritual and sacrifice; on inward disposition rather than on outward acts. Above all, the primary requirement of God and the end of the Law is a personal relationship between man and God, a relationship of thoroughgoing integrity and unlimited generosity, which is nothing less than a demand for the human limitation of God. The logical culmination of Jesus' entire teaching is summed up in the Sermon on the Mount: "You, therefore, must be perfect, as your heavenly father is perfect" (Matthew 5:48; cf. Leviticus 11:45b).

This staggering demand is, of course, bound up with Jesus' vivid sense of the impending end of the present aeon, and men ever since have been reflecting on its content and relevance to the practical world of affairs. Albert Schweitzer's answer is well known: it is an "interim ethic" applicable only to the brief interval until the kingdom comes. Others regard it as defining the quality of life *in* the kingdom; and in another connection there is Reinhold Niebuhr's oft-quoted "impossible possibility."[16] The main point of such an ethic in its New Testament context probably lies in its vivid imperatives which are relevant for every age, not because they can be fulfilled, but because all of the standards by which history, society, and men are judged are set not by what is customary in each age, but by the perfection of God which confronts men at all times.

JESUS AS SUFFERING MESSIAH. Scholarly opinion on the question of what is called Jesus' "messianic consciousness," whether or not Jesus accepted for himself in some form the role of messiah, is widely divided. It is certain that the Christian community was thoroughly convinced that he *was* the Messiah, especially after the resurrection, but the gospel tradition probably is the reflection and interpretation of the post-Easter Church. Did he think of himself not only as announcing the crisis in history but as being himself a factor in that crisis? That he might have come to regard himself as the Messiah is conceivable—such claims were not at all unusual in Palestine, both preceding and following him. It is significant, however, that he never clearly makes the claim for himself, nor directly acknowledges the title when bestowed upon him by others. His only response is to bind them to secrecy (cf. the "Messianic secret" in Mark 8:27–30).

However, if the term Messiah were taken in the general sense of "one appointed of God" to proclaim the nearness of the kingdom of God, then he may well have thought of himself as being related in some unique way to the coming crisis and judgment. In any case, he seemed convinced that he faced inescapable suffering and death at the hands of the ruling powers. Certainly he awakened such messianic expectations. The faith which is expressed by the two disciples at Emmaus: "we hoped that he was the one to redeem Israel" (Luke 24:21) seems to express accurately the conviction of the followers of Jesus before his death. But the traditional views of the messiah had no place for such humiliation. The concept of a suffering Messiah was to the Jews "a scandal," as Paul was later to say, although there are later and scattered talmudic references to a suffering forerunner to the Messiah (Sukkah 52a). But this idea developed later (second century c.e. and was not the figure of Messiah which was decisive for Judaism. The death of Jesus conformed to no previous pattern, and certainly was not understood by his immediate followers, who are pictured as trying to dissuade him from "going up to Jerusalem" to meet his fate. Perhaps he hoped that his suffering and death would be vindicated by the inaugural of the new age. He certainly did not think of himself as a messiah in the Davidic, Maccabean warrior-king pattern, but as a suffering servant and son of man, and thus his death would be a call to his disciples likewise to prepare for martyrdom.

In any case, this death has always been the object of special attention, and it has a place of special significance. This significance of the symbol of the cross as the center of memory and faith, symbolizes the fact that it was in connection with his death that the whole concrete meaning of Jesus' life as a human being comes clear.

THE RESURRECTION.   While the form critics assure us that the passion narrative is among the earliest of the oral traditions and, being at the heart of the earliest Christian witness, is the focal point of attention in New Testament literature, the synoptic records of Jesus' trial and death are nonetheless filled with difficulties for historians. Yet there emerges clearly from the welter of detail the impression of a panic-stricken return of disillusioned, despondent disciples to their Galilean homes. Their great hope had been quenched. The enemies of their Master had proved the stronger, and the new age after all had not come. Then in familiar places in Galilee, on hillsides, by the lake where they lived and worked with Jesus and had learned from him, to one and then another of them, to individuals and groups, there came the conviction of his living presence. He was not just a memory but he "was known still." Indeed, there came upon these despairing folk a new sense of power which was actually greater than any had experienced while he was alive in the flesh. In this conviction the early Christian community had its beginning.

These people who had left Jerusalem in despair now reappeared as preachers of a new gospel. The primary affirmation was the familiar one of the declaration of the sovereignty and fatherhood of God, and yet this ancient tenet is set in a new perspective. The God of Abraham, Isaac, and Jacob is now in a special sense the God and father of Jesus, the Messiah. The God who had raised him from the dead had vindicated him before men. The traditional Hebrew monotheism has still its customary elevation and force, but in addition there is a new immediacy of contact with the contemporary scene.

No doubt the declaration that "God raised Jesus from the dead" is baffling to historians. Although it refers to an event, it is not strictly speaking a historical report at all, but a statement of faith and proclamation. No one had seen Jesus being raised. However, historians can deal with the occurrences or visible signs through which Jesus' followers came to believe that he was risen. The evidence is of two sorts: the appearance of Jesus to his disciples in Jerusalem and Galilee, and the tradition of the empty tomb. The earliest evidence of the fact of the resurrection is, however, that of Paul, in which he cites the evidence that he had received:

> For I deliver it to you as the first importance what I also received, that Christ died for our sins in accordance with the scriptures, and that he was buried, and that he was raised on the third day in accordance with scriptures, and that he appeared to Cephas and then to the twelve. Then he appeared to more than five hundred brethren at one time, . . . Then he appeared to James, then to John, then to all the apostles. Last of all, as to one untimely born, he appeared also to me (I Corinthians 15:3–8).

He was known to have been raised from the dead because he was known as living. One must consider this statement in its Hebraic context, for the resurrection must be understood in the light of the messianic interpretation of history. In the first century of the common era the belief in the resurrection of the dead was inseparably related to the messianic hope for the future; Jewish messianic expectations, particularly of the apocalyptic type, pointed to the consummation of history when God would establish His rule over the whole of creation. Then it was believed that God would raise up the dead, so that all preceding generations, as well as those present and living, would witness God's final triumph in the historical drama. This belief was elaborated during the intertestamental period and, as we have noted before, was championed by the Pharisees during Jesus' day. The resurrection therefore does not so much deal with the problem of the afterlife, nor does it imply an escape from history. Quite the contrary, the emphasis is upon this world and is associated with the conviction that God's kingdom would come, at which time His will would be done on earth. The resurrection, according to this way of thought, occurs at the final end or goal of history, so that the resurrection is an expression of God's triumph in history.

The primitive Christian community then was not just a memorial society, and the resurrection is not to be thought of as mere belief which arose as a result of a projection of hopes. It is true that it is not an objective event capable of being seen by everyone. Jesus appeared only to his followers, and it was only in faith that men beheld the miracle of the resurrection. The truth of the resurrection lies not in the field of factual inquiry but in the field of historical interpretation and as an answer to the question: Was Jesus truly God's Messiah? In this context the resurrection is a genuine occurrence and a supremely momentous event. It is a part of and belongs to the event itself—the Christ event.

The Nature of Christ

Christian theology or the interpretation of the Christ event, properly speaking, begins after Jesus' death. It begins not as a system of thought but rather as a spontaneous, enthusiastic, and irrepressible proclamation on the part of his followers. Their primary affirmation, as we have seen, arose from the conviction that the content of traditional monotheism was to be seen now with special force as the God of Jesus, and the pages of the New Testament reveal a gradually developing doctrine of the nature of Jesus as Messiah. This thought does not advance in a straight line but moves out simultaneously in all directions.

But both the faith and the interpretation of the first generation of Christians faced a serious problem: the death of Jesus on the cross. The idea of a suffering and dying Messiah was difficult enough, but worse still was the fact that his death had been the most shameful and humiliating known to the ancient world. It was not only that Rome reserved this form of public execution for the most depraved criminals but that it did the greatest violence to human dignity. The naked victim, hung up to die of slow exhaustion with no concealment of his agony, no protection from the stares and jeers of the mob, became a grotesque and obscene figure. This was the death to which Jesus was subjected. How could one who suffered so ignominiously be the Messiah? It was not only his death itself but the manner of his death that made it even more an obstacle to faith and the central theological problem confronting the early Church.

It was the faith of his followers that God Himself had supplied the answer. By raising Jesus from the dead (resurrection), by his continuing presence in the community, by receiving him in the heavens (ascension), God had put the unmistakable stamp of approval upon his life and message, thus showing him to be God's "anointed." Thus, what was once a scandal became the center of the Christ event, the focus of their memory and interpretation, and the symbol of the whole meaning of the event. They became convinced that, in Paul's words, "God was in Christ reconciling the world to himself" (II Corinthians 5:19) and, moreover, "God shows his love for us, while we were yet sinners Christ died for us" (Romans 5:8). These two sentences typify New Testament Christological thought.

Since its thought grew out of its experience within the Jewish matrix with its Tanakh, apocalyptic writings, and rabbinical sayings, the members of the early Christian community already had a pattern of received ideas, thoughts, prayers, and religious vocabulary. It is not therefore surprising that this tradition formed early Christian thought, especially since they had not themselves any self-sufficient metaphysical system divorced from this historic matrix. Christological development is, of course, conceptual development, and they needed categories to describe this Christ of their experience. This Christ was the historical Jesus of Nazareth, was the exalted Messiah or Lord, and was foreshadowed in the Old Testament. This conviction was applied like a magnet to the Hebraic text for passage after passage which would yield meaning for the Christ event.

MESSIANIC TITLES.   But the role of Jesus could not be contained in ordinary categories. Unhesitatingly, his followers attributed to him a medley of titles. He was prophet, teacher, son of David, Son of Man, Son of God, Lord and Savior, Word, Logos, Suffering Servant, High Priest, all of which were within the Hebrew compass. A dozen different interpretations are distinguishable and, therefore, the Christologies are many. But how can Jesus be "Prince of the House of David" and the "Son of Man" of Ezekiel's lowly prophet, and at the same time the supernatural "Son of Man" of Daniel or the Similitudes of Enoch riding on the clouds? At first, these seeming contradictions mattered little. The numerous titles and expressions simply are indicative of the sweeping rushes of thought trying to articulate the deep conviction and devotion, but not making for distinctions or clear ideas. All these titles represent his followers' endeavor to interpret Christ in terms that had meaning and associations with themselves and their contemporaries. They were all necessary in order to convey their own sense of Christ's significance.

Believing themselves to be living in the Messianic Age, the fulfillment of Israel's national hopes and expectations, they viewed the Christ event as of one piece with Israel's past, and Christ's vocation is pictured in categories which were previously only applied to the people of Israel. Jesus is thus the second Adam and his birth inaugurates a new era, a new creation. He is the new Moses, the new gospel, the new Law. He is "the Christian rabbi." As the Exodus delivered Israel from bondage, Jesus' death is the "new Exodus," delivering from the bondage of sin and death. At his birth, he and his parents flee from Herod, as Moses had to flee from Pharoah, and then return, for "out of Egypt have I called my son" (Hosea 11:1). He is the "Son of David," the Messiah inaugurating the kingdom. He is "Son of Man," the "elect one" and the "suffering servant" of deutero-Isaiah, which referred only to the elect and suffering people. The Church is the "new creation" and the "new Israel" which had undergone the "new Exodus." In brief, Jesus is sort of a "one-man Israel" who recapitulates the whole history of Israel. Thus they interpreted the Old Testament typologically (see Chapter 3).[17]

This was all very well for the Jewish context, but as the apostles turned toward the gentile world a different kind of interpretation was required. To such congregations it appeared more meaningful to say that "*Jesus was Lord*" (Greek: *kyrios*) and the confession "Jesus Christ is Lord" (Philippians 2:11) is the simple proclamation. To a world accustomed to the language of mystery religions, however, this would mean that Jesus was the lord of their cult offering assurance against the powers of death. The people of the Mediterranean world knew many such cult deities, and one more would not raise apprehensions. But the Christian use of the term *kyrios* came out of Jewish tradition and had almost always been a translation of the tetragrammaton, YHWH. In the Septuagint the term *kyrios* was a translation of "Adonai"—Lord—which referred only to YHWH.[18]

Another title came into use about the same time and under similar circumstances: *Son of God*. Like the familiar messianic name, Son of Man, this title could also be understood in two quite different ways. Son of Man could mean, generically, any human being or, specifically, the celestial messianic figure of the books of Daniel and of Enoch. Likewise, the phrase Son of God could mean, generically, a faithful Israelite or an angelic being. But, as it is used in the New Testament, it means, first of all and uniquely Jesus Christ and then Christian believers who, through him, are enabled to become sons of the Most High—"sons of God" (cf. Romans 8:14). As applied to Jesus, the title left room for diverse conceptions. It is with the use of these two titles that we begin to see the rise of a problem which is to occupy a Christian discussion for the next four hundred years.

But there was also a fourth view which held that he was the Son of God even before the beginning of his earthly life. This doctrine of preexistence used as its medium the concept of Wisdom in the book of Proverbs and in various later Jewish works, particularly the writings of Philo, and affirmed that Jesus Christ was the Wisdom of God who had been present at the creation of the world. But there is no indication of a fixed terminology at these early stages. Even after the title Logos, or Word, came to be the preferred mode of expression, the early Christians continued to use words like Wisdom and Word.

Whether or not the early Christians affirmed that Jesus Christ is God is probably unknowable. Certainly by the second century this affirmation comes to be explicit. In any case, at this point the Jewish Christians are faced with a difficulty of reconciling traditional monotheism with the increasingly high Christological affirmations being made about Jesus. As we shall see, this central theological problem received no solution until the middle of the fifth century.

We have been able only to hint at the considerable variety of modes of thinking in the New Testament about the person of Christ. The variety is even greater beyond the reach of the New Testament. This variety is significant, for it shows that no category was felt to fit exactly, and all of them together failed to exhaust their sense of his full significance. Paul's effort to be "all things to all men" apparently exemplifies the way the early Christians were prepared to use concepts of wisdom, of logos, of substance, and of anything else as pedagogical points of contact with people of diverse backgrounds. They combine Jewish monotheism, the traditions of the historical Jesus, and Hellenistic philosophy, apparently with no thought of the logical problems involved in such combinations. Their thought runs primarily in personal and in religious terms which enabled them to think of God and Christ as real and distinct, yet somehow uniquely related.

Christology was not precisely formulated, therefore, in the first century. Such primitive formulations as there were are in forms of letters and early efforts, for example in Hebrews and Romans. In its beginnings Christian doctrine simply developed out of direct living experience; the doctrinal attempts were attempts to overcome difficulties of language and explain the nature of the new experience through missionary apologetics. They were not a system of theological speculation.

It would help us, however, to see that every statement about Christ in the New Testament is the attempt to say something about God. Here God revealed His own nature through the person of Christ: that is the theme of every New Testament writer. How could the glorious Son of God who dwelt at the Creator's side in eternal glory have been a village carpenter who ultimately came to a convict's end? To this they recited the simple story of the passion as sufficient apologetic which needed no elaboration or rhetorical skill. Or, the question was put another way: How could a Galilean have become the ascended Messiah? How could the Son of God have been a carpenter, suffering the death penalty between two robbers? These questions had a simple appeal. One answer was simply to identify Jesus with the suffering servant of Isaiah 53. To Paul, approaching from another angle, the answer was that Jesus

. . . who, though he was in the form of God, did not count equality with God a thing to be grasped, but emptied himself, taking the form of a servant, being born in the likeness of men. And being found in human form he humbled himself and became obedient unto death, even death on a cross. Therefore God has highly exalted him and bestowed on him the name which is above every name, that at the name of Jesus every knee should bow, in heaven and on earth and under the earth . . . (Philippians 2:6–10).

The ancient world knew many gods, demigods and human beings who wanted to be equal with God. The novelty about the early Christian view of the Incarnation is that it tells of one who is equal with God yet had not considered it anything to boast about. Rather he turned aside from the divine prerogative and did not shrink, even from public execution. This is the manifestation of God's character and love—and power. He showed power and weakness, majesty and humility. His power was revealed in the weak things of the world (I Corinthians 1:27).

To put this in more technical language, the New Testament writers have a functional theology. They think concretely and write their narrative in which the significance of the person is seen in what he does. They are rarely concerned with abstract, philosophical questions. Their main concern is in what Christ is for man, what role he fulfills in the history of salvation. They were not concerned with the question of what he was in his inmost being (that is, in metaphysics or ontology).

EARLY CHRISTOLOGICAL DEVELOPMENT.   In the first centuries after the New Testament there are no striking new developments of Christological opinion. The major lines have been set by Pauline and Johannine thought, which had developed rather naturally from the wisdom literature of Judaism. But the lines of Judaism and Christianity began to diverge. Jewish messianic thought tended to place more emphasis upon the character of the messianic age that was to come, and less upon the character of the messiah. Christian thought tended to place more and more emphasis on the person of Christ. Although variously stated, Christianity made a seemingly paradoxical assertion: Jesus was in every sense a real human being, a historical individual, and he was at the same time the eternal son of God. Man was in Christ—man as God intended him to be; and God was in Christ restoring His lost creation. Christianity rested upon both claims. Jesus was the true son of Israel whose parentage was known by his contemporaries (John 7:27), and he was a man of unique significance to be understood only by tracing his line to Adam, the creation of God.

This affirmation distinguished Christianity both from Judaism and from the competing cults of "lords many and gods many" already abounding in the Mediterranean world. It was its conflict with paganism, much more than with Judaism, that forced the Church to formulate its doctrine of the God-Man which so sharply distinguished it from the savior gods and "divine men" of purely discarnate deities. The distinctive and unique contribution of Christianity is inseparably bound up with incarnation, the actual appearance of God on earth.

CHRISTOLOGY IN THE PATRISTIC AGE[19]   From the second century on, Christianity moved more and more from the Semitic world of Palestine to the Hellenistic world of both Jew and Greek. There was a natural shift in what Christians thought about and the way they expressed themselves. The Hellenistic mind raised questions not adequately answered in the experiential, functional language of the biblical ethos. They ask not only, "What is Christ for us?" but "Who and what is he in himself?" "Is he God, creature, or both?" "If both, how do we conceive of the relationship of the divine and human? Are they identical, distinct, or both? If both, explain that." This period is the era in which the Church groped for appropriate conceptual and linguistic tools to explain what they conceived to be essentially mystery.

Such questions and much of the discussion sound remote and abstract— even "nit-picking"—and not exactly gripping or even graspable to the modern religious imagination. It is only fair to see that this could not be avoided in a profoundly theological age. Moreover, the discussions were inspired by a very practical import: the salvation of man. They were based upon an analysis of man's plight and how he could be rescued from the absurdities of human existence. Consequently the context of the onto-logical (What is he in himself?) question was always functional (salva-tional). What is the message of redemption? These were questions of cosmic significance which called for right answers.

THE CULTURAL CONTEXT.   Not only do the questions seem remote, but the atmosphere is strange to a nontheological age. Religious questions were burning questions felt by every part of the society, low and high, poor and uneducated, scholars and rulers. In the Byzantine particularly, religion entered every aspect of life. Holidays were religious festivals; circuses began with the singing of hymns. Trade contracts invoked the Trinity and were marked with the sign of the cross. Gregory of Nyssa describes the atmosphere in Constantinople at the time of the Second General Council (A.D. 381): "The whole city was full of it, the squares, the market places, the crossroads, the alley ways, old-clothes men, money changers, food sellers: they are all busy arguing. If you ask someone to give you change, he philosophizes about the Begotten and the Unbegotten; if you inquire about the price of a loaf, you are told by way of reply that the Father is greater and the Son inferior; if you ask 'Is my bath ready?' the attendant answers that the Son was made out of nothing."[20]

More seriously, the Church faced these questions under severe pressure which was not only doctrinal but also pastoral, political, and cultural. For an institution which had undergone persecution and martyrdom and through which apostasy was the major sin, heresy was not just an intellectual deviation but a frightening moral and religious spectre. The term "heresy" (*hairesis*, from the verb meaning "to choose") was not originally a derogatory word. It simply referred to sects or bodies or was used for those who followed particularly any strongly held opinion. A theological model tries to describe the antinomies of reality and hold them in tension. Heresies tend to choose one pole or the other and therefore are attempts to solve the paradox and relieve the tension. Therefore, too many opinions, each firmly held, produces sectarianism and divisions. Thus, heretics always contribute greatly to the theological process by the pressure which they bring, and some of the noblest thinkers at some time or another in history have been declared heretics. If their ideas were valid they sooner or later entered into the mainstream of western thought. Therefore, to us today it is not a particularly frightening word. It is not even a possibility in the twentieth century, when men no longer believe that there can be a final and complete theology and the Church does not have the power to enforce its dogma.

To a religious community, however, living in an alien world, the menace of internal conflict and the oppression of hostile opinion tend to force precise formulation of the convictions and attitudes firmly and deeply held. Moreover, schism was to them the wounding of the body of Christ. They therefore were acutely aware of the meaning of orthodoxy—right Christian doctrine—as against heterodoxy, which was any doctrine alien to Christianity. They did not live in an ivory tower, nor were their actions against their opponents exactly saintly. The burning concern they had for rightness of teaching accounts for the vehement, even violent tone of the polemics of the time, for political machinations and force which was employed in the defense of faith. In an age where theological heresy was tantamount to political conspiracy in our day, it is not surprising that their passionate dedications to Christian truth led, sometimes, to monks emerging from their cloisters and lay people from their homes to take up cudgels in the struggle for one dogmatic position or another.

Furthermore, the Age of Constantine (A.D. 312) ushered in an age of imperial expansion of the Church in which Christianity, instead of being persecuted, became fashionable. Many were baptized as a mark of respectability. Consequently, the Church was crowded with the half-converted, the socially ambitious and the ill-instructed. It was therefore natural that pagan ideas penetrated the Christian presence. In the half-century after the Council of Nicea (A.D. 325) the whole world took sides. The Church was rent asunder. There were court scandals, political intrigues, adulation of the emperor, and many, many other degrading features appeared before orthodoxy was finally established.

THE INCARNATION: TWO NATURES.   From the beginning, the Christian problem was to maintain that Christ was God-man, truly God and truly human. It is not difficult to maintain one or the other, but to hold both integrally and together—that is the problem. This problem had come to sharp focus in a controversy which led to the First Ecumenical Council at Nicea in 325. Arius, a priest of Alexandria, affirmed that the Logos (Word) is a created being, therefore essentially other than God. The Council approved a creed which affirmed the full deity of the Son and his sharing of one essential being (*homoousia*) with the Father. This formula had to be reaffirmed at the Second General Council of Constantinople in 381. The solution succeeded only in posing another problem: the humanity of Jesus. Having asserted strongly his deity, there appeared the powerful tendency to declare that being wholly God, he was man, if at all, only in some partial sense.

Two answers are logically possible and, historically, these two answers took the form of two Christologies which were represented by the rival schools of Alexandria and Antioch (see Chapter 3). Each represents both positive contributions and polar extremes (heresies) which were issues at the first three ecumenical councils and finally came to a head at the Fourth Ecumenical Council at Chalcedon in A.D. 451. The ensuing arguments are complex, involving disputes about natures, wills, bodies, souls, realities and appearances—issues which were debated from the second century but discussion of which would take us too far afield for our present purposes. In brief, the Alexandrians (word-flesh) emphasized the divinity of Christ and tended to minimize his humanity. The Antiochenes (word-man) stressed the reality of Christ's human nature and so intended to de-emphasize the divine nature. The characteristic formula of the Alexandrians was "the Word became flesh" (John 1:14), while for the Antiochenes it was "man assumed" by the Word. This latter formulation has had the greatest influence in the west.

In any case, the insights of Alexandria and Antioch were incorporated in the Chalcedonian formula in 451:[21]

We, then, following the holy Fathers, all with one accord teach men to acknowledge one and the same Son, our Lord Jesus Christ, at once complete in Godhead and complete in manhood, truly God and truly man, of a reasonable soul and body; consubstantial (*homoousia*) with the Father according to the Godhead, and consubstantial with us according to the manhood, in all respects like us, apart from sin; begotten of the Father before the ages according to the Godhead, but yet according to the manhood born in these latter days of the Virgin Mary, the Mother of God (*Theotokos*), for us and for our salvation; one and the same Christ, Son, Lord, Only-begotten, in two natures without confusion, unchangeably, indivisibly, inseparately, the distinction of natures being in no way annulled by the union, but rather the characteristics of each nature being preserved, and coming together to form one person (*prosopon*) and on subsistence (*hypostasis*), not parted or divided into two persons, but one and the same Son and Only-begotten, God the Word, the Lord Jesus Christ; as the prophets from the earliest times spoke of him, and the Lord Jesus Christ himself taught us, and the creed of the holy Fathers has handed down to us.

This definition established the western view as normative. In the man, Jesus Christ, the fathers asserted, is the incarnation of God. Unhappily, the controversy dragged on for two centuries more in the East, but the Chalcedonian formula finally prevailed and remains to this day the touchstone of Christological thought. The medieval thinkers developed their thought from this definition. The Protestant reformers, being more interested in the functional questions, simply accepted the patristic formulas as the basis for their thought.

Exceptions to the normative views are represented in the varieties of "unitarian" thought current in the "left wing" of the Reformation in groups like the Anabaptists, spiritual reformers, Socinians in Poland, and in exceptional individuals such as the Spaniard, Miguel Servedo (Servetus). Servetus, a man of genuine mystical piety, wanted to recover a thoroughgoing monotheism with stress on the immanence of God which he felt had been lost in the dogmatic elaborations from Nicea onward. The Word was a divine emanation, present in Adam, in the theophanies of the Old Testament, and in Jesus Christ as the son of the Eternal God, but he could not accept Christ as God incarnate.

The Socinians, organized into a well-established ecclesiastical community in Poland by their leader, Faustus Sozzini (Socinus), in a more rationalistic temper emphasized the transcendence of the Creator, and the moral responsibility and freedom of man. While Jesus Christ came as man's savior, he was in fact a marvellously endowed human being, not divine, fully in accord with the will, purpose, and action of God. "The Word became flesh" means not that a divine being takes on flesh, but that the revelation comes in one who is fully human, albeit with a God-given power that sets him above the ordinary range of human capacity. It is from this strain of thought that modern Unitarianism has been most strongly influenced.

Whether or not the insights of Chalcedon are valid principles is not to be decided here. Perhaps, one can say that the solutions adopted then were probably the right answers to the questions then being asked. Even in the patristic era the answers were understood to be preliminary and were stated primarily in negative terms. As Athanasius said of the Nicene Creed, these definitions are "signposts against all heresies." And Karl Rahner, the distinguished Roman Catholic theologian, who is exercising great influence on modern thought, has said often that "Chalcedon is both end and beginning." That is true not necessarily because the formula is to be regarded as final or complete, but because it provides the data or the postulates from which any Christology must proceed. This is a considerable accomplishment in and of itself.

Whitehead, whose metaphysics is the basis for many contemporary theological formulations, has said of the schools of Alexandria and Antioch: "The originality and value of their contribution to the thought of the modern world has been greatly underestimated." That is partly their own fault, he observes, because they insisted that they were "only stating the faith once delivered to the saints," when really what they were doing, he thinks, was "groping after the solution of a fundamental metaphysical problem." He then adds, "These Christian theologians have the distinction of being the only thinkers who in a fundamental metaphysical doctrine have improved upon Plato."[22] We need not accept this assessment as valid in every respect, but we do need to see that successive ages have the responsibility to think out the meaning of these events in their own terms.

For our time other modes of reflection than the ones employed by the church fathers are doubtlessly required, modes of thought which will employ distinctively modern contributions to human thought. Instead of concepts of substance, person, and nature, there may be models from history and faith which will be more useful. Rather than "two natures" it may be more to the point to talk about "two histories," to use H. Richard Niebuhr's terms, where Jesus Christ is seen as the point at which "outer" history has come together with "inner" history.[23] In any case, there is little doubt that modern thought requires a shift in the terms with which this question can be discussed.

SOTERIOLOGY

Recognition that the relationship between God and man has been impaired, and that man stands in radical need of the proper means of restoring that relationship, is an integral aspect of western man's religious consciousness and a major goal of his religious striving. Understanding the ways and means of reconciliation and atonement has varied in different periods, but neither Judaism nor Christianity has ever adopted one theory of salvation or atonement. That God is in covenant with His people and that His people have violated that covenant and must somehow atone is deeply embedded in Jewish history. That God became incarnate in Jesus Christ for the sake of man's salvation is an intellectual formulation of the experience of forgiveness and reconciliation which Christians affirm. In the evolution of their thought many theories have been held, sometimes simultaneously in the thought of one man, but always in the terms of the particular world view at any given time.

Particular terms are used in reference to the understanding of God's character and purposes and to the diagnosis of man's flaws, defects, or plight as these are seen in contrast to the perfection (holiness) of God understood either as the ground or as the goal of existence. The technical term for this idea is *soteriology* (from the Greek *soter*, savior, *sozein*, to save, and *logos*, discourse). A discussion of soteriology would include such ideas as sin, the means of grace, and man's final destiny. Traditionally certain nearly synonymous terms have been used soteriologically in the Scriptures and theological writings of Jews and Christians. *Redemption* is a financial term which refers to the act of paying for the restoration of property stolen. It is the redemption of bond or of a note. Thus God redresses, ransoms, delivers Israel out of bondage; or Christ pays the price which restores men to freedom and new life. *Atonement* (at-one-ment) is a psychological term meaning the restoration of a relationship, the overcoming of separation, or the reconciliation of alienation. *Salvation* (*salus*) is a medical term meaning health or healing. A physician tries to restore health, sin is sickness, salvation is healing; lostness is to be found, to recover identity or to be restored wholly. *Justification* is a legal term meaning to make expiation for or to propitiate a wrong. All of these concepts have historical grounding in both the Jewish and the Christian traditions.

In Judaism: Atonement

To many readers these words will have a Christian "feeling tone," but at the outset it is important to realize that every one of them belongs to the vocabulary of Judaism. The crucial event of deliverance is, of course, the Exodus and the establishment of the covenant relationship. Israel is rescued from bondage, freed for the Promised Land, the people a new creation. The Exodus is a focal point of Hebrew history because it is the clue to the meaning of Jewish existence. The Law is both the terms of the

Covenant and the means for keeping it. By obedience to the Law YHWH restores man to a new relationship celebrated and symbolized in the Passover.

A second figure is the Day of Atonement (Yom Kippur). The word originally meant to cover or to remove or to wash away the guilt. It is a ritual purgation whereby expiation takes place, resulting in purification and reconciliation. Expiation takes place by the letting of blood, and by the shedding of blood one atones for and thus achieves forgiveness. The chief symbol for this is the *sacrifice*. Wherever the nature of blood is sacrosanct it is because it is the vehicle of life and covenantal in character. The shedding of blood restores the blood bonds of fellowship with God (Leviticus 16).

A third and very important idea of atonement is found in vicarious atonement or suffering. In a marvelous story in Exodus, Moses pleads with YHWH to pardon his people's sins even if it meant the erasing of his name from the Book of Life (Exodus 32:10). After this pleading God reveals Himself in a renewal of a covenant ceremony (Exodus 34:6–7) and reveals Himself in His thirteen attributes of mercy which form the basis of grace. In the Prophets the sacrificial ritual is based on ethical foundations, and atonement means spiritual regeneration and true penitence (Psalm 51). But by all means the Hebraic concept reached its zenith in deutero-Isaiah (Isaiah 53) in the idea of righteous suffering for the world. The ideal Israel bears the penalty of sinful nations and atones for them. This "Servant of the Lord," poetically described by the prophet, is without doubt the personification of Israel, or at least the faithful remnant in Israel. This is the Israel which suffers, waiting and hoping for the salvation of the Lord. Whether or not the suffering servant is an individual will probably always be a moot question. The personification is, of course, carried to a high pitch of intensity and if the prophet had in mind some individual, he saw him as the representative of man or the "corporate personality."[24] In any case, the rabbis saw Israel's historical destiny as suffering predicted here, and this remains the pervading interpretation of the majority of Jewish exegetes (e.g., Rashi). The point is that suffering has an atoning power, especially the death and suffering of the righteous on behalf of other people.

This idea of vicarious suffering develops into a kind of theology of martyrdom is illustrated vividly in IV Maccabees, which dates either from the late first century B.C.E. or the first century C.E. This idea forms a basis for Paul's theory of atonement through the death of Jesus.[25] It refers to the effectiveness of the death of the Maccabean martyrs at the time of the persecution of the Jewish people by the Greco-Syrian ruler Antiochus Epiphanes. These martyrs preferred death at the hands of a tyrant to apostasy from Judaism and allegiance to YHWH. Antiochus Epiphanes proposed to eradicate Judaism and replace it with the Hellenistic cult of the worship of Zeus-Uranus. The Maccabean books are the narratives of the fidelity of the Jews of this period to their religious faith and practice at the cost of their lives. The death of the martyrs broke the power of the tyrant over the minds and hearts and wills of the Jewish people. IV Maccabees uses this language:

These, therefore, having been sanctified for God's sake, were honored not only with this honor, but also in that for their sake the enemies did not have power over the nation, and the tyrant was punished, and the fatherland purified, they having become, as it were, a substitute, dying for the sake of the nation; and through the blood of these godly men and their propitiatory death, divine Providence saved Israel, which was before in an ill plight (17:20-22).

The martyrs through their death deliver Israel, their suffering and death a vicarious atonement for the sins of their people. As God raised up Moses and delivered the people from Egypt, so God raised up the martyrs and delivered the people from tyranny and apostasy. This theology of martyrdom has two leading ideas: the contribution made by a minority of persons to the providential preservation of the Chosen People, and especially the atoning and redemptive value of the innocent sufferings of the just.

This concept further stresses the sense of the corporateness of the people and hence of their salvation and atonement. This corporate sense is deeply embedded in Judaism, which is not an individualistic religion in the "atomic" sense which characterizes much of our modern world. The people were, so to speak, an organic group responsible to God as a total society. God dealt with the people not only as individuals but as a nation. Therefore, the faithful Jew understood that as an individual he was an integral part of a people the whole direction of which might be against or for the will of God. It is as members of the human race, in this case as members of the Jewish people, that the martyrs take upon themselves this corporate identity and thus atone for humanity.

These basic themes continued and were refined during the rabbinic period although the destruction of the temple in 70 C.E. produced radical changes in their expression. Two illustrations will be sufficient for our purpose. Suffering as a means of expiation preparatory to the advent of the Messiah achieved prominence and was regarded as a more effective means of atonement than ritual sacrifice. Moreover the act of expiation was associated with a suffering Messiah. The Talmud often refers to the sufferings of the Messiah as for example in the following reference: "The Messiah as it is written, 'and the Spirit of the Lord shall rest upon him, the spirit of wisdom and understanding . . . and shall make him of quick understanding in the fear of the Lord.'" Rabbi Alexander said: "This teaches that he loaded him with good deeds and suffering as a mill" (b. Sanhedrin 93b). In the same literature the Messiah is described as sitting at the gates of Rome attending to the wounds of lepers. Again he is called the "leper scholar." And in a talmudic passage which comes out of the first half of the second century, the King Messiah is directly identified with the suffering servant of deutero-Isaiah.

Second, the fall of the temple brought about the cessation of ritual and animal sacrifice altogether, and Jews to their great consternation and dismay were forced to find effective substitutes. The import of this is illustrated in a story of a rabbi and his disciple going out of Jerusalem one day. At the sight of the temple in ruins the disciple exclaimed, 'Woe to us, for the place where the iniquities of Israel were atoned for is destroyed!" The rabbi replied, "Do not grieve, my son, for we have an atonement which is just as good, deeds of mercy, as the Scripture says, 'For I desire mercy and not sacrifice.' " (Hosea 6:6).[26] This story exemplifies a return to the prophetic teachings for an understanding of the relative merits of ritual sacrifice and moral regeneration as means of atonement, a theme which dominates the history of Judaism. In addition, Torah, prayer, and fasting assumed atoning power because they lead men to repentance and the confession of their sins. These ideas continue to form the bases of Jewish understanding.

The Cross: The Pivotal Point of Christian History

This analysis of Hebraic-Jewish context sheds considerable light upon the New Testament interpretation of the relation of atonement to Jesus' death on the cross. There is a commonly held theory that all of the Christian sacrificial rites and understanding of redemption are wholly Hellenistic in origin and cannot be understood apart from the influence of mystery cults of the Roman Empire. In view of the complexity of developments in the first centuries of the common era there is doubtless a modicum of truth in the theory. However, recent scholarly discoveries have pointed up the difference in climate between the mystical pantheistic world of the mystery cults and the ethical and legal outlook of Judaism and Christianity, and have revealed how thoroughly the method and thought of the new Testament writers were influenced both by their Old Testament background and contemporary practices in Judaism. These influences provided at least the beginning point of their thought on the work of Christ (the second question in Christology: What did he do?).

The dark shadow of the crucifixion required for Christians a re-evaluation of Jesus' life and messiahship. Not only was such an appalling form of death an embarrassment hard for them to overcome, but it seemingly wrecked any association with the contemporary messianic hopes. Vindicated however by the resurrection, their understanding was transformed to the point that the cross became not a mere disgraceful accident, but the crucial point of the Christ Event. Jesus was "delivered up according to the definite plan in the foreknowledge of God" (Acts 2:23).

In interpreting this event the New Testament writers—and this is especially true of Paul and the writer of the Epistle to the Hebrews—at first find their clues in biblical and contemporary Jewish thought patterns, especially in ideas like the suffering Messiah, sacrifice, and the atoning power of blood, in the efficacy of the obedience and death of one man for the benefit of all. To be sure, these views were to be transmuted and transformed almost beyond recognition to their Jewish contemporaries, but the figures were to be found on biblical soil.

Paul's Theology of Reconciliation

We will confine our analysis to Paul. There are difficulties in that procedure because it is difficult to systematize Paul's thought. He is never a painstaking or systematic thinker, and his thought moves in powerful, sweeping rushes that cut through customary patterns of religious thought. Moreover, we know his thought only through some of his letters, which are genuine pieces of personal correspondence, probably never intended to be read publicly. Yet his principles are so radical and massive that most later systems of Christian thought are simply commentary and fresh elaboration of his understandings.

MAN'S SITUATION. To appreciate fully his theology of reconciliation we should begin with an analysis of "man's sinful plight," but our exposition of the nature of man in Chapter 8 will serve to provide the base for our present discussion. It can be characterized here in one sentence as an extreme statement of the rabbinic conception of the two opposing tendencies in man: the *yetzer ha-ra'* and *yetzer tov* (see Romans 7). To Paul's mind this tragic plight is universal. Moreover, the present age is beset by powers of darkness—unseen hosts of "principalities, powers, world rulers of this darkness" which prod man from all sides. Like man, the "whole creation groans and travails" in desperate hope (Romans 8). The holy God stands in radical opposition to what man and creation have become, and His wrath and Law must be satisfied. Yet it is this very God Who in mercy opens a new way of life by and through the crucified Messiah. Paul devotes little attention to speculative problems of Christology and is prepared to use many images, but there is little doubt that he regards Christ as the Son of God who has come in life and death from a preexisting personal life with God (Philippians 2:6–11). Rather he rivets his attention on the sacrifice of the cross, the obedient servant, and the suffering Messiah.

SACRIFICE.   Much of Paul's understanding of sacrifice is spelled out with reference to the Last Supper or the Eucharist. The Jewish festivals, particularly the Passover and the Day of Atonement, fascinate him (see Romans 3 and 6). "Christ our Passover is sacrificed for us," he writes, and the meaning of the festival is applied to the work of Christ. For Paul, Christ is the perfect sacrifice and his blood efficacious for atonement. The new covenant is inaugurated by Christ's death: "To reconcile to himself all things . . . making peace by the blood of his cross" (Colossians 1:20). By this power men become new creatures through this new principle of action becoming dominant in their lives: "They are justified by his grace as a gift through the redemption which is in Christ Jesus whom God put forward as an expiation by his blood to be received by faith" (Romans 3:25). Thus the penalty is paid in a wholly new way.

OBEDIENCE.   The efficacy of obedience is stated explicitly in Romans 5:17–19:

If, because of one man's trespass, death reigned through that one man, much more will those who receive the abundance of grace and the free gift of righteousness reign in life through the one man Jesus Christ.
Then as one man's trespass led to condemnation for all men, so one man's act of righteousness leads to acquittal and life for all men. For as by one man's disobedience many were made sinners, so by one man's obedience many will be made righteous.

Paul's analogy is to the disobedience of the first man, Adam, which in his view has involved all mankind in sin. So the obedience of Christ, the second Adam, has the power to raise all men to righteousness. Says he, "While we were yet helpless, at the right time, Christ died for the ungodly" (Romans 5:6). If the solidarity of all men involves them in Adam's disobedience, this same solidarity makes it possible for the action of one man to be efficacious for the whole human community.

THE SUFFERING MESSIAH.   The idea that martyrdom is the supreme act of obedience is the theme of an oft-quoted passage in Philippians 2: ". . . in human form he humbled himself and became obedient unto death, even death on a cross (v. 8). Doubtless, Paul is here identifying Jesus, the Messiah, with the suffering servant of deutero-Isaiah (52:13–53:12). It is this identification of the suffering servant with the Son of Man figure in Daniel and Enoch widely associated with the messianic age, a figure oft attributed to Jesus by early Christians ("The Son of man must suffer" [Mark 8:31]), that is unique to Christian interpretation.

Hence, man himself is not only liberated from the power of sin as a new creature but the whole of mankind is given this status. Moreover it is God Himself who took the initiative and freely offers to man forgiveness and new life. "God commands his own love towards us in that, while we were yet sinners Christ died for us" (Romans 5:8). The result is that a new norm is established in Jesus Christ which provides a new spring of action. The risen Christ himself becomes the indwelling power by which believers now live. So to those who respond in faith and love there is an influx of energy that vitalizes and guides the believers' minds and wills. In fact, men become adopted sons of God. The consequence of a permanent transformation in their lives, as Paul put it, is that, "It is no longer I that lives, Christ liveth in me" (Galatians 2:20). That is the distinguishing mark of a community of Christian believers who have transformed lives and who are henceforth known as "the body of Christ." This applies not only to members of the Christian community, not only to the universality of men, but even to creation itself (Romans 8). The description of the whole creation being transformed fits the popular figure of the Messiah as "a man from heaven," a transcendent messenger in whose coming the whole world order would be transmuted, even nature itself would be changed. This implies the second advent of Christ, the *Christus victor* overcoming all of the powers that be.

Historical Views of the Atonement

All Christian literature from the New Testament onward is unanimous: God became incarnate in the person of Jesus Christ "for our salvation." Clement of Alexandria, writing at the end of the second century, said: "The word of God became man, in order that thou also mayest learn from men how man becomes God."

The cross is the pivotal point in Christian history. The meaning of the cross as Christians understand it is that the almighty God took upon himself man's nature and went to this extreme to reconcile man to affect his at-one-ment. It was reconciliation, achieved at great cost—redemption means agony and sweat, the cross, the passion, and death. In contrast to the standard of the love of God, man stands in a state of guilt, guilt meaning to be wrong by the standard of God's law of love. The cross is both the tragic and the transforming symbol that human existence is in such deadly enmity with God's righteousness that humanity crucifies the standard in the person of Jesus; so that man is definable as the crucifier of Christ and all men are enmeshed inextricably in this Christ-crucifying world.

Throughout history the Christian mind has struggled with systematic attempts to explain this phenomenon, but there has never been a consensus on any elaborate theory. In the history of Christian thought there have been five main ways of conceiving the atonement.

The first is *deification* (Greek *theosis*). This is a view held mainly by the eastern Church and given classic expression by Athanasius. "God became man that we might be made God." The Greek fathers read St. John literally —"The glory which thou hast given me I have given to them, that they may be one even as we are one, I in them and thou in me, that they may become perfectly one, so that the world may know that thou hast sent me" (John 17:22–23), and argued that if he is to be perfectly one with God this means, in effect, that man must be deified. He is called to become by grace what God is by nature.

Second, there is what Gustaf Aulen calls the *classical* view.[27] According to Aulen, the crucial idea is that God Himself is the chief actor in the drama. Man is enslaved by sin, death, and the devil, which are regarded in the ancient world view as objective power. God in Christ defeats these powers in a decisive battle so that they no longer have power over men. Here the graphic portrayal is that of *Christus Victor* or *Christus Regnans*— conqueror and king. His victory is achieved, his work accomplished, and men share in this victory and enjoy the fruits of his work. Redemption is deliverance from cosmic powers, forces of evil. In this way the ancient expressed his experience of direct, personal release. Aulen thinks this view is characteristic of Paul and Luther as well as the early Greek fathers.

The third view is the *ransom* theory, held variously by Origen, Irenaeus, and Luther, that the death of Christ was a ransom paid by God to the devil. This is sometimes very crude in expression. Christ, being divine, could not be conquered by death and so the deceiver was, by an act of poetic justice, deceived. The deity of Christ was veiled in his humanity, and in the infinite wisdom of God the devil received his due. Christ's flesh is the bait which lured the devil, his divinity is the net in which he was caught. The strangest form of this metaphor was found in Augustine, who likens the cross to a mousetrap baited with the blood of Christ! Nonetheless this is a theory which has held sway throughout the history of Christian thought. Its main theme is the costliness of redemption bought in Christ's death.

The fourth is known as the *satisfaction* theory given classical expression by Anselm's *Cur Deus Homo* (Why the God man?) and held by Calvin in the past and by Emil Brunner in our own day. Anselm repudiated the ransom theory as unworthy of God and tried to express a new theory in the thought forms of the Middle Ages, where God was thought of rather naturally as the supreme feudal overlord to whom all beings owed allegiance and honor. Man owed honor to God as a squire or serf might owe it, but by his sin he had so dishonored God that he was powerless to render satisfaction. According to the code of chivalry one could pay for an offense either by receiving the due punishment or by rendering "satisfaction," that is by restitution of the honor which had been outraged. Man is unable to render satisfaction to God, therefore, God in His infinite mercy sent His son, who assumes manhood and who as man rendered ample satisfaction by his innocent death. That is why God became man. The debt of honor was paid. This view won universal acceptance in the Middle Ages and became the basis upon which the theologians of the Reformation built. The reformers added the penal element. Christ is believed to have taken upon himself the punishment properly due man and to satisfy God's just demands.

The fifth theory is sometimes called the *"moral influence* theory" given expression by Abelard (1079–1142). Abelard held that the cross is the most appealing exhibition of God's love. The appeal of suffering love, of Jesus crucified by man's folly, pride, and sin, converts the sinner as no other appeal could do. So men are saved by the appeal of Christ's self-giving love, and they are freed from the fear of God's so that they can respond personally. Jesus brought home by his death what he could not succeed in doing by his teaching, that the greatest thing in life is self-giving love and that true greatness consists of the ability to become the servant of all. The cross, therefore, has become the most powerful moral influence in history, bringing men to repentance, which renders them able to be forgiven. Abelard's favorite New Testament text and the key to his understanding of the atonement is: "We love, because he first loved us" (I John 4:19).

The death of Jesus was and is so significant because it is the symbol of the meaning of his humanity. Many of these historical descriptions seem incredible today, perhaps even crude and elementary. But they must be seen as earnest attempts at interpretation in the thought forms of their times. Certainly there are other modes of reflection than the insights of Plato or Aristotle or Hegel and Heidegger. Perhaps new insights can come from twentieth-century understanding of cosmic and human evolution and its restatement of one of Judaism's and Christianity's central understandings, that the human person is a conscious and free subject. Or perhaps contemporary man may discover that true objectivity is in Kierkegaard's phrase, "inter-subjective subjectivity." In any case, every age will deal with the question in the terms which seem natural to it.[28]

Thus far we have discussed two aspects of Christianity's distinctive motif as it developed within and from its historical matrix in Judaism. We have seen both the essential Semitic substructure of Christian thought and the differences which developed in the genius of both traditions. It is important to stress that Judaism is not just the matrix from which Christianity emerged. We have two self-contained and self-justifying entities, each an authentic tradition in its own right and not just to be understood by using the other as a foil. Not only is Christianity to be seen as a new and original emergent from Judaism which understands itself to be in a direct line and continuous with the Old Testament, but we must also see that rabbinic Judaism represents a similar kind of emergent and has equal claim to continuity with the Tanakh.

Precisely where and when the turning point occurred is probably unknowable, but we have seen the shape of some of the issues—and the central issue between the two was the Christian evaluation of the historical Jesus as the Messiah who both had come and was to come. Within their Jewish matrix Christians affirmed that as YHWH had made a covenant with Israel on Sinai, He now makes a new covenant for the world on Golgotha. Judaism was and is unable to believe that its expected Messiah has already come in Jesus of Nazareth because the anticipated signs and promises related to the advent of the Messiah had not been fulfilled. As Reinhold Niebuhr puts it: "though expected, he proves not to be the kind of Messiah who was expected."[29] Furthermore, the Christian interpretation of Jesus as one of more than human significance created an impassable gulf between the two peoples which resulted in the development of separate histories and theological understandings of history.

By now we may be able to see what was fundamental both to first-century Judaism and to primitive Christianity, what the latter took for granted as true within that tradition, and what was new and distinctive in New Testament thought. In the next chapter we will discuss the third element in the Christ Event, the new community, and consider further Jewish estimates of that complex of events. We will discuss further the process of transition of the Church as the eschatological community (in its orientation) from its Jewish beginnings.

NOTES

1. Among many sources see especially Herman Strack, *Introduction to the Talmud and Midrash*, Philadelphia: Jewish Publication Society, 1931). W. D. Davies, *Christian Origins and Judaism* (London: Darton, Longman & Todd, 1962); *Paul and Rabbinical Judaism* (London: SPCK, 1962), and *The Sermon on the Mount* (Cambridge: Cambridge University Press, 1966); Leo Baeck, *The Pharisees and Other Essays* (New York: Schocken, 1966), and *Judaism and Christianity* (New York: World, and Philadelphia: Jewish Publishing Society, 1958, Meridian, 1961); Jean Daniélou, *The Dead Sea Scrolls and Primitive Christianity* (New York: New American Library, Mentor, Omega Edition, 1962). Joseph Klausner, *From Jesus to Paul*, trans. W. S. Stinespring (London: Allen and Unwin, 1946), Marcel Simon, *Jewish Sects at the Time of Jesus*, trans. James Farley (Philadelphia: Fortress, 1967); Samuel Sandmel, *A Jewish Understanding of the New Testament* (Cincinnati: Hebrew Union Press, 1957).

2. George Foot Moore, *Judaism* (Cambridge: Harvard University Press, 1958), I, 193.

3. W. D. Davies, *Paul and Rabbinical Judaism*, has revolutionized our understanding of Pauline thought by pointing out that Paul was grounded in essentially the rabbinic world of thought, a rabbi become Christian and primarily governed by Pharisaic concepts.

4. Sandmel, *A Jewish Understanding of the New Testament*, p. 28.

5. Abba Hillel Silver, *Messianic Speculation in Israel* (Boston: Beacon, 1959).

6. We are, of course, deeply indebted to Professor John Knox's schema as described in his *Jesus: Lord and Christ* (New York: Harper, 1958), p. 217.

7. See *ibid.*, pp. 66–67.

8. R. H. Lightfoot, *History and Interpretation in the Gospels* (London and New York: Harper, 1938).

9. Maurice Goguel, *The Life of Jesus*, trans. Olive Wyon (London: Allen and Unwin, second impression, 1954). Chapter 6 reviews the external evidence.

10. Albert Schweitzer, *The Quest of the Historical Jesus*, trans. W. Montgomery (London: Adam and Charles Black, 3rd ed., 1954), p. xix.

11. A review of the differences in issues in the nineteenth and twentieth centuries would take us too far afield, but for a description of the recent efforts see James M. Robinson, *New Quest of the Historical Jesus* (London: Student Christian Movement Press, 1959).

12. See Henri Daniel-Rops, *Jesus and His Times* (New York: Doubleday Image Book, 1958). 2 vols.

13. The establishment of present calendar division, B.C. and A.D., goes back to a Roman abbot in A.D. 525 who reckoned backward to what he thought was the date of Jesus' birth, and so developed the custom of dating western history from "the year of our Lord." However, he made a slight error in his calculations. If Jesus was born during the reign of Herod the Great, as the New Testament states, the date must be ca. 8–4 B.C.E.

14. Joseph Klausner, *Jesus of Nazareth* (Boston: Beacon, 1964), p. 384. Rudolph Bultmann in *Jesus and the Word* (New York: Scribner, 1958), and Henri-Rops, *Jesus and His Times, op. cit.*, vol. II, make similar judgments.

15. Klausner, *Jesus of Nazareth*, p. 389.

16. For a penetrating analysis, which we cannot pursue here, see "The Relevance of an Impossible Ideal" in Reinhold Niebuhr, *An Interpretation of Christian Ethics* (New York: Harper, 1935), Chapter 4.

17. This in itself is a fascinating study which cannot detain us here, but for further explication see Davies, *Paul and Rabbinical Judaism*, and for a study of Matthew's use of Scripture see his *Sermon on the Mount*. For a terse but accurate explanation of Christological titles, see Millar Burrows, *An Outline of Biblical Theology* (Philadelphia: Westminster, 1946), pp. 83–112.

18. There is one exception in the Old Testament: Psalm 110:1. Here the term applies both to God Himself and to His anointed one. Without much doubt the term, as it was used by Christians, was originally intended as a term for Christ, but it does mark the beginning of some confusion.

   The problem of translation is nicely illustrated in this development. The translation of the Old Testament into Greek, known as the Septuagint, greatly influenced the meaning of words so that they acquired a new sense and overtone. Recent scholarship has demonstrated that the language of the mysteries had little influence on Jewish or Christian thought, as has been widely held. As Herman Cohen once pointed out in another connection, a translation introduces an alien spirit and is, in itself, a form of commentary. It makes for a "different connotation and feeling tone." One of the results has been that Jews have tended to give up words that have taken on Christian overtones (i.e. Redeemer, Lamb of God). See S. H. Bergman, *Faith and Reason: An Introduction to Modern Jewish Thought* (Washington, D.C.: B'nai B'rith Hillel, 1961), p. 53.

19. The patristic ("fathers of the church") era is usually dated from A.D. 100 (Clement of Rome) to the middle of the eighth century (John of Damascus). This era stands as an intermediary between the New Testament and the first centuries, when the doctrines were not defined precisely or defined at all, and the Scholastic thought of the Middle Ages, which was seemingly possessed with the necessity of precise definition. Theology in the scholastic environment was concerned with metaphysics—essence and existence, nature and person, substance and accident, intellect and will—in an atmosphere where philosophical speculation abounded and abstractions seemed almost a way of life. Since we cannot discuss this development in any detail, see Robert Barr, S.J., *Main Currents in Early Christian Thought* (Glen Rock, N.J.: Paulist Press, 1966); James M. Carmody, S.J. and Thomas E. Clarke, S.J., *Word and Redeemer* (Glen Rock, N.J.: Paulist Press, 1966). See also Alan Richardson, *Creeds in the Making* (London: Student Christian Movement Press, 1951).

20. "On the Deity of the Son," quoted from Timothy Ware, *The Orthodox Church* (Harmondsworth: Penguin, 1964), pp. 43–44.

21. Other translations can be found in Carmody and Clarke, *Word and Redeemer, op. cit.*, pp. 104–105; or in Henry Bettenson, ed., *Documents of the Christian Church* (London: Oxford University Press, 1963), 2nd ed.

22. Reprinted with permission of The Macmillan Company from *Adventures of Ideas* by Alfred North Whitehead. Copyright 1933 by The Macmillan Company, renewed 1961 by Evelyn Whitehead.

23. See H. Richard Niebuhr, *The Meaning of Revelation* (New York: Macmillan, 1955).

24. See H. Wheeler Robinson, *Corporate Personality in Ancient Israel* (Philadelphia: Fortress, 1964).

25. Beryl D. Cohon, *Judaism in Theory and Practice* (New York: Bloch, 1954), p. 297.

26. Moore, *Judaism*, I, 503.

27. Gustaf Aulen, *Christus Victor* (New York and Toronto: Macmillan, 1931).

28. For surveys in short compass of modern Christologies see Daniel Day Williams, *What Present-Day Theologians Are Thinking* (New York: Harper, 1952); D. M. Baillie, *God Was in Christ* (New York: Scribner, 1948); John McIntyre, *The Shape of Christology* (Philadelphia: Westminster, 1966); *The Idea of Catholicism*, ed. Walter J. Burghardt and W. F. Lynch (New York: Meridian, 1960), pp. 104–253.

29. Reinhold Niebuhr, *The Nature and Destiny of Man* (London: Nisbet, 1948), II, 16.

SELECT BIBLIOGRAPHY

ANDERSON, HUGH. *Jesus and Christian Origins.* New York: Oxford University Press, 1964.

BAILLIE, D. M. *God Was in Christ.* London: Faber and Faber, 1948.

BARR, ROBERT, S.J. *Main Currents in Early Christian Thought.* Glen Rock, N.J.: Paulist Press, 1966.

BORNKAMM, GUENTHER. *Jesus of Nazareth.* New York: Harper and Brothers, 1960.

BULTMANN, RUDOLF. *Jesus and the Word.* New York: Charles Scribner's Sons, 1958.

CARMODY, JAMES M., S.J. and THOMAS E. CLARKE, S.J., eds. *Word · and Redeemer*. Glen Rock, N.J.: Paulist Press, 1965.

DANIEL-ROPS, HENRI. *Jesus and His Times*. New York: E. P. Dutton, 1954. 2 vols.

DANIÉLOU, JEAN. *The Theology of Jewish Christianity*. Trans. John Baker. London: Darton, Longman and Todd, 1964.

DAVIES, W. D. *Christian Origins and Judaism*. London: Darton, Longman and Todd, 1962.

GOGUEL, MAURICE. *The Life of Jesus*. Trans. Olive Wyon. London: Allen and Unwin, 1933.

GRAHAM, DOM AELRED, O.S.B. *The Christ of Catholicism*. New York: Longmans, Green, 1947.

GRANT, FREDERICK C. *An Introduction to New Testament Thought*. Nashville: Abingdon, 1950.

GUIGNEBERT, CH. *The Jewish World in the Time of Jesus*. Trans. Sidney Hook. London: Routledge and Kegan Paul, 1939.

KLAUSNER, JOSEPH. *Jesus of Nazareth*. Trans. Herbert Danby. London and New York, 1925.

KNOX, JOHN. *Jesus: Lord and Christ*. New York, Harper and Brothers, 1958.

LIETZMANN, HANS. *A History of the Early Church*. Trans. Bertram Lee Woolf. New York: World, Meridian Books, 1961. 2 vols.

McINTYRE, JOHN. *The Shape of Christology*. Philadelphia: Westminster Press, 1966.

SANDMEL, SAMUEL. *We Jews and Jesus*. New York: Oxford University Press, 1965.

SCHUERER, EMIL. *A History of the Jewish People in the Time of Jesus*. New York: Schocken Books, 1961.

SCHWEITZER, ALBERT. *The Quest of the Historical Jesus*. Trans. W. Montgomery. London: Adam and Charles Black, 1910.

TILLICH, PAUL. *Systematic Theology*. Chicago: University of Chicago Press, 1957. Vol. 2.

WEISS, JOHANNES. *Earliest Christianity*. New York: Harper Torchbook, 1959. 2 vols.

X

The People of God

THE religious faith of the Jew is inextricably woven with the concept of the Jewish people. Certainly the traditional Jew could never conceive of his achieving salvation or self-fulfillment apart from his people. This idea is based on the biblical and rabbinical accounts of Israel's history and mission in the world. The Jew is a man under commandment since the command was given to the first Jew, Abraham (Genesis 12:1–4); this command to become a holy people (Exodus 16:6) is like the command at creation and therefore constitutes Israel as a unique people. To be an integral part of the life and history of Israel is to play a strategic role in the drama of history. As the world is the center of the universe, so Israel is the center of the world and, sooner or later, the covenant (*b'rit*) between Israel and her God will encompass the whole race. Enslaved in Egypt, they were delivered, and a covenant on Sinai set the terms for the inheritance of the Promised Land. With David they became a new nation. Jeremiah had a vision of a new man (31:31). Deutero-Isaiah had a vision of a restored people from exile by which suffering and tragedy would be transmuted into the messianic hope (Isaiah 42:6–7). Israel has a messianic role in world history. From exile (*galut*) would come redemption and return with the coming of the Messiah, and the nations would recognize Israel's hegemony and the sovereignty of the God of Israel.

After 200 B.C.E. more formal conceptions of the messianic age began to appear, as we have seen, which anticipated a number of events to happen which would reaffirm the ancient prophets' faith in the direction of history. Redemption would extend to all nations; the Kingdom of God would appear on earth. From time to time men arose who claimed to be either the Messiah or his forerunner. But they proved to be false; false because their objectives were not fulfilled. Men must work and wait for the messianic era, they learned. And a popular legend pictured the Messiah as bound in fetters, ready to come, yet held back by God, Who alone knows the secret of the right time. Even though the rabbis forbade all speculation about the day and the hour, calculations were many. "The Messiah will arrive when the world has become good enough to make his coming possible; or evil enough to make it necessary. Men must act as though all depended on them; and wait and pray as though all depended on God."[1]

This introduction provides a background for understanding the events of the first century of the Common Era. Within the Hebraic-Jewish stream of history there existed in this period two religious communities: the synagogue and the church. The synagogue ("gathering") had become the real center of Jewish religious life. The word *synagogue* is the translation in the Septuagint for Hebrew nouns meaning congregation or assembly of Israel. The same words are rendered *ekklesia,* and Proverbs 5:14 in the Septuagint reads, "In the midst of the *ekklesia* and the *synagoge.*" The first word became the standard word for church, and the second the usual designation for the Jewish organization or place of worship and study. But both the Jews in the Diaspora and Greek-speaking Christians found the two words used interchangeably in the Greek Bible for the congregation of Israel. In brief, both the synagogue and the church become the historical continuation and successors to the Old Testament congregation. To put it another way, the congregation of Israel, the people of God, is now divided between the synagogue and the Church. The Epistle of James actually refers to a "Christian *Synagoge*" (2:2). The difference consists in the fact that the Church is now the community of those who have recognized and accepted Jesus as the Messiah and Lord, and they think of themselves as continuous with the "Israel of God."

THE NEW COMMUNITY: THE NEW TESTAMENT SETTING

This brings us now to the third element of the Christ event: the New Community; a community established with a common memory and shared history around a historical person who is now experienced in a new order of relationships. The community is an integral part of the Christ Event; it came into existence with and is the continuation of the event. Hence, the chief difference within the Hebraic-Jewish stream of history between the beginning and the end of the first century c.e. was the existence of the

Christian Church, a new kind of human community, the sole residuum of the memory of the historical Jesus, his life, death, and resurrection. The New Testament, the only record of that event, is the product of this community.

Of no less importance than concern with the Christological problem was the primitive Christian community's concern to interpret adequately the new age and its place in it. The Jewish messianic hope, as we have seen, had looked forward to a future transformation of society. They were confronted with the problem of interpreting the actual presence of the new order. What was the evidence that the Messianic Age had come? What are its primary characteristics and demands?

The first main theme of the primitive Christian community centered around the outpouring of the spirit of God. That the Messianic Age had been inaugurated with the resurrection, that the spirit had descended with power at Pentecost (Acts 2) as the prophet Joel had promised seemed evidence enough that the new age had dawned. They had become the new Israel and the true heir of the promises made to Abraham and his descendents. The Messiah was enthroned in heaven and they could pray "Thy will be done on earth as it is in heaven." But the Messiah both had come and is to come in the future (Acts 3:19–21). He has come in Jesus' life, death and resurrection, and Jesus is to be appointed Messiah for the age to come (Parousia). This conviction of a future consummation, "Thy kingdom come," was a faith devoutly shared with the Jewish community. Therefore the message is "repent . . . that the time of refreshing may come from the presence of the Lord, and that he may send the Christ appointed for you, Jesus whom the heavens must receive," until the consummation.

In the meantime they experienced the power of the spirit of Christ. They had become sons of God, not as those being saved out of a perishing world but as those who know that the world was being saved. They were empowered with heightened imagination and insight, with persuasive and forceful speech, courage, mastery of physical weakness. The new age meant the burning up of tawdry works, the healing of a miasmic ocean of diseases, the resurrection of the dead, the forgiveness of sins. It meant also a unity affirmed in word and action. So they put goods in a common pool, cared for the poor, and above all elevated their common meal to a central place in their lives "till he come"—Maranatha. These all seemed appropriate expressions of their conviction and hope.

That human frailty marred these expressions of common life is evidenced by the story of Ananias and Sapphi'ra (Acts 5) and Paul's earnest admonitions to those who disrupted the fellowship of the table (I Corinthians 10). Even when the second advent was expected in any day or hour the empirical Church was not exactly a communion of saints. Nonetheless, these earliest Christians felt themselves a unified company set apart from the world and standing at the threshold of tremendous consummation of all of their hopes.

At the same time, they were also aware of the dangers of the undisciplined enthusiasm of antinomianism (against the law). Many of Paul's letters (see especially I Corinthians 7), the Pastoral Epistles, the Epistle of James, and the Gospel of Matthew make this abundantly clear. In fact, in Matthew, a neolegalistic society begins to emerge. The Christian counterpart of the rabbi and the law become regulatory. There is evidence to think that the early Church in Jerusalem conceived of the Christian Gospel primarily as a new and higher law. A forceful statement of this view is found in the letter of James, which characterizes what may have been a highly influential opinion. Thus there developed a kind of unity in the face of diversity which is described by Paul: "Now there are varieties of gifts, but the same spirit; and there are varieties of service, but the same lord; and there are varieties of working, but it is the same God who inspires them all in everyone. To each is given the manifestation of the spirit for the common good" (I Corinthians 12:4–7).

The Continuing Incarnation

The community is the legacy of the Incarnation apprehended as the continuing incarnation of the spirit of Christ. It is known as the "fellowship of the holy spirit," "body of Christ," or the "mystical body," and those within the community are "in Christ."[2] Described thus, the third element of the Christ Event puts man immediately in contact with the stream of history and is closely connected with the modern world. The Christ Event is not just a historical memory but "is known still"; it could not be known apart from the presence in human history of a tradition or church.

To the great surprise of the primitive Christian community, what happened through Christ did not come to an end when "the days of his flesh" had ended, though they were appalled at his death. On the contrary, there was the *Presence* continuing independent of Jesus' actual existence, but stemming from his having lived, and furthermore this experience was not confined to a small circle who had known him. Just as God had established the people of Israel as the nucleus of mankind in the Covenant, the early Christians believed, so now He had created a new nucleus by becoming incarnate Himself in a man of that same people. This perception of the grace of God came into sharp focus in the Christ Event. "The Christ-event was a revelatory moment in history summoning the motives, the intellectual vision, and the imagination of men to a new center of focus as truly as the heralding of atomic energy was a radical disclosure of a new level of physical powers, altering materially the structural experiences of men."[3] Here was a real man in real human existence—Christ as the incarnate pattern and historical action which directed man toward God and God toward men, actualizing in a brief, concrete life the intent of the Creator for all men and breaking into the world with new power. "He is . . . an eruption of history in which the good that is in God and the tenderness of man's life itself came physically to view."[4]

This perception of grace was like the primordial movement at creation "In the beginning God"—the Word. The miracle of creation was being repeated as the second Isaiah said, "Behold, I am doing a new thing. Do you perceive it?" And St. Paul said, "God who said, 'let light shine out of darkness' has shined in our hearts." "If any man be in Christ, he is a new creature." It was perfectly clear to the early Church that this re-creation was every bit as much of a miracle as the first creation itself, in fact was grounded there. The Sabbath was from the foundation of the world. Christ was the second Adam. These redemptive events were the renewal of a relationship with God known as Creator. They were the redemptive occasions which throw light on every other occasion and event. They were the light of meaning that illuminated the meaning of every other moment of existence.

THE TRIUNITY OF GOD

By this time it may be evident that we have been discussing the doctrine of the Trinity, as these phenomena are known in traditional theology. The idea of the Holy Spirit was integral to the creedal discussions at all of the major ecumenical councils, and was analyzed and reflected upon in much the same way as we have seen in the discussions of the Incarnation.[5] The classic expressions appear in the Nicene Creed, written in the fourth century:

We believe in the Holy Spirit, the Lord and Giver of life, who proceedeth from the Father, who with the Father and the Son together is worshipped and glorified, who spake by the prophets.

and in the famous *Quicunque Vult* (so-called Athanasian Creed) which dates from the middle of the fifth century:

The Father is God; the Son is God; and the Holy Spirit is God. And yet they are not three Gods, but one God.

So the Holy Spirit is an aspect of both the character (the inner life) and the modality of God.

The Concept of Spirit

The concept of spirit has a way of slipping out of hand when one tries to grasp its meaning. In spite of apparently clear definitions, the doctrine of the Holy Spirit is the most undeveloped in Christian thought, and it is the most easily abused. In all their variety, the ideas of God's spirit in the Tanakh, the rabbinic writings, and the New Testament have one common theme: the Spirit of God is at work in human affairs, present, active, creating and fulfilling human possibilities; and yet is strangely immune from human manipulation and exploitation. It is not contained by religious events, but, like the wind, "it blows where it wills"; not dependent upon the ways of men, it is free to work in the spirit of men everywhere, in every human situation. It is the objective side of man's spirit. It is the sense in which man actually transcends himself to become aware of meaning which can become a good not his own.

The word *spirit* (Hebrew: *ruach*; Greek: *pneuma*, word or breath) appears repeatedly in the Bible from the Book of Genesis to the Book of Revelation, and has the same connotation as "the Spirit of God moved upon the face of the deep" and "breathed into his nostrils the breath of life." Although the spirit is frequently mentioned as Holy Spirit, "Spirit of God," "Spirit of the Holy One," it sounds strange to modern ears, especially when it is called the "Holy Ghost," as it was frequently called in the past. In function it is sometimes like the wind—a storm grand and devastating. Sometimes it is like breath. Sometimes, as the Bible says, it "rushed upon him"; at other times it "clothed" a person. Mostly, like the air, it is always present but not always noticed. It is mostly quiet, entering life to keep it alive. Sometimes it rushes into the great moments of history, but mostly it works hiddenly in daily encounter.

It is understood as a new state of things, a new covenant, a new relationship between God and man. It is the power in man qualifying him for a new state. This is the work of the spirit. Wherever there is creativity, discovery, aspiration toward righteousness, scientific quest for truth—that is the movement of God's spirit in the world, so Jews and Christians believe. It is the power which drives the human spirit beyond and above itself toward what it could not attain by itself. It is the truth, and within the depths of being it opens to man the "Holy," the manifestation of ultimate presence. It consists of the depth that forms the matrix of all relationships in which man's life is cast. In short, the spirit is God Himself in action, immanent in the world, at work in the world with a purpose for the world and for man.

Doctrines of the Trinity

The doctrine of the Trinity is not explicitly stated in the New Testament. Although it seems implicit in the experience of the primitive Christian experience, the community held fast to the Jewish conception of the unity of God. The idea of spirit stands for God at work in the Church, in their hearts, in historical crises. It is the manifestation of the divine mystery in the Torah and in Christ.

The evolution of the idea follows the typical course of theories striving for articulation in the midst of confusing pressures, heresies, and feeble attempts at definition, so that there developed several doctrines of the Trinity both prior to and after the definitions we have quoted above. With the conviction that their life in the Church was the work of the living God, eventually the Holy Spirit came to be affirmed as sharing with the Son in the divine mystery—and was called the third "person" of the "Blessed Trinity." The Trinity is not a mathematical formula, neither is it logically necessary to Christian experience. It is a way of speaking analogously about the experience of God as Father, Son, and Spirit. It is expressed variously in the history of Christian thought, but essentially it affirms that the Father is the Lord and Source of the universe, from which all proceeds, the condition of there being anything whatsoever; apart from whom nothing or any possibility exists. The Son is the expression of God's being, His Self-revelation incarnate in the historical person of Jesus, the Christ. The Holy Spirit is the movement from God to man, the Presence of God in the world, and present in the new community.

The intention of the doctrine even when it attributes the most explicit personal existence to the Holy Spirit is to express all the data of revelation and the Christian experience without infringing on the idea of the unity and oneness of God. Contrary to all distortions of the doctrine, it is not tritheism or a definition of a "committee God." As it developed in the patristic period it safeguarded the fundamental unity of God against all attempts of Hellenistic pluralism.

In sum, the doctrine of the Trinity, as Christians have attempted to formulate it through the centuries, asserts the utter transcendence of the living God Who is essentially unknowable and beyond the reach of any definition; this transcendent One becomes immanent in a man of His own choosing in a particular time and place; this Wholly Other is present in history as the ground of reality and process. In the language of creed and liturgy, therefore, the Christian Church affirms three axioms: (1) radical monotheism, the firm conviction that there is one God; to worship anyone or any other is idolatry; (2) God is incarnate in Jesus Christ; and (3) God is Spirit immanent in creation, and actively at work therein. They speak of the Being, Purpose and Activity of God. God is known *as* Father *in* the Son and *through* the Holy Spirit. This is the triunity of God.

This is the God, as Christians understand it, whose Spirit called the Community into being—the Spirit is God Himself in action, immanent in the world, not as an impersonal force but as Being who possesses a character as clearly defined as Christ. The Community is the instrument through the ages with the perennial function to proclaim by word, sacrament, and deed that "God was in Christ, reconciling the world unto himself." That is the Christ Event.

JUDAISM AND THE CHRIST EVENT

In these two chapters we have spent considerable time discussing the meaning of the Christ Event not only because it is so central to Christian thought and experience, but also because this complex of events and their interpretations represent the real distinctions between Judaism and Christianity. Throughout this book we have stressed both the common and particular genius of these two traditions, but we need now to be especially clear about the fact that Christian modes of interpretation as they developed after the first century represent a radical departure from Jewish modes of thought. We would therefore be doing violence to the customary Jewish categories were we to force them into the Christian mold. We turn then to discuss in brief compass some Jewish interpretations.

Method

A Jew reading the synoptic Gospels would find himself in familiar territory.[6] On the other hand, as Samuel Sandmel[7] points out, a Palestinian Jew who happened to overhear the Christian debates from the third century onward would have found them completely incomprehensible. This would have been true not only because rabbinic Judaism and Christianity had become self-contained entities, isolated from each other, but also because of the nature of the Jewish mentality. While Jewish religious philosophy, which developed apologetically in the medieval period in response to Christian attack and debate, represented comparable intellectual exercises to the Christian theological disputes of the patristic and medieval periods, it is generally true to say that Jewish thought is concrete and practical. And in any case these Jewish theological writings are ancillary. Certainly Jews would not have conceived of calling a council of authoritative persons to debate and decide the definition of some article of belief. Whereas for the Christian tradition right faith required as precise a definition as possible, and this faith is revealed, defined, and mediated by the Church, the rabbis seemed content to leave the content of faith implicit, requiring only common consent to the tradition, not explicit dogmatic formulation. The "tradition" interpreted the Torah.

Interpreting the Torah is a matter of special concern. As we have seen, there are clearly parallels in talmudic and Christian exegesis. The Christian claim for the uniqueness of its typological and allegorical exegesis will not stand when compared to talmudic and midrashic exegesis (cf. Chapter 3). Rabbinic Judaism understood the community to be the authoritative bearer and interpreter of the religious truth, and the Jewish tradition for ages has viewed the possession of the Torah to be the guarantee of its election. Therefore they had to take serious issue with the Church's claim to be the New Israel in possession of the New Covenant. Disagreeing violently with what they believed to be the Christian misinterpretation of the Scriptures, they held that God, having foreseen the possibility of such misinterpretation, had given the teaching in two parts: in addition to the Torah in writing there was the oral tradition, without which the Torah could not be understood at all. "The oral tradition was not given in writing, lest the Gentiles should falsify it, as they have done with the written tradition, then asserting that they are Israel" (Bamidbar Rabbah, Chapter 14). It was also said that God had denied Moses' request to reduce the Mishnah to writing, because He foresaw that the Gentiles would translate the Scriptures into Greek and say, We are Israel (Tanhum Wayera 5). These passages and many others in the Talmud or Midrash are directed toward the Christian polemic. Israel remains the people of God; the Covenant cannot be nullified.

Monotheism

At the heart of Jewish faith is the *Sh'ma:* "Hear, O Israel, the Lord is our God, the Lord is one" (Deuteronomy 6:4). An assertion of radical monotheism, it was and remains the central "dogma" of Judaism. When, therefore, the Jew confronts the doctrine of the Trinity, he assumes, at the very least, that the Christian is hopelessly confused about the nature of Deity, introducing a plurality into the Oneness of God. Not only is he convinced that Christianity is not monotheistic, but that the God of Jesus Christ is not the God of Israel. Add to the "mystery of the Blessed Trinity" the "mystery of the Incarnation," a man put on the same plane with God, and the confusion borders on blasphemy. Christological doctrine in itself was, as Paul said, a "stumbling block" to the Jews; and after the Church began to develop such doctrines there are statements in the

Midrash and particularly in the Amoraim intended to illustrate the impossibility of such ideas for strict Jewish transcendental monotheism (cf. Midrash Samuel V:4).

With reference to the idea of the Trinity, Christian exegetes were inclined to fasten on a tendency found in the late parts of the Tanakh and in contemporary Judaism, for example in the Targums, to hypostatize (to individualize or personalize; to give "substantial" existence) the divine powers. In the New Testament period both Jew and Christian attribute *hypostasis* to such terms as Word, Wisdom, Spirit of God. It is also true that there was and is within Jewish tradition triadic formulations such as God, Israel, Torah; Creator, Lawgiver, Redeemer; or Creator, Teacher (giver of the Torah), and Redeemer. But these are terms to describe the utter inviolability of God in relationship to His world and people. Jewish monotheism is not to be understood mathematically as setting the One over against the many, but as the uniqueness of the God of Israel and the contrast between Him and the world. Yehezkel Kaufmann claims this is the original meaning of Jewish monotheism. He writes, ". . . it is a mistake to think that a merely arithmetical difference sets off Israel's religion from paganism. . . . The Israelite conception of God's unity entails His sovereign transcendence over all."[8] Yet the Jewish tradition affirmed both the wholly otherness and the absolute nearness of God. His fearful otherness is symbolized in his Holiness (Kadosh). It is said that it was after hearing the chanting of "Kadosh! Kadosh! Kadosh!" in a Moroccan synagogue that Rudolf Otto, the German Protestant theologian, arrived at his understanding of God as the "Mysterium Tremendum."[9] This utter separateness is seen in the use of surrogate names for God. For the tetragrammaton, YHWH, Jewish traditions substituted "Adonai" (Lord) or "Adonai Elohenu" (Lord our God). Yet the tradition affirmed at the same time the nearness and presence of God by the use of the name, *Shekhinah*, the Present One (from *shken*, to dwell); thus God is "He who dwells with us" continuously. It is this relationship which Martin Buber describes in *I and Thou.* Thus God is "Thou." It is this "Thou," so Jewish tradition affirms, Who has made Himself known in Israel's history and in men's lives, standing over against the community and the individual as a living Person. This is what gives meaning to the Torah and promises redemption.

Jewish Estimates of Jesus[10]

Since the young Church was not taken very seriously during the first century of the Common Era, there are very few clear references to Jesus in contemporary literature, and almost nothing in the Talmud that refers to him with real certainty. The Gospels are the primary sources and, as we have noted before, they reflect the opinions of later decades. They cannot therefore be taken as reflecting accurately Jewish opinion. Our discussion of Jewish attitudes toward Jesus will of necessity deal with later, and for the most part, modern evaluations.

Because the "problem" of Jesus for Jews has been so overlaid by a dismal history in which both Jew and Christian have felt their relationship to one another to be one of true faith versus false faith, a proper assessment of Jewish opinion would require that dispassionate skill of the scholar who can get beneath popular folklore and its misrepresentations to evaluate what happened when the young Church emerged from its Jewish matrix; to penetrate beyond the alienating factors in later developments in an effort at least to get the record straight. Even then estimates will vary greatly depending upon the questions asked. For our purposes there are two main sets of questions. First is the historical question: Who was Jesus? a question about his person, time, and place. Second are the interpretative questions: What was he? What did he do? and What is the significance of his person and career?

On the historical question Jewish opinion varies considerably. There are those who see Jesus as a man with a personality striking enough to be something of a leader, a Jewish loyalist yet a martyr to his patriotism; something of a teacher although not unique; a courageous witness to truths he passionately held, but to which most of his contemporaries in Pharisaic Judaism subscribed. There are others who own great admiration for him and are high in their evaluation of the intensity of his thought, which had a prophetic quality about it. Klausner concludes his book with the question, "What is Jesus to the Jews?" He answers that Jesus is for the Jewish nation "a great teacher of morality and an artist in parable."[11] Nearly all see him as a person within Jewish compass and, so far as it can be ascertained through the layers of tradition, an authentic teacher within the rabbinical tradition. Leo Baeck finds Jesus to be a Jew in every trait and feature of his character. In the Gospels "we encounter a man with noble features who lived in the land of the Jews in tense and excited times and helped and labored and suffered and died: a man out of the Jewish people who walked on Jewish paths with Jewish faith and hopes. . . . Jewish history and Jewish reflection may not pass him by nor ignore him. Since he was, no time has been without him; nor has there been a time which was not challenged by the epoch that would consider him its starting point."[12]

When we turn to the second set of questions, however, the story is different. Samuel Sandmel puts the matter succinctly: "When we Jews have understood Christian explanations, and when we have not, we have consistently rejected the Christian claims about Jesus. We have not believed that Jesus was the Messiah; we have not been willing to call him

Lord; we have not believed that the *Logos* became incarnate in Jesus; we have not believed that Jesus was, or is, the very Godness of God."[13]

It is the Christological doctrine, the interpretation of the significance of the person and the career of Jesus, which was and has remained alien to the realistic expectations of the Messiah of the Jews. In the first century the Sadducean High Priest, it was reported, rended his clothing in horror at hearing the assertion of an incarnation of the eternal God. Jesus could never be other than a man. The Christian view of soteriology, a single individual suffering vicariously as a propitiation for the sins of his fellow-men, seems so much "Greek" speculation. The crucifixion as an atoning death for the redemption of men is equally alien.

The sum of the matter is that neither classical or modern Judaism has encountered the Christ Event with faith, nor did it then or now feel obligated to give reasons for this lack, in spite of the fact that this only made the Jew in Christian eyes an obdurate fellow. Jews are prepared to acknowledge that here was a historical event external to Judaism in which something of great significance to the Gentile world took place, an event which assumed visible form in the Christian churches. Therefore, Jesus is a concrete fact of western history and insofar as Jews are part of western culture, it is a fact with which they are continually confronted.

Law and Gospel

As important as many other differences may be, all issues recede in significance to the contrast between Law and Gospel, Law and Grace, Faith and Works. There is a classic and familiar oversimplification of the relationship between the two traditions which can be stated: "Judaism is a religion of law, Christianity of grace." For the Christian who holds such a view, Judaism requires an almost unbearably difficult observance of a huge number of unimportant laws, while the Christian has his existence in grace and merely opens one's being to receive forgiveness and justification which comes from the atoning act of Christ on the cross. For the Jew, with an equally simplified view, Paul is the culprit and renegade who held that the law was abolished by faith in Jesus Christ. Willfully misunderstanding his Jewish heritage, he turned the teachings of Jesus into a mystery religion and claimed it to be a superior religion, setting aside the whole corpus of Halakhah, its ritual and ceremonial prescriptions. As we have seen, there has been a tendency to recognize that Jesus is somewhere within the pale of Judaism, perhaps even as one of the great teachers in the prophetic tradition. This recognition comes very often at the expense of Paul. This attitude can be summed up in a saying: "A Jew named Saul, later called Paul, came and spoiled it all!"

Thoughtful students of the Talmud and New Testament will recognize the misleading if not erroneous character of these statements. For classical Judaism obedience to the Law was the unique and indispensable instrument for doing the will of God. Far from being a joyless exercise, observance of the Law is a kind of holy joy one shares in living, acting, and performing according to the standards prescribed by a loving and immanent as well as an aweful God. Otherwise the Jew could not sing, "Oh, how I love thy law! It is my meditation all the day" (Psalms 119:27). The Law is then the pathway to God, given not to make one righteous and acceptable, but because it proclaims the will of God. Existence under the Law is existence in grace. God's choosing to bring Israel out of Egypt was an act of grace; grace is allied with the Covenant, and the Covenant is the basis of the Law. Law is the response to grace on the part of the faithful Jew, and at the same time it is judgment. Yet the God of the Torah is merciful and gracious, slow to anger and abounding in steadfast love . . . (Psalms 103:8). Law is his duty and it is also the way he responds to God's steadfast love.

Nor is the Gospel to be understood apart from the Law. It is as much of a misapprehension to see only an antinomian strain in the New Testament as it is to see only joyless burden and narrowness in the best of the rabbinic tradition. The law reformulated by Jesus (cf. Matthew 5–7) is not the same as rabbinic law, yet it shares many basic elements; in some ways it is even more stringent. Likewise, Paul's arguments for justification by faith without the Law must be judged in the light of exegetical principles of Judaism as a way of defending his mission to the Gentiles.

This argument will proceed for a long time. As Robert Gordis says, "No matter how much one may reduce the importance of the loyalty to the Law in Judaism and stress the value of law in Christianity, a substantial margin of difference will remain."[14] The Jew will continue to love the Law and do it with little sympathy for the Christian's doubt about his ability to keep the Law. For him the nature of man is such that he needs the Law as a guide in making his moral decisions, but the Law is to be studied and loved for its own sake and not for any hope of reward. Our discussion in the next section will throw further light on Jewish and Christian understanding of this relationship.

TORAH, GOSPEL, AND PRESENT EXPERIENCE

Already we have faced the question of how an ancient historical event can be of significance now. In any study of religions, one must deal both with the primordial or classical revelatory event and the present experience of that particular tradition. Certainly, the past would not be significant were it not a part of man's present experience. But, likewise, man's present experience is "controlled and given its form by the primordial revelation."[15] The disclosure granted to the founder or founders becomes the paradigm for the repeated experiences of the Holy. That experience, powerful enough to found a community of faith, can be made accessible to the present through repeated reenactments and thus become normative experience. This is the meaning of tradition, and tradition means both interpretation and reenactment. Each generation must appropriate that tradition for itself by interpreting the ancient revelation in its own terms. We are using the terms, Torah and Gospel, to symbolize the content of the traditions.

Torah is the "Way" of Jewish existence, and Jewish existence is the way of the Torah. "Salvation is of the Jews" because the history of Israel is redemptive history for the world. The Church is the "extension of the incarnation" and its function is to re-present Christ to the world as his "ambassador." To perform these functions each tradition employs particular forms or vehicles which are fitting to its own history and symbols. By such symbols, the religious community believes that it can realize the divine presence (Sh'kinah). They become, so to speak, "means of grace," and grace and salvation are paradigmatic of the experience of Jew and Christian. "Consciousness of sin and assurance of grace are the two great motive powers in the working of religion,"[16] is the ways Solomon Schechter expresses it. This "gestalt of grace" has application both within the life of the traditions in Mitzvoh (commandments), word and sacraments, and to the problems of human existence in ethics.

Grace and Salvation

Grace is probably the most crucial concept in western religious thought because it refers to the free and unmerited act by and through which God restores man. In essence grace is a paradox which affirms that every good in man and every good act is somehow from God rather than from the self. The paradox consists in this: that the "God of Israel is he who in his transcendent otherness does not need man and yet chooses to need him; who in his love makes man free and responsible, and thus as commanding demands free response."[17] In technical language, grace is prevenient in that the good was God's before it was man's, but neither God's actions or man's acts are delimited by one another. A person is never more free, in this context, than when he is wholly dependent. All man's choices are his alone. No one else can make them. The errors are also his. Yet, of every good thing and deed man can only say, "Not I, but the grace of God."

Grace and Torah

In the perspective of Judaism the Call of Abraham and the Exodus-Sinai events made Israel God's covenant people. The election of Israel is a constant theme in the Tanakh and rabbinic literature. There is, however, never a suggestion that the election came through any merit of Israel. On the contrary, "it attributes the election to a mere act of grace or love on the part of God."[18] Grace (Hebrew *Hesed* and *rahamim*) refers to God's "loving-kindness" and "mercy" and His constant faithfulness to His covenant people; to His beneficences bestowed upon man without his merit. Grace, then, is closely associated with the Covenant and finds its expression in the Law.

To be a Jew means to stand in Abraham's place and at the foot of Sinai receive the Torah. The Covenant binds Jews to the task of being a corporate priesthood. The Law is both his duty and the means of grace through which he responds to this call. God wants to redeem man, but man must make the beginning. Through the Law man enters a partnership with God as a man under commandment, yet free. Grace as it is manifested in and through the commandment does not diminish man's freedom. As the rabbinic sage declared, "When Torah came into the world freedom came into the world" (Midrash Genesis Rabbah Wayyera LIII. 7). Thus man's freedom is established. And "He who submits to the yoke of the Torah liberates himself from the yoke of circumstance" (Ethics of the Fathers). Man's freedom is expressed in choosing to live by the commandments.

The Torah not only establishes man's freedom; it is the means by which man is enabled to fulfill the Law. Since the Law is concerned not only with man's acts, but also his thoughts and intents of his heart; and since the demand is for perfection and holiness ("You shall be holy; for I the Lord your God am holy" Leviticus 19:2), man's defects disable him from fulfilling the Law. Although desires for yielding to temptation are ever present, it is the Jew's experience that God's grace is ever available through the Torah, which is a very present help for him in his hour of decision. "The *yetzer* has no power against the Law, and he who has the Law in his heart, over him the *yetzer* has no power" (Midrash on Psalm CXIX, 10).

This fundamental experience is expressed in that part of the Torah known as the *Halakhah*, and particularly, within the context of our discussion, in the ritual observances—Sabbath, circumcision, Passover, dietary laws (Kashrut), and the traditional holidays and festivals. Here we will be brief and defer a lengthier discussion to Chapter 12. The degree of literal observance of the ancient Mitzvoh and the extent of changing forms vary within the Jewish community from Orthodox, Conservative, Reform, and Reconstructionist. The halakhic code of ritual observance is the "acting out" of the Jew's convictions about the Torah and became a reenactment of the election of Israel. "I have separated you from among the nations that you should be mine" (Leviticus 20:26).

Grace and Christianity

In the Christian understanding, dependence upon grace is even more explicit. Having real doubt about man's abilities to achieve anything on his own, it is the Christian's fundamental experience that man is saved by faith and grace alone. Yet man is not a lifeless, passive stone. The effect of grace is a re-ordering of man's powers and faculties which awakens and summons him to new acts of faith, understanding, and love. Grace and justification establish not only a new relationship but a new attitude. This is due to no merit of his own. God not only demands obedience but also supplies obedience. Man then can "work out (his) own salvation with fear and trembling," but it is God who does both the willing and the working (Philippians 2:12–13). For Christians this reality of grace is vividly symbolized in Word and Sacrament. We will first discuss the contrasting theories of grace and salvation as they are related to word and sacrament. Then we will describe the sacraments as they are understood by Roman Catholics and Protestants.

For the Roman Catholic, grace as a gift of God is an energy-giving virtue which is infused into the soul sacramentally. The sacraments are the effective signs of grace—grace made visible. Through the sacraments actual grace (that is, the general statement above) becomes sanctifying or habitual grace by the infusion of the virtues of faith, hope, and love and by receiving the "gifts of the Holy Spirit." In this view it is possible to speak of the infusion of grace which regenerates and makes man worthy of his Creator. This is the grace of justification and sanctification by which man is saved. Sacraments are therefore vitally necessary for salvation. In the case of baptism, confirmation, and ordination, indelible characteristics are conferred upon the recipient. The Eucharist is the drama of advent wherein Christ gives himself to man.[19]

For the Protestant, the sacraments are not infusions of renovating grace which make one objectively worthy of forgiveness. Through Christ's sacrifice the act of forgiveness means that man's guilt is no longer reckoned against him. For example, Martin Luther, following Bernard of Clairvaux, rediscovered the astonishing biblical paradox that justification does not mean distributive justice which rewards the good and punishes the evil; it is not a judge's merciless verdict against man, but the father's costly gift to man. Ultimately the righteousness of God is not punitive but redemptive.

Thus man is justified by grace through faith alone. In grace God in His deepest being is performing a completely gratuitous act. There are no degrees of grace; either one is forgiven or one is not. Therefore the Protestant rejects the notion of the sacrament as infusion of any substance. The heart of the sacrament is divine action received only by active faith. The function of the sacramental act is similar to the function of the word (preaching): they confirm, proclaim, and seal the promises of God (Calvin). But they are not the sole means of grace, nor are they necessarily efficacious. One cannot speak of imparting indelible characteristics or infusion of energy. The sacraments rightly administered and rightly received do embody the promises of God, but grace is not thereby restricted.

Salvation

The differences between Roman Catholic and Protestant views are related to their views of salvation. We shall have to speak here of tendencies; these differences are not absolute; indeed they are overlapping. The Roman Catholic view places major emphasis on the Incarnation (but not to the exclusion of the salvific) and salvation is basically the deification of man by participating in a supernatural God. Therefore the Church and sacraments play decisive roles as divinely appointed instruments for mediating the "medicine of the soul" (Augustine). The idiom is in the language of substance, nature, and supernature.[20]

The Protestant, on the other hand, tends to emphasize the atonement (but not to the exclusion of the Incarnation). Salvation is the restoration of broken relationships, grace is divine favor, and man's destiny is in forgiveness and personal communion with God. The sacraments are important primarily for the communication of the Word, calling for repentance, promising forgiveness, and liberating man to be a responsible and responsive creature who can and will serve the neighbor. Here the idiom is in the language of personal existence—covenant, promise, faithfulness, righteousness.

We emphasize that these are descriptions of tendencies. To put them in sharpest form, these tendencies can be seen in their polar extremes: in Catholicism the monastic life—an ordered round of prayer and sacrament; in Protestantism the moralization of belief and the reduction of the content of faith to moralistic conduct.

Word and Sacrament

This analysis may help us to see how the various ways symbols are used and interpreted provide a key to the deeper understanding of tradition; and how seemingly similar experiences are indicative of fundamental differences. The Eucharist and Passover, for example, are likewise similar experiences, yet they have become symbols of fundamental differences between the traditions. We turn now to examine the specifically Christian symbols in word and sacrament. There is, of course, no reason why the whole of reality, the wide world of nature or any material thing could not mediate these experiences since the whole universe is sacramental. The Second Vatican Council said, "there is hardly any proper use of material things which cannot thus be directed toward the sanctification of men and the praise of God."[21] But "in the word and sacrament the divine presence is focused so as to communicate itself to us with directness and intensity like that of the incarnation itself, which indeed is re-presented in the proclaiming of the word and in the celebration of the sacraments."[22]

Word. By the Word we mean, in this connection, the Bible, its proclamation, its explanation, and the creeds—in other words, those means by which the content and the tradition come to be heard, reflected upon, and understood. These constitute the kerygma, which, along with the sacraments, are the historical media of the Holy Spirit.

Sacrament. The sacraments are the historic points at which the diverse rays of religious life are brought in focus by a combination of *things* possessing symbolic significance—wine, bread, water—with *words* of authority which bring sacramental *acts* into relation with the event and so mediate the fellowship with God. Sacraments, in this sense, can apply even to those traditions which have no sacramental tradition or practice (Judaism and Quakerism). These traditions, seemingly the antithesis of sacramental tradition, are steeped in images and convictions which have grown up and which have been handed down by concrete historical acts (Quaker silence), men, and institutions. Sacraments, generally, are symbolic of those important experiences of life which, in the human community, are marked by rites of passage such as birth, naming, adulthood, marriage, vocation, and death. A sacrament, in the Christian sense, is a rite in which it is believed God's saving grace is uniquely active. John Calvin, following Augustine, defined a sacrament as "an outward sign by which the Lord seals in our consciences the promises of his good will towards us to support the weakness of our faith;" or "it (is) a testimony of the grace of God toward us, confirmed by an outward sign." Either definition, he felt, would be in accord with Augustine's definition "a visible sign of a sacred thing, or a visible form of the invisible grace."[23]

The two sacraments having clear New Testament warrant and celebrated by almost all of the Christian bodies are *baptism* and *the Lord's Supper*. The ancient Church felt that all sacred actions were sacramental. The Scholastics enumerated as many as thirty at different times. But during the medieval period many thinkers felt the need for a clearer definition. Abelard had suggested five, and Peter Lombard suggested seven. The fourth Lateran Council in 1215 established the number of seven for Roman Catholics: baptism, confirmation, the Lord's Supper, penance, extreme unction, ordination, and matrimony. Each sacrament consists of two elements which are defined in terms of form and matter—a material portion (water, bread, wine, etc.); and a formula conveying a sacred use, for example (I baptize thee . . .). The administrant must have the intention of doing what Christ and the Church appoint, and the recipient must have a sincere desire to receive the benefit of the sacrament. In the case of the Roman Catholic, these conditions fulfilled, the sacrament conveys grace by the fact of its reception—*ex opere operato*. God is the principal cause of this grace, the sacrament itself is the instrumental cause. We shall later point out the important Protestant qualification upon the efficacy of this definition of sacrament.

BAPTISM.   The ritual use of water for purification for initiation is a widespread practice in many religions. Baptism generally is a rite of initiation, of repentance and purification, of identity and vocation. By it the recipient is initiated into the Church with the remission of sins, and in the case of christening receives his name; and vocationally it is the layman's equivalent of ordination. Christian baptism has its origin in Jewish proselyte baptism of the early centuries of the Common Era, especially the rite of John the Baptist. In the early Christian ceremony, individual believers were to undergo the experience of dying and rising with Christ. This experience of the believer is mirrored in the practice of baptism. Going down into the water is like going down into the valley of death and into the tomb, and rising from the water is like emergence from death (Romans 6).

This symbolizes one of Paul's most significant concepts—"in Christ" (Galatians 2:20). It is a social concept which signifies becoming a part of new humanity, the true Israel. To be "in Christ" is to discover the new community. It is not, as some have maintained, a mysto-magical flight into ecstasy, but indicates a most intense personal relationship to the new creation by invoking identity of experience with Christ, his life and death and resurrection.[24]

CONFIRMATION.   Confirmation is a Roman Catholic sacrament. Although it is not strictly a sacrament for Protestantism it has sacramental value in many Protestant churches, especially those which practice infant baptism. While baptism can be administered by a priest in any of the traditions, confirmation in episcopal-type churches must be performed by the bishop. Confirmation is a complement to baptism and is intended to

underscore the seriousness of the commitment; the confirmand is expected
to have a conscious understanding of the faith and its meaning and be
aware of the serious import of the act.

The Eucharist. The Eucharist is the holiest and most venerated of
the sacraments because of Jesus' last supper with his disciples which was
probably the *Seder*, the *paschal meal*; and because, more than any other
rite, it is a celebration of Christ's passion and death. It clearly represents
one of the earliest Christian practices of the community.

In the early Church, the common meal had two phases closely knit
together. In one, the Christians came together, rich and poor, bringing
food to be spread on the common table and shared as by members of a
single family. These meals were given the picturesque name *Agapae* ("love-
feasts"). After the manner of the paschal meal or the common meal there
was the habitual blessing of wine and broken bread, in a formal observance
called *eucharistia* ("thanksgiving"). Besides this stress upon unity in the
group, the eucharist was regarded as an expression of gratitude for God's
favor already granted and of eager and confident expectation of the age to
come. Gathered around the table they felt themselves pilgrims alert and
ready for their Lord to come again and lead them to the Promised Land.
The spirit characterized by the primitive Eucharist at its best is exemplified
by a prayer in the *Didache* of the second century, a prayer used at the
breaking of bread:

We thank thee, our father, for the life and knowledge which thou madest
known to us through Jesus thy servant; to thee be the glory forever. Even as this
broken bread was scattered over the hills, and was gathered together and
became one, so let thy church be gathered together from the ends of the earth
into thy kingdom.

Likewise it is inextricably related to the symbol "the body of Christ." As
Adam is the generic term for the unity of mankind by virtue of the
creation, so Christ is the symbol of the new humanity by virtue of his
death and resurrection. As Jesus' words and actions at the Last Supper
indicate, Christians are united with Christ and with each other share one
corporeity—body. "A new corporate personality is created in Christ."[25]
"As in Adam all men die, so in Christ shall all be made alive" (I Corinthians 15:22).

There are many names for the eucharistic rite—Holy Communion, Last
Supper, Lord's Supper, Love Feast (agape), the Sacrifice of the Mass—and
each title indicates a different theory of what happens in the sacrament. At
the two extremes are receptionism and transubstantiation. In the first,

sacramental action is subjective, dependent on the mind or faith of the recipient. The Roman Catholic theory of the sacrifice as transubstantiation was defined by the Fourth Lateran Council and confirmed by the Council of Trent (1562); the Second Vatican Council reaffirmed the principles of the Council of Trent.[26] At the consecration a miracle takes place, according to this theory, whereby the "accidents" (shape, taste, etc.) remain unaltered, but the "substance" is transformed into the very body and blood of Christ.

Positions between these two poles include: a *symbol* and memorial (Zwingli); a doctrine of *real presence* of Christ (Calvin, Anglican) which is never really defined beyond saying that Christ is really and truly present; *consubstantiation* (Luther) affirms the "true body and blood" of Christ "in and under the bread and wine." The chief distinction from transubstantiation seems to reside in the power of the priest. To Luther, it is dependent solely on a divine act.

The other sacraments we will review more briefly.

ORDINATION.   The rite of ordination is practiced by all churches but it is sacramental only in the Roman Catholic branch. It confers a special status by the laying on of hands of persons chiefly for administering the Word and sacraments and such other sacerdotal functions the church practices. It is in three degrees: deacon, priest, and bishop.

MARRIAGE.   At first sight, it seems strange that this should be a sacrament since it is a "natural" institution formed by contract. But since it is the basic institution of social life, and protects and controls the sexual function, the Church affirms the importance of divine grace for this vital institution.

PENANCE.   Baptism remits sins, but where righteousness and sins are viewed as special acts rather than states, penance is required. In the early Church public confession was the practice, but in the thirteenth century it became a private rite required before receiving the sacrament of Communion. According to Aquinas the rite involves the acts of contrition, confession, satisfaction, and absolution.

HOLY UNCTION.   Holy unction, sometimes called extreme unction, is the practice of anointing with oil or laying on of hands of the sick or the dying. In practice it has been a rite for those on the point of death, but the Second Vatican Council urged it to be called "anointing the sick" or the elderly or seriously ill. The rite is practiced for healing in some Protestant churches (James 5:13–16).

"Mysteries" of Christ as Symbols of Devotion

In this discussion of ritual observance, word, and sacrament one may begin to sense the import of Frederick C. Grant's statement: "If one wishes to feel the very pulse beat of any high religion, it must as a rule be sought in its liturgy."[27] In addition to word and sacrament there are "events" celebrated in the liturgy of the Church. It may be appropriate in this connection to consider the character of the stories of the birth and resurrection of Jesus, and the role of the Virgin Mary in Roman Catholic devotion. We might have discussed these earlier in connection with the Christ Event, but we postponed discussion because they are best apprehended, we think, in the language of symbol and devotion. They are sometimes treated as "mysteries" of Christ—those critical moments in the revelation of Christ which may be more or less historical but which are so elaborated by legendary tendencies that it is almost impossible to know what happened. Among these mysteries are the birth stories, the baptism of Jesus, the temptation, the transfiguration, and the resurrection.

If the best guide to the essence of any religion is its liturgy then it is not an accident that these "moments" in the life of Jesus have been major occasions for the Church's life and devotion. They stress the immanence of God—those relational and responsive aspects of the character of God subsumed in traditional theology under the work of the Holy Spirit. In the context of a Hebraic mode of thought and devotional language characteristic of the synagogue these ritual acts embody some of the unmistakably human events in the life of Jesus as effective symbols for those crucial turning points in human life. Thus, for example, Jesus' baptism is the prototype for the Christian baptismal rite pointing to the Christian vocation of the child or adult. Lent begins with the temptation stories, not to psychoanalyze Jesus but to emphasize the universal human problem of temptation in the fact of decision and suffering.

THE BIRTH AND RESURRECTION STORIES.   The two greatest festivals of the Christian calendar, Christmas and Easter, are respectively symbols of birth and death. Whatever their event character may be, they are not to be taken literally as religious explanations of biological anomalies. In the New Testament world, birth and death were "mysteries" that were "numinous" in character, not matter-of-fact biological explanations of conception or resuscitation of cellular structures as understood in later biology. Such attempted explanations say nothing essentially religious at all. For example, if the Virgin Birth could be explained by parthenogenesis, then Jesus would be part human and part divine (Arianism) which is precisely what the Church has always maintained that he is not. Christ is not, according to Christian belief, a "third something" composed of a fusion of God and man. On the contrary, according to orthodox belief, in him the divine nature in its distinctiveness and human nature in its distinctiveness are united; and their perfect union manifests the divine through the whole and complete humanity. The resurrection does not assert that a dead Jew was photographically and publicly observable for a time and then went up into the sky in a cloud. The New Testament stories make perfectly clear that these were not empirically observable events in that sense, since Jesus appeared only to his disciples. Rather, against all docetic and gnostic assertions, these are symbols or stories meant to say something about the import of Jesus' whole life—the pathos and joy of coming into this world with its tragic antinominies in suffering and death, hope and victory of the cosmic significance of life. The Christian assertion is not that a Jew named Jesus was born without a human father but that the Son of God of one substance with the Father became man. The resurrection experience likewise is one of the whole living personality of Jesus united with God and apprehended as the risen Christ. The living Lord of the Universe conquered destruction and death and united humanity with himself as a symbol of the sure and certain promise of the high destiny of mankind.

All this is portrayed in the picturesque language of creed, canticle, and poetry which are event statements. "He was conceived by the Holy Ghost —he comes by the action of God; and "He sitteth at the right hand of God"—he reigns over the universe. The nativity story with its annunciation by angels, the mother, the child, lowly at birth in a manger, the wise men discovering the cosmic import of the child and then a man with a message of peace and love, his suffering and death, final despair and the supreme victory—all of these are sung and told in legend and poetry. But note that these are songs not just about the past events but about the human situation in every generation. There are always cruel Herods, flights into Egypt, and deliverances therefrom. These are all events unmistakably human and yet pointing to situations where God is present and manifest. As history, legend, or myth, they can be subjected to historical scrutiny or interpreted in abstract faith statements, but these human episodes are best comprehended in worship, song, and prayer.

THEOTOKOS: THE MOTHER OF GOD.   "Of Mary the Virgin, theotokos as to his manhood." This formulation at the Council of Ephesus in A.D. 431 indicates a doctrine and symbol of similar character. The veneration of Mary is integral to both Orthodox and Roman Catholic liturgies. Mariology is often a very controversial subject, but it is one very germane to the ecumenical discussions of the present age, since Protestants do not share in the dogma.

Both the dogma and devotion so important to Catholics especially are the outcomes of many centuries of development and practice. References in the New Testament are obscure but theologians defend the doctrine by implicit reference in Scripture. Although veneration of the Virgin as the "Mother of God" or "Mother of Christ" emerged in the Church as early as the second century, was defined at the Council of Ephesus in 431, and was reaffirmed in the Chalcedonian formula, it was not until the Middle Ages that Mariology appeared as an indispensable expression of piety. In 1854, Pius IX promulgated the dogma of the immaculate conception of Mary—that she was naturally conceived but from the first was exempt from original sin "full of grace" and "innocent." This is not to be confused with the "virgin birth" of Jesus. In 1950, as a logical consequence of this dogma, Pius XII proclaimed the dogma of the *assumption* of Mary: "The immaculate mother of God, ever a virgin, at the end of the course of her earthly life was raised with her body and soul to heavenly glory." In 1964, at the closing session of the Second Vatican Council, Pope Paul VI proclaimed her "Mother of the Church."

The Catholic Church has assigned to Mary many titles, but the most significant one is mediatrix. As Mother of God, Catholics believe that she plays an indispensable role in Incarnation. As chief of the saints, she is believed to be closest to the sources of divine love and aid so that prayers addressed to and through her carry a fervent hope of fulfillment. Mary as mediatrix should be understood in the role of intercessor rather than as coredeemer or mediator. She is to be venerated for those acts of intercession which belong with the intercession of the saints, and these are the counterparts of the Comforter or the Holy Spirit as these have been understood historically.

Ethics and Grace

By now we may be able to see more clearly the fallacy of supposing that Judaism is a religion of law, Christianity of grace. Both law and grace are in both, with varying emphases, to be sure, but grace is in the commandment and the response to grace is in law. We turn now to apply these principles to wider questions of the human condition and particularly to the responsibility of the Jew and Christian in the world. Technically, this comes under the heading of Ethics or Moral Theology. However, it is not our purpose here to describe, in any formal sense, the fields of ethics or social ethics. Our discussion takes as its starting point the stance of Jews and Christians in the world. The term *ethics* comes from the Greek word

Ethos, stable, meaning the place where one stands. This provides our clue: How does a Jew or Christian, taking his stance in faith and grace, respond fittingly both to the demands of the will of God and the situation which confronts him? In more formal terms, what is the good to be sought, the imperative to be obeyed, in what situation? Or, how can one decide and act responsibly?

MYSTERY AND COMMANDMENT.   The *Ethics of the Fathers* says that the world rests upon three foundations: the Torah; divine service; and the practice of loving-kindness between man and man. This is both mystery and commandment; mystery because the infinite God is in relationship with finite man, to whom he gives the commandment. To receive the commandment man must remain man. The giving of the commandment accentuates the humanity of man because it assumes that he is responsible. "How does a man find his Father who is in heaven? He finds him by good deeds and the study of the Torah. The Holy One Blessed Be He finds man through love, brotherhood, truth, peace, humility, study; through a good heart; through a NO that is a firm NO, and a YES that is a firm YES" (Seder Eliahu Rabbah 23).

This is described as the *righteousness of God*, which is both judgment and steadfast faithfulness to the Covenant. The righteousness of God is usually distinguished from justice (mishpat), but the two are also closely related. The divine righteousness determines the nature of human justice, and justice is concerned with salvation. The revelation of God's righteousness means the enactment of salvation.

> In thy righteousness, rescue me and deliver me,
> Incline thine ear unto me and save me (Psalms 71:2)

Apparently, the Psalmist is convinced that God will reply to his petition, so that when God is bent on salvation to men, His righteousness is operative. Likewise, injustice is unrighteousness, unfaithfulness, lack of mercy. Doing justice (Micah 6:8) means doing God's will. Hence, a violation of the covenant relationship and a sin against mercy is a sin against God.

To the prophets, a single act of injustice was a disaster. They speak and act as if the heavens were about to collapse because Israel had become unfaithful to God (Jeremiah 2:12–13). The standard is a "supernatural measure," remembering that Israel herself was once a sojourner in Egypt and God had a care for her which did not calculate her merit. Indeed, the motive for action cannot be limited to respect for divine authority. The people of the Covenant responded to God in a way which may be described as grateful obedience or obedient gratitude; and gratitude was more fundamental, since God had first delivered Israel out of Egypt before ever there was a nation to receive the Law. This love of God—God's love of man and man's responsive love of God—is the source of man's power to love his neighbor, that is, it is the source of his ethics. Man can refuse this grace or love, refuse to enter into this relation because of self-will and self-sufficiency. That is sin. Yet God seeks man out and offers him salvation. God wishes to redeem, but only with man's consent. Without this grace there is nothing, but man must make the beginning. The Law is his duty and it is also the way he responds to God.

FAITH AND WORKS.   When we turn to the Christian understanding of grace and law, we come upon one real difference: for the Christian, the stress is not upon the law as response by man to God, but upon the perception of God's ways by man. Consequently there is real doubt about man's ability to keep the law. Nonetheless, he takes the divine law, the moral law, very seriously. The difficulty with obeying the law is not so much in its commandments; one presumably could keep the Ten Commandments. But law is concerned with the thoughts and intents of the human heart. Man's impulse to self-love, even in his quest for salvation, is too subtle and self-deceiving to be disinterested. Luther rediscovered the astonishing paradox in the biblical meaning of righteousness, that it does not mean distributive justice which rewards the good and punishes the evil. Ultimately the righteousness of God is not punitive but redemptive. It is not a judge's merciless verdict against us, but a father's costly gift to us. This led Luther to the famous notion of justification by grace through faith.

This was not a new notion. Actually, Luther learned it from St. Bernard of Clairvaux who had held that justification by faith was the only basis for new life in God; that no moral achievement was possible except by grace. One place where Luther differed with many of the medievalists was in the conception of the importance of natural or moral law. Aquinas regarded the natural law as that form of the eternal law by which man, through the exercise of his powers of reason, may be directed toward his earthly end and to a knowledge of his otherworldly end. Such a knowledge in either respect is limited; hence it is necessary that the divine law be given to man to perfect his pursuit of his earthly end, and his knowledge and his attainment of his supernatural end. Luther held that the law has three functions: as a mirror to show us our deceitful, impotent selves; as a hammer to break us down, reducing us to despair—as grace is defined as love in action, so law is wrath in action; and as a mask, since the sinner's despair is part of God's beneficent intention. It is only then that grace can do its proper work, for God gives man freely and utterly what man can never earn or compel. Thus God's grace works through His righteousness, for it is His nature to have mercy and to forgive.

Augustine put it this way:

Now the love of God is said to be shed abroad in our hearts, not because He loves us, but because He makes us lovers of Himself; just as the righteousness of God is used in the sense of our being made righteous by His gift; and the salvation of the Lord, in that we are saved by Him; and the faith of Jesus Christ, because He makes us believers in Him. This is that righteousness of God, which He not only teaches us by the precept of His law, but also bestows upon us by the gift of His Spirit."[28]

Only through the forgiveness of sins are good works possible; and only through the grace of God may one be assisted so that eternal life may be won as reward.

So for Christians as for Jews the gift of grace involves responsive human activity. Justification, so far from implying quietism, is the source of morality. It is the impulse to action. Faith without ethical consequences would be no faith. Luther in his famous *Preface* said that true faith was a work of God in man which transforms and regenerates his heart and faculties: "Faith does not ask whether there are good works to be done; for, before one can ask, it has already done them . . . It is always in action. . . . One can no more separate works from faith than one can separate light and heat from a flame. . . . Faith is a living and unshakeable confidence, a belief in the grace of God so assured that a man would die a thousand deaths for its sake."[29]

Religion and morality, therefore, are not only indissociable; it is religion which makes morality real. How does one describe this obligation to love? First, it is springing and overflowing and requires no stimulus. It does not calculate, ask for security, or guarantee for the future. Tillich interprets justification by faith as a willingness to live in the "boundary situation"— that is, in the knowledge "that his existence can at no time and in no way be made secure." Second, love is the love of neighbor. A Christian is a channel, Luther said, open upward to heaven by faith, and outward to the neighbor in love. All that he possesses has been received from God, that he may pass it on. Thus he is called to be a Christ to his neighbor. What we do to our neighbor therefore we do not only in this world order, but in the eternal order.

The Christian position, with all the variations and shadings aside, can be stated as "Justification by grace . . . through faith . . . unto good works" (Ephesians 2:8–10). Forgiveness stands and needs to stand over the best of human hopes, aspirations, and activities. Through God's unqualified acceptance of man, man is freed from calculation, terror, and self, and set free to love his neighbor and to work responsibly in the world. For both Jew and Christian, perhaps, we can say that the divine will or purpose defines the positive meaning of human life, which is to do the will of God. And the content of this will is ethical action.

The ethical obligations of their faith for Jews and Christians ought to be clear: the sovereignty of God, His actions in history, the demand for obedience, and the hope of the coming kingdom—all are relevant for the moral life. The primary questions are, What is God doing in the world? and How do I respond? They still leave the ambiguities and complexities of man's situation for ethical decision. A search for ethics is a search for meaning, an integrative relationship, a frame of reference. The question for man is, What am I, as a Christian or a Jew, to do? This makes it necessary for one to follow the demands of his particular faith. I do what I am. Whatever is done must be done in relation to one's faith—what is God doing?—or the Law, or principles derived from faith in relation to the concrete situation. The facts are important. Faith and facts determine one's ethical decisions and actions.

Social Ethics

All that we have been saying about faith applies to the social and political structure as well. If God works in history, then He is at work in the great political and economic struggles of the time. This has not always been clearly seen. Too often moralistic ethics have been more concerned with personal habits than with such relationships as those of Negroes and whites. Love of neighbor is equally applicable to problems of the South— and North; war and peace; surpluses and starvation; the use of nuclear energy; Israelis and Arabs. The Jew or Christian dealing with such questions must respond not only as a Russian, American, or Indian, not only as politician, businessman, or teacher, but as Jew or Christian, whose understanding of all experience and being is illumined by his faith.

Finally, it is the conviction of both Jews and Christians that God the Creator wills to bring to perfection nothing less than the whole of His creation. This is symbolized in the messianic hope and in the idea of the Kingdom of God, a political symbol. The Messianic Age may come with an ideal leader, the universalism of faith, the action of God, or the unification of mankind. It is a hope and goal. For Christianity, the kingdom concept is a symbol for the victory or reign of God. It has little to say about how the end (if any) will come; it has the conviction that history has a purpose which will be, and is being, completed and fulfilled. God's purpose for mankind and the world is illuminated in the mythology of the creation on the one hand, and in the Last Judgment or Second Advent, on the other. The ultimate issue of history or the end of the world is the final victory of God. It is both hope and promise in the future, and power and vision in the here-and-now. But that is the subject of the next chapter.

NOTES

1. Emil Fackenheim, "Judaism." From *The Meaning of Life in Five Great Religions*, edited by R. C. Chalmers and John A. Irving. Published in the U.S.A. by The Westminster Press, 1966. Copyright by The Ryerson Press, Toronto, 1965. Used by permission.

2. See Walter J. Burghardt, S.J., and William F. Lynch, S.J., eds., *The Idea of Catholicism* (Cleveland and New York: World and Meridian, 1964), pp. 143 ff.

3. Bernard Meland, *The Reality of Faith* (New York: Oxford University Press, 1962), p. 258.

4. Bernard Meland, *Faith and Culture* (London: Allen and Unwin, 1955), p. 183.

5. For a concise discussion of this development see Gerard S. Sloyan, *The Three Persons in One God* (Englewood Cliffs, N.J.: Prentice-Hall, 1964).

6. See "The Gospel as a Document of the History of the Jewish Faith" in Leo Baeck, *Judaism and Christianity* (New York: World, and Philadelphia: Jewish Publication Society, 1961).

7. See Samuel Sandmel, *We Jews and Jesus* (New York: Oxford University Press, 1965), especially Chapter 3.

8. See Yehezkel Kaufmann, "The Biblical Age," in Leo W. Schwarz, ed., *Great Ideas and Ages of the Jewish People* (New York: Random House and Modern Library, 1956), p. 12.

9. See Rudolf Otto, *The Idea of the Holy* (London: Oxford University Press, 1923), Chapter 4.

10. For further reading see especially Joseph Klausner, *Jesus of Nazareth*, trans. Herbert Danby (Boston: Beacon, 1964); Sandmel, *We Jews and Jesus*, and Samuel Sandmel, *A Jewish Understanding of the New Testament* (Cincinnati: Hebrew Union College Press, 1957); Hans Joachim Schoeps, *The Jewish-Christian Argument*, trans. David Green (New York: Holt, Rinehart and Winston, 1963); and Baeck, *Judaism and Christianity*.

11. Klausner, *Jesus of Nazareth*, p. 414.

12. Baeck, *Judaism and Christianity*, pp. 100–101.

13. Sandmel, *A Jewish Understanding of the New Testament*, p. 44.

14. Robert Gordis, *Judaism in a Christian World* (New York: McGraw-Hill, 1966), p. 158.

15. John MacQuarrie, *Principles of Christian Theology* (New York: Scribner, 1966), p. 397. In this section we are deeply indebted to this book, especially Chapter 19.

16. Solomon Schechter, *Studies in Judaism* (Philadelphia: Jewish Publication Society, 1945), second series, p. 178.

17. Emil Fackenheim, "On the Self-Exposure of Faith to the Modern World: Philosophical Reflections in the Light of Jewish Experience," in *Daedalus*, Winter, 1967, p. 210.

18. Schechter, *Studies in Judaism*, p. 61.

19. See Burghardt and Lynch, eds., *The Idea of Catholicism*, pp. 184 ff.

20. See P. Gregory Stevens, O.S.M., *The Life of Grace* (Englewood Cliffs, N.J.: Prentice-Hall, 1963).
21. Walter M. Abbott, S.J., ed., *Documents of Vatican II*, trans. Very Rev. Msgr. Joseph Gallagher (New York: America Press, 1966), III, 61, 158.
22. Macquarrie, *Principles of Christian Theology*, p. 398.
23. *Institutes*, IV, 14–1, trans. by John Sclen (London: 1813), 3 vols., Seventh American edition (Philadelphia: Presbyterian Board of Christian Education, 1945), 2 vols.
24. Cf. A. D. Nock, *Conversion* (London: Oxford, 1961), pp. 144 ff.; and E. R. Goodenough, *By Light, light; the mystic gospel of Hellenistic Judaism* (New Haven: Yale University Press; London: H. Milford, Oxford University Press, 1935).
25. C. H. Dodd, *The Epistle of Paul to the Romans* (London: Collins-Fontana, 1960), pp. 99 ff. See also II Esdras, 3–21 ff.
26. Abbott, ed., *Documents of Vatican II*, p. 156.
27. Frederick C. Grant, *An Introduction to New Testament Thought* (New York and Nashville: Abingdon, 1950), p. 101.
28. St. Augustine, *Of Spirit and Letter*, 56.
29. Quoted from John Dillenberger, ed., *Martin Luther: Selections From His Writings* (Garden City, N.Y.: Doubleday Anchor Book, 1961), p. 24.

SELECT BIBLIOGRAPHY

BAECK, LEO. *Judaism and Christianity*. Trans. and intro. Walter Kaufmann. New York: World; and Philadelphia: Jewish Publication Society, 1961.

BOUYER, LOUIS. *Life and Liturgy*. London & New York: Sheed and Ward, 1956.

S. S. COHON. *Judaism: A Way of Life*. New York: Schocken, 1962.

CONGAR, YVES. *The Mystery of the Temple*. Trans. R. F. Trevett. London: Burns & Oates, 1962.

DIX, GREGORY. *The Shape of the Liturgy*. London: Dacre Press, 1945.

GASTER, THEODOR. *Passover, Its History and Tradition*. Boston: Beacon, 1962.

GLATZER, NAHUM N., ed. *The Dynamics of Emancipation: The Jew in the Modern Age*. Boston: Beacon, 1965.

JOSEPH, MORRIS J. *Judaism as Creed and Life*. London: Routledge and Kegan Paul, 1958.

MACQUARRIE, JOHN. *Principles of Christian Theology*. New York: McGraw-Hill, 1966.

NOCK, A. D. *Conversion*. London: Oxford University Press, 1961.

PETUCHOWSKI, J. J. *Ever Since Sinai: A Modern View of the Torah*. New York: Scribe, 1961.

RICHARDSON, CYRAL. *The Doctrine of the Trinity*. New York and Nashville: Abingdon, 1958.

ROBINSON, H. WHEELER. *The Christian Experience of the Holy Spirit*. London: Nisbet, 1928.

SANDMEL, SAMUEL. *We Jews and You Christians*. Philadelphia and New York: Lippincott, 1967.

SCHARPER, PHILIP, ed. *Torah and Gospel*. New York: Sheed and Ward, 1966.

SCHILLEBEECK, E. *Christ the Sacrament of the Encounter With God*. New York: Sheed and Ward, 1963.

SCHOEPPS, HANS J. *The Jewish-Christian Argument*. New York: Holt, 1963.

SILVER, A. H. *Where Judaism Differed*. New York: Macmillan, 1956.

STENDAHL, KRISTER, ed. *The Scrolls and the New Testament*. London, 1958.

VAN DER LEEUW, GERARDUS. *Sacred and Profane Beauty: The Holy in Art*. Trans. David E. Green. New York: Holt, 1963.

WEIGLE, GUSTAVE. *Where Do We Differ: Catholic Theology in Dialogue*. London: Burns & Oates, 1961.

XI

Eschatology and History

IN this chapter we shall examine in some detail the general meaning and the place of eschatology in Judaism and Christianity. Our concern will be directed toward the fundamental eschatological symbols[1] that appear in these religious faiths. The specific problems arising from these symbols as they affect either Judaism or Christianity will be dealt with in their proper context. Thus, the different meanings of the Messiah for Judaism and Christianity will be noted, and this will lead to the different interpretations each faith places upon such symbols as the Last Judgment, the Resurrection, Heaven, and Hell. Similarly certain differences within Christianity on the interpretation of these symbols will also be pointed out. Above all it will be emphasized that many of the conclusions concerning the basic symbols of either Judaism or Christianity are highly speculative and frequently admit of more diversity of opinion than agreement.

THE MEANING OF ESCHATOLOGY

Eschatology is that branch of theology concerned with last things, such as, death, resurrection, judgment, the Messiah, and immortality. The term "eschatology" is derived from the Greek *eschatos*, meaning "furthest" or "last." The Oxford English Dictionary defines it as "the science of the four last things: death, judgment, heaven, and hell." Paradoxically, although it is concerned with "last things," as with the termination of this world and this life, the religious meaning of the term emphasizes at the same time that it will deal with a new life and a new world. The old world—this present world—will give way to the ushering in of the new world of eternity. The Old Adam of man is replaced in Christian thought by the new man in Christ. The instrument for effecting this momentous change will be God, Who having created the world can also bring it to an end. But at the end of this world, He creates the new world of His kingdom, realized either in *this world* or in *another world*—the world of Israel redeemed or the world of the Kingdom of God established by Jesus Christ.

Eschatology is essentially a religious symbol. Dealing as it does with the symbols of the religious experience, it is not conducive to philosophical conceptual analysis. Nor can it be reduced to scientific knowledge, for scientific knowledge is conceptual and factual. Eschatology transcends both philosophy and science; it relates to a cosmic reality based upon revelations apprehended and accepted by the individual. Occasionally, of course, it may touch upon certain problems frequently treated within philosophical investigation, such as the demonstration of the immortality of the soul, or the attempt to discover the laws of history. For the most part, however, eschatology remains fundamentally religious. Its symbols are the symbols of religious experience, its premises are the truths that man accepts as revealed, and its method is essentially the explication and interpretation of such truths and symbols.

As a religious symbol eschatology is concerned with the interpretation of history as meaningful, purposeful, and ethical. This interpretation of history contrasts sharply with the views of many historians and philosophers. The historian usually looks upon his task as a scientific or humanistic study. As a social scientist the historian views historical research as necessary to obtain a better understanding of man's past. The past is something to be ordered and investigated so that probable predictions can be arrived at with respect to the future course of human history. From the humanistic point of view the historian is concerned with the values that can be learned and applied from the study of man's past. In any event, the historian is not concerned with the end of history, nor does he strive to transcend history and relate it to some higher cosmic reality.

Philosophers are agreed that the study of history does not yield demonstrative knowledge and that to determine its purposes is a hazardous undertaking. But these considerations have not prevented many philosophers from speculating about the nature and course of human history. Such speculations have been embodied either in many utopian myths of the wave of the future or in the outright rejection of any vistas of the future. Like the writer of Ecclesiastes, the philosopher of history may contend that "there is nothing new under the sun."[2] With the historians Spengler and Toynbee he may contend that history is completely cyclical, cultures and civilizations succeeding one another in unending cycles of time.

The Cyclical View of History

The cyclical view, or the myth of the eternal recurrence, holds that history is endlessly repetitive, directionless, devoid of end or purpose. History, it is claimed, moves in cycles of time throughout eternity, rather than in a linear time that culminates in some specific goal.

The cyclical view may be all-embracing in its scope. In the Hindu mythologies the cycles of birth and rebirth, the wheel of death and birth, apply to the life of the individual, the life of society and the state, and the life of the universe. These cycles are usually divided into four stages marked by periods of moral progress and decline.[3] A complete cycle is usually computed in terms that stagger the imagination of the western mind. Such a cycle is said to cover 4,320,000,000 years. Obviously the place and the importance of man and his values are dwarfed within such a world, especially since there is no finality to the process.

Greek mythology is also dominated by this notion of cycles or the myth of the eternal recurrence. The content of the Greek mythology differs from that of the Hindu, but the most marked differences between the two views is that the cycles and the stages in Greek mythology are far more limited in time. Thus in Plato's odyssey of the soul, the total lapse of time for one cycle in the transmigration of the soul is only 10,000 years—and even less for the soul of the philosopher.[4] Greek mythology also seems less concerned with the extension of the cycles to the cosmos and the birth and rebirth of the universe. The Greek cycles are applied more to man and society. Thus the various forms of government are assumed to undergo a cyclical change. In the *Republic* Plato describes the process by which the form of government moves successively from aristocracy (the best) to timocracy, from timocracy to oligarchy, from oligarchy to democracy, and from democracy to tyranny (the worst). Then it is assumed that the process will be begun all over again.

Although there is an ethical element present in both mythologies, the stages within the cycles representing different moral levels, the cyclical view as a whole offers no real finality of happiness or salvation for the individual. The cyclical view negates the virtue of hope for man. And without hope the future has no significance and history is without meaning. St. Paul reminded the Christians of Ephesus that when they were Gentiles they had no hope.[5]

That history is meaningful, that it has a purpose and a goal, and that it holds out hope for man is nowhere better exemplified than in the whole Jewish-Christian tradition. Judaism and Christianity are unique in their conception of history. Following certain interpretations of Judaism, the hope of man lies in God and in the conviction that God's purposes are realized in history. The people of Israel place their hopes in the expectation of a great good, the coming of the messianic kingdom. In such a kingdom the ultimate happiness and salvation of man will be achieved. With Christianity there is another and a marked change in the interpretation of history. Jesus as the Messiah *has* appeared in history. The hope of man is now directed toward a salvation promised by Christ and to be realized through his redemption and in a life to come. For the Christian the spiritual progress of man begins with a faith in God. With this faith the individual is moved by a desire for salvation and an expectation that God will fulfill His promises to man. Charity or the love of God perfects the faith and hope of the individual and leads him to the love of God in an eternal happiness. Once such happiness in eternity is achieved, faith and hope are no longer needed.

The rejection of the cyclical version of history was very well stated by Augustine when he wrote:

> What pious ears could bear to hear that after a life spent in so many and severe distresses . . . that after evils so disastrous . . . and when we have thus attained to the vision of God and have entered into bliss by the contemplation of spiritual light and participation in His unchangeable immortality, which we burn to attain—that we must at some time lose all this . . . and that this will happen endlessly again and again, recurring at fixed intervals, and in regularly returning periods? . . . Who, I say, can listen to such things? Who can accept or suffer them to be spoken? . . . For if in the future world we shall not remember these things and by this oblivion be blessed, why should we now increase our misery, already burdensome enough, by the knowledge of them? If, on the other hand, the knowledge of them will be forced upon us hereafter, now at least let us remain in ignorance, that in the present expectation we may enjoy a blessedness which the future reality is not to bestow; since in this life we are expecting to obtain life everlasting, but in the world to come are to discover it to be blessed, but not everlasting.[6]

History as Meaningful: Conclusion

For the religious concept of eschatology the meaning of history is revealed in Scripture rather than in the attempted speculations of the philosopher. The true meaning of history may be said to be contained in a theology of history. Such a theology of history would have a certitude not found in a philosophy of history and a meaningfulness based upon the faith of the individual. Within Judaism and Christianity the meaning of creation is revealed in its end, and only the valuation of creation as good makes creation meaningful. As Tillich puts it: "Between the questions 'wherefrom' and 'whereto' lies the whole system of theological questions and answers."[7]

What is said of the beginning and the end of the universe is necessarily highly symbolical or speculative. For the meaning of the end of history there are many symbols in the Jewish-Christian tradition, symbols that must be held together in a kind of syndrome for their total understanding. In addition, they must be placed within an ordered structure, which is history itself.[8] For the Jews the meaning of history centers upon the covenants God made with Noah and Abraham and ratified in the Covenant with Moses at Sinai. The Law given to Moses gives meaning to history, for by the observance of the Law man perfects himself and society. The Law will disappear with the consummation of history and the realization of the Kingdom of God. For Christians, Christ is the principle of the fulfillment of the goal and the consummation of all existence. For Christians the cross becomes the pivotal point in the Christian examination of the meaning of history, its beginning and its end. The Jew looks forward to the future consummation of history; the Christian sees its consummation in the Christ event, so that time is divided between "B.C." and "A.D.," facing in two directions, looking backward to creation and forward to the consummation of all things. The meaning of history in the Jewish-Christian ideology must be seen against the understanding of what the eternal has to do with the temporal. The Jewish-Christian understanding of historical reality refers not so much to the relations of nations and of persons as it does to their relationship to God. History, therefore, is not reduced to mere human happenings; this would undermine man's sense of personality, his significance in the ebb and flow of events. The importance of being a person is to take one's place, one's role in the drama of man in the presence of God. In that drama no individual is a mere thing or event. Each individual is a subject of unlimited destiny and great significance, and each individual is challenged to make a decision which will make history so far as that individual is concerned. This is the discernment of the eternal in time, which gives to the idea of time an incomparable significance. If, for example, the period A.D. 1–30 is a time of great destiny in the world, or if 1250 B.C.E. in the lunar calendar of Judaism is a moment of great destiny, then every moment is of great worth. It is the Kairos which gives meaning to the Chronos, for the Kairos is the intersection of our time with eternity, making every moment of time significant. With the manifestation of God in and through history every moment of time is charged with significance and value.

This, then, is the symbol and the meaning of eschatology. The development of the various symbols contained within eschatology we shall consider next by examining in order the basic eschatological symbols that appear in Judaism and in Christianity.

The Eschatology of Judaism

As we have observed in previous chapters, Judaism is essentially a historical religion. God reveals Himself to the Jewish people in history and He intervenes in history for His people and for all men and nations. God has covenanted with His people. He is concerned with the welfare and the salvation of His chosen people, and He has led them out of Egypt to the Promised Land. This recital could be continued at length, but it should be obvious that Israel has a future, that God has given the history of Israel a meaning and endowed it with His promises and hopes. These promises and hopes center upon the central symbol of the Jewish eschatology: the Messiah and the messianic kingdom.

The Messiah and the Messianic Kingdom

For Judaism there is a Messiah and a messianic kingdom. Both are intimately connected and bound up within history. The Messiah *will* appear in history and the messianic kingdom *will* appear within history. This contrasts sharply with Christianity, which teaches that the Messiah as Jesus has appeared and that he has established his kingdom both now and in the future. The future messianic kingdom foretold in the Hebrew Scriptures envisions the destruction of all present evils and the realization of a whole new set of values. It is important to stress this point, for Jewish eschatology (like the Christian) is through and through ethical. The vision of the messianic kingdom as one in which the highest ethical values will be achieved is the logical consequence of the belief in a personal God Who has established a moral relationship with His people. Furthermore, to say that the Messiah and the messianic kingdom will appear in history means for the Jewish tradition that the Messiah and the messianic kingdom are essentially of *this* world although their realization lies in the future.

The coming of the Messiah and the messianic kingdom is closely bound up in the early development of Judaism with the Jewish monarchy. The term "Messiah" means anointed, and in the early monarchy it referred to the person anointed with the holy oil (II Kings 5:3). In the early history of Israel the monarchy, especially under King David, attained considerable prestige. Thus the monarchy established by David becomes not merely an ideal for the future, but it is given a religious sanction and ratification. It has the duty of maintaining the Covenant and preparing for the future salvation of man in the messianic kingdom that is to come. The close relationship between the Davidic monarchy and God is clearly evident in much of the second book of Samuel, which covers the reign of David. In particular the divine character and direction of the monarchy is very marked in the words of God as reported by the prophet Nathan.

When your days are fulfilled and you lie down with your fathers, I will raise up your son after you, who shall come forth from your body, and I will establish his kingdom. He shall build a house for my name, and I will establish the throne of his kingdom for ever. I will be his father, and he shall be my son. When he commits iniquity, I will chasten him with the stripes of the sons of men; but I will not take my steadfast love from him, as I took it from Saul, whom I put away from before you. And your house and your kingdom shall be made sure for ever before me; your throne shall be established for ever (II Samuel 7:12–16).

Of verse 12, in which it is said "I will raise up your son after you, who shall come forth from your body, . . ." the immediate reference is to the reign of King Solomon. Jewish theologians would add that this verse also refers to the sanctification of the coming rule of the Messiah as King. Some Christian theologians would interpret the verse as referring more to the coming of Jesus as the Messiah, since Jesus is called the son of David. However this may be, the entire chapter certainly ratifies the Davidic monarchy and establishes its messianic character for all time to come.

Furthermore, the very prosperity and greatness of the Davidic monarchy is a type of what is to come in the future realization of the messianic kingdom. The religious character of the monarchy, evident in its important role in the maintenance of the Covenant, was coupled with its political prestige and its economic prosperity. All these factors contributed not only to the strong sense of nationalism in Israel but served as the basis for certain nationalistic hopes that came to be centered on the vision of the messianic kingdom. In particular such hopes included the strong conviction that the new kingdom would be of this world and that it would be especially marked by material blessings and prosperity.[9]

Despite the ratification of the Davidic monarchy and its more immediate and phenomenal successes, its increasing failures in the years to come led to prophetic criticism and denunciation. One of the strongest and most significant critics of the monarchy in this later period was the prophet Isaiah. The prophecy of Isaiah for the future of the monarchy is the vision of an ideal monarchy, of a kingdom of God ruled over by the Messiah, who shall be a descendant of David. For Isaiah the Messiah as an ideal king will come to rule over an ideal kingdom, one which will restore the golden age of man, an age in which there is no evil, no sickness, and no death. All this is clearly brought out in the following frequently quoted passage:

There shall come forth a shoot from the stump of Jesse, and a branch shall grow out of his roots. And the Spirit of the Lord shall rest upon him, the spirit of wisdom and understanding, the spirit of counsel and might, the spirit of knowledge and the fear of the Lord. And his delight shall be in the fear of the Lord.

He shall not judge by what his eyes see, or decide by what his ears hear; but with righteousness he shall judge the poor, and decide with equity for the meek of the earth; and he shall smite the earth with the rod of his mouth, and with the breath of his lips he shall slay the wicked. Righteousness shall be the girdle of his waist, and faithfulness the girdle of his loins.

The wolf shall dwell with the lamb, and the leopard shall lie down with the kid, and the calf and the lion and the fatling together, and a little child shall lead them. The cow and the bear shall feed; their young shall lie down together; and the lion shall eat straw like the ox. The sucking child shall play over the hole of the asp, and the weaned child shall put his hand on the adder's den. They shall not hurt or destroy in all my holy mountain; for the earth shall be full of the knowledge of the Lord as the waters cover the sea (Isaiah 11:1–9).

Some Christian theologians regarded this prophecy of Isaiah as a fore-telling of the coming of Jesus as the Messiah. For Jewish theologians the coming of the Messiah is still a part of the dream of Israel. Also, the Messiah expected by the Jews is a person, a human being and not a god. The human nature of the Messiah is often signalized in terms of "the suffering servant of the Lord" (Isaiah 52–53). The Messiah will also be poor and humble and despised. But he will be a concrete reality and his appearance will come in God's own time, and that will be the end of time and the establishment of God's kingdom. The knowledge of the end of history lies with God, and He and not man will consummate the end of history with the coming of the true Messiah.

In the historical development of this notion of the Messiah, it should be observed that a transition is made from the conception of the Messiah as a political ruler and liberator, one who will merely free the Jews from the oppressive rule of others, to the conception of an ideal monarchy, one who will effect the spiritual regeneration of all people. Although originally only a national savior, the Messiah now becomes the perfect type of ruler who will sanctify and establish the rule of God's law for all men. The particularism and nationalism involved in the original conception of the Messiah merges into the conception of a Messiah for all mankind, one who will redeem not merely Israel but the whole world. With this conception of a more universalistic religion, the emphasis upon the Messiah is replaced more and more with an emphasis upon the messianic kingdom, the benefits of which will extend not merely to the Jewish people but to all peoples and for all times. This new conception of the Messiah and the messianic kingdom is present in the revelation of the prophet Daniel:

I saw in the night visions, and behold, with the clouds of heaven there came one like a son of man, and he came to the Ancient of Days and was presented before him. And to him was given dominion and glory and kingdom, that all peoples, nations, and languages should serve him; his dominion is an everlasting dominion, which shall not pass away, and his kingdom one that shall not be destroyed (Daniel, 7:13–15).

That the religion of Israel is to be world encompassing is revealed also in the fact that Israel is to be not only a witness to God, a partner of God in a historical relationship, but that Israel is also concerned to bring its truth to other nations. For if there is but one God, why should there not be one mankind, one law, one justice, one set of moral values for all men and not simply for a chosen few?

At this point it would be in order to note some essential principles of agreement and disagreement between the Jewish and Christian conceptions of the Messiah and the messianic kingdom. For Christians there is an equal emphasis placed upon the historical Jesus as the Messiah and the kingdom of God that he established. For Judaism there would appear to be perhaps more emphasis by contemporaries upon the messianic kingdom than upon the Messiah. Noting what he considers some differences between the Jewish and the Christian positions, Leo Baeck states:

> Judaism's messianic conception may also be contrasted with that of Christianity. Judaism stressed the kingdom of God not as something already accomplished but as something as yet to be achieved, not as a religious possession of the elect but as the moral task of all. In Judaism man sanctifies the world by sanctifying God and by overcoming evil and realizing good. The kingdom of God lies before each man so that he may begin his work; and it lies before him because it lies before all. For Judaism, the whole of mankind is chosen; God's covenant was made with all men.[10]

This statement requires certain qualifications. It is not accurate to say that in Christianity the kingdom of God is only for the elect. As St. Paul says: "God will have all men to be saved"; He wishes that all men would accept His grace for their salvation. Since this grace is offered to all men, it is the duty of all men to accept this grace and with it to fulfill their moral obligations and work out their salvation. For Christianity the kingdom of God is not to be attained through the individual's own efforts. The individual requires the grace of God, whereas Judaism leaves the attainment of such an end up to the individual. Again, the Christian may regard the kingdom of God not only as something already accomplished by Jesus but as something to be realized in the world to come. Christianity identifies Jesus with the divine figure portrayed in the apocalyptic imagery. For Judaism the Messiah will be either a wholly human person or a symbol of the product of the collective endeavors of all men to bring the Messianic Age into being.

In concluding this topic, it must be emphasized that the messianic expectation, despite differences of opinion among Jews, is a vital and living thing for the Jewish believer. Not only is it stated frequently in Scripture; it is diffused throughout the Jewish holy days, the Sabbath, and indeed throughout the whole calendar of Judaism. As Maimonides expressed this expectation: "He may come on any day." A contemporary Jewish rabbi and editor expresses this messianic expectation as follows:

> The chief features of the belief in the Messiah can then be summarized: 1) his rule of truth and goodness will extend over all mankind; 2) Israel will be restored to its pristine glory and security; 3) his sovereignty will be ushered in by God's enactment, not by human achievement; 4) the Messiah will be a single human person through whom God will perform the ultimate miracle.[11]

Lesser Symbols of the Jewish Eschatology

The symbols of hell, heaven, resurrection, and immortality are of less significance in Jewish eschatology in comparison to the all-important symbol of the Messiah and the messianic kingdom, and therefore they are considered "lesser symbols." There is much less agreement among Jewish theologians and believers on any one of these lesser symbols, whereas there is a virtual unanimity of faith in the Messiah and the messianic kingdom, however these may be conceived. The evidence, both scriptural and traditional, for the lesser symbols is less substantial, and is often a matter of differences of interpretation. It does not matter with which of these lesser symbols we begin, for it is extremely difficult to give them an essential historical coherence with one another. We shall confine our attention to the symbols of hell, heaven, resurrection, and immortality in that order. All these symbols and the beliefs associated with them acquire their significance from the moral requirements upon which they are based, upon the need to affirm a moral retribution for the individual. Actually, the way in which this moral retribution may be worked out is of much less importance than the idea of moral retribution itself. This explains why, once the symbols are affirmed, little more is said of them. In this connection it should be pointed out that for some scholars the more significant doctrine in Judaism is that of the redemption of man to be effected by the Messiah in days to come. This important ethical notion we have already commented upon in the preceding chapter.

HELL: SHE'OL AND GEHINNON.   As in Christian belief, Jewish belief in heaven and hell is bound up with the moral conviction that God will mete out retribution to the individual in accordance with his actions in this life.

In Judaism the notion of retribution in association with the afterlife develops gradually.

The death of the individual in the early Jewish belief centers on the term *nefesh* (Genesis 2:7; Leviticus 7:20–21). Death is conceived as a virtual ebbing away of the life force of the individual person so that he becomes a mere shadow of his former self (nefesh). Such a shadow or "shade" reflects the notion of the dead as leading a kind of drab, ghostly existence. The abode of the dead in this sense was called she'ol, apparently derived, according to some, from "hole" or "pit." Thus in Psalm 30:3 we read: "O Lord, thou hast brought up my soul from Sheol, restored me to live from among those gone down to the Pit."

She'ol is clearly subterranean and is similar to the Hades described by Homer. In the early development of Jewish doctrine, roughly to the third century B.C.E., there is little emphasis placed upon rewards and punishments in the afterlife for the individual. Rather it is assumed that such rewards and punishments are to be meted out in this life and in the justice imposed by the community. After the Exile there came a breakdown in the social justice imposed by the community. This led to an affirmation and an emphasis upon a retribution for each individual in the afterlife. Only in this way was it felt that divine justice could be maintained. Apparently, too, there is little relation between Yahweh and the inhabitants of she'ol in the pre-exilic period. But after the Exile, the rule of Yahweh over she'ol is asserted, each individual is judged by Yahweh and made subject to the divine justice. Sh'eol disappears as an important concept. There appears to be no description of the final judgment in the Old Testament. In the apocryphal Book of Enoch 45:69, final judgment is turned over to the Messiah.

After the Exile the term "Gehinnon" (or Gehenna) becomes prevalent. For now that the wicked must suffer individually for their misdeeds, they are no longer mere shades living a dull existence with their equals in she'ol. The term "Gehinnon" is taken from Ge-Hinnon, the valley of Hinnon, apparently located just outside Jerusalem, where the pre-Israelites were believed to have sacrificed children to the fire god Moloch. The early Jews were said to have used it to dispose of the bodies of criminals and animals, which were left to decay and to be burned. The descriptions of such a place—the fire and smoke, the sufferings and cries—easily came to be identified with the horrors of hell. The rabbinic writings and the New Testament identify it as a place of punishment ('Erubin 19a, Sukkah 32b; Matthew 5:22, 29). The closing verse in the prophecy of Isaiah apparently affirms an endless punishment for the wicked: "And they shall go forth and look on the dead bodies of the men that have rebelled against me; for their worm shall not die, their fire shall not be quenched, and they shall be an abhorrence to all flesh" (Isaiah, 66:24).

In later talmudic times the School of Hillel taught a much more moderate and humane conception of Gehinnon. Premising their argument upon the compassion of God, they held that after retributive justice of God was satisfied and all sinners purified, then Gehinnon would cease and all souls would share in the world to come. A more profound interpretation of this doctrine was that Gehinnon, like Gan Eden, is made by man and exists in man. The saying of the School of Hillel that "Gehinnon will cease" means that man will abolish it by righteous living.

HEAVEN: GAN EDEN.   The *Gan Eden* (Garden of Delight) in early Jewish writings was regarded as an abode of bliss. It may have been derived by linguistic analogy from the account of the Garden of Eden in the Book of Genesis. The Garden of Eden was regarded by many as a prototype of a heavenly paradise. Although early Jewish writers tended to treat the descriptions of heaven and hell in the literal sense, later writers interpreted them in a figurative sense and considered them primarily as exemplifying the divine justice. As M. Friedlander puts it:

As the life of Adam and Eve in the Garden of Eden was free from care and trouble, and such a life was the ideal of human hopes and wishes, the Garden-Eden [literally, the "garden of pleasure"] became the symbol of man's happiness in its perfection, such as will fall to the good and the righteous. On the other hand, the valley of Hinnom, near Jerusalem, was a place of horror and disgust; a place where at one time children were burned to Moloch, and where later the refuse of the city was cast. Dwelling in the valley of Hinnom became the symbol of the punishment to be inflicted on the wicked. Gan-Eden or Paradise, and Gehinnon or Hell, are thus mere figures to express our idea of the existence of a future retribution, and must not be taken literally as names of certain places. The detailed descriptions of Paradise and Hell as given in books both profane and religious are nothing but the offspring of man's imagination.[12]

RESURRECTION.   The idea of the resurrection appears occasionally in the Hebrew Scriptures, and it is certainly a part of the Jewish tradition. One of the more frequently cited passages from Scripture is the vision of Ezekiel in the Book of Ezekiel, 37:1–14. This has been interpreted as symbolical of the future restoration of Israel. More positive affirmations of a belief in the resurrection are to be found in Daniel 12:1–3 and perhaps in Isaiah 26:19. Jewish prayers and services also emphasize the resurrection of the dead. Thus: "There is none but Thee, oh our Redeemer, even in the days of the Messiah, and there is none comparable to Thee, oh our Savior, [who is capable of bringing] about the resurrection of the dead."

To perceive more clearly the nature of the resurrection, we shall raise a number of specific questions concerning it. Thus: Does the resurrection apply to all people? What form does the resurrection take—does it apply only to the spirit or to the body as well? What specific relation does it have to the symbol of immortality, and how is the latter interpreted?

To the first question no clearcut answer can be given. There are texts in the extracanonical books which unequivocally exclude the wicked from the resurrection. This seems to be the meaning of chapters 3 and 4 of the Book of Wisdom, at one time attributed to Solomon. And in the extracanonical book of the Psalms of Solomon we are told: "The destruction of the sinner is forever, And he shall not be remembered when [the Lord] visits the just. This is the portion of sinners for ever; But they that fear the Lord shall arise to eternal life."[13] However, there seem to be no indubitably clear and explicit statements on this question in the Hebrew Scripture. Hence it is difficult to decide these matters, and certainly not on the basis of a few texts and the difficulties of exegesis. Once the messianic symbol is considered as universal in scope then the resurrection would apply to the righteous of all peoples.

The second question opens the way to similar difficulties. Some early writers interpreted the symbol of the resurrection as meaning literally a physical resurrection. The reasoning was that since God has created man, He can re-create him. God repeats the miracle of creation, he re-creates the physical body and unites it with the soul. This is well brought out in the prophecy of Ezekiel 37:10–14. The physical resurrection of the body (there seems to be no specific teaching of a spiritual body) also involves a return to this earth in the messianic kingdom of the future. Most contemporary Jewish writers reject any literal interpretation of the resurrection of the body.

IMMORTALITY.   Second in importance only to the belief in the Messiah and the messianic kingdom is the belief in immortality. Without this belief there would be little meaning to such doctrines as the resurrection, retribution in the hereafter, and other eschatological notions. The belief in immortality probably arose during the Second Temple period. At any rate it was not held at the time the Book of Job was written, for Job does not have the consolation such a belief might offer. The Pharisees were primarily responsible for the development of this belief. In opposition to the Sadducees, who emphasized a national God for Israel alone, the Pharisees affirmed the existence of a universal God of all mankind. Stressing the relation and the responsibility of the individual to God, they argued to the necessity for the survival of the soul and its reward or punishment in the hereafter.

Among the medieval Jewish philosophers the notion of immortality is fairly prevalent. Generally they tend to regard immortality as wholly spiritual and as applicable to the soul rather than to the body. In this way Maimonides might be said to give a figurative interpretation to what others regard as a physical resurrection. Maimonides teaches that the functions of the body are no longer needed (but he does not teach that the body is evil) and that immortality applies only to the soul. In his *Essay on the Resurrection of the Dead* he describes this immortal existence:

> In the world to come there is no bodily form. . . . Nor can any of the accidents to which bodies are subject in this world occur there. Perhaps that bliss will be lightly esteemed by you, and you will think that the reward for fulfilling the commandments and for being perfect in the ways of truth consists in nothing else than indulging in fine food and drink, enjoying beautiful women, wearing raiment of fine linen and embroidery, dwelling in apartments of ivory, and using vessels of silver and gold and similar luxuries, as those foolish and ignorant Arabs imagine who are steeped in sensuality. But wise and intelligent men know that all these things are nonsense and vanity and quite futile. . . . As for the great bliss which the soul is to enjoy in the world to come, there is no possibility of comprehending it or knowing it in this world; because in this world we are only cognizant of the welfare of the body and for that we long. But the bliss of the world to come is exceedingly great and cannot bear comparison with the happiness of this world except in a figurative manner. . . .[14]

This conception of immortality involves more than a mere survival beyond the grave. It calls upon man to cooperate with God and to continue the divine relationship. Man must merit immortality—"and the dust returns to the earth as it was, and the spirit returns to God who gave it" (Ecclesiastes 12:7).

In conclusion let us note very briefly some of the basic beliefs of contemporary Judaism on these issues. For Orthodox Judaism the Jewish tradition on all of the symbols of the eschatology is generally accepted, but individual differences of belief on each of the symbols is acknowledged. For Conservative and Reform Judaism a belief in the resurrection is rejected, but generally some form of belief in immortality is essential. Usually both groups reject the beliefs in heaven and hell. In contrast to the Orthodox, who emphasize a belief in both a personal Messiah as well as in a messianic kingdom, the Conservative and Reform groups emphasize more the belief in a messianic kingdom of universal scope.

For all groups there would appear to be common agreement upon the notion of retribution associated with these symbols, for Judaism has always emphasized the ethical aspects of religion. The important thing is the fulfillment of the moral law, the punishment and rewards due the individual, rather than precisely where and how this retribution will be meted out. The doctrine of retribution usually implies a belief in immortality, and this is why most Jewish thinkers accept such a doctrine even though they generally do not concern themselves with the ways of implementing or demonstrating it. It is the belief in retribution that is important, not the means of effecting it in a future life.

The Eschatology of Christianity

The lines of eschatological development within Christianity can be best seen, if we parallel our treatment of them with that of Judaism. That is, we shall begin our study with the Christian point of departure from the Judaic conceptions of the Messiah and the messianic kingdom. For Christianity the basic departure rests with the doctrine of Jesus as the Messiah and the kingdom of God that Jesus established. From this belief there follow all the symbols of the Christian eschatology: the Resurrection, the Last Judgment, the Parousia, death and immortality, the particular judgment, heaven, hell, and purgatory. Not all of these symbols are articles of faith for both Protestant and Roman Catholic. The differences in the beliefs of Catholic and Protestant respecting these symbols of eschatology, as well as differences of interpretation, will be noted in the account that follows.[15]

The Kingdom of God

This is one of the most difficult and at the same time controversial ideas in Christianity. Its source lies in Judaism and in the notion of the messianic kingdom. As we have seen, the Jews believe that the Messiah and the messianic kingdom have yet to appear. Christians believe, however, that it was the essential mission of Jesus to proclaim that he was the Messiah and that the kingdom of God was at hand. Although the expression "the kingdom of God" has political overtones connoting political rule and sovereignty, these remain expressions that are more or less intimately bound up with the Old Testament and its emphasis upon law and obedience, and the relations between God and the Davidic monarchy.

In the Pentateuch God is sometimes referred to as the "Father of Israel." In the prophetic writings the expression "husband of Israel" appears. The dominant theme of the Old Testament, however, is that of the "Lord Yahweh." The expression "God the Father" appears in many instances and typifies what is to be the dominant theme of the New Testament. There is a real continuity between the Old and the New Testaments. Jesus does not proclaim another God than that of Israel, and the concept of "God the father" is the same in both Testaments. But in the New Testament the emphasis is always upon God as "the father." Jesus constantly speaks of God as "the Father" or "my Father." Even a casual reading of the New Testament reveals the importance of this theme. Thus the Lord's Prayer, which Jesus taught to his disciples, begins: "Our Father who art in heaven, hallowed be thy name" (Matthew 6:9). Jesus commands his disciples to be perfect in love, "as your heavenly Father is perfect" (Matthew 5:48). The story of the prodigal son conveys that profound message that both sons are blessed with the divine love of the father. The universality of God's love and His fatherhood to all men is clearly portrayed in the parable. Many additional examples could be given, but the more significant difference that emerges in the New Testament is Jesus' identification of himself with God the Father. "I have been with you so long and you do not know me? When you see me, you see the Father" (John 14:8–9).

THE KINGDOM OF GOD AS THE NEW PEOPLE

Behold, the days are coming, says the Lord, when I will make a new covenant with the house of Israel and the house of Judah, not like the covenant which I made with their fathers when I took them by the hand to bring them out of the land of Egypt, my covenant which they broke, though I was their husband, says the Lord. But this is the covenant which I will make with the House of Israel after those days, says the Lord: I will put my law within them, and I will write it upon their hearts; and I will be their God, and they shall be my people. And no longer shall each man teach his neighbor and each his brother, saying, "Know the Lord," for they shall all know me, from the least of them to the greatest, says the Lord; for I will forgive their iniquity, and I will remember their sin no more" (Jeremiah 31:31–34).

This passage is repeated in its entirety by St. Paul in Hebrews 8:8–12. He hails it as an anticipation of the new covenant or new testament to be instituted by Christ. Hence, for the people of the Old Covenant, of the Chosen of Israel, was to be substituted a New People including all mankind. Thus there is a real historical continuity between the two testaments, the two covenants, and the two peoples. Jesus as the Messiah constitutes the new covenant and the new people and effects the continuity of the saving work of God. This does not mean that in the new dispensation effected by Jesus the Jews are to be abandoned, but rather that the new people will include all people (cf. Romans 11:25–32).

THE KINGDOM OF GOD AS THE CHURCH. This heading represents another fairly common description of the kingdom of God. The term "church" as used in the New Testament never refers to a building but always to an assembly or congregation. The Church as the Kingdom of God means essentially the community of the faithful with the mission of bringing the message of Jesus to all people. In this sense the kingdom of God is a reality that has been achieved and not simply some "far-off divine event." Matthew 3:2 says that "the kingdom is at hand"; in Luke 17:21 that "it is in the midst of you." These passages and others illustrate what the Gospels all proclaim, namely, that the kingdom of God, that for which Israel prayed, has actually come to pass in Jesus Christ. The ethical significance of this event must not be overlooked. With the kingdom of God at hand, the hopes of man can be fulfilled; a new way to a life of righteousness and salvation is open to all. To become members of the kingdom of God means to accept the Christian way of life, to preach the "good news" of the gospels, and to rest our faith in Christ as God. The spiritual nature of the kingdom of God, that which has been termed the invisible Church or community, is brought out most markedly in the words of Jesus to his disciples in the fifth chapter of Matthew and the teaching of the Beatitudes.

The kingdom of God is also represented by the conception of the visible Church. The evidence for this visible Church is most clearly set forth in Acts 2 with the description of the descent of the Holy Spirit upon the apostles on the day of Pentecost. This event affirmed the intention of Jesus to establish a Church that would carry out his mission. The Greek term for "church" as used in the New Testament, *ekklesia*, designated all who were committed to the teachings of Christ. Christ himself used this term and apparently considered that his apostles formed a religious community or church dedicated to his messianic mission. With few exceptions this description of the early Church as the community of the faithful, as both visible and invisible, would be accepted by both Catholic and Protestant theologians. In time, however, this early religious community was enlarged and assumed different forms. For Catholics the Church was identified with the Catholic Church at Rome. Protestants reject this interpretation of the meaning of the Church and define differently its nature and its functions. The nature of these different forms of the Church and the conflicting definitions given to it will be discussed in a later chapter. But we may note briefly that the basic issue separating Catholic and Protestant is not quite as sharp as it used to be. This is evident in a recent pronouncement of the Second Vatican Council:

According to the Constitution, the Church of Christ survives in the world today in its institutional fullness in the Catholic Church, although elements of the Church are present in other Churches and ecclesial communities—a point which will be more fully developed in the Decree on Ecumenism. These "ecclesial elements" in other Churches, far from shattering the unity of the Mystical Body, are dynamic realities which tend to bring about an ever greater measure of unity among all who believe in Christ and are baptized in Him.[16]

THE TWO KINGDOMS.   That the kingdom of God is at hand, that it constitutes a present reality, that it appeared as both a visible and invisible Church, and that the kingdom for which Israel prayed has come to pass, is so clearly affirmed in the New Testament that we may overlook what is also equally justified by the New Testament, namely, that the kingdom of God exists in the future as well. Just before his death Jesus speaks of the kingdom of God as an event that God will bring to pass at the end of time, an event both outward and visible. Matthew 24:29–31 describes this apocalyptic event: "Immediately after the tribulation of those days the sun will be darkened, and the moon will not give its light, and the stars will fall from heaven, and the powers of the heavens will be shaken; then will appear the sign of the Son of man in heaven, and then all the tribes of the earth will mourn, and they will see the Son of man coming on the clouds of heaven with power and great glory; and he will send out his angels with a loud trumpet call, and they will gather his elect from the four winds, from one end of heaven to the other." This passage, and others (see also Mark 9:1 and Luke 13:28–30) emphasizes that the Kingdom of God is an eschatological event of profound importance. It introduces not only the notion of a second kingdom to be realized in the future, but it confers upon Christianity its distinctively other-worldly and supernatural character. And it introduces the notion of a new way of life for the individual, an eternal life in the kingdom of God that will be effected with the second coming of Christ.

Some Christian theologians have rejected this notion of the two kingdoms of God and maintain either that the kingdom of God is wholly present or that the kingdom of God is wholly eschatological and lies exclusively in the future. These contrasting views may be illustrated from the writings of C. H. Dodd and Albert Schweitzer.

"Realized" Eschatology

This is the position put forward with considerable force by C. H. Dodd,[17] who maintains that the purpose of history has already been achieved in the realization of the teachings of Jesus and that by comparison all history from this point on is insignificant. The kingdom of God, then, is wholly present. "It is not merely imminent, it is here."[18] We cannot set forth in detail Dodd's theory. It relies upon his own interpretation of various scriptural passages. He observes, and rightly, that there are many passages which clearly affirm the presentness of the kingdom of God: "Whatever we may make of them, the sayings which declare the Kingdom of God to have come are explicit and unequivocal. They are moreover the most characteristic and distinctive of the Gospel sayings on the subject. They have no parallel in Jewish teaching or prayers of the period. If, therefore, we are seeking the *differentia* of the teaching of Jesus upon the Kingdom of God, it is here that it must be found."[19]

With respect to those passages that clearly seem to indicate a future kingdom of God, for example Mark 1:15 and Mark 9:1, Dodd's procedure is to translate and interpret these passages in such a way as to eliminate any implication of the notion of a future kingdom. We cannot in our limited space enter upon the dispute between Dodd and his critics on the exegesis of the New Testament passages and upon the parables. Without rendering any judgment of our own we can at least point out that there are theologians, Catholic and Protestant, who disagree with Dodd's "realized" eschatology. Thus Reinhold Niebuhr states: "The modern interpretation of the coming of Christ in the theory of 'realized eschatology,' according to which all symbols of the second coming in the New Testament are without general significance, cannot effectively destroy or obscure either the historic validity or the systematic relevance of the strain of thought in the Gospels embodied in the idea of the 'second coming.' It is as indispensable for a gospel interpretation as for a true understanding of the Gospels."[20]

And Fr. Jean Daniélou points out that there is much truth in Dodd's view, for with the Incarnation and the Resurrection the real significance of history has been reached: "Indeed the essence of the Gospel message is to declare the accomplishment of prophecy in Jesus Christ, the new Adam of the new Paradise, and the New Moses of the true Exodus.

"But in Dodd's eyes this essential truth fills the whole picture, to such an extent as to leave no room (now that the end has come) for any further useful activity. History since Jesus is a sort of remainder, and theologically insignificant."[21] This conclusion is rejected by Fr. Daniélou. He prefers what he calls "initiated" eschatology, a formula taken from Fr. Donatien Mollat: "With Christ, the time of judgment has really started, the last days really begin. These are days of crisis and decision, which we have to recognize and appreciate. . . . They continue so long as the Son of Man is present in his brethren and in his fellowship. . . . They will be completed by the Second Coming, with the establishment once for all of God's Kingdom."[22]

"Consequent" or Futuristic Eschatology

In sharp contrast to the position taken by Dodd is the still influential thesis of Albert Schweitzer[23] that the kingdom of God is wholly eschatological, that the future kingdom of God and the coming of Christ are imminent. That the kingdom is future is implied in one of the petitions of the Lord's Prayer: "Thy kingdom come." And Schweitzer points out that it is also affirmed in the very real importance attached to the symbols of the Last Judgment and the Parousia. What Schweitzer apparently does is to emphasize exclusively all those passages in Scripture which refer to the immediacy of the Second Coming, of the imminence of the kingdom of God and the Last Judgment.

Schweitzer further argues that at the beginning of his ministry Jesus proclaimed the coming of the kingdom of God in that same year. The disciples were sent out by Jesus with this message. They were to call upon all for repentance in the imminent expectation of the kingdom and in the revelation of Jesus as the Son of Man. However, when the disciples had returned and the prediction of the coming of the kingdom had not been realized, Jesus is said to have changed his outlook. According to Schweitzer, Jesus now sees that he alone must endure the messianic woes stated explicitly in the Jewish revelation (Isaiah 53) and predicted in Matthew 10. Thus through the sufferings of Jesus and his death on the cross, he will precipitate the coming of the kingdom of God. In this manner he fulfills the messianic vocation and his manifestation of it as the Son of Man.

This interpretation of Schweitzer is subject to the same criticism that applies to Dodd, namely, that the validity of his theory depends completely upon his own interpretation of Scripture, and especially of Matthew 10 and 11. Schweitzer arrives at his position primarily through a rather one-sided interpretation of the life of Jesus. As Lundström observes: "The decisive criticism of Schweitzer is, however, that even if the Gospel does express the Jewish hope of the future, the centre of interest is Jesus' work among His people, in the light of which the picture of Jesus as a whole must be seen. The center of interest is thus the overwhelming happenings which the Historical Jesus saw taking place before His eyes as He went about His mission: 'The blind receive their sight and the lame walk, lepers are cleansed and the deaf hear, and the dead are raised up, and the poor have the good news preached to them' (Matt. XI. 5)."[24]

Finally, the number of passages in the Gospels dealing with the Kingdom of God as realized or present cannot be excluded. Nor can they be made to yield even by the cleverest exegesis an interpretation of the kingdom of God as wholly future.

Actually, then, if we accept the New Testament statements at their face value instead of trying to prove a specific thesis, there are two kingdoms of God. The one is the kingdom of God realized through the Incarnation and the Resurrection, the Kingdom as present. For the individual believer in this kingdom, life now takes on a wholly new meaning and purpose. He becomes radically transformed through the essential Christian categories. Yet the believer also hopes that through his faith he can attain the eternal happiness promised by Christ. This hope opens another dimension of time, for hope has meaning only within the dimension of the future. Hence there will also be an "anticipated" eschatology, a concern for that which is yet to be, the future kingdom of God. In a word, there are two kingdoms, one of the present, the other of the future; the one realized, the other anticipated; the one symbolized by the Incarnation and the Resurrection, the other by the Parousia and the Last Judgment.

That there are two kingdoms may be taken as revealing again the paradoxical nature of Christianity rather than as an inconsistency. If the mystery
of the Incarnation and the paradox it offers is granted, then the paradox of
the two kingdoms may be accepted upon faith, for it may be argued that
the testimony of Scripture amply supports the notion of the two kingdoms.
Since, however, we should strive where possible to explicate faith, to seek
an understanding of it, we may next consider a distinction that may possibly
make the paradox of the two kingdoms a little less obscure. We refer to the
distinction between chronos and kairos.

Chronos and Kairos

The distinction between chronos and kairos is one between time as
impersonal, objective, and secular, and time as personal, subjective, and
religious.[25] Thus chronos is a neutral term; it has no reference to God or
to human purposes. The New Testament writers used the term kairos for
time because they wished to emphasize time in the religious sense as
including purposes both human and divine. Time in this sense is a
determinant, revelatory of moral events; whereas time as chronos manifests
only the duration of impersonal things or events, determining nothing.

The distinction can be further clarified with respect to the relation
between time and prediction and prophetic and apocalyptic predictions. To
predict a religious or moral event depends upon the moral purposes of God
or the individual. Without a knowledge of such purposes the prediction of
events is fruitless, for time as chronos predicts nothing. The fact that a
thousand years have elapsed or that we are close to realizing the two
thousandth year of our existence since the time of Christ has no special
historical significance. A certain day in time determines nothing, but a
certain day in time may be that time in which a divine purpose is achieved.[26]
Isaiah prophesies the coming of the Messianic kingdom but he does not
predict an exact date for it. This would be to place a restriction on the
freedom of God. On the other hand, the enthusiasm of the Apocalyptist
betrays him into the prediction of an exact date or time for the end of
human history.

Whatever occurs and the time at which it occurs will depend upon the
divine and human factors in history, upon the personal rather than the
impersonal element. Time as chronos is strictly subordinate to these
factors. To say that the world must come to an end at such and such a date
or that Christ will appear for the second time at some precise date, is to
make time in the sense of chronos a determining factor rather than a subordinate factor. Time as chronos is a creature and subject to the divine
purposes. Bishop Robinson illustrates the difference in the two conceptions

of time with the simile taken from William James' "The Dilemma of Determinism." Robinson states: "God, the master chess-player, takes on the novice, representing man. All moves are open to man and God does not know exactly which he will make. But he knows that, *whatever* the other may do, He will be able to counter it and to win. That is the prophetic position. The apocalyptist goes on to say not simply, 'God will win,' but, 'God will win at move 30.' And between these two is all the difference between freedom and determinism. In the one *kairos* determines *chronos,* in the other *chronos* determines *kairos.*"[27]

To God it is quite unimportant whether His purposes are to be achieved in a day or in a thousand years. To Him the important thing is the realization of His purposes and not the time (for He is above time) in which they are achieved. In other words the notion of a "date" is irrelevant of God's purpose. Hence, although the establishment of His kingdom through His Son came at a certain time in history, the important thing was the purpose realized and not the moment of time in which it was realized. We should regard the Second Coming of Christ in a similar manner, in terms of *kairos* and not *chronos.* As Robinson clearly and succinctly states:

Consequently, the Christian era and the Christian life are viewed in the New Testament as set between two poles, between the fact that the end has come and the fact that the end is yet to be. Every great New Testament phrase reflects this double reference: the Kingdom of God, eternal life, salvation, justification, sanctification, perfection, even glorification, are all spoken of as being at one and the same time present possessions based on past fact and objects of full attainment only in the future. Sunday is at once a remembrance of the first Lord's Day and a foretaste of the last: it symbolizes the eschatological time between the Resurrection and the Parousia.[28]

With some exceptions, then, most Roman Catholic and Protestant theologians would accept the notion of the two kingdoms and the two advents of Christ. There would probably be less unanimity on the distinction between the kairos and the chronos. But on another—the chiliastic— interpretation of the kingdom of God and the Second Coming, both Protestant and Catholic theologians would be almost unanimously opposed.

The Chiliastic Eschatology

To affirm the two kingdoms of God does not mean that there exists a spiritual gap between the two. There is a very real continuity between the kingdom of God established by Christ and that kingdom of God which is to appear at the end of all history. For Christ himself is always present and his judgment is always upon man. However, there were in the early history of the Church (and a few even now) many speculative dreamers who, in the intensity of their hope for a better world, conceived that such a world was not only imminent but that it would constitute a kind of earthly paradise ruled over by Christ and all the blessed for a period of a thousand years. Such believers and dreamers were called "chiliasts" from the Greek word for "thousand." Sometimes their view is termed the "millennarian," a term derived from the Latin word for "thousand."

This dream of the chiliasts generally supposed that a fairly precise time or date could be set for the Second Coming of Christ and the establishment of his kingdom. It also supposed that this kingdom would be an earthly one and that it would appear after the General Resurrection. It would be composed of all the saints or blessed who would reign with Christ for a thousand years. After the consummation of all things the saints would enter heaven for an eternal life of bliss. The sinners would apparently remain in a state of punishment during and after the millennium.

The origins of this belief are many, but the principal source is the Apocalypse or Book of Revelation.[29] The nature of this millennium is prophesied with the most vivid imagery in the last several chapters of the Apocalypse. Here St. John presents a series of visions prophesying the course of events for the immediate future (A.D. second century). After many wars, afflictions, and tribulations, Christ will triumph over Antichrist[30] and the Kingdom of the New Jerusalem will descend from heaven and Christ will rule over the blessed for a thousand years.

This revelation of John was taken quite literally by many people. It led almost immediately to the origin and development of the Montanist heresy. In A.D. 156 in Phrygia a certain Montanus asserted that he was empowered to reveal all things through the Holy Spirit. Claiming to be virtually the Incarnation of the Holy Spirit, he predicted the imminent end of the world and the Second Coming of Christ. Tertullian, one of the great western theologians of this period, joined the movement. He, too, predicted the imminence of the Parousia or Second Coming, and wrote that in Judaea a portentous sign had appeared in the heavens every day for forty days. The sign was a vision of a walled city prophetic of the imminent descent of the City of the New Jerusalem. Over the years numerous other signs were reported by other believers in the millennium.

Another characteristic of the chiliastic description of this kingdom of the New Jerusalem are the material blessings and joys that are to be realized. Lactantius describes the advent and the joys of such a kingdom in the following words:

When peace has been brought about and every evil suppressed, that righteous and victorious King will carry out a great judgment on the earth of the living and the dead, and will hand over all heathen peoples to servitude under the righteous who are alive, and will raise the [righteous] dead to eternal life, and will himself reign with them on earth and will found the Holy City, and this kingdom of the righteous shall last for a thousand years. Throughout that time the stars shall be brighter, and the brightness of the sun shall be increased, and the moon shall not wane. Then the rain of blessing shall descend from God morning and evening, and the earth shall bear all fruits without man's labor. Honey in abundance shall drip from the rocks, fountains of milk and wine shall burst forth. The beasts of the forests shall put away their wildness and become tame . . . no longer shall any animal live by bloodshed. For God shall supply all with abundant and guiltless food.[31]

And Irenaeus (ca. 136–203) gives the following citation from a *Fragment of Papias*, one of the apostolic fathers:

Then creation, reborn and freed from bondage, will yield an abundance of food of all kinds from the heaven's dew and the fertility of the earth (Gen. 27:28), just as the seniors recall. Those who saw John, the Lord's disciple [tell us] that they heard from him how the Lord taught and spoke about these times: Days will come when vines will grow each with ten thousand shoots, and on each shoot ten thousand branches, and on each branch ten thousand twigs, and on each twig ten thousand clusters, and on each cluster ten thousand grapes. Each grape, when pressed will yield twenty-five measures of wine. And, when anyone of these saints will take hold of a cluster, another cluster will cry out: "I am a better cluster. Take me and give thanks to the Lord through me."[32]

Many more descriptions of the millennium could be cited, and from many different sources, because for over a century the belief in it was very strong, remaining so until the time of Constantine. With Constantine and the legal sanction given to Christianity by the Roman Empire, the belief in the millennium no longer was quite so important. The more evident reasons are that the dream was not realized, and more significantly that the persecution of Christianity had ceased and the empire was not overthrown. Furthermore, an interpretation of this strange book of the Apocalypse was put forward by Augustine and the reasonableness of his interpretation as well as his authority prevailed for many centuries.

Augustine admitted that at one time he had been attracted to this chiliastic eschatology, but then he reacted as strongly to it as he did to the cyclical view of history. This was not merely because the chiliastic view had been largely discredited by this time, but also because so many of those who represented this position interpreted it in materialistic terms. Augustine states his reaction to this interpretation very positively.

And this opinion would not be objectionable, if it were believed that the joys of the saints in that Sabbath shall be spiritual, and consequent on the presence of God; for I myself, too, once held this opinion. But, as they assert that those who then rise again shall enjoy the leisure of immoderate carnal banquets, furnished with an amount of meat and drink such as not only to shock the feeling of the temperate, but even to surpass the measure of credulity itself, such assertions can be believed only by the carnal.[33]

For the most part Augustine gave the Apocalypse an allegorical interpretation. He rejected it as a mirror of temporal history. In fact Augustine rejected any philosophy of history; he refused to speculate or make predictions of future history. Following Scripture, he held that although there will be a Second Coming of Christ, such an event cannot be calculated by man. The events in the Apocalypse will occur, but at what precise time we cannot say. The only certitude we have with respect to historical events are those already revealed by God.[34] Hence a theology of history has a limited possibility, but not a philosophy of history. The position of Augustine is far more reasonable than that taken by many of his successors, who all too often could not avoid the temptation to read the secrets of the Book of the Apocalypse and to prophesy in exact terms the date of the Second Coming. Even now, no doubt, some false prophet may somewhere be predicting the imminent destruction of the universe and the Second Coming of Christ.[35]

Lesser Symbols of the Christian Eschatology

PAROUSIA.   In the light of our analysis of the kingdom of God any further account of the Parousia (from the Greek meaning "presence") would seem to be redundant. If one grants that there is a second or future kingdom of God, then the Second Coming of Christ, the Parousia follows. Today most theologians—Catholic and Protestant alike—follow the Pauline and the Augustinian traditions in holding not only that there will be a Second Coming but also that it is impossible to establish with certitude any particular time for this event. That Christ will appear for the second time is a symbol of hope for Christians, but when he will appear is beyond comprehension. As Jesus himself testifies: "But as for that day and that hour you speak of, they are known to nobody, not even to the angels in heaven, not even to the Son; only the Father knows them" (Mark 13:32).

DEATH.   For the Christian, death takes on a profound meaning that can in no way be discovered in the interpretations given to it by the biologist or the philosopher. For the biologist death is a universal natural phenomenon affecting all living creatures and caused by the disintegration of the chemical and functional unity of the living organism. For the philosopher death may be looked upon as an event of which man alone among all living creatures is aware, an event which man faces with dread or with equanimity and which affects his outlook upon the world and the self. For the Christian, death includes these notions but it also embraces something far more significant—the relation of man to his Creator. The Christian believes that man was not only given life by God, but that originally he was exempt from death. Now through the sin of Adam he is subject to death, but at the same time through the resurrection of Christ he has been liberated from death. "I am the resurrection and life: he who believes in me, though he is dead will live on, and whoever has life, and has faith in me, to all eternity cannot die" (John 11:23–26). For the Christian, then, the mystery of death is wrapped in the mystery of the Resurrection, for him death means the beginning of a new life in eternity.

IMMORTALITY. To be immortal means, strictly speaking, the negation of mortality or the possibility of death. Somehow man, it is said, will survive death and go on to a new form of existence. This conception of immortality—the mere survival of the individual—has been common to many primitive religions. If the individual is considered to be a wholly physical being, then the new life differs but little from the old. As we noted in early Judaism the conception of She'ol was that of a place of habitation by the shadows or shades of individuals who had died. This type of immortal existence was still wholly material, even though the shade was a mere "ghost" of the former self. On the other hand, the life of the individual in the world to come may be thought to be wholly spiritual in nature. The soul no longer has any relation with the body, which does not survive in any way. This view of an immortal and wholly spiritual existence is common to present-day *Spiritualism*.

The philosophical conception of immortality, which is more sophisticated than the type just described, takes its origins largely in Greek philosophy. The influence of Platonism has been persistently strong upon Christian doctrine in this respect. If the average Christian were asked of his belief in the afterlife he would probably express it in the proposition of the immortality of the soul. Yet there is no evidence whatsoever in Scripture for a doctrine of the immortality of the soul. Christian immortality is an immortality of the whole man, of the individual person. In Platonism there is a sharp dualism between soul and body, with the latter regarded as inferior and even evil.[36]

This dualism of soul and body, mind and matter, is continued in Plotinus and the Neoplatonic philosophy. The soul of man is now held to be an emanation from the World Soul, which in turn emanates from the Nous and the One. As in Platonism the soul is temporarily imprisoned in the body, but it will eventually be reunited with the World Soul, the Nous, and finally the One. In this view as in Plato's there is no conception of a personal God, of creation *ex nihilo*, or of a final end to all things. The life of the soul is that of an eternal emanation and return, of never ending cycles of existence.

For Christianity the soul of the individual was created in the image of God. The immortality of the individual—of the whole person and not just the soul—participates in an eternal life with God. That is, there was a time when we were not, but once created, we are destined for an eternal life with God or to a second death and an alienation from God. True immortality for the Christian involves the whole of man; it is an immortality of the person and not just the psyche or soul.

Most Christian theologians would agree that by immortality is meant the immortality of the person, of man as both body and soul. For the most part Protestant theologians are not inclined to speculate beyond the biblical account of resurrection. They explicitly reject any Neoplatonic or Platonic conceptions of the soul. Also they would reject the Thomistic interpretation of immortality and would certainly balk at the statement that "death consists in the separation of the body and soul," which is rather explicit in Catholic tradition.

Roman Catholic theologians for the most part have long accepted the definition of the person given by Boethius that "a person is an individual substance of a rational nature." They follow Catholic tradition in affirming that death consists in the separation of the body and soul, although acknowledging that the most that Scripture states is that God has withdrawn the life (breath) of the body. They point out, however, that Scripture does not deny the separation of the soul from the body. Perhaps most important of all, the majority of Catholic theologians follow the Thomistic analysis of the nature of the soul and body and their relationship. As we have noted in a previous chapter, the Thomistic conception of man is based upon the Aristotelian doctrine of hylomorphism. No matter how adequate this doctrine may be for an explanation of man in this life, it does give rise to some difficulties concerning the nature of the person in the life to come. These difficulties are with the nature of the separated soul, for thre is no problem of the resurrection of the body which is quite compatible with both Scripture and hylomorphism.

The principal difficulty is that the soul apart from the body would appear to lack any basis for personality and identity. For the person consists of both body and soul, and the identity of the person depends in the Thomistic doctrine upon the body and the knowledge and memory derived from the senses. Some would contend that to insist upon this separation of body and soul is to deny personal immortality. The problem for Thomists is to mitigate this rather serious difficulty. Just how this might be done would lead us too deeply into philosophical issues, but although there are difficulties present in Thomism, this does not mean that St. Thomas denied immortality even in terms of the whole person. In any event, for Thomism the resurrection of the body restores the full personality of the individual. For prior to the resurrection of the body the soul maintains some kind of existence until the union with a spiritual body. A serious theological problem for both Catholics and Protestants lies in any attempt to account for the state of the person after death. If there is no separation of the soul from the body, just what is the nature and status of the person? If there is such a separation, and the nature of the person depends upon *both* body and soul, what is the status of the person? And finally, what is the nature of that interim state between death and the resurrection? Is it one of sleep, or does the soul somehow continue to exist and to await the reunion with the spiritual body? No one view is without difficulty, and none gives a complete and satisfactory answer.

One last consideration is of some importance. In the philosophical conception of immortality, such immortality is not only restricted to the soul, but it may be made possible for the individual apart from any relation to God. In Christianity immortality depends upon God rather than upon man; it is a goal that is open to all and not merely to those who have perfected themselves by some philosophical discipline, for example yoga or the anagogic path of Plotinus, in order to achieve such an end. For Christianity all men have died in Adam and all men will be given a new life in Christ. This new life is made possible through the resurrection of Christ.

THE RESURRECTION.   The story of the resurrection as an event in the life of Jesus has already been considered in the chapter on Christology. Here we wish to comment solely on the resurrection as one of the symbols[37] within the whole context of the symbol of eschatology.

In our account of original sin we had noted that one of its consequences was the introduction of death in the nature of man. Now just as the sin of Adam introduced death into the world, so the resurrection of Christ extinguishes death. The testimony of Jesus is quite specific on this point: "I am the resurrection and life: he who believes in me, though he is dead, will live on, and whoever has life, and has faith in me, to all eternity cannot die" (John 8:51).

The resurrection of Christ stands out then as one of the key symbols of Christian belief. Just as the Incarnation reveals that Jesus as the Messiah has appeared to effect man's redemption and salvation, to establish his kingdom, so in the resurrection of Jesus man's resurrection may be said to be prefigured and his salvation assured in an eternal life in the world to come. In effect what Jesus accomplished through his resurrection was man's resurrection and our immortality. Just as the resurrection of Jesus included the resurrection of his body, so man's resurrection involves the resurrection of man's body. The message of the Gospels on the resurrection of the body of Jesus is quite clear and explicit. When the disciples went to the tomb to look for the body of Jesus they found only the grave clothes, but no body. However, they are assured by angels that Jesus is risen from the dead as he had promised. A short time later Jesus appears before them (Matthew 28:1–11; Mark 16:1–14; Luke 24:1–12; John 20:1–18).

That our bodies will be resurrected is a rule of faith. As St. Paul puts it: "If what we preach about Christ, then, is that he rose from the dead, how is it that some of you say the dead do not rise again? If the dead do not rise, then Christ has not risen either; and if Christ has not risen, then our preaching is groundless, and your faith, too, is groundless" (I Corinthians 15:12–15). And in the Apostles' Creed Christians say: "I believe in the resurrection of the body and the life everlasting."

Recalling what was said earlier on immortality, it should be evident now that any immortality of man apart from the resurrection of the body is unthinkable for the Christian. The evidence of the New Testament on the resurrection of the body is overwhelming. But although the New Testament attests primarily to the resurrection of the body, such a resurrection applies to the whole being of the individual, soul as well as body. Man as a person is resurrected with the resurrection of the body. This is why the New Testament virtually equates resurrection with immortality.

So far we have noted principally that the resurrection of the body is a matter of belief—an article of faith for all Christians. Now we have to consider how the resurrection is effected. Clearly it is not a natural process, and it cannot be explained in accordance with natural laws or scientific knowledge. Most Christian theologians would maintain that the resurrection of the body transcends all scientific knowledge, that it is in the realm of the miraculous, and that it is effected by the omnipotence of God. If there is to be life after death, if the creation is to be re-created, this can be effected only by an act of God Himself. The contemporary mind may find this a rather difficult idea to accept. Logically it is no more difficult than the notion of immortality and certainly no more difficult to accept than creation itself. As Augustine puts it:

Therefore, brother, confirm yourself in the name and help of him in whom you believe, so as to withstand the tongues of those who mock at our faith, out of whose mouths the devil speaks seductive words, desiring especially to ridicule the belief in the resurrection. But from your own experience, perceiving that you now exist although you once were not, believe that you will exist hereafter. For where was this mass of your body, and where was this form and structure of your members a few years ago, before you were born? Did it not come forth to light, out of the secret places of creation, under the invisible formative power of God? Is it then in any way a difficult thing for God to restore this quantity of your body as it was, seeing that he was able to make it formerly when it was not?"[38]

St. Paul resorts to an analogy to stress not only the resurrection but also the real continuity that exists between the dead body and the resurrected body: "But some one will ask, 'How are the dead raised? With what kind of body do they come?' You foolish man! What you sow does not come to life unless it dies. And what you sow is not the body which is to be, but a bare kernel, perhaps of wheat or of some other grain. But God gives it a body as he has chosen, and to each kind of seed its own body" (I Corinthians 15:35–38).

Without a real continuity between the old body and the new, we would have to speak of the assumption of a new body. But if this new body is not identical with the old but in some manner continuous with it, just what is its precise nature? Again this is a problem to be answered by Scripture and theological opinion. In Scripture we find one of the most explicit statements in the chapter just cited from St. Paul. To the question "With what kind of body do they come?" he answers: a spiritual body. The assertion that the risen body is of a spiritual nature has led to considerable speculation among theologians. Catholic theologians in particular have been concerned with the problem of just what qualities such a spiritual body might be said to possess. Aquinas held that such spiritual bodies are wholly perfect, but that all purely physical functions are excluded. Scholastic doctrine, following the leadership of Aquinas, attributed four principal qualities to the spiritual body: impassibility, clarity, agility, and subtlety. Space does not permit a discussion of these qualities. The whole issue of the nature of the spiritual body continues to be highly speculative.

Two questions remain: Who shall be resurrected? When will the resurrection occur? To the first question St. Paul seems to give an explicit answer: "Lo! I tell you a mystery. We shall not all sleep, but we shall all be changed" (I Corinthians 15:51). Implicit in this answer is the Christian belief that there is no individual resurrection apart from a general resurrection.

That all men will be resurrected may be interpreted to mean that there will be two resurrections: the resurrection of those who are dead and the resurrection of those who are living at the time of the Second Coming. There is also the question raised by St. Paul's statement whether this means that not only will all men be resurrected but also whether all men will die. Much depends upon the text of the passage, as Fr. Knox points out. Commenting on verse 51, he says: "The Greek manuscripts are here strangely divided; some read the text given here, but there is better support for the reading 'We shall not all fall asleep but we shall all be changed.' The sense in that case would be, that those of the elect who are still alive at the Day of Judgment will pass into a heavenly existence without undergoing death. According to the text here given, which is that of the Latin versions, the sense is rather that all men will die, but only the elect will be glorified after death. Owing to this textual doubt, the generally received view that those who are alive at the Second Coming will experience physical death is not certain, but only a more probable opinion."[39]

To the second question, "When will the resurrection occur?" the answer is on the Day of Judgment, the Last Judgment.

THE LAST JUDGMENT.   Although the symbols of the Parousia, the Resurrection, and the Last Judgment may be set forth successively in a given order of time, actually they constitute a single unique moment in which our days upon earth will be closed out and the kingdom of God will be open to all the elect. Creation comes to an end in the re-creation and consummation of all things in God. It would be a mistake, however, to think of the Last Judgment as literally the last in the sense of the only time at which man is to be judged. For the Christian is always under the judgment of God. As Fr. Molliat puts it: "Between the inauguration of judgment at the time of Christ's coming, and its fulfillment at his coming again, Christian life in its entirety is thus a continual judgment. The mystical presence of the Son of Man in all men imports an unsuspected eschatological dimension into all human relationships, that is to say, into all history at all time. Man is now face to face with the Son of Man at every moment of existence: the judgment is now. . . . The resurrection of Christ is presented as the first and decisive act of the last day . . . everything essential has been secured already.[40]

The Day of the Last Judgment cannot be foretold. It is clear, however, that Christ will be the Judge, and that the Judgment will occur upon his Second Coming. Hence, Christ's statement (Mark 13:32) that only the Father knows the day and the hour when He will appear, applies equally to the Last Judgment. The reality of the Last Judgment is amply attested to in the New Testament, notably in: "When the Son of man comes in his glory, and all the angels with him, then he will sit on his glorious throne. Before him will be gathered all the nations, and he will separate them one from another as a shepherd separates the sheep from the goats, and he will place the sheep at his right hand, but the goats at the left" (Matthew 25:31–34). Other passages include John 5:21–24; II Corinthians 5:10; II Timothy 4:8.

It should be observed that this Last Judgment is general or universal in scope; it applies to all men and to both the living and the dead. As general it must be distinguished from the particular judgment[41] which is imposed upon each man at the time of his death. Catholic theology teaches that the particular judgment is immediate and irrevocable. Upon the death of the individual person his soul is at once judged and then either condemned to hell or allowed to purge itself of all sinful inclinations before being permitted to enter heaven. With the resurrection of the body the soul is again a complete personality. The Last Judgment reaffirms the particular judgment. Related as it is to Catholic theology's conception of immortality, the idea of a particular judgment presents similar difficulties. Yet if we regard the particular judgment as emphasizing primarily the personal character of our redemption, then it presents a needed supplement to the collective judgment explicit in the Last Judgment.

HELL.   The attitude of Christian theologians on the mystery of *hell*, the abode of the damned and the demons, has revealed diverse and contrary views. In the early history of the Church the tendency was to treat of hell in a very literal sense, especially with respect to its precise location and the punishment by fire. Some believed that the punishment of hell would be postponed until the day of the Last Judgment, although the wicked in the interim would be given some kind of punishment which would not necessarily be final and irrevocable. Occasionally, too, there were those who would reject the eternity of hell, as does Origen,[42] or that the wicked would be annihilated rather than punished eternally, as Arnobious speculates. Within the Christian tradition there have always been theories of eternal punishment and the existence of hell, but there is no definitive statement of faith on the precise nature of the punishment. Generally the punishment is spoken of in terms of fire, but the exact meaning for this term is unclear and is still a matter of debate. Why, then, should the term "fire" be retained in any description of hell? Because it has scriptural justification, being mentioned at least seventy times in the Bible. Until the contemporary period, the symbol of hell was commonly accepted by both Protestant and Catholic theologians. Although some endeavored to mitigate the realities of hell and eternal punishment, generally the theologians interpreted both more or less literally and objectively.

More recently it may be said that most Protestant theologians tend to reject the earlier views on the nature of hell. Some deny it completely or mitigate it to a temporal form of retribution for sinners. Fundamentalists among Protestant theologians accept the traditional account with little change.

For the most part Catholic theologians accept the reality of hell and its punishments even though many Catholic believers may tend to be somewhat skeptical. One Catholic theologian expresses his astonishment at this rejection of hell in the following statement: "This rejection of hell is indeed a remarkable development, more important than the capture of Constantinople or the discovery of America. Why has no one ever written, besides the history of battles and treaties, the inner history of man? When once man ceased to admit, as a self-evident truth, that his deeds in this life entail dire consequences in the next, he was no longer the same. Henceforth, a sin or a crime, provided they remained hidden or did not become amenable to justice, no longer moved him to remorse or atonement. Unbelief guaranteed his impunity. This was a spiritual revolution more momentous than the intellectual revolution we owe to Galileo and Copernicus."[43]

Catholic theologians usually describe the punishment of hell as a pain of loss and a pain of sense. The pain of sense is the punishment by fire, although there is no definitive meaning given to fire. More emphasis is placed upon the pain of loss by which is meant the loss of the beatific vision ("then we shall see God face to face"), the eternal joy that will come with a union with God in the hereafter.

That hell exists and that the punishment of hell is everlasting is a dogma of the Catholic faith. As to whether hell is actually a place, this is a matter of opinion rather than faith. Some Catholic theologians prefer to describe it more as a state of the soul. Any description, however, encounters the usual difficulty attendant upon the effort to describe the spiritual phenomena which transcend the physical in physical terms and categories. This applies also to any description of purgatory and heaven. And it has led to some rather striking descriptions of hell. Thus in the *Diary of a Country Priest* we are told: "Hell is not to love any more, Madame, not to love any more. . . . The sorrow, the unutterable sorrow of these charred stones which once were men, is that they have nothing to be shared."[44] Rondet characterizes hell as "the land of dispersion and solitude. Hell is the antithesis of the communion of saints."[45] We may also recall Sartre's famous definition of hell as "other people."[46]

Although the notion of eternal punishment is a dogma, there are some Catholic theologians who would mitigate the punishment applied to particular sins. And others have held out the hope of a grace of conversion to the sinner at the time of death or the possibility of a gradual diminution of the punishment of hell. The notion of a grace of conversion, a kind of last reprieve, sounds rather plausible when first considered. Yet would God's grace be effectual in a case where the individual has already through a lifetime of sin made an irrevocable decision against God? In other words, the choice has already been made by the sinner and it is an irrevocable choice. The separation and alienation from God is so complete that any offer of grace would be meaningless.

Among Protestant theologians one view which has recently won some support is that known as "universalism." It accepts both the reality of the Last Judgment and of hell, but holds that eventually all men will be redeemed. Hell is not truly eternal, for this would negate the divine love and all that Christ means.[47]

PURGATORY.   There is no mention of *purgatory* in the Bible. But the Roman Catholic Church through its Magisterium has declared that there are temporal punishments that must be undergone by the sinner before he is granted the happiness of the beatific vision. Purgatory is a kind of intermediate state in which the individual suffers the pains of a fire which purifies the soul from its venial sins or from the punishment of those mortal sins which have not been sufficiently expiated for. The "time" of purgatory is understood in a spiritual rather than a literal sense. It is a period of spiritual progress for the individual and a time in which while afflicted with the temporal punishments he has the joy of anticipating his ultimate reward. It has been likened to a "hell where the souls are happy and a heaven where they suffer." To this description of purgatory Catholic teaching adds that the faithful may pray for the souls in purgatory. In this way they may approach more closely to God through them. Does this mean that the souls in purgatory can pray for men on earth? Some Catholic theologians have urged this since such souls are close to God and could intercede for them.

As we have observed, Protestant theologians usually reject the whole idea of purgatory, on the grounds that it lacks scriptural justification. They also point out that the term "purgatory" is not used in II Maccabees 12:39–46, a scriptural passage that Catholic theologians say can be interpreted as justifying purgatory.

HEAVEN.   On this last symbol of the Christian eschatology, there is not much difference of opinion among theologians. Generally all would admit that heaven lies beyond our comprehension. All would probably admit that it involves some kind of union with God, a state of joy and love in relation to God. Such a love, it is held, will be completely satisfying and will know no end. It will constitute an experience of ineffable happiness for each person. Heaven is simply God. As St. Paul tells us, "What no eye has seen, nor ear heard, nor the heart of man conceived, what God has prepared for those who love him" (I Corinthians 2:9).

NOTES

1. "By *symbol* we mean that which represents or expresses some form of reality, whether that be a particular thing, person, or action in the past, present, or future. The religious use of symbols excludes the conceptual for the existential. In the words of Mircea Eliade: 'Symbols still keep their contact with the profound sources of life; they express one might say, the "spiritual as lived" ' (*le spirituel vécu*). That is why symbols have, as it were, a numinous aura; they reveal that the modalities of the spirit are at the same time manifestations of life, and, consequently, they directly engage human existence. The religious symbol not only unveils a structure of reality or a dimension of existence; by the same stroke it brings a *meaning* into human existence. This is why even symbols aiming at the ultimate reality conjointly constitute existential revelations for the man who

deciphers their message." M. Eliade and J. Kitagawa, *The History of Religions* (Chicago: University of Chicago Press, 1959), p. 100.

2. For a defense of the writer of Ecclesiastes see Augustine's *City of God*, XII, 14.

3. For an excellent view of the Hindu myths see "The Wheel of Rebirth" from Joseph Campbell, ed., *Myths and Symbols in Indian Art and Civilization* (New York: Pantheon, 1946), pp. 11–19.

4. Cf. Plato's *Phaedrus*.

5. Ephesians, 2:11–13.

6. St. Augustine, *The City of God*, trans. Marcus Dods (Edinburgh: T. & T. Clarke, 1887), XII, 21.

7. Paul Tillich, III, 299.

8. See our comments in Chapter 4 on "Event and Interpretation."

9. This notion of material prosperity as a concomitant of spiritual values is not an uncommon one. It is present, for example, in the beliefs of certain Puritan theologians of the seventeenth century who identified material wealth as a sign that the individual who possessed it was one of the elect, whereas poverty was a sign of future damnation.

10. Leo Baeck, *The Essence of Judaism* (New York: Schocken Books, 1961), p. 252.

11. *Great Jewish Ideas*, edited by A. Millgram (B'nai B'rith, Wash., 1964), from chapter on "The Messianic Decline in Contemporary Jewish Thought," by Steven S. Schwarzschild.

12. M. Friedlander, *The Jewish Religion* (London: Shapiro Vallentine & Co., 1937), p. 223.

13. Quoted from Edmund F. Sutcliffe, S.J., *The Old Testament and the Future Life* (London: Burns, Oates and Washbourne, 1947), p. 170.

14. Quoted from Ben Zion Bokser, *Judaism: Profile of a Faith* (New York: Alfred A. Knopf Incorporated, 1963), pp. 142–143.

15. Since there are wide divergences of opinion among Protestant theologians on the whole subject of eschatology, it will be impossible to state of any one belief that it is subscribed to by all Protestant theologians. To a lesser extent the same may be said to be true of Catholic theologians.

16. Walter M. Abbot, S.J., ed., *Documents of Vatican II*, trans. Very Rev. Msgr. Joseph Gallagher (New York: Guild Press, 1966), p. 23, n. 23. This paragraph was especially written for this publication by Avery Dulles, S.J.

17. C. H. Dodd, *The Parables of the Kingdom* (New York: Charles Scribner's Sons 1941), p. 49.

18. *Ibid.*, p. 49.

19. *Ibid.*, p. 49.

20. Reinhold Niebuhr, *The Nature and Destiny of Man* (New York: Charles Scribner's Sons, 1941), II, 50.

21. Jean Daniélou, *The Lord of History*, trans. Nigel Abercrombie (Harlow: Longmans, Green, and Chicago: Regnery, 1958), p. 271.

22. *Ibid.*, p. 272.

23. See especially Albert Schweitzer, *The Quest of the Historical Jesus*, trans. W. Montgomery (London: Adam and Charles Black, 1954, 3rd ed.).

24. Gösta Lundström, *The Kingdom of God in the Teaching of Jesus*, trans. Joan Bulman (Richmond, Va.: John Knox Press, 1963), p. 75.

25. An excellent illustration of this distinction is to be found in the famous analysis of time that St. Augustine gives in Book XI of the *Confessions*. To many it has seemed that Augustine is primarily concerned with the analysis of time as merely physical or psychological. But this is to misinterpret him and to overlook the very profound influence that Scripture had upon him. The Augustinian philosophy may

be said to be God-oriented rather than self-centered. The ultimate explanation of the mystery of time is to be found only in God and His purposes. For Augustine time is essentially a religious category.

26. To further illustrate this point it might be observed that as the year 1000 approached many people in the Middle Ages in Europe felt that the end of the world was at hand and that the second coming of Christ was imminent. As it turned out the first day of the year 1000 was uneventful. Time alone is not a determining factor in human history.

27. J. A. T. Robinson, *In the End, God* . . . (London: James Clarke & Co., Ltd., 1950), p. 48.

28. *Ibid.,* p. 61. We are much indebted for the distinction between *chronos* and *kairos* to Bishop Robinson's penetrating analysis. Although there are difficulties in the distinction, the distinction does, we feel, make more intelligible the problems at hand.

29. Obviously an important source is to be found in the Jewish apocalyptic literature, in the Prophetic Books and the Vision of Daniel, and generally in the whole eschatological symbol of the Messiah. Another important source is to be found in the sayings of Jesus which reveal the influence of the Jewish apocalyptic teaching. Thus there is the prophecy stated in Matthew 24:29–31, cited on p. 349, and Mark 13:24–31.

30. Usually pictured as Satan or the Son of Perdition, who claims to be divine and who would destroy the redemptive mission of Christ. In the account of the apostle there is also a political note. The description of the great Beast is thought to represent Nero. In succeeding centuries the Antichrist was identified with the Jews, Mohammed, the Papacy, Phillip II of Spain, Napoleon, Hitler, Stalin, and even the World Council of Churches.

31. From Norman Cohn, *The Pursuit of the Millennium* (New York: Harper and Row, 1961), p. 12.

32. *The Apostolic Fathers: The Fragments of Papias*, trans. Joseph M.-F. Marique, S.J. (New York: Fathers of the Church, 1947), p. 375.

33. St. Augustine, *The City of God*, trans. Marcus Dods (Edinburgh: T. & T. Clarke, 1887), XX, 7.

34. Augustine divides the epochs of history into six: (1) from Adam to the Flood; (2) from Noah and the Flood to Abraham; (3) from Abraham to David; (4) from David to the Babylonian exile; (5) from the Babylonian exile to the birth of Christ; and (6) from the Incarnation to the Parousia and the end of the world. The first five epochs are accounted for in the Old Testament. But the period of the sixth epoch cannot be calculated. The most he can say is that Christ will come again.

35. One of the most interesting of the many interpretations of the millennium is that of Joachim of Flore (1132–1202). Joachim divides all history into three ages: (1) the Age of the Father and the Law of the Old Testament; (2)the Age of the Son and the Law of the New Testament; (3) the Age of the Holy Spirit, which is implicit in the work of St. Benedict and which will be marked by the Eternal Gospel. By the grace of the Holy Spirit the Eternal Gospel will transform the Gospel of Christ. Joachim develops in considerable detail this highly speculative account of the three ages of the world. He even estimated that the New Age of the Holy Spirit would replace the Age of Christ around the year 1260. At this time the Church would be overthrown and the leadership of the Third Age would fall to the monks (later identified by the Spiritual Franciscans with themselves). Out of all the fantasy and imagery connected with this vision of Joachim the most significant feature is that in the new millennium there would be no place for Christ. The Holy Spirit and not Christ now stands at the center of history. This extreme apocalyptic view is wholly irreconcilable with the Augustinian view and has been virtually unanimously rejected by Christian theologians.

36. This kind of dualism, especially as it appears in the philosophy of Descartes, led the British philosopher Gilbert Ryle to refer to it as the doctrine of the "ghost in the machine" (Cf. his *Concept of Mind* [London: Hutchinson, 1949]).

37. Augustine refers to the Resurrection in terms of Confession of Faith, Rule of Faith, and Symbol.

38. Quoted by Justin McCann, O.S.B., in *The Teaching of the Catholic Church* (New York: Macmillan, 1949), II, 1219–1220.

39. *The New Testament*, trans. R. A. Knox (New York: Sheed & Ward, 1952), p. 372 n.

40. Quoted by Daniélou, *The Lord of History*, p. 272.

41. The notion of a particular judgment is found more within Catholic theology than in Protestant theology. This is because Catholic theologians continue to stress immortality as involving a separation of soul from body. Another factor undoubtedly is the Catholic teaching on purgatory and hell. Purgatory is unacceptable to Protestants and hell no longer receives the emphasis it once did.

42. "Origen argues for the universal restoration of all things in Christ and thus the eventual salvation of all men. 'The end of the world and the consummation will come when every soul shall be visited with the penalties due for its sins. This time, when everyone shall pay what he owes, is known to God alone. We believe, however, that the goodness of God through Christ will restore his entire creation to one end, even his enemies being conquered and subdued'. . . . Seeing, then, that such is the end, "When all enemies shall have been subjected to Christ," when "the last enemy shall be destroyed, that is, death," and when "the kingdom shall be delivered up to God and the Father by Christ, to whom all things have been subjected," let us, I say, from such an end as this, contemplate the beginning of things. For the end is always like the beginning. . . .' " From *Origen: On First Principles*, trans. G. W. Butterworth (New York: Harper and Row, 1966), pp. 52–53.

43. Quoted by H. Rondet, S.J., *Un seul corps. Un seul esprit. La communion des saints.* Taken from the book *Life After Death* by Maurice and Louis Becque, vol. 28, of The Twentieth Century Encyclopedia of Catholicism; © 1960 by Hawthorn Books, Inc., 70 Fifth Avenue, N.Y.C. 10011.

44. G. Bernanos, *Diary of a Country Priest*, trans. P. Morris (New York: Macmillan, 1937), p. 177.

45. Rondet, *Un seul corps*, p. 10.

46. See especially Sartre's play *No Exit*. Two of C. S. Lewis' works are well worth reading relative to this topic: *The Screwtape Letters* and *The Great Divorce*.

47. For an excellent exposition of this position, which appears to owe much to Origen, see Robinson, *In the End, God* . . . , pp. 99–124.

SELECT BIBLIOGRAPHY

Becqué, Maurice, C.SS.R., and Louis Becqué, C.SS.R. *Life After Death.* Trans. P. J. Hepburne-Scott. New York: Hawthorn Books, 1960.

Bokser, Ben Zion. *Judaism: Profile of a Faith.* New York: Alfred A. Knopf, 1963.

Cohn, Norman. *The Pursuit of the Millennium.* New York: Harper and Row, 1961.

Cullmann, O. *Christ and Time.* Philadelphia: Westminster Press, 1950.

CULLMANN, O. *Immortality of the Soul or Resurrection of the Dead?* London: Epworth Press, 1958.

DANIÉLOU, J., S.J. *The Lord of History.* Trans. N. Abercrombie. London: Longmans, 1958.

DODD, C. H. *The Parables of the Kingdom.* London: Fontana, 1935.

EPSTEIN, ISIDORE. *Judaism.* Hammondsworth: Penguin, 1959.

GUARDINI, R. *The Last Things.* London: Burns and Oates, 1954.

NIEBUHR, RIENHOLD. *Faith and History.* New York: Charles Scribner's Sons, 1951.

RAHNER, KARL. *On the Theology of Death.* Trans. Charles H. Henkey. London: Nelson, 1961.

ROBINSON, J. A. T. *In the End, God.* . . . London: James Clark, 1950.

SCHWARZSCHILD, STEVEN S. "The Messianic Doctrine in Contemporary Jewish Thought," in A. MILLGRAM, ed. *Great Jewish Ideas.* (B'nai B'rith) New York: Tetlinger Co., 1964.

SCHWEITZER, ALBERT. *The Quest of the Historical Jesus.* London: 1906.

SHINN, ROGER L. *Christianity and the Problem of History.* New York: Charles Scribner's Sons, 1953.

SUTCLIFFE, EDMUND F., S.J. *The Old Testament and the Future Life.* London: Burns, Oates and Washbourne, 1947.

WILDER, AMOS N. *Eschatology and Ethics in the Teaching of Jesus.* New York: Harper and Brothers, 1950.

Foreword to Chapter XII:
The Institutional Character
of Western Religion

IN the concluding chapters of this book we have the manifold task of showing how the doctrines and ideas, the symbols and the mysteries expounded in the preceding chapters all find expression in one way or another in the institutional character of western religion. Here we shall be concerned with some of the more fundamental and practical manifestations of religion, with religion as a way of worship and devotion, a way of life, rather than a matter of history, philosophy, and theology. The title of this foreword aptly introduces and characterizes the subject matter of the following two chapters. The definition of "institutional" as applied to religion is given as follows in the Oxford English Dictionary: "Of religion: Expressed by means of or taking shape in definitions, as a church, a hierarchy, sacramental ordinances." Expanding somewhat upon this definition, we shall regard our task as involving a study of such topics as Church and Synagogue, Liturgy, Law, Prayer, and Rites. Since a great deal can be said about each of these and related topics, we shall endeavor to reduce the magnitude of our task by singling out the more important features of each topic for study and supplementing where necessary with tabular outlines. As a guide for the more convenient ordering of our subject matter we shall devote Chapter 12 to the structures of western religious institutions, that is, their organization, the locus of authority, and the nature and function of law. Chapter 13 will consider the functions of these institutions: their liturgies and related practices which more often reveal the differences in their beliefs that are not as readily apparent in their theologies and creeds.

XII

The Structures of Western
Religious Institutions

THE terms *church* and *synagogue* each have several distinctive meanings that more or less parallel one another. Thus church may mean a building or place of worship. The same applies to synagogue. Again, church may refer to those who are associated in some way with the building or place of worship. With respect to those who participate in the purpose to which the building is dedicated, church designates the congregation or assembly of believers. Similarly the synagogue has been defined as "a congregation of Jews for worship and study." Obviously the distinguishing characteristic of church or synagogue is in the purposes to which it is dedicated. Essentially they are religious institutions and their basic purpose is the worship of God. Characterizing them also as assemblies or congregations brings out another important aspect: that this worship is social in nature.

Church and synagogue may also be considered in relation to those who are more actively and permanently concerned with the organization and administration of the various functions of church or synagogue. In the Christian churches we have ministers, priests, pastors, deacons, bishops, elders, cardinals, and others. In Judaism at one time there were both priests and rabbis, but now there are only rabbis. Occasionally the representative officers of Roman Catholicism, Judaism, and Protestantism are loosely referred to as priests, rabbis, and clergymen. Further differentiations of a more accidental nature may appear within the meaning of church or synagogue relative to geographical considerations or minor differences of belief. Thus we may have Southern Baptists, Byzantine Catholics, or Reform Jews.

The development and elaboration of the principal characteristics as well as the lesser differences that appear in the structures of church and synagogue will appear more clearly as we examine in some detail, first the synagogue, and second the Christian church.

THE SYNAGOGUE

To understand more clearly the nature and purpose of the synagogue we must observe that historically Jewish worship came to be centered first in the temple. The term "synagogue" does not even appear in the Hebrew Scriptures. However, in the course of Jewish history the synagogue gradually replaced the temple, especially after the destruction of the latter. Today the sole Jewish institution for public worship is the synagogue. Among Reform Jews it is true that the term "temple" is used in place of "synagogue," but this is done in commemoration of the temple and the past glories of Judaism associated with it.

In the history of Judaism there were two successive temples that served as places of worship. The first was the great temple built by Solomon at Jerusalem. One of the most magnificent structures of antiquity, it became a national sanctuary for the Jews and a great unifying force in the life of Judaism. Much of the Jewish liturgy and ritual came into being with the temple, particularly a sacrificial ritual which was common to all antiquity. It was this liturgy and ritual that manifested so clearly Jewish belief and contributed to the development and the strength of Jewish nationalism.

In 586 B.C.E. after some four centuries of existence, the Temple of Solomon was destroyed by Nebuchadnezzar, the King of Babylonia, and the Jews were driven into exile. In 519 B.C.E. after the exile had ended, work was begun on a restoration of the temple, and was completed in three years. Finally, in 20–19 B.C.E. the temple was again rebuilt by Herod, the King of Judaea. It lasted about a century and was destroyed by Titus, the Roman Emperor, in 70 C.E.[1]

Formal Jewish worship first became institutionalized with the erection of the Temple of Solomon. Before that period we know little of the nature of Jewish public worship. From the Torah we know, however, that there did exist a priesthood, drawn from the tribe of Levi. The functions of this priesthood were largely the performance of sacrificial rites. Before the temple these were carried out by the priests at different sanctuaries. In the very early period of Jewish history such religious functions were carried out principally by the patriarchs.

The development of the priesthood, concomitant with the rise and the fall of the Jewish theocracy, was always closely identified with the temple.

Actually, the priesthood lasted up to the time of the destruction of the temple. It may also be noted that the relation of the priesthood and the Jewish monarchy was at one time exceptionally close. David and Solomon not only appointed priests but even performed some of the priestly functions themselves. In his own temple Solomon acted as High Priest. After the time of Solomon the priesthood gradually won a measure of independence from the crown, and before long it possessed a monopoly on the various functions of the temple. The priesthood was in charge of all sacrifices; they expounded the Law and they conducted the liturgical services and rites of the temple. They had complete charge of the levying of tithes upon the people for the financial support of the temple.

One of the most important functions of the priests was the observation of the laws of purity that applied to the priesthood. Such laws are stated in Leviticus, and also in parts of Genesis, Exodus, and Numbers, and from early times they set the priests apart from the rest of the people. Their more specific applications concerned the life of the priest. For example, the priests could not be deformed; although marriage was an obligation for them, they could not marry divorced women; they had to be of high moral character; they could never touch a corpse. It should be pointed out, however, that the observance of laws of purity to varying extents are also incumbent upon all Jews, for the assumption is that spiritually speaking every Jew is a priest since he is chosen by God to serve Him.

Although the priesthood no longer exists in Judaism, remnants of it survive in the person of all those Jewish men who are of priestly descent. Such descent is determined upon the basis of the names of the individuals. Many Jewish men with names such as Cohen, Cahan, Kohn, Kahn, Kagan, Kogen, and the like—names which indicate a relation to *Cohanim* (priests)—continue to follow certain Levitical laws relating to the priesthood, for they are expected to resume their priestly functions when the Messiah appears and a new temple is established on Mount Zion. Today they are accorded certain privileges during the traditional Jewish services. For example, they have a priority in any public reading from the Torah and in the recitation of the Priestly Blessing before the Ark of the Torah. Such privileges would not be found in the more liberal synagogues.

In Hebrew the term for "synagogue" is *Bet Ha-Knesset*, meaning "House of Assembly." The term "synagogue" does not appear in the Hebrew Scriptures, although it does appear frequently in the New Testament, which explains the Greek origin of the term. Historically, the synagogue came into existence about 2500 years ago. Its actual origins are unknown, but many believe that it first arose in Babylon among those Jews who had been reduced to captivity in 586 B.C.E. by Nebuchadnezzar. It was these exiled Jews who kept alive the Jewish traditions and Jewish religious life and custom. Apparently they also contributed a good deal to the liturgy and the literature of Judaism in this period. It was these contributions on their part that made the eventual transition from the temple to the synagogue as the central place of worship of the Jewish people relatively easy. After the exile and for a number of years the temple and the synagogue existed side by side until the temple was destroyed in 70 C.E. From that time to the present the synagogue has been the place of public worship for the Jews.

An appropriate contemporary description of the synagogue is that given by Steinberg:

> Whatever spot Jews set aside for their religious exercises, wherever they put up an Ark containing the Torah-scroll, source and symbol of the Tradition, there is a synagogue. No dedicatory rites or sacramental procedures are required to hallow the place. The Tradition insists that the synagogue be cleanly; it urges that it be beautiful. Yet many a synagogue is little more than a bare room and is not a whit diminished in holiness on that account. For, it is the Jewish teaching concerning God that, since He is present everywhere, He may everywhere be invoked.[2]

The synagogue has three principal functions: it serves as a school or "house of study," as a chapel or "house of prayer," and as a social or communal center. Some of its principal features may be drawn out by contrasting it with the temple which it replaced. One significant change is that the priesthood has been dropped; the individual Jewish worshiper has been brought into direct relation with God. He no longer requires the sacrificial offerings and the mediation of the priests. In the synagogue there is no place for an ecclesiastical hierarchy, an official priestly class, and the elaborate rites which were so characteristic of the temple. The result has been the increasingly democratic and independent character of the synagogue. The members of the synagogue are free to choose the rabbi and the other officers of the synagogue. These characteristics as well as its success as a school, a chapel, and a social center have contributed to the great strength of the synagogue. Through the synagogue Judaism has been able to maintain its unity and its identity, often in the face of a hostile world. Its importance has been well stated by G. F. Moore:

> Its (Judaism's) persistent character, and, it is not too much to say, the very preservation of its existence through all the vicissitudes of its fortunes, it owes more than anything else to the synagogue. . . . Nor is it for Judaism alone that it had this importance. It determined the type of Christian worship, which in the Greek and Roman world of the day might otherwise easily have taken the form of a mere mystery; and, in part directly, in part through the church, it furnished the model for Mohammed.[3]

A synagogue officially comes into being with a *minyan*—a quorum of ten men.[4] The contemporary synagogue divides into the Orthodox, the Conservative, and the Reform. Despite these divisions, there is an overall unity within Judaism. The differences in the interpretation of the Law and the way of life do not lead to separation but only to division.

Of these divisions the Orthodox adhere very strictly to the divine revelation, to the Torah and the Talmud, to the written and the oral Law. For them the Law is complete and final—nothing in it can be changed. In the Orthodox synagogues certain practices are prevalent which identify the Orthodox mode of worship: the use of the Hebrew language, the segregation of the sexes during worship, the absence of instrumental music, the head coverings of male worshipers, and the use of the historic prayer books.

The Reform Synagogue rejects many of the practices of Orthodox Judaism. It permits an equal place to women in the formation of a synagogue, and generally it does not follow most of the dietary laws. Reform worship has tended to use more of the English language than the Hebrew. The divine authority of the Torah, the belief in a personal Messiah, and a personal resurrection are generally denied. Much emphasis is placed on Jewish cultural values, and in the present century considerable support has been given to the ideals of Zionism.

The Conservative Synagogue compromises between the extremes of the Reform and the Orthodox. Conservative Judaism emphasizes Jewish traditionalism and modernism. For all observances it stresses the spirit rather than the letter of the Law. Some practices of Orthodoxy are retained, for example, the use of the Hebrew language, the covering of the head by men, and somewhat relaxed dietary laws. In general, Conservative Judaism adheres to traditional practices as far as practicable. On the other hand, it permits instrumental music, uses the English language for many prayers, permits riding to the synagogue on the Sabbath, and excludes the segregation of the sexes during worship. More so than either Orthodox Judaism and Reform Judaism, Conservative Judaism has sought to unify Jewish cultural values, Jewish religion, and the political ideals and aspirations of Judaism. Like Reform Judaism, it has given strong support to the Zionist movement.[5]

THE SYNAGOGUE AND LAW AND AUTHORITY.   It should be evident from what has been brought out in Chapter 3, and in some things that have been said here, that the Law as embodied primarily in the Torah and secondarily in the Talmud occupies a very large place in the Jewish religion. Law is basic to Judaism, for the Law is the divine law. Furthermore Judaism was originally a theocracy, and the development of the Law followed the needs of a theocratic state. It is also true, in the history of the Jewish people after the destruction of the temple and the dispersal of the Jewish communities throughout the world, that the Jewish people have found themselves more or less isolated from other groups. Hence the necessity for the continuing development of the Law, not merely concerning the forms of belief and worship, but even more as a guide for the moral behavior of the individual Jew. Furthermore, it became evident that in the observance of certain religious practices Jewish religion and group identity could best be preserved. This helps to explain the great authority given to Jewish law, the reverence for and study of the Torah, and the strict observance of all rites and ceremonies. It is little wonder that the Jewish Law assumed so complex and diversified a character. For it is actually made up of thousands of laws added in virtually every century of Jewish history. The result is an astonishing kind of "code of codes" including all manner of injunctions, prohibitions, regulations, and statutes. This tendency toward the ever increasing number of laws was heightened in the Middle Ages in Europe and brought about by the isolation of the Jewish communities. The very complexity and cumbersomeness of the Jewish laws led to many efforts to codify them. The most ambitious of all these efforts was undoubtedly that undertaken by Maimonides, who codified all the accumulated Jewish laws of the previous centuries in his Mishnah Torah. Although quite valuable, it tended to be overly philosophical and too elaborate. It was replaced in the early modern period by the more practicable codes of Rabbi Jacob ben Asher (d. 1340) and Rabbi Joseph Caro (1488–1575). This last code has been very influential, and among Orthodox Jews it still has a place of considerable importance.

The adoption of these codes was brought about in part by the increasing integration of the Jewish peoples in the European community, and in part by the Reform and Conservative movements in Judaism. Although much of the traditional customs and religious practices persist, and although the study of the Torah is still emphasized, the strict and literal interpretation of the Torah and the Jewish laws has broken down. Today there seems to be an almost imperceptible shift in the locus of authority in Judaism. Authority now appears to lie more in the Tradition and what this means for Judaism rather than in a concept of authority centered in the Torah as divine revelation. This would not be true, of course, for Orthodoxy; but in varying degrees it would probably be true for Reform and Conservative Judaism. Finally, in relation to the synagogue the place of authority lies with the Law and tradition. It does not extend to the synagogue and its officers. What authority the rabbi may have is due solely to his knowledge, his prestige, and his capacity for spiritual leadership rather than for any office he may hold. As we shall see after an examination of the role of law and authority in Roman Catholicism and Protestantism, Judaism presents a much simpler concept of authority than those of these other religions. In Judaism authority rests entirely upon the Law, however this may be interpreted.

The Rabbinate

In the Hebrew the term "rabbi" means "teacher." The principal and essential function of the rabbi was that of instructing others in the Torah and its applications to everyday life. The ideal teacher was Moses— Mosheh Rabbenu ("Our Teacher Moses"). In the early history of Judaism the rabbi remained primarily a dedicated teacher of the Torah. He exercised few other functions and he received no salary for his religious leadership in the community. It was this dedication to the study of the Torah and the concern for the preservation of Judaism in the years of the Exile that led to the creation of the Talmud by the Rabbinic Sages, as they came to be called.

Until the modern period the title of rabbi was conferred by the laying on of hands. To attain the title an individual had to prove himself learned in the Torah and the Talmud. There was no requirement for any particular course of study or for any kind of academic degree. Individual study, a disinterested devotion to the religious values of Judaism, and a high moral character were the only prerequisites for a strictly nonprofessional office. By the thirteenth century and after, as his duties multiplied, and more and more was demanded of him, it became necessary for him to be given some compensation for his work. By this time he was not only a teacher of the Torah and Talmud. He also supervised the education of the young, interpreted the law, settled disputes, and supervised the observance of the dietary laws and the Sabbath. He officiated or participated in many of the religious ceremonies; he confirmed (Bar Mitzvah), he married, and he buried.

More recently the cultural changes of contemporary society, the influence of other religious organizations, and the demands made upon the rabbi for leadership not only within his own group but in the larger community as well, has led to certain important changes in the position of the rabbi. Today the rabbi is expected to have a rather broad intellectual competence and the kind of educational training that assures such competence. It is no longer sufficient for him to have simply a good understanding of the Jewish tradition such as can be acquired by private study. He must know more than the Hebrew language, the Torah, and the Talmud. Today a rabbi is expected to have an academic degree and a thorough training in a rabbinical seminary or *yeshivah*. Today he is well paid, more broadly cultured, and likely to be a leader not only in the

Jewish community but in the larger communities of city, state, and nation. Like that of the Christian clergyman, his career is professional.

Finally, we should observe that the modern rabbinate possesses both an intellectual and a spiritual independence. Except for the period of the Great Sanhedrin[6] the rabbi, either singly or as a group, has not exercised any great authority. The present-day rabbi has no superior, and each rabbi is free and bound only to his own conscience and to the Jewish tradition. There is no hierarchy in Judaism. Rabbis are chosen by the congregation, but they are not "called" in the evangelical sense to a given synagogue. Furthermore, the rabbi is not marked off from the other members of the congregation by the possession of any spiritual powers given through ordination. He differs from the others only in the possession of a superior knowledge of all that constitutes Judaism. He has no special privileges in the conduct of the ritual or the ceremony of worship. As a rule any member of the congregation can fulfill this role. In practice, however, this role belongs primarily to the rabbi.

THE CHRISTIAN CHURCH

In our discussion of the kingdom of God in Chapter 11, on eschatology, we noted that the term *ekklesia* or Church designated all who accept the teachings of Christ and that Christ himself used this term and considered his apostles as constituting a religious community or church dedicated to carrying out his messianic mission. From this very simple beginning the Christian Church eventually came to assume many different forms. It is in these different forms that the major differences exist between Roman Catholic and Protestant notions of the Church as well as those existing among the many Protestant churches. To the differences arising out of the historical development of the Church must be related the differing conceptions of its structure—its organization, its laws, its conception of authority. The differences relevant to Protestantism will be based upon an examination of contemporary American Protestant churches.

First, let us point out in a very general fashion the principal points of agreement and disagreement between the Roman Catholic and the Protestant notions of the Church. After this very brief introduction we shall examine in more detail the major points of difference. Both Catholics and Protestants accept the origin of the Church in Christ and his apostles. Catholics contend that Christ transferred his spiritual authority to Peter and the other apostles, and that Peter established the Church at Rome. Thus the Roman Church is identified as the visible Church here upon earth, and the head of that Church today is a successor of Peter. Protestants reject this contention and the New Testament passage (Matthew 16:18–19) upon which it is based. They emphasize that the Church is represented by all the faithful and that it is not centered in any one organization. Some would declare that there is only an invisible Church.

With respect to the principal functions and activities of the Church there are again points of agreement and difference. Both Catholics and Protestants accept the Church as fundamentally a place of worship but they differ on the forms that that worship takes. Both accept the social character of the Church. The Catholic Church is more highly organized and authority is rather highly centralized. In Protestantism authority as a general rule rests more with the congregation than with a hierarchy. Some Protestant churches retain a hierarchical form of organization, but without the same concentration of authority found in the Catholic Church. The decentralized character of most Protestant churches undoubtedly has led to a greater latitude of freedom for the individual. Ecclesiastical laws are much more highly developed in the Catholic Church. This is because of the long history of the Catholic Church, its international character, and the requirements of a complex administration.

The Roman Catholic Church

Roman Catholics maintain that the Church was established by Christ in his word, in his works, and in his presence. The Church has a divine foundation, and insofar as it is divine the Church is a mystery and beyond the complete understanding of man. Catholics emphasize the unity of the Church as developed in the Pauline doctrine of the Mystical Body. The Church is the Mystical Body and Christ is the head of that Church. "There is one body and one Spirit, just as you were called to the one hope that belongs to your call, one Lord, one faith, one baptism, one God and Father of us all, who is above all and through all and in all" (Ephesians 4:4–6). This Church of Christ was turned over to Peter. "And I tell you, you are Peter, and on this rock [Latin *petra*] I will build my church, and the powers of death shall not prevail against it. I will give you the keys of the kingdom of heaven, and whatever you loose on earth shall be loosed in heaven" (Matthew 16:18–19). After the Resurrection, Peter and the others were commanded by Christ: "Go therefore and make disciples of all nations, baptizing them in the name of the Father and of the Son and of the Holy Spirit, teaching them to observe all that I have commanded you; and lo, I am with you always to the close of the age" (Matthew 28:19–20).

In these words of St. Matthew, Christ is addressing the eleven apostles who are to be the living authority of the Church in the immediate future. They formed the beginnings and the nucleus of the Church and its teaching authority that was to exist for all time. Christ informs them that following his ascension they will be visited by the Holy Spirit (Acts 1:4–8). This significant event is described in Acts 2:1–4:

> When the day of Pentecost had come, they were all together in one place. And suddenly a sound came from heaven like the rush of a mighty wind, and it filled all the house where they were sitting. And there appeared to them tongues as of fire, distributed and resting on each one of them. And they were all filled with the Holy Spirit and began to speak in other tongues, as the Spirit gave them utterance.

From this time Peter and the other apostles carried out the mission of Christ; they organized and established the visible Church. According to Catholic belief the Catholic Church today is this same Church that Peter and the other apostles established through the instructions given them by Christ. There are ecclesial elements in the other churches, as we noted in Chapter 11;[7] but the teaching of the Catholic Church is very explicit on the issues of the primacy of Peter and the succession through Peter of the popes at Rome. On this point the Church appeals not only to scriptural authority (Matthew 16:18–19, Luke 22:31–32, John 1:42), but also to the historical evidence. Thus, Peter resided in Rome and was martyred in Rome under Nero. The names of his immediate successors, Linus and Cletus, are known. And there is the statement attributed to Clement, the successor of Cletus, who writes to the Corinthians: "If indeed, there are some who will not listen to what He (Jesus Christ) has said through us, let them bear in mind that they will come to sin and great danger."[8]

THE HIERARCHY.   Out of the frequently unclear references in the Book of the Acts of the Apostles the structure of the early Church gradually emerges. First appear the bishops, who are identified with elders (Acts 14:23) and with guardians or overseers (Acts 20:28). The Greek term for overseer is *episkopos* (bishop). The bishops derived their authority directly from the apostles by the laying on of hands (ordination). In turn they consecrated others to the office. ("Hence I remind you to re-kindle the gift of God that is within you through the laying on of my hands," II Timothy 1–6.) The letters to Timothy and Titus bring out more clearly the organization of the early Church. Timothy and Titus acted as delegates of St. Paul to the churches in Crete and Ephesus. Their status was evidently that of bishops, and they were advised and assisted in the conduct of their office by elders or *presbyters*. The office of priest and the use of the term does not seem to have arisen until the second century. In apostolic times their position might be said to be that of the presbyters. The qualifications of bishops and deacons are clearly set forth in I Timothy 3:1–13.

From the very beginning of the history of the Church there has been no doubt concerning the validity of the office of bishop. That bishops succeeded to the offices and powers of the apostles has been affirmed by successive church councils. It should be emphasized here that the authority of the bishop is spiritual and is one of service rather than domination. The title of the pope as the Bishop of Rome is "the servant of the servants of Christ." Again, with respect to the authority of the bishops, it should be pointed out that with the pope they constitute the supreme power in governing the Church. This is the meaning of what is termed "the principle of collegiality" in the Church. The exercise of this power is effected in various ways, one of which is through an ecumenical council. At first glance it might seem that the principle of collegiality would have the effect of limiting the power of the papacy. However, the intention of the principle is a sharing of the papal power with that of the other bishops without any lessening of the primacy of the papacy. To the extent that this is effected and precisely how it will be worked out is a matter for future decisions.[9]

The functions of the bishop are manifold. He enjoys all the ordinary functions of the priesthood—celebrating Mass, hearing confessions, distributing the sacraments. He also administers the sacrament of confirmation, ordains to the priesthood, and consecrates to the episcopacy. Of singular importance is his function of preaching the gospel and clarifying the faith for all those under his guidance. In the matter of faith and morals the teaching of a bishop is as authoritative as that of the pope. Infallibility is not, however, the right of an individual bishop, although together in a council with other bishops their collective judgment is regarded as infallible in matters of faith and morals. Finally, the bishops have the power of governing a number of particular churches within a district termed the *diocese*. In his own diocese the power of the bishop to govern is absolute. In this respect he is a vicar of Christ and on an equal basis of authority with the pope as the Bishop of Rome. Frequently associated with the bishops are coadjutor bishops and auxiliary bishops. Both assist the bishop in the performance of his duties, but the former have the right of succession to the bishopric. Auxiliary bishops are now named episcopal vicars and given specific duties for a certain part of the diocese. Recently, in the New York Archdiocese, six episcopal vicars were named to assist the cardinal, whose role will be described later.

In the larger urban areas a number of contiguous dioceses may be brought together into an archdiocese under the leadership of an archbishop. One of the bishops in such an area is named as the archbishop, but each individual bishop within such an area remains the master of his own diocese. Archbishops may convene councils, they may hear appeals from their bishops, and they may appoint a vicar capitular to succeed a deceased bishop. In the past, archbishops were more commonly known as *metro-*

politans, and their jurisdiction and powers generally were greater than they are today.

Apart from the papacy the highest jurisdictional office in the Church is that of the patriarch. Originally a patriarchate was any great see, but by the time of the fourth century the term applied to the cities of Rome, Alexandria, Antioch, Jerusalem, and Constantinople. After the Islamic conquest most of these patriarchates were lost, although the papacy has followed the practice of nominating bishops to these posts. The pope is known as the Patriarch of the West as well as Bishop of Rome and the Metropolitan of the Province of Rome.

THE PRIESTHOOD.   Like the bishop, the priest is a representative of Christ and of the Church. In rank among holy orders within the Church he is second. His priestly functions are to offer the sacrifice of the Mass, to bless and to rule the people within his jurisdiction, to preach, and to administer the sacraments. He is subordinate in jurisdiction to the bishop. Since a diocese consists of a number of churches, frequently a great many, it is impossible for the bishop to govern each church and to carry out the functions of the priestly office for each church. The jurisdictional area of each church is known as a *parish,* and the number of parishes or sub-divisions of a diocese may vary. To the parishes are assigned the priests. The number of priests assigned to each parish church depends upon the size and the needs of the parish. In large city parishes there may be several priests attached to a given church. The priest in charge of the parish is generally known as the pastor and he is usually appointed to such a post only after considerable service as an assistant pastor in one or more churches in the diocese. In some of the larger city parishes it is not un-common for a priest to remain as an assistant pastor until he is fifty years old or more. In less populated areas they may become pastors while rela-tively young. As pastors they exercise a governing authority in the parish, supervising and directing the activities of their assistants and serving as the spiritual leader of all the parishioners in the parish. Of primary adminis-trative importance is their duty of establishing and financing the church and school buildings of the parish. They are subject to the rule of the bishop; they are appointed to their parishes by the bishop and they may be removed by him. The financing of parish buildings is supervised by the bishop and he holds title to the property of the parish. A portion of the revenue of each parish is turned over to the bishop; he in turn pays the salaries of all the priests and other officers under his jurisdiction.

Immediately below the office of priest is that of the deacon. Until quite recently deacons did not constitute a separate order within the hierarchy. Their functions were usually assumed nominally in ecclesiastical rites and ceremonies by the priests, or the title of deacon might be bestowed upon seminarians just prior to their ordination. Today it is very likely that the order of deacons will be established as a permanent grade within the Church and there is even a likelihood of the future ordination of married assistants to the priests—administering baptism, reading the Scripture to the congregation, or assisting in dispensing the Eucharist.

CARDINALS.　The term "cardinal" is formed from the Latin *cardo*, the hinge of a door. On this interpretation it could be said that the rule of the Church turns on the cardinals as a door on its hinges. The term is also interpreted as synonymous with "principal." As such it was used in the early Church to designate the principal priests and deacons within a given diocese. In the metropolitan area of Rome those bishops closely associated with the papacy were frequently designated as cardinal bishops. In the course of time the use of the term "cardinal" came to be restricted to those clergy—bishops, priests, and deacons—in the diocese of Rome who rendered special assistance to the pope. Thus by the ninth century there were three orders of cardinals in Rome: cardinal bishops, cardinal priests, and cardinal deacons. In the historical development of this office within the Church we may note two major changes. First, as a result of various rulings by the popes, the three orders of the cardinals were given the privilege of electing the popes. The first pope so elected was Innocent II in 1130, and from that time the cardinals as a group have continued to exercise this privilege of electing popes. In 1179 at the third Lateran Council this privilege was made official, and the three orders of cardinals now became known as the Sacred College of Cardinals, a designation which reflects their corporate and religious character. By the end of the twelfth century the College of Cardinals also assumed a position of importance in the government of the Church. Dante refers to them as "rowers in the bark of Peter." Today they occupy a position of primary importance in the government and the administration of the Church.

Cardinals are appointed solely by the pope and it is now customary that they have episcopal consecration. In recent years the number of cardinals has generally approximated eighty. They now take precedence over bishops, archbishops, and patriarchs. Their duties are twofold: first, to govern the Church during a vacancy of the Holy See and to elect in solemn conclave a new pope; second, to participate in the administration of the Roman Curia, which consists of all those authorities and functionaries who are associated with the executive, legislative, judicial, and administrative powers of the papacy. The papal or Roman Curia consists at present of twelve sacred congregations and several tribunals, offices, and secretariats. The function of the sacred congregations is obvious from their names. Thus there is the Congregation of Rites, the Congregation of the Consistory, the Congregation for the Propagation of the Faith, and the

Congregation for the Eastern Church. The tribunals are courts, such as the Sacred Roman Rota, which hears appeals on sacramental judgments. Of the offices there are, for example, the Secretariat of State who acts as a prime minister for the pope in his relations with foreign states, and the Camera, which is concerned with the temporal affairs of the Holy See. In addition there are numerous commissions which are usually appointed for some specific purpose, for example the Biblical Commission, and which go out of existence once their purpose is accomplished. Since the cardinals are in charge of the various congregations, tribunals, and offices of the Curia, their influence has become highly important.

AUTHORITY AND LAW IN THE ROMAN CATHOLIC CHURCH.   In Chapter 4 we commented upon the authority exercised by tradition and upon the Magisterium or teaching authority of the Catholic Church. Here we shall restrict our account to the ways in which this teaching authority is manifested and applied: through the papacy, the councils, and in the canon law of the Church.

INFALLIBILITY AND THE PAPACY.   We have observed the preeminent position occupied by the pope and the rather considerable administrative and spiritual power which he exercises as both pope and bishop. To avoid any possible confusion and misunderstanding it must be borne in mind that the infallibility attributed to him is not consequent upon the authority he wields as person. Rather, as Catholics emphasize, it is a gift of grace by which the Holy Spirit safeguards him from error in his capacity as spiritual leader of the Church, and only in those cases that involve questions of *faith and morals*. This power or charisma of infallibility does not mean that the pope is free from all error. A great deal of what he says may be subject to error. He may express opinions in encyclical letters, and in certain pontifical decrees, that are subject to error. And like you or me he can make mistakes in more mundane matters, such as adding sums or predicting the weather. Again, infallibility does not mean impeccability. A pope can sin just like any other human being. Finally, even on matters of faith and morals, the pope is infallible only when he is speaking for the Church and as the head of the Church, that is, when he speaks *ex cathedra* (from the papal chair).

Individual bishops, aside from the pope, do not possess the charisma of infallibility. But as members of a general or ecumenical council they possess infallibility when the teaching authority of such a council is shared with the papacy. Provincial councils of bishops do not have this power. Again, papal infallibility is neither arbitrary nor absolute. Before he arrives at any doctrinal decisions the pope consults with other bishops who advise him but who do not validate the decisions.

CANON LAW.   Taking Aquinas' definition of law "as an ordinance of reason made for the common good and promulgated by the person who has care of a community," the Roman Catholic Church, like any comparable institution or organization, requires certain rules or laws. The term "canon" in Greek means a rule. In the early history of the Church a distinction was drawn between the *leges* of the State and the *canones* of the Church. Hence the practice arose of designating the law of the Church as the *jus canonum* or *jus canonicum*. Canon law, then, is the legislation of the Church. For some time the terms "canon law" and "ecclesiastical law" were used interchangeably, but today ecclesiastical law refers more to the law concerning the Church issued by civil authority.

The canon law originates with all those within the Church who have the authority to enact legislation for the benefit of those under their jurisdiction. Consequently, canon law may be based upon the juridical powers of the pope, the ecumenical council, and the Roman congregations. A certain amount of legislative power is also possessed by bishops and abbots but generally it is carried out within the framework of the more universal laws issued by the higher authorities. The legislative power of bishops and abbots are applicable to their specific jurisdictions, that is, dioceses and provinces. Their legislative power is limited, of course, by the higher laws of the Church. Plenary and provincial councils may enact legislation, but again only in conformity with the universal laws of the Church. The lesser officials within the Church—priests, vicars, generals, or deans—have no legislative power.

Some legislation may be issued directly by the pope. This consists of *apostolic constitutions* or *decrees motu proprio*. The former term applies principally to the more important documents the pope is called upon to issue. The latter term applies to the less important statements and those undertaken solely on his own initiative.

The legislative power of an ecumenical council may be best exemplified by the work of the Second Vatican Council. The Dogmatic Constitution recently issued by this council forms a part of the body of canon law of the Church. With respect to the congregations, these bodies have been delegated legislative power by the papacy; acting in the name of the pope they may issue decrees concerning the matters under their jurisdiction.

In principle the laws of the Church are binding upon all those who are baptized. Dispensations from the laws may be granted; a dispensation from all the laws of the Church could conceivably be granted by the pope. Bishops and abbots have a limited power of dispensation applicable when recourse to Rome is very difficult, when a delay in the granting of a dispensation may cause serious hardships, and if the question is one upon which the papacy has been in the practice of granting dispensation.

The extensive character of the canon law of the Church may be seen from a consideration of the Code of Canon Law which was issued in 1917. This code brought together all the laws of the Church which had not been codified since 1317. It is modeled on the Code Napoleon and contains in all some 2,414 canons, dealing with benefices, clergy, canonization, sacraments, rules for the religious life, divine worship, and penal laws.

The Protestant Conception of the Church

With few exceptions, Protestants, like Catholics, maintain that the intention of Jesus was to found a Church, that this intention finds ample justification in the New Testament, and that this Church in the beginning was simply the community of the faithful. Precisely how the scriptural references are to be interpreted with respect to later developments in the form that the Church would take is a matter of dispute among Protestants and Catholics. But the common ground is the conviction that the Christian Church was founded by Jesus, that it is apostolic in origin, and that it continues to be directed by the Holy Spirit. In the words of Daniel Jenkins, "Modern orthodox Protestantism is at one with all forms of Catholicism in saying that the Church knows Jesus Christ principally through the testimony of the apostles, and of those prophets who were forerunners of the apostles. The Church is, above all else, apostolic."[10]

One of the basic divisive issues between Catholicism and Protestantism is that of the apostolic succession. This is a fairly complex theological problem that requires far more study and attention than we can give to it here. However, we may note a few of the major differences of interpretation on this issue.[11] For example, the Anglican Church has always claimed the validity of its orders, namely, that its church, despite the break with Rome, is the same Church that Christ established through his apostles. Anglicans have frequently observed of the Elizabethan settlement that one of its important features was the affirmation that the Church of England was neither Catholic nor Reformed!

Those Protestant churches that follow the inspiration of reformers like Calvin and Zwingli also claim that their churches are in a true line of succession to the Apostolic Church. But generally they also deny that the Roman Catholic Church was ever the true Church. On the other hand, the Lutherans accept the Roman Catholic Church as the true Church down to the period of the Reformation; however, they insist that because of the abuses in the Catholic Church a new Church based more truly upon the spirit of the Apostolic Church was required.

Another significant issue that divides the Protestant churches from the Roman Catholic Church is the question of authority. One of the basic Protestant principles to come out of the Reformation was that of the authority of Scripture over against other claims of authority that might be attributed by the Catholic Church to the papacy, the magisterium of the Church, and to church councils. In fact, Luther and Calvin both explicitly rejected any appeal to conciliar authority. With this rejection of any Roman Catholic authority there also occurred the frequent affirmation by the Reformers of the freedom and the right of the individual and his conscience in the interpretation of Scripture. Protestants usually reject the implication that this freedom of the individual leads to an absolute right of private judgment for each individual. Rather:

The Protestant idea of faith does not entitle a man to believe what he pleases, for every man must think in accordance with the truth. But the principle of the Reformation is that the truth of the gospel is made known to faith by the inward working of the Holy Spirit. This truth is therefore received only in decision, in personal acceptance, in an obedience to the Word of God which no man can perform for another.[12]

In Protestantism there is a need for authority. Although that authority is primarily scriptural, the emphasis upon the freedom of the individual and at the same time the revolt against the authority of the Catholic Church has led to certain tensions within Protestantism between the "Catholic" elements and the "Protestant" elements.[13] The former may be said to express the need for unity and authority, the latter the desire for freedom of individual decision and autonomy. It is out of these tensions that two paradoxical characteristics of Protestantism have come: the ecumenical movement and the struggle toward unification, and, on the other hand, the proliferation of churches within Protestantism.[14]

The more specific points of division between the Roman Catholic Church and the Protestant churches, and also the basic divisions within Protestantism, can be best seen by an examination of some of the Protestant churches in the United States at the present time. Because of the very considerable number of Protestant denominations we must limit our selection somewhat arbitrarily to five of the larger and more influential Protestant churches. Our selection is also restricted to those churches that are wholly within the traditional meaning of Christianity and to those churches that are most closely related to the reformation tradition. Therefore, we shall consider in order the Baptist Church, the Lutheran Church, the Methodist Church, the Presbyterian Church, and the Protestant Episcopal Church. In the brief descriptions that follow, some theological distinctions will be noted, but the major emphasis will be placed on the origins and the structure and institutional characteristics of each church. Liturgical characteristics and differences among the liturgies will be observed in Chapter 13.

THE BAPTIST CHURCHES.   It is generally held by Baptists that their church had its origin in the work of John Smyth (1570–1612), an Anglican clergyman who established the first Separatist Church in Amsterdam in 1609.[15] A year later after further study of Scripture he came to the conclusion that only adult believers should be baptized. Baptism was more a rule of faith than a sacramental means of grace. The first Baptists to emigrate to the United States were led by Roger Williams, a Separatist minister who left the Massachusetts Bay Colony and established a Baptist church at Providence, Rhode Island, in 1639. By 1707 the first Baptist association of churches was formed in Philadelphia. The rise of the Baptist groups in the United States was rapid over the next century, but their traditional sentiments for "independence" more often than not led to division rather than unity among them. Although temporarily united by the missionary ideal and their formation of the General Missionary Convention, the Baptists, like the other religious groups in America, became subject to the divisive influence of the slavery question. Today they are still fragmented into numerous sects and divided into two large groups —the Northern and the Southern Baptists. Yet they are united spiritually on the doctrine of baptism. They emphasize the primacy of faith and Scripture; like the Anabaptists they reject infant baptism and require a rebaptism of those who were baptized in infancy. They also regard baptism as invalid unless performed by one of their own members, and most of the sects require baptism in the form of total immersion. On the doctrines of the fall, justification by faith, the authority of Scripture, and the rejection of tradition, the Baptists are within the reformation tradition. They depart from the tradition by holding that baptism is not a sacrament but an ordinance and a symbol by which faith in Christ is shown. Baptism provides a regeneration of the faith of the individual but it does not provide for salvation. Frequently baptism by total immersion is required for communion at the Lord's Supper.

The structure of the Baptist churches is along democratic lines.[16] The fundamental unit of government in the Baptist community is the local congregation. Much emphasis is placed upon the freedom of the congregation to govern itself and to carry out its own functions. The congregations may unite in associations and conventions. The two largest Baptist conventions are the American Baptist Convention (originally the Northern Baptist Convention) and the Southern Baptist Convention. The former is the more liberal of the two. The differences between the two are more social and cultural than doctrinal, although it can be said that the Southern Baptists reflect more the spirit of revivalism and fundamentalism. There is more theological agreement among Southern Baptists than among Northern Baptists. In addition to these two major conventions there is a rather large group of Negro Baptists organized into the National Baptist Convention, U.S.A., Inc., and the National Baptist Convention of

America, the first organized in 1895, the second in 1915. Finally, there are the Baptist Associations, the most prominent of which are the Free Will Baptist Association, the American Baptist Association, and the General Association of Regular Baptist Churches.

Generally speaking, Southern Baptists have tended to shy away from ecumenical movements, fearing that these might endanger the independence of their congregations. Traditionally they have associated themselves with the cause of religious liberty and are firm believers in the separation of Church and State. They contributed substantially to the development of the spiritual democracy of the American frontier by their emphasis upon freedom and equality, the value of the individual, and his redemption.

THE LUTHERAN CHURCH. In Chapter 2 we commented upon the place of Lutheranism in the development of the Reform Movement of the sixteenth century. Here we shall restrict our account to the Lutheran Church in America, its principal beliefs, its divisions, and its structure and the place of authority in its churches.

The principal doctrines of Lutheranism are to be found in the Augsburg Confession (1530), the Apology for the Augsburg Confession (1531), the Catechisms of Luther (1529), the Schmalkald Articles (1537), the Formula of Concord (1577), and finally the Book of Concord (1580), which contained all of the preceding and came to constitute a kind of "summa" of theology for Lutherans. Today it is more or less standard for the majority of Lutherans, although a number of them prefer to follow only the Augsburg Confession and Luther's Small Catechism.

The more salient features of the theology contained in the various Lutheran creeds and adhered to with some deviations and exceptions by contemporary Lutherans are: the acceptance of Scripture as the sole authority for faith and practice, justification by faith and the priesthood of all believers, and salvation by faith and not good works. There is much less acceptance of the Lutheran doctrine of free will and the contention that man is utterly corrupt because of original sin. The number of sacraments is regarded as unimportant, but baptism and the Lord's Supper are affirmed, as is the doctrine that the Church is the "assembly of all believers" both visible and invisible. On the doctrine of the Church as visible and invisible there is a considerable difference of opinion. More liberal Lutherans maintain that the Church is invisible and that the Church is "Wherever the Word of God is preached and the sacraments are administered." Evangelical Lutherans hold that the Church exists only in the heart of the believer and this is known only to God and is invisible to men.

The beginnings of Lutheranism in America occurred as early as 1637, when a number of Lutheran immigrants from Sweden settled near Wilmington, Delaware. In 1699 Old Swedes Church was established; it is now a historic shrine. These early Lutheran immigrants later became affiliated with the Episcopal Church. The real beginnings of Lutheranism and the first systematic organization of the Lutheran Church in America was undertaken by Henry Melchior Muhlenberg (1711–1787), known as the "patriarch of the Lutheran Church" in America. He established the first Lutheran synod (known as the Ministerium of Pennsylvania) and his son set up a second synod (also known as the Ministerium of Pennsylvania) about twenty-five years later. Immigration and linguistic differences caused some divisions in the movement, and to establish greater strength and unity a General Synod for all Lutherans in America was established in 1820 by Samuel Schmucker. However, the more conservative Lutherans resisted this movement and the trend toward an American type of Lutheranism. This difficulty in the formation of a national united body of Lutherans was increased with the slavery issue and the Civil War. Eventually the breach between the conservatives and liberals of the northern and southern synods was healed, and in 1918 the United Lutheran Church in America came into being and is now the largest Lutheran organizaton in the United States.

In the meantime new waves of immigrants from Central Europe came over in increasingly large numbers and settled mainly in the American Middle West. They were very conservative and uncompromisingly loyal to the basic Lutheran confessions. They soon formed synods of their own in Missouri and Wisconsin. The Missouri Lutherans were the most conservative of these groups. They established their own parochial school system and adhered literally to the Scriptures and the confessions (even to the statement that the pope was Antichrist). In 1868 they joined the Wisconsin Synod and later embraced other Lutheran groups to form the Lutheran Synodical Conference of North America.

Other smaller bodies of Lutheran churches should be mentioned. The Swedish Lutherans formed the Scandinavian Augustana Synod in 1860. It is now known as the Augustana Synod. In 1930 the American Lutheran Church was developed out of Ohio, Buffalo, and Iowa synods. Finally, the Evangelical Lutheran Church was formed from the Norwegian Lutheran Church in 1947. The latter had been created in 1917 from several Norwegian synods.

The fundamental unit of the Lutheran churches in America is the congregation. For all Lutheran churches the pattern of organization on the parish level is fairly similar. The congregation calls and elects the pastor. In cooperation with a council of laymen designated as elders, deacons, or trustees the pastor administers the affairs of the church. Above the parishes are the synods. Some synods, like the Missouri or Norwegian, are made up of local pastors and delegates from the different congregations. Other synods, such as the American Lutheran Church, are designated as churches, but their organization is similar to that of the synods. In either case they constitute the juridical character of the denomination. Generally, such an organization is directed by a president and a number of boards and commissions and meets every three years.

Beyond the level of the synod or church there exists the council. Today the council is composed of the following major bodies: (1) The American Lutheran Church, formed in 1960 of the American Lutheran Church, The Evangelical Lutheran Church, and the United Evangelical Lutheran Church; (2) The Lutheran Church in America, formed by a consolidation in 1963 of the American Evangelical Lutheran Church, the Augustana Evangelical Lutheran Church, the Finnish Evangelical Lutheran Church, and the United Lutheran Church in America; (3) The Lutheran Church —Missouri Synod, the leader of the conservative Lutheran groups. Recently this group reaffirmed the synod's traditional doctrines, such as, that God "created all things in six days," that Adam and Eve were "real, historical beings," and that sin had its origin in "one man, Adam."

Although the locus of authority in Lutheranism lies with the congregation, any tendencies of a seriously divisive nature have been largely curbed by reason of certain unifying factors that continue to persist in strength in Lutheranism. The authority of the confessional norms generally accepted by most Lutherans is a strong factor making for unity. On the other hand, this authority tends to be weakened by controversies over the nature of the Church and the sacerdotal character of the ministry.

THE METHODIST CHURCH.   When we speak of "Methodism" in the United States we shall mean principally that form of Methodism represented by the Methodist Church in America, which has close to nine and one half million members in contrast to approximately two and one half million for the other Methodist churches. In addition, the *Doctrines and Disciplines of the Methodist Church* is a compendium of belief subscribed to even by those Methodists who are not members of the Methodist Church in America.

Methodism had its origins in the evangelical revival movement within the Anglican Church in the eighteenth century. Its outstanding leader was John Wesley (1707–1788), and the success of the movement was due almost entirely to the inspiration of his preaching and teaching. With the help of his brother Charles Wesley, a great hymn writer, he evangelized the masses of England. A measure of Wesley's evangelizing zeal can be obtained from the fact that during his life time he traveled 250,000 miles and delivered on the average of one sermon a day. The first Methodist chapel was founded by Wesley in 1739 at Bristol. Upon his death in 1791 there were approximately 75,000 Methodists in England and an equal number in North America.

The first Methodist missionary to the United States was Robert Strawbridge, who came to Maryland. Others soon followed and in 1769 Wesley despatched Francis Asbury to direct the missionary activity in the United States. Asbury soon became the genius and outstanding leader of American Methodism. He surpassed Wesley in missionary activity, riding 270,000 miles and preaching 16,000 times before his death in 1816. It was Asbury who founded the Methodist Episcopal Church[17] in the United States. Actually, Methodism achieved ecclesiastical identity in the United States before it did in England. For a number of years Wesley considered himself a member of the Anglican Church, and it was not until 1784, when the Bishop of London refused to ordain a number of Methodist ministers, that Wesley took matters into his own hands and after careful study of Scripture decided that he had the right to ordain. It was upon this occasion that Wesley ordained three ministers and sent them to the United States with orders to ordain Asbury and appoint him as Superintendent of the Church in America. Asbury subsequently assumed the title of "bishop" on his own authority, and since then the title has been retained.

Methodists usually contend that they have very little theology. Wesley stated that the "distinguishing marks of a Methodist are not his opinions of any sort." Prospective members are simply asked to confess their faith in Jesus Christ and to repent of their sins. However, when the American Methodists separated from Wesley following the American Revolution, Wesley saw fit to send them an abridgement which he wrote of the Thirty-nine Articles of the Anglican Church. This abridgement was published in 1784 and called the *Articles of Religion*. Methodists also reply upon other writings of Wesley, particularly his *Sermons* and his *Notes Upon the New Testament*. The doctrine based upon these treatises follows the traditional Protestant viewpoint. Thus Luther's doctrine of justification by faith alone, and the Reformed position on the authority of Scripture are accepted. The appeal to tradition as authoritative is rejected and several books of the Old Testament are rejected, notably the Book of Wisdom and the two Books of Maccabees. In their theology Methodists also tend to be Arminian, that is, they insist on the free will of man and universal redemption. Thus Calvin's views on predestination were rejected. On the concept of the Church the Methodists emphasize that the Church is universal, visible, and local. The universal Church is composed of all who affirm their belief in Jesus Christ. The visible Church is that organization which establishes a common worship and discipline. The local Church consists of those who have accepted membership in the Methodist Church. Finally, the Methodist discipline has always emphasized the central importance of the religious experience in the faith of the individual. As Wesley himself put it: "I *felt* my heart strangely warmed. I *felt* I did trust in Christ, Christ alone for salvation: and an *assurance* was given me that he had taken away my sins. . . . . I then testified openly to all there what I now first *felt* in my heart."[18]

It should also be pointed out that there is a considerable amount of tolerance and latitude in the attitude of the Methodists. On baptism they accept any form and recognize the rule performed by other churches. No question is ever raised concerning the validity of the orders of other churches. And they admit all Christians to Communion at the Lord's Supper.

One of the more significant aspects of the organization of the Methodist Church is the role assigned to the laity. Laymen serve as trustees and stewards and supervise the property and finances of the parish. A layman may also serve as pastor although not ordained as elder or deacon. However, he must be licensed for such a position.

The Methodist Church is organized along episcopal lines, but the role of the bishop is administrative rather than sacramental in character. With the advice of the district superintendents he appoints pastors and ministers, but this power may be challenged. He consecrates bishops and ordains elders and deacons; deaconesses are consecrated, commissioned and licensed. The real power of the bishop rests with his qualities of personal leadership, his place and role in conferences, and in his relations with other officials in the church. He holds office for life, is an elder, and also acts as a superintendent within his geographical district.

Next in rank is the elder, who is ordained by the bishop and other elders through the laying on of hands. Below the elder is the deacon, who is also ordained by the bishop. Deaconesses are salaried; they are dedicated women who serve in an educational, missionary, or social capacity in the activities of the Methodist Church.

At the top of the Methodist hierarchy are the conferences, which number six in all. The General Conferences is the supreme legislative body in the Methodist church and meets every four years. The Annual Conference is the principal administrative unit in the church. It is restricted to a specific territory but within that territory has supervision over the affairs of the church. It also elects delegates to the General Conference. The Jurisdictional Conference is a representative body of the Annual Conferences. It is composed of an equal number of lay and ministerial delegates. One of its chief functions is the election of bishops. The District Conference is a further subdivision of the Annual Conference. It is authorized by the Annual Conference and meets each year in a given district. Its principal concern is with the examination of candidates for the ministry, the support and promotion of missions, and education in the district. The quarterly Conference is "the governing body of the pastoral charge" and relates the affairs of the parish to the church. It is made up of local preachers and lay leaders. The Church Conference is an assembly of the members of any one church that reviews the work of the church and elects church officers. Its meetings are presided over by the pastor.

THE PRESBYTERIAN CHURCH.   The Presbyterian Church derives its name from the structure of the church rather than with the name of a founder, as in Lutheranism, or by association with a sacrament, as in the Baptist Church. The Presbyterian Church derives its name from the Greek word *presbuteros,* which means elder and which is usually understood as synonymous with bishop. In the Presbyterian churches today the elders are elected representatives of the church, and together with the minister they govern the church. The ecclesiastical polity of the Presbyterian church is a compromise between episcopacy and congregationalism, although it was not intended as such.

Presbyterianism had its origins in the teachings of John Calvin, whose place in the Reform movement we have already noted in Chapter 2. The essential teachings of Calvin are present with some modification in the Westminster Confession of Faith, which defines Presbyterian doctrine for the Scottish, British, and American forms of Presbyterianism. Through the influence of John Knox, the most famous disciple of Calvin, Presbyterianism was established as the state religion of Scotland in 1560. From here its influence spread to England and Northern Ireland. In England the Puritans followed for the most part Calvinist principles. Under their leadership an Assembly of clergymen was called together by the Puritan Parliament and produced along with other documents the famous Westminster Confession of Faith.

In the United States Presbyterianism began with the migrations of the English Puritans to Massachusetts, the Dutch members of the Calvinist Reformed Church to New York, and the Scotch-Irish to Pennsylvania under the leadership of Francis Makemie, who became known as "The Father of American Presbyterianism."[19] Under his leadership the first presbytery was organized. During the eighteenth century Presbyterianism experienced a very successful and rapid growth. Two factors were responsible for this success: the increasing numbers of Scottish-Irish immigrants and the unifying influence of the Westminster Confession of Faith. By 1716 the original presbytery established by Makemie had grown to four presbyteries with some forty churches. By 1789 there were sixteen presbyteries and over four hundred churches. This year also witnessed the organization of the first General Assembly of the Presbyterian Church.

The unity of Presbyterianism was first seriously disrupted with the Cumberland schism of 1810 and the Old School-New School schism of 1837. This last schism eventually expanded into a division of policy concerning slavery and the Civil War. At the close of the war the southern synods and presbyteries merged into the Presbyterian Church in the United States. To this day it exists as a separate organization, conservative in theology and until recently following a policy of segregation with respect to its Negro churches and presbyteries. Presently it is joining in the creation of a joint Christian education curriculum with the United Presbyterian Church, U.S.A. and the United Church of Christ.

A second major Presbyterian group in the United States is the United Presbyterian Church, U.S.A. This church was formed as the result of the merger at Pittsburg in 1958 of the United Presbyterian Church and the Presbyterian Church, which until then had formed the two northern branches of Presbyterianism in the United States.

We have mentioned rather frequently the Westminster Confession of Faith. This document, which has been accepted with varying degrees of modification by the different Presbyterian groups, gives a clear picture of the essential beliefs of Presbyterians. This confession of faith,[20] as with the confessions of other Protestant groups, is based solely upon the authority of Scripture. On the meaning of the Church it is held that the Church is both invisible and visible:

1. The catholic or universal church, which is invisible, consists of the whole number of the elect, that have been, are, or shall be gathered into one, under Christ the head thereof; and is the spouse, the body, the fullness of Him that filleth all in all.
2. The visible church, which is also catholic or universal under the gospel (not confined to one nation, as before under the law), consists of all those throughout the world that profess the true religion, together with their children, and is the Kingdom of the Lord Jesus Christ, the house and family of God, through which men are ordinarily saved and union with which is essential to their best growth and service.[21]

Furthermore, "The Lord Jesus Christ is the only head of the Church, and the claim of any man to be the vicar of Christ and the head of the Church is unscriptural, without warrant in fact, and is a usurpation dishonoring to the Lord Jesus Christ."[22]

Predestination is still an embarrassing issue for contemporary Presbyterians, but in 1903 the decree of predestination was modified to read:

. . . that concerning those who perish, the doctrine of God's eternal decree is held in harmony with the doctrine that God desires not the death of any sinner, but has provided in Christ a salvation sufficient for all, adapted to all, and freely offered in the gospel to all; that all men are fully responsible for their treatment of God's gracious offer; that his decree hinders no man from accepting that offer; and that no man is condemned except on the ground of his sin.[23]

The Presbyterians accept two sacraments: baptism and the Lord's Supper. However, the sacraments are treated wholly as signs and with no intrinsic efficacy of grace. More will be found on this point in the chapter dealing with sacraments and grace.

The government of the Presbyterian Church is exercised by sessions, presbyteries, synods, and general assemblies. Their power is wholly spiritual or moral, but they can require obedience to the laws of Christ and exclude individuals from the privileges of the Church. The *session* is the smallest unit of government and consists of the pastor and the ruling elders of a particular church. The pastor acts as the moderator. The function of the session is the spiritual government of the congregation. The *presbytery* "consists of all the ministers, in number not fewer than twelve, and at least one ruling elder from each church, within a certain district which includes at least twelve churches."[24] The presbytery has a number of functions which make it an important unit in the government of the church. It hears all appeals and complaints; licenses and examines candidates for the ministry; forms, unites, and divides congregations; ordains and removes ministers; visits particular churches; and in general seeks to do all that may be in the spiritual welfare and interests of the churches under their control. The *synod* consists of the ministers and ruling elders of not less than three presbyteries within a certain geographical area. The members of the synod are elected by the presbyteries. The synod meets once a year; it hears appeals and complaints addressed to it, and it decides upon the creation of new presbyteries. The *General Assembly* is representative of most Presbyterian churches in the United States and is the highest judicatory body of that church. It consists of an equal number of ministers and ruling elders from each presbytery. It meets once a year. It has the power to create new synods and it may hear appeals and complaints affecting the doctrine or the interpretation of the Constitution of the Church that may be referred to it by the lower judicial bodies.

Three ranks of church officers are provided: the bishops or pastors (teaching elders), the ruling elders, and the deacons. The office of the pastor (or ministry) is the highest in dignity and usefulness. The pastor has several titles expressive of his different duties. "As he has the oversight of the flock of Christ, he is termed bishop. As he feeds them with spiritual food, he is termed pastor. As he serves Christ in his church, he is termed minister. As it is his duty to be grave and prudent, and an example of the flock, and to govern well in the house and Kingdom of Christ, he is termed presbyter or elder."[25] His principal function is that of teaching, expounding and preaching the Word of God. The ruling elders are the immediate representatives of the people and are elected by them. In association with pastors or ministers they have charge of the government and the discipline of the particular church. They may also visit the people of the congregation in their homes in their fulfillment of Christian duties and charities. The deacons are the lowest in rank of the officers of the church. Their principal function is to minister to the sick and to all those in need or distress. They are also concerned with the finances and properties of the church and with its missionary and education programs and policies. At the wish of the congregation these functions may be carried out by a board of deacons.

THE PROTESTANT EPISCOPAL CHURCH.   More commonly known as the Episcopal Church, the Protestant Episcopal Church is an American branch of the Anglican Communion, which numbers over forty million adherents, the great majority of whom belong to the Church of England. The Anglican Church originated in the sixteenth century. As we have seen it developed out of Henry VIII's difficulties, with the papacy and his subsequent revolt and declaration that he was the supreme head of the Church in England. The breach with Rome continued to widen and became complete in 1563 with the Elizabethan Settlement. This established the Church as a National Institution. A Book of Common Prayer containing Thirty-nine Articles was promulgated as the new faith. Even so, the Elizabethan Settlement was not as radical as the Reform movements on the Continent or that which had taken place under Edward the Sixth.

It was a deliberate compromise, providing the legal settlement and secular framework within which Anglicanism could develop as a *via media*. This characteristic note of Anglicanism was struck early in the Queen's reign by legislation which declared in effect that the Church of England was both Catholic and Reformed. Reflecting the sovereign's temperate mind and moderate policy, the Church was neither to revert to Rome nor to advance to meet Protestant Geneva. . . . It gave outward shape to what has since been recognized as essential in the nature of Anglicanism—loyalty to a Catholic past in creeds and polity, and glad appropriations of the fruits of reform not only in freedom from papal control but in the central place assigned to the scriptures and in definite changes in doctrine and ritual.[26]

The Protestant Episcopal Church in the United States came into existence during the period of the Revolutionary War. At the outbreak of that war all Anglican clergy were required to take an oath of allegiance to the King. Many refused and seceded, and in 1785 they officially adopted the name of the Protestant Episcopal Church. After obtaining for some of their outstanding clergy ordination as bishops in Scotland and England, the new church held a General Convention in Philadelphia in 1789. This was the most important General Convention of the Church, for it set up a constitution which contained the following important provisions. A liturgy similar to that of the Anglican Church was adopted. It was decided that there should be three orders of the ministry: bishops, presbyters, and deacons. It provided for a House of Bishops as the supreme legislative body of the Church. Some revision was made in the English Book of Common Prayer, but primarily in matters of discipline and worship. In 1928 the Book of Common Prayer was again revised, this time more thoroughly; some ultra-Protestant statements were eliminated and the liturgy was enriched and completed.

Recalling Addison's statement that Anglicanism represented "a kind of compromise between Catholicism and Protestantism," it is not surprising to find that in the United States its history has manifested this character and that at the present time we find three rather distinct forms of Episcopalianism: High, Low, and Broad. High Church Episcopalianism emphasizes liturgy and much of the "Catholic tradition." Historically the High Church element was strongly influenced in America by the English Oxford movement. Similarly, the Low Church reflects the influence of the various evangelical movements in the United States during the nineteenth century, as well as the highly Puritan character of the early Low Church. The Low Church has little use for elaborate liturgy; it calls for a simple service and more emphasis upon the Gospel; but the Low Church does not reject episcopacy. The Broad Church represents a mean between the High and the Low. Modernist in attitude, it is generally liberal and somewhat critical of what it regards as the extremes of Low Church and High Church. Such divisions, however, should not lead one to overlook the essential unity that Episcopalianism has managed to retain despite these divisions. As Pittenger puts it: "They all use the Book of Common Prayer; they are all in communion with the Archbishop of Canterbury; they all recognize bishops as their chief pastors."[27]

In structure the Protestant Episcopal Church is hierarchical but it does not acknowledge any one bishop or archbishop as having supreme authority. Although a member of the Anglican Communion, it is not subject in any way to the Anglican Church or the Archbishop of Canterbury. In this country no one bishop is supreme.

Nationally there are two executive-legislative bodies, the National (executive) Council and the General (legislative) Convention. The former represents the national Church; it is headed by a Presiding Bishop and is composed of bishops, priests, and lay members from the various dioceses of the country. The National Council has charge of the missionary, educational, and social work of the Church. At the present time the constitution of the National Council provides that the Presiding Bishop should hold office until his sixty-eighth year and that he is to be relieved of diocesan responsibility during his term of office.

The General Convention has direction of all the legislative activities of the Church. It is composed of a House of Bishops, which includes all the bishops of the Church, and a House of Deputies representing each diocese and composed of eight representatives from each diocese. For legislation to be valid it must be passed by both houses. This is not an easy task because of the cumbersomeness of the General Convention—it has a membership of more than one hundred bishops and more than seven hundred deputies.

Provinces constitute the first major subdivision of the National Church. There are eight in all, each representing a number of dioceses. Their organization is similar to that of the National Church. The Provincial Synod is divided into a House of Bishops and a House of Clerical and Lay Deputies. Generally, their legislative tasks are few and they may be said to exist primarily to help carry out regionally the various functions of the National Church.

The *diocese* is the basic ecclesiastical unit in the Protestant Episcopal Church. The bishop in charge has somewhat restricted power in comparison to that which prevails in the Roman Catholic Church. The Episcopal bishop governs his diocese in conjunction with the Diocesan Convention. He may appoint ministers to missionary parishes, but in regularly established parishes he recommends a candidate for the post of rector and discusses the candidate with the vestry. The parish is a legal entity composed of the rector, the wardens, and the vestrymen. The rectors in all cases must be ordained priests, but all matters of temporal administration are in the hands of the wardens and vestrymen of the parish. The rector cannot be removed except by the bishop, and this only after due consideration. The rector cannot resign unless the vestry is willing.

On the cause of Christian reunion the Episcopal Church initiated an important step when it proclaimed the Lambeth Quadrilateral in 1888. This document sets forth some of the basic principles of the Episcopal position and continues to this day to represent the official position of the Episcopal Church on union with other Protestant churches. These principles are:

I. The Holy Scriptures of the Old and New Testaments, as "containing all things necessary to salvation," and as being the rule and ultimate standard of faith.

II. The Apostles' Creed, as the Baptismal Symbol; and the Nicene Creed, as the sufficient statement of the Christian faith.

III. The two sacraments, Baptism and the Supper of the Lord, ministered with unfailing use of Christ's words of institution, and of the elements ordained by Him.

IV. The Historic Episcopate, locally adapted in the methods of its administration to the varying needs of the nations and peoples called of God into the unity of His Church.[28]

Notes

1. For a brief but excellent account of the physical structure of the Temple see Nathan Ausubel, ed., *The Book of Jewish Knowledge* (New York: Crown, 1964), pp. 460–465.
2. Milton Steinberg, *Basic Judaism* (New York: Harcourt, Brace, 1947), p. 150.
3. Quoted by Beryl D. Cohon in *Judaism in Theory and Practice* (New York: Bloch Publishing Co., 1954), p. 14.
4. "When ten people sit together and occupy themselves with the Torah, the Shechina abides among them, as it is said, 'God standeth in the congregation of the godly' " (Berakhoth 28b).
5. For further details on the beliefs of these divisions of Judaism see Chapter 3 for the statement of the creed by Maimonides, which is followed by Orthodoxy.
6. A religious and political body of some seventy elders, composed mostly of the members of the nobility and the higher temple priests.
7. Cf. page 348.
8. N. G. M. Van Doornik, S. Jelsma, and A. Van De Lisdonk, *A Handbook of the Catholic Faith* (Westminster, Md.: Newman, 1956), p. 110.
9. For a further account of collegiality see Walter M. Abbott, S.J., ed., *The Documents of Vatican II*, trans. Very Rev. Msgr. Joseph Gallagher (New York: Guild Press, 1966), pp. 42–44.
10. Daniel Jenkins, *The Strangeness of the Church* (Garden City, N.Y.: Doubleday, 1955), p. 63.
11. It is pertinent and of interest here to recall that one of the simplest statements of the meaning of the apostolic succession is that given by Newman in the first of his Tracts of 1833: "Christ gave His Spirit to His apostles; they in their turn laid their hands on those who should succeed them; and these again on others, and so the sacred gift has been handed down to our present bishops. . . ."
12. John Dillenberger and Claude Welch, *Protestant Christianity* (New York: Charles Scribner's Sons, 1954), p. 287.
13. When we speak of "authority" in the Roman Catholic Church and its various expressions, we should keep in mind that the basic and primal authority in Catholicism is Scripture as the word of God. As Hans Kung well notes: "If, therefore, the Church draws a sharp line between the word of God and the word of man, the commandment of God and the commandment of man, and the law of God and the law of man, she speaks on the basis of the Gospel. The commandment of God is fundamentally absolute and inalterable. The commandment of man is fundamentally conditional (it is perforce relative, related to the commandment of God and superposed by it) and alterable (in the course of history it can be established and disestablished, formulated, spoiled, distorted, and newly formulated)." *Structures of the Church* (Camden, N.J.: Thomas Nelson and Sons, 1964), p. 321.
14. Sometimes the term "church" is identified with "denomination" or "sect." Strictly speaking, the term "Church" is usually applied to the whole assembly of the faithful in the universal or catholic sense. Roman Catholics speak of it in this sense and also identify it with the Church of Rome. Protestants usually accept the term "Church" as applying to all the faithful but of course do not identify it with the Roman Church. When the term is not capitalized it usually applies to a less universal assembly of the faithful, e.g. Baptists, Lutherans, Episcopalians. Each of these groups may also be spoken of as "denominations," for they are

religious groups whose *names* indicate their origin: Baptists from certain views on the sacrament, Episcopalians from the acceptance of the rule by bishops. The term "sect" is somewhat narrow and usually applies to smaller groups which have cut themselves off (Latin *secare*, to cut) from a larger group. Thus we may have Free Will Baptists, Hard-Shell Baptists, Southern Baptists, etc.

For the definitive discussion of the terms "Church" and "sect" see Ernst Troeltsch, *The Social Teachings of the Christian Churches*, trans. Olive Wyon (London: Allen and Unwin, 1949), 2nd ed., Vol. II, Chapter 3. For American interpretations see H. R. Niebuhr, *The Social Sources of Denominationalism* (New York: Holt, 1929, republished as a Living Age Book by Meridian Books, 1957); and H. Shelton Smith, Robert T. Handy, and Lefferts A. Loetscher, *American Christianity: An Historical Interpretation with Representative Documents* (New York: Charles Scribner's Sons, 1960), 2 vols.

15. The Separatists (in the seventeenth century known as Independents) were those congregations who dissented from the Anglican Communion and established separate or independent churches of their own.

16. For a contemporary study of Baptist organization see Paul M. Harrison, *Authority and Power in the Free Church Tradition* (Princeton: Princeton University Press, 1959).

17. Episcopacy is an office and not an order in the Methodist Church. The title of "bishop" is retained but in rank is no different than that of elder.

18. Quoted by Elmer T. Clark, "Methodism," in Vergilius Ferm, ed., *The American Church of the Protestant Heritage* (New York: Philosophical Library, 1953), p. 325.

19. The New England settlers included both Puritans and Pilgrims. The latter were Separatists and with the Puritans formed the first Congregational Church in America. Later the Puritans went back to Presbyterianism.

20. However, a new Confession of Faith was proposed in 1966 and will probably be adopted in 1967.

21. From the Constitution of The United Presbyterian Church in the United States of America, copyright © 1966, p. 36. Used by permission.

22. *Ibid.*, p. 37.

23. *Ibid.*, p. 44.

24. *Ibid.*, p. 127a.

25. *Ibid.*, p. 122.

26. J. T. Addison, *The Episcopal Church in the United States* (New York: Charles Scribner's Sons, 1951), p. 8.

27. W. Norman Pittenger, "What is an Episcopalian?", in Leo Roster, ed., *A Guide to the Religions of America* (New York: Cowles Publishing, Inc., 1955), p. 48.

28. Addison, *The Episcopal Church in the United States*, p. 277.

SELECT BIBLIOGRAPHY

ABBOTT, WALTER M. S.J., ed. *The Documents of Vatican II.* Trans. Very Rev. Msgr. Joseph Gallagher. New York: Guild Press, 1966.

AUSUBEL, NATHAN, ed. *The Book of Jewish Knowledge.* New York: Crown, 1964.

COHON, BERYL D. *Judaism in Theory and Practice.* New York: Bloch, 1954.

DILLENBERGER, JOHN and CLAUDE WELCH. *Protestant Christianity.* New York: Charles Scribner's Sons, 1954.

FERM, VERGILIUS, ed. *The American Church of the Protestant Heritage.* New York: Philosophical Library, 1953.

HORTON, WALTER. *Christian Theology: An Ecumenical Approach.* New York: Harper and Row, 1955.

JACQUET, CONSTANT H., JR., ed. *Yearbook of American Churches.* New York: National Council of the Churches of Christ in the U.S.A., 1967.

JOURNET, CHARLES. *The Primacy of Peter.* Trans. John Chapin. Westminster, Md.: Newman Press, 1954.

KÜNG, HANS. *Structures of the Church.* New York: Thomas Nelson and Sons, 1964.

MOORE, GEORGE FOOT. *Judaism.* Cambridge: Harvard University Press, 1927. 3 vols.

STEINBERG, MILTON. *Basic Judaism.* New York: Harcourt, Brace, 1947.

WHALE, J. S. *The Protestant Tradition.* Cambridge and New York: Cambridge University Press, 1955.

XIII

The Liturgies of Western Religion

THE term liturgy is taken from the Greek word *Leitourgia,* meaning public service; originally it was used to indicate both an official service and a religious service. The liturgies of the Christian churches and the synagogue constitute those forms of worship that are performed by the community and officially sanctioned or ordered by those who direct the public worship. In Judaism the liturgy is the order and form of public worship carried out in the synagogue; the liturgy reflects in word (prayer) and act (mitzvoh) the basic beliefs of Judaism. As we shall see, the sum and substance of the Jewish liturgy is now contained in the Siddur or Prayer Book, of which there have been many editions. The prayer literature of Judaism is the creation of successive ages and is ever expanding. In the Christian churches the order and form of worship[1] are incorporated in their constitutions, their laws, their books of Common Prayer or Common Worship, and most recently in the Constitution on the Sacred Liturgy issued by the Second Vatican Council.

Some of the common features of the three liturgies—Roman Catholic, Jewish, and Protestant—may be briefly noted. First, they all exemplify in a very concrete way the beliefs of the worshipers. Second, they emphasize the importance and the use of prayer in their services; they employ rather extensively psalms, hymns, and chants. Third, they follow a specific calendar of worship. The principal features of such a calendar of worship are the inclusion of a weekly Sabbath or Sunday service and the designation of a number of days of special worship dedicated to or representing certain beliefs or events essential to the faith of the believer. Thus in Judaism there are the solemn festivals of the New Year and the Day of Atonement; in Christianity, there are the great feasts of Christmas and Easter, representing the birth and the resurrection of Jesus. The function of the calendar of worship is educational. By the repetition and commemoration or sacramental participation in the great events associated with a religious belief, the individual worshiper achieves not only a better understanding of his faith but a constant renewal of that faith. Fourth, all three liturgies employ certain rites and ceremonies. Even the exclusion of rites is in itself a ritual.

The distinction between rite and liturgy is frequently obscure. Generally, liturgy is the more inclusive term. Rite is a formal observance of a particular religious function that may fall within the liturgy. Thus the different ways of praying—kneeling, standing, the use of silent prayer, making the sign of the cross—may all be regarded as rites. Similarly the various practices associated with the Communion service may be regarded as constituting ritual. And somewhat apart from the liturgy of worship there are rites for the consecration of a church, rites for marriage, cemetery rites, and others.

Finally, there is a very close historical relation among the three liturgies. The Christian liturgy is very much indebted to the Jewish, particularly in the Liturgy of the Word of God and in the use of many Jewish psalms, prayers, and practices.[2] Among Christians the Protestant liturgy frequently takes over unchanged a great deal of the liturgy of the Roman Catholic Church.

In the descriptions that follow of the liturgies of the three faiths we shall concentrate upon the following major characteristics: the nature of worship and prayer in the synagogue and the church; the calendar of worship and the more important holy days and festivals celebrated by Jews and Christians; and the Sabbath service as celebrated by the Jews and the Sunday service as it is celebrated by the principal Christian groups.

The Liturgy of Judaism

Most historians are agreed that the forms of Jewish worship developed over a long period of time and that its beginnings are to be found very early in Jewish history. Like many other primitive peoples, the Jews of the patriarchal period incorporated sacrifice as an important part of their form of worship of Yahweh. In Genesis 22:13–14, Abraham sacrifices a ram as a burnt offering to Yahweh in place of his son Isaac. Even earlier, Noah "offered burnt offerings on the altar." (Genesis 8:20). The form of prayer seems to have followed a similar pattern. Frequently prayers are offered for protection, as in Jacob's prayer in Genesis 32:12, or the prayer of Samson for strength that he might have vengeance upon the Philistines. Sacrifice and prayer were closely related in the early days of Judaism and Christianity, as Hedley points out:

> What seems unquestionably to be true is that at the beginning, and far into the period of recorded history, sacrifice was understood to be a necessary condition of effective prayer. "Thou shalt not take the name of the Lord thy God in vain" seems to have meant at the outset neither the taboo on pronouncing the sacred Name which Judaism developed, nor the rule against profanity which we have thought it to be. Rather it should be read, "Thou shalt not call upon Jahveh thy God when thou art empty-handed." Sacrifice thus appears to have been integral to Israelite worship from the earliest days, even as it was to continue central so long as Jewish nationality was maintained.[3]

Temple Worship

Not much is known of the liturgy of the Temple of Solomon, which was destroyed by the Babylonians in 586 B.C.E. However, it does seem fairly evident and also rather significant in contrast with later Judaism, that prayer was definitely subordinated to rather elaborate sacrifices consisting of slaughtered animals—usually cattle or sheep—fruit and other forms of food, and incense offerings. To the later prophets the slaughter of animals in the temple was a barbarous practice possessing no spiritual value. The condemnation of such practices is voiced by Micah 6:6 and by Jeremiah 21:22: "For in the day that I brought them out of the land of Egypt, I did not speak to your fathers or command them concerning burnt offerings and sacrifices." The prophets also protested against the subordinate role assigned to the people in the temple worship. It appeared that the only function of the people during the service was to give an occasional response to the prayers of the priests. The description given in Exodus 25–40 of the pattern of worship in the Tabernacle is essentially that followed in the temple.

During the period of the second temple the sacrifice of animals at the altar was practiced on a lesser scale, and more emphasis was placed upon prayer. The role of the priest became less influential and his place was gradually taken by a rabbi who was both a scholar and a teacher. In this period the number of synagogues continued to increase in Jerusalem until, according to the Talmud, they numbered close to 400. With the destruction of the temple in 70 C.E. the whole system of sacrifices and offerings was dropped from Jewish worship and replaced by the liturgy of the synagogue.

Synagogue Service

It is generally held that Jewish worship in the synagogue began during the period of the Babylonian captivity. However that may be, the characteristic feature of the synagogue service was the elimination of the temple sacrifices and offerings and a renewed emphasis upon the other elements in the service, namely, readings from the Torah and the Prophets, Psalms, and prayers. Hedley notes that "Late in the first century after Christ, the Rabbi Gamaliel II set forth the order of worship that has been the basis of synagogue practice ever since: Psalms, the *Sh'ma* ("Hear, O Israel: the Lord our God, the Lord is one"), the "Eighteen Benedictions" or prayers, and reading (always) from the Law and (often) from the Prophets."[4]

Before we look in more detail at the nature of the Jewish liturgy it is necessary to observe that it augments and supplements in a most important manner the beliefs of Judaism. In our earlier discussions of the meaning of faith in Judaism we have observed the lack of a systematic theology, of precisely defined dogmas and beliefs. Occasionally, of course, as with Maimonides, Saadia, and others, Jewish philosophers used the vehicle of Greek philosophy to explain some of the beliefs of Judaism. But such explanations and the creeds arising from them are not binding; there is no one uniform creed to which all Jews must subscribe as all Christians subscribe to the Apostles' Creed. However, the fundamental beliefs of Judaism, although not appearing in a formally written creed or text, do find expression in the Jewish liturgy. Judaism, then, may be said to be a liturgical religion rather than a creedal religion. In the words of Rabbi Arzt:

> In his prayers, the Jew gave voice to his yearning for God, to his deep sense of moral accountability, to his ecstatic love for the Torah, and to his invincible faith in his people's rehabilitation in a peaceful world. It was the liturgy in word (prayer) and in act (*mitzvah*) which gave our forbears high hope in the face of despair, and perseverance in the midst of persecution. . . . Because the Prayer Book reflects the beliefs about God, man, and the universe which are distinctive of historic Judaism, it is the most authentic source book for an understanding of the faith which animates it and the people that poured its spirit into it.*[5]

Central to the Jewish liturgy since the time of the temple has been the Prayer Service. In fact the Jewish liturgy may be designated as the Prayer

---

* From *Justice and Mercy: Commentary on the Liturgy of the New Year and the Day of Atonement* by Max Arzt. Copyright © 1963 by Max Arzt. Reprinted by permission of Holt, Rinehart and Winston, Inc.

Service. This service in the synagogues has been more or less formalized and standardized with the introduction of the Prayer Book (Siddur) and the development of the order of services for the Sabbath and the Holy Days. Before describing such services in any detail we must first say something of the nature and the place of prayer in Jewish worship.

Prayer takes on a highly social significance in Jewish worship. Only occasionally are Jewish prayers, for instance, expressed in the first person singular. Far more frequent is the use of "we" and "us." The Jew prays not so much for himself but for all Israel, for the collective good. As Heschel puts it: "Judaism is not only the adherence to particular doctrines and observances, but primarily living in the spiritual order of the Jewish people, the living *in* the Jews of the past and *with* the Jews of the present. . . . The Jew does not stand alone before God; it is as a member of the community that he stands before God. Our relationship to Him is not as an I to a Thou, but as a We to a Thou."[6]

As in all religions, prayer in Judaism takes on different forms. The prayers of the Psalms exhibit not only an extraordinarily fine poetic achievement, but they exemplify great spirituality and represent a very high stage of spiritual development. Centuries later, in a curious contrast, we find in the incantations and exorcisms of the Kabbalistic prayers a reversion to a quite primitive form of religious expression. Frequently, too, the early prayers of the Jews, like those of other peoples in a comparable stage of religious development, are almost exclusively petitionary and materialistic in character. They exhibit a kind of *quid pro quo* relationship with Deity in which the worshiper expects in return for his prayers that God will secure his material welfare, protect him from evil, and assist him in obtaining vengeance upon his enemies.

On the other hand, the petitionary prayer in a higher stage of religious development generally emphasizes the need of man for spiritual values. In the Amidah or "Eighteen Benedictions" the people call upon God for knowledge, understanding, repentance, the restoration of Zion, the coming of the Messiah, and the desire for peace. Another type of prayer that is greatly emphasized in Jewish worship is the prayer of praise and thanksgiving. This type of prayer is an expression of thanksgiving by man for the good that God has bestowed upon man. It is a prayer of praise and adoration, of appreciation for a universe that God created as good. It is an acknowledgment of the infinitude and omnipotence of God, a praise of His greatness. The Psalms are replete with this type of prayer. Jewish prayer is also didactic, for prayer has a teaching function. In addition to devotional material the Jewish Prayer Book will contain citations from the Talmud, texts from the Prophets, Maimonides' Thirteen Principles, didactic hymns, and of course readings from the Torah ("He who turns his head in order not to hear Torah, his prayer too is an abomination" Proverbs

28:9). The language of prayer is still predominantly in the Hebrew but in English-speaking countries in particular the use of the vernacular is becoming more and more popular.

Regarding the posture of the Jews at prayer, one of the earliest statements is that made by Moses in Exodus 9:29 when he declared: "As I go out of the city, I shall spread out my hands to the Lord." Later the Jews were influenced by the customs of their Babylonian captors and adopted the practices of kneeling and prostrating themselves. At the time of Jesus they folded the hands in prayer (this became a Christian practice) and also observed the postures of standing, kneeling, and prostrating. When kneeling at prayer became firmly established in early Christian worship, this rite was abandoned by the Jews except at certain times during the celebration of the High Holy Days. Reform congregations do not adhere to the practice. Today prayer is said while seated on benches or chairs except during the more solemn portions of the prayer service, such as the Eighteen Benedictions, which are read while standing. Among the Orthodox Jews prostration is continued only on the High Holy Days of Rosh Hashanah and Yom Kippur.

THE PRAYER SERVICE.   The Jewish liturgy, like the Bible and the Talmud, developed over a long period of time. The liturgy of the synagogue began during the period of the First Exile. It took over many of the practices of the temple, such as the reading of the Torah, the use of Psalms and the Psalter, the hours of worship, and many of the basic prayers. Originally, there were three prayer services in the synagogue: the morning service, the afternoon service, and the evening service. To these was soon added the Mussaf, or "Additional Service," recited immediately after the morning service on the Sabbath and on festivals.

With the continuing evolution of the liturgy and the religious life of the community a very real need arose to codify and standardize what was becoming a very complex liturgy. In 856 c.e. the first comprehensive prayer book or siddur comprising all these developments was completed by Amram Gaon. In time other siddurim appear. In the twelfth century the predominant liturgies were those of the Sefardim (used by the Jews of Spain, Portugal, North Africa, and Greece) and the Ashkenazim (used by the Jews of Northern France, Germany, Austria, and Bohemia). The Sefardim based their liturgy and prayer book on the siddur of Amram Gaon. The Ashkenazim created their own prayer book, the Machzor Vitry, which emphasized the prayers for the yearly cycle of holy days and also made considerable use of liturgical poems. At the present time in America the Jewish prayer books in use reflect to some extent the divisions within contemporary Judaism. However, the use of one prayer book for the Sabbath and the daily prayers (siddur) and another for the festival prayers (machzor) has continued. And as Rabbi Arzt so well points out, there is both unity and variety in the Jewish liturgy: "What is intriguing and even astonishing about Judaism's liturgy is that although it has over fifty different rites, they all contain a common core of standard prayers which gives them all an identifiable, though not identical, schematic structure. The basic unity among all the liturgical rites is the result of the authority enjoyed by the liturgical material in the Babylonian and Palestinian Talmuds."*[7]

A brief look at some of the basic Jewish prayers will exemplify what Rabbi Arzt has pointed out. The Sh'ma is a standard prayer, mandatory in the prayer service, and stipulated to be performed at all morning and evening services. It is the prayer most reverenced by Jews and it is their confession of faith. The Sh'ma consists of a series of statements from the Torah. Thus in Deuteronomy 6:4–7 we read:

Hear, O Israel: The Lord our God is one Lord; and you shall love the Lord your God with all your heart, and with all your soul, and with all your might. And these words which I command you this day shall be upon your heart; and you shall teach them diligently to your children, and shall talk of them when you sit in your house, and when you walk by the way, and when you lie down, and when you rise.[8]

The *Amidah* (literally, "standing," to indicate the posture assumed while reciting it) as referred to by the Sefardim, or *Shemoneh Esreh* as designated by the Ashkenazim, consists of nineteen (originally eighteen) benedictions. It forms a central and very sacred part of the liturgy and is recited during the three services on the Sabbath, and on holy days. The first three benedictions are in praise of God and his attributes, the next thirteen are for a variety of human needs, and the last three are in thanksgiving to God and for peace.

Two additional prayers may be noted. These are the *Alenu*[9] and the *Kaddish*. The Alenu, which expresses the messianic hopes of Israel, is recited at the conclusion of each of the daily services. The Kaddish, derived from the Aramaic and meaning "holy," was originally a hymn of praise, sanctifying the name of God and the coming of His kingdom. It is recited only within the congregation. Today it is known as the prayer for the dead, and the mourner is required to recite it with others at the synagogue. Paradoxically, the prayer itself does not contain any reference to the judgment of the individual nor even to the name of the departed. Actually, the prayer may be said to transfigure the grief of the individual into a

* From *Justice and Mercy: Commentary on the Liturgy of the New Year and the Day of Atonement* by Max Arzt. Copyright © 1963 by Max Arzt. Reprinted by permission of Holt, Rinehart and Winston, Inc.

sanctification of God and His kingdom to come. The doxology passages in the Kaddish later were taken up into the Gloria and the Sanctus of the Mass. The passages concerning the messianic kingdom are related to the Lord's Prayer.

The *piyyutim* (from the Greek meaning "poem") are liturgical poems and form an important part of the Mahzor prayer book as well as an addition or embellishment of the basic prayers of the Siddur. They consist of the prayers, poems, and hymns used on holy days and festivals. Their use is voluntary rather than mandatory as are the Sh'ma and Amidah. These devotional poems are said to have their source in the writers of the Talmud and Midrash. A great number of them were created in the post-talmudic and medieval periods, perhaps as many as 34,000. In time many of them were put to music and rather frequently the music was borrowed from non-Jewish sources. The hymn "El Norah Alilah" ("God, Mighty in Thy Deeds") is said to be quite similar to Martin Luther's famous hymn "A Mighty Fortress Is Our God."[10]

THE LITURGICAL CALENDAR.   The Jewish calendar is essentially lunar and was taken from Babylonian sources. The year is divided into twelve months and each month has a little more than twenty-nine and one half days, necessitating the addition from time to time of an extra month. The week is divided into seven days and each seventh day is celebrated as the Sabbath. Within this calendar of worship, which began by Jewish reckoning at the creation and whose date in 1968 C.E. is 5728, there developed in the course of time many religious festivals and holy days. The holy days have always exerted a strong impetus to the maintenance of Jewish unity and spirituality. Despite persecutions and times of trouble they have served to maintain the permanence and the stability of Jewish life and devotion.

In the account that follows we shall begin with a consideration of the Sabbath service and then discuss the High Holy Days of Rosh Hashanah (New Year) and Yom Kippur (Day of Atonement). Following that discussion a brief description will be given of some of the lesser festivals or holy days in the religious calendar. The Sabbath (from *Shabbat*, meaning "rest") may be said to be the most ancient of the Jewish holy days. The scriptural source for the Sabbath is to be found in Exodus 20:8–11:

Remember the sabbath day, to keep it holy. Six days you shall labor, and do all your work; but the seventh day is a sabbath to the Lord your God; in it you shall not do any work, you, or your son, or your daughter, your manservant, or your maidservant, or your cattle, or the sojourner who is within your gates; for in six days the Lord made heaven and earth, the sea, and all that is in them, and rested the seventh day; therefore the Lord blessed the sabbath day and hallowed it.

The observance of the Sabbath by the Jews has ranged (as within the Christian churches) from a very strict interpretation of the injunction to rest to a very liberal and more spiritual interpretation of the significance and purpose of the Sabbath. In the past, Orthodox Judaism followed a very rigoristic interpretation of the Sabbath regulations. In this they inspired some of the Christian sects of the Reformation. Among the Orthodox Jews (and to a certain extent this is true even today) the injunction to rest was followed very literally; no work of any kind could be done. Food had to be prepared the night before; riding was prohibited, and even walking was restricted. As an extreme example of some of the minute regulations, one was even forbidden to untie a knot on the Sabbath. In case of serious illness a physician, however, was permitted to treat his patient, for the saving of a human life takes precedence over the observance of the Sabbath.

This strict interpretation of the Sabbath regulations by Orthodox Judaism should not be taken to imply that they regarded the Sabbath as a joyless occasion or a kind of punishment for man. Jews hold that the statement attributed to Jesus that "the Sabbath was made for man" was the view of the Pharisees of that time. One Pharisee teacher states: The Sabbath was handed over to you, not you to the Sabbath. In keeping with this injunction Jewish tradition has regarded the Sabbath as a day of joy. There must be no mourning on the Sabbath, and all fasts are excluded. Three good meals are to be taken, and wine is regarded as appropriate. Among contemporary Jews, Reform Jews and Conservative Jews tend to disregard some of the ritualistic observances and prohibitions. All branches of Judaism, however, dedicate themselves to the spiritual meaning and the values of the Sabbath.

THE SABBATH SERVICES.   The Sabbath services begin on Friday evening not later than eighteen minutes before sunset according to the regulations followed by Orthodox Judaism. Reform and Conservative Judaism permit the service to begin at a later hour in the evening. The synagogue service opens with hymns welcoming the Sabbath, followed by prayers of praise and the recitation of the Sh'ma. Then the recitation of the Amidah, interspersed with prayers for special occasions, begins. Next the Kiddush, the prayer of sanctification, is recited ("Remember the Sabbath day to sanctify it"), followed by the delivery of a sermon. At the conclusion of the sermon the Alenu is recited, and this brings the service to an end.

The Sabbath morning service is usually more elaborate. Its service centers around the reading from the Torah as well as the recitation of the Sh'ma and the Amidah. In the reading of the Torah, by the rabbi or by a member of the congregation, a special ritual and certain prayers are designated. The Torah itself is written upon scrolls and is contained in a chest representing the Ark of the Covenant. The Ark is on a raised platform and stands against that wall of the synagogue which faces Jerusalem. The reading of the Torah is divided for all the Sabbaths of the year into certain fixed lessons or *sidrots*. To such lessons are customarily added lessons from the other books of the Bible, especially the Prophets. The prophetic reading is termed the "Haftarah." Blessings and prayers follow these readings and the Torah is then returned to the Ark. The service then concludes with the Mussaf or "Additional Service," which has its own Amidah and in which is added the recitation of the Kidusha, another prayer of sanctification.

The afternoon service of the Sabbath is traditionally spent in the reading of devotional literature, particularly at certain times of the year, of selections from the Sayings of the Fathers, a collection of ethical maxims and traditions forming part of the Mishnah. The afternooon service in the synagogue is also marked by a reading of the first portion of the Torah for the following week.

The Sabbath day concludes with an evening service called *Maariv* including the *Havdalahl*, a ceremony memorializing, so to speak, the departure of the peace of the Sabbath. Except by Reform congregations, the Torah is not read at the evening service.

The Holy Days

Of the Jewish holy days, two—*Rosh Hashanah* and *Yom Kippur*—are known as High Holy Days.

ROSH HASHANAH.   Literally meaning "head of year" or "New Year," this designation is not relevant to the Jewish calendar, for Rosh Hashanah actually occurs on the first day of the seventh month (September–October). It is sometimes called the "Day of Remembrance" and the "Day of Judgment," for God is said to "remember" the deeds of the individual and to prepare his "judgment" accordingly. In his prayers the worshiper implores God to remember him with mercy and kindness and to remember His covenant with Israel. Thus Rosh Hashanah is a time of commemoration, of self-examination, and of repentance. There is no "celebration" of the New Year as in the secular tradition. Recently, however, the exchange of greeting cards has become common.

Originally Rosh Hashanah was observed in one day. Now it is a two-day observance, although Reform Jews usually limit the observance to one day.[11] The synagogue services for Rosh Hashanah follow the customary order of the liturgy with the recitation of the Sh'ma, the Amidah, and the reading from the Torah, but some additional distinctive features of this service may be noted. Since there are two days of observance there are two readings from the Torah and two readings from the prophets. The service is generally interspersed with many piyyutim. But most important of all is the blowing of the *shofar* or ram's horn, a symbol of Rosh Hashanah, which is sounded after the reading of the Torah and during the recitation of the Mussaf Amidah. The three notes of the shofar signify the sovereignty of God, divine justice, and revelation. Their purpose is to awaken the sinner to his need for repentance. As Maimonides put it: "Awake, ye sleepers, and ponder your deeds; remember your Creator and go back to Him in penitence."

YOM KIPPUR.   The most solemn of all the Jewish holy days, Yom Kippur ("Day of Atonement") is frequently termed the "Sabbath of Sabbaths." It is a strict fast day; no food or water may be taken from sundown to sundown:

And it shall be a statute to you for ever that in the seventh month, on the tenth day of the month, you shall afflict yourselves, and shall do no work, either the native or the stranger who sojourns among you; for on this day shall atonement be made for you, to cleanse you; from all your sins you shall be clean before the Lord.
It is a sabbath of solemn rest to you, and you shall afflict yourselves; it is a statute for ever (Leviticus 16:29–31).

Some scholars believe that the word *kippur* is derived from the Babylonian meaning "to purge." In the early history of Judaism atonement was carried out by the sacrifice of a "scapegoat." In accordance with Jewish law forbidding the sacrifice of human beings, the sacrifice was transferred to an animal, usually a goat, although in Galicia in the eighteenth century a chicken was frequently used. In this manner a collective forgiveness of sins was obtained. After the destruction of the temple this form of atonement was given up for one based upon a *repentance* by the individual for his own sins. As Maimonides expressed it: "Every man should confess his sins and turn away from them on that day." Some have expressed the aim of atonement as "at-one-ment" among man and neighbor and God.

One of the chief features of the services in the synagogue on Yom Kippur is the recitation of the litany of sins, the confession by the individual of his sins. In this confession there is no intermediary; the rabbi does not hear the sins of the individual or perform absolution. The sins are confessed directly to God. In the recitation of his sins (of which there are 56 categories) the individual observes certain formulas that are strikingly similar to the Roman Catholic sacrament of confession. The formula for each sin confessed begins: "For the sin which we have sinned against Thee by . . ." Beating his breast for each sin enumerated, the penitent declares (in unison with the entire congregation): "For all these sins, O God of forgiveness, bear with us! forgive us!" The formula of confession is known as the *Al chet* and its resemblance to the *mea culpa* is quite noticeable.

Kol Nidre is an ancient hymn which, chanted by the cantor, opens the evening service on Yom Kippur. Kol Nidre is an Aramaic term meaning "all vows." In the early history of Judaism the inclusion of the Kol Nidre in the liturgy for Yom Kippur was strongly opposed. However, it became increasingly popular with the people, particularly since the sixteenth century, when it was adapted to a beautiful, sad, and inspiring melody. The prayer itself is a rather uninspiring legal formula:

All vows (kol nidre), oaths, and anathemas, whether called konam, konas, or by any other name, which we may vow or swear, or pledge, or whereby we may be found, from this Day of Atonement until the next (whose happy coming we await), we do repent. May they be deemed absolved, forgiven, annulled, and void, and made of no effect; they shall not bind us nor have power over us. The vows shall not be reckoned vows, the obligations shall not be obligatory; nor the oaths be oaths.[12]

Here the Jew is petitioning that he be forgiven as a transgressor in not having fulfilled the various promises and vows that he has made to God from one Day of Atonement to the next. Throughout history this has often been grossly misinterpreted as giving the Jew the right to violate his promises and vows whenever it pleased him. However, such vows are religious and wholly between the individual and God.

At the conclusion of the evening service in the synagogue many worshipers remain for the entire night, reading and meditating.

In contrast to the High Holy Days, three great festivals are times of pilgrimage and celebration. In ancient times they were joyous occasions, times when the Jewish worshipers traveled to the temple to offer up the fruits of the harvest and their prayers of thanksgiving. Their original agricultural basis eventually merged into events of historic significance.

PASSOVER.   The oldest of all Jewish festivals and holy days, symbolically represents freedom and is called "The Season of Our Freedom." The term "Passover" is from the Hebrew verb *pesach* (Gr. *pasch*) meaning "to pass over." Its source is to be found in the account in Exodus 12:21–34 in which the Destroyer "passed over" the houses of the Israelites and destroyed the first born of the Egyptians. The principal feature of this festival is the celebration of the escape of the Israelites from the bondage of Egypt. Originally, it was wholly a festival of spring commemorated by the sacrifice of lambs and the eating of the *matzot* or unleavened bread. In time the eating of the unleavened bread continued as a memorial of the escape from Egypt, hence the festival is sometimes called "the festival of freedom" or "the festival of the unleavened bread." The festival lasts for seven or eight days.

PENTECOST.   This festival is frequently termed "the Season of the giving [to us] of [our] Torah." Its importance lies in the commemoration of that event. The festival is celebrated fifty days after the Passover and represents the completion of the grain harvest. Originally, it was termed the "Feast of Weeks," that is, seven weeks from the beginning of the Feast of the Passover. In the synagogue on this festival the Book of Ruth, because of its agricultural context and the moral it conveys, is read aloud.

SUCCOT.   The term *Succot,* or the Feast of Tabernacles, is derived from *sukkah,* meaning "hut." This harvest festival apparently had its origins in the injunction of God to Moses: "And you shall observe the feast of weeks, the first fruits of wheat harvest, and the feast of ingathering at the year's end" (Exodus 34:22). And in Leviticus 23:42: "You shall dwell in booths for seven days. . . ." The Feast of Tabernacles is held four days after Yom Kippur and lasts for seven days. Precise instructions are given for building the booths, which are temporary dwelling places that may be constructed within or outside the synagogue, although few but the very orthodox construct them outside their homes. Such booths are symbolical of man's dependence upon God and of the tents used by the Israelites in the wilderness as they fled from Egypt. During the festival food and drink may be taken in the booths, although today more emphasis is placed upon the study of the Torah in the booths by the participants. The seventh day is one of great sanctity and known as *Hoshanah Rabbah,* the Great Hosanna, on which the ceremony culminates with a hymn, "A Voice Brings Glad Tidings," promising the coming of the Messiah and the establishment of God's kingdom upon earth.

CHANNUKAH.   The Feast of Dedication or the Feast of Lights, the source of Channukah is to be found in the Jewish Apocryphal Books of the Maccabees. The festival lasts for eight days and is a commemoration of the victory of Judah the Maccabee over the Seleucidae on December 25 of the year 165 C.E. In celebration of his victory Judah re-dedicated the Temple on Mount Zion and kindled the lights of the great menorah. He enjoined the Jewish people to celebrate this festival for eight days every year until the end of time. The outstanding feature of the present celebration is the lighting on successive evenings of the several branches of the menorah or candlestick. The festival is a happy one in which the Jewish family participates both at home and in the synagogue by the lighting of the menorah, the recitation of benedictions, and prayers of thanksgiving.

PURIM.   Concerning the religious festival Purim there is some doubt of its historical character and authenticity. It is based upon events that are recorded in the Book of Esther of a plot by Haman, the chief minister of the Persians, to destroy the Jews. Some have regarded the events as wholly fictional; others have insisted that the inauguration of Purim was merely a Jewish rationalization for their adoption of a pagan form of carnival. However, devout Jews for the past twenty-two centuries have accepted as authentic the events recorded in the Book of Esther. They believe that the designs of Haman were discovered in time, and that instead of being exterminated, the Jews turned the tables on Haman and routed his forces and hanged him. The celebration of Purim is somewhat of a carnival affair. Celebrations in the Orthodox synagogues have usually been somewhat noisy.

THE CHRISTIAN LITURGY

Just as the Jewish liturgy centers on God and His relations with His chosen people, so the Christian liturgy centers on Jesus as the Son of God and the meaning and purpose of his incarnation, his sacrifice, and his resurrection. Just as the beliefs of Christians owe much to the origins of Christianity in Judaism, so its liturgy is seriously indebted to the Jewish liturgy. The point of departure in the two liturgies is simply, Jesus Christ. Christians accept him as the primised Messiah and the Jews do not. In the Christian liturgy that part which is called the "Liturgy of the Word" is derived in part from Jewish sourcés. That part of the Christian liturgy which centers on the Eucharist or the Lord's Supper is wholly and essentially Christian; it has no counterpart in the Jewish liturgy.

The historical development of the Christian liturgy is an enormously complex and fascinating subject. At best we can merely give a brief outline of that development, for our principal concern in this chapter is with the Christian liturgy as it is found today in the Roman Catholic Church and in those Protestant churches described in Chapter 12.

The scriptural basis of the Christian liturgy is found in the life of Jesus. From the Gospels and the Epistles we know that Jesus was a Jew, that he had been brought up in the Jewish tradition, that he had been educated as a Jew, and that he had studied and taught in temple and synagogue. In particular he was well acquainted with the services of the synagogue and so were his disciples, who, with the exception of Luke, were also Jews. It was only natural then that many of the elements of the Jewish liturgy, as well as some of the beliefs, should have been taken over into the first beginnings of the Christian Church. It was in this manner that the readings from the Law and the Prophets, the commentaries on them, the recitation of the Psalms, the chants, and many of the briefer prayers became a part of the Christian liturgy. To these elements the Christians later added readings from the New Testament and from the Epistles and the Gospels. All of this later came to be known as the "Liturgy of the Word."

For what has been termed the "Mass of the Faithful," the "Liturgy of the Eucharist," the "Lord's Supper," and "Holy Communion," the scriptural basis is to be found in several places in the New Testament. As St. Paul describes it:

> For I received from the Lord what I also delivered to you, that the Lord Jesus on the night when he was betrayed took bread, and when he had given thanks, he broke it, and said, "This is my body which is for you. Do this in remembrance of me." In the same way also the cup, after supper, saying, "This cup is the new covenant in my blood. Do this, as often as you drink it, in remembrance of me." For as often as you eat this bread and drink the cup, you proclaim the Lord's death until he comes (I Corinthians 11:23).[13]

At the time of the apostles the commemoration of the Last Supper was celebrated in the evening and it was not preceded by any fast. The supper consisted of food supplied by some of the wealthier Christians to which many needy Christians came. Thus it seems to have been a charitable affair and came to be termed the "Agape" or "love feast." In Jerusalem the apostles may have found the upper room not large enough and the supper was frequently celebrated at different homes in the city. Apparently, too, the supper was often confused by some with the ordinary meals of the day. The participants failed to perceive then its true spiritual significance. This is observed by St. Paul: "When you meet together, it is not the Lord's supper that you eat. For in eating, each one goes ahead with his own meal and one is hungry and another is drunk. What! Do you not have houses to eat and drink in? Or do you despise the church of God and humiliate those who have nothing?" (I Corinthians 11:20-22). And after censuring them he says: "So then, my brethren, when you come together to eat, wait for one another—if any one is hungry, let him eat at home—lest you come together to be condemned" (I Corinthians 11:33-34). In time the material and spiritual elements involved in the Last Supper, the distinction between the Agape and the Eucharist, came to be definitively established. And apparently it was not until the second century that the Lord's Supper was instituted as a morning service.

Apparently there were no written liturgies during the first three or four centuries in the history of the Church.[14] Consequently, it is extremely difficult to try to put together any orderly development of the liturgy in the early history of the Church. Each Christian community tended to commemorate the Lord's Supper in its own way. Generally, however, the services began with readings from the Prophets, the Epistles, and the Gospels. These readings were followed by a sermon and then certain prayers were said over the catechumens—those being instructed in the faith—and they were dismissed. In a letter to his sister Marcellina in A.D. 386, St. Ambrose reports that after the lessons and the sermons he dismissed the catechumens, then gave an exposition of the creed to those awaiting baptism, and finally proceeded to the celebration of the Mass of the Faithful.[15] This is said to be one of the earliest accounts revealing the division of the Mass into the Mass of the Catechumens (Liturgy of the Word) and the Mass of the Faithful (Liturgy of the Eucharist). It also explains the origin of the term "Mass," which is derived from the Latin and means *misse*, or dismissed. Thus after the catechumens were instructed in the Word of God they were dismissed and the Lord's Supper was celebrated for the faithful. By this time the Mass of the Faithful contained most of the elements of the more formalized Mass of later centuries. Thus, the Sursum Corda, the singing of verses from the Psalms, the Preface followed by the Sanctus, the recitation of the Lord's Prayer, the consecration of the bread and wine, the Communion, and closing prayers were all present.

By the late sixth and early seventh centuries during the pontificate of St. Gregory the Great, the order of the Mass took on more definitive form. St. Gregory added the traditional entrance chant and he simplified the Mass by reducing the number of variable prayers to three (collect, secret, and post-Communion), limited the number of prefaces, and substituted verses for entire psalms.

In this early period there were several groups or families of liturgies—the Syrian, Alexandrian, Roman, Gallican, and their derivatives. Eventually the Roman liturgy came to dominate the West, and the West Syrian (the liturgies of St. Basil and St. Chrysostom) came to dominate the East.

In the later Middle Ages to the time of the Council of Trent the development of the Roman liturgy was characterized by some rather serious changes that had an impact not only upon the Roman Church but upon the Reformation churches as well. The most serious change was that the celebration of the Mass seems to have become less of a corporate affair, a matter of public worship such as existed in the early history of the Church. Private Masses became increasingly common, partly due to the lack of education of the laity and their inability to understand the Latin of the rite. The worshipers tended to assume more and more of a passive role in the celebration of the Mass. It still remained true, of course, that the function of the priest to say Mass continued to be an obligation; nor was there any lack of devotion on the part of the people. Nevertheless the inevitable result was that the people were left to their own prayers and devotions and the priest to his. Although the Council formalized the liturgy of the Mass as it was used down to the time of Pope Pius XI, there have been some significant changes in recent years. Before examining these changes as they appear in the present liturgy of the Roman Church, and also certain significant changes that have occurred in the Protestant liturgies in recent years, we shall first say something of the Christian liturgical year and of the meaning and place of prayer in the Christian liturgy.

The Christian Calendar

The Christian year exemplifies in its various festivals the essence of all Christian teaching. The central figure in the Christian drama is that of Christ. What the Christian liturgy does throughout the year is to commemmorate his birth, his life, and his resurrection. Presently there is a liturgy for every day of the year, which is why the Christian calendar is also referred to as the liturgical calendar. Originally, only a few festivals were celebrated in the Christian year; the sources for some of these festivals are to be found in the Jewish calendar. The earliest Christians knew well the Jewish Sabbath, the Passover—at which time Jesus was tried and crucified —and the Pentecost. Jesus and his disciples observed the Jewish Sabbath, the Passover, and undoubtedly the other Jewish festivals.

The first great change in the worship observed by the apostles came with the institution of Sunday as the beginning of the Christian week, a day of worship which took the place of the Jewish Sabbath. The origin of Sunday as the "first day" is based upon the known chronology of events connected with the death of Christ, which took place on Friday, the eve of the official Pasch (Passover). The Resurrection occurred two days later, the day after the Sabbath, which was the seventh day of the week. Hence, Sunday is the first day of the week, the day of the Resurrection. The Gospel of St. John, 20:19–30 appears to offer the earliest evidence for the apostolic Sunday. St. Paul states: "On the first day of the week, when we were gathered together to break bread . . ." (Acts 20:7).[16] Thus each Sunday became a little Easter, just as each Friday became a day of special memorial for the death of Christ. The term "Sunday," which replaced the expression "the first day" by the second century, was derived from Roman sources and referred to the day of the sun, or the day after the day of Saturn. In the Christian era Christ is often symbolized by the sun.

At first the Christians rejected the legal observances imposed by the

Jewish Sabbath. Sunday was not declared a day of rest principally because the Roman law did not permit it and most of the early Christians were members of the lower classes and had to work. The spiritual devotions of these early Christians took place in the early morning or the early evening before or after work. With the conversion of Constantine the Sunday rest became a matter of law. By the end of the sixth century even agricultural work was prohibited. Today necessary servile work is permitted, but a more positive emphasis is placed upon the importance of spiritual devotions on Sunday, such as attendance at church or Mass.

ADVENT.   Originally the "first day" of the Christian year was Christmas Day. From the eighth century the beginning of the Christian year is dated from Advent Sunday, which is that Sunday nearest to the Feast of St. Andrew (November 30). The season of Advent is one in which the Church prepares for the coming of Christ. A period lasting three or four weeks, originally it was a time of fasting and abstinence. Today there are no special fasts except on Christmas Eve and the Ember Days.[17] The lessons (passages from the Old & New Testament) read during Advent are usually taken from Isaiah and his prophecies of the coming of the Redeemer, and from the Gospels, emphasizing the advent of the Last Judgment.

CHRISTMAS.   The Feast of Christmas (Mass of Christ) commemorates the Incarnation or birth of Jesus. It is the central event in what has been termed the "Christmas cycle" which includes Advent, Christmas, and Epiphany. This is termed a "cycle" because, like the Easter cycle, it is repeated every year in the services of the Church to remind the faithful of the coming of Christ and to instruct them in what is necessary for their salvation. Such cycles of Christian festivals will terminate only with the Second Coming of Christ.

The Feast of Christmas is one of the "fixed" feasts of the Church. Independent of Easter, it always has a definite date, December 25, originating in the Roman calendar. In the later days of the Roman Empire the worship of the sun god (Osiris) was taken up by the Roman emperors, and the date of the feast of this god was December 25. With the conversion of Constantine this day was transformed into a memorial for the birth of Christ, for whom the sun was to be a mere symbol in the heavens. The actual date of the birth of Christ is not known. Clement says that some thought it to be April 20. In Egypt the date of January 6 was accepted. Others accepted the date of May 20. However this may be, the celebration of Mass on the birthday of Christ was well established in the West from early times. In the East Christmas did not become an established feast until the fourth century. The first written record of the feast of Christmas

Day appears in the Philocalin calendar, the first Christian calendar, compiled by a Greek artist, Philocalus, in 354.

EPIPHANY.   Taking its name from the Greek word meaning "manifestation," this feast was celebrated as a great feast in the East prior to A.D. 300. Thus in the East it was actually celebrated as a feast before the Christmas feast became a matter of custom. Like the celebration of Christmas at Rome, the feast of the Epiphany in the East had certain associations with pagan worship and undoubtedly represented in part an effort by the Church in the East to find a Christian substitute for a pagan festival. The date of the festival was fixed for January 6, which in Egypt corresponded to the Roman December 25. The Feast of the Epiphany was devoted to three manifestations or *miracula* of the glory of Christ: the adoration by the Magi; the baptism of Christ when he was proclaimed as the Son of God; and the miracle at Cana, where Christ transformed water into wine.

EASTER.   The celebration of Easter, the Feast of the Resurrection, is one of the "movable" feasts of the Church. The greatest feast day in the Church, it sanctifies the entire Christian year, for all other movable feasts are based upon it. The name "Easter," of Germanic origin, comes from Eastre, the name of a Saxon goddess. Those Christians who have not taken over the German expression usually refer to Easter in some modification of the term "pascha," which originally designated the Pasch or Jewish Feast of the Passover. This was a feast that Christ himself observed on the eve of his death.

Historically Easter is the first feast day of the Church. From the very earliest days all the evidence indicates that the Christians celebrated Easter as the Feast of the Pasch. Toward the close of the second century Tertullian notes the celebration of two Pasches, the first marked by fasting and the other corresponding to our Easter. Other writers in these early days refer to the Pasch of the Crucifixion and the Pasch of the Resurrection.

The problem of determining the date of Easter is a very complex issue; it is the subject of much dispute and has given rise to varying practices in the history of the Church. The major difficulty in determining the date of Easter lies in its relation to the Jewish Passover, the date of which is based upon the lunar calendar of Judaism. Yet there is nothing in Christianity itself which requires that Easter be celebrated on the Sunday following the first full moon of spring. Hence, since most of the feasts of the Church are fixed and attached to the solar calendar, it may be argued that the old controversy of the Easter date could be easily resolved by assigning a fixed date to Easter and abandoning all calculations based on a lunar calendar. In fact, Christianity in its early history readily adapted itself to the solar calendar once it had broken away from its early Jewish origins. The practical value of a more stable calendar might be said to outweigh whatever values are associated with the traditional Easter reckoning.

THE LENTEN SEASON.   The word "Lent" is derived from the Dutch *Lente*, meaning spring. The Greek and Latin names ($\tau\epsilon\sigma\sigma\alpha\rho\alpha\kappa\sigma\sigma\tau\grave{\eta}$, *Quadragesima*) are more precise because they designate the number of days—40—in Lent. Lent, then, is a period of forty days of fast preceding Easter. It commemorates the fasts performed by Moses, Elias, and above all Christ. It would appear that the Lenten fast existed from the earliest days even though there is no scriptural mention of its observance. At first the fast period consisted principally of the two days from Good Friday to Easter. By the time of St. Athanasius there was a whole week of fasting, and by the beginning of the fourth century this period had been extended at Rome to three weeks. By the time of St. Leo (440–461) the Lenten fast— had been extended to six weeks. Finally, by the ninth century, in the West four additional days were added to the Lenten fast by marking the beginning of the period on Ash Wednesday four days prior to the beginning of the traditional six-week period.

Space does not permit a full account of the Lenten fast. Briefly, however, we may note that the Lenten fast reaches a high point with Palm Sunday or Second Passion Sunday. On Palm Sunday the Church commemorates the entry of Christ into Jerusalem by the distribution of palms to the faithful.[18] On Palm Sunday the liturgy provides for the entire reading of the Passion of Christ as described by Matthew 26:36–75 and 27:1–60.

Holy Week begins on the Monday following Palm Sunday. It is a week in which the Church commemorates the trial, crucifixion, death, and burial of Christ. Holy Week, or the Week of the Holy Passion, is mentioned as early as the second century. It is characterized by strict fasting and the singing of the Tenebrae.[19] On Maundy Thursday[20] the altars are stripped of all ornament, and this rite is followed by that of the washing of the feet in emulation of Christ's washing the feet of the apostles.

GOOD FRIDAY.   The most solemn day of the Christian year, Good Friday commemorates the Passion of Christ. No candles are lit, and the clergy are clothed in black vestments. It is the only day in the year in which the Mass is not celebrated. In the Catholic Church there is the Mass of the Presanctified, but the bread and the wine have been previously consecrated. The services on Good Friday begin with solemn prayers, followed by the veneration of the cross by the priest and the congregation. The Mass of the Presanctified completes the service.

Holy Saturday, the Vigil of Easter, is the last day of Holy Week.

Formerly the services began in the afternoon and were climaxed by the midnight Mass, which belonged to Easter Sunday. Today the services begin early on Saturday morning with the blessing of the new fire for the lighting of the Easter candle, symbolic of the presence of Christ in the Easter mystery and of his mission. It is designated as "the Service of Light" and is based upon the statement of Jesus: "I am the light of the world; he who follows me will not walk in darkness, but will have the light of life" (John 8:12). The reading of the twelve prophecies (originally designed for the instruction of catechumens) follows upon the blessing of the candle. After the procession and the blessing of the font (the baptismal water to be used during the year) the recitation of the Litany of the Saints is begun. The concluding Mass of Holy Saturday is a jubilant Mass, since it was originally the midnight Mass of Easter Sunday.

Easter Sunday is a day of rejoicing and thanksgiving, a day in which through the resurrection of Christ is celebrated the victory over death and the promise of eternal salvation. The services on Easter reflect these joyous and triumphant notes, especially in the chanting of the hymns and the repetition of the "Alleluia."

PENTECOST.   This feast day occurs fifty days after Easter. In Judaism it was termed the "Feast of the Weeks" and was a harvest feast commemorated fifty days after the first day of the Passover. For Christians the Feast of Pentecost is especially sacred, for it is on that day that the Holy Spirit descended upon the apostles. Pentecost is also known as "Whitsunday" in England and means literally "white Sunday." It is thought that the name is derived from the white robes worn by the candidates for baptism on that day. The Sunday after Pentecost is known as Trinity Sunday. The Anglican calendar numbers consecutively all Sundays from Trinity Sunday to the first Sunday in Advent; the Roman calendar numbers the Sundays from Pentecost to the first Sunday in Advent.

Christian Prayer

Many of the comments previously made concerning Jewish prayer are equally applicable to Christian prayer. Thus, Christian prayers may be petitionary and intercessionary. They may be prayers of praise, of thanksgiving, and of adoration. Petitionary prayers may be for material values or for spiritual values. In Catholic practice the prayers or the Masses offered by individuals are frequently termed "special intentions." They may be offered for a variety of reasons—for the recovery of a sick friend, for success in finding employment, for assistance in reaching a decision of great consequence. Protestant petitionary prayers are similar in nature, although not designated as special intentions, nor do Protestants (with the exception of High Episcopalians) have Masses said for individuals. The scriptural basis for the Christian petitionary prayers is to be found, among other places, in the Gospel of Matthew 7:7–9, but with reference to this type of prayer the Christian should always be mindful of the admonitions for prayer given by Jesus in the preceding chapter of Matthew.

The prayer of thanksgiving may be offered by an individual for some spiritual or material benefit he believes God has bestowed upon him.[21] The prayer of thanksgiving may also be of a more general nature. All the Christian liturgies provide for a prayer of thanksgiving after the Communion and in the eucharistic prayer. In fact all through the liturgy of the Mass there are many different types of prayers—the prayers at the foot of the altar, the prayer before the Gospel, the prayer to the Holy Trinity, the prayer over the gifts, the prayer for peace, and others. Typical of the variable post-Communion prayers is the one offered on Christmas Day: "Almighty God, we pray thee grant that the Saviour of the world, whose birth on this day has brought about our own rebirth in godliness, may also bestow on us immortal life." In the Presbyterian liturgy the prayer of thanksgiving after the Lord's Supper reads: "O, God who hast so greatly loved us, long sought us, and mercifully redeemed us: give us grace that in everything we may yield ourselves, our wills and our works, a continual thank offering unto thee; through Jesus Christ our Lord. Amen."[22]

Most of the great prayers of the Christian churches are concerned with the spiritual edification of the individual. Christians pray that their wills may be identified with God, that they may become dedicated to His service, that they may receive His grace. Christian prayer in its highest form aspires to what St. John Damascene calls "a lifting up of the mind to God." Christian prayer should be a conversation, a dialogue with God. As St. Teresa of Avila expressed it, "a prayer is an intimate friendship, a frequent conversation held alone with the Beloved." To pray that man's will should be God's will, that His will be done, should prepare him for the unexpected—that his prayer may be denied. There can be no obligation upon God to grant every wish. As Hedley puts it: "Prayer according to the will of God can mean no other. Even the inner blessings we seek may not be those which he intends for us; and if he gives us continuing problems instead of resolutions, and a sense of failure rather than an unbroken joy, we still must say, 'Thy will be done.' "[23]

What of extemporaneous prayers? These are a fairly common feature of Protestant worship. Undoubtedly extemporaneous prayer possesses a freshness and an inspirational quality that is all too often lacking in the continued repetition of the formalized prayers of the Christian liturgy. But the advantage of the extemporaneous or "free prayer" is too often restricted to the minister. Except for the "amen" the congregation merely listens, sometimes edified and sometimes not. The true devotional quality of prayer for the congregation is best brought out in the recitation of the Lord's Prayer or in the recitation of the prayers given in the prayer book. One of the objections to the recitation of prayer formulas has been removed now that the Roman Catholic liturgists have restored the use of the vernacular in the service, thus making the content of the prayers more meaningful to the worshiper.

The silent prayer also has a proper place in the liturgy and should be used. Again, however, there is the possibility of abuse. To resort too often to the silent prayer is apt to make it meaningless. And the suggestion that silent prayer be used in the public schools strikes us as nothing less than the evasion of a problem. Since the silent prayer would be the only prayer offered, it is doubtful if it would accomplish any real purpose. The silent prayer loses its value if it is taken out of the context of prayer itself. Indeed, the highest value of prayer would seem to be found in the prayers that are recited with others in the spirit of congregational worship, for worship is essentially corporate, and it is as members of the Church that Christians pray.

Christian prayer is based upon faith. It is faith that gives meaning to prayer, for it is through faith that God is known. Christian prayer is also distinctive because it is prayer that is addressed not merely to God the Father, but to God the Father through the Son and the Holy Spirit. In contrast to Jewish prayer, Christian prayer in all its appearances in the liturgy is uttered "through Jesus Christ." The principle of Christian prayer may also be said to be the Holy Spirit, for it is the Holy Spirit that makes the believer one with Jesus Christ.

Finally, that prayer which more than any other is truly Christian, is that known as the Lord's Prayer. In Matthew 7 Jesus says:

> Pray then like this:
> Our Father who art in heaven,
> Hallowed be thy name.
> Thy kingdom come,
> Thy will be done,
>   On earth as it is in heaven
> Give us this day our daily bread;
> And forgive us our debts,
>   As we also have forgiven our debtors;
> And lead us not into temptation,
>   But deliver us from evil.[24]

The Mass Today

The liturgy of the Mass as it exists today incorporates many changes of a revolutionary nature which distinguish it sharply from the liturgy that was formalized by the Council of Trent. In addition to the Dialogue Mass established by Pope Pius XI, the Second Vatican Council has gone much further and introduced into the Mass a more extensive use of the vernacular, other forms of music than the Gregorian, and a greater participation in the singing of hymns by the congregation. An increased emphasis has been placed upon Scripture so that the faithful may take a more active and fruitful part in the Mass. The celebration of the Mass takes place with the priest facing the congregation rather than the altar, the laity assumes a more active role through the offices of the lector and the commentator, and certain changes have been effected in the liturgical year.

By describing the Mass in the Roman Catholic Church today we shall be in a position not merely to set down in some detail such a service, but also to show later by contrast and comparison the essential features of the Sunday service of the principal Protestant churches. Just as the Roman Church has placed renewed emphasis on certain didactic functions of the Mass as well as on greater congregational participation, so the Protestant churches have restored in their services many of the features of the liturgy of the Eucharist formerly absent or rejected. The net result has been that, except for some major differences based on the interpretation of the Eucharistic sacrifice and a number of minor semantic differences, there is considerable accord among the Christian churches today on the liturgy.

Let us first summarize some of the more important decisions and changes effected in the liturgy of the Roman Catholic Mass by the Second Vatican Council. The division of the Mass into two parts—the Liturgy of the Word of God (Mass of the Catechumens) and the Liturgy of the Eucharist (Mass of the Faithful)—has been reaffirmed.

The number of participants in the Mass will depend upon the kind of Mass that is being offered. Fundamentally, of course, the participants are the priest and the people. However, both the priest and the people have assistants. The assistants to the priest are the deacons, subdeacons, and servers (or altar boys). The deacon may read the Gospel, and helps in the distribution of Communion. The subdeacon may read the Epistle and otherwise assists the priest and deacon. The servers assist the priest in various ways, as by responding to the prayers offered by the priest at the foot of the altar and by assisting in the distribution of Communion.

The assistants to the people are the lector, the commentator, and the cantor. The lector leads the congregation in the recitation of many of the prayers, and all readings except from the Gospel are read by him. The office of the commentator is to instruct the people when to sit, stand, or kneel, and to comment on the various rites of the liturgy so that the people may have a better understanding of it. The two offices of lector and commentator may be combined. Both the lector and the commentator must be laymen. In those cases where it is not possible to have one or both of these officers, their role is assumed by the priest. The function of the cantor is to lead the congregation in singing. His task is particularly important because he must develop a nonsinging congregation into a singing congregation. His function may also be assumed by the priest, the lector, or the commentator.

OUTLINE OF THE LITURGY OF THE MASS[25]

I. Liturgy of the Word
   A. Entrance Rite (Hymn, in English, sung with congregation)
      1. Prayers at the foot of the altar (confessions of sins, prayers for pardon and absolution)
      2. Reading of the *Introit* (verse of a Psalm)
      3. Kyrie Litany ("Lord, have mercy")[26]
      4. *Gloria* ("Glory to God"). At the conclusion of the Gloria, the priest greets the people with "the Lord be with you" (*Dominus vobiscum*), to which they respond "And with your spirit" (*Et cum spiritu tuo*). Following a silent prayer by the congregation the priest then recites the
      5. *Collects* (brief prayers) for the day
   B. *The Word of God* (from the Epistle to Prayer of the Faithful)
      1. Reading of the *Epistle* (or selection from Old Testament)
      2. Gradual, Alleluia, or Tract[27]
      3. *Gospel* (read by priest or deacon)
      4. Homily or Sermon (traditionally a commentary on one of the lessons of the Mass, for example, Epistle, Gospel)
      5. Nicene Creed (recited by all)[28]
      6. Prayer of the Faithful (includes a petition for all the members of the Church)
II. Liturgy of the Eucharist
   A. Preparation of the Gifts (the Offertory)[29]
      1. Offertory Hymn
      2. Prayers at the offering of the Host
      3. *Lavabo* (washing of the fingers) and prayer to Holy Trinity
      4. Prayer over the Gifts (introduced by the "oratre fratres")
   B. Eucharistic Prayer (Preface–Canon)[30]
      1. Sanctus
      2. Eucharistic Prayers–Remembrance of the Church, remembrance of the living faithful, remembrance of the saints.
      3. Consecration (recited by the priest making present the Eucharistic sacrifice).[31] During the recitation of the consecration the celebrant raises both the Host and chalice
   C. Eucharistic Banquet (Communion rite)
      1. Preparation
         a. Lord's Prayer (led by priest with hands outstretched)

TABLE 3

ORDER OF THE LITURGY

ROMAN CATHOLIC[1]	LUTHERAN[2]	EPISCOPALIAN[3]	METHODIST[4]	PRESBYTERIAN[5]	BAPTIST[6]
Entrance Rite (Hymn)	Invocation	Hymn	Hymn of Praise	Call to Worship	Prelude
Prayers at Altar (Confession, Absolution, Pardon)	Confession of Sins / Declaration of Grace		(Scripture Sentences)[7] / Greeting[8]	Hymn of Praise / Prayer of Confession (Kyrie)	Processional Hymn / Call to Worship / Invocation
				Declaration of Pardon	Lord's Prayer
Introit	Introit				Hymn (Youth Choir)
Kyrie	Kyrie				
Gloria	Gloria			Gloria	Hymn (Adult Choir)
Collect	Collect	Collect for Purity	Collect for Purity	Prayer for Illumination (Collect)	
Epistle (or Old Testament)	The Lesson	Decalogue	Lord's Prayer	Old Testament Lesson (Anthem, Psalm)	Bible Reading
	Psalm	Collect for Day	Gloria		Prayer
Gradual, Alleluia, or Tract	Epistle for Day	Epistle	Confession	New Testament Lesson	Worship (with offering)

Gospel	Gradual or Alleluia	Gradual	Prayer for Pardon Comfortable Words	Sermon (Ascription of Praise)	Hymn
Homily	Gospel	Gospel	Litany of Intercession	(Invitation)	Prayer of Dedication and Doxology
Creed (Nicene)	Creed (Nicene)	Creed (Nicene)	Epistle	Creed (Nicene or Apostles')	Informal Words of Pastor
Prayer of Faithful	Hymn	Hymn	Gospel	Intercessions (Prayers) Invitation to Lord's Table Announcement of Communion	Hymn of Month Communion Meditation (Sermon)
Offertory	Sermon Votum	Sermon	Creed (Nicene or Apostles') Sermon	Offering (Anthem)	Deacon's Fund
Lavabo	Offertory	Words of Institution	Offertory	Words of Institution	Unison Prayer
Prayer over Gifts	Prayer of Church	(Hymn or Doxology)	Hymn	(Hymn, Doxology)	
	Sursum Corda	The Peace	Sursum Corda		

Roman Catholic	Lutheran	Episcopalian	Methodist	Presbyterian	Baptist
Sursum Corda	Preface and	Offertory: Kyrie	Preface	The Peace Sursum Corda	Words of Institution (Hymn, Doxology)
Preface	Proper Preface	Doxology and Prayer for Country	Sanctus	Eucharistic Prayers (Preface)	
Sanctus	Sanctus	Prayer for Church	Consecration	Sanctus	
Eucharistic Prayers	Lord's Prayer	Invitation			
Consecration	Prayer of Thanksgiving	Confession	Prayer of Humble Access	Lord's Prayer	Offering of Bread
Lord's Prayer	Words of Institution	Absolution		Breaking of Bread	Offering of Cup
Libera	The Pax	Comfortable Words Sursum Corda		Pouring of Wine	Hymn
Breaking of Bread		Preface			
Commingling		Sanctus			Benediction
Agnus Dei	Agnus Dei	Consecration	Agnus Dei	Agnus Dei	Postlude

Prayer for Peace	Administration of Sacrament	Lord's Prayer	Communion	Communion
Communion	Nunc dimittis	Prayer of Humble Access	The Peace	Thanksgiving after Supper
Post-Communion Prayer (Thanksgiving)	Post-communion Prayer	Agnus Dei	Prayer of Oblation	Prayer of Communion of Saints
		Communion	Communion	
Blessing	Benediction	Prayer of Thanksgiving	Hymn	Hymn
Dismissal		Benediction	The Blessing	
Hymn	Hymn	Hymn	Hymn	Charge and Benediction

1. Abbreviated from pages 427 and 432.
2. Taken with some abbreviations from Edward T Horn, III *The Church at Worship* (Philadelphia: Muhlenberg Press, 1957), pp. 20–21.
3. Based on the Book of Common Prayer and with some modifications taken from the Sunday service of Saint Andrew's Episcopal Church in State College, Pennsylvania.
4. Based on the report of the General Conference of the Methodist Church and a commentary on the Sacrament of the Lord's Supper by a committee of St. Paul's Methodist Church in State College, Pennsylvania.
5. Taken with some abbreviations from *The Book of Common Worship*, edited by the Joint Committee on Worship of the Presbyterian Church (Philadelphia: Westminster, 1966), p. 17.
6. Taken with slight modifications from the *Order of the Communion Service* (October 4, 1964) of The University Baptist Church of State College, Pennsylvania.
7. Throughout this table the use of parentheses indicates additional or alternative forms that may be used.
8. This corresponds to: "The Lord be with you. And with your spirit. Let us pray." which appears after the Gloria in the Mass.
9. The broken line indicates the division between the Liturgy of the Word and the Liturgy of the Eucharist.

        b. *Libera* (or embolism—from *embolismus* meaning a prayer thrown in) [32]

        c. Fraction or breaking of the bread. The host is divided, one part placed on paten, another in chalice. This is the commingling of the body and the blood [33]

        d. Agnus Dei ("Lamb of God") [34]

        e. Final Prayer for Peace

    D. Communion [35]

        1. Prayers before Communion

        2. Communion of the Celebrant. Recites three times the prayer of the centurion from Matthew 8:8 substituting the word "soul" for "servant"

        3. Communion of the faithful (who at the conclusion of the "Lord, I am not worthy" recited by the celebrant and people together have assembled at the communion rail). The prayer of the centurion is again repeated and Communion is distributed by the priest or deacon by placing the host on the tongue of the communicant and saying: "The Body of Christ," to which the communicant responds, "Amen" [36]

        4. Ablutions, followed by silent prayers

    E. Thanksgiving or post-communion prayer

    F. Dismissal—"The Mass is ended" (*ite missa est*)

        1. Final prayer to the Trinity and blessing of the faithful

        2. Closing hymn

A careful comparison of the preceding table with the explanation of the Liturgy of the Mass should bear out what was previously stated, namely, that the differences in the liturgy within Christianity are rather slight. A major difference still lies in the emphasis that is placed on the Communion service by the Christian churches. Here we find, perhaps, the greatest disparity between the Baptist Sunday Service and the others. Basically, this is due to the emphasis placed upon the interpretation of the sacrament of baptism by the Baptists and to the fact that Baptists, so to speak, are "free wheeling," that is, the rules and order of worship are left largely to the individual congregations. With the Methodists and the Presbyterians, Communion service may still be optional, although both churches are encouraging a frequency of Communion by the laity.

It may also be noticed that the greatest similarity both in the order and the features of the service obtain between the Roman Catholic and the Lutheran churches. Of some surprise here, however, is the rather astonishing changes that have recently been made in the Presbyterian service. It is now far more liturgical than it has been in the past. With respect to the Episcopalian service the order of the service departs rather sharply in some ways from that of the Roman Catholic or the Lutheran, and even the Presbyterian service. In other respects, however, the Episcopalian service is just as liturgical and in the High Episcopalian service it is difficult to distinguish this service from that of the Roman Catholic. The Methodist service has also become much more liturgical than it has been in the past. Like the Episcopalian, of which it is a derivation in its Anglican sources, the order of service differs from the Catholic, but in other respects it is much the same although perhaps less detailed.

A careful study of the differences in the expressions used throughout the liturgy would reveal that the differences are largely semantic and do not involve substantial doctrinal differences. Most of the prayers and psalms in any of the liturgies are usually variable in any event. And the prayers of Consecration, the Agnus Dei, the Sursum Corda, and others are fairly uniform.

Concerning the meaning of some of the expressions that appear fairly commonly and which were not previously explained in connection with the Roman Catholic Mass, we may observe the following: What are termed "Intercessions" or "Litany of Intercessions" are simply prayers offered up for the faithful, for the Church, or for any other noble end. The expression "Comfortable Words" usually consists of a verse from the New Testament emphasizing that God intends to save all sinners. The Prayer of Oblation is a prayer accompanying a dedication or sacrifice. It corresponds to the Prayer of Thanksgiving in several of the services. The Prayer of Humble Access is a prayer offered up before Communion.

NOTES

1. "Worship" is derived from "worth-ship" and signifies an honor or devotion to God.
2. To attempt to show the full indebtedness of the Christian liturgy to the Jewish would require a separate study. Insofar as it is feasible within this limited exposition we shall make occasional references to the Jewish liturgy where this has influenced the Christian.
3. George Hedley, *Christian Worship* (New York: Macmillan, 1956), p. 12.
4. *Ibid.*, p. 15.
5. Arzt, Max, *Justice and Mercy* (New York: Holt, 1963), pp. 7–8.
6. Abraham Joshua Heschel, *Man's Quest for God* (New York: Charles Scribner's Sons, 1954), p. 45.
7. Arzt, *Justice and Mercy*, p. 15.
8. Cf. also Deuteronomy 11:13–21 and Numbers 15:39.
9. See Chapter 8, p. 262.
10. For a further account on the Jewish hymns see Nathan Ausubel, ed., *The Book of Jewish Knowledge* (New York: Crown, 1964), pp. 220 ff.
11. For an explanation of the number of days of observance see Artz, *Justice and Mercy*, pp. 25–26.
12. From *The Book of Jewish Knowledge* By Nathan Ausubel. ©, 1964 by Nathan Ausubel. Used by permission of Crown Publishing Co.

13. See also Matthew 26–30; Mark 22–26; Luke 14–24.

14. There are the so-called Liturgies of St Mark, or "of St. James," etc., but there is no evidence to connect such liturgies with the apostles themselves.

15. St. Ambrose, *Letters* (New York: Fathers of the Church, Inc., 1954), XXVI, p. 366.

16. See also Luke 24:1 and I Corinthians 16:2.

17. "Ember" is possibly derived from *ymbren* meaning a circuit; it is unlikely that the term is derived from "ash." The Ember Days are observed as fast days on the Wednesday, Friday, and Saturday following the first Sundays in Lent and Pentecost as well as on September 14 and December 13.

18. Palm Sunday has also been termed "Pascha Floridum," and it may be of interest to point out that the State of Florida derives its name from the fact that it was discovered on Palm Sunday.

19. Literally, shadows. This chant is the matins or lauds usually sung for the following day on the afternoon or evening of Wednesday, Thursday or Friday in Holy Week.

20. The English equivalent of Holy Thursday. The term "maundy" is derived from "Mandatum," the first word of the antiphon "A new commandment I give to you, that you love one another; even as I have loved you, that you also love one another" (John 13:34).

21. Among Catholics such prayers may be a response to a petition addressed to a saint or to the Blessed Virgin and which the petitioner believes has been granted.

22. From *The Book of Common Worship Provisional Services*. The Westminster Press. Copyright © 1966, W. L. Jenkins. Used by permission.

23. Hedley, *Christian Worship*, p. 139.

24. Other authorities, some ancient, add in some form: *For thine is the kingdom and the power and the glory, forever. Amen.*

25. What is described here is a typical Sunday Mass without the use of the choir. The Mass may take several different forms: the private devotions of the priest, usually celebrated at a side altar; Week Day Masses; Sunday Masses; Holy Day Masses; Funeral Masses; Wedding Masses, and other special Masses.

26. An ancient Eastern litany chanted by deacons and petitioning Christ as Lord *Kyrios*) for the many needs of the Church.

27. Originally psalms sung as part of the service. Now they are shortened to a few verses and either sung or said. The Gradual is the oldest, taking its name from "gradus," meaning an elevated step. It was sung at one of the steps of the *ambe* or pulpit. The *Alleluia* (from the Hebrew meaning "praise Yahweh") was originally a chant of joy. From Septuagesima to Easter a psalm (or tract) replaces the *Alleluia*.

28. At present the sign of the cross at the end of the recitation is omitted. For the genuflection at the "Incarnatus est" a bow of the body has been substituted.

29. In the past an antiphonal psalm was chanted while the faithful in procession presented their offerings of bread and wine to the celebrant at the altar. In this manner the people presented outward gifts of bread and wine (which are to be transformed into the perfect sacrifice) to symbolize the interior gifts of themselves. Today the Hosts are presented to the priests by the servers, who in turn may receive them from members of the congregation who bring them to the altar.

30. The Preface is a part of the canon or rule of the Mass. A brief dialogue with the people precedes the Preface, which is variable for the day and which initiates the Eucharistic Prayer or Canon of the Mass, which continues and is invariable down to its conclusion at the Communion.

31. The words of consecration are:

The day before he suffered
he took bread,
and looking up to heaven,
to you, his almighty Father,
he gave you thanks and praise.
He broke the bread,
gave it to his disciples and said:
Take this and eat it, all of you;
this is my body.

When supper was ended,
he took the cup.
Again he gave you thanks and praise,
gave the cup to his disciples and said:
Take this and drink from it, all of you;
this is the cup of my blood,
the blood of the new and everlasting covenant—
the mystery of faith.
This blood is to be shed for you and for all men
so that sins may be forgiven.
Whenever you do this,
you will do it in memory of me.

32. The Prayer of the Roman rite is: "Deliver us, we beg you, O Lord, from every evil, past, present, and to come; and by the intercession of the blessed and glorious ever-virgin Mary, Mother of God, Of the blessed apostles Peter and Paul, of Andrew, and all the saints, in your mercy grant peace in our days, that by your compassionate aid we may be ever free from sin and sheltered from all turmoil. Through Jesus Christ, your Son, our Lord, who lives and reigns with you in the unity of the Holy Spirit, God, forever and ever. Amen."

33. The prayer of the celebrant is: "May this mingling and consecration of the Body and Blood of our Lord Jesus Christ be for us who receive it a source of eternal life. Amen."

34. The celebrant and the congregation recite: "Lamb of God, who take away the sins of the world, have mercy on us. Lamb of God, who take away the sins of the world, have mercy on us. Lamb of God, who take away the sins of the world, grant us peace."

35. Since the Council of Trent required of all the faithful at least once a year. The prevalent opinion in the Church today holds that participation in the Mass without communicating is incomplete.

36. Communion with wine in the Roman Church was finally abolished in the year 1415. Many difficulties were attendant upon its use: the danger of spilling, the difficulty in estimating the amount needed, the scarcity of wine in northern countries. Even in early Christianity communion in both kinds was never an absolute principle. Only wine was given to small children and usually only the Host to the dying and to prisoners.

SELECT BIBLIOGRAPHY

ABBOTT, WALTER M., S.J., ed. *The Documents of Vatican II.* Trans. Very Rev. Msgr. Joseph Gallagher. New York: Guild Press, 1966.

ARZT, MAX. *Justice and Mercy.* New York: Holt, Rinehart and Winston, 1963.

AUSUBEL, NATHAN, ed. *The Book of Jewish Knowledge*. New York: Crown, 1964.

COHON, BERYL D. *Judaism in Theory and Practice*. New York: Bloch, 1954.

DILLENBERGER, JOHN, and CLAUDE WELCH. *Protestant Christianity*. New York: Charles Scribner's Sons, 1954.

FERM, VERGILIUS, ed. *The American Church of the Protestant Heritage*. New York: Philosophical Library, 1953.

HEDLEY, GEORGE. *Christian Worship*. New York: Macmillan, 1956.

HESCHEL, ABRAHAM JOSHUA. *Man's Quest for God*. New York: Charles Scribner's Sons, 1954.

JUNGMANN, J. A., S.J. *The Mass of the Roman Rite, Its Origins and Development* (Missarum Solemnia). Trans. F. A. Brunner, C.SS.R. New York: Benziger, 1951, 1956. 2 vols.

KÜNG, HANS. *Structures of the Church*. New York: Thomas Nelson and Sons, 1964.

MICKLEM, NATHANIEL, ed. *Christian Worship*. London: Oxford University Press, 1954.

SPERRY, WILLARD. *Reality in Worship*. New York: Macmillan, 1955.

STEINBERG, MILTON. *Basic Judaism*. New York: Harcourt, Brace, 1947.

XIV

Epilogue:

Religion in American Life and Thought

WE have come at last very near to the end of our study. Our task, however, would not be complete without some description of the contemporary situation and some indications—or more probably, questions—about future directions. We can best do that by focusing on the American scene and see there how Judaism and Christianity have come to terms with the vitalities and structures of one particular culture. We will of necessity do this with a broad and general sweep, ranging over a vast field of complicated relationships and differences of considerable importance, in which we will indicate how Jews and Christians have made commendable efforts with a high degree of success to find areas of mutual cooperation and to create sound bases for reciprocal understanding.

In this final chapter we will discuss the American context, the character of its religious and cultural pluralism, the forms of religious structure, the role of religion in the public domain, and the climate for religious thought. We will then discuss the present relationships between Judaism and Christianity, with particular attention to the problems and possibilities of a Jewish-Christian tradition, and then conclude by taking a look at the ecumenical movement and its implications for the worldwide role of Judaism and Christianity.

THE AMERICAN CONTEXT

The cosmopolitan and pluralistic character of American culture confronts religion with wholly new problems and opportunities. It is a society of people with extraordinarily diverse cultural, religious, philosophical, and racial backgrounds and beliefs learning and living together. Here for the first time in history there is a diverse complex of traditional living religions and new religions having the distinct experiene of living among political, economic, social, and cultural institutions together. Within this setting the fundamental problem of American society has always been, and is now, how to establish a basis for social existence. How can men of such great differences live together in peace?

When Goethe came to America in the nineteenth century he was very surprised, we are told, to observe the peaceful coexistence of this multifarious complex. The United States had then, and has now, every Protestant sect under the sun; the fastest growing and most disciplined Roman Catholic community; the largest and most creative Jewish community; and a plethora of other sects and religions which do not fit easily into the tripartite scheme of Protestant, Catholic, and Jew. All these "have had to come to terms with the vitality and structures of American society. . . . What is peculiarly American is just this experience of living together in a situation where every tradition has its open hearing."[1]

Religious Pluralism

In the United States under the principle of separation of Church and State—or better, the principle of religious liberty—a special form of religious pluralism and a characteristic form of religious structure have developed which enables all religious groups of all types to exist together as equals, where no one group dominates. Since no particular form of religion is normative for the entire society, some cooperation is by definition necessary in the good society. The historic doctrine of religious liberty assumes that "a state represents a basic interest which is common to conflicting religious codes, and which arises from the fact that men must live together as men."[2] Democracy therefore poses the question of how these diverse groups can live together in dignity, without the violation of their integrity, and still arrive at a sufficient consensus to contribute to the common good. What happens to Protestants when they are no longer in the majority? What happens to Roman Catholics when they are under open scrutiny and criticism in a culture where dogma tends to develop by consensus? Can Jews transcend their habitual exclusivism enough to support the articulation of some basic Jewish-Christian motifs in the culture?

This effort to define the common good and to accommodate religious differences to the requirements of the social order means that every religious body must analyze the American community, find its place within it, and define the contributions it can make to the foundation of an ethical order. How do these diverse theologies come to terms with democracy's vision of its national mission and destiny? The answer to these questions requires a maturing doctrine of religious pluralism which regards pluralism as not only necessary, but also desirable. It is *necessary* because in the "limited warfare of democracy" there is always the possibility of error lurking in truth. All historical points of view are fragmentary and do not exhaust the truth. Therefore, there must be at least a toleration of disparate views. As the Puritan mystic of the seventeenth century, John Saltmarsh, said, "My truth is as dark to thee as thy truth is dark to me, until the Lord enlightens all our seeing." In American Jewish and Christian thought and experience this is assumed, and it is understood in the light of the inevitable limitation that befalls men. The testimony of every institution, including religious ones, is conditioned by fallibility. Reinhold Niebuhr puts it cryptically: "The truth as it is contained in the Christian revelation includes the recognition that it is neither possible for man to know the truth fully, nor to avoid the error of pretending he does."[3]

Pluralism is not only a necessity, it is also the *sine qua non* of creativity. To be creative the community must be convinced that religious loyalties do not detract from national and cultural unity. Such pluralism does not only allow for a variety of religious versions. It also gives full scope to the secular protest. The secular protest is necessary for scientific inquiry, for pragmatic achievements of social ends, and as a moral vanguard against false religious absolutes. In cultures which do not allow for secular criticism, historical religions tend to become moribund. On the other hand, it is worth noting that secularism can also erect false absolutes in such forms as rigid rationalisms or demonries like Nazism, unless there is a vital religious criticism of culture as well.

Under the aegis of religious pluralism some compatible goals have developed in spite of dogmatic and traditional differences. This has not been easy to achieve, for men suffer from what John Courtney Murray calls "a stain on our imaginations" so that Protestants sometimes fear Roman Catholic domination and are suspicious even of their most recent definitions of their relationship of Church and State—a fear, incidentally, which might be allayed by an open-minded reading of the documents from the Second Vatican Council. Roman Catholics are often resentful of the WASP (White Anglo-Saxon Protestant) establishment and its supposed political power which makes them victims of distributive injustice. Jews, with good historic reason, fear any Christian establishment or ecumenical unity. Also, generally speaking, the culture has a fear of religious divisions as a block to social achievement. In spite of these difficulties, Judaism and Christianity have in the last twenty years moved from tolerance to mutual cooperation to something like symbiosis. They have seen that they have much in common, that they have originated and formed many of the fundamental aspects of the culture, and in turn that they have been influenced and shaped by the science, philosophy, history, politics, and art of America.[4]

FORM OF THE RELIGIOUS STRUCTURES.   In the context of the historic doctrine of separation of Church and State and this special form of pluralism, a particular type of religious structure has developed in the United States. The basic structure is *denominationalism,* an institution which is formed by voluntary association in "fellowship" for the achievement of certain ends.[5] The commonly accepted categories of church and sect, as defined by the famous German historian Ernst Troeltsch to describe types of religious organization, are really not descriptive of the American scene.[6] Essentially, denominationalism is sectarian in character since no one "church" is representative of the body politic or even a geographic area. To be sure, one can talk about Roman Catholics, Orthodox, Episcopalians, or Lutherans being more like a church, and left-wing Protestants and Jewish synagogues as being more like sects, but the term *denomination* is applicable to all. Judaism, for example, is organized into three denominations: Orthodox, Conservative, and Reform. There are many types of Catholics, Lutherans, Baptists, and others. Each denomination, presumably, is a product of its own history, founded upon its own theology, which for the most part predates its American experience. What they have in common is their American experience, and this has shaped both their theologies and their institutional forms. This relatively easy form of association accounts in large part for new American denominations, like the Mormons or the Disciples of Christ, and for the plethora of smaller sects. It also contributes to an aspect of religious liberty—the right which each group claims for the practice of its faith without interference from others.

This seeming anarchy of religious bodies is somewhat mitigated by various efforts at cooperation, and a limited ecumenism. The three Jewish synagogues come together in the Synagogue Council of America; the Roman Catholic Diocesan Bishops are united in the new National Conference of Bishops (formerly the National Catholic Welfare Conference); and many Protestants are federated in the National Council of Churches of Christ. In addition, recent decades have seen the merger of several denominations, for example the United Church of Christ, a union of four denominations. All of the Presbyterian bodies, as well as the Methodists, are now unified. But the most ambitious effort now under way is the Consultation on Christian Unity, an attempt to merge several Protestant bodies with a total membership of twenty-five to thirty million members.

RELIGION IN THE PUBLIC DOMAIN.   The other characteristic of American religious life is the existing harmony between the *religious institution and its secular context.* This theme would in itself make for an interesting historical study. This relationship so impressed that astute observer of American culture Tocqueville, on his visit in 1835 that he was anxious that the statesmen and scholars of Europe should learn from the American experience. He sensed keenly the problems in Europe that were occasioned by the rise of democracy and the attitudes toward it, and he looked to the United States of America as a kind of laboratory. What had religion to hope for or fear from democracy? He recalled the eighteenth-century theory of the Philosophes that religion would fade as liberty advanced and enlightenment prevailed. But on the contrary here was occurring a wholly new thing. On the American continent, liberty, democracy, and religion were intimately associated and were prospering together.[7]

Tocqueville was right in that there has been little hostility between church and state and no inherent fear of the religious denomination. Since religion is thought of as a personal and inward phenomenon rather than as purely institutional, there is underneath all the institutional differences a devotion to the common good which deemphasizes peculiar items of belief. This can be seen in two dimensions. First, there is a "public domain" to which all men belong and in which they act. Men are simultaneously Jews or Christians, and local, state, national, and world citizens. They function in a variety of cultural contexts in which they are inextricably involved. To each of these areas—and simultaneously—they bring their own history and commitments. Second, there is a religious substratum in American national life which Professor Bellah has labeled "civil religion."[8] Civil religion does not mean a concordat between Church and State, but rather represents the inwardness of the citizen who is at work in the secular realm. This faith is expressed in the myths, symbols, ceremonies, and rituals of the national life. It has, for example, been expressed in presidential proclamations from Washington to Johnson. These proclamations and political addresses express certain elements of religious orientation which most Americans share, which have played significant roles in history, and which provide some dimension to the fabric of American life. As Bellah points out, "the separation of church and state has not denied to the political realm a religious dimension."

An anatomy of religious life in this public domain would show a remarkable blend of religious faiths agreeing on paramount political, social, and moral issues. This has been dramatically illustrated in the civil rights movements, for example, when priests and nuns, rabbis and Protestant clergymen found themselves walking arm in arm to Selma and to Washington, in Harlem and in Watts, and lobbying for civil rights legislation in the halls of Congress. In instances like these, high religion witnessed to the racial universalism of faith and united in common humanity despite theological differences.

The belief that the "religious life" is not confined to the religious institution has characterized religion's role in the public domain throughout American history. Religious organizations have spawned voluntary associations to fight against some social evil, or for some cause, be it slavery, liquor, war, or Sunday observance. Judaism has its Anti-Defamation League, its B'nai B'rith and hosts of others; Protestantism has its YMCA's and YWCA's, it has had its abolitionist societies or peace unions; Roman Catholicism has had its Holy Name societies, its Mariological societies, and many other forms of expression for the lay apostolate. Indeed the voluntary character of the denomination as an organization of purposeful activity has placed great emphasis on pragmatic achievement.

Not only has this resulted in strong social action measures but it has also developed a strong institutional flavor which expends vast energies and monies on the institution itself in building programs which some have called its "edifice complex"; and it has become an organization of immense power and prestige, characterized largely by social values. Whether or not this means the bringing of the dimension of the Holy to American life is another question. But there is impressive evidence that the influence of religious institutions has been pervasive in political life.

Indeed, one of the most influential theologians in America defined the goal of the Church "as the increase among men of the love of God and neighbor." He went on to say that these "two loves" are inseparable; they are Law and Gospel. "Historically they are associated in Judaism and Christianity, in the two tables of the Ten Commandments, in the double summary of the law offered by Jesus, in apostolic preaching, in the theology and ethics of Catholic and Protestant churches."[9] This definition has been widely accepted by both Jews and Christians as a proper definition of their purposive goal.

THE CLIMATE OF RELIGIOUS THOUGHT.   One would expect the American context to have profound influence also on the basic themes and shape of religious thought, since as we have said theological discourse has no discontinuous mode of existence; and this is the case. Of course, the basic shape of theological thought in America has been determined by those social and intellectual forces that have shaped all western thought. But this unique context has given American religious thought its own special style and provided it with its specific themes. Traditionally, American religious thought has been characterized by a special genius for drawing its main strength from the categories of the western intellectual tradition: the biblical and theological mythos. It has then turned to an analysis of the American scene, an analysis carried on with the help of all other available disciplines such as philosophy, art, literature, and politics. And with these two sources of knowledge it has attempted to reexpress its motifs in categories and modes of thought relevant to its time and place. This has given American thought a pragmatic character which has as often as not turned to analyzing the American community and its destiny and to a preoccupation with ethical questions. All of the great native American theologians, including the greatest of them all, Jonathan Edwards, have dwelt upon or included the moral or ethical conclusions in their reflections, as the writings of the Niebuhr brothers will testify. An interesting illustration of this tendency occurred in a recent newspaper story about John Courtney Murray, the distinguished Jesuit theologian "Father Murray's lifelong study was the interaction of his native America and Roman Catholicism, which caused some of the critics in his church to complain . . . that the Jesuit was more American than Catholic. It was a point Father Murray did not argue. It was his view that Catholics should make a major contribution to American society in its spiritual crisis and once . . . observed 'the question is not whether Catholicism is safe for democracy, but whether democracy is safe for Catholicism.' "[10]

Contemporary Religious Thought

When we attempt to analyze the contemporary scene it soon becomes apparent that it is easier to make historical comments and describe trends of the past than it is to say anything definitive about what is now going on. The vagaries and diversities of current developments and reactions in western religious thought are simply too great for more than mere mention. This fact becomes patently clear when one confronts the American situation. Comments are almost bound to appear inconsistent and contradictory. With that reservation in mind, however, we can then make several random observations. First, the theologians and philosophers who have most influenced the present climate of thought are now either very old or deceased; and this is basically true for all three traditions. We need only mention in passing those on the American scene: Paul Tillich and H. Richard and Reinhold Niebuhr among the Protestants; Jacques Maritain, John Courtney Murray, and Gustave Weigle among the Roman Catholics; and Kaufmann Kohler, Solomon Schechter, and Mordecai Kaplan among the Jews. If we assay the European influences on American thought the same thing is true. Among the Protestants, Karl Barth, Rudolf Bultmann, and Dietrich Bonhoeffer; in Judaism, Martin Buber, Franz Rosenzweig, and Leo Baeck; and while the statement is not quite so valid for Roman Catholicism we can still mention the names of Gabriel Marcel and Henri de Lubac, for example. By and large these are among the seminal thinkers who have set the basic tone of twentieth-century theological thought. Their successors, if any, are not yet identifiable.[11]

Second, as paradoxical as it may seem, theological thought has never been as vibrant, as popular, or as relevant as it is now. ". . . there is a new sense of the importance of theological questions, a new concern for fundamental issues, and a new desire to think things out creatively from the very beginning, for ourselves and for our own ages," says one of the rising younger theologians.[12] Again, this is true for all three traditions. But, interestingly enough, this concern for theological issues is not confined to religious traditions. Our observation that religious action is not confined to religious institutions can be said with equal cogency about religious thought. The intellectual enterprise in religion has widespread appeal and validity for many people beyond the bounds of the church, synagogue, or theological seminary. Religious thought has become a respectable academic discipline in universities—and especially in state universities; and, moreover, religious thought and literature are now being introduced in the curriculum of many public secondary schools. The reasons for this development is a subject for considerable speculation. Whatever the reason, it is still true that many people who have never regarded the religious life of institutions as a possibility for themselves, in fact have evaluated them as altogether moribund and intellectually stagnant, still find the "objective" study of religion a fascinating and worthwhile endeavor. In any event, we see here a happening that is not altogether dissimilar to the movement of religious scholarship into the academies during the Middle Ages.

Then, too, the ecumenical movement, associated as it is with the technological and moral revolution of the twentieth century, has contributed to the changed intellectual climate both within and beyond the religious communities. Jews and Christians, like everyone else, take for granted that the old, familiar institutional symbols have lost or are fast losing their significance, and they are asking what can take their place. What Judaism or Christianity means is as much of a problem for them as for others. Even the nonreligious, for whom active participation in one of the religious traditions was nonessential but who regarded the institution as an important conserving element in the culture, are now alarmed about the state of the Jewish-Christian tradition. What is to fill the void in the heart of the culture if Church and Synagogue cease to be significant? Both, faced with the unique historical possibility of a totally humanized and technically controlled world where the distinctions between sacred and profane— between the unknown, mysterious and unpredictable on the one hand and the new, controllable and predictable on the other—are fast disappearing, see that the deepest ecumenical problem is the common search for intelligible meaning for believer and nonbeliever alike.

With these general comments we may now proceed with some trepidation to single out some specific themes from the many and conflicting strands of present-day theological reflection and discussion. It is difficult to isolate clearly discernible themes, but from the many possible we will choose three as somewhat indicative of the contemporary theological climate. They are: the "problem" of God, the importance of tradition, and myth and symbol as characteristic terms.

THE "PROBLEM" OF GOD.   The "problem" of God is one basic theme clearly discernible in all theological writing and discussion. The word "problem" is used advisedly, for this is precisely what the idea of God has become for modern man. It is exceedingly difficult, if not impossible, for man in this era to discern any dimension of the "Holy" or of transcendence in the world. Therefore, it has become commonplace to assert that the God of Judaism, Christianity, and Islam is unbelievable to the contemporary mind for whom such talk is clearly absurd. America is without a single holy place or pilgrimage; the plains, the cities, indeed the universe itself is devoid of mystery, free from any sense of transcendence customary to primitive man. If the Middle Ages was a time when man had just about all the answers to all the worthwhile questions, now he not only doubts the answers, but has lost faith in the questions. So the argument goes.

This theme was most strikingly expressed in the letters and papers of Dietrich Bonhoeffer, a German martyr to Hitler, and a seminal influence today. Following Pierre Simon LaPlace, Bonhoeffer asserted that God is an unnecessary hypothesis for the man of today. In "a world come of age," man must learn to get along without God and develop a nonreligious interpretation of life.[13] These startling and unsystematic statements started a whole train of writing known variously as "Secular Christianity," "Honest to God," and "Death of God" theologies.

Whether or not T. S. Eliot was correct when he wrote: "But it seems that something has happened that has never happened before: . . ./ Men have left God not for other gods, but for no god; . . ."[14] is a subject for lively debate. As Bonhoeffer himself observed, the present situation is the completion of a process that began in the thirteenth century with an emphasis on the autonomy of man. The theme resounded in the nineteenth century, especially with Nietzsche, and it may go back to the Psalmist in Babylon. What is new, however, and therefore all the more interesting, is the extent of the theme in contemporary popular writing and conversation. One of the ironies, however, surrounding all of the "God is dead" talk is that "God" has never been so much alive in the intellectual world. Once again the doctrine of God has become a lively subject of theological reflection and discussion in ways seldom known since the medieval period.

THE IMPORTANCE OF TRADITION.   Within the religious traditions, however, there is growing dissatisfaction with the "secular" and "new" theologies with which many theologians were once fascinated. They are now seen to be not so much theologies as the raw material from which theology must work. The "aggiornimento" of the Second Vatican Council has unleashed a flood of theological writings, especially among younger thinkers of all traditions, concerned with the nature of the Church and its relationships to the modern world. There is a new sense of the importance of tradition which prompts the exploration of the idea of Christian community and its future development and relevance to a modern technological society.

This concern is clearly manifest in Judaism. Traditionally, Jews have frowned upon theology as a "Christian pastime," but that there is a rising tide of theological interest among Jews is beyond quesion. *Commentary*, one of the most influential Jewish periodicals, recently ran a symposium on "The State of Jewish Belief," in which 38 rabbis participated.[15] Although no entelechy is clearly discernible in their statements, they do give indications of the shape of Jewish thought. On the one hand, Jewish thought is formed by the indescribable suffering and fate of the Jewish people in tragic events of the twentieth century symbolized by that deadful name of Auschwitz, a suffering mitigated in part by a hope fulfilled in establishment of the State of Israel; and on the other hand, by the erosive effects of emancipation. These concerns are expressed in theological terms. Arthur Cohen indicates why this is so.[16] "The Dynamics of Emancipation" makes this the first generation of Jews who are free to choose *not* to be Jews. It is therefore possible that Jews could survive, but not Judaism. But Cohen believes that Judaism has a mission to complete and it is, consequently, crucial for Judaism as well as for Jews to survive. This means a return to the sources of Judaism, to a tradition which in its classical sense understood itself to be a revealed religion realizing its present meaning out of a memory which goes back to Abraham and forward to the Messianic Age for the whole of humanity.

This last comment is indicative of the new sense of the importance of tradition which characterizes not only Jewish thought, but much Christian thought as well. Tradition is the sense of the total past as being present now. It is a time bond, so to speak, with the most ancient past which points the way to the future through the present. In short, there is a growing recognition that contemporary statements are meaningless apart from their classical understandings. In this perspective, the present is not definable and the future direction is not clear apart from an understanding of the genesis of the tradition.

MYTH AND SYMBOL.   There are those, of course, who think of the twentieth century as a completely novel epoch for which historical understanding is irrelevant, or at least an uncertain guide. But there are an increasing number of scholars who are convinced that the present era in its formal structures, if not in concrete detail, is very much more like the first-century world than it is like the rational world view which has been the mainstream of man's recent heritage. It is not strange, then, that a dominant interest of recent religious thought should center around biblical science and theology, with a special emphasis upon historical studies, hermeneutical problems, and a new understanding of the relevance of myth and symbol as the language of interpretation.

This is a generation, as these thinkers interpret it, which thinks in gestalts and is looking for a holistic view of human identity and the future of man. This is a point of view to which the Hebraic and Christian messianic elements are not foreign; and the present world situation makes the apocalyptic perspective on history rather appealing. In brief, say these Jewish and Christian thinkers, this is a generation which can take myth and symbol seriously. Therefore, myth and symbol must be the characteristic terms of theological thought and discourse. Today, theological thought "views symbols as the logically indispensable way for the whole of being to be represented to man and man to develop total responses, total attitudes toward reality. . . . The question is . . . which set of symbols is most appropriate to the fathomless mystery which lies at the heart of things. . . ."[17]

THE JUDEO-CHRISTIAN TRADITION

The preceding description of the American matrix sets the stage for a further discussion of the relationships between the Jewish and Christian communities. As we have seen, the American community accepts not only the validity but also the desirability of religious and cultural pluralism as the condition for the emerging human community, a condition which can provide a genuine dialogue for the cross-fertilization of a variety of points of view and the salutary correction of each. Throughout this book we have placed equal emphasis upon the common documents, the common background, and the common beliefs held by Christians and Jews as well as upon the vast gulfs which separate the traditions intellectually and religiously. For nineteen hundred years the relationships between the two have been subtle and shifting, and for most of that time each has faced the other as an enemy. It is only in the last two hundred years that a radical change has marked the attitude of the two with the development of something like mutual tolerance. In view of this history and the vast gulfs which have separated the traditions, is it possible to speak meaningfully of a Judeo-Christian tradition?

The term, Judeo-Christian tradition or heritage, has received currency only in the modern period and has gained in usage in the twentieth century. Matthew Arnold first popularized the idea that the two sources of western culture were Hebraism and Hellenism, a point of view which has widespread acceptance, but which also is subject to considerable misunderstanding. To the Jew, for example, the term is often nothing more than a polite euphemism for "Christian culture." This is illustrated in two recent books by prominent Jewish authors: Ben Zion Bokser, *Judaism and the Christian Predicament* and Robert Gordis, *Judaism in a Christian World.*[18] Then too it is sometimes used as a polite term to cover the embarrassment of a culture that deemphasizes the importance of particular beliefs and differences. This point of view widely held in the eighteenth and nineteenth centuries particularly is illustrated dramatically in a story about Moses Mendelssohn, one of the prominent fathers of Jewish modernity. About two hundred years ago, so the story goes, Moses Mendelssohn was trying to secure the right of residence in the city of Berlin, where Jews were not allowed to live. The cultural adviser to Frederick the Great asked the King to grant Mendelssohn the right of residence in the following words: "An intellectual who is a bad Catholic begs an intellectual who is a bad Protestant to grant the privilege of residence in Berlin to an intellectual who is a bad Jew. There is so much intellectualism in all this that reason must be on the side of the request." Here of course is a common assumption that reason is the enemy of tradition and must overlook subtle or profound differences.

But the Judeo-Christian tradition is a valid term only if it symbolizes the symbiotic (living together in harmony to mutual good) existence of both Judaism and Christianity. The only basis for understanding, let alone living together, is to recognize that Judaism and Christianity are both authentic traditions in their own right, not foils for one another, and therefore each has genuine claim to legitimacy. It is of decisive importance for the dialogue between Judaism and Christianity to understand both the elements of identity and similarity and the elements of difference and opposition, and for each to forego any claims to objective superiority or incomparability. Judaism and Christianity must both be seen as authentic manifestations of religious truth, that are not so much opposites as on the same side, and not so much opposed as different. Neither can give up the claims laid upon it by its separate witness to truth. They represent one truth, although their modes of participation in truth may differ, and they have irreducibly different, yet organically related, functions in the divine economy. Franz Rosenzweig, a German Jew who has had seminal influence on recent American Jewish thought, and who was once himself tempted to convert to Christianity, puts it this way: "Israel: to represent, in time and history, the eternal Kingdom of God, Christianity: to bring itself and the world toward that goal."[19] Thus the meaning of the Judeo-Christian tradition does not lie in a completely secularized and traditionless society, but in one in which, as the prophet put it, the farmers will "write the name of YHWH on the bells of the horses" (Zechariah 14:20). There are, of course, people who deny the authenticity of this linkage, but the frightful events of the twentieth century are causing more and more Jewish and Christian thinkers to become aware of the bond between Judaism and Christianity, in spite of the continued existence of some tragic barriers.

In the continuing discussion more highly sophisticated theological understanding would be useful to both Jews and Christians. It would be helpful to recognize that American denominations of whatever tradition are not intellectually disciplined theological communities. Therefore each particular denomination is often as diversified internally as the whole Church or all the synagogues would be. These differentiations are internal and very often institutions are capable of holding together tremendously conflicting points of view. The time when one could identify theological position by ecclesiastical label is gone. It is possible for example on the theological level for Rabbi A. J. Heschel and the Reverend Paul Tillich and Father John Courtney Murray to have as much or more in common with each other than they each have with members of their own tradition. But as Rabbi Gordis points out: "A living tradition is never monolithic, but will always contain currents and crosscurrents, and even strongly antagonist tendencies within itself which nevertheless are authentic components of the tradition."[20] A cursory study of western history, and especially of the last decade, should convince everyone of that. We now know about the interplay of sects and sectarians in the first century, and of the vast variety of thought within Judaism. Of all the sects in the Judaism of the first century only two have survived in our time: rabbinic Judaism and Christianity, each of which is a distinctive way of human existence. Whether one is better or worse than the other neither Jews nor Christians are in a position to say. Hence they must resist the temptation to substitute defense for interpretation.

The tendency to emphasize the uniqueness of one over the other, to define one as "true" as against the other, is to erect unnecessary walls of division. Not only does overemphasis upon the conflicting strands of the traditions confuse the proximate with the ultimate, but it makes it impossible for men to understand that these strands simply constitute part of a larger pattern. This fact at least about Judaism and Christianity has been demonstrated by the scholarly enterprise when it has been freed of its dogmatic presuppositions. A person raised in a nonwestern culture, for example, would doubtless be more impressed by the elements of identity and similarity than by the divergent elements. He would be able to see the common history, common Scriptures, the character of God revered, and the common ethical codes. He would see these monotheistic traditions in marked contrast to his own eastern religio-philosophical traditions and its variety of forms. When, therefore, Christians are tempted to picture the synagogue with a sacred scroll in her hand and a bandage over her eyes, they should remember that they too belong to this prophetic tradition which prays for the day when "God shall be One and his name one" (Zechariah 14:9), which signifies that one God is really worshiped under many forms, in very different but authentic cults. The question is whether Jews and Christians can stand together in a Judeo-Christian tradition and thus enrich each other's experience in that tradition and respect it and each other even more. This is the thrust of Martin Buber's moving statement made before a German missionary organization in 1930:

It behooves both you and us to hold inviolably fast to our own true faith, that is to our own deepest relationship to truth. It behooves both of us to show a religious respect for the true faith of the other. This is not what is called "tolerance," for our task is not to tolerate each other's waywardness but to acknowledge the real relationship in which both stand to the truth. Whenever we both, Christian and Jew, care more for God himself than for our images of God, we are united in the feeling that our Father's house is differently constructed than our human models take it to be.[21]

The Messianic era will see the unity of the traditions and worship realized. "In those days ten men from the nations of every tongue shall take hold of the robe of a Jew saying, let us go with you, for we have heard that God is with you" (Zechariah 8:23).

THE ECUMENICAL THRUST

The term ecumenical, from the Greek word, oikoumenikos, meaning universal, world-wide, is a household word in Christian circles. It refers to a movement of the last two hundred years, and especially of the last fifty years, for unification of all Christian bodies. William Temple, the former Archbishop of Canterbury, said it was the "great new fact of our time" and it is widely regarded in the West as "The greatest event of our century in the field of religious history."[22] This is the assessment of George Tavard, himself an active participant and *Peritus* (expert) in the Protestant-Roman Catholic conversations of the last decade. He goes on to say that "If Catholic and Orthodox would unite tomorrow, it would be the best thing that would have happened in the last nine hundred years. If Catholics and Protestants would unite, it would be the best thing that would have happened in the last five centuries."[23]

The ecumenical movement, then, refers first of all to the movements among Protestants for unification and especially the actions of the World

Council of Churches. But in the last five years it has been associated more dramatically with the Second Vatican Council, which was called by Pope John XXIII as an "aggiornamento" or the updating and internal renewal of the Roman Catholic Church. It must be called a movement for unification rather than reunification, since none of the ecumenical councils in the first seven centuries of the Christian era were totally ecumenical or totally successful (see Chapter 2).

But the term not only refers to the unification of a worldwide Christian Church including Orthodox, Roman Catholics, and Protestants, but it has come more and more to mean also a genuine dialogue with Judaism. And as we have seen, this must be a dialogue with a living Judaism, that is, the contemporary Jew, who is no more exclusively a product of the Old Testament than is the Christian himself, and who has a postbiblical history obviously as long as that of the Christian.

But the ecumenical movement cannot stop with the federal union of Christians nor even with the Christian tradition. It has also to search together with leaders of Islam, Hinduism, Buddhism and the world's other living religions to see if there is any way of translating the great conceptions of Judaism and Christianity in such a way that genuine exchange can take place in the spirit of authentic catholicity. Genuine catholicity means that the dialogue must rise above the temptation of Jews and Christians to consider themselves first of all as members of the national and cultural society rather than of the worldwide community. Nor should ecumenical dialogue devolve into a weapon for the defense of western civilization or a bulwark for the western way of life. Even more, ecumenism must mean a radical grappling with the spiritual and cultural revolution of our time. All religious faiths must face their responsibility to share in man's struggle for a world neighborhood.

For there is a pervasive conviction that twentieth-century man is living in a time of general shift in culture more fundamental then any since agriculture and herding replaced food-gathering and hunting. And this revolution is not only in the outward forms of culture, but in standards of value, thought, and conduct. Men everywhere are becoming conscious of new dimensions of human existence which form the matrix for ferment and revolution. Men have a new consciousness of history, not only the universal history of mankind but also the special historical struggles of each nation, race, and group to define its particular missions and vocation in the world. An ecumenicity that is real must grapple with this radical fact.

It is not enough to talk about ecumenicity among Protestants in defense of Protestantism; it is not enough to talk of ecumenicity between Jews and Christians in defense of the Christian tradition. It is not even enough to talk about ecumenicity among all religions against the forms of secularism in defense of religion. Such attempts are largely irrelevant. This revolution in standards of value, thought, and conduct involve criteria of judgment so that all yardsticks—all canons of culture—are changing. The canon of the west is being displaced by the canon of the globe; a hierarchy of values is being displaced by a spectrum of values. All of these changes point not only to the fact of globalism but also voice an aspiration for the unity of mankind.

How effective can Judaism and Christianity be in contributing to this aspiration? The biblical religions have had their moments of finest insight in just such cultural revolutions. Historically, they have had the energy and imagination to develop belief systems, ritual patterns, and institutional strength to contribute to the coherent ordering of life, clarity of thought, and direction of human conduct in ways that came to have universal validity. Monotheism, the legacy of Israel, asserts that there is a unity which pervades existence; that above and beneath all particularisms and finite forms there is the loftiest of all unities, the unity of God, bound to no locale or people. And Christianity, emerging from Judaism with this conviction, expanded in larger and larger concentric circles to become a religion embracing the world.

If God is, as biblical faith believes, the God of truth, then all truth must be of one piece. It is the function of any religion to affirm this truth that transcends man and to direct man toward that truth. As the content of religious truth transcends historical forms, so must its expression in western religions, and in all other religions, be freed from their accidental links in such a way as to be translatable in all cultural contexts.

The worldwide consciousness of the twentieth century confronts religion with a theological task which must take seriously the root meaning of the ecumene, a task which is universal in scope. It is a task no less than that of showing the profound relevance of God's acts and man's responses to a technological culture which now embraces the world.

NOTES

1. Daniel D. Williams, "Tradition and Experience in American Theology," in James W. Smith and Leland Jamieson, eds., *The Shaping of American Religion* (Princeton: Princeton University Press, 1961), pp. 446–447.

2. Ralph Barton Perry, *Puritanism and Democracy* (New York: Harper Torchbook, 1944), p. 349.

3. Reinhold Niebuhr, *The Nature and Destiny of Man* (London: Nisbit, 1948), Vol. II, p. 225.

4. Cf. John Courtney Murray, *We Hold These Truths* (New York: Sheed & Ward, 1960), Part I; and his *The Problem of Religious Freedom* (London: Geoffrey Chapman, Deacon Books, 1965). See also Walter M. Abbott, S.J., general editor, *The Documents of Vatican II*, trans. Very Rev. Msgr. Joseph Gallagher (New York: America Press, 1966), pp. 672–696; and John Cogley, ed., *Religion in America* (New York: America Press, 1958).

5. See Sidney Mead, *The Lively Experiment* (New York: Harper, 1963), p. 104 for a definition of denomination as "a voluntary association of like-hearted and like-minded individuals, who are united on the basis of common beliefs for the purpose of accomplishing tangible and defined objectives."

6. See Ernst Troeltsch, *The Social Teachings of the Christian Churches* (London: Allen and Unwin, 1931), Vol. II, Chapter 3.

7. See Alexis de Tocqueville, *Democracy in America* (New York: Knopf, 1956), I, 3–14.

8. Robert N. Bellah, "Civil Religion in America," in *Daedalus*, Winter, 1967, pp. 1–21.

9. H. Richard Niebuhr, *The Purpose of the Church and Its Ministry* (New York: Harper, 1956), pp. 31, 33.

10. From his obituary in *The New York Times*, August 17, 1967.

11. Titles from the works of nearly all of these will be found in the Select Bibliography following each chapter.

12. Langdon Gilkey, "Sources of Protestant Thought in America," *Daedalus*, Winter, 1967, p. 97. This whole issue is devoted to "Religion in America," and should be read for clues to the new voices in theological thought.

13. Most of Bonhoeffer's writings have been collected and are being translated posthumously. See especially *Letters and Papers From Prison*, ed. Eberhardt Bethge, trans. R. H. Fuller (London: Student Christian Movement Press, 1953), pp. 145–146; 162–163; 178–81.

14. From T. S. Eliot, "Choruses from 'The Rock,'" VII, *The Complete Poems and Plays*, (New York: Harcourt, Brace, 1952), p. 108.

15. *Commentary*, August, 1966.

16. See Arthur A. Cohen, "Why I Choose to Be a Jew," in Nahum Glatzer, ed., *The Dynamics of Emancipation* (Boston: Beacon, 1965), p. 251. For a review of Jewish thought see Cohen's *The Natural and Supernatural Jew* (New York: Random House, Pantheon Books, 1962).

17. George A. Lindbeck, "The New Vision of the World and the Ecumenical Revolution," in *Religious Education*, LXII, No. 2 (March–April, 1967), p. 87.

18. Ben Zion Bokser, *Judaism and the Christian Predicament* (New York: Knopf, 1967), and Robert Gordis, *Judaism in a Christian World* (New York: McGraw-Hill, 1966). The latter book, however, accepts the authenticity of the term and we are greatly indebted to it for profound insights into the meaning of the Judeo-Christian tradition.

19. Quoted from Samuel Bergman, *Faith and Reason: An Introduction to Modern Jewish Thought*, trans. and ed. Alfred Jospe (Washington: B'nai B'rith Hillel Foundations, 1961), p. 69.

21. Martin Buber, "The Two Foci of the Jewish Soul" in *Israel and the World* (New York: Schocken, 1963), p. 40.

22. George Tavard, *Protestant Hopes and the Catholic Responsibility* (Notre Dame, Ind.: Fides, Dome Edition, 1964), p. 9.

23. *Ibid.*, p. 29.

SELECT BIBLIOGRAPHY

COGLEY, JOHN, ed. *Religion in America*. New York: Meridian Books, 1958.
Daedalus, Winter, 1967. "Religion in America."

GORDIS, ROBERT. *Judaism in a Christian World*. New York: McGraw-Hill, 1966.

MARTY, MARTIN E., and DEAN G. PEERMAN, ed. *New Theology Nos. 1, 2, 3, 4.* New York: Macmillan, 1964–67. 4 vols.

MELAND, BERNARD E. *The Realities of Faith: The Revolution in Cultural Forms.* New York: Oxford University Press, 1962.

MURRAY, JOHN COURTNEY, S.J. *We Hold These Truths.* New York: Sheed & Ward, 1960.

NIEBUHR, H. RICHARD. *The Kingdom of God in America.* New York: Harper Torchbook, 1959.

NIEBUHR, REINHOLD. *The Irony of American History.* New York: Charles Scribner's Sons, 1952.

NOVECK, SIMON, ed. *Contemporary Jewish Thought.* Washington, D.C.: B'nai B'rith, 1963.

OLMSTEAD, CLIFTON E. *History of Religion in the United States.* Englewood Cliffs, N.J.: Prentice-Hall, 1960.

SCHARPER, PHILIP, ed. *Torah and Gospel.* New York: Sheed & Ward, 1966.

SMITH, H. SHELTON, ROBERT T. HANDY, and LEFFERTS A. LOETSCHER. *American Christianity: An Historical Interpretation with Representative Documents.* New York: Charles Scribner's Sons, 1960. 2 vols.

SMITH, JAMES W., and LELAND JAMIESON, eds. *Religion in American Life.* Princeton, N.J.: Princeton University Press, 1961. 4 vols. See Vol. I, *The Shaping of American Religion.*

TAVARD, GEORGE H. *Two Centuries of Ecumenism.* Notre Dame, Ind.: Fides, 1960.

Glossary of Terms

This Glossary is designed to give ready access to brief definitions of some terms which are frequently used in the study of religions in general and Judaism and Christianity in particular. The words within each entry which are capitalized refer to other entries in the Glossary.

AGGIORNAMENTO.   Italian for a "bringing up to date" or "making contemporary," used specifically to refer to certain "progressive" developments within the Roman Catholic Church in recent decades.

ALEXANDRIA, SCHOOL OF.   This term refers to several Christian biblical scholars and EXEGETES who were related to the principal CATECHETICAL school there during the second and third centuries C.E. and whose work was united by a common methodology. They practiced largely ALLEGORICAL EXEGESIS, which had been introduced into the Jewish-Christian tradition principally by Philo Judaeus of Alexandria (first century), in order to make biblical Christianity intelligible to the Hellenistic intellectual world. The most important members of this school were Clement of Alexandria (d. ca. 215) and Origen (ca. 182–251). The latter especially sought to give Christianity full scientific credence in terms of the dominant Neoplatonic philosophy.

ALLAH.   Arabic for "god," divine being, a word used by Moslems to refer to the One God of the Patriarchs, Moses and the other prophets, Jesus, and Mohammed, His true Prophet.

ALLEGORY, ALLEGORICAL EXEGESIS.   Allegory is a method of literary presentation wherein one thing is said but another is meant to be understood. An allegory is a construction of this sort in which every detail is meant to be read in a symbolic fashion. Allegorical EXEGESIS is a method of interpreting biblical texts which assumes this manner of presentation to have been that of the authors of Scripture. The allegorical exegete therefore looks everywhere for a hidden, more sublime meaning than that presented in the plain sense of the text. This method was first used by the Stoics to interpret away the anthropomorphisms of Homeric myths, by Philo Judaeus to do the same for the Hebrew Scriptures; it enjoyed great currency in Christian circles in the Middle Ages and thereafter. See ALEXANDRIA, SCHOOL OF.

AMORAIM (sing. AMORA). Hebrew for "speakers," rabbis so called because
they addressed themselves orally and extemporaneously (though not im-
promptu) to the MISHNAH and to the written TORAH. The Amoraim flourished from the closing of the MISHNAH (ca. 200 C.E.) to the fifth century
C.E. They were instrumental in bringing to completion the TALMUDIC
tradition: the conversations and disputations which they carried on in the
YESHIBOT (Academies) of Babylonia and Jerusalem are recorded in the
GEMARA or Talmud proper; they were also responsible for many of the major
MIDRASHIM. In addition to the SOPHERIM (scribes) who recorded their
disputations, they were assisted by "living memories," men called TANNAIM,
whose task it was to recall the tradition of the great Tannaitic rabbis. The
Amoraim generally carried on the mishnic attempt to render Torah intelligible and relevant in the new Hellenistic cultural situation, but they
emphasized HAGGADAH as well as HALAKAH.

ANTIOCH, SCHOOL OF. A school and a tradition of EXEGESIS and biblical
scholarship which flourished in Antioch during the fourth and fifth centuries
C.E. The members of this school were under the influence of Jewish exegetes
and therefore practiced a more TYPOLOGICAL and literal kind of exegesis than
the SCHOOL OF ALEXANDRIA, whom they opposed. Diodorus (?–394), Theo-
dore of Mopsuestia (d. 428), Chrysostom (346–407), and Nestorius were
among the most prominent members of this school; and their methodology
was heavily influential upon Jerome, great exegete and translator of the Bible
into the Latin version known as the VULGATE.

APOCALYPSE, APOCALYPTIC. *Apocalypsis* is Greek for REVELATION. As well as
denoting in particular the last book of the NEW TESTAMENT, apocalypse
refers more generally to any work of a genre of writings which flourished
between ca. 200 B.C.E. and 350 C.E. in and around Palestine. These writings
usually portrayed the imminent ESCHATON in fine detail, but in highly
symbolic, allusive, and ALLEGORICAL language.

APOCRYPHA, APOCRYPHAL LITERATURE. The Greek *apokryphos* means hidden;
its English equivalent, apocryphal, usually means "of dubitable authenticity
or authority" and is usually applied to literature or tradition. "*The* Apocrypha" refers to a discrete body of sacred literature of contested authenticity
and antiquity which is often included along with the canonical books of
Judaism and Christianity because of its moral and spiritual worth.

APOLOGETICS, APOLOGISTS. Apologetics, taken from the Greek word *apologia*,
"a speech in defense," is the theological discipline of reasonably defending or
justifying a religious position or conviction. "*The* Apologists" usually refers
to a group of second century (C.E.) Christian writers, the most important of
whom is Justin Martyr, who aimed to defend the new religion against certain
Roman and pagan slanders.

ATONEMENT (at-one-ment). Atonement, in both Christianity and Judaism,
connotes the restoration of a broken relationship between God and man. The
doctrine of atonement is as rich as the many ways in which divine-human
alienation and the overcoming of it are conceived. In Jewish theology TORAH
is the principal agency by which atonement for sins is accomplished; the

Christian doctrine of atonement focuses upon the righteous work of Jesus Christ.

BISHOP. In some parts of the early Christian church local leadership and governance were invested in one *episcopos* or "overseer." The "bishops" of prominent congregations tended to have influence and oversight over several lesser or newer congregations. Thus the episcopal form of church governance grew up: in the bishops have been traditionally vested the functions of assuring the ORTHODOXY of teaching and the general well-being of each congregation in his diocese. See also PRESBYTER and DEACON.

CANON (Greek for "measuring rod"). Canon means specifically that standard or norm of accepted tradition, especially written tradition ("Scripture") by which the development of additional subsequent tradition is sifted and judged.

CASUISTRY. In religion, cauistry is the application and adaptation of general moral principles to specific instances in which moral decisions must be made. Casuistry often results, therefore, in very fine distinctions and discriminations being made between cases: such extreme hairsplitting has been practiced in various periods by both Christians and Jews and has given the notion of casuistry negative connotations.

CATECHISM, CATECHUMENS. A catechism is usually a summary of Christian DOCTRINE and instruction in question and answer form; therefore, a course or book of doctrinal instruction in such form. Catechumens are those undergoing such a course of instruction.

CHRIST, CHRISTOLOGY. *Christos* is the literal Greek equivalent of the Hebrew MESSIAH; both mean "Anointed One (of God)." Most specifically, Christology denotes the DOCTRINE of the person, activity, and mission of Jesus of Nazareth, understood by Christians to be God's Messiah (Christ). More generally, however, Christology may be understood to mean the doctrine of the specific agency of God's salvation activity.

DEACON. The title *diakonos* was first applied in early Christian congregations to any "one who served"; it later came to be applied to a subordinate position, to those who assisted the PRESBYTER or the BISHOP in the administration of the congregation's affairs and who especially helped look after the material welfare of the members of the congregation.

DIASPORA. The Greek for "dispersion" (Hebrew *galut*) refers to those places outside Palestine to which Jews have been scattered over the centuries due to the vicissitudes of history. One can begin speaking of a Diaspora already in 721 B.C.E. with the deportation of the Samaritans; however, Diaspora refers especially to the Judaism-in-exile after the destruction of a Jewish national life in 70 C.E.

DOCTRINE. In general any instruction or thing which is taught may be called "doctrine"; therefore the term may apply to any part of a religious tradition. Those teachings or doctrines which are essential to a tradition are called DOGMA.

DOGMA, DOGMATICS. Dogma is religious DOCTRINE which defines, constitutes, is essential to a particular tradition. Therefore, adherence to the dogma of a tradition usually defines membership in that tradition. Judaism, however, has tended to have an a-dogmatic, even an anti-dogmatic tradition. Hence, *dogmatics*, the systematic study of those articles of doctrine which are dogma, has tended to be a peculiarly Christian discipline.

ECUMENICAL COUNCILS, ECUMENICAL MOVEMENT. Ecumenical means "universal" or having to do with "the whole (civilized) world" (Greek: *oikoumene*). In the PATRISTIC AGE "ecumenical" came to refer to the world of the whole Church. Thus, those councils are termed ecumenical which have involved all the BISHOPS of the (Roman Catholic) Church. The ecumenical movement aims variously at reconstituting, in some form, a unity among the whole Christian world, or at constituting a unity among the religions of the whole world.

EPISTLE. Greek for "letter." The epistolary form, used by Paul to communicate with early Christian churches, developed into a genre adopted by the authors of other didactic writings included in the NEW TESTAMENT.

ESCHATOLOGY, ESCHATOLOGICAL. Eschatology is the teaching or knowledge about the ESCHATON, the "last things"; in Western religions usually a doctrine describing the perfection of nature and history by God's activity at the end of historical time. Therefore, that which is eschatological has to do with the final perfection of creation, including humanity.

EUCHARIST. The principal Christian SACRAMENT and central drama of Christian LITURGICAL life is called by a name which comes from the Greek meaning "to give thanks," and it has a wealth of meaning for various traditions: the elements of bread and wine stand for material sustenance but also for the sacrificed body and blood of Jesus the Christ which give spiritual sustenance; celebration of the Eucharist is variously understood as a re-enactment of the Last Supper which Jesus shared with his disciples (Communion) and as the "unbloody" reenactment of the sacrifice of Jesus (esp. Roman Catholic). See TRANSUBSTANTIATION.

EXEGESIS. Generally the activity of interpreting any document; most properly applied to the activity and results of interpreting biblical and other sacred and authoritative texts. Exegetical methodology is called HERMENEUTICS.

FATHERS. In both Judaism and Christianity those who exercised a formative influence on the tradition are known as "the Fathers": among Jews the term refers to the great TALMUDIC RABBIS, especially the TANNAIM; among Christians the term refers to the great theologians and churchmen of the first five centuries C.E. See RABBINICAL AGE, PATRISTIC AGE.

GEMARA. Records of the discussions of the Palestinian and Babylonian AMORAIM on specific Tractates of the MISHNA, the Gemara ("completion") is the second and concluding part of the TALMUD. The Palestinian rabbis discussed more Tractates numerically, but some of their concerns were appropriate only to the Holy Land and their discussions were relatively briefer. Both groups of AMORAIM attempted to elaborate upon and interpret the Mishnah in such a way that it might be harmonized more both internally and also externally in relation to the written TORAH and the ever-changing cultural situation. The definition of Gemara is less clear than that of the written Torah and the Mishnah: the Amoraitic tradition continues only sporadically after the fifth century until the tenth century.

GNOSTICISM. Gnosticism, which flourished in the eastern part of the classical world during the second century C.E., may perhaps best be characterized as an ideology claiming that salvation is achieved primarily through *gnosis*, "(supernatural) knowledge." This ideology took on mystical, occult, or philosophical form as it attached itself to the established religions; for a time it threatened to swamp the claims of young Christianity that salvation was achieved through *pistis*, "faith." Gnostic tendencies have continued, from time to time, to plague both Christian and Jewish ORTHODOXY.

GOSPEL. This English term is used to translate the Greek *evangelion*, "good news," and designates: (1) the KERYGMATIC message of Christians about Jesus of Nazareth, the proclamation of salvation in his name; and (2) a genre of Christian writings which clothed the gospel message in a quasi-biographical form. Four specimens of this genre are considered authoritative by Christians and are included in the NEW TESTAMENT.

HAGGADAH. Generic term for all parts of the Scripture and the TALMUDIC literature which are not HALAKHA, it also describes that part of MIDRASH which is sheerly homiletical or narrative in character. Therefore, any nonlegal discourse in Scripture or in the rabbinical literature may be classified as HAGGADAH.

HALAKHAH (pl. HALAKHOT). Hebrew for, literally, a "walking," this term means "law." The imagery of Halakhah refers to that authoritative norm, to that which one must do in order to stay on the "way" or the "path" set out by God. Halakhah is, therefore, a genre of discourse which results in positive injunctions, distinctions, and exhortations relating to behavior. See HAGGADAH.

HASIDIM (Hebrew for "pious ones"). The name for the adherents of three different movements in Judaism: (1) a party during the Hasmonean period who observed the commandments of the TORAH rigorously; (2) an ethical movement in twelfth- and thirteenth-century Germany; (3) a modern religious and social movement spiritually revitalizing Eastern European Jewish piety. Hasidism emphasizes the omnipresence and omnipotence of God and attempts to give a mystical depth to ethical action. Hasidism has influenced such modern Jewish saints as Martin Buber.

HEBRAISM. This term describes the religion of the Hebrew patriarchs and the Hebrew people from the Call of Abraham (ca. 1750 B.C.E.) to the Mosaic Covenant and the explicit dedication of the people Israel to the God Yahweh. Hebraism was characterized by devotion and sacrifice to a God Who had not yet identified himself but who had revealed himself to the successive generations of Abraham, Isaac, and Jacob; it was succeeded by what may best be called YAHWISM.

HEBREW BIBLE. See TANAKH.

HERESY. What constitutes heresy is definable in a number of ways: heresy may be simply a doctrine which is not in conformity with ORTHODOXY; it may be a conscious and deliberate rejection of orthodox teaching and dogma; it may be the unbalanced and imprudent magnification of part of orthodox teaching to the slight of the rest of it.

HERMENEUTICS. Hermeneutics are generally the principles of interpretation of any document or work of literature; it has come to mean more specifically the principles by which Scripture is interpreted and understood. See EXEGESIS.

INCARNATION. The Christian DOCTRINE that in the person of Jesus of Nazareth the divine principle (however it may be conceived) took human shape and became flesh (Latin *carnis*). Since the fourth and fifth centuries the articulation of this doctrine has remained a central concern of CHRISTOLOGY.

JUDAISM. This term recognizes the religious nature of the development in Hebrew tradition following the Exile (after ca. 450 B.C.E.). It is from this period that one can talk properly about Judaism, a religion differentiating a more or less discrete tradition (TORAH). Judaism extends, therefore, from the inauguration of the Torah as the norm for Israel's total life under the leadership of Ezra, down through the classical period of Israel's religious development—the development of RABBINICAL JUDAISM and the TALMUDS, which have remained normative for Orthodox Jewry—to the present modern developments (Reform, Conservative, and Reconstructionist movements).

KABBALAH, KABBALISTS (Hebrew for "reception [of oral tradition]"). The Kabbalah is a body of mystical teaching and a mystical practice handed down orally in Judaism until the later Middle Ages, at which point the Kabbalah entered into the broader Western mystical and occult tradition. Kabbalistic theoretical teaching represents a secret WISDOM concerning the relationship of the divine being to the world and the quasi-alchemical relationship among all things; kabbalistic practice is a secret discipline in achieving mystic unity with the divine being and consequently with all things.

KERGYMA. A "proclamation"; specifically, the core of the original Christian proclamation affirming the saving life, death, and resurrection of Jesus of Nazareth.

KORAN. The sacred book of Islam, compiled by Mohammed's spiritual heirs from fragments of his inspired writings, the Koran is believed by Moslems to contain the completion of the revelation of ALLAH to men, a revelation which was contained in part in the TANAKH and in the NEW TESTAMENT.

LEGEND. A legend is a poetic portrayal of heroic deeds or lives such that historical truths may be illumined.

LITURGY (from the Greek for "public worship or service"). A liturgy is any particular form of public exercise or worship; a form of communal religious ritual. Sometimes liturgy refers especially to some form of EUCHARISTIC worship.

Logos. Greek for "word, discourse, reason," this term was used by early Christian writers to refer to the eternal and preexistent aspect of the nature of Christ, the second Person of the Trinity. The Logos is also that through which "all things were made" (John 1:3). The Logos in Christian thought has tended to take on some attributes of the Hebraic wisdom and Torah.

Masoretes (from the late Hebrew *masora*, "tradition"). During the period ca. 500–1000 C.E. the Masoretes, "traditionalists," were responsible for the maintenance and transmission of the text and tradition of the Tanakh. In order to make sure that none of the text was lost or altered in copying, the Masoretes divided it by chapters and verses and utilized various statistical devices.

Messiah. The title of Messiah, "Anointed One (of God)," was applied in ancient Israel to those chosen by God to conserve His people, for example, certain kings. During and after the Exile in Babylon and under the Roman rule, many Jews anticipated the coming of such a One to complete creation and initiate the Reign of Yahweh on earth. Christians believe Jesus of Nazareth to be this Coming Messiah ("Christ").

Midrash (pl. Midrashim). Hebrew for "study," "investigation," or "exposition," the term especially means a didactic interpretation or commentary upon Scripture, written Torah. Midrash may be either technical expository exegesis, or it may be homiletical narrative; but it is more often Haggadah than Halakhah. In general, "Midrash" can apply to any nonhalakhic commentary on Scripture, including most Christian commentary. It is frequently used in contrast to Mishnah, a method which has more to do with Halakhot as such. "*The* Midrash" applies particularly to, and sometimes is part of the titles of, certain specific books of commentary that are the literary deposit of the Tannaim and the Amoraim, the talmudic rabbis.

Mishnah. Literally "repetition," Mishnah is a technique and a curriculum for comprehensive study and instruction in Halakhah of some antiquity, developed to a high degree of systematization by the Tannaim. Instruction in the mishnic manner was particularly carried on in the Yeshibot, the Academies, and was introduced by rabbis of the Pharisee party into the synagogues. Mishnah is often contrasted to Midrash because of the former's preoccupation with halakhic form and substance. Halakoht were divided for convenience approximately according to subject matter into six Orders, subdivided into Tractates (63) and Chapters (523). The schema of Orders is attributed to the great rabbi Akiba (fl. 110–135); the Mishnah was definitively collated by Judah ha-Nasi (Judah the Nasi), a teacher so formidable that he is simply known as rabbi, about 200 C.E., marking the conclusion of the Tannaitic period. The authoritative Mishnah is the cornerstone of all other Talmudic literature and the common starting-point for both Talmuds.

MYTH, MYTHOLOGY.   A myth is a story about the activities of the gods or of God which portrays that Being or beings as entering into the course of human history and natural events. A myth is a story told to portray an existential truth, a truth that may be portrayed in no other way. Mythology is therefore a system of thought, a world-view, which supports and legitimates such a portrayal.

NEW TESTAMENT.   *Testamentum* is a Latin translation of the Greek word for "covenant." The early Christians called their writings by this name because they believed that in the blood of Jesus of Nazareth God had made a new covenant with His people, fulfilling the old Covenant. The TANAKH to which the new writings were joined, thus became the books of the old covenant or the OLD TESTAMENT. The New Testament contains books in historical form (4 GOSPELS plus Acts, the completion of Luke), didactic works (21 EPISTLES), and one APOCALYPSE.

OLD TESTAMENT.   The early Christians called the TANAKH the book of the "old covenant" or "testament" to indicate what they understood to be its relationship to the books of the NEW TESTAMENT.

ORDINATION.   Among Jews and Christians, ordination is the general term for the consecration of individuals (especially clergy) to a special office, task, or role performed for the religious community. Some Christian communions count ordination as one of the SACRAMENTS.

ORTHODOX, ORTHODOXY.   This term comes from the Greek word meaning "sound or correct opinion," and applies especially to religious or theological doctrinal opinion. It is therefore definable in dialectical relation to *heterodoxy* ("variant opinion") and HERESY. Orthodoxy has some special meanings in special contexts; it may mean: conforming to the accepted teaching, especially, in Christian theology, to the ecumenical church councils of the fourth and fifth centuries; pertaining to any of the (Greek, Russian, Syrian, etc.) Orthodox churches; pertaining to the (traditionalist) Orthodox movement in Judaism.

PASSOVER.   In Hebrew *pesach:* the festival celebrating and commemorating the sparing of Israelite first-born in Egypt during the plagues inflicted on the land by the wrath of YAHWEH.

PATRISTIC AGE, PATRISTICS.   The patristic age is the formative period of the great fathers (Latin *patri*) of the Church, roughly the second through the fifth centuries C.E.; patristics is the study of their theological writings.

PHARISEES (from the Hebrew *perushim,* "separated ones"). In postexilic Judaism the Pharisees were the party of religious liberalism and political idealism. They represented the democratizing influence of the SYNAGOGUES, the opening of the TORAH to include the oral tradition (issuing in the TALMUDS), and took a hard line against Roman oppression. In all this they opposed the patrician SADDUCEES over whom they triumphed after the fall of the Temple in 70 C.E. Normative JUDAISM is accordingly essentially Pharasaic. The anti-Semitism of early Christian writings was therefore frequently expressed as a polemic against the Pharisee party.

PRESBYTER. The first-century SYNAGOGUE congregations were governed by a body of men called *zaken*, "elders"; the earliest church adopted the Greek equivalent, *presbyteros*, to refer to one who performed an analogous role in the church congregation, namely the role of "oversight," a role which later and more generally became invested in BISHOPS.

RABBI (Aramaic meaning "my Master"). This title was used first during the first century to refer to a teacher of the TALMUD tradition who had been ORDAINED in Palestine itself; but it was later used to refer to anyone versed in the Talmudic learning who had been ordained by another rabbi to the function of jurist-scholar. The title now applies to one who may also perform the function of clergyman within the Jewish community.

RABBINICAL AGE, RABBINICAL JUDAISM. These terms refer to the period (ca. 500 B.C.E.–500 C.E.) and the religious outlook of the TANNAIM and AMORAIM who were responsible for the final codification of the TALMUD.

REVELATION. Revelation is the disclosure or "unveiling" of a mystery. Judaism and Christianity use the term to signify the self-disclosure of God's truth and person in certain paradigmatic historical events (special revelation) and through the regular processes of history and nature (general revelation).

SACRAMENT. A ritual or symbolic act, a visible sign which is believed by Christians to convey, to be a channel for the working of God's grace when it is performed according to the rubrics and ordinances established by church authority. Catholics designate seven sacraments—baptism, confirmation, confession, the eucharist, marriage, ordinations, extreme unction—and many Protestant churches count only two—Communion (Eucharist) and baptism. Judaism has no sacraments. The unqualified phrase *"the* Sacrament" refers ordinarily to the EUCHARIST.

SADDUCEES (from the Hebrew *zadokim*, "descendants of Zadok," high priest under David). In postexilic times during the Second Temple period, the Sadducees comprised the priestly and military ruling classes among the Jews. They were realists and "collaborators" with the Romans in politics, fundamentalist in religion. They opposed the religious liberalism of the PHARISAIC SCRIBES and rabbis who added the oral TORAH to the written; but when the temple was destroyed in 70 C.D., the Sadducee party fell permanently from influence in Judaism.

SAGA. An imaginative portrayal of heroic deeds and the movements of peoples illumining historical roots and the relationships between peoples. See LEGEND.

SANHEDRIN. A body of elders, largely from the SADDUCEN party, who seem to have exercised some religious and juridical and some quasiautonomous political powers among the Palestinian Jews from the third century B.C.E. to ca. 57 B.C.E., at which date the Sanhedrin was divided into several sub-assemblies and became an instrument of Roman rule.

SCRIBES. See SOPHER.

SEPTUAGINT (abbr. LXX, seventy). The LXX is a Greek translation of the

TANAKH and APOCRYPHA made in Alexandria in the third century B.C.E. (Old Testament) for the great library at Pharos by—as tradition has it—seventy-two Jewish elders in as many days (*septuaginta* is Greek for seventy). This translation became the foundation of Alexandrian DIASPORA Hebrew culture and became that version of the OLD TESTAMENT used by the earliest (Greek-speaking) Christians as their Bible.

SOPHER (pl. SOPHERIM). The scribes in the Judaic tradition are called literally "book-men" because their ultimate responsibility is to preserve and hand-copy the Scripture, the TORAH. In origin the remnants of a class of scribal civil servants, the Sopherim emerged into social and religious prominence during late exilic times (fifth century B.C.E.) as the keeping of the tradition assumed an importance apart from the disrupted temple worship. Ezra, promulgator of the Second Law (*Deutero-nomos*) was a scribe. The scribes figured prominently in the development of universal education through the SYNAGOGUE system, acting in concert with the rabbis. They acted as secretaries to the TANNAIM and AMORAIM, copying and disseminating their discussions. The sheerly technical aspects of copying became their preoccupation after the great RABBINIC AGE (ca. sixth century C.E.), and they continue to fulfill their function of hand-copying TORAH.

SOTERIOLOGY. This term especially denotes doctrine concerning the savior (Greek *Soter*), although it more generally refers to the whole of the activity of God on behalf of the salvation of His people and of mankind.

SYNAGOGUE (Greek for "assembly"). The principal institution of Judaism's communal religious life since the fall of the TEMPLE in 70 C.E. The synagogue had its roots in the experience of the Babylonian exile (586 B.C.E.). Gradually the local Sabbath prayer services and the study of TORAH carried on in the synagogue replaced temple sacrifice as the center of gravity of Jewish religiosity, especially in the DIASPORA.

SYNOPTIC GOSPELS (the SYNOPTICS). The GOSPELS of Matthew, Mark, and Luke are called the synoptic Gospels because they have among them a similar general view of the life and activity of Jesus; the fourth Gospel, John, has a very distinct and theological way of presenting the Gospel story.

TALMUD. This term itself is rich in English cognates: in its various aspects it connotes "study" as a theoretical activity in contrast to practice, but also "instruction" or "exposition," particularly of matters related to Scripture. There are two Talmuds, which have the MISHNAH in common: the one also contains the discussions of the Babylonian AMORAIM, the other the discussions of the Palestinian (Jerusalem) Amoraim. Therefore, Talmud refers properly to GEMARA, these later rabbinic discussions. The Babylonian Talmud is both the more extensive and the more authoritative of the two. The Talmud as a whole contains both HALAKHAH and HAGGADAH, by which means it serves as a norm for Jewish interpretation of the written TORAH. The talmudic literature as a corpus may be seen as an attempt on the part of the rabbis to comprehend and explicate the meaning of an originally agrarian Torah in the emergent urban and cosmopolitan culture, and the meaning of Judaism and Israel-in-Diaspora in the pluralistic Hellenistic world.

TANAKH. An acronymic term for the Hebrew Bible, whose principal divisions are the TORAH ("the Law" or the Pentateuch), Nebi'im ("the Prophets") and Khethubim ("the Writings"). This is the body of literature Christians call the OLD TESTAMENT.

TANNAIM (sing. TANNA). Hebrew for "those who hand down (tradition)": (a) the rabbis who are mentioned in the MISHNAH, whose discussions of HALAKAH indeed comprise the Mishnah, therefore the prominent scholarly rabbis in the SYNAGOGUE and in the YESHIBOT from the third century B.C.E. until about 200 C.E.; also (b) those who passed down the mishnic, tannaitic tradition to the AMORAIM. The Tannaim were guardians and cultivators of an oral tradition which was supposed to have been handed down parallel to the written TORAH from the time of Moses. By relating Mishnah to the written Torah, the Tannaim also preserved and created an important body of MIDRASH.

TEMPLE. Worship in the temple in Jerusalem was the center of HEBRAIC religion from the time of Solomon and of JUDAISM in its earliest period. The three successive structures to bear this name were: The Temple of Solomon, razed by Nebuchadnezzar at the beginning of the DIASPORA (586 B.C.E.); the Second Temple, built by the returning exiles; and the Third Temple ("of Herod") that supplanted it. The Third Temple was destroyed in 70 C.E. by the Romans. See SYNAGOGUE.

THEOPHANY. A theophany is literally an appearance (*phania*) of God or of a god (divine being or *theos*) to man; any manifestation of the divine.

TORAH. Most literally and most generally, "Torah" may be rendered "instruction," "direction," or "law"; but it is a term used with a wide range of degrees of specificity. Thus, Torah may be all religious instruction and custom, or the body of all rabbinical and priestly teachings; it may connote particular statutes, or a particular body of statutes—e.g. the "Covenant Code" (Exodus 20:23–23:19), the Ezraic Deuteronomic code, or the law of the priestly code. Torah often refers to the first five books of the Hebrew Bible, the Pentateuch. In the Jewish tradition, Torah is preeminently that body of tradition which is traced back to Moses and which may be conveniently divided into the *Torah sheh-bi-Ketab* ("Torah which is written," i.e., the Pentateuch) and *Torah be-al-Peh* ("oral Torah," including the MIDRASHIC tradition). But it is the authority of this body of tradition as Torah which renders all tradition that submits to its authority Torah also. In rabbinical theology Torah is, therefore, the complete and eternal Word of God which is continually fulfilling itself, the instrument of God's government of the world in which the Jew participates by submitting himself to it.

TRANSUBSTANTIATION. The Roman Catholic DOGMA that the substance (the actual reality) of the EUCHARISTIC elements of bread and wine become the actual body and blood of Jesus Christ in the celebration of the Mass, although the accidents (the outward appearances) of the bread and wine remain unchanged.

TRINITY. The doctrine of the Trinity is the Christian attempt to explicate its understanding of the divine nature and self-REVELATION as threefold. The one primary being of God is believed to be tripersonal, Father, Son, and Holy Spirit. The persons are coequal in power and dignity (are of "one substance"), but have different roles (function as different "persons") in the divine scheme of creation and revelation. This doctrine is perhaps the central "mystery" of the Christian faith.

TYPOLOGY, TYPOLOGICAL EXEGESIS.   Typology is the prefiguring of one event or historical configuration by another in such a way that the juxtaposition of both of them adds depth and understanding to the interpretation of each of them. Typological EXEGESIS thus uses events or conditions separated in time and space to illumine one another, e.g., the saving action of YAHWEH in leading Israel out of bondage in Egypt and the saving action of Jesus Christ in leading men out of the bondage of sin. This method has been used particularly by Christian exegetes, but one can find it already in the prophets. See ANTIOCH, SCHOOL OF.

VULGATE.   A translation of the whole Christian Bible from texts in the original Hebrew and Greek made by Jerome (340–420 C.E.) into Latin, the Vulgate remained the standard Bible of the western Church until the time of the philological renaissance in the sixteenth century and the Reformation. It is still employed as a standard of ecclesiastical and liturgical use in the Roman Catholic Church.

WISDOM, WISDOM LITERATURE.   The "wisdom literature" refers primarily to those books among the part of the TANAKH known as the "Writings," which contain practical wisdom in either a positive (Proverbs, etc.) or negative (Ecclesiastes) form. Wisdom is also used in Jewish Scripture and in the RABBINICAL writings to refer to the Wisdom of Yahweh, by which He created the world and sustains it. Wisdom therefore became identifiable in some respects with TORAH and by Christians with the divine LOGOS.

YAHWEH.   So far as is known, Yahweh is the correct vocalization and transliteration of the proper and personal name of the God of Israel, written in the Hebrew texts with the four letters YHWH (q.v.) and often mistakenly transliterated into English as "Jehovah."

YAHWISM.   The second phase in the development of Hebrew religious tradition, this term denotes Israelite religion from the Mosaic dedication of the people Israel to the God YAHWEH at Sinai, through the "classical" period of Israel's political history—the Davidic kingdom and temple worship centered on Jerusalem—to the inauguration of the second temple and the second Law under the leadership of Ezra and Nehemiah (ca. 450 B.C.E.). From this latter date we may speak properly of JUDAISM as a discrete religious tradition.

YESHIBA (pl. YESHIBOT).   "Academies" or "Talmudic colleges," institutions for the study of Torah which arose first in postexilic Babylonia and Palestine-Syria as Torah gradually superseded temple worship as the center of gravity of Jewish religiosity, the yeshibot first flourished with the perfection of the MISHNAH curriculum (second and third centuries C.E.). Study was presided over by a rector (Gaon) under whose supervision public disputation was carried on. Yeshibot formed around master-rabbis flourished especially again during the late Middle Ages and Renaissance in Islamic and southern European countries, and in the sixteenth and eighteenth centuries in central and eastern Europe.

YHWH.   The *tetragrammaton* or *shem ha-mephorash* ("four letters") used in Hebrew Scripture to designate the personal, mystic, almost ineffable name of God. It is ordinarily paraphrased and euphemistically read as *adonai*, "My Lord"; therefore it is often written LORD in English translations of the Bible. Pronunciation of the sacred name (YAHWEH) has generally been avoided by the pious Jew—in ancient and medieval times in part because it was believed to unleash superhuman powers, but also out of reverence for the holy.

Index